ECONOMIC ISSUES and POLICY

Third Edition

Jacqueline Murray Brux
University of Wisconsin-River Falls

THOMSON

™

SOUTH-WESTERN

Australia · Canada · Mexico · Singapore · Spain · United Kingdom · United States

THOMSON
™
SOUTH-WESTERN

Economic Issues and Policy, Third Edition

Jacqueline Murray Brux

VP/Editorial Director:
Jack W. Calhoun

VP/Editor-in-Chief:
Mike Roche

Publisher of Economics:
Michael B. Mercier

Acquisitions Editor:
Peter Adams

Developmental Editor:
Sarah K. Dorger

Marketing Manager:
Lisa L. Lysne

Production Editor:
Cliff Kallemeyn

Manager of Technology, Editorial:
Vicky True

Technology Project Editor:
Peggy Buskey

Media Editor:
Pam Wallace

Designer/Illustrator:
Tippy McIntosh

Manufacturing Coordinator:
Sandee Milewski

Production House:
BookMasters, Inc.

Printer:
Phoenix Color, Hagerstown, MD

Cover Photo Images:
PhotoDisc

For permission to use material
from this text or product, contact
us by
Tel (800) 730-2214
Fax (800) 730-2215
http://www.thomsonrights.com

For more information
contact South-Western,
5191 Natorp Boulevard,
Mason, Ohio 45040.
Or you can visit our Internet site at:
http://www.swlearning.com

International Icon: Artville
Viewpoint Icon: Eyewire
Map art: Cartesia

BRIEF CONTENTS

CHAPTER 1   Introduction   2

CHAPTER 2   Crime and Drugs   34

CHAPTER 3   The Environment   56

CHAPTER 4   Education   80

CHAPTER 5   Discrimination   108

CHAPTER 6   U.S. Poverty   130

CHAPTER 7   World Poverty   162

CHAPTER 8   Market Power   186

CHAPTER 9   International Trade   210

CHAPTER 10   Housing   236

CHAPTER 11   Health Care   260

CHAPTER 12   Agriculture   282

CHAPTER 13   Social Security   306

CHAPTER 14   Unemployment and Inflation   326

CHAPTER 15   Government Macroeconomic Policy   352

CHAPTER 16   Taxes, Borrowing, and the National Debt   380

CHAPTER 17   Globally Free Markets for the Twenty-First Century?   408

EPILOGUE   427

GLOSSARY   429

INDEX   438

CONTENTS

Preface   xv

CHAPTER 1 Introduction   2
Economics and Scarcity   4
Economics and Distribution   9
Demand and Supply   9
Efficiency and Equity   25
A Glimpse of the Future   25
Public Goods and Services   25
Spillovers   26
Equity   26
Market Power and Trade   27
Special Markets   27
Stability   27
Some Final Comments to Students   28
Summary   30
Notes   30
Discussion Questions   30
Appendix   32

CHAPTER 2 Crime and Drugs   34
Crime Prevention   36
Crime Prevention as a Public Good   36
Crime Prevention Measures   37
Evaluation by Cost-Benefit Analysis   37
Benefits and Costs of Crime Prevention Activities   37
Increased Costs of Our Prison System   38
Empirical Studies of the Trend Toward Higher Incarceration
    Rates   39
Decreasing Violent Crimes Against Persons   39
White-Collar Crime   40
Should Drugs Be Legalized?   41
Background on the Legal Status of Drugs   41
The War on Drugs: U.S. Antidrug Policy   42
The Argument Against Legalization of Drugs   43
The Argument for Legalization of Drugs   44
The Economics of Prohibition or Legalization   46
The Legalization of Other Victimless Crimes   51

Summary 51
Notes 52
Discussion Questions 52
Appendix 53

CHAPTER 3 The Environment 56
The Problem of Pollution 58
Spillover Costs and Benefits 58
Inefficient Resource Allocation 59
Environmental Policies and Politics 62
Environmental Legislation 63
Methods of Regulation 65
The Standards Approach 65
Pollution Fees 66
Marketable Pollution Permits 67
Evaluation of Environmental Policies 68
Conservation and Recycling 68
Economics of Conservation 69
Economics of Recycling 71
Innovative Policies 73
The Effects of Environmental Policy
on the U.S. Economy 73
International Aspects of the Environmental
Problem 74
Criticism of U.S. Environmental Policy 75
Summary 77
Notes 77
Discussion Questions 78

CHAPTER 4 Education 80
Education's Spillover Benefits 82
Kindergarten through Grade 12 (K–12) Education 84
The Quality of K–12 Education 86
Proposals for Improving K–12 Education 87
No Child Left Behind 92
Final Words on Public K–12 Education 92
Higher Education 93
Public and Private Higher Education 93
Higher Education as an Investment in Human Capital 96
Who Benefits from State Government Support of Public Higher
Education? 99

Decreasing State Government Support for Public Higher
    Education   100
Different Tuition for Different Programs   101
Financial Aid: What About Low-Income Students?   103
Affirmative Action: What About Underrepresented
    Groups?   104
Summary   105
Notes   105
Discussion Questions   106

CHAPTER 5 Discrimination   108

The Diversity of the U.S. Population   110
  Hispanics   111
  African Americans   111
  Asian or Pacific Islanders   111
  American Indians, Eskimos, and Aleutian Islanders   111
  Trends in Population Growth   111
What Is a Minority?   112
Earnings and Income   113
  Types of Earning Discrimination   113
  Earnings and Education   115
  Earnings and Unemployment   116
  Earnings and Experience   116
Some Explanations of Discrimination   116
  Statistical Discrimination   117
  Occupational Crowding   117
Effects of Labor Market Discrimination   118
  Effects on the Economy   119
  Effects on Individuals   120
Problems in Measuring Discrimination   121
  Rational Individual Choice   121
  Choice, Discrimination, and Culture Intermingled   121
Policies to Eliminate Discrimination   122
  The Equal Pay Act of 1963   122
  The Civil Rights Act of 1964   122
  Executive Orders   122
  Indirect Labor Market Policies   124
Other Forms of Discrimination   124
  Residential Segregation   125
  Educational Segregation   125
Affirmative Action in Education   126
Summary   127

Notes   128
Discussion Questions   128

CHAPTER 6 U.S. Poverty   130

Relative Poverty   132
Measuring Relative Poverty   132
Trend in the U.S. Distribution of Income   132
International Comparisons   134

Absolute Poverty   134
Measuring Absolute Poverty in the United States   134
Trends in Poverty Statistics   135
The Incidence of Poverty   137
Who Are the Poor?   137
The Implications of Poverty   139

Causes of Poverty   140
Recession   140
Labor Productivity   141
Structural Changes in Our Economy   141
Personal Factors   141
Demographic Trends   142
Budget Cuts   143
Additional Causes of Poverty   143

Solutions to Poverty   144
Macroeconomic Policies to Relieve National
    Unemployment   144
Microeconomic Policies to Improve Labor
    Productivity   144
Universal Entitlements   144
A Negative Income Tax   145
Miscellaneous Solutions   146
Welfare and Other Government Programs   146

Welfare Reform   148
Controversy over Welfare   148
The Personal Responsibility and Work Opportunity
    Reconciliation Act (PRA)   149

The Role of Economic Growth Versus
    Government Programs   153

Complexity of Poverty   155

Summary   155

Notes   156

Discussion Questions   157

Appendix   158

CHAPTER 7 World Poverty   162

GNI per Capita   165
Economic Growth   166
  Problems in Measuring Well-Being   167
  Income Distribution   168
Economic Development and Standards of Living   170
Growth and Development   172
  Agricultural Development   173
  Access to Inputs, Extension, and Markets   173
  Agricultural Prices   174
  Export Cropping   176
  International Role   176
  Human and Natural Resource Development   177
  Women's Role in Development   178
Population Growth   179
Urbanization and Rural–Urban Migration   180
AIDS   182
A People-Oriented Strategy   183
Summary   183
Notes   183
Discussion Questions   184

CHAPTER 8 Market Power   186

Competition   188
Monopoly and Oligopoly   190
Measuring Bigness and Concentration   192
Barriers to Entry   194
  Economies of Scale   194
  Exclusive Franchises   195
  Control of Essential Raw Materials   195
  Patents   195
  Product Differentiation   196
  Licensing   196
  Behavior of Established Firms   196
Effects of Market Power   197
  Collusion   198
  Inefficiency   199
  Price Discrimination   200
Forces that Decrease Market Power   201
  Technological Change   201
  The U.S. Antitrust System   201
  Regulation and Deregulation   203
  Import Competition   204

Extent of Market Power   204
One Final Comment   205
Summary   206
Notes   206
Discussion Questions   207
Appendix   208

CHAPTER 9 International Trade   210
The Importance of Trade   212
The Benefits of Trade   213
    Absolute Advantage   214
    Comparative Advantage   214
    The Basis for Advantage   218
    All of the Benefits of Trade   218
The Distribution of Benefits   219
Restrictions to Free Trade   221
The Rest of the Controversy   223
    Less-Developed Countries   223
    Politics and Trade   226
    International Trade Agreements   227
Summary   229
Notes   229
Discussion Questions   229
Appendix   231

CHAPTER 10 Housing   236
Housing Markets: Is Home Ownership Within Our
    Reach?   237
    Trends in Housing   239
    Factors Influencing the Affordability of Housing   240
    Government Policy Toward Home Ownership   243
Housing for Low-Income Families   244
    Rental Ceilings   245
    Programs to Increase Supply   247
    Programs that Affect Demand   249
    Adequacy of Current Programs and New Directions
        for Policy   249
Housing Segregation   250
Homelessness in the United States   252
    Government Policy Concerning the Homeless   253
Summary   254

Notes   255
Discussion Questions   255
Appendix   256

CHAPTER 11 Health Care   260

U.S. Health Care Expenditures   262
Social Significance of Increased Expenditures   262
Outcomes of Health Expenditures   264

U.S. Health Care Problems   265
Escalating Health Care Costs   265
Lack of Access to Health Care   269

The Rationing of Health Care   272

Alternatives for Health Care in the United States   274
Privatization and Increased Competition in Health Care   274
Curtailment or Elimination of Medicare and Medicaid   274
Medical Savings Accounts   275
Privatization of the Supply of Medical Services   275
Group Practices and Managed Care   276
National Health Insurance   276

Recent Policy and Proposals   277
Recent Policy Change   277
Recent Proposals   278
Compromise?   279

Summary   280
Notes   280
Discussion Questions   280

CHAPTER 12 Agriculture   282

Characteristics of Agriculture   284
Inelastic Demand for Farm Products in the Short Run   284
Price Instability   284
Farm Income   285
Extensive Technological Change in the Past Half Century   286
Immobile Farm Resources   286

Government Policy Toward Agriculture   287
Price Supports   288
Programs to Restrict Supply   291
Efforts to Increase Demand   292
Recent Agricultural Policy   293

An Evaluation of U.S. Farm Policy   294
Treating a Symptom   295
Increasing Concentration in Agriculture   295
Harmful Environmental Effects   295

Farmworkers and Native Americans   296
Biotechnology   296
Agriculture and Less-Developed Countries   297
The Politics of U.S. Agricultural Policy   298
Summary   300
Notes   300
Discussion Questions   301
Appendix 1   302
Appendix 2   304

CHAPTER 13 Social Security   306

Social Security: A Social Insurance Program   308
Social Security Taxes and Benefits   310
Social Security Taxes   310
Social Security Benefits   312
Problems and Issues   313
The Long-Run Problem: An Aging Population   313
Should Social Security Be Made Voluntary?   315
The "Bad Buy" Issue: Is Social Security Unfair to Younger
    Workers?   317
Social Security's Treatment of Women   318
Does Social Security Decrease Savings?   319
Common Misconceptions About Social Security   320
**What Does the Future Hold for the Social Security
    System?   320**
Altering the Social Security Tax   321
Cutting Current Social Security Benefits   321
Taxing All Social Security Benefits   322
Increasing Retirement Ages   322
Investing Social Security Taxes in the Stock Market   323
Partial Privatization   323
Summary   324
Notes   324
Discussion Questions   325

CHAPTER 14 Unemployment and Inflation   326

The Macroeconomy   328
Unemployment   328
The Labor Force Participation Rate   328
The Unemployment Rate   330
The Data   331
Problems in Measuring Unemployment   334

The Effects of Unemployment   334
Types of Unemployment   335
Employment Effects of Immigration   338
The Minimum Wage   340

Inflation   342
Inaccuracy of the Inflation Rate   343
The Data   344
Hyperinflation   344
The Effects of Inflation   345
Types of Inflation   347

Which Problem Is More Serious: Unemployment or
    Inflation?   348
Summary   349
Notes   349
Discussion Questions   350
Appendix   351

CHAPTER 15 Government Macroeconomic
    Policy   352
Graphing the Macroeconomy   353
Gross Domestic Product   355
A Definition of GDP   355
Real Versus Nominal GDP   357
Flaws of GDP   357
Nonmarket Activities   358
Underground Activities   358
Composition and Distribution   359

Aggregate Demand and Supply   359
What Sectors Are Represented by Aggregate Demand?   359
Shifts in Aggregate Demand   362
Shifts in Aggregate Supply   362

Inflation Revisited   362
Demand-Pull Inflation   363
Cost-Push Inflation   363
Profit-Push Inflation   364

Government Macro Policy   365
Fiscal Policy   365
Monetary Policy   367
Supply-Side Policy   369
Effects of Supply-Side Policy   371
Trickle-Down   372
Economic Policy for the New Century   373
Summary   374

Notes   374
Discussion Questions   375
Appendix   375

CHAPTER 16 Taxes, Borrowing, and the National Debt   380

Government Taxes   382
Federal Taxes   382
State and Local Taxes   384
Effects of Taxes on the Macroeconomy   386
Effects of Taxes on the Income Distribution   387
Effects of Taxes on the Microeconomy of Individual
    Markets   390
Government Borrowing   392
Effects on the Macroeconomy   392
Effects on the Income Distribution   393
Effects on Interest Rates   394
Effects on the Government Budget and the National Debt   396
The National Debt   398
The Size of the National Debt   398
Who Owns the National Debt?   399
The Impact of the National Debt   400
Proposals to Require a Balanced Budget   400
Summary   402
Notes   403
Discussion Questions   404
Appendix   405

CHAPTER 17 Globally Free Markets for the Twenty-First Century?   408

Markets   409
The Western Industrialized World: Economic Growth   411
Economic Growth Rates   411
Aggregate Supply and Production Possibilities   412
Policies to Achieve Economic Growth   413
Implications of Growth for the Twenty-First Century   416
The Formerly Socialist Industrialized World:
    Economic Transition   417
Market-Determined Prices   418
Privatization   418
Effects of the Transition   419
The Twenty-First Century?   420

The Less-Developed World: Economic Reform   420
    The 1970s: Oil Crisis   420
    The Early 1980s: U.S. Reaction   421
    The 1980s: International Debt Crisis   421
    The 1990s: Economic Reform   423
    The Twenty-First Century?   424
Summary   425
Notes   425
Discussion Questions   426

Epilogue   427
Glossary   429
Index   438

PREFACE to the Instructor

This text is intended for a non-technical, issues-oriented economics course, usually a 100-level course in four-year universities. It is often a general education course. The book is also appropriate for two-year colleges and other institutions, as well as economic education programs for secondary teachers. Chapters are designed so that they can be taught in any order after Chapter One. Each chapter includes references to other chapters that mention similar topics.

I have almost 20 years of experience teaching issues-oriented economics. Usually my students are not economics majors, although many decide to major or minor in economics after taking this course. Some of my students are recent high school graduates and incredibly naive about the workings of the economy. Others are non-traditional students who know only too well how the economy works. They also understand how disadvantaged they are without a college degree. This book aims to reach both groups of students and those in between.

My goals in writing the book were to make students aware of social issues in the world around them and to facilitate their understanding of these issues and their related policy options from an economic perspective. Students are often unaware that the important issues of our day, even ones that directly affect them—the environment, our health care programs, our educational system, crime and drugs, and matters as weighty as war and peace—are rooted in economics. Furthermore, students often set aside as too complex the issues that *are* recognized as economic, such as unemployment and inflation or trade and budget deficits. They believe that these issues are better left to the experts. Students need to know that these issues are indeed relevant and within their ability to understand. They need to comprehend these issues to make sound choices and form intelligent opinions. Of course, before students are willing to commit themselves to the life-long learning of economics, they first need to be convinced that it is relevant to their lives and that it *is* interesting!

Recent studies suggest that today's youth are disinterested in the world around them and are focused instead on more personal concerns such as getting good grades, paying for education, and acquiring a job. Students must be shown the connection between themselves and their world. In the post 9-11 era, students are indeed beginning to look at the world around them. In a functioning democracy, they need to understand the relevance of social issues to their lives, and the impact their lives can have on these issues. This book is an effort to demonstrate that relevance and suggest that impact. Indeed, its Epilogue, "You and the World around You," invites the student to address many of the matters raised in the text.

The discussion of issues in this book is lively and current. I have deliberately included issues of gender, race, and ethnicity. And, because the world is so rapidly becoming thoroughly interdependent, I have also provided plenty of discussion of international topics throughout the book and in specific chapters. Even if you rarely have time to include international topics in your course, I encourage you to read all three chapters that specifically address international topics (Chapters 7, 9, and 17) before you decide to skip them. I think you will find them quite relevant and interesting, and the issues are presented in such a way that students can understand them.

In this book, economic theory is used to analyze social and economic issues and the implications of potential policies. The level of technicality is deliberately appropriate for an economic issues course with no prerequisites, unlike other issues texts that attempt to incorporate all relevant principles and theory into pages better focused on the issues themselves. The text is written in a clear and student-friendly manner. Graphs are clear and normally illustrate only one concept per graph. Except for the appendices, there are only two basic types of graphs used in the text: production possibilities and demand and supply (and aggregate demand and supply). Every effort has been made to place the graph and the discussion of the graph on the same or adjacent pages. More technical material and additional examples are frequently placed in appendices.

This text generally presents economic theory in a straightforward, market-oriented framework, but the policy discussion is not limited to such a narrow context. Instead, diverse policy perspectives are offered. As a result, the book contains a more liberal orientation than one that would rely on market analysis only. Indeed, the careful presentation of both conservative and liberal viewpoints is one of the unique characteristics of this book. Students often have opinions, and they often consider themselves to be either conservative or liberal, but they rarely have the sophistication to understand the economic meaning of these terms and how their viewpoints tie into one or the other general philosophy. The Viewpoint section at the end of each chapter clarifies these notions, giving students a framework within which to understand their own economic philosophies. Please point out to your students the importance of reading the Viewpoint sections, which clarify the conservative versus the liberal economic views on the topics in the chapter. The Viewpoint section of Chapter One is especially important insofar as it introduces students to what it means to be an economic conservative and an economic liberal. It sets the stage for further discussion of this topic in relation to the issues in chapters to come.

CHANGES IN THE THIRD EDITION

The third edition of the text is extensively updated. It has a new design and artwork that will be more appealing to the student. Revised "Roadmaps" demonstrate how economic issues are interrelated throughout the book. The new Economic Toolbox at the beginning of each chapter lists the key economic concepts addressed in the chapter, providing instructors with a helpful course-planning tool and students with a proven effective pre-reading strategy. Additional Internet exercises are included in the Discussion Questions at the end of each chapter to help students learn to use the Internet for data collection and research.

I have reorganized the chapters so that three issues that generally interest students the most (crime and drugs, the environment, and education) are placed up front immediately after introductory Chapter One. The first of these chapters involves a public good (criminal justice), followed by the next two chapters that present examples of a negative externality (environmental pollution) and a positive externality (education). The next three chapters deal with "equity issues" (discrimination, U.S. poverty, and world poverty). The first of the chapters on market power presents the problem of market power; the second provides an answer (international trade). Following these are chapters pertaining to "special markets" (housing, health care, agriculture, and social security) that economists often believe are too important to leave entirely to private markets. Stability issues are then covered in the chapters on unemployment and inflation; macroeconomic policy; and taxes, borrowing, and the national debt. As in the second edition, the final chapter, "Globally Free Markets for the Twenty-First Century?" remains at the end of the book, inviting students to synthesize all they have learned about conservative and liberal economic philosophies and to put it to the test of predicting the future of the world economy. It also enables them to define their own personal economic philosophies. I believe this reorganization of chapters provides a more logical order and addresses early on issues that directly affect students.

Theoretical discussion in certain chapters has been streamlined and reduced, and the more technical material has been placed in appendices. Examples of new appendix material include the production possibilities curve with increasing opportunity costs, the construction of the consumer price index, and the detailed discussion of elasticity. New material is placed in appendices as well, such as the relation between elasticity, monopoly revenue, and price discrimination. Other material has been eliminated from the book, such as details of regulation and more complex graphs of perfect competition, monopoly, and economics of scale.

The new edition contains updates in data, as well as new, current topics. These topics include the new economy that is partially attributable to 9-11, including the dramatic increase in U.S. government spending on national defense, homeland security, and the invasions of Afghanistan and Iraq. The third edition also takes us away from the glowing economy described in the previous edition (with economic growth, budget surpluses, and relatively low poverty rates) to the more recent problems of economic recession, large budget deficits, and rising poverty rates. New topics also pertain to the dramatic conservative shift in the economic policies and proposals of President George W. Bush from those of the previous administrations: deregulation, cuts in domestic programs, the "No Child Left Behind" agenda, the partial privatization of Social Security and Medicare, changes in our federal tax system, and many more. In short, just a few short years have resulted in radical changes in this nation's policies and issues.

In addition, students are invited to broaden their sensitivity and understanding of multicultural and global issues through new references to topics such as migrant farm workers, Colombian coca growers, immigrants to the United States, West African "cocoa slaves," court rulings on vouchers and affirmative action in school admissions, charges of racist statements by former Senate Majority Leader Trent Lott, "freedom fries," Native Americans, and others. As with previous editions, students are encouraged throughout the text and in the Epilogue to use the knowledge they gain about the economics of social issues to try to make the society in which they live a better place. In summary, the third edition of the textbook provides students with more effective, attractive, interesting, and relevant study of economic issues and policy.

ANCILLARIES

I have authored two ancillary volumes for the text, the *Instructor's Manual with Test Bank* and the *Study Guide*. I have revised these volumes to complement changes in the third edition of the text to ensure that the ancillaries are consistent with the third edition in both vocabulary and content.

The *Instructor's Manual with Test Bank* reveals the goals and objectives on a chapter-by-chapter basis. The manual contains teaching and lecture suggestions (based on my own education in how students think), as well as additional discussion or lecture examples to use in class. It also contains some answers and comments on the discussion questions at the end of each chapter in the textbook. The instructor's manual also contains sample multiple-choice, true-and-false, critical thinking, and short-answer (including graphical) exam questions, providing instructors with plenty of choices for assessment. The manual also includes suggested Web sites for instructors and/or students. Whether you are a novice or a seasoned teacher, you will find material in the instructor's manual that is beneficial to you.

The *Study Guide* also presents the goals and learning objectives. Study suggestions and practice exercises are included on a chapter-by-chapter basis, reflecting the years I've spent getting to know the problems and confusion often faced by students. I also provide a self-test of multiple-choice and true-and-false questions (and answers).

PREFACE to the Student

This book focuses on the economics of social issues. It includes those issues that you would normally consider to be economic by nature, such as unemployment and inflation. But it also includes a variety of other social issues that you might not ordinarily think of as economic ones: illegal drug use, the plight of our nation's homeless, the degradation of our environment, the problems in financing your higher education, and the issue of affirmative action. These and many other issues are addressed in this book.

The basic economic tools in the text can be used as a framework for understanding the various social issues in the world around us. They can provide greater insight into issues such as health care, poverty, and discrimination. They can help us understand government policy within our nation. They can help us understand economic events in other countries, including those countries making a transition from socialism to capitalism in Eastern Europe and those countries struggling to develop in the less-developed world. In short, these tools can be used again and again to examine problems and issues present in our world today as well as in the future.

The book is intended to be student-friendly. The graphs are straightforward and clear. You may be relieved to know that these graphs boil down to just two basic types: production possibilities and demand and supply. The definitions of economic vocabulary in the margins of each chapter help you cut through any economic jargon. The issues are current. The text is clear, lively, and to the point, with a minimum of technicality. The material is presented in a way that you should find relevant to your personal life. It includes issues of gender, race, and ethnicity. And because the world is so rapidly becoming interdependent, there is plenty of discussion of international topics.

The book is intended to get you to think. As you acquire a basic understanding of economics, you also acquire a framework within which to form and justify your personal opinions about social issues. Are you a conservative or a liberal? Do you even know what these terms mean in the context of economics? Briefly, by conservative we mean a view that *less* government involvement in the economy is best. By liberal, we mean that *more* government involvement is best. Both of these are further explained in the Viewpoint section of Chapter One, and the Viewpoint sections in subsequent chapters focus on specific issues and policies from both a liberal and conservative perspective. You will do yourself a great service by carefully reading the Viewpoint section in each chapter.

Finding solutions to economic problems is not easy. People of different philosophies can hold very different viewpoints, despite a common understanding of economic concepts. Here is where you, the student, come in. This book will provide a basic economic framework for discussing social issues and problems, but *you* must determine your own viewpoint on these issues and problems. It is my hope that you will use your new knowledge to try to make a difference in the global society in which we live.

Each chapter opens with two features that will help you prepare for the material in the chapter: a chapter "Roadmap" and the "Economic Toolbox." The "Roadmap" demonstrates how the economic issue discussed in the chapter is related to the other chapters' issues. The "Economic Toolbox" lists the key economic concepts addressed in the chapter. Reading this list prior to your reading of each chapter will improve your reading comprehension in two ways: if you are unfamiliar with any of the concepts listed, you can mentally prepare for taking in new information; if you are familiar with some of the concepts (and you will find as you work through the chapters that concepts are often repeated), you can use your prior knowledge to deepen your understanding of the concept as it is presented in a new context.

Within your new textbook, you will find an e-con @pps card. It provides the serial number to gain access to the e-con @pps Web site (*http://econapps.swlearning.com*), where you will find hands-on exploration and analysis of the latest economic news stories, policy debates, and data. It also offers an excellent research starting point for class assignments such as papers, projects, and presentations. In addition, I have included boxes in the margins of your textbook that will point you to a specific e-con @pps feature that relates directly to the text discussion at hand.

Discussion questions at the end of each chapter will stimulate your thinking about what you have just read. Many of the questions direct you to Web sites that provide a wealth of economic information and perspectives. If you do not use the questions in class, try one or two on your own or with a classmate. You will find that your understanding of the issue will grow and the relevance of the issue to your world will increase.

I have authored a study guide for use with this textbook to aid you in your study of economic issues and policies. It presents the purpose and learning objectives for each chapter. It also includes, on a chapter-by-chapter basis, many study suggestions that reflect my long-standing experience with problems faced by students. Practice exercises are also available, as well as self-tests with multiple-choice and true-and-false questions (and answers).

Now enjoy your discovery of the world of economic issues!

ACKNOWLEDGMENTS

I owe a debt of gratitude to many people. First, thank you to the thousands of students who have allowed me to experiment on them. As a result of their enthusiasm and idealism, they are responsible for my love of teaching. I could never have written a book without them!

Second, I appreciate the support provided by some wonderful student assistants, especially Tabitha Dziak and Christina Brux. Look out world, because these young people will barrel us into the future with their gifts of friendship and energy. There is no such thing as a lost generation!

Third, the comments of my colleagues guided me in this revision. I am grateful for their perspectives and the extensive sharing of their experience and recommendations: Ed Ford (University of South Florida), Alan Grant (Eastern Illinois University), Chiara Gratton-Lavoie (California State University-Fullerton), John Nader (Grand Valley State University), and Raymond A. Pepin (Stonehill College). Critical to decisions on the text's reorganization were the comments of colleagues that participated in a survey: James H. Holcomb, Jr. (University of Texas-El Paso), Edward Lyell (Adams State College), Orhan Kara (University of North Dakota), Bonnie Orcutt (American International College), Roberta Biby (Grand Valley State University), Gary L. Hodgin (Belmont University), Ken Peissig (College of Menominee Nation), and Glenn Potts (University of Wisconsin-River Falls).

I am grateful to the team at South-Western, especially Peter Adams, Sarah Dorger, Cliff Kallemeyn, Tippy McIntosh, and Lisa Lysne.

And finally, I am grateful for the love and support of family and friends. To Keith and Christina, thank you for your gift of love. And to Corey and Emily, thank you for your gift of new life. To little Asher, thank you for your gift of hope for the future!

Jacqueline Murray Brux

ABOUT THE AUTHOR

Jacqueline Murray Brux received her Ph.D. in economics in 1983 from the University of Michigan in Ann Arbor, and is a professor of economics at the University of Wisconsin-River Falls. Her area of expertise is the economic development of less developed countries. Her research encompasses the area of economic development, with special focus on women in development and the effects of structural reforms. Dr. Brux's international experiences include work and research in the countries of Burkina Faso and Ghana in West Africa; Mexico, Chile, and Cuba in Latin America; Russia; and Vietnam.

ECONOMIC
ISSUES and
POLICY

Third Edition

CHAPTER ROADMAP

Inequality
Ch. 5: Discrimination
Ch. 6: U.S. Poverty
Ch. 7: World Poverty

Market Power and Solutions
Ch. 8: Market Power
Ch. 9: International Trade

Externalities
Ch. 3: Environment
Ch. 4: Education

Public Goods and Services
Ch. 2: Crime and Drugs

Chapter 1 Introduction

Special Markets
Ch. 10: Housing
Ch. 11: Health Care
Ch. 12: Agriculture
Ch. 13: Social Security

What Is Your Responsibility?
Epilogue: You and the World Around You

Global Synopsis of Liberal Economics vs. Conservative Economics
Ch. 17: Globally Free Markets for the Twenty-First Century?

Stability Issues
Ch. 14: Unemployment and Inflation
Ch. 15: Macroeconomic Policy
Ch. 16: Taxes, Borrowing, and the National Debt

THE ECONOMIC TOOLBOX

The Economic Toolbox is a feature of each chapter. It points out specific economic topics that will be covered, alerting you to watch for these concepts in the chapter.

- scarcity
- resources
- production possibilities
- microeconomics
- macroeconomics
- unemployment
- economic growth
- opportunity cost
- demand and supply
- equilibrium

INTRODUCTION

In economics, hope and faith coexist with great scientific pretension and also a deep desire for respectability.
—John Kenneth Galbraith, U.S. economist, *New York Times Magazine,* June 7, 1970

Welcome to economics! Welcome? To the dismal science? To the colorless pages of the *Wall Street Journal*? To the realm of boring statistics, intimidating jargon, complex graphs, and middle-aged men and women in three-piece business suits carrying leather briefcases?

Welcome? To terms such as *budget deficit, balance of trade, national debt, inflation, money supply, unemployment rate, labor force,* and *market equilibrium*? Do we really want to know what these phrases mean? Do we really want to look at the graphs, charts, numbers, and newsprint? Can these possibly have meaning for our lives? Can they possibly be understood by average citizens such as those right here in this classroom?

Perhaps surprisingly, the answer to all of the preceding is a resounding yes . . . not because we enjoy jargon and numbers, but because we want answers to important questions. Will I be able to get a job when I graduate? Why does a marketing professor make more than an English professor? Will I be helped or hurt by a raise in the minimum wage? Why are college costs so high? Should students receive greater financial aid? Why do female workers earn only about three-quarters as much as male workers? Why do we go to war? Why have we encouraged farmers to produce huge surpluses through government subsidies? Why does hunger persist in a world of plenty? Why does poverty exist in the midst of affluence? Who will eat, and who will not? Who will find jobs, and who will not? Whose children will have quality education and health care, and whose children will not?

Scarcity
Limited resources relative to wants and needs.

If you've wondered about these or similar questions, then you are interested in economics. This is because economics deals primarily with **scarcity**: how shall we allocate our limited resources to satisfy seemingly unlimited human wants and needs? Once you understand a little economic reasoning, you will be able to answer the world's (and your) pressing questions better than most of the politicians, newscasters, and opinionated people who persistently tell you what to believe. Survival in the face of scarcity is what economics is all about. Understanding a few economic concepts allows you to analyze these issues yourself and come up with your own answers to these questions. So, let's get started.

ECONOMICS AND SCARCITY

Resources
Land, labor, machinery, and other inputs used to produce goods and services.

Let us begin by discussing scarcity. **Resources** (land, labor, factory buildings, timber, minerals, machinery, and the like) are the basis for producing the food, shelter, medical care, and luxury goods that we want. These resources are scarce in the sense that there are not enough of them to produce everything we need and desire. Even when using all resources as efficiently and completely as possible, and using all modern technology to its fullest extent, there is some limit to the amount we can currently produce. Scarcity forces us to choose among competing uses for society's resources. What to produce and how to distribute this output to society's citizens are the most basic economic choices to be made.

Production possibilities curve
An economic concept explaining scarcity and the need for choices; a graph showing alternate combinations of the maximum amounts of two different goods that can be produced during a particular time period if the economy's resources are efficiently and fully employed.

The easiest way to think about the problem of societal choice is by looking at a basic economic concept and graph called the **production possibilities curve**. (We promise that only two basic graphs will be used to analyze the issues in this book.) The production possibilities curve shows the maximum amounts of two different goods that can possibly be produced during any particular time period using society's scarce resources. Because reality is complex, economists try to simplify it by making assumptions about the basic elements involved in analyzing an issue. In examining production possibilities, we must make these simplifying assumptions about our economy:

1. All available resources will be used fully.
2. All available resources will be used efficiently.
3. The quantity and quality of available resources are not changing during our period of analysis.
4. Technology is not changing during our period of analysis.
5. We can produce only two goods with our available resources and technology.

Let's consider the implications of these simplifying assumptions. First, all available resources are used fully, so that no workers are unemployed, no factory buildings sit idle, and so forth. (This does not mean that we fail to conserve some of our resources for the future. If we think that the habitat of the snowy owl is important ecologically, we simply do not make that part of the available resources.) Second, *efficiency* means that we use our knowledge and technology to produce the maximum amount of output with these resources. These first two assumptions mean that our economy is doing the best that it can; it is operating fully and efficiently. Third, the quantity and quality of our resources are not changing. This means that over the current time period, workers do not begin new training programs to make them more productive, new natural resources are not discovered, and so on. The next assumption is similar. Technological change—which might give us a better means of producing more goods with the same resources—is not occurring. We make these last two assumptions to deal with the world as it is right now, and not how it might become in the future. And finally, to simplify our analysis (and because here we graph in only two dimensions), we assume that we can produce only two goods with our resources. Let's pick bread and roses as the goods.

One of our choices is to put all of our resources and technology into the production of bread. This choice might give us 150 units of bread. Whether these bread units are loaves, cases, truckloads, or tons is irrelevant here. Let's suppose they are tons.

Two old adages suggest that man (and woman) cannot live by bread alone and that life is richer if we stop and smell the roses. So, let's allow another choice and take some resources and some technology out of bread production and use them to produce roses. Now, we might end up with 20 units of roses and only 120 tons of bread. Again, the nature of the units is irrelevant; our rose units might be bouquets, boxes, truckloads, or tons. Let's suppose they are tons. (Note, however, that we had to give up 30 tons of bread production in order to produce the 20 tons of roses.)

Another alternative might be to give up even more bread, leaving us with bread production of only 90 tons, in order to produce 40 tons of roses. (Note that, once again, we had to give up 30 tons of bread production in order to get the additional 20 tons of roses.) The alternatives could go on and on and might be summarized in a production possibilities table such as Table 1-1 on page 6. Note that each alternative A through F represents one possible combination of bread and roses that we could produce.

The information in Table 1-1 can be easily displayed in a production possibilities curve, or graph. Don't let graphs intimidate you. They can be very useful. Every graph has just two axes, and each axis shows the amounts of one variable. As you move along the axes away from the origin, the amounts of the variables increase. In Figure 1-1 on page 6, the horizontal axis represents tons of roses, and the vertical axis represents tons of bread. Each point in the graph represents a row in the table, and the labeling of the points corresponds to the alternatives in the table. Connecting all points gives us a production possibilities curve, which shows the alternative combinations of maximum quantities of bread and roses that our country is capable of producing. (Even though we end up with a straight line, we still call it a production possibilities *curve*. The appendix to this chapter considers the more realistic production possibilities curve that is actually bowed outward.)

A number of important concepts are illustrated by the production possibilities curve. The most basic concept is that there is some limit to what we can produce. Thus, to produce more of one good, we must give up production of something else. This reality is what economists refer to as **opportunity cost**. Opportunity cost is the best alternative that is forgone in order to produce or consume something else. The

Opportunity cost
The best alternative forgone in order to produce or consume something else; what you give up to get something else.

TABLE 1-1 Production Possibilities Table

Alternative	Bread (tons)	Roses (tons)
A	150	0
B	120	20
C	90	40
D	60	60
E	30	80
F	0	100

FIGURE 1-1 Production Possibilities Curve

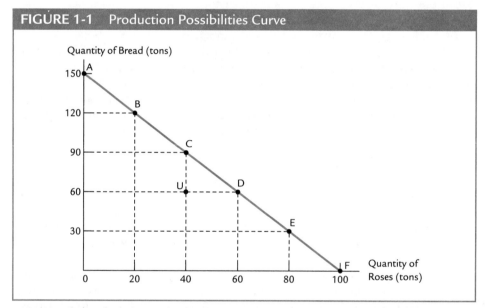

Points A through F show alternative combinations of bread and roses that the economy can produce, whereas point U represents unemployed resources.

opportunity cost of producing roses is not measured in dollars but in the bread that we give up when we produce these roses. And the opportunity cost of producing bread is the roses we give up when we produce this bread. As economists are fond of saying, there is no free lunch! There is an opportunity cost to everything.

The second economic concept that is illustrated by production possibilities is that of **unemployment**. Realize that our alternative combinations of the two products represent possible quantities. We have explicitly assumed the full use of our resources, knowledge, and technology; hence, the phrase production *possibilities*. In actuality, we rarely if ever produce to our full potential. In reality, some resources may go unused: factories are idle and workers are laid off. Nor do we always use resources in

Unemployment
A situation in which resources are not fully used in production.

the most efficient manner. In these cases, we will not be on the production possibilities curve, but at some point below it, such as U (representing unemployment) in Figure 1-1. At point U, we are producing only 40 tons of roses and 60 tons of bread, though we could produce more of both if we had full employment. Clearly, we could do much better by putting idle resources to work and moving our way back out to the production possibilities curve.

Finally, it is evident that our country need not be restricted to a single production possibilities curve forever. Economies may grow, and the variables that we assumed are unchanging (resources and technology) certainly *do* change over time. **Economic growth** may occur if the quality or quantity of society's resources increases, or if new technologies are developed so that we can produce more output with our available resources. Such growth would be reflected in an outward shift of the entire production possibilities curve, as illustrated in Figure 1-2. Such a shift would enable us to move to a point such as point G (representing growth) on the new production possibilities curve. Clearly, point G (with 80 tons of roses and 90 tons of bread) is superior to a point such as D (with 60 tons of roses and only 60 tons of bread) on the original curve. Such growth is possible only over time, and not in the current time period illustrated by the first production possibilities curve.

Of course, our country and world are capable of producing more than just two goods. We produce trucks, spaghetti, gasoline, VCRs, swimming suits, and a

EconDebate

"Is There a New Economy?"

Read the full debate on the changes between the economy of the 1990s and today's economy. Did unemployment increase or decrease? Why?

Find the full debate under the Macroeconomics Employment, Unemployment, and Inflation category.

http://econapps. swlearning.com

Economic growth
A sustained increase in production, represented by an outward shift of the production possibilities curve.

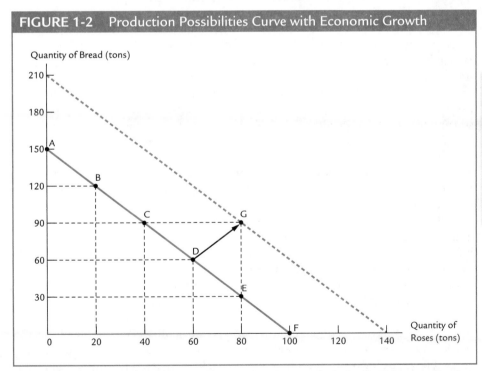

FIGURE 1-2   Production Possibilities Curve with Economic Growth

Note that more of both bread and roses can be produced when the production possibilities curve shifts outward as a result of economic growth.

Services
Activities such as haircuts, health care, and education that are consumed (used) by consumers.

Consumer goods
Goods that are consumed (used) by consumers.

Capital goods
Goods such as machinery and factories that are used to produce other goods.

Private goods
Goods provided by business firms.

Public goods
Goods provided or paid for by government.

bewildering array of merchandise that fills our shopping centers. We also produce **services** such as health care, education, road repair, and telephone installation. We can easily imagine infinite combinations of all the goods and services that an economy can potentially produce. We cannot graph these infinite combinations, however, because our graphs have only two axes. So, bread and roses simply represent one of an infinite set of choices. We can make our graph a bit more realistic by redefining the axes. We might redefine the horizontal axis as staple goods and the vertical axis as luxury goods. Or we could divide our economy's output into agricultural goods and manufactured goods, or **consumer goods** (goods that are purchased by consumers) and **capital goods** (goods such as factory buildings and machinery that are used to produce other goods). We may examine the choice between military goods and civilian goods. Or we may look at the production possibilities for **private goods** (such as CD players and hamburgers, which are provided by businesses) and **public goods** (such as police and fire protection, which are provided by government). Thus, we can realistically consider many choices involved in the production of various types of output.

We hope you don't suspect that the purpose of the production possibilities exercise was merely to illustrate some economic concepts and drawings. It wasn't. It has very important real-world relevance. It suggests to us first of all that we can never be absolutists when it comes to our nation's spending priorities. If we wish to devote more of the country's current resources to environmental protection, for example, we may have to give up part of our space program. If we wish to expand public education, we may have to give up some of our national defense. Or if we wish to have more government goods and services overall, we must give up some private goods. We can't have more of everything. We can't insist on any spending priority without limit, because there are always opportunity costs to consider.

The production possibilities curve also helps us realize that the costs of unemployment are not limited to personal hardships experienced by the unemployed person and his or her family, although these personal costs may be severe. Costs are also borne by our nation and our world as a whole in the form of reduced production. If we waste our resources through inefficient production techniques, output is similarly reduced. In a world of scarcity, we must see to it that our resources are fully and efficiently employed in the present, and we can then seek to expand our productive potential in the future.

And the problem of scarcity is real. Worldwide, more than 15 children die every minute from lack of adequate nutrition and health care. Many of the world's citizens lack basic education, shelter, clothing, clean water, and hygiene as well. Many of the world's nations lack basic infrastructure in the form of communications, transportation, sanitation, and electricity. Any time a poor country makes a decision to improve transportation, for example, as an investment in the future, many of its citizens may die of hunger in the present. Even in a prosperous country such as ours, some 12 percent of the population is poor. As we shall see in Chapter 6 on U.S. poverty, these people do not receive adequate food, shelter, health care, clothing, and other necessities. Our nation as a whole lacks sufficient environmental protection, first-rate educational opportunities, and quality health care for all. Choices as to what we produce and how much we produce are clearly important to our citizens.

ECONOMICS AND DISTRIBUTION

Although production choices are important, they really tell us only half of the story. At least as important are choices relating to the distribution of goods and services. The reason there is hunger in a world with plenty of food is not a problem of production but of distribution. Poor people and poor governments lack the ability to purchase the food that is produced. In terms of our current example, who shall receive the bread and roses after they are produced? Shall the decision be based on equality so that everyone receives the same amount of every good that everyone else does? Shall people receive a share of the goods and services that is proportional to their contribution to producing those goods and services? Shall the government make the distribution decisions, perhaps giving higher rations to those most "deserving" (however that might be determined)? On what basis shall distribution choices be made?

As we shall see, in a market-based economy such as ours, the choices of distribution as well as production are based primarily on prices. And prices are determined by demand and supply.

Demand and Supply

Demand

Have you ever had to hire a tutor to help with your coursework? (We hope you haven't had to in economics, at least not yet!) What are some of the factors that would determine the number of tutoring hours you would wish to purchase? Probably the degree of difficulty of the coursework is important, and so is your income, which will determine how much tutoring you can afford. Most likely, the price of tutoring services is important to you as well. All other things being equal, you would probably be inclined to purchase more tutoring service hours at $1 per hour than at $5 per hour. Most of us tend to behave in the same way. At very high prices, we tend to be frugal in our use of tutoring services. We will ask more questions in class, study with a friend, or visit the teacher during office hours (maybe bringing along an apple or two). We will perhaps study harder (or take the consequences) rather than pay the fee for many hours of tutoring services if the price is high. At lower prices, we are willing and able to purchase more hours of tutoring. Let's focus on the price variable for a moment.

Let's assume that you attend a large university where there are many students who want tutors as well as many students willing and able to tutor. Suppose we consider all your school's students and their desire to purchase tutoring services. Let's assume that the time period is one week and that all factors other than price (such as course difficulty and student income) are held constant. (Economists usually say "all other things equal" to specify that all other factors that might influence the quantity demanded are unchanging.)

To illustrate this example further, let's put this information into a tabular format. Let's consider people's willingness to buy tutoring services, where P stands for alternative possible prices of tutoring services and Q^D (quantity demanded) stands for the amounts of tutoring that students are willing and able to purchase at these various

TABLE 1-2   Demand Schedule for Tutoring Services, One Week

Alternative	P ($ per hour)	Q^D (hours)
a	$1	100
b	$2	80
c	$3	60
d	$4	40
e	$5	20

prices. This is reflected in Table 1-2, which shows alternative prices and the quantities that people are willing and able to purchase at these prices. This is called a **demand schedule**. It is clear that if tutoring prices are low (say, $2 per hour), the quantity demanded will be high (80 hours). If tutoring prices are higher ($4 per hour), the quantity demanded will be lower (40 hours). This simple commonsense idea that people will be willing and able to buy more of a good or service at low prices than at high prices is a fundamental economic principle, the law of demand, which is usually stated as follows: *price and quantity demanded are negatively related, all other things equal.* This means that when price goes up, quantity demanded goes down, and vice versa.

We can place the information from Table 1-2 into a graph of demand, illustrated in Figure 1-3. A graph of demand is referred to as a demand curve (even though demand curves are often drawn as straight lines). The price of tutoring services (P) is on the vertical axis, and the quantity of services demanded (number of hours) is on the horizontal axis, which is labeled Q for quantity. Plotting the information in each of the rows a through e in the table gives us points a through e in the graph. Connecting these points gives us the demand curve in Figure 1-3. The **demand curve** (labeled D for demand) indicates all possible combinations of alternative prices and

Demand schedule
A table showing the quantities that consumers are willing to buy at alternative prices during a specified time period.

Demand curve
A graph showing the quantities that consumers are willing to buy at alternative prices during a specified time period.

FIGURE 1-3   Demand for Tutoring Services, One Week

TABLE 1-3 Increased Demand Schedule for Tutoring Services, One Week

Alternative	P ($ per hour)	Q^D (hours)
a′	$1	140
b′	$2	120
c′	$3	100
d′	$4	80
e′	$5	60

quantity demanded, assuming that all factors except price that could affect quantity demanded are held constant.

Note that the demand curve is downward sloping, reflecting the **law of demand**. A higher price is associated with a lower quantity demanded (40 hours at $4 per hour), whereas a lower price is associated with a larger quantity demanded (80 hours at $2 per hour).

What if one of the other factors affecting demand was to change? Course difficulty might increase, for example. Or student incomes might increase, making students better able to afford tutoring. Each of these examples would increase the demand for tutoring services. You probably can add to the list of things that would increase the demand for tutoring.

An increase in the demand for tutoring services will result in an entirely new demand schedule, such as the one in Table 1-3. We can plot this new information in the same graph as before, and we end up with an entirely new demand curve, D′. (See Figure 1-4.) Demand has increased so the demand curve has shifted forward,

Law of demand
There is a negative relationship between price and quantity demanded.

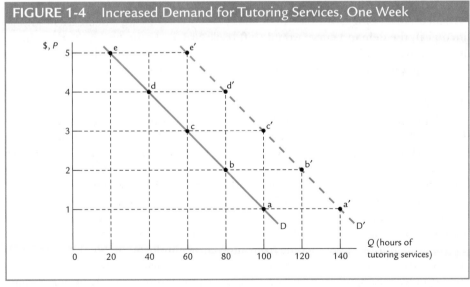

FIGURE 1-4 Increased Demand for Tutoring Services, One Week

Demand curve D′ represents larger quantities demanded at each price than does demand curve D.

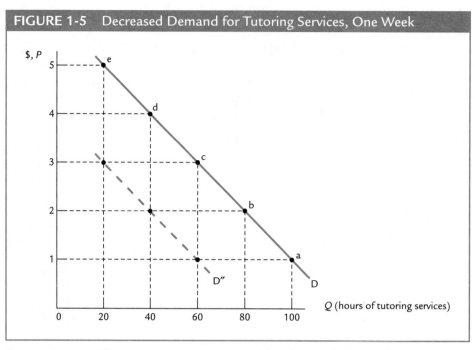

FIGURE 1-5   Decreased Demand for Tutoring Services, One Week

Demand curve D″ represents smaller quantities demanded at each price than does demand curve D.

or to the right. Note that for every price that existed before, a higher quantity demanded now exists.

If an event causing a decrease in demand were to occur (say, a decrease in student incomes), the demand curve would shift backward, or to the left. A decrease in demand is shown in Figure 1-5. Note that for every price on both demand curves, a smaller quantity is shown on D″ than on the original demand curve D.

Supply

Now let's consider the other side of the market for tutoring services, the supply side. Imagine the students at your school who not only don't need tutoring but who are actually able to tutor. This is the group of students who might supply tutoring services for a fee. What are the factors that influence these students' willingness to offer their tutoring services for sale? Probably the costs associated with providing the service are important. The most obvious cost is the value of the tutor's time. Remember that opportunity costs are always important. The opportunity costs of a tutor's time may be quantified easily if an adult tutor hires a baby-sitter while he or she tutors or if the tutor forgoes income from alternative employment. Some costs that are less easy to quantify are just as real. The tutor might be giving up precious study time, quality time with friends and family, or simply valued leisure time. Although it's hard to attach a dollar value to these costs, they remain important. Remember that there is no free lunch; *every choice has an opportunity cost; every activity chosen entails another activity given up.*

Another factor affecting the total quantity of tutoring services supplied will be the number of tutors available. If we experience an increase in enrollment of top-notch students who are dying to become tutors, we can expect more tutoring services suddenly to be supplied.

The price that tutors can receive for their services will also be an important determinant of their willingness to supply these services. Let's focus our attention on this price variable for a moment. Let's look at the supply of tutoring services in a one-week time period, when all the factors except price that might affect the number of tutoring hours supplied are held constant. It is realistic to assume that individual tutors will be more willing to provide tutoring services at a high price than at a low price. The higher price will allow them to cover their baby-sitting expenses more easily or will serve as a stronger inducement to give up leisure or time with friends and family. It will compensate them better for other job prospects they don't pursue because they are tutoring. In simple terms, the higher the price, the greater the incentive to provide tutoring services. Tutors (and business firms) will offer for sale a larger amount of the good or service at higher prices rather than at lower prices. This is known as the law of supply, which is usually stated as follows: *price and quantity supplied are positively related, all other things equal.* This simply means that price and quantity supplied (the amount offered for sale) change in the same direction. If price goes up, so does quantity supplied; if price goes down, so does quantity supplied.

The behavior of all tutors as a group might be summarized in Table 1-4 on page 14, which is a **supply schedule** showing different quantities of tutoring hours supplied (Q^S) at the alternative prices that the tutors might receive. The quantities represent the total number of hours supplied by the group as a whole at each alternative price over the specified one-week time period. All the factors other than price that might affect the tutors' willingness to tutor do not change. Thus, the only thing changing is the price determinant.

We can place the information from the supply schedule in Table 1-4 into a graph of supply, or a **supply curve**. The axes are identical to those in the demand graphs with price on the vertical axis and quantity on the horizontal axis. Plotting the information in each of the rows v through z gives us points v through z on the graph. Connecting these points gives us the supply curve S in Figure 1-6 on page 14. The supply curve indicates all possible combinations of quantity supplied and alternative prices with the assumption that all other factors affecting supply are held constant. Note that the supply curve is upward sloping, reflecting the **law of supply**: price and quantity supplied increase together.

What if one of the other factors affecting supply was to change? Baby-sitting costs might decrease so that some tutors would be more willing to provide tutoring services, for example. This would increase the supply of tutoring services. You can probably list other factors that would increase the supply of tutoring. Changes in the costs

Supply schedule
A table showing the quantities that suppliers are willing to sell at alternative prices during a specified time period.

Supply curve
A graph showing the quantities that suppliers are willing to sell at alternative prices during a specified time period.

Law of supply
There is a positive relationship between price and quantity supplied.

TABLE 1-4 Supply Schedule for Tutoring Services, One Week

Alternative	P ($ per hour)	Q^S (hours)
v	$1	20
w	$2	40
x	$3	60
y	$4	80
z	$5	100

FIGURE 1-6 Supply Curve for Tutoring Services, One Week

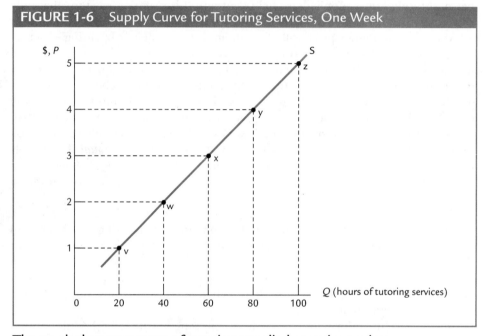

The graph shows amounts of tutoring supplied at various prices.

of producing or supplying a product are among the most important factors causing a shift in the supply curve.

An increase in the supply of tutoring services as a result of lower baby-sitting costs will result in an entirely new supply schedule, such as the one shown in Table 1-5. Note that for each price, a larger quantity supplied now exists. Lower costs always cause a forward shift in the curve, whereas higher costs always cause a backward shift in the curve.

If we plot this new information on the same graph as the original supply curve, we have an entirely new supply curve S′, as indicated in Figure 1-7. Supply has increased, and the supply curve has shifted forward, or to the right, showing increased quantities supplied at each of the given prices.

TABLE 1-5	Increased Supply Schedule for Tutoring Services, One Week	
Alternative	P ($ per hour)	Q^S (hours)
v'	$1	60
w'	$2	80
x'	$3	100
y'	$4	120
z'	$5	140

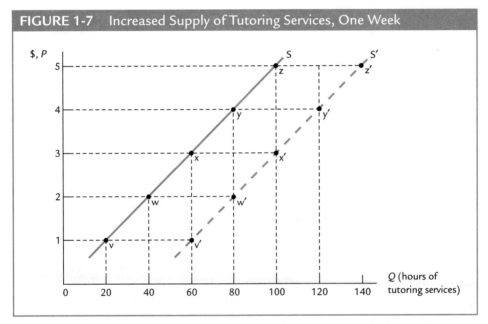

FIGURE 1-7 Increased Supply of Tutoring Services, One Week

Supply curve S' represents larger quantities of tutoring supplied at each price than does supply curve S.

If an event (such as an increase in baby-sitting costs) causing a decrease in the supply of tutoring were to occur, the supply curve would shift backward, or to the left. Figure 1-8 on page 16 shows a decrease in supply. The original supply curve is S. Note that there is a smaller quantity supplied at every price on supply curve S″ than on S.

Putting Demand and Supply Together

We can now consider the entire market for tutoring services at your school for the time period of one week. We have a demand schedule (or curve) that reflects the buyers' (students') attitudes toward purchasing tutoring services. And we have a supply schedule (or curve) that reflects the sellers' (tutors') attitudes toward supplying tutoring services. We simply have to put demand and supply together. Let's put them

FIGURE 1-8   Decreased Supply of Tutoring Services, One Week

Supply curve S″ represents smaller quantities supplied at each price than does supply curve S.

together graphically first. We will consider the original demand curve D and the original supply curve S, which are shown together in Figure 1-9.

As you can see, there is only one point in the graph (point E) where quantity demanded (which we read off the demand curve D) is equal to quantity supplied (which we read off the supply curve S). This point occurs at the intersection of demand and supply and corresponds to a price of $3 and quantities demanded and supplied of 60 hours a week. At point E, the market for tutoring services is in **equilibrium**, or a state of balance, because the amount of tutoring services that students are willing and able to purchase is identical to the amount that tutors are willing to provide. This equilibrium can also be seen in Table 1-6, which shows

Equilibrium
A state of balance; a point at which quantity demanded equals quantity supplied.

TABLE 1-6   Supply and Demand for Tutoring Services, One Week

P ($ per hour)	Q^S (hours)	Q^D (hours)
$1	20	100
$2	40	80
$3	**60**	**60**
$4	80	40
$5	100	20

FIGURE 1-9   Market for Tutoring Services, One Week

EconNews

"Students Learn
The Hard Way"

How has rising tuition affected the
supply and demand
for higher education?

Read a brief
summary when
you navigate to
Equilibrium under
Economic
Fundamentals.

*http://econapps.
swlearning.com*

The market will clear at point E. At $3, quantity demanded equals quantity supplied.

the original supply and demand schedules and (in bold) the equilibrium price and quantity.

The market for tutoring services naturally tends to move toward the equilibrium point. To illustrate this tendency, consider what would happen if tutors were charging less than the equilibrium price of $3 an hour. Suppose that the tutors were charging only $1 an hour. At $1, the quantity demanded (100) exceeds the quantity supplied (20) by 80 hours. There would be a **shortage** of tutoring services of 80 hours, because at $1, buyers regard tutoring as a bargain, whereas sellers have little incentive to provide tutoring. Students will bid for the tutoring services that are available, and in the process the price will be bid up. Put yourself in the position of a student who needs tutoring. You would quite likely offer slightly more than $1 to a tutor so that you would receive the tutoring instead of your friend. Your (former) friend would probably be trying to do the same. In this process, the average price of tutoring would be pushed up. The bidding up of the price will continue only as long as the shortage exists, and as the price rises, the shortage will disappear. Two things happen as price increases: (1) buyers decrease the quantity they demand, and (2) sellers increase the quantity they offer for sale. This process of rising price, decreasing

Shortage
A situation in
which quantity
demanded is
greater than
quantity supplied. This occurs only when
the price is
lower than the
market level.

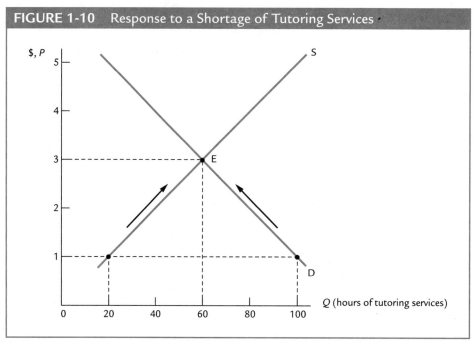

FIGURE 1-10   Response to a Shortage of Tutoring Services

At a price of $1, quantity demanded exceeds quantity supplied by 80 hours. The 80-hour shortage will cause price to rise to the equilibrium price of $3.

quantity demanded, and increasing quantity supplied is shown in Figure 1-10. The process will come to a screeching halt when equilibrium is reached at point E. Because the shortage no longer exists, the price will rise no higher. Economists usually refer to this phenomenon as the rationing function of price. This means that the movement of the price has ultimately rationed away the shortage. Without the ability of prices to adjust by moving upward, the shortage would have persisted indefinitely. Socialist countries had often done just that—they had prohibited prices from adjusting upward. As a result, shortages had been commonplace.

Now consider the opposite possibility. Tutors might be charging a price—say, $5—that is above the equilibrium price. Perhaps they feel that they can make a lot of income at this high price. There is, however, a problem in the market at this price. At $5 an hour, the quantity (20 hours per week) of tutoring services demanded will be very small. But tutors will be willing to supply a large quantity (100 hours per week) because they have so much incentive. The difference between the quantity that tutors supply and the amount that students actually buy (quantity demanded) is a **surplus** of unsold services in the market. Surpluses cause price to fall. Tutors will undercut one another's price to get some business, and the price will fall until it reaches the $3 equilibrium. As the price decreases, quantity demanded will increase, quantity supplied will decrease, and the surplus will disappear. This process is illustrated in Figure 1-11. The process comes to a halt when equilibrium is reached. The falling price has rationed away the surplus.

Surplus
A situation in which quantity supplied is greater than quantity demanded. This occurs only when the price is higher than the market level.

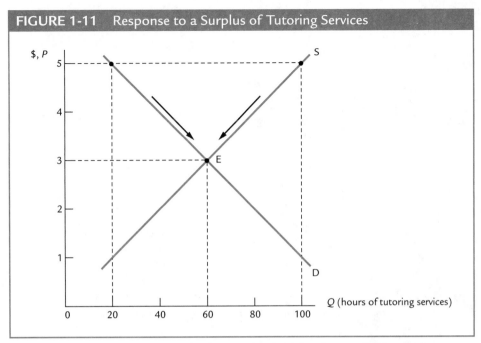

FIGURE 1-11 Response to a Surplus of Tutoring Services

At a price of $5, quantity supplied exceeds quantity demanded by 80 hours. This 80-hour surplus will cause price to fall to the equilibrium price of $3.

Shifts in Demand and Supply

The market for tutoring services will remain in equilibrium at point E unless some other factor affecting the market changes. Because things rarely remain unchanged, it is important to consider what might happen if the variables affecting either the demand for or the supply of tutoring services were to change.

Consider our earlier example in which an increase in student incomes caused an increase in the demand for tutoring services. The only thing that we are doing differently now is considering this shift in demand in the context of demand, supply, and equilibrium. The demand curve will shift forward to D′, as illustrated in Figure 1-12 on page 20. *Note that the supply curve will not shift.* The old demand curve D becomes irrelevant, and a new equilibrium E′ exists at the intersection of the new demand curve D′ and the old supply curve S. By reading the new equilibrium price and quantity off the respective axes, we see that price has increased to $4 an hour and quantity has increased to 80 hours per week. Because demand has increased, the market price has increased, and suppliers have moved up their supply curve and increased the amount that they are willing to offer for sale (the quantity supplied). The increased demand curve and the unchanged supply curve have thus caused an increase in both equilibrium price and equilibrium quantity.

The opposite phenomenon would have occurred if there had been a decrease in demand. Such a decrease is shown in Figure 1-13 on page 21. If student incomes had decreased, causing a decrease in demand, the demand curve would have shifted

FIGURE 1-12   Effects of Increased Demand for Tutoring Services

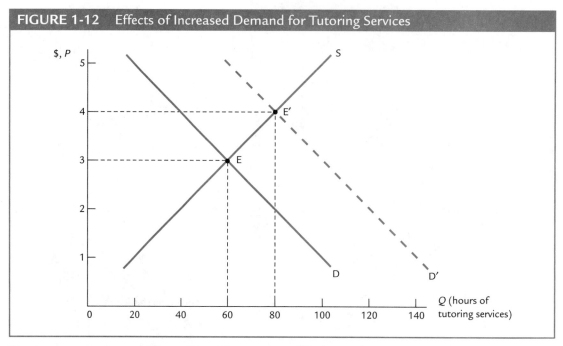

The increase in demand from D to D′ causes equilibrium price to increase from $3 to $4 and equilibrium quantity to increase from 60 to 80 hours.

backward to D″. The new equilibrium point would be E″ at a price of $2 an hour and a quantity exchanged of 40 hours per week. Both price and quantity would have decreased.

Now consider the supply side of the tutoring market. Recall that a decrease in baby-sitting costs causes an increase in the supply of tutoring. If this increase occurs, the supply curve will shift forward *but the demand curve will not shift*. This phenomenon is illustrated by the shift of supply from S to S′ in Figure 1-14.

The new equilibrium E′ is found at the intersection of the original demand curve D and the new supply curve S′. We see that the price has decreased to $2 an hour, while the quantity has increased to 80 hours per week. As a result of an increase in supply, market price went down, so students (consumers) moved down along their demand curve, increasing the amount of tutoring services that they were willing and able to buy. Because supply increased, price decreased and the quantity exchanged increased. The increased supply curve and the unchanged demand curve have caused a decrease in equilibrium price and an increase in equilibrium quantity.

If supply had decreased because baby-sitting costs had increased, causing tutors to desire a higher price for tutoring services, the opposite phenomenon would have occurred. As shown in Figure 1-15 on page 22, the supply curve would shift backward to S″ resulting in a new equilibrium E″. The price would be $4 an hour, and the

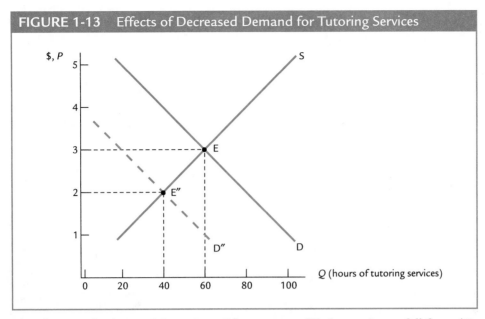

FIGURE 1-13   Effects of Decreased Demand for Tutoring Services

The decrease in demand from D to D" causes equilibrium price to fall from $3 to $2 and equilibrium quantity to fall from 60 to 40 hours.

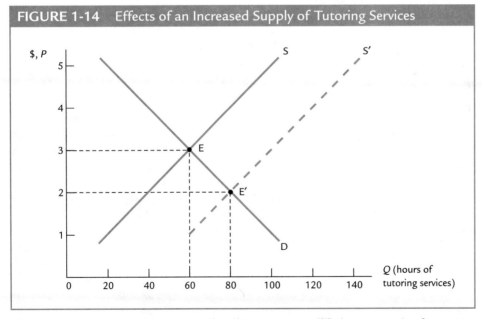

FIGURE 1-14   Effects of an Increased Supply of Tutoring Services

The increase in supply from S to S' will increase equilibrium quantity from 60 to 80 hours but decrease equilibrium price from $3 to $2.

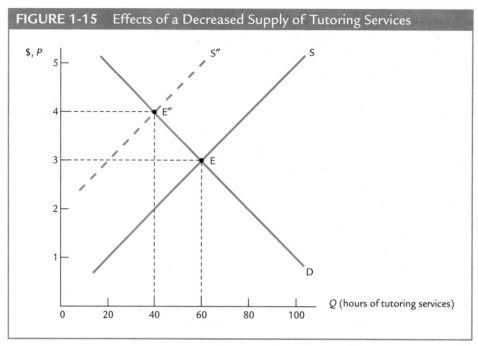

FIGURE 1-15   Effects of a Decreased Supply of Tutoring Services

The decrease in supply from S to S″ will increase equilibrium price from $3 to $4 and decrease equilibrium quantity from 60 to 40 hours.

quantity bought and sold would be 40 hours per week. The market price would be higher, but the equilibrium quantity would be lower.

The Real World

Whew! What a lot of graphs! But you now have learned the basic tools to answer many of life's economic questions. All markets have a demand (buyer's) side and a supply (seller's) side. And the things that affect supply and demand are the commonsense sorts of things described in the tutoring market example. Demand curves shift if the number of buyers changes, if consumers' incomes change, if consumers' tastes change, or if the prices of other goods that the consumers regard as substitutes or complements change. In our tutoring example, a substitute for tutoring might be buying and using the study guide that goes along with the textbook. Substitute relationships occur when the consumer substitutes one good for the other good. A classic example of substitutes is butter and margarine. Complements are the opposite of substitutes. If the consumer uses more of one good, he or she will also use more of the other. A good example of complementary goods is cameras and film. If the price of cameras goes down, all other things constant, more cameras will be purchased. With more cameras in the hands of consumers, there will be a greater demand for film.

Supply curves shift if the number of sellers changes or if the factors that affect the producers' (sellers') costs change. So, a rise in the energy costs of a manufacturer will decrease the supply of manufactured goods. If businesses must pay higher wage rates to produce the same amount of output, the supply of output will decrease. On the other hand, if the price of raw materials goes down, the supply of the product for which the materials are used will increase. If the government taxes the production of a good or service, the supply of output will decrease; if the government provides subsidies (which lowers costs), however, the supply of the product will increase. Technological change that increases business efficiency and lowers the cost of producing each unit of output will increase the supply of output.

Figure 1-16 shows the factors that commonly cause real-world demand or supply curves to shift. Assume that you wake up some morning and read the following newspaper headlines: "Drought in Brazil destroys coffee crop. Coffee prices skyrocket!" "Harry Potter book craze sweeps the country. Prices of Harry Potter books soar!" "Boycott of chocolate drives chocolate prices down.[1] Chocolate growers dismayed." "Great weather results in bumper crop of pumpkins. Pumpkin prices plummet!" How would you explain these price changes?

If you follow a step-by-step procedure, it is not hard to answer this question. First, draw a graph showing the particular market (coffee, books, chocolate, etc.) in equilibrium. Always label your equilibrium price along the vertical axis (label it P) and equilibrium quantity along the quantity axis (label it Q). Second, consider the situation that is occurring. Decide whether its first and primary effect is on consumers or suppliers. Your answer will determine whether the demand or supply curve will shift. *You will shift only one curve in each graph!* Determine whether this curve should increase or decrease, and shift the curve accordingly. Third, find the new point of

---

FIGURE 1-16   Factors That Cause Real-World Demand and Supply Curves to Shift

Factors That Cause Real-World Demand Curves to Shift

1. Changes in the number of consumers who wish to purchase the product.
2. Changes in the tastes of the consumers in the market.
3. Changes in the prices of complements or substitutes.
4. Changes in consumers' incomes.
5. Changes in consumers' expectations about the product's future price or availability.

Factors That Cause Real-World Supply Curves to Shift

1. Changes in the number of sellers in the market.
2. Changes in the prices of resources used to produce the product.
3. Changes in the technology used to produce the product.
4. Changes in the prices of other products that could be produced with the same resources.
5. Changes in government taxes or subsidies.
6. Changes in sellers' expectations about the product's future price.

FIGURE 1-17 Newspaper Headlines: Demand and Supply

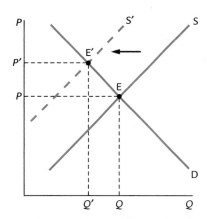

Drought in Brazil causes coffee supply to decrease, which causes a rise in coffee prices.

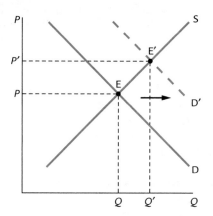

Harry Potter craze causes demand to increase, raising the price of Harry Potter books.

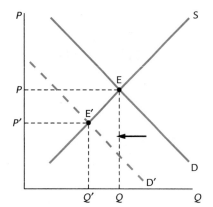

Boycott of chocolate will decrease the demand for chocolate, which causes the price of chocolate to fall.

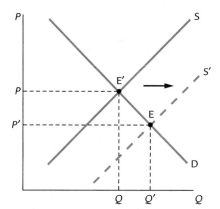

Great weather causes an increase in the supply of pumpkins, which causes a decrease in their price.

equilibrium and label the new equilibrium price and quantity along their respective axis. Finally, compare the new quantity with the old quantity and the new price with the old price. It's as easy as pumpkin pie when there is a bumper crop of pumpkins! See Figure 1-17 for the analysis of these newspaper headlines.

Which Comes First?

Which came first, the chicken or the egg? Which comes first, the price or the quantity? We know that price determines both quantity demanded and quantity supplied. Yet demand and supply together determine the market price of the product. In a market economy, it is the simultaneous interaction of all prices, quantities, demands, and supplies that ultimately determines the final market price and the market quantity exchanged.

EFFICIENCY AND EQUITY

Understanding demand and supply gives us greater insight into the working of the market economy and its production possibilities, because demand and supply determine how much of each particular good or service is produced. High prices encourage frugality. Only those most willing (with the greatest desire) or most able (with the greatest income) will purchase the product at high prices. The marketplace sifts out those with lesser preferences or lesser ability to afford the product and the market thus serves as an allocating mechanism. High prices also encourage producers to offer more for sale.

In many ways, this function of market prices is desirable. Prices encourage thrift and careful choices among competing goods. Goods and services are allocated to those most willing to pay. Thus, the market is an effective allocative device. Without prices, products might go to people who do not strongly desire them and might be wasted. Shortages of highly desirable goods and surpluses of less desirable ones might occur. But in the market, prices ration away these shortages and surpluses, suggesting that the marketplace is very **efficient** as a means of allocation and distribution.

Efficient Using resources in such a way as to maximize the desired output.

On the other hand, the distribution of goods and services may not be equitable. **Equity** is a value-laden concept, and economists cannot say whether a particular distribution is fair. But some of the results of market activity may not seem fair to some of us. A student may truly need tutoring services but not be able to afford them and thus fail the course. Children may go without milk, the homeless without shelter, and poor pregnant women without prenatal care because their low incomes render them unable to pay the prices that the market determines for these products. We might summarize by saying that the market entails both positive and negative aspects. It is often efficient, but not necessarily equitable.

Equity Fairness.

A GLIMPSE OF THE FUTURE

Most economists agree that the marketplace performs many useful functions. As just described, the marketplace is considered efficient. Market prices provide proper incentives for producers to supply desired products and for consumers to choose their purchases wisely. A market-based economy tends to be highly productive. The combination of competition and proper price signals encourages efficient production of the products desired by consumers in the least costly manner.

Despite the benefits of a market economy, most economists also recognize that the marketplace can also fail. The existence of many market failures does not necessarily imply that the marketplace itself is a failure. Rather, it points to ways that the government may become involved in the marketplace to assure that all societal needs are met. The following list of market failures also provides a glimpse into the chapters yet to come in this textbook.

Public Goods and Services

Public goods and services have unique characteristics that make it unlikely that the market will provide enough of them. As a result, the government often provides them. Public goods and services include national defense, police and fire protection, public libraries, highway construction, crime prevention, and others. At least to some point, the use of public goods and services by some of us does not keep others from using them. Your driving on the highway does not keep others from driving along it, for example. Public goods and services are unlikely to be provided by the marketplace because they cannot be divided into small segments and offered for sale. For example, it doesn't make sense for each individual consumer to purchase one mile of a highway. Furthermore, if a private consumer does buy such a good or service, it is difficult to keep people who do not pay for the product from using it. Take fire protection, for example. Suppose the 100 merchants in the downtown section of your town decide to pay a fee for fire protection. Suppose that one merchant refuses to pay for fire protection, and that the place of business of this individual starts on fire. Even though this person has not paid the fee, the other businesses cannot afford to let it burn. If it burns, it will endanger the properties of the other businesses. Fire protection is thereby provided. Most economists agree that the provision of public goods and services is an appropriate role for government. Our disagreement concerns just what goods and services these will be, and how much of them we want. These disagreements are not trivial; they are taken up in Chapter 2 on crime prevention activities. They are also addressed in topics involving education, health care, and others.

Spillovers

Spillovers
Costs or benefits of private market activity shifted onto society at large.

Economic efficiency and equity cannot occur when spillovers exist. Economic **spillovers** occur when some cost (or benefit) related to production or consumption "spills over" onto people not involved in the production or consumption of the good. Pollution of our environment is the most obvious example. If a manufacturer pollutes our air and water in the process of production, we will bear the costs of this pollution even if we don't own the company, work for the company, or buy its products. We bear the costs of pollution in terms of greater risk of illness, less aesthetic beauty, and lower-quality environment. The manufacturer has shifted part of the costs of production to society at large. Our natural resources are not being used appropriately, and our economy is not addressing our real needs and concerns. Our own dissatisfaction with the degraded environment will not remedy the problem unless collectively we are able to channel our concern through active government involvement. Issues surrounding pollution and government response are addressed in Chapter 3. Other goods and services provide spillover benefits to society. Education, discussed in Chapter 4, provides significant spillover benefits to society. The educated person is likely to be a more productive worker and to contribute more than the uneducated person to the economy. The educated person is more likely to vote and otherwise participate in government and public affairs. The educated person is less likely to be chronically unemployed or to commit a violent crime. He or she is more likely to pay taxes and less likely to be on welfare. The market will not, by itself, provide sufficient levels of education, because the market does not reflect these spillover benefits.

Equity

We've already noted that the marketplace is not necessarily equitable. Discrimination is an issue of equity and is addressed in Chapter 5. Poverty and inequality of income distribution are also issues of equity. We may argue that the inability of low-income people to meet their basic needs is unfair. We may also argue that the extreme inequality of income distribution within the U.S. economy is unfair. These issues are addressed in Chapter 6 on U.S. poverty. Other topics in other chapters, such as housing and health care, also raise issues of equity. In addition, the problem of poverty at the global level, as well as how to reduce it, is addressed in Chapter 7.

Market Power and Trade

Our example of the demand and supply of tutoring services at a large university is one that approximates **pure competition**. There were many suppliers of tutoring services so that no single tutor could dictate the market price. If 1 of 100 tutors were to charge an exorbitant price, students would seek the services of the other 99. Competition protects us from unreasonable prices. We would not be protected if there were only one tutor. This monopoly supplier of tutoring services could charge a high price and consumers desiring the service would be forced to pay it. Even if there were a few more tutors available, this small group could hold back-alley meetings and fix the price of their services at a very high level.

Pure competition
A market in which many independent producers compete to sell a standardized product to many independent buyers.

Without competition, we would be at the mercy of this group. We would say that the single supplier and the price-fixing group possess **market power**, which is the ability of a supplier to influence the market price of its product. It is only with a large number of tutors—so many that it is unrealistic for them all to come to agreement about prices and so many that no individual supplier produces for a large share of the market—that market power is absent. To the extent that many industries in the United States consist of just a few dominant producers (examples are the automobile, steel, and breakfast cereal industries), competition is reduced and society's well-being suffers. This problem of market power is discussed in Chapter 8.

Market power
The ability to influence the market price of a product.

Since market power arises when a small number of suppliers influence the market price of their product, it is reasonable to conclude that a larger number of suppliers, whether these are domestic or foreign producers, will serve to reduce market power. Many people are unaware of the important contribution of international trade in enhancing competition and reducing market power. Nevertheless, international trade is controversial, and these issues are explored in Chapter 9.

EconNews

"Winn-Dixie Loses in Dixie"

This news story gives a real-life example of perfect competition. Find it by navigating to Perfect Competition under Microeconomics.

http://econapps. swlearning.com

Special Markets

The markets for some products are often considered too important to be left alone to the marketplace. These markets include housing, health care, agriculture, and the care of the elderly. Most societies have concluded that government involvement is necessary in most or all of these markets. Certainly, housing and health care, addressed in Chapters 10 and 11, are too important to human well-being to be left to the vagaries of the marketplace. Similarly, food production, addressed in Chapter 12 on agriculture, and care of the elderly, addressed in Chapter 13 on Social Security, are also areas that our government involves itself in the marketplace.

Stability

Finally, we return to the topic of production possibilities and employment. The factors that determine whether our nation will be *on* the production possibilities curve (operating at full employment) or *below* the production possibilities curve (with unemployed resources) are very volatile. Thus, at times we may have very low employment, and at other times we may have high employment. Closely related are the factors affecting the average level of prices throughout our economy. When the average price level rises, we say that we have **inflation**. Because prices and employment tend to fluctuate a great deal, we say that our market economy is inherently unstable. We address these issues in Chapter 14 on unemployment and inflation, Chapter 15 on government macroeconomic policy, and Chapter 16 on taxes and borrowing. In the process, we discover how our government and our central banking system can intervene in many ways to ensure greater stability of prices and employment.

Inflation
A rise in the average price level in the economy.

Some Final Comments to Students

We've examined the production possibilities curve as a means of discussing scarcity. And we've studied the graphs of demand and supply to understand distribution. We will use these topics throughout the text to analyze a variety of microeconomic and macroeconomic issues. **Microeconomics** deals with individual activity within the economy, whereas **macroeconomics** deals with the economy as a whole. Microeconomics covers topics such as the distribution of income within the country and the nature of individual markets such as agriculture, whereas macroeconomics covers topics such as total income and total output in the economy. When we speak of total output, we are really referring to gross domestic product. More specifically, **gross domestic product (GDP)** is the value of an economy's total output of goods and services produced within a particular year. GDP will be a very useful concept throughout the textbook because we often use it as a frame of reference. For example, it is somewhat meaningless to talk of the millions of dollars spent on health care when a more meaningful topic of discussion is the expenditure on health care relative to GDP. This is because GDP is really the nation's capacity to generate income that can be spent on health care or on any other good or service.

Micro-economics
The study of individual areas of activity within the total economy.

Macro-economics
The study of the total economy.

Gross domestic product (GDP)
Total output of an economy.

The terms private and public are also used throughout the text. The term **private** refers to individual people and businesses. It relates to *private* markets, which reflect consumer demand and producer supply. We speak of *private* spending (by people and businesses) and *private* ownership (by people and businesses). On the other hand, the term **public** refers to the government. Thus, we can speak of *public* spending and *public* ownership. Recall that we have already used these terms as we considered private and public goods.

Private
Individual people and businesses.

As our world becomes increasingly internationalized, awareness of the economics of domestic social issues is insufficient. We must also be aware of our international economy. We must enter into the exciting world of international trade and finance, the devastating presence of international poverty, and the fascinating set of international issues addressed in Chapter 17. The world is alive on our TV sets and computer screens, in our travels and contacts with international students and faculty, and in our jobs of the future. We must be aware of our global world!

Public
Government.

And now we've come back to the topic we started with: that is, *you,* the student. How do *you* fit into this world of economic problems and issues? What do these problems and issues mean for *your* life and well-being? And how can *you* affect the world around you? The Epilogue tackles these questions. The way to begin making changes is to educate ourselves. With that in mind, let's begin to address our social and economic concerns!

VIEWPOINT: CONSERVATIVE VERSUS LIBERAL

This book is intended to get you to think. As you acquire a basic understanding of economics, you also acquire a basic framework within which to form and justify your personal opinions about social issues. Are you a conservative or a liberal? Are you conservative on some issues and liberal on others? Do you even know what these terms mean in the context of economics? From a U.S. perspective, being an **economic conservative** generally means believing in only a limited role for government in the economy. In the conservative view, the free market operates relatively well by itself, so that little government intervention in the form of regulations, taxes, and programs is needed. Indeed, conservatives believe that if left alone, the market will solve most economic problems. The conservative view exists on the right end of the economic philosophical spectrum. Being an **economic liberal**, on the other hand, generally means supporting far greater government involvement in the economy. In the liberal view, the marketplace entails many shortcomings, shortcomings that can be rectified only by government involvement. The liberal view is on the left end of the economic philosophical spectrum.

We have already discovered that although the marketplace tends to be efficient, it is not necessarily equitable. We've recognized that many market failures exist and that many goods and services are considered too important to leave solely to the market. All of these suggest some proper role for government in the economy. Nevertheless, there is probably no debate more contentious in our economy than the ideal *degree* of government involvement in our economy.

The Viewpoint boxes at the end of each chapter clarify the positions of both liberals and conservatives in order to help you formulate your own beliefs. Keep in mind that while this section is intended to show opposite viewpoints, economists and policymakers often find themselves closer to the middle. On many issues, agreement among economists is widespread. Also keep in mind that an economic conservative or liberal is different from a social conservative or liberal. Social conservatives, for example, may oppose gun control and support prayer in schools. A social conservative (or liberal) may be entirely different from an economic conservative (or liberal).

Now, enjoy the discovery of your own opinions about government involvement in the economy in the chapters to come!

Economic conservative
A person who believes in very low levels of government involvement in the economy.

Economic liberal
A person who believes in high levels of government involvement in the economy.

SUMMARY

Economics deals primarily with scarcity: how shall we allocate our limited world resources to satisfy our seemingly unlimited human wants? Limited resources translate into limited production possibilities. The production possibilities curve shows us the alternative combinations of the maximum amounts of two different goods that can be produced during any particular time period, assuming full use of our technology and resources. Unemployment of resources results in production levels lower than those possible. Economic growth over time results in increasingly higher levels of production of all goods.

Our output and distribution decisions are mostly made in the markets for individual goods and services. Demand for a product by consumers and supply of a product by producers both hinge on the prices that must be paid or received. Demand and supply together determine the market equilibrium, establishing the going market price and the quantity exchanged. Our market economy ensures that goods and services are distributed only to those most willing and able to pay the market price. Markets are often considered to be efficient, but inequitable.

Market failures include the problem of public goods and services, the existence of spillovers, the issue of equity, the presence of market power, and the lack of stability in our economy. An important issue is the role of government versus the free market. Economic liberals prefer a large role for government in the economy, and economic conservatives prefer a small role. As you continue your reading, you will make your own decisions about whether you are liberal or conservative on certain issues. Finally, you will consider your role within our world economy.

NOTES

1. Many activists are encouraging a boycott of chocolate that has been produced with cocoa beans from West Africa. The situation of "cocoa slavery" will be discussed more in Chapter 9 on international trade.

DISCUSSION QUESTIONS

1. Suppose your friend is a hawk on defense and insists that we must bolster our national defense, whatever the cost. How can you use economic logic to make him aware of the opportunity costs associated with his objective?

2. Unemployment imposes serious hardship on out-of-work individuals and their families. What are the costs of unemployment to society as a whole? (Keep in mind the production possibilities curve.)

3. Why, in a rich nation, is it important that we fully use our resources and technology to maximize our nation's output? Is it only the level of *total* output that is important, or are the *types* of output that we produce also important? Do you think that the *distribution* of this output (and the income generated by its production) is just as important as its total amount?

4. How do you think our nation's output should be distributed—according to income or according to some other standard (such as basic human need)?

5. Equilibrium implies that quantity demanded equals quantity supplied at a particular price. Must consumers and producers actually sit down to discuss and decide on an equilibrium market price, such as we may see in a farmers' market or a flea market? Why or why not?

6. Does the efficiency of the price mechanism ensure that our market-based economy is an equitable one? Why or why not?

7. The following schedules are for bushels of apples in a local market. Graph the supply and demand curves. What are the equilibrium price and quantity?

Price	Quantity Demanded	Quantity Supplied
$20	200	1,000
$18	400	800
$16	600	600
$14	800	400
$12	1,000	200

Now assume that an early freeze has decreased the apple harvest, and the new supply schedule is as follows. Has supply increased or decreased? What are the new equilibrium price and quantity? (Note that the demand curve is unchanged.)

Price	Quantity Supplied
$20	600
$18	400
$16	200
$14	0

8. Go to the Web site at **www.netec.mcc.ac.uk/ JokEc**, find a good economics joke, and share it with your teacher!

9. Become familiar with the EconApps Web site at **http://econapps.swlearning.com** and explore some of the topics mentioned in the margins of your book. This site includes South-Western's dynamic Web features: EconNews Online, EconDebate Online, and EconData Online. Organized by pertinent Economic topics and searchable by topic or feature, these will deepen your understanding of theoretical concepts through hands-on exploration and analysis of the latest economic news stories, policy debates, and data. You, the student, will find this site invaluable.

10. One additional source that may be useful if you need to do research on economics topics is the Web site of the British periodical, *The Economist*. Its articles on various topics can usually be understood by beginning students of economics. You can find this site at **www.economist.com**.

CHAPTER 1 APPENDIX: INCREASING OPPORTUNITY COSTS

The production possibilities curve that we've considered is actually a simplified representation of the real world. Recall that for each additional 20 units of roses that were produced, society had to give up the production of 30 units of bread. This ratio of 20 units of roses to 30 units of bread remained constant, regardless of how much bread and roses were actually produced. In the real world, this ratio usually is not constant, but rather it is increasing. In other words, as we produce larger quantities of roses, we must usually give up increasingly larger quantities of bread. This is another way of saying that the opportunity cost increases as we produce more of one particular good. It increases because we ultimately use resources that are less well suited to producing more of this particular good. In our example, we would begin production by using those resources that are best suited for each product. As we produce more roses, we would eventually need to use resources that are more suitable for bread production so that we would need to use larger and larger quantities of these resources to make up for their lower productivity. In other words, we must give up increasingly larger amounts of bread production in order to produce additional roses. And this means that the opportunity cost of rose production increases as we produce more and more of it. The same would be true for the production of bread.

Increasing opportunity costs
As more of one good is produced, society must give up increasingly larger amounts of the alternative good.

Table 1-7 shows the production possibilities for bread and roses, under the more realistic assumption that opportunity costs are increasing. We note that if we begin with alternative A, 150 tons of bread and 0 tons of roses are produced. If we increase rose production by 20 tons, we will give up 5 tons of bread. If we produce 20 more tons of roses, we will give up 15 tons of bread. And if we produce 20 more tons of roses, we will give up 20 tons of bread. In other words, we have **increasing opportunity costs**: as more and more of one good is produced, society must continually sacrifice increasingly larger amounts of the other good.

TABLE 1-7	Production Possibilities Table with Increasing Opportunity Cost	
Alternative	**Bread (tons)**	**Roses (tons)**
A	150	0
B	145	20
C	130	40
D	110	60
E	70	80
F	0	100

FIGURE 1-18 Production Possibilities Curve with Increasing Opportunity Costs

Points A through F show alternative combinations of bread and roses that the economy can produce.

CHAPTER 2 ROADMAP

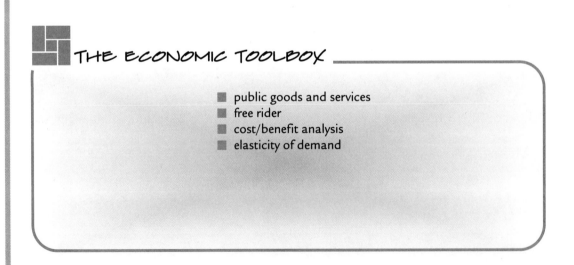

Chapter 5
Discrimination
Drug laws may result in discriminatory incarceration

Chapter 7
World Poverty
U.S. efforts to fumigate drug sources worsens health and poverty in less developed countries

Chapter 2
Crime and Drugs

Chapter 11
Health Care
Drugs have public health consequences and so would the legalization of drugs

Chapter 10
Housing
Public housing concentrates poverty and leads to dysfunctions such as drug use

THE ECONOMIC TOOLBOX

- public goods and services
- free rider
- cost/benefit analysis
- elasticity of demand

CRIME AND DRUGS

Corporate corruption has struck at investor confidence, offending the conscience of our nation . . . The era of low standards and false profits is over; no boardroom in America is above or beyond the law. No more easy money for corporate criminals—just hard time.

—President George W. Bush, July 6, 2003

oes the opening quotation to this chapter surprise you? When we speak of crime, we must be sure to include all types of criminal behavior, from drug possession and violent crimes, to the white-collar crime to which President Bush refers. Indeed, the publicity surrounding corporate crime has reached such a level as to suggest that this form of crime is the status quo for the new millennium. But first let's consider more conventional crime.

Consider the statistics on crime in the United States, as documented by The National Center for Victims of Crime. One murder is committed every 33 minutes, one rape or sexual assault every 2 minutes, one burglary every 10 seconds, and one theft every 2 seconds. Additionally, sixty-two women are victimized by an intimate person every hour, a person is killed in an alcohol-related traffic crash every 41 minutes, identity theft is reported every 6 minutes, three women and/or men become victims of stalking every minute, and a child is abused and/or neglected every 36 seconds.[1] Given these statistics, it's no wonder that some of us are very concerned about the social problem of crime in the United States.

Crime, broadly defined, imposes huge costs on the United States each year. These costs include both the damage to property and to people, as well as the cost of policies undertaken by government to prevent and punish criminal activity. Not all these costs can easily be assigned a monetary value. We can calculate the replacement cost of a building destroyed by arson, but what is the cost of an assault victim's trauma and pain? One element of these costs that is relatively easy to measure is the cost of administering the criminal justice system, which consists of police, courts, and prisons. This system, intended to prevent and punish crime, was responsible for expenditures of $147 billion annually by federal, state, and local governments by the new millennium.[2] Indeed, expenditures for the criminal justice system are an increasingly important item in state government budgets over time. Resources absorbed by the criminal justice system cannot be used for tax relief, education, housing, health care, or any other worthwhile purpose, so it is important that these resources be used wisely. Economics may help us to analyze the effectiveness of our policies to combat crime.

When we think of crime, we usually think of violent crimes such as murder, rape, robbery, and assault. Perhaps we also include various offenses against property, such as arson and theft. However, a crime is any action that is forbidden by law and carries criminal penalties, which often include imprisonment. Among other crimes in the United States are gambling, prostitution, possession of and trafficking in drugs, and sales of pornography. These are crimes because society, or a significant portion of society, thinks they are bad and has prohibited them by law.

The Federal Bureau of Investigation (FBI) reports the number of serious crimes that occur per hundred thousand people in the country. These crime rates indicate that as of the year 2000, crime had fallen for the ninth year in a row. However, the decline in 2000 was the smallest drop during this nine-year time period. More disconcerting is the fact that the *serious* crime rate increased in 2001. More specifically, serious crimes increased by 2.1 percent in 2001, including a 2.5 percent increase in murders, a less than 1 percent increase in forcible rapes, and a 3.7 percent increase in robberies.[3] Although it is too early to discern whether these increases represent a trend, we can certainly ascribe part of the problem to the failing economy, which is discussed in more detail in Chapter 14 on unemployment and inflation. Despite the earlier years of improvements in crime statistics, the level of crime still seems high and people indicate in opinion surveys that they do not feel safer.

In this chapter, we will look at several issues involving crime and economics. We will begin by examining the economic characteristics of crime prevention and the proper focus for evaluation of our criminal justice system. Then will consider the issue of white-collar crime and analyze the controversy over legalization of so-called victimless crimes, using drugs as an example.

CRIME PREVENTION

Crime Prevention as a Public Good

Police activity and other crime prevention measures are examples of **public goods and services**. These goods and services, first discussed as market failures in Chapter 1, have characteristics that make private market production of them inefficient. First of all, public goods are **indivisible**, which means that they cannot be divided reasonably into small enough units to be sold in a market to individual consumers. (It doesn't make sense for each of us to purchase 1/100 of a criminal justice system, for example.) Second, up to a point, public goods and services are **nonrivalrous**. This means that the protection afforded to one citizen by a police officer on patrol, for example, does not "use up" the benefits of police protection and prevent other citizens from receiving the same benefits. (Most goods are rivalrous. Consider a hamburger: if you eat it, no one else can.) Finally, public goods are **nonexcludable** in that we cannot prevent specific citizens from deriving benefits from crime prevention activity. This last characteristic of public goods means that they are subject to the **free rider problem**—for example, if police protection was provided by the private market, we would be unable to withhold the benefits of safer streets from those who refuse to pay. (Most goods, on the other hand, are excludable, so no free rider problem exists. A good example is a theater seat; you can't get one if you don't have a ticket.)

The private market is extremely efficient in providing hamburgers and theater seats and many other goods that are divisible, rivalrous, and excludable. The intersection of demand and supply at the equilibrium price results in neither shortages nor surpluses, and both buyers and sellers agree that the value of the product is the equilibrium price. But the private market is not efficient in providing public goods. Therefore, we usually have the government provide public goods and services and we finance them with tax revenues.

There are many examples of public goods and services besides crime prevention. Examples of these include fire protection, public libraries, public schools and universities, national defense, the space program, highway construction, and public parks. What other examples can you think of?

Crime Prevention Measures

Crime prevention measures are undertaken by the police, the criminal courts, and our prison system. Police cars patrolling our neighborhoods, police-sponsored activities for young people, the support of neighborhood watch programs, and the investigation of crimes are among the duties of the police. The courts are responsible for bringing to trial those who have been accused of violating criminal law and who have been apprehended by the police. The prison system exists to incarcerate, punish, and sometimes rehabilitate those convicted of crimes. Some practices, such as the operation of programs for disadvantaged youth, are preventive in that they may keep crime from occurring. Other activities involving the investigation of crimes, trial of suspects, and sentencing of those found guilty are crime prevention measures because they have a deterrent effect.

Evaluation by Cost-Benefit Analysis

The appropriate method, to evaluate government policy is **cost-benefit analysis**. Using this method, we add up the benefits from a particular course of action and compare them to the costs. The activity is justified only if the benefits are greater than the costs. Furthermore, if two policies both have greater benefits to society than their costs, the one with the larger **net benefits**, or excess of benefits over cost, should be adopted. Cost-benefit analysis is also discussed in the context of environmental protection policies in Chapter 3.

Benefits and Costs of Crime Prevention Activities

In the context of anticrime policy, the benefits of crime prevention activities include the value of property damage that is prevented, as well as the medical expenses, psychological trauma, loss of income, and other expenses that are *not* incurred when criminal assaults are prevented. Costs of anticrime activity include the costs of

Nonexcludable
A characteristic of public goods in that their benefits cannot be kept from persons who do not pay for the goods' provision in a private market.

Free rider problem
A situation in which individuals that do not pay their share for a good or service nevertheless enjoy its benefits.

Cost-benefit analysis
A study that compares the costs and benefits of a policy or program.

Net benefits
The excess of benefits over costs.

equipment, such as squad cars and prison cells; the salaries and fringe benefits of police, court, and corrections personnel; and the costs of administering the system. Can you think of other costs?

Our direct expenditures on the criminal justice system have increased markedly during the past three decades. For the period between 1982 and 1998, for example, spending on police protection increased by 244 percent, expenditures on our judicial system increased by 314 percent, and expenditures on corrections increased by 442 percent. Even after adjusting for inflation, these increases mean that far more resources are allocated to today's criminal justice system. In terms of the production possibilities curve introduced in Chapter 1, resources used in the criminal justice system are not available for other uses. Figure 2-1 shows a production possibilities curve with crime prevention on the vertical axis. The curve illustrates that resources used for crime prevention are not available for other uses such as education. Furthermore, we have moved from a point such as A to one such as B, which indicates increased criminal justice activity relative to other goods and services over the past quarter century or more.

Increased Costs of Our Prison System

The greatest percentage increase in spending on the criminal justice system is for corrections activities. The increase in resources devoted to our prison system mainly reflects a change in the thrust of our crime control policies. We now lock up in prison, or incarcerate, far more people than we did in the past. In 1999, we had nearly five times as many prison inmates as we had in 1970, and the incarceration rate has

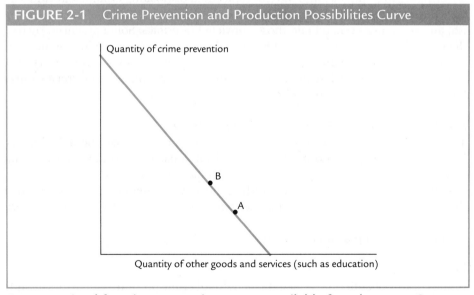

FIGURE 2-1   Crime Prevention and Production Possibilities Curve

Resources used for crime prevention are not available for other uses. Over time, the United States has moved from a point such as A to a point such as B on the curve.

continued to grow. The U.S. incarceration rate of 682 inmates per 100,000 people is the second-highest incarceration rate reported by any country; it is second only to Russia's rate of 685.[4] Higher levels of incarceration and longer prison sentences are supposed to reduce crime in two ways. They deter would-be offenders from committing crimes because of the increased likelihood of a prison sentence. And they physically prevent convicts from committing new crimes while they are in prison. This movement toward prison expansion and greater incarceration is perhaps the most controversial aspect of our current crime prevention activities. As a result, there has been significant effort to rationally evaluate this policy by cost-benefit analysis. The results of the studies, however, are not conclusive. Let us see why.

Empirical Studies of the Trend Toward Higher Incarceration Rates

The discussion of our imprisonment policy is usually couched in terms of (1) decreasing violent crimes against persons or (2) prison overcrowding and the nature of the prison population. We all agree that we want to prevent rapes, murders, and muggings. Whether harsher sentences and more prisons prevent these and other crimes is the question.

Decreasing Violent Crimes Against Persons

Some researchers have indicated that the violent crime rate has indeed gone down as a result of our tougher policy; others have disagreed. These conflicting conclusions are the result of differences in research methods. Specifically, some studies control for age, whereas others do not.

Ages 15 to 29 are violence-prone years in our society. As people mature, they are less likely to commit violent acts. The average age of the U.S. population is increasing, which in itself should cause a decrease in our violent crime rate. Age adjustment of data takes into account this changing demographic characteristic of the population in an attempt to rid the data of age bias. When the data are adjusted for the age distribution of the population, results indicate that a relatively small amount of crime is reduced by "get-tough" policies. When the data are not adjusted, the results indicate a larger reduction in crime.

In terms of cost-benefit analysis, studies that use age-adjusted data tend to find few benefits and great costs associated with higher incarceration rates. Studies without age adjustments find that the benefits of increased incarceration greatly exceed the costs. Thus, conflicting research methods lead to uncertain conclusions.

Prison Overcrowding and the Nature of the Prison Population

The second aspect of our incarceration policy concerns prison overcrowding and the need to continually build more prisons to accommodate the increased number of prisoners. This need will, of course, lead to a still greater allocation of resources to corrections. Although crime rates fell throughout the 1990s, the prison population soared. A number of factors contributed to this increase. Let's consider three of these.

First, mandatory minimum sentences have been established for drug violations, and now one in four prisoners is a drug offender. These laws were established in response to the epidemic use of illegal drugs in the 1970s and 1980s, in an effort to "get tough" with drug offenders. The outcome, though, is that there is less discretion for judges in individual situations. Some commentators believe that the population that has been harmed most by mandatory sentences has been women. Often these women become involved in relationships with criminal men, and they may become peripherally involved with drugs as a result. Although these women are not serious offenders, they and their children suffer from the women's long incarcerations. Indeed, research by the Department of Justice and other agencies has documented that many prisoners with mandatory sentences are low-level offenders whose continued imprisonment is extremely costly and wasteful of prison space.

The second factor in rising imprisonment is the 1994 federal crime bill, which contained a Truth in Sentencing provision. Under this law, half the states have qualified for federal prison funding by changing their sentencing laws to require that certain offenders serve at least 85 percent of their prison sentence before being considered for parole.

Third, the federal government and nearly half the states have passed "three strikes and you're out" laws that require sentences of life for a third conviction of certain crimes. This movement originated in California, where a three-strikes law was passed almost 10 years ago after the kidnapping and murder of a 12-year-old California child. Other states have passed similar laws as a result of public outrage over repeat offenders. However, despite good intentions, these laws have resulted in life imprisonment of many people for relatively minor crimes. For example, the California law has resulted in bizarre situations. One man whose third crime was stealing videocassettes and another man whose third offense was stealing golf clubs were both given life sentences in prison. Many other Californians have received life sentences as a result of other nonviolent crimes such as drug possession. As of this writing, the Supreme Court will soon decide whether the California law violates the Eighth Amendment's protection against cruel and unusual punishment in these types of cases. Those involved with the criminal justice system are anxiously awaiting this decision, which may have ramifications for criminal justice decisions around the nation.

U.S. Attorney General John Ashcroft stepped up the pressure of the U.S. Justice Department on federal judges in August 2003. He directed government lawyers to report to him any federal judge who hands out sentences that are softer than federal sentencing guidelines. Many federal judges in turn argue that this prevents them from dealing individually with individual cases.

As a result of all three of these policies, the national prison population rose to nearly two million by 2002.[5] States have built new and larger prisons, but the prison population has been increasing as rapidly as has prison capacity.

WHITE-COLLAR CRIME

The term *white-collar crime* is generally used to describe crime by business managers, as well as their supporting structure of boards of directors, accountants, investment bankers, lawyers, and other professionals who engage in dishonest practices for financial gain. Since it is a nonviolent crime, many people are less concerned about white-collar crime than some of the other crimes we've discussed. Nevertheless, white-collar crime is real and seems to be growing in epidemic proportions. Certainly, the individuals and businesses that are victims of white-collar crime experience as great a loss as those who are victims of outright thievery. And the ability of our federal, state, and local governments to provide basic services is threatened by the tax evasion that is often part of the white-collar criminal activity.

The early 2000s arose as banner years for white-collar crime, with revelations of outrageous compensation packages for managers, loss of pensions and savings funds for employees, and allegations of abuse by large corporations including Enron, World-Com, Tyco, Global Crossing, and others. In addition, campaign financing has been exploited by corporate financiers in a manner that threatens the very meaning of democracy. In the midst of his second year in office, President George W. Bush signed a corporate responsibility law that he vowed would improve oversight over business practices and create sanctions for white-collar criminals. In the context of a grand White House ceremony to commemorate his signing of this law, President Bush stated his opposition to corporate crime in the quotation that opens this chapter.

SHOULD DRUGS BE LEGALIZED?

According to the findings of the 2001 National Household Survey on Drug Abuse, which asks people age 12 or older about their drug use in the month prior to the survey, the percentage of people that said they were marijuana users increased from 4.8 percent in 2000 to 5.4 percent in 2001. Prior to this, the numbers had held roughly steady between 1996 and 2000. In addition, some 7.1 percent of the same population reported using some type of illicit drug in 2001. This compares with 6.3 percent in 2000. Nearly one-fifth of young people age 18 to 25 said that they had used illicit drugs.[6]

One of the most controversial topics in the issue of drug use, and in the entire field of crime and criminology today, is legalization or decriminalization of illegal drugs. If we were to legalize these drugs, we would simply repeal the laws that make possessing and selling drugs a crime. If we were to decriminalize the possession or selling of drugs, we would reduce the severity of the laws against these offenses, making them misdemeanors punishable by modest fines. Economic theory can add another dimension to the discussion of this emotionally charged subject. Furthermore, the economic analysis we use here can be extended to other related topics. Let us begin by discussing the possibility of legalizing drugs.

Background on the Legal Status of Drugs

The United States has a history of prohibiting or regulating the use of mind-altering substances. Laws and public policy concerning these substances do, however, change over time. Opiates have been illegal since 1914 and marijuana since 1937. Alcohol was entirely prohibited between 1920 and 1933. Currently, alcohol and tobacco are legal but cannot be sold legally to minors. All of these substances are at least somewhat addictive, and our dominant attitude is that, at a minimum, they should be regulated. Legalization of drugs is therefore unlikely, but at least partial decriminalization might be politically feasible.

Despite widespread opposition to legalization of drugs in the United States, drug laws and policy have been much more relaxed in many European countries. In addition, Canada is now considering the legalization or decriminalization of marijuana

EconLinks

"Should Marijuana Be Decriminalized?"

Read the full debate under the Scarcity, Choice, and Opportunity Cost category.

http://econapps. swlearning.com

possession. These countries may provide better evidence of whether legalization of drug use is beneficial.

The War on Drugs: U.S. Antidrug Policy

In the last half of the twentieth century, two U.S. presidents have declared war on drugs: Richard Nixon in 1971 and Ronald Reagan in 1982. The drug war has been one of the most popular of our recent conflicts. The majority of the populace supports the concept. *In economic terms, the so-called war on drugs involves measures to decrease both the supply of and the demand for drugs.*

Decreasing the Supply of Drugs

Among the measures designed to decrease the supply of drugs have been (1) efforts to prevent drugs from entering the country and (2) increases in the severity of the punishment for selling drugs. We have hired more personnel: federal agents for the FBI and Drug Enforcement Agency (DEA), U.S. attorneys to prosecute drug cases, and clerical staff. We have given drug enforcement agencies more money with which to operate, and we have redirected dollars formerly allocated to drug treatment programs and research into law enforcement programs. We have built more prison cells to accommodate more people with drug-related convictions. We have passed stricter laws and cut through bureaucracy in the attempt to decrease the supply of illegal drugs on the streets of our cities.

Since the 1980s, efforts to stem the supply of drugs coming into this country from abroad have involved the U.S. military. The century-old Posse Comitatus Act, which prohibited the military from enforcing civil laws, was amended in 1982 to permit the war chest of the U.S. military to be used for drug enforcement. As a result, the military is now involved in drug enforcement training, intelligence gathering, and detection. Military personnel operate navy, army, and marine corps equipment for these purposes under the direction of civilian agencies.

Decreasing the Demand for Drugs

To decrease demand, we have instituted drug awareness and education programs for our youth. To deter our citizens from experimenting with drugs, we have increased the penalties for the possession of illegal drugs. Our prisons have drug treatment programs for offenders. Any education or treatment program is designed to act on the demand side of the drug market.

In 1988, the White House policy of zero tolerance of drug use was announced. This policy appears to be based on the belief that drug abuse starts with a willful act on the part of the drug user and that without users there would be no drug problem. The underlying idea is that the market is created not only by the supply of drugs but also by the demand for them. The public perception that drug addicts are unable to control their drug habits is presumed to be wrong, and it is held that users could stop their drug use and must be held accountable if they do not. Therefore, the public tolerance for drug use has been reduced to zero. From this position come more severe penalties for drug users in an attempt to reduce the demand side for drugs.

Although these policies were initiated under Republican presidents, the War on Drugs is bipartisan. The Clinton administration's "drug czars" Lee Brown and Barry

McAffrey oversaw one of the world's strictest drug prohibition programs. About 70 percent of the money spent on the War on Drugs has been directed toward activities designed to decrease supply; the remainder has targeted programs to decrease demand. The Bush administration continued to focus on decreasing the supply of illegal drugs.

The Argument Against Legalization of Drugs

The argument against the legalization of drugs is based mainly on (1) the adverse public health consequences of drugs, (2) the uncertain link between drug use and criminal behavior, (3) the expected increase in drug-related social problems if drugs were to be legalized, and (4) the successes of the War on Drugs.

Public Health Consequences

Proponents of continued drug prohibition argue that there is solid evidence that the legalization of drugs would have great public health consequences. Some studies indicate that marijuana is at least as harmful to the lungs as tobacco—maybe more harmful—because it delivers more concentrated tar than do filter-tipped cigarettes. Moreover, the potency of marijuana has increased in recent years, so its effects persist longer. Marijuana is thought to inhibit personal growth and effective coping with personal problems. Furthermore, marijuana may serve as a "gateway drug" from which the inexperienced user advances to more harmful substances. Marijuana may not be physically addictive, but many of the other drugs available are addictive. Opponents of legalization believe that drug use would soar if we were to legalize drugs.

Criminal Behavior and Drug Use

The link between criminal behavior and drug use is uncertain. Proponents of legalization argue that the high cost of illegal drugs leads to criminal behavior by drug users who finance their drug habits through criminal activity, but recent research casts doubt on this relationship. It's obvious, however, that some crimes are committed by individuals under the influence of drugs. Opponents of legalization are concerned about this fact but allege that although many criminals have a history of drug use, the high cost of illegal drugs cannot be shown to cause the crime. Instead, they argue, the drugs may be merely a symptom of an established pattern of antisocial behavior: these drug-using criminals would be crooks whether drugs were legalized or remained illegal.

Drug-Related Social Problems

Opponents of legalization also argue that because more people would use drugs if they were legal, we would have more drug-related problems. Like alcohol use, drug use contributes to higher worker absenteeism and lower productivity. Driving under the influence of alcohol contributes to car wrecks, injuries, and loss of life, and so would driving under the influence of legalized drugs. And like alcohol, drug use may contribute to birth defects or miscarriages. Alcohol currently contributes to many antisocial behavior patterns; legalized drugs would contribute to such patterns as well.

Successes of the War on Drugs

The War on Drugs is certainly not an unqualified success, but it assuredly has had some limited victories. Use of marijuana and cocaine in the United States fell during the 1980s, as did the use of most other drugs. Opponents of drug legalization argue that we certainly should not adopt any policies that would conflict with this trend. Because most people in the United States oppose legalization anyway, legalization would be politically impractical.

Other Arguments against Legalization

Proponents of drug legalization argue that our current drug laws infringe on our individual liberties and our right to make our own choices, even if these choices are self-destructive. Opponents of drug legalization argue that society has always regulated our choices to protect itself and individuals from harm. Allowing us access to addictive, harmful substances would really be a perversion of liberty. Note that virtually no one who provides treatment to crack cocaine addicts recommends the legalization of currently illegal drugs.

Opponents of legalization argue that we should strengthen supply-side programs that keep heroin and cocaine from crossing our borders. Furthermore, they believe that we should commit more resources to drug education and treatment programs. The emphasis on supply-side programs instead of demand-side programs has been largely political, since arrests and seizures of drug shipments are widely publicized measures of success that are used to justify the resources devoted to drug control. Data indicate that students 12 to 17 years old who have more positive school experiences are less likely to have used alcohol or illicit drugs than those students without positive school experiences. Although we cannot presume that positive school experiences *cause* lower drug use, we can at least recognize that the two are correlated. Furthermore, the rates of alcohol and illicit drug use were lower for youths who had seen or heard drug or alcohol prevention messages at school than youths who had not.[7]

The Argument for Legalization of Drugs

Proponents of drug legalization argue that efforts to restrict the supply of drugs have largely failed. They also maintain that our drug laws result in costly and harmful effects on society and that there are many benefits of legalization of drugs.

The Failure of International Drug Control

Many U.S. experts on drug control have emphasized international drug control efforts, because domestic efforts to control the supply have been virtually futile. Marijuana and opium can be grown almost anywhere, and the coca plant (from which cocaine is produced) is now grown in environments that were once thought inhospitable to it. Whenever supply from one area of the globe is disrupted, other areas rush to fill the void. It has been likened to pushing in on a balloon. For example, successful eradication of marijuana from Mexico in the 1970s led to greater importation of marijuana from Colombia and expanded marijuana production in the United States.

Controlling drug supply at the source faces many other obstacles. In some of the Third World countries that export drugs, political parties are involved in the production and sale of these commodities. In others, drug cartels have power rivaling

EconLinks

"A Tale of Two Countries: Hemp Farming"

Canada farmers are able to grow hemp, but drug enforcement authorities will not permit hemp growing in the United States. Find out what worries U.S. farmers. Navigate to the Equilibrium category for more information.

http://econapps. swlearning.com

that of the government. Low-income peasants producing raw drugs cannot switch to legal crops and make nearly as high a profit. In some cases growing and using the products are cultural: some Andean natives, for example, grow and chew coca leaves. These producers do not perceive themselves as criminals who hurt the U.S. people through their endeavors. So long as Americans demand drugs, there will be producers who try to meet that demand. It has been estimated that we have managed to stop only about 10 percent of drug shipments that originate from abroad. A major source of illegal U.S. drugs has been the South American country of Colombia, where the United States has attempted to halt the production of coca and to encourage alternative crops. So far this effort has not been successful, partly because the alternative crops have not proved viable for Colombian farmers. In addition, the U.S. government fumigation of Colombian coca fields has caused health problems and has rendered some of Colombia's food crops inedible.

The Costs of Prohibition

Proponents of drug legalization argue that our current drug laws not only are ineffective in controlling supply but also have unintended and huge costs. First, because drugs are illegal, they are provided by an illegal, or underground, economy. Therefore, the major beneficiary of drug prohibition is organized crime. Organized crime is the major source of illegal drugs, and it has been estimated that sales of illegal drugs account for half the revenues of organized crime in the United States. Drugs command a high price on the street, but this price is not based on high costs of manufacture. Instead, the price is largely attributable to the risks that traffickers take, risks for which they charge a high premium. These risk premiums are like an illegality tax that swells the coffers of organized crime.

Second, drug prohibition may contribute to crime in other ways. Because the street price of illegal drugs is so high, addicts may commit crimes to buy their drugs. And much violent crime results from turf wars among drug dealers. A real victim of drug prohibition may be the law-abiding citizen hurt in the crossfire of a drug turf war.

Third, the taxpayers bear the burden of the criminal justice system. The War on Drugs has increased both the absolute dollar expenditures on the criminal justice system and the percentage of our resources devoted to drug violations. About 25 percent of the convicts in state and federal prisons are there for drug law violations. The more effective our current drug laws, the more prison cells we will need. The burden on taxpayers will escalate as we build and equip more prisons to accommodate drug violators. Furthermore, drug laws may result in discriminatory incarceration. The mandatory sentence for possession of crack cocaine, often used by blacks, is higher than the mandatory sentence for powdered cocaine, which is more often used by whites. Finally, resources used in the War on Drugs cannot be used in alternative activities, such as investigating violent crimes and crimes against property. There is a conflict here. In some localities, law enforcement has come to mean drug law enforcement.

Fourth, proponents of legalization argue that another cost of drug prohibition is its contribution to the corruption of the police and others in the criminal justice system. All vice-control efforts are particularly susceptible to bribes, and bribes are difficult to detect because there is no victim of bribery to file a complaint. Police may be disillusioned by the widespread use of illegal drugs. The financial temptations are enormous and understandable, given the difficulty involved in enforcing our drug laws.

Fifth, another cost of drug prohibition may be the violation of our constitutional rights. Proponents of legalization argue that roadblocks and random searches of automobiles are violations of constitutional rights. The same may be true of exclusionary rule exceptions that allow authorities to use illegally seized evidence in court and of random drug testing. These actions are, however, accepted by society because public opinion so greatly favors drug-law enforcement.

Finally, proponents of legalization argue that although drugs may have adverse public health consequences, so does drug prohibition. Because drugs are illegal, we cannot regulate their safety. Users cannot tell if the drugs are pure or adulterated or what their strength is. Marijuana may have been sprayed with the dangerous herbicide paraquat or grown with dangerous fertilizers that are more hazardous to the user than the marijuana. Some argue that drug prohibition also keeps us from adopting sane policies to combat the spread of AIDS through the use of shared needles. Although some governments of the world have instituted policies to exchange needles as a means of controlling the spread of AIDS, our government has not. The prevailing belief is that to support needle exchange programs is to support, or at least to condone, the use of illegal substances.

The Benefits of Legalization

Proponents of legalization argue that repealing drug prohibition laws would provide many advantages. First, net financial benefits to the government from legalization would be considerable. We could tax the producers of the formerly illegal substances, generating many tax dollars for the government. Enforcement expenditures could be cut or redirected toward more serious crime. And we would be able to halt the constant expansion of the prison system at the expense of other social programs. Second, drugs would be safer if they were legal. We could regulate quality and institute needle exchange programs in good conscience. Third, the risk premium that stems from the illegality of drugs would disappear. As a result, drugs would not be such a profitable business for organized crime. We could expect that organized crime syndicates would exit the drug industry and be supplanted by legal pharmaceutical firms. Fourth, we would expect less criminal activity on the part of users who engaged in crime to finance their expensive drug habits when drugs were illegal. Finally, some of the resources saved could be directed toward education and treatment programs. This emphasis on the demand side of the drug market may well be more effective than the historical emphasis on supply-side programs.

The Economics of Prohibition or Legalization

Having laid out the cases for and against legalization, let us now add careful economic analysis to this discussion. The tool we will use is supply and demand analysis. Let's initially focus our attention on the demand for drugs. Figure 2-2 analyzes the effect of legalization on the demand for drugs. The graph shows supply and

EconLinks

"The Economics of Drug Dealing"

Read the full article under the Monopoly category.

http://econapps. swlearning.com

FIGURE 2-2   Effect of Legalization of Drugs on the Demand for Drugs

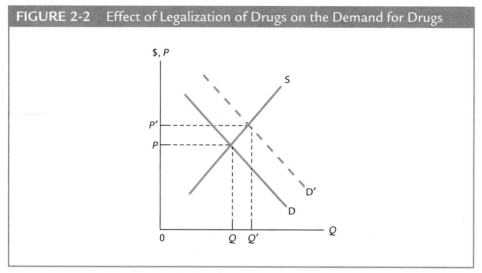

Legalization would increase demand from D to D', which would increase price to P' and quantity to Q'.

demand in a market for a particular drug, where D and S are the demand and supply curves if drugs are illegal. When drugs are prohibited by law, some potential users are deterred from using the drugs by the drug law penalties. Others simply prefer to act legally regardless of penalties. In these cases, demand for the drug might increase if drugs became legalized. The increase in demand is shown in Figure 2-2. When demand increases from D to D', price and quantity increase to P' and Q', respectively.

Now let's consider the effects of legalization on supply. Note that the original supply curve S incorporates a risk premium to the drug traffickers, as well as the high costs of bribing the local police. (It is pushed backward because of the higher costs of supplying the product when the product is illegal.) With legalization of this drug, supply will increase because the higher costs of production (bribery and risk premium) would no longer exist. As a result, the price of the drug would decrease. This price decrease might indeed cut into profits enough to cause organized crime syndicates to look elsewhere for profits. But the equilibrium quantity would increase; we cannot ignore the fact that the use of drugs would increase with legalization.

How much the use of the drugs would increase depends on an important characteristic of the demand for the drug. The demand for highly addictive drugs is said to be inelastic. An **inelastic demand** means that consumers are relatively unresponsive to changes in price: when prices go either up or down, quantity demanded doesn't change very much. This is certainly the case for a user who is physically addicted to a drug such as cocaine. For even large increases in the price of this drug, the user will scarcely reduce his or her usage. We represent an inelastic demand with a relatively steep demand curve.

Inelastic demand
Demand in which buyers are relatively unresponsive to changes in price.

FIGURE 2-3   Effect of the Legalization of Drugs on the Supply of Drugs

Inelastic Demand
In the case of the inelastic demand for drugs, the same increase in supply resulting from legalization, would result in a smaller increase in drug usage.

Elastic Demand
In the case of an elastic demand for drugs, legalization would shift the supply curve forward and result in a larger increase in drug usage.

Legalization of drugs would increase supply from s to S′. The effect of the new equilibrium quantity (drug use) and the new price depends on the elasticity of demand.

Elastic demand
Demand in which buyers are relatively responsive to changes in price.

Figure 2-3 shows both an inelastic demand curve and a flatter (elastic) demand curve. **Elastic demand** means that buyers are relatively responsive to changes in price. Thus, quantity demanded changes a lot for even small changes in price. This is the case for less physically addictive drugs, such as marijuana. (Elasticity of demand is discussed in greater detail in the appendix to this chapter.)

Note that equilibrium quantity (use) of the drug increases in both cases when supply increases. However, drug usage increases just a little when demand is inelastic, but it increases significantly when demand is elastic.

The fact of the matter is that we do not know whether the demand for most drugs is inelastic or elastic. Because drug markets are illegal, we lack information about price–quantity combinations in the real world. Although we would expect those addicted to a narcotic to have a highly inelastic demand, we do not know much about the responsiveness of casual users to changes in the price of controlled substances. What little experimental knowledge we have comes from the decriminalization of marijuana by several U.S. states and the legalization of drugs by the Netherlands. The states that decriminalized marijuana in the 1970s experienced the same usage patterns as neighboring states that continued to prohibit it. And the Netherlands' legalization was not accompanied by greatly increased drug use, if we adjust for the international movement of addicts from more restrictive countries into the Netherlands. Assuming that drug prices fell in both of these cases, the findings that drug use did not greatly increase in either case is somewhat reassuring and indicative of inelastic demands.

Note that the increase in supply decreases the price of drugs and that the increase in demand increases their equilibrium price. The changes are offsetting, so the effect on equilibrium price is really quite difficult to predict. Most experts, however, predict that the price of drugs would go down at least somewhat with legalization. But note also that both the increase in demand and the increase in supply would both increase equilibrium quantity so that it is quite clear that drug use would increase with legalization.

Regulation through Economic Policies

Economists who favor drug legalization or decriminalization often also suggest economic means of influencing the legal markets for drugs. First, they argue that a much greater percentage of the government's expenditures on drug-related programs should be directed toward demand-side treatment and education programs. As we have already noted, only 30 percent of drug-related expenditures are directed to demand-side policies. By decreasing demand, we can decrease use.

Second, a system of excise taxes can be levied on the legal drugs. (An **excise tax** is like a sales tax, except that it is imposed on only specific goods and services such as cigarettes, alcohol, and gasoline.) The effect of these excise taxes would be to decrease the supply of the drug, since we view the excise tax as an additional cost of production to the supplier. This is the case since it is the supplier of the drug who pays the tax dollars to the government. (Remember that an increase in the costs of production shifts the supply curve backward.)

Excise tax
A tax applied to the purchase of a specific good or service.

Figure 2-4 shows a hypothetical market for a legalized drug with a public health excise tax levied on suppliers. The decrease in supply caused by the excise tax causes an increase in the drug's price and a decrease in its use.

FIGURE 2-4   How an Excise Tax Can Decrease the Use of a Legalized Drug

The excise tax causes a backward shift in the supply of the drug, resulting in a higher price and lower quantity (usage).

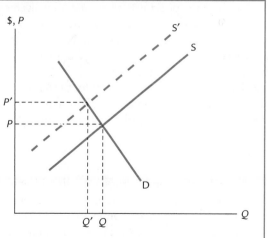

EconLinks

"Coco Leaf Prices Reach a High"

The emergence of new trafficking routes have reduced supply and caused a greater demand for cocaine. Read more under the Equilibrium category.

http://econapps. swlearning.com

The level of the tax on each drug should be correlated with the drug's harmful public health effects. If the clinical evidence indicates that the consequences of using cocaine are more severe than the consequences of using marijuana, the tax levied on cocaine should be higher. Furthermore, revenues from the excise tax could be earmarked for treatment and education programs. In addition to the excise taxes, the substances would be regulated and kept out of the hands of minors, as we currently attempt to keep both alcohol and tobacco from being purchased by teenagers. Furthermore, drivers under the influence of any drug could be arrested, as should drivers under the influence of alcohol. So, legalization and the imposition of the taxes would not eliminate the need for policing the market for drugs entirely. The policing burden would, however, be far lighter than it is under prohibition.

Illegal Use of Legal Drugs

Although our discussion in this chapter has focused on illegal drugs, another issue is the illegal use of *legal* drugs. For example, many people have become addicted to prescription drugs, such as the pain reliever Oxycontin. Others abuse these drugs to

VIEWPOINT: CONSERVATIVE VERSUS LIBERAL

When discussing emotionally charged social issues such as the control of drugs, pornography, and prostitution, it is especially important to apply care in the way we use the terms *liberal* and *conservative*. These terms often have opposite meanings when we are considering government involvement in our daily lives (social liberals and conservatives) versus government involvement in the economy (economic liberals and conservatives). Let's try to understand the distinction.

Economic conservatives support less government involvement in economic realms. They favor a market-oriented approach to most situations. Thus, economic conservatives would support the legalization of drugs and other victimless crimes. (Note that social conservatives would not support such legalization.) The economic conservative would value the efficiencies attained when market forces shift demand and supply curves if legalization occurs. Furthermore, they would prefer excise taxes and other market approaches to account for the harmful community effects of drugs and other victimless crimes, instead of the prohibition of the activity itself.

Economic liberals, on the other hand, favor greater government intervention in the marketplace. They would favor the criminalization and prohibition of drug use and other victimless crimes. They might especially favor efforts to reduce the supply of drugs and would support the law enforcement expenditures needed to increase the effectiveness of the War on Drugs. (Note that social liberals are more likely to support legalization of drugs.) We should point out, however, that economists, like the rest of our society, usually hold opinions about the legalization of drugs and other victimless crimes that are not based solely on economic principles. And, both economic and social conservatives and liberals may be conservative on some issues and liberal on others.

get an artificial "high." Both Brett Favre (quarterback for the Green Bay Packers) and Rush Limbaugh (conservative radio and TV host) have admitted addiction to prescription drugs, as have many more celebrities. Proper treatment is essential for all drug abusers, whether the drugs are illegal themselves, or are legal drugs being used illegally, since both of these can be very dangerous to the user.

THE LEGALIZATION OF OTHER VICTIMLESS CRIMES

The economic analysis (and many of the noneconomic arguments) we have used to examine the controversy over the legalization of drugs can also be applied to arguments about the legal status of other so-called victimless crimes such as pornography and prostitution. These are considered crimes not because of violence against persons or property, but because of public censure and disapproval. It can be argued that, like drug use, the purchase of pornography or the services of a prostitute are a consensual transaction. That is, both buyer and seller consent to the trade. Thus, there is no victim (though some will argue that this type of behavior may create victims, such as by increasing violence against women, for example). Certainly child pornography should always be illegal. Policing by the vice squad for these victimless crimes is difficult because there is no victim to file a complaint. Corruption of police working the vice squad is thought to be higher than of police working details such as robbery. The same arguments for legalization, regulation, and taxation therefore can be made for these offenses. As with drugs, the equilibrium quantity would undoubtedly increase with legalization, but regulation and taxation for regulatory purposes might well be more efficient than prohibition. But as with drugs, social issues related to legalization may outweigh the economic issues.

SUMMARY

A crime is any activity forbidden by law and punishable by criminal penalty. Our expenditures on our criminal justice system, which includes police, courts, and prisons, have increased greatly in the past 20 to 25 years. The greatest increase has occurred in the prison system.

The appropriate methodology to evaluate crime prevention measures is cost-benefit analysis. A policy should be adopted only if its benefits are greater than its costs. The results of cost-benefit studies on our prison expansion are contradictory and inconclusive.

Some crimes are victimless because they are the result of consensual transactions between two parties. These crimes are illegal only because society, or a significant group in society, disapproves of them on moral, health, or ethical grounds. Therefore, we have passed laws prohibiting them. Legalizing these victimless crimes may be more efficient than prohibiting them. Both demand and supply would increase, price would decrease at least slightly, and equilibrium quantity would increase. Although use would increase, the goods and services involved would be provided legally and earn lower profits, so their provision would be less attractive to organized crime. If these victimless crimes were made legal, we could regulate them, in part through taxation.

NOTES

1. The National Center for Victims of Crime, **www.ncvc.org**.

2. These and other statistics in this chapter (unless otherwise noted) are from the U.S. Department of Justice, Bureau of Justice Statistics, **www.ojp.usdoj.gov/bjs**.

3. U.S. Department of Justice, Federal Bureau of Investigation, Uniform Crime Report, **www.fbi.gov**.

4. The Sentencing Project, **www.sentencingproject.org**.

5. Substance Abuse and Mental Health Services Administration (SAMHSA), **www.drugabusestatistics.samhsa.gov**, and Health and Human Services, **www.hhs.gov/news/press/2002pres**. SAMHSA is an agency in the Department of Health and Human Services and is the federal government's lead agency for improving the quality and availability of substance abuse prevention, addiction treatment, and mental health services.

6. SAMHSA, **www.drugabusestatistics.samhsa.gov**.

DISCUSSION QUESTIONS

1. What is the definition of a public good or service? Name some other public goods and services in addition to crime prevention.

2. What is the free rider problem? Why does it exist? What are other examples of free riders?

3. What is meant when we say that a public good is indivisible, nonrivalrous, and nonexcludable?

4. Discuss cost-benefit analysis. What are the benefits of crime prevention? What are the costs? Are all the benefits and costs easily measurable? Are there situations in which cost-benefit analysis is inappropriate?

5. Of what significance is the elasticity of demand for drugs in the debate about legalization of presently illegal substances?

6. How could taxes be used to regulate legal drug markets? How is the issue of excise taxes and drugs similar to the issue of excise taxes and cigarettes? Why are excise taxes on cigarettes and alcohol sometimes called "sin taxes"?

7. Is it possible to be a social liberal and an economic conservative (or vice versa) with regard to victimless crimes?

8. Go to the Federal Bureau of Investigation Web site (**www.fbi.gov**), click Uniform Crime Report, and find the latest statistics on violent crime. Has violent crime increased or decreased in the latest year available?

9. Go to the Web site for the National Center for Victims of Crime at **www.ncvc.org**. How might this Web site be used by someone who has been a victim of crime?

10. Go to **www.albany.edu/sourcebook**, which is the Web site for the Sourcebook of Criminal Justice Statistics. Try to find updated statistics on crime rates in the United States.

11. The Sentencing Project has a Web site at **www.sentencingproject.org**. Try to discover the underlying view of the Sentencing Project toward expansion of prisons and incarceration in the United States. What is their view toward gender and racial issues?

12. The Bureau of Justice Statistics of the Department of Justice has a Web site at **www.ojp.usdoj.gov/bjs**. Try to find information on the number of prisons and prisoners in the United States.

CHAPTER 2 APPENDIX: ELASTICITY

Elasticity of demand is the responsiveness of buyers (in terms of their buying decisions) to changes in the price of the product. When buyers are relatively responsive to changes in the product's price, we say that demand is elastic. When buyers are relatively unresponsive to changes in the price of the product, we say that demand is inelastic, as described earlier in the chapter.

When we say that buyers are relatively unresponsive to a change in price, we mean that a change in price has little effect on the quantity that consumers are willing to buy. If demand is elastic, and buyers are more responsive to changes in price, a change in price has a significant effect on quantity demanded. Economists frequently describe elasticity by calculating an elasticity coefficient. The formula for the elasticity coefficient is as follows:

$$\frac{\text{Percentage Change in Quantity Demanded}}{\text{Percentage Change in Price}}$$

If demand is elastic, the coefficient will have an absolute value greater than 1, indicating that any percentage change in price causes a larger percentage change in quantity demanded. However, if demand is inelastic, the coefficient's absolute value will be some fraction less than 1, indicating that any percentage change in price causes a smaller percentage change in quantity demanded. (Since a rise in price usually causes a reduction in quantity demanded and vice versa, the elasticity coefficient always has a negative value. However, in order to avoid confusion, we express the coefficient in absolute value; that is, we ignore the minus sign.)

The graphs in Figure 2-5 show the theoretical extremes of elasticity: perfect inelasticity and perfect elasticity. The demand in the graph on the left is perfectly inelastic. Regardless of any price

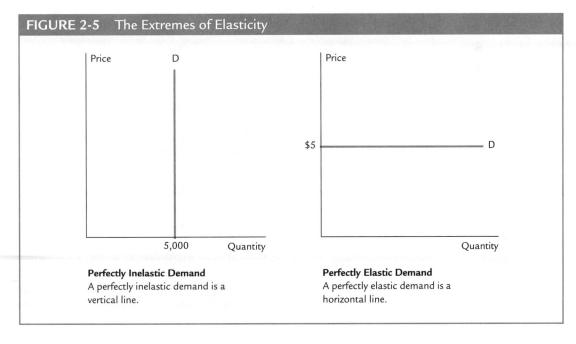

FIGURE 2-5 The Extremes of Elasticity

Perfectly Inelastic Demand
A perfectly inelastic demand is a vertical line.

Perfectly Elastic Demand
A perfectly elastic demand is a horizontal line.

change, quantity demanded does not change, but remains at 5,000. Since there is no response to a change in price, we say that demand is perfectly inelastic. Perfectly inelastic demand curves are always drawn as vertical lines, and they have an elasticity coefficient equal to zero. The graph on the right in Figure 2-5 is a perfectly elastic demand curve. Perfectly elastic demand curves are always horizontal lines. Although price does not vary from $5, quantity demanded varies infinitely. This is the ultimate in responsiveness, with an elasticity coefficient equal to infinity.

Most demand curves are neither perfectly elastic nor perfectly inelastic. The more typical case of elasticity is related to both the location of the curve on the graph and its slope. If two demand curves intersect so that their location on the graph is very close, we can compare their elasticity in the region near their intersection by comparing their slopes. The flatter (closer to horizontal) curve will be more elastic. The steeper (closer to vertical) curve will be more inelastic.

Figure 2-6 shows two demand curves that intersect at $4 and a quantity of 200 units. Demand curve D_1 is more inelastic at prices near $4 and quantities near 200 than is D_2, which is flatter.

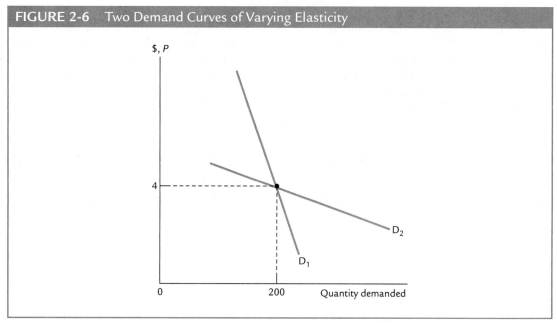

FIGURE 2-6 Two Demand Curves of Varying Elasticity

D_1 is less elastic than demand curve D_2 at prices near their $4 intersection.

Elasticity has interesting implications when an excise tax is imposed on the sale of a good or service. In the case of a physically addictive drug, such as cocaine, demand is inelastic. In the case of a less physically addicting drug, such as marijuana, demand is elastic. Figure 2-7 represents these differing elasticities by the slopes of the two demand curves. If supply decreases (shifts to the left) by the same amount in both cases, because of the imposition of an identical excise tax, equilibrium quantity of the drug changes very little in the case of inelastic demand, and it changes much more in the case of elastic demand. In addition, the price of the drug increases by a larger amount in the case of the addictive drug with inelastic demand and a smaller amount in the case of the less-addictive drug with elastic demand. Since the amount of the excise tax is the vertical distance be-

FIGURE 2-7 Two Demand Curves of Varying Elasticity with the Imposition of an Excise Tax

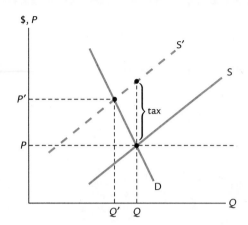

A relatively inelastic demand will have a large increase in price if supply is reduced because of the imposition of an excise tax. The greater burden of the tax falls upon consumers.

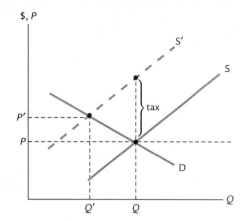

A relatively elastic demand will have a small increase in price if supply is reduced because of the imposition of an excise tax. The greater burden of the tax falls upon suppliers.

tween the two supply curves, we see that the price of the drug increases by almost the full amount of the tax in the case of inelastic demand. This means that the greater burden of the tax falls upon the consumer in the form of the higher price of the drug. In the case of elastic demand, the price of the drug rises very little. This means that the greater burden of the tax falls upon the supplier of the drug in the form of lower profits. *In general, we say that the burden of the tax falls most heavily on that group (consumers or suppliers) with the more inelastic curve.*

Can you explain the relative burden of an excise tax in the case of the perfectly inelastic demand curve and the perfectly elastic demand curves of Figure 2-5? In both cases, simply add a normal upward sloping supply curve and then add a new supply curve as a parallel backward shift. In the first case, the price of the drug increases by the full vertical distance between the two supply curves. In other words, the entire burden of the tax falls upon consumers of the drug. In the second case, the price does not increase at all. In other words, the entire burden of the tax falls upon suppliers of the drug. These are the extreme cases of the general observation that the burden of the tax falls most heavily on that group with the more inelastic curve. The phenomenon of elasticity and excise taxes is revisited in the appendix to Chapter 16, which discusses inelasticity in greater detail.

**Chapter 9
International Trade**
Much pollution is global in nature

The different environmental regulations of different countries can foster trade

Trade agreements and policies can encourage environmental destruction

**Chapter 12
Agriculture**
Chemical runoff from farms is a source of pollution

Some of our agricultural policies foster environmental harm

**Chapter 3
The Environment**

**Chapter 17
Globally Free
Markets for the
Twenty-First Century?**
Do free markets and increased trade have environmental consequences?

**Chapter 7
World Poverty**
Environmental protection is a luxury good that is not affordable in poor countries

Environmental issues are increasingly important as poor countries seek economic development

THE ECONOMIC TOOLBOX

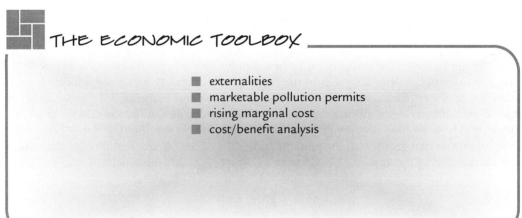

- externalities
- marketable pollution permits
- rising marginal cost
- cost/benefit analysis

THE ENVIRONMENT

We are all stewards of this planet, and we all share responsibility for protecting and preserving a precious heritage for our children and grandchildren. As long as we work together and stay firmly focused on our goals, I am confident we will continue to make our air cleaner, our water purer, and our land better protected for future generations.

—Christine Todd Whitman, Administrator of the Environmental Protection Agency, 2003, **www.epa.gov**

The opening quotation to this chapter suggests a sense of optimism: if we all work together we can improve our environment. Do we indeed have grounds for optimism? What are our pressing environmental issues? What has been the role of President George W. Bush regarding the environment? What is the role of the consumer, the firm, and even the international community?

Are you concerned about global warming? Acid rain? Ozone depletion? Deforestation of the rain forests? Desertification of once-productive land? Pollution of our air and water? Extinction of species of animals and plants?

Do you recycle? Do you try to conserve our natural resources? Do you support government policies to protect the environment? What are *you* doing to protect our environment?

Most (probably all) of us are concerned to some degree about environmental issues. In this chapter, we will consider the economics of the environment. Let's start by saying that economic activity affects the environment, often in a harmful manner. Production of goods often causes pollution. Consumption of goods can also pollute. We often use our scarce resources inefficiently and unwisely.

In this chapter, we will discuss the pollution created as a by-product of production, as well as policies to deal with this pollution. We will also consider the environmental effects of consumption, conservation, and recycling; and the international dimensions of the environmental problem.

THE PROBLEM OF POLLUTION

Pollution
Waste that is not recycled.

Let's consider the global problem of pollution. We will define **pollution** as waste that is not recycled. Motor vehicles and industrial plants emit carbon monoxide, sulfur oxides, nitrogen oxides, and other hazardous compounds into the atmosphere, thereby polluting our air. The burning of fossil fuels releases carbon dioxide, which, along with other greenhouse gases, traps heat within the earth's atmosphere, thereby contributing to global warming. Deforestation of the rain forests causes the loss of precious biodiversity while removing vegetation that could otherwise absorb the carbon dioxide that leads to global warming. Desertification occurs when deforested areas no longer prevent the shift of desert sands onto previously fertile soil. The release of certain chemicals, primarily chlorofluorocarbons (CFCs), damages the ozone layer of our atmosphere, thereby allowing in dangerous levels of ultraviolet radiation from the sun. Industrial wastes, leaking septic tanks and landfills, and pesticides contaminate aquifers and threaten our water supply.

In all of these cases, environmental damage is an unplanned and harmful by-product of economic activity. The problems caused by pollution are twofold: spillover costs and inefficient resource allocation. These problems are discussed in the sections that follow.

Spillover Costs and Benefits

Externality
The cost or benefit of an economic activity that spills over onto the rest of society.

Pollution is the classic example of an economic externality. An **externality** is simply a cost or benefit of an economic activity that spills over onto the rest of society. Externalities can be positive or negative. Pollution represents a negative externality, or a **spillover cost**. Although firms that pollute incur the private costs of production such as wages and energy costs, they do not bear the entire cost of production. A portion of the production costs, specifically the pollution, spills over onto society. The polluter's accounting books do not take into account the effects of pollution. Instead, society bears the burden of this pollution cost in the form of poorer health and productivity, higher health care expenses, greater cleaning costs, damage to buildings and forests, aesthetic displeasure, and so on. Other businesses bear the burden of the pollution cost in the form of damage to capital structures and machinery, damage to crops and needed resources, and so forth. We, as a society, either tolerate the environmental degradation or clean up someone else's mess with our tax dollars. This inequitable burden of costs is one of the chief economic characteristics of pollution. All negative externalities involve costs created by an economic activity and shifted to other firms or individuals outside that economic activity. This situation is not an equitable one.

Spillover cost
A negative externality in which costs are shifted from the private market onto society.

Pollution is not the only negative externality that is common in our lives. Consider your dismay if you live near a newly constructed airport or highway. You will bear the burden of the noise pollution that results. Or imagine living in a heavily populated area, driving on heavily congested streets and freeways, and experiencing time delays and a greater probability of accidents. You would bear costs of congestion. These, too, are negative externalities.

Not all spillover costs are caused by businesses. We consumers create some negative externalities. A good example is our use of the automobile. As you know, Americans love their cars and as a result are reluctant to carpool or take public transportation. We incur private costs associated with driving: car payments, insurance, gas, oil, maintenance costs, taxes and license fees, and parking expenses. Society, however, bears a portion of the total costs of our driving in the form of the air pollution caused by auto emissions. Another example might be our use of throwaway bottles and cans. We consumers pay for the product, but society bears a burden in the form of litter, solid waste, and an inefficient use of scarce resources. All negative externalities involve costs imposed on others who do not benefit from the production or consumption of the product.

Externalities can also be positive. We call positive externalities **spillover benefits**. Education is a classic example of a service that yields spillover benefits. You, the student, will benefit most directly from your education. You are likely to earn a higher income, to have a job you enjoy, and to have a richer intellectual life if you are educated. But society also benefits. College graduates tend to be better-informed citizens. They are less likely to be chronically unemployed. They are more likely to vote. They are less likely to commit crimes, or at least violent crimes. They often are more productive workers. So, spillover benefits are conferred on society. Because society receives these benefits, most people feel that society is justified in bearing part of the costs of education through tax revenues. We will address this issue of education in greater detail in the next chapter.

> **Spillover benefits**
> A positive externality in which benefits are shifted from the private market onto society.

Another spillover benefit comes to society through immunization of children against common childhood diseases. Families pay for the shots and vaccinations and receive most of the benefits in the form of decreased risk of measles, smallpox, and polio. Others in society benefit as well, however. Other children, even if not immunized, are less likely to contract these diseases because the diseases will not be so prevalent. The families of nonimmunized children benefit without bearing any of the cost. Society benefits in terms of lower medical expenses. The burden of costs is inequitable if you are not in some way compensated for the benefits you provide society.

Inefficient Resource Allocation

As we have noted, externalities can shift costs to groups that did not incur them and benefits to groups that did not earn them. In addition, externalities can cause resources to be inefficiently allocated. Simply put, we produce and consume too much (overallocate resources) if negative externalities are present, and we produce and consume too little (underallocate resources) if positive externalities (such as benefits to nonimmunized children) exist. Let's look at the effects of pollution on the market for a good produced by firms that hypothetically pollute the environment. Let's use spring vacation air travel to the Bahamas during one week in March as the product.

The Effects of Pollution in a Single Market

First consider the hypothetical market demand curve for air travel to the Bahamas. Remember that demand reflects the value of the product to consumers in society, because it represents the prices that consumers are willing to pay for a ticket to the Bahamas. D is the market demand curve in Figure 3-1 on page 60.

FIGURE 3-1 Allocative Effects of Pollution in a Hypothetical Market for Spring Vacation Air Travel to the Bahamas

Hypothetical air and noise pollution increase the social costs above the private costs of providing travel. This rise in social costs causes the private market equilibrium price to be too low, resulting in the overallocation of resources to air travel.

Now let's consider the supply of air transportation to the Bahamas. Remember that we defined pollution as waste that is not recycled. The amount of pollutants emitted by firms will increase proportionately with output. But low levels of output will not result in spillover costs, because the natural processes of the earth can absorb and reprocess a certain amount of waste (pollutants). If production increases beyond the level that natural processes can handle, we incur pollution and spillover costs.

Suppose that natural processes can absorb the hypothetical air and noise pollutants that we create if we provide 2,000 units of output (passenger tickets), but that if we provide more than 2,000, we exceed the earth's capacity to cleanse itself. (Pretend that college students flying to the Bahamas during this particular week in March represent the only people traveling to the Bahamas by air.) After the production of 2,000 units of output, we have a negative externality.

Curve S^P in Figure 3-1 is the hypothetical private market supply curve. This curve is based on firms' (airlines') private costs of production but does not reflect the full **social costs of production** when pollution occurs. These social costs of production include both the private costs to the producer and the spillover costs borne by society. Curve S^S is the hypothetical social supply curve. This curve is higher in the graph (in terms of the dollar axis) than the private supply curve, reflecting the higher so-

Social costs of production
The total costs of production, including private costs and spillover costs.

cial costs of production. The vertical distance between S^P and S^S at each level of output is the hypothetical amount of the spillover cost.

The private market supply curve intersects with the demand curve at a quantity of 5,000 units (tickets to the Bahamas) and a price of $400 per person. Note, however, that the social supply curve intersects with demand at only 4,000 units and a price of $500. The private market supply curve results in output that is too high, because it is based on a cost that is too low. When markets base their output decisions on their costs of production they do so on the basis of private costs of production only, and not on the full costs of production. However, the socially optimal level of output is based on the full social costs of production. This is because we wish to balance our desire for the product with the *full* social costs of production.) Because the free market results in too much output, we say there is an **overallocation of resources** to the production of this product. Too much output may not sound like a problem, but remember that society has scarce resources. Too much production of a product that society doesn't want (especially when it causes pollution) means too little production of products that society does want. Inefficient allocation of resources means that society's preferences are not being met.

Note an essential difference between the economist's view of the market and the environmentalist's. The socially correct quantity in Figure 3-1 is 4,000 units, and at this quantity, we will have some pollution. The environmentalist's goal would be to eliminate all pollution, but if we do that we have to cut production to 2,000 units. Most economists believe that if all costs are accurately reflected in the supply curve, and society's values are accurately reflected in the demand curve, the market output is efficient and desirable. Society values those extra 2,000 units enough to be willing to bear the cost of the pollution that accompanies them. In the region between 2,000 units (no pollution) and 4,000 units (socially desirable output), the demand curve is above the social supply curve, indicating that society values these units of the good more than it costs to manufacture them, including the costs of pollution. Thus, economists would not recommend cutting back production to 2,000 units to eliminate all pollution. (And students heading for the Bahamas during spring break can breathe a collective sigh of relief!)

> **Overallocation of resources**
> The production of more than the socially optimum amount of a good or service.

The Effects on One Market of Pollution in Another Market

Now let's consider a hypothetical case of resource allocation between two industries, the paper industry and the beer industry, to understand how the actions of firms in one industry can affect those in others. To simplify, the demand and supply curves for the two industries are drawn identically in Figure 3-2 on page 62. Initially, we assume no pollution and no spillover costs. The market equilibrium of price P and quantity Q in each market is the socially desirable price and quantity. Now suppose that firms in the paper industry decide it is too expensive to prevent pollution, and they begin to dump by-products and waste into the river nearby. They save on production costs, but cause water pollution. Decreased private costs of production in the paper industry will shift the firms' supply curve forward to S' (for the firms' private costs will not include the costs of pollution). The market equilibrium price and quantity are now P' and Q', respectively. Too much paper is being produced and consumed at a price that does not reflect the costs of pollution.

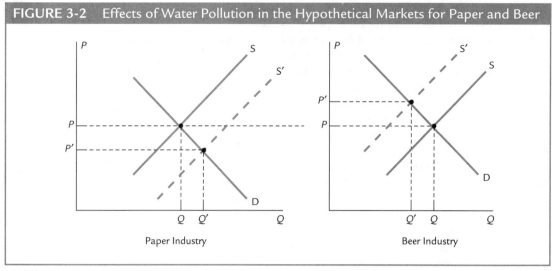

Paper Industry

Beer Industry

Pollution causes overallocation of resources to the polluting industry (here, the paper industry). As a result, resources are underallocated to other industries (here, the beer industry).

The beer industry, which uses water as an input to beer production, will be adversely affected by the paper companies' actions. Assume that the beer industry has breweries located downstream on the river. Because polluted water will not produce beer that is safe and good-tasting, beer producing firms in the formerly land of sky blue waters have to clean up the water before they use it for brewing. The beer industry therefore incurs private costs in purifying the water, shifting the beer industry's supply curve back to S'. This decrease in the supply of beer causes an increase in equilibrium price to P' and a decrease in equilibrium quantity to Q'. We consume less beer at higher prices.

Underallocation of resources

The production of less than the socially optimum amount of a good or service.

Thus, the externality in the paper market not only shifts the pollution costs to society at large, but also causes a distortion of resource allocation in other markets, namely, the **underallocation of resources** in the beer market. We are consuming more paper and less beer than we would if not for the pollution. To most economists, an essential problem with pollution (or any other externality for that matter) is that it causes resource allocation to be distorted. We can summarize the discussion so far by stating that externalities cause both problems of inequity (unfairness) and inefficiency (improper allocation of resources).

ENVIRONMENTAL POLICIES AND POLITICS

Air and water pollution are certainly not new phenomena. In 1858, London was stricken by the "Great Stink" caused by the dumping of wastes and garbage into the Thames River. We tend to romanticize the past as a cleaner, better environment, but this view ignores much of our environmental history. The horse-drawn carriage left its own brand of pollution behind it.

Widespread concern about environmental quality is a recent phenomenon, despite our history of environmental problems. It began in the 1960s and was confined mainly to the United States and other economically advanced countries. Why did environmental concern occur so late, and why was it localized in these countries? First, growth in population, accompanied by increases in output, has greatly increased the amounts of pollutants released into the air and water. Inevitably, the quantity of these pollutants has exceeded the natural cleansing abilities of the earth. And the effects are pervasive. The cities of Victorian England may have been grimy, unpleasant, and possibly hazardous to inhabitants' health, but the middle and upper classes could easily avoid these effects by moving to the pleasant, agrarian countryside. This strategy no longer works. Pollution follows us to our rural hideaways.

Second, the degree of peril occasioned by pollutants is greater today than it was in preceding centuries. Nuclear wastes and polychlorinated biphenyls (PCBs) are significantly different from the pollutants that plagued our grandparents. Complex technologies have produced pollutants they never dreamed of. The news that the polar ice cap seems to be melting and the very real threat of global warming are problems of a different magnitude than those experienced by previous generations.

Finally, we have become more affluent, and the demand for environmental quality has increased markedly. Environmental quality is a **luxury good**, or a commodity with a demand extremely sensitive to increases in income. Once society's basic needs for food, clothing, and shelter have been met, citizens begin expecting other things, such as a healthier and higher-quality environment. These three factors explain why the environmental movement is both recent and a product of affluent, economically advanced countries.

Luxury good
A commodity for which demand is highly sensitive to changes in income.

ENVIRONMENTAL LEGISLATION

Environmental legislation is based on the fact that spillover costs and misallocation of resources result from externalities unless the government takes an active role in controlling the situation. We cannot expect business firms, which are motivated by profit maximization, to take a strong stand against pollution if they are not compelled to do so through regulation or encouraged to do so by economic incentives. Nor will most consumers make major efforts to reduce their pollution unless forced to do so or provided with economic incentives.

Environmental regulation grew out of a grassroots movement, and therefore many initiatives were at the local level. Chicago and Cincinnati enacted laws to control smoke emissions from factories and power plants in the 1880s, before there was an environmental movement as such. Many other cities subsequently followed their lead. In fact, the federal government did not become involved in controlling air pollution until the 1950s. The Air Pollution Act of 1955 was a federal call for research into the problem. This call was followed by the Clean Air Act of 1963 to control air pollution and the Clean Air Act of 1970 to enforce national clean air standards. Of special concern at that time were automobile emissions, which contributed greatly to the smog plaguing the nation's cities. The Clean Air Act was further amended in 1977 and in 1990.

The Environmental Protection Agency (EPA) was formed by executive order in 1970 to administer all the environmental laws. The Federal Water Pollution Act of 1972 mandated that the EPA also reduce discharges into the nation's waterways, and the mission of the EPA was subsequently amended to add protection of land and other environmental issues to its jurisdiction. Christine Todd Whitman, whose quotation opened this chapter, was the Bush administration's Administrator of the EPA from 2000 to mid-2003.

The environmental disaster of the Love Canal made the nation aware of the problem of hazardous waste. Throughout the 1950s, the Hooker Chemical and Plastics Company, as well as certain federal agencies, put waste into an old canal excavation near Niagara Falls, New York. Eventually the landfill was sealed, and a school and housing development were built in the area. Toxic wastes bubbled to the surface and ended up in storm sewers, gardens, basements, and the school playground. In response to the environmental disaster of the Love Canal, the Comprehensive Environmental Response, Compensation, and Liability Act of 1980 established the Superfund to clean up hazardous waste. It also gave the EPA significant enforcement authority to hold identified responsible parties liable for the cost of cleanup.

More recently, activists have publicized the environmental horrors that have surrounded the border area between the United States and Mexico. As a result of poor environmental regulation and enforcement, toxic chemicals have filled landfills and rivers, creating significant health hazards for citizens of both the United States and Mexico. The North American Free Trade Agreement (NAFTA), which removed trade restrictions and was put into effect on January 1, 1994, included a "side agreement" designed to protect the environment. As discussed in Chapter 9 on international trade, many believe that the environmental protections built into NAFTA are not being enforced adequately on either side of the border. Horror health stories in the border area continue to fill our newspapers.

Because the federal government as well as state and local governments have been involved in regulation for environmental protection, it is important to address the issue of the proper level of government to handle environmental regulation. Some people argue that the federal government is characterized by a huge bureaucracy that is far from the people it governs and unresponsive to the people's needs. The EPA, they argue, is slow to respond to local needs and insensitive to local opinion. They feel that local, or regional, regulation would be more sensitive and responsive. Conservative representatives to Congress have generally taken a strong stand against federal regulations, including those that protect the environment. Mike Leavitt, President George W. Bush's pick to head the EPA after the resignation of Christine Whitman, strongly favors giving states a bigger role in environmental regulation.

Although local regulation keeps government closer to the governed, the federal level may be the more appropriate level of government to regulate the environment. One reason is that whatever the source of air and water pollution, the problem affects neighboring communities, states, and even countries. Acid rain originating in the United States but damaging property in Canada has become a heated issue between the two nations. Global warming, ozone depletion, and loss of biodiversity are also global phenomena.

At the same time, local communities, acting in their own perceived self-interest, may be lax in setting standards to control air and water pollution. By tolerating pollution, they may attract industry and increase the jobs available for their citizens. As long as some pollution affects other jurisdictions, localities have an incentive to under-regulate their own pollution sources. Indeed, a major cause of acid rain is the sulfur dioxide emitted into the atmosphere by the tall smokestacks of coal-burning electric utilities. The smokestacks were built to conform to local standards for air pollution, and they protect the local community but emit pollutants that damage distant communities. They were (and are) considerably less expensive than scrubbers, which are designed to eliminate most of the pollutants at the source. The localities export the problem rather than solve it. Federal legislation helps minimize the disparity of pollution control standards that would exist if regulation were left to individual localities and states.

Furthermore, the states have widely differing resources. The federal government has a larger tax base than any state, and it has greater ability to finance pollution control activities. It can also mitigate the burden of pollution control by transferring income from affluent states to poorer states. *Although pollution control policy might be administered at a variety of government levels, the jurisdiction for setting pollution control standards should be large enough to capture all the negative spillovers. Thus, decisions about pollution control are most appropriately made at the national, or even international, level.*

EconDebate

"Should Antipollution Standards Be Strengthened?"

Read the full debate under Economics and the Environment.

http://econapps. swlearning.com

METHODS OF REGULATION

Government agencies, at any level, use the following methods to limit adverse environmental effects: (1) standards, (2) pollution fees, and (3) pollution permits.

The Standards Approach

Let's look at the standards approach to pollution control first. This approach is the easiest to understand and the one originally used by environmental agencies.

Using the Standards Approach

With the **standards** approach, maximum acceptable levels of pollutants are established, and firms that exceed these levels are punished, usually by fines. Firms can thus be forced into compliance with the standard.

Standards
Maximum levels of pollutants that are acceptable by law.

The logic of the standards approach is clear, and the process appears simple. But this approach is more complex than it at first appears. The agency must first set the standards, and then enforce them. In addition, it should continually explore new technical possibilities and evaluate its programs.

Standards may be broad or narrow. A broad water-purity standard might be "swimmable rivers." A narrow standard might be "less than 0.5 percent lead" in paint. The broad standard is vague and general; a statement of what is desirable. As a result, it is not possible to enforce on an individual-firm basis. For enforcement and prosecution, narrow standards are necessary. A firm producing paint that contains more than a half percent of lead is obviously in violation of the narrow lead-content standard.

Standards may also be classified as performance standards or design standards. A **performance standard** specifies a certain level of performance or compliance that must be met. It does not specify the means by which that level must be reached. The regulating agency might require the firm to reduce the pollutants emitted in a combustion process by 10 percent, without specifying the means by which this standard will be met. A **design standard**, on the other hand, specifies not only the required level of performance but also the means to reach that level. Control of auto emissions by the installation of catalytic converters is an example of a design standard. A performance standard leaves the compliance method up to the regulated firm. It is more flexible than the design standard and may encourage research into new technologies and lower-cost methods by business firms to meet pollution reduction goals. In practice, both types of standards are used.

Technology Forcing

Agencies are criticized for setting standards that force firms to use specific pollution control technologies. This is the situation when design standards, rather than performance standards, are used. A good example is the emissions standard for automobiles. It requires the installation of catalytic converters, which are expensive bits of technology. Emissions could be cut by the use of diesel engines or other experimental engine designs, but because car emission standards require the use of catalytic converters, research into other emissions control methods has been stymied. The general problem with **technology forcing** is that techniques that could control pollution more cheaply are not being encouraged, developed, or used.

Given the very real problems with the standards approach to environmental regulation, many economists propose that we use pollution fees or pollution permits instead. Both methods are more flexible than standards and rely on the market to control pollution more efficiently than standards regulation can. Let us look now at how these methods of regulation can achieve our environmental goals at less cost than can standards regulation.

Pollution Fees

There are two types of pollution fees. **Effluent fees** are taxes on production that causes water pollution, whereas **emissions fees** are taxes on production that causes air pollution. If the amount of the pollution fee is at least equal to the social spillover cost, the imposition of the tax will correct the overallocation of resources that results from pollution. It does this by giving firms an incentive to change their behavior. They can either pay the fee or find a new process of production that is less harmful to the environment.

Refer back to the polluting paper company in Figure 3-2. If the company continues to pollute, it must pay the effluent fee, which can be viewed as an additional cost

Performance standard
A regulation that specifies the required level of performance but not the means of compliance.

Design standard
A regulation that specifies both the required level of performance and the means of compliance.

Technology forcing
Standards that force firms to use specific pollution control technologies.

Effluent fees
Taxes on production causing water pollution.

Emissions fees
Taxes on production causing air pollution.

of production. Supply will decrease in the direction of the original curve. Consumers will pay a higher price for the polluters' products because of the effluent fee. They will also consume less. In these ways, they will bear some of the burden of pollution control. If the company chooses to eliminate its pollution, the higher costs of doing so will also cause supply to decrease. The important point is that fees do not force technology. Instead, they give firms an incentive to look for least-cost techniques to cut pollution and fees. From the view of enforcement and administration, pollution fees are easier to administer than are standards. From society's view, they result in least-cost—and thus more efficient—pollution control.

Marketable Pollution Permits

Under the **pollution permits** approach, the maximum level of pollution acceptable to society is divided into units, and the government issues permits that allow business firms to produce these units of pollution in their production process. These permits can be bought and sold. They will eventually wind up in the hands of firms for whom the costs of reducing pollution are the highest. In economics, we often identify small changes in some variable with the word *marginal*. When we are referring to changes in cost, we use the term *marginal cost*. Hence, **marginal cost** is the additional cost of one additional unit of change (in this case, the additional cost of reducing one additional unit of pollution). As is often the case in economics, the additional cost of reducing the first unit of pollution is lower than the additional cost of reducing the few remaining units of pollution. The more general term for this type of situation is **rising marginal cost**. This means that business firms causing small amounts of pollution will have the highest marginal costs of pollution control (because they are closer to removing their last additional units of pollution). Business firms causing large amounts of pollution will have lower marginal costs of pollution control, since they will be far from removing their last units of their pollution. Firms with high marginal costs will prefer to purchase a permit rather than reduce their levels of pollution. Purchasing the permit will raise their costs of production, thereby increasing the price of their product. Consumers will then buy less of this product that causes pollution.

On the other hand, firms that can reduce pollution relatively cheaply (that is, those firms causing the greatest amount of pollution) will choose to reduce their pollution rather than purchase a high-priced permit. In both cases, the pollution is decreased and the resource misallocation is corrected as well. Society receives greater pollution control in a least-cost process of doing so.

In 1979, the EPA established on an experimental basis its first marketable pollution permits. The earliest experiments focused on individual firms that caused pollution at various points in each of their production processes. Amendments made to the Clean Air Act in 1990 extended the concept industry-wide, creating pollution permits for coal-burning utilities.

Pollution permits and pollution fees are incentive-based regulation schemes. Studies indicate that these schemes do work. They are less expensive than standards regulation and do not stifle technological change. Instead, they encourage research and the development of new pollution control technologies.

Pollution permits
Tradable permits that allow the owners of the permits to produce a given amount of pollution.

Marginal cost
The additional cost of one additional unit of change (in this case, it refers to the additional cost of reducing one additional unit of pollution).

Rising marginal cost
The rising additional cost of making each additional unit of change.

EconNews

"An International Market in Pollution"

Read more on the U.S. proposal of international trading of pollution permits under the International Trade category.

http://econapps. swlearning.com

EVALUATION OF ENVIRONMENTAL POLICIES

Pollution affects our lives. And policies to prevent or reduce pollution also affect our lives. Whatever the method used by regulators, regulation raises the firm's production costs and increases the price we pay for the products we buy. These policies also, of course, result in air, water, and soil of higher quality. It is important that the policies used are efficient. The framework for evaluating public policies of all types is cost-benefit analysis.

Cost-benefit analysis
A study that compares the costs and benefits of a policy or program.

Cost-benefit analysis is the systematic comparison of all the costs of a program with all of the benefits. The program should be undertaken only if the benefits are greater than the costs. From the perspective of the environment, let's look at the costs and benefits of environmental protection programs. The costs of these programs are the costs incurred by government in regulating business, in running public recycling programs, and in any other activity that cuts down on or cleans up pollution. Business firms also incur costs of environmental protection. If they adopt a more expensive but less-polluting process, their increase in cost is an environmental protection cost. If they use less-polluting but more costly raw materials, the difference in cost is also an environmental protection cost. If they install and maintain pollution control equipment, such as scrubbers in smokestacks, they incur an environmental protection cost. Consumers can also incur environmental protection costs if they install high-efficiency, less-polluting furnaces and other appliances, or if they incur the expense and inconvenience of recycling. The environmental protection costs are the total of all these costs, whether incurred by government, businesses, or households.

The benefits of environmental protection are the improvements in our environmental quality that result. Some of these benefits are quantifiable. We save on cleaning costs if air pollution is reduced. Businesses save on repair costs when acid rain no longer damages their structures. We save on medical costs when people no longer suffer the ill health that results from pollution.

However, many of the benefits of environmental programs cannot be calculated in monetary terms. The personal benefits of improved health and longevity go far beyond the savings on medical costs. The biodiversity of our rain forests is expected to yield yet-undiscovered products to benefit humankind. And there is no way to place a price on a stream used for trout fishing or a lake used for swimming that might otherwise be too polluted for use.

In reconciling the costs with the benefits of environmental protection, we must take a wide view and a long view. We must consider the monetary and nonmonetary benefits of environmental protection, and we must consider the benefits to future as well as current generations.

EconNews

"Reducing Airline Emissions: The Future is the Past"

Find a summary of this news story under Economics and the Environment in the Microeconomics category.

http://econapps.swlearning.com

CONSERVATION AND RECYCLING

Pollution by producers is an important facet of our environmental problem, but consumers also contribute to the problem. As the world's population increases, we exhaust nonrenewable resources such as copper, oil, and coal at an increasing rate. The danger is that supplies will be depleted to the point at which these resources cannot be extracted economically from the earth.

Population creates environmental strain in two ways. From an ecological viewpoint, a country is overpopulated if (1) its people outnumber its ability to sustain them, or (2) its people consume so great an amount of resources that they stress the global environment. The first condition is the problem of many countries in Asia and Africa, where resources are often inadequate to meet the needs of a growing population. The second condition applies to our own country, which, on a per capita basis, uses an inordinate share of the world's resources. With only 4.7 percent of the world's population, the United States produces 29 percent of all goods and services, uses 23 percent of the world's energy, and produces 22 percent of the world's carbon dioxide emissions.[1] Given its consumerism, U.S. society stresses the environment far more than does an overpopulated less developed country. The attitude reflected in the bumper-sticker quotation, "The one who dies with the most toys wins," results in wasteful consumption of resources and energy. We live in a society characterized by a throwaway mentality, planned obsolescence, and the production of unnecessary and ecologically harmful products. The antithesis of this attitude is one of conservation and recycling. Let us look first at the economics of conservation, then that of recycling. Then let's examine a few innovative policies to reduce pollution by consumers.

Economics of Conservation

As a starting point, let us review the law of demand from Chapter 1. Price and quantity demanded are inversely related. Consumers will buy more at low prices than at high ones. It therefore follows that raising the price of a product will result in less consumption of it, whereas lowering the price will cause greater consumption. The market can act as a mechanism to encourage conservation. And the government can influence the market by taxes or by **subsidies**, which are payments to producers or consumers of the product.

Subsidies
Payments from the government for some given action, such as recycling.

Let's look at a few examples of such policies, beginning with a hypothetical market for gasoline. The United States is castigated by environmentalists for being the world's largest importer of oil. Much of the oil we consume is in the form of gasoline to power cars, sport utility vehicles, and light trucks. Despite having only 4.6 percent of the world's population, the United States has 35 percent of the world's cars.[2] The price per gallon of gasoline in the United States is unrealistically low because it is not fully adjusted to account for pollution costs and depletion of natural resources. When the price of gasoline is adjusted for the effects of inflation, we see that it has not changed much since 1940. Further, gas prices in the United States are much lower than in the rest of the industrialized world, where countries impose gasoline taxes higher than those in the United States. Such taxes increase the price of a gallon of fuel, giving consumers an incentive to conserve gas.

Let's consider two hypothetical countries, illustrated in Figure 3-3 on page 70. Let's assume identical demand and supply curves in each hypothetical market. These identical curves result in an initial equilibrium price of $1 per gallon, and an initial equilibrium quantity of four million gallons in each country.

Recall that an excise tax is an additional cost of production that must be paid to the government by the sellers of the product. The tax will thereby cause a backward shift in supply.

Low-Tax Country

High-Tax Country

The higher ($1.00 per gallon) gasoline tax results in the consumption of only two million gallons of gas and thus encourages greater conservation than the lower ($.50 per gallon) tax.

Now suppose that the first country (the low-tax country) imposes a gasoline tax of $.50 per gallon, and the second country (the high-tax country) imposes a tax of $1.00 per gallon. The supply curve in the low-tax country shifts back (upward) by $.50 per gallon to S'. The new equilibrium price to consumers is $1.25 per gallon, and the new equilibrium quantity is three million gallons. The imposition of the tax has increased price slightly and resulted in a decrease in consumption of one million gallons of gasoline.

In the case of the high-tax country, the supply curve shifts back (upward) by $1.00 per gallon to S''. The new equilibrium price is $1.50 per gallon, and the new equilibrium quantity is two million gallons. The imposition of the tax has increased price greatly and has resulted in a decrease in consumption of two million gallons of gasoline. In both cases consumption decreases, but far more significantly where gasoline taxes are higher.

How does this conservation occur? In many ways. Drivers are less likely to make unnecessary trips. They are more likely to take public transportation if it is available. They carpool. When purchasing a car, they compare the gas efficiency of various models and weigh this information heavily in their decision to buy. Higher gasoline prices give individuals an incentive to make many independent decisions that result in conservation of oil supplies. Conversely, a low price encourages us to waste gasoline. (Americans do not vote for politicians who campaign on the promise to raise gasoline taxes, although it might be in our long-run best interest to do so.)

Other examples of using economic incentives to conserve scarce resources come from our agricultural policy. We will see in Chapter 12 that one aspect of farm policy is to reduce the supply of farm products by taking land out of production. We pay farmers *not* to farm their agricultural land. It makes ecological sense to require that highly erodible land be taken out of production, and it makes sense for the farmer to be paid to leave such land uncultivated. It also makes sense to eliminate government payments to farmers who cultivate wetlands or other environmentally fragile acreage.

The bottom line with regard to conservation is that taxes increase market prices and therefore lead to efforts to conserve. The marketplace, combined with taxes, is an effective tool for implementing conservation policy.

Economics of Recycling

It is also possible to save and reuse some of our natural resources. Many communities and business firms have established recycling programs in an effort to reduce the strain on our landfills and resources. Recycling has many dimensions and many economic aspects.

Recycling programs vary throughout the nation. Communities commonly recycle aluminum and newspapers. Some communities also recycle cardboard, magazines, tin cans, glass, plastics, scrap metal, and used oil. Recycling keeps these commodities out of landfills. As our population has grown, so have the wastes we produce. Landfills have filled up. Old landfills, in which everything (including hazardous waste) has been dumped, are recognized as environmental hazards that pollute the land and water supply.

The problem of garbage was brought home to many of us in 1987 as we followed the news story of the barge named *Mobro*, which was loaded with 3,190 tons of garbage at Long Island, New York, and sent out to find a garbage dump that would accept its cargo. It was refused permission to unload in North Carolina, Florida, Louisiana, the Bahamas, Mexico, and Honduras. After a 6,000-mile journey lasting about half a year, the barge returned to New York City, where it was refused permission to dock. After three months in the New York harbor, the garbage was incinerated in Brooklyn, and the ash was shipped back to the originating community, which buried it in its landfill.

Although modern, state-of-the-art landfills are environmentally safe if located and monitored properly, their use is nevertheless controversial. If you have ever followed the local political wrangling over the site of a proposed new landfill, you are aware of this. No one wants the landfill anywhere near his or her property, and citizens' groups form to fight landfill siting projects. Reducing the bulk of our garbage through recycling is therefore a popular alternative to landfilling.

The two most pressing problems faced by recycling programs are (1) motivating consumers and businesses to recycle and (2) developing markets for recyclable goods.

Motivation to Recycle

Studies have found that people are more willing to recycle if it is convenient for them to do so. Collecting recyclables at consumers' homes (curbside recycling) or establishing numerous neighborhood drop-off points makes recycling easier and more convenient for people.

Although some people recycle because they are environmentally conscious, others are willing to do so only if they are given sufficient economic incentives. These incentives can take a variety of forms.

Many households pay for waste disposal services by a fixed fee to a public or private garbage collection service. A family might pay $10 a month to have its garbage collected. The charge is the same whether the family has 1 bag or 12 bags of garbage per week. There is no incentive to reduce the amount of waste that is collected.

On the other hand, some communities have begun to charge households for each bag or can of garbage they discard. A charge of $2 per bag of garbage provides an incentive to decrease the number of bags disposed of. Households can save money by buying products with less packaging or by recycling or composting their waste. Although such programs hold much promise for motivating consumers to recycle, they also may create some less desirable effects. They may motivate some people to dispose of their garbage illegally by dumping it in vacant lots or along country roads or by burning it themselves.

Under another type of incentive system, the government sets a target for recycling a product, and producers are responsible for ensuring that their product is recycled. Producers are required to buy "credits" from firms that recycle their type of product. For example, if a 50 percent recycling target were set for newspaper, the local newspaper company would be required to buy 500 pounds of credits for every 1,000 pounds of newspapers it produces. It would buy its credits from firms such as cardboard box producers that can use old newspapers in producing their product. Because the box producer is paid for using old newspapers, it has an incentive to use recycled newsprint instead of new paper pulp.

The price of the recycling credit is set by market forces. If the box manufacturer can use the newspapers at low cost, the price of the credit will be low. If a second firm can use old newsprint at a still lower cost, it will sell the credits to the newspaper at a still lower price. The old newspaper will go to the firm with the lowest use costs, and society's recycling costs will be minimized. As with taxes and subsidies, recycling credits are most appropriate for particularly troublesome items in our waste stream.

A final example of an economic incentive to reduce waste by recycling is the beverage container deposit, which is legally required in several states. Consumers pay a deposit of 5 or 10 cents per can or bottle when they buy beer or soda pop. Their money is returned when they bring the containers back to the store or a redemption center. A similar situation exists for plastic milk and water containers. It is estimated that the 10 states with beverage deposit laws recycled more containers than all other 40 states combined and achieved an overall recovery rate of 72 percent compared to 28 percent in nondeposit states. The bottom line is that economic incentives can motivate us to recycle and reuse materials, which extends the life of our resources and landfills.

Markets for Recyclable Products

A serious problem faced by recycling programs is lack of markets for recyclable materials. Old newspapers can be used to make paper or cardboard, or they can be shredded for animal bedding. Glass can be used as an additive for asphalt paving. Other recyclable materials have similar uses. But the firms that produce recycled products often face an uncertain demand. They may therefore suspend the purchase of the recyclable materials, and recycling centers will build up inventories of these articles. When we drop off our recyclables at the recycling collection point, we assume that these articles will be put to some appropriate use. In fact, they sometimes go to landfills because there is no user for them. The EPA has awarded numerous grants to local governments so they can develop additional markets for recyclables. Further uses of recycled products must be found, and consumers, governmental units, and business firms must be given incentives to choose products made with recycled material, if such a choice is available. Many people are averse to buying products made with recycled materials (for example, retreaded tires) because they view the products as inferior to those made with new materials. If there are quality differences between recycled products and new ones, price differences should be consistent with the quality differences. Last, we must also raise the issue that sometimes recycling is simply not an efficient choice in the context of the resources used in recycling, the negative by-products created in the process, or the possible lack of safety of recycled products.

Innovative Policies

Beginning on February 17, 2003, motorists driving into central London were charged $8 per day for the privilege. While controversial, the goal of the policy is to reduce the volume of traffic in the area, ease congestion, and raise money for investing in public transportation. Those who support this policy believe that the costs of pollution should be placed back on those who cause the pollution, thereby giving them an incentive to change their ways. Those who oppose the policy believe that it is misguided and will never work. Because of the controversy surrounding the policy, it is not clear at this time whether the policy will stay in place, be altered, or be eliminated. Regardless of public opinion, it is definitely an innovative effort to reduce the pollution caused by consumers. Similar type policies, such as raising the excise tax on gasoline and increasing parking fees, offer similar incentives to reduce reliance on the automobile.

THE EFFECTS OF ENVIRONMENTAL POLICY ON THE U.S. ECONOMY

The environmental movement and our environmental policies are not uncontroversial. Environmental regulation has increased the costs of American business and has therefore been accused of the following adverse effects on the U.S. economy. Critics argue that by increasing costs, environmental regulation has contributed to inflation, which is a general increase in the average level of prices. They also argue that environmental regulation has increased unemployment because the equilibrium output sold by firms is lower (and fewer workers are needed to produce it).

Moreover, they argue that because output is lower, economic growth, which is the increase in national production, will slow down. U.S. firms will be less competitive than their international competitors because they face stricter environmental regulations than many firms abroad. This was certainly the concern in the controversy mentioned earlier with the North American Free Trade Agreement.

Several studies have estimated the effect of pollution control on these macroeconomic variables. The consensus is that inflation is only slightly affected by environmental regulation and that employment has actually increased as a result of the regulations because the decrease in jobs in polluting firms has been offset by an increase in jobs at firms formerly harmed by pollution (remember the paper and beer industries?) and by the creation of jobs in pollution control. Furthermore, our competitive position in the world has not been harmed by our environmental protection.[3] Last, keep in mind the production possibilities curve introduced in Chapter 1. Although there may be some short-run cost of environmental protection on our economy, over the long run, we know that without environmental protection, the production curve would actually shrink inward as our resources are depleted. This would be the opposite of economic growth. Hence, the long-run and short-run benefits of environmental protection must be considered along with the short-run costs.

INTERNATIONAL ASPECTS OF THE ENVIRONMENTAL PROBLEM

Just as local governments do not effectively control local pollution that affects the nation, individual nations do not effectively control national pollution that affects the world. As we have seen, environmental policy should be made by decision-making groups that include all those affected by negative spillovers. Environmental problems such as loss of biodiversity, ozone depletion, and global warming are international issues. International action is therefore necessary. Many experts believe that the major environmental issue of the twentieth century was pollution, but the principal issue of the twenty-first will be global warming.

Several international environmental summits have been held to try to deal with some of these problems. Participants have sought environmental treaties modeled after our international trade treaties and have sought to reform and strengthen the United Nation's powers with regard to the environment. These summits include the Rio Earth Summit in Brazil in 1992 and the follow-up summit in Kyoto, Japan, in 1997. The result of the Kyoto summit was a treaty designed to reduce global warming. This Kyoto Accord, named after the location of the summit, would require industrial countries to substantially reduce industry-generated heat-trapping gases that cause global warming.

The 10-year anniversary of the Rio Summit took place in Johannesburg, South Africa, in 2002. This latter summit presented an opportunity for governments, United Nations agencies, global financial institutions, nongovernment organizations, and others to work to achieve sustainable development. Approximately 60,000 people from all over the world attended this summit, and it was hoped that negotiators would modify the Kyoto Accord in such as way as to increase support for the treaty. A major problem is President George W. Bush's opposition to the Kyoto Accord, which has angered and frustrated many environmentalists at home and abroad. The Bush administration acknowledged for the first time in June 2002 that human activity is indeed causing global warming. As of late 2003, however, the Bush administration still opposed to the Kyoto treaty and instead supported voluntary restraint among U.S. companies. Indeed, the EPA ruled in August 2003 that carbon dioxide is not even a pollutant, thereby eliminating the opportunity of the EPA to regulate carbon dioxide.

An additional global issue is that of ozone depletion. In contrast to the problem of global warming, efforts to reduce ozone depletion have been viewed as one of the greatest environmental success stories over the past few decades. Unfortunately, as of this writing, President George W. Bush is seeking to perpetuate the use of methyl bromide, the most ozone-destructive chemical still used in developed countries, otherwise slated to be phased out. It is ironic that President Bush's father, as vice president during the Reagan administration, supported the protocol that restricted the use of this ozone depleting chemical.[4]

In addition, environmental activists argue that some provisions of the World Trade Organization interfere with and weaken environmental protection standards in developed countries. Others maintain that the world community, through the World Bank and International Monetary Fund, is forcing less developed countries to increase their export earnings by selling timber and by producing other export crops on previously forested areas. The result is deforestation of parts of Africa, Asia, and Latin America. (We will discuss these international organizations in greater detail in Chapter 9 and Chapter 17.) And, as mentioned before, many people are concerned about the pollution caused by the maquiladoras (U.S.-owned assembly operations) along the Mexican side of the U.S. border. They are also concerned about pesticides that are banned by the United States but are exported by U.S. corporations to Central American countries, where the chemicals contaminate groundwater and harm the health of farmworkers. Similarly, U.S. waste and environmentally harmful products are often shipped to other countries.

One of the most notorious global examples of industrial pollution occurred in 1984, when a Union Carbide subsidiary plant accidentally released toxic emissions in Bhopal, India. More than 1,000 people were killed, and more than 200,000 were injured. It was the worst industrial accident ever recorded until then. The official death toll of the 1986 Chernobyl nuclear accident in Russia is 3,576, but Greenpeace Ukraine, an environmental organization, estimates that by 1995 the total death toll from the accident approached 32,000. Many people were killed, many more were injured, women are still bearing deformed children, and contamination in the Ukraine and neighboring countries continues to this day. Clearly, there are many aspects of the global pollution problem.

CRITICISM OF U.S. ENVIRONMENTAL POLICY

As a conservative president with a conservative administration, George W. Bush has been strongly criticized by environmentalists for his environmental policies. As mentioned earlier, he wants voluntary restraint by businesses that contribute to global warming, rather than mandatory restraints. President Bush has repeatedly called for more research into the problem of global warming, whereas his critics charge that this is just a delaying tactic. We've also noted that President Bush may be backing away on the issue of the ozone layer. In addition, critics charge that the widespread use of the hydrogen fuel cells that President Bush made a centerpiece of his energy plan might not be as environmentally friendly as Bush wants to believe. Scientists say that the new technology could lead to greater destruction of the ozone layer. President Bush has also supported the approval of a federal dump for nuclear waste at the Yucca Mountain in Nevada and has proposed the drilling for oil and gas in the Arctic National Wildlife Refuge, both to the chagrin of environmentalists. Bush has also reversed prior policy in many areas, including the loosening of environmental restrictions on logging and mining on federal property, the easing of rules that require an environmental impact assessment before thinning our national forests, and the pushing of a comprehensive energy plan that stresses reliance on fossil fuels, which are known to cause global warming and air pollution.

A recent Knight Ridder analysis of data concluded that polluters have paid 64 percent less in fines for breaking federal environmental rules under the Bush administration than they did in the last two years of the Clinton administration.[5] Furthermore, the Bush administration is requiring violators to pay much less for environmental improvement projects, such as restoring wetlands, that they are ordered to undertake as part of their settlements. The value of extra projects plummeted 77 percent during the first 20 months of the Bush administration. Their value averaged $2.6 million per month versus $11.6 million per month, during the last 28 months of the

VIEWPOINT: CONSERVATIVE VERSUS LIBERAL

Economists often make decisions about environmental matters on noneconomic grounds, as they do with certain other issues (such as crime) discussed in this book. It is possible for both liberal and conservative economists to care deeply about the environment.

Because conservatives want to limit the role of government in the economy, they are more likely than liberals to oppose environmental regulation. They will be more likely to favor pollution control policies that utilize market forces rather than other methods. Thus, they favor pollution fees and marketable pollution permits over the regulation of pollution by means of standards. Conservatives may also prefer state and local solutions to environmental problems over policies developed at the federal and international levels.

Liberals, on the other hand, are less averse to government intervention in the economy and the regulation of private businesses. As such, liberals are also more likely to favor standards regulation. They may also be more favorable to policies drafted at the national and international levels. Liberals may well take the position that we should do whatever it takes to get the job done and not worry about the government's expanding role in the economy.

Clinton administration. Current EPA officials responded by saying that it is unfair to compare the first months of the Bush administration to Clinton's second term insofar as Clinton's administration had already achieved many years of experience in comparison to Bush's fledgling administration.

Also in support of the current administration, Bush argues that environmental policy must be carried out in a way that blends the needs of the environment with the needs for economic growth. His administration cites a new approach that embraces "a new way of thinking that is results-oriented." Furthermore, his administration believes that the Clear Skies Act of 2003, presented to Congress by the Bush administration, will, according to the EPA, "significantly improve air quality across the nation, resulting in enormous health and environmental benefits." And, of course, as a conservative politician, President Bush generally prefers voluntary compliance with environmental protection rather than mandatory compliance through government regulations. Similarly, he prefers that environmental regulations take place at national or lower levels of government, and not at the international level. He also favors market-oriented solutions, such as pollution fees and pollution permits, to more heavy-handed solutions such as standards.

SUMMARY

Economic activity causes pollution. Pollution is a spillover cost of production that distorts the allocation of resources in the economy. Pollution causes resources to be overallocated to the market in which it occurs and underallocated to other affected markets. Government therefore regulates private business by the standards approach, pollution fees, or pollution permits.

The standards approach has been criticized, especially when it forces certain types of technology on producers of the product. Conservation and recycling programs also reduce pollution. Such programs are most effective when they give individuals and businesses some economic incentives for participation. Environmental programs should be evaluated by cost-benefit analysis, and these programs should be used only if benefits are greater than costs. Benefits must be broadly considered and include the monetary and nonmonetary benefits to current and future generations.

Many environmental problems are, in fact, international in nature. Thus, international cooperation will be necessary to solve these problems.

NOTES

1. United Nations Development Program, *Human Development Report 2000* (New York: Oxford University Press, 2000).

2. G. Tyler Miller, Jr. *Living in the Environment*, 8th. ed. (Pacific Grove, Calif.: Brooks/Cole, 2001), p. 227.

3. For a discussion of these studies, see Adam B. Jaffe, Steven R. Peterson, Paul R. Portney, and Robert Stavins, "Environmental Regulation and the Competitiveness of U.S. Manufacturing," *Journal of Economic Literature* (March 1995): 132–163; Michael Porter and Claas van der Linde,

"Toward a New Conception of the Environment-Competitiveness Relationship," *Journal of Economic Perspectives*, 9, no. 4 (Fall 1995); and Robert Repetto, "U.S. Competitiveness Is Not at Risk in the Climate Negotiations" (Washington, D.C.: World Resources Institute, 1997).

4. Geoffrey Lean, Environment Editor, *The Independent*, July 20, 2003,

news.independent.co.uk/low_res/story.jsp? story=425893&host=3&dir=507.

5. The data are based on a Knight Ridder analysis of statistics compiled from the Federal Register by the Rockefeller Family Fund's Environmental Integrity Project, published in November 2002.

DISCUSSION QUESTIONS

1. Why do polluters pollute? Consider various reasons for both individuals and businesses.

2. How does pollution distort resource allocation in the economy? Consider both overallocation and underallocation of resources.

3. What are some of the costs of pollution control? Should we be willing to pay anything and sacrifice everything to eliminate all pollution?

4. What do you think is the appropriate level of government to deal with pollution? Does it matter what type of pollution we are considering? Why?

5. Can you think of examples of negative or positive externalities not mentioned in the text?

6. Compare the various incentive-based environmental policies to the standards approach. What are the strengths and weaknesses of each?

7. Do you think it is appropriate that the consumer bears part of the burden of effluent or emission fees in the form of higher prices? Why or why not?

8. Explain cost-benefit analysis. Would the results of cost-benefit analysis ever be different in the short run than in the long run? Why or why not?

9. Do you think that we are a throwaway society? Are your attitudes toward consumption the same as your parents'? Your grandparents'?

10. Is it efficient to convert food (corn) into ethanol to burn in our cars and trucks? Would

this be economical if the government taxed the use of gasoline and subsidized the use of ethanol? How might the government justify these taxes and subsidies?

11. Keeping in mind that environmental regulation is a luxury good, would you expect American attitudes to be the same as attitudes of citizens of Third World countries?

12. Go to the Environmental Protection Agency Web site (**www.epa.gov**). Click Where You Live, go to Search Your Community, enter your zip code, and find current environmental issues in your geographical area.

13. Consider the pollution, gasoline use, and other problems associated with our cities that are congested. People often demand additional roads and parking structures to handle these problems. How might these measures be self-defeating? What are other (incentive-based) policies that might be used to reduce automobile use and/or increase mass transit?

14. The Web site for the World Business Council for Sustainable Development is **www.wbcsd.ch**. Go to this Web site to discover the coalition of some 165 international companies that are united by a shared commitment to sustainable development through economic growth, ecological balance, and social progress. It concerns itself with issues such as poverty and other social justice issues and it provides an extensive list of publications. After "surfing," do you find yourself to be in general agreement with the World Business Council, or do you find that you largely disagree?

15. The Johannesburg Summit was mentioned in the text of this chapter. The Web site for the summit, **www.johannesburgsummit.org**, provides much information, including surveys, documents, publications, and summaries of the summit. What were some of the major accomplishments of the summit?

16. The U.S. Environmental Protection Agency (EPA) provides much information about EPA policy and environmental issues. Check out its Web site at **www.epa.gov** and report on some of the information that pertains to human health.

17. The Web site for Resources for the Future, an environmental research group, is **www.rff.org**. Use this Web site to browse for information on research topics such as the environment, natural resources, and methods of environmental protection. Are there any environmental protection tools or techniques that seem particularly useful to you?

18. The Environmental News Service has up-to-date information on environmental issues at its Web site, **www.ens-news.com**. Use this Web site to find examples of the latest news on environmental issues.

19. Are you a liberal or a conservative on issues of environmental protection? Why?

CHAPTER 4 ROADMAP

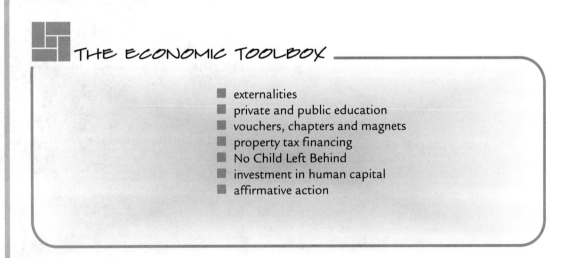

**Chapter 6
U.S. Poverty**
Lack of education is a cause of poverty
Investment in human capital is one remedy for poverty

**Chapter 7
World Poverty**
Lack of investment in human capital is a serious problem for poor countries

**Chapter 5
Discrimination**
Human capital discrimination affects minorities in the labor market
Inner-city schools tend to be underfunded
Will "No Child Left Behind" aid minority children?

**Chapter 4
Education**

**Chapter 10
Housing**
Residential segregation contributes to low-quality inner-city schools

**Chapter 2
Crime and Drugs**
Demand-side policies, such as education, are a method of treating the drug problem

**Chapter 17
Globally Free Markets for the Twenty-First Century?**
Investment in human capital creates economic growth
Education budgets in poor countries are cut due to "economic reforms"

THE ECONOMIC TOOLBOX

- externalities
- private and public education
- vouchers, chapters and magnets
- property tax financing
- No Child Left Behind
- investment in human capital
- affirmative action

EDUCATION

I have something to say to every family listening to us tonight. Your children can go on to college. If you know a child from a poor family, tell her not to give up—she can go on to college. If you know a young couple struggling with bills, worried they won't be able to send their children to college, tell them not to give up—their children can go on to college. If you know somebody who's caught in a dead-end job and afraid he can't afford the classes necessary to get better jobs for the rest of his life, tell him not to give up—he can go on to college. Because of the things that have been done, we can make college as universal in the twenty-first century as high school is today. And, my friends, that will change the face and future of America.

—President William Jefferson Clinton, State of the Union Address, 1998

I'm here to say . . . We care about your children. Each child matters. We believe every child can learn. We're going to challenge the soft bigotry of low expectations in the Nation's Capital and around the country, because we know a more helpful America depends on this nation's capacity to educate each and every child.

—President George W. Bush, Speech in Washington, D.C., July 1, 2003

Clearly, both of our nation's most recent presidents have made strong statements about education, and both seem to want it to be provided universally to all young people. However, as we shall see, the two presidents vary considerably in their approach to improving education, both representing opposite ends of the liberal and conservative spectrum.

Historically, the United States has valued education highly. We provide public primary and secondary education (kindergarten through high school, or K–12) free to the student and the student's family. Higher education (postsecondary) public colleges, universities, and vocational schools are partly financed by tax revenues so that tuition is affordable for the average student. Public education is viewed as the force that levels the playing field and ensures that all Americans have an equal opportunity to succeed in our society. Historically, it has been one of our most important antipoverty policies. Furthermore, our economy reaps the benefits of education in the form of literate, productive workers. Education is the classic example of a good or service that creates positive externalities, as we will discuss shortly.

In this chapter, we will look at the U.S. education system. First, we will discuss the spillover benefits of education, including both K–12 and higher education. Next, we will focus on K–12 education and pay special attention to the financing of K–12 education, the quality of K–12 education, and various proposals for improving K–12 education. We will consider both public schools and private schools. **Public schools** are those that are financed by taxes and operated in large part by government. **Private schools** are not owned and operated by government but by churches, businesses, or other groups in the private sector. They are largely financed by tuition and endowments, which we will discuss shortly.

Next, we will focus on higher education, including both public and private universities. We will discuss higher education as an investment in human capital, as well as other issues in higher education.

EDUCATION'S SPILLOVER BENEFITS

The provision of education creates private benefits that go to the student and the student's family. The educated, skilled individual is able to earn higher wages than the uneducated, unskilled worker. The educated worker is less likely to be frequently unemployed and is more likely to find a job that is intellectually rewarding. He or she may be exposed to a wider variety of aesthetic experiences that enrich life. These are the private benefits of education that the student receives. We imagine that you and your family considered many of these factors while you were deciding whether to go on to college.

The provision of education also creates benefits for society. Educated citizens are more likely to vote and otherwise participate in public life. They have more productive skills and contribute more to the economy's output. They earn more and therefore may pay more income taxes. They are less likely to be chronically unemployed than are uneducated workers. They are less likely to go on welfare and less likely to commit crimes, or at least violent crimes. Therefore, society receives spillover benefits from education, and the educated person receives private benefits.

These benefits to society are examples of externalities. As discussed in Chapter 3 on the environment, **externalities** are benefits or costs of an economic activity that spill over from the private market (or individual) onto society as a whole. These externalities can be either negative or positive. A positive externality provides a benefit to society and is called a **spillover benefit**. A negative externality imposes a cost on society and is called a **spillover cost**. The classic example of a spillover cost is pollution. The classic example of a spillover benefit is education. Externalities tend to create some degree of **inequity**, which we have defined as unfairness. Externalities also cause society's resources to be inefficiently allocated. Our economy will produce either too much (overallocate resources) or produce too little (underallocate resources) when externalities occur. This improper allocation of resources is an example of **inefficiency**. *Externalities thereby create inequity and inefficiency.*

Figure 4-1 shows the underallocation of resources that results from education's spillover benefits. D^p is the demand for education in the private market. The bene-

Public schools
Schools that are operated by the government and are financed by tax revenue.

Private schools
Schools that are not operated by the government and that are mainly financed by student tuition.

Externalities
The costs or benefits of an economic activity that spill over onto the rest of society.

Spillover benefit
A positive externality in which benefits are shifted from the private market to society.

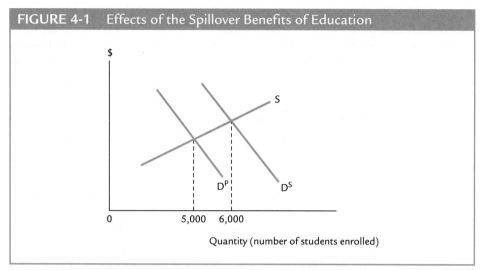

FIGURE 4-1 Effects of the Spillover Benefits of Education

Quantity (number of students enrolled)

Because the private market does not reflect the spillover benefits of education, the number of students enrolled in college (5,000) is less than the socially optimum number (6,000).

fits that students and their families perceive they will receive determine this demand. The supply curve intersects the demand curve at an equilibrium quantity of 5,000. Thus 5,000 students would enroll.

But the private market demand curve is not the socially correct demand curve, because it does not reflect the benefits gained by society from education. If we take the spillover benefits into account, demand would be greater. So, the true socially correct demand curve, based on the benefits received by students and by society, is D^S. D^S intersects supply at an equilibrium quantity of 6,000, which is the socially optimal amount. Because the private market demand does not reflect the positive externalities, the market will produce too little education. We say that the market underallocates resources whenever spillover benefits exist. The market equilibrium is not efficient, or optimum for society, when this occurs.

The spillover benefits justify the government's provision of K–12 education, subsidization of college education through grants and financial aid to students, and establishment of public colleges and universities. These policies correct the underallocation of resources. If the government's contribution toward the student's education is just equal to the spillover benefits that society receives from education, the socially optimum amount of education will be produced and consumed in our economy.

Different levels and types of education yield different amounts of private and spillover benefits. Most people agree that the spillover benefits of K–12 education are tremendous, because basic literacy is developed through such education. The provision of primary and secondary education free to the student is therefore justified by the societal spillover benefits. Some argue, however, that most of the benefits of postsecondary education are private and that spillover benefits from college

Spillover cost
A negative externality in which costs are shifted from the private market to society.

Inequity
Unfairness.

Inefficiency
Using resources in such a way as not to maximize the desired output from them.

education are few. They therefore feel that the primary burden of college costs should be borne by the student and the student's family. What do you think?

Our nation incurs large government expense for our nation's educational system, spending 5.2 percent of gross domestic product on education. This is about average for the industrialized countries shown in Table 4.1. Clearly, some countries spend a much higher share of GDP on education, whereas others spend much less.

KINDERGARTEN THROUGH GRADE 12 (K–12) EDUCATION

Primary and secondary education in the United States may be free to the student, but the government incurs great expense for them. In 1998–1999, spending for public K–12 education was $347.4 billion.[1]

Of this amount, local, state, and the federal governments each contributed part. Figure 4-2 shows the percentages paid by each level of government. Note that the federal government contributes a very small share, whereas local and state governments bear the principal burden for funding primary and secondary education. Indeed, spending for the local public school system is the largest item in most municipal (city) budgets. As we shall see, the financing of K–12 education raises difficult issues.

As far as K–12, education is heavily funded by the local property tax, this creates a problem of many underfunded schools in our nation and poor education in these

TABLE 4-1	Total Public Direct Expenditures on Education as a Percentage of Gross Domestic Product for Selected Industrialized Countries, 1998		
Country	**Spending as % of GDP**	**Country**	**Spending as % of GDP**
Australia	4.8	Japan	3.6
Austria	6.3	Korea	4.4
Belgium	5.0	Luxembourg	4.2
Canada	5.7	Mexico	4.5
Czech Republic	4.3	Netherlands	4.3
Denmark	8.3	New Zealand	6.1
Finland	6.2	Norway	6.6
France	6.0	Poland	5.8
Germany	4.6	Portugal	5.8
Greece	3.5	Spain	4.7
Hungary	4.6	Sweden	6.8
Iceland	7.1	Switzerland	5.4
Ireland	4.5	United Kingdom	4.6
Italy	4.6	United States	5.2

Source: U.S. Department of Education, www.ed.gov.

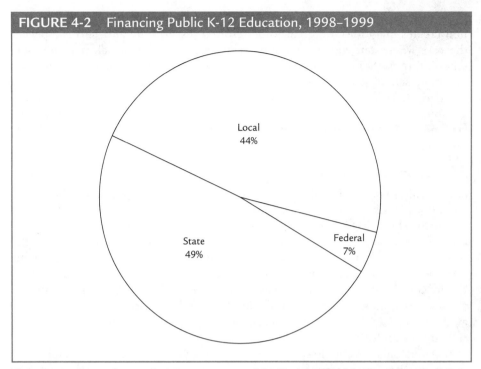

FIGURE 4-2   Financing Public K-12 Education, 1998–1999

Local
44%

State
49%

Federal
7%

The above chart shows the percentages of funds provided by each level of government to public elementary and secondary schools in the United States.

*Source: U.S. Department of Education, **www.ed.gov**.*

schools. The amount of property taxes that can be collected to support the schools depends on the **tax base** and the **tax rate**. The tax base is the value of taxable property (land, homes, other buildings, and so on) in the school district, whereas the tax rate is the percentage of the tax base that is collected as property tax. Property in the suburbs has a high value. Industrial plants, stylish shopping centers, and $500,000 homes add up to a large tax base. But decaying inner-city slums have little value. Moreover, a large percentage of inner-city property is exempt from the property tax. Tax is not collected on municipal buildings, colleges, hospitals, and art museums. The tax base to support the city schools is thus relatively small compared with tax bases in the suburbs. If the tax rate is the same, the suburbs will collect many more tax dollars per student. In fact, tax rates are usually higher in the cities, but because of their inadequate tax bases, inner cities cannot come close to matching the suburbs in educational spending per student.

The state's contribution toward public K–12 education is meant to enrich and equalize education within a particular state. Since there are rich and poor communities in every state, and since local property tax revenues vary greatly, state aid is intended to provide more equal funding and educational opportunities among rich and poor communities.

Tax base
Value of income, earnings, property, sales, or other variables to which a tax rate is applied.

Tax rate
Percentage of the tax base that must be paid to the government as tax.

Nevertheless, the heavy reliance on the local property tax to fund K–12 education creates inequities too great to be resolved just by state aid. This is especially the case when state aid distribution formulas provide aid to all, not only poor, school districts. Some rural school districts are severely underfunded, as are most inner-city school districts. Inner-city school districts are terribly underfunded in comparison with suburban public schools. Spending per student varies widely. Low spending often means shoddy facilities, inadequate supplies, and understaffed classrooms. In turn, these conditions contribute to high dropout rates and functional illiteracy.

The Quality of K–12 Education

Social critic Jonathan Kozol shocked the nation when he reported on the terrible conditions in six inner-city school systems in the early 1990s. He described these inner-city schools in his book, *Savage Inequalities: Children in America's Schools*.[2] In each case the physical facilities were dreadful. He observed schools with holes in their roofs (and no means of repairing them), vocational classes in which young people were being taught typing on old manual typewriters in the age of computers, libraries converted to classrooms because schools housed half again as many students as they were built to house, and classes in which students had to share the few books available. Such basics as working toilets, toilet paper, soap, and chalk were in chronically short supply.

Teachers' salaries were lower in these underfunded school districts than in other school districts. Young teachers tended to burn out and quit, either to find teaching jobs in better-paying, better-supplied suburban districts or to leave teaching altogether. The top salary in one Chicago high school that Kozol visited was two-thirds what Chicago suburban school districts paid teachers. To cut costs, the inner-city school districts often hired "permanent subs" at still lower salaries and without benefits. Even that measure was not enough to stretch the budget to cover the entire year, and some classes simply went unstaffed, especially in the spring when funds were exhausted.

Many students observed in Kozol's study were chronic truants by the time they reached eighth grade. In effect, they had dropped out before they even reached high school. High school dropout rates, which measure the percentage of freshmen who do not finish high school, were high. Dropout rates were in the neighborhood of 50 to 60 percent in the schools Kozol visited. Nor did graduating mean much. The quality of education was so poor that a high school diploma did not guarantee literacy. Kozol noted that in Chicago, 27 percent of high school graduates read at the eighth-grade level or below. At the city's community colleges, which received most of their students from the Chicago public schools, the noncompletion rate was 97 percent.

There is, of course, a racial dimension to this phenomenon. The overwhelming majority of the students in the inner-city schools described were either African American or Hispanic. Whites have moved to the suburbs, leaving the inner cites to minorities who lack the means to escape. This migration means that our public education system is still largely segregated in fact, even if not by law. Minority children receive inferior education because they must attend these poor schools. They emerge inadequately prepared to enter our labor markets or to go on to college. This is a form of discrimination discussed in Chapter 5.

In a landmark state supreme court ruling in 1989, the school funding system of the state of Texas was found to be unconstitutional. Spending per pupil ranged from $2,112 in the poorest district to $19,333 in the richest. The property tax base in the poorest district was only $20,000 per pupil, whereas in the richest district it was $14,000,000. Although the spending figures include property taxes plus the state and federal contributions, it is obvious that the citizens of Texas inner cities taxed themselves to finance their schools by much higher rates than the citizens of suburbs. The problem was their extremely low tax bases.

Other areas of the country were also found to have significant differences in property tax bases and spending per student. For example, the tax base per student in Camden, New Jersey, was only 10 percent of the state average. In 1989–1990, the property tax base per pupil ranged from $39,000 to more than $340,000 in Kentucky. In Kentucky, however, some of the poorest districts were rural.[3] These disparities in spending per pupil have led to numerous court cases in which low-property-value school districts have challenged their state's school-financing system. Several of these cases, such as one in Kentucky, resulted in changes in the way that states finance K–12 education. Many states have revised the formulas by which they distribute funds to equalize spending per student. Federal funds have also been designated to improve education in our poorest school districts. Although some terribly underfunded inner-city school districts remain, the picture is somewhat brighter than it was in the early 1990s.

Unfortunately, many problems remain today in our nation's public K–12 schools, especially when we compare some of our educational outcomes with other Western industrialized countries. Overcrowding is one concern, as demonstrated by the number of pupils per teacher in our schools. For elementary schools, the average number of pupils per teacher is 16.3 in the United States; whereas countries such as Denmark, Italy, and Norway have much lower numbers.[4] In addition, children in other countries such as Singapore, South Korea, Japan, the Netherlands, and the Czech Republic scored better on math tests than U.S. children (though U.S. children generally did better than other countries on science tests).

As a result of poor test results, high dropout rates, differential access to quality schools, and disparities in the funding of suburban versus inner-city schools, our nation has begun to debate the issue of education. President George W. Bush has made educational "reform" a major centerpiece of his domestic policy. Indeed, he has referred to the No Child Left Behind Act of 2001 as "the cornerstone of my administration." We will look at Bush's proposals for education, including the No Child Left Behind Act, as well as other proposals for improving K–12 education in the United States.

Proposals for Improving K–12 Education

Many of us are dissatisfied with the performance of our public K–12 school system, and different proposals abound in the media. The two most common types of policy proposals focus on either an increase in the competition among schools or reform of the tax system through which we support our public schools. We will look at these in turn.

Proposals to Increase Competition among Schools: Charters, Magnets, and Vouchers

Advocates of policies designed to increase competition among schools note that competition in markets for goods and services results in greater efficiency in the production and allocation of resources. They argue, therefore, that measures to increase the competition among a city's schools can be expected to improve performance and simultaneously cut costs. Competition presupposes that consumers can choose among various suppliers. However, public education has traditionally operated on a take-it-or-leave-it basis: a student could either attend the public school in his or her school district or attend a private or parochial school. Traditionally, there have not been choices among public schools for students, and frequently private or parochial schools are expensive or inaccessible. Proposals to increase competition therefore aim to increase choice. Three types of programs to provide such choice are charter schools, magnet schools, and school vouchers.

Charter Schools   Charter schools are public schools that operate with freedom from many of the regulations that apply to traditional public schools. According to the U.S. Charter School Organization, "The charter that establishes each such school is a performance contract detailing the school's mission, program, goals, students served, methods of assessment, and ways to measure success."[5] The length of time for which charters are granted varies, but most are granted for 3 to 5 years (renewable at the end of the contract). Charter schools are typically sponsored by states or local school boards. The basic concept underlying charter schools is that they have greater autonomy in exchange for accountability.

Charter schools offer an alternative to public schools. Those who favor competition in education argue that charter schools can provide such competition. Just like market demand and supply for any other good or service, the demand for education by good schools will be high, with students and their families willing to pay the cost of the school. Schools that provide a poor service will lose their "customers" and will eventually fail unless they decide to improve their quality. Hence, competition among schools theoretically assures that the outcome is high-quality education for all.

Magnet Schools   Another means through which cities have increased the choices of students and their families is the establishment of so-called magnet schools. Magnet schools are public schools that focus on some particular type of curriculum in an attempt to excel in that aspect of education. The city of St. Paul, Minnesota, offers magnet schools that focus on international business, the sciences, and the fine arts. Parents and students can choose any one of them, regardless of the school district in which they reside.

The major argument in favor of magnet schools is that if a school's specialty is desired by families and if it does a good job of providing an education, the school's enrollment will grow; conversely, if a magnet school's specialization is in low demand or it does a poor job of educating, its enrollment will decline. Money to run the schools depends on enrollment. The school with increasing enrollment will be allocated more resources. The budget of the school with decreasing enrollment will decrease. Just as with charter schools, the competition provided through magnet schools will theoretically improve the quality of education for all.

Vouchers   Another proposal to increase consumer choice is the tuition voucher. In such a program, each student would be given a voucher for some particular amount of money to apply toward tuition in qualified public or private schools. The student's family would choose the school it likes best. If parents are satisfied with their child's public school, they would use their voucher to keep their child in that school. Parents who are dissatisfied with the local public schools could enroll their children in private schools, including parochial schools, and tuition could be paid with the voucher. Funding would be withdrawn from the poorer-quality schools and transferred to the better schools through the vouchers. Proponents of vouchers argue that the increased competition would be healthy for our educational system. We would tear down the financial barriers between public and private schools. Good schools should prosper, and really bad schools should go out of business. School vouchers were an important issue in the 2000 presidential campaign. Support for vouchers was part of the Republican Party platform advocated by George W. Bush, whereas vouchers were opposed by the Democratic candidate Al Gore.

In 2002, the United States Supreme Court ruled that an Ohio school voucher program was constitutional. In Cleveland, Ohio, over 5,000 students now receive up to $2,250 per year toward tuition at private schools. Since then, support for similar programs in other states has spread only slowly, partly because of opposition to public subsidies for religious education and partly because of current state fiscal crises that reduce their ability to fund such programs. In addition to Cleveland, voucher programs exist in Milwaukee, Wisconsin, and in Florida.

Since the Supreme Court ruling, President Bush has come out strongly in favor of school vouchers and charter schools. In July 2003, he spoke to a group of educators in Washington, D.C., to announce his proposal to provide vouchers in the nation's capital and elsewhere. The president's request for $75 million from Congress would be used as a "choice incentive fund," a new and perhaps less controversial name for vouchers. The value of vouchers would range up to $7,500 per student per year. If the private school charges less than that, the remainder of the money would go back into the voucher program. The president did not expand on what would happen if there were more applicants for vouchers than the number of vouchers available.

Opposition to Charters, Magnets, and Vouchers   There are many opponents of the types of policies just discussed. Despite the argument that these alternatives provide more competition in our nation's schools, many believe that these programs will in fact endanger our existing public school system. The concern is that our poorest school districts simply cannot compete with the better-off charter, magnet, and private schools. For one thing, popular charters, magnets, and private schools must often close enrollment early because they run out of space, so that students who want to enroll in them often cannot do so. Second, the better schools may be located some distance from the student's home, making it difficult or impossible to arrange transportation. Third, consumers of education (students and their parents)

EconNews

"Do School Vouchers Improve the Quality of Education?"

Given the choice between a public or private school, which would lead to a better education? Read about the government's experiments with vouchers and their debated results by navigating to the Scarcity, Choice, and Opportunity Cost category.

http://econapps. swlearning.com

may not be sufficiently informed about educational options for any of these programs to result in an efficient market. And most important, these programs would likely shift funds from public schools to private ones. Poor public schools would receive fewer resources and become even poorer. With respect to vouchers, a realistic outcome (regardless of the ideal theory) is that the size of the voucher will not cover the entire tuition at an alternative school. This means that low-income students will be forced to remain in poor-quality public schools, from which funding will be transferred in the form of vouchers to the better schools. One educator refers to vouchers as "financial aid for the rich." Many opponents also argue that vouchers for private religious schools violate our nation's separation of church and government. Because of these objections, we must also consider the alternatives.

Proposals for Tax Reform

As we noted in our discussion of inner-city schools, property-tax financing of public education results in unequal spending per student and unequal tax burdens throughout states. The redistributing of funds through state equalization measures and federal grants to poor school districts is one way to alleviate this problem, though this would need to be expanded in order to fully reduce inequity. Tax reform is another option. Let's first address the issue of property tax reform.

Property Tax Reform: The Michigan Experiment   In 1993, the state of Michigan changed the way it finances education, and the rest of the country has been watching the results. If the Michigan experiment works, other states may follow. Here's how the Michigan experiment evolved.

Although Michigan was a national leader in economic growth and high living standards in the 1960s, it became an economic laggard in the decades thereafter. The primary reasons were the restructuring of the U.S. economy and profound changes in the automobile industry, on which Detroit's economy is based. High-paying jobs in manufacturing have disappeared, while lower-paying service sector jobs have been created. It was argued that Michigan's high average property tax rate caused businesses to locate in other states.[6]

Michigan's average property tax rate was about 30 percent above the national average, but the property tax rates of school districts in the state varied. Businesses tended to locate in districts with low property tax rates, because lower taxes meant lower costs of doing business. These districts spent considerable sums per pupil on education, but their large tax bases enabled them to do so at low tax rates. At the same time, Detroit, which in 1990 had a high property tax rate of 4.40 percent (compared with the national average rate of 1.67 percent), could not attract new business investment and was forced to postpone government expenditures of all types. Local spending per Michigan student ranged from $3,000 in property-poor districts, such as Detroit, to $11,000 in property-rich districts. The state needed to reform its tax laws to encourage economic development as well as to provide more equality in educational opportunity throughout the state.

Michigan's new tax plan replaced the property tax with a blend of tax sources to finance education. More specifically, the new law raised the state sales tax by 2 percent, increased the tax on cigarettes by 50 cents, and levied a new real estate transfer tax and a new 6 percent tax on out-of-state telephone calls.

This new tax scheme involved some redistribution of funds from rich to poor districts. Revenues raised from local property taxes were pooled and distributed to the schools by the state. Minimum per-student funding was increased from $3,000 to $4,200 the first year. High-spending districts could increase their spending per pupil only by a local referendum in which the citizens of the district voted to increase spending.

Property taxes to finance education were not fully eliminated, but locally determined rates were replaced by statewide tax rates that vary for different types of property. The new rates were, on average, lower than the property tax rate on businesses. Because the rates were the same throughout the state, businesses' locational decisions would not be distorted.

Critics of the Michigan plan argue that it threatens local autonomy. Local school boards have traditionally controlled public education. Critics fear that state funding will inhibit local choice. Proponents argue that something had to be done to attract business and equalize education throughout the state. Because the property tax burden is high and educational opportunities are unequal in many other states, these same arguments are heard elsewhere. If the Michigan experiment is a success, other states are more likely to revise their tax systems.

Federal and State Corrective Funding   An alternative to property tax reform is to shift the major burden of financing public education to the state and federal levels. This can be done through state equalization measures and federal grants to poor school districts. Property taxes would provide little if any financing for public schools and the problem of differential property tax bases would disappear. There are many merits for this approach. First, unequal funding between poorer and richer school districts would be eliminated. Children would be treated more equally throughout the state and throughout the country. Second, larger expenditures for disadvantaged children could be used to address their needs for the highest possible corrective educational efforts.

There are two obvious problems with this approach. One is that state governments throughout the country have been experiencing worsening budget crises. Partly as a result of a poor national economy and partly because of reduced federal transfers to state governments, most states are in no shape to expand their funding of public education. Alleviating this problem would require higher state taxes or greater federal expenditures on public education and assistance to state governments. The other problem involves the common view that local citizens and their school boards should be making decisions involving their schools. The fear is that if the federal and state governments finance a larger share of public education, the autonomy of local decision making will be lost. Although there is no automatic relationship between funding and autonomy, enough people believe there is and will object to a shift in funding away from local school districts.

The Issue of Funding   The financing of education has been a major part of our discussion of public K–12 education. Aside from the source of funding, some have argued that the level of spending per student doesn't matter much. Some research has indicated that increased spending per student does not by itself improve average student performance by very much. Instead, the research shows that the best predictor of student performance is the school's poverty rate. Simply put, students from schools with high poverty rates generally do not perform as well on standardized tests as students from schools in more affluent areas. The issue is not so much the spending per student on education, but whether the student lives in a poverty-stricken area. As we discuss in Chapter 10 on housing, residential segregation creates inner-city ghettoes, concentrates poverty, and contributes to the creation of an underclass. The poor performance of students from these areas reflects a host of economic and cultural factors outside of school. Increased spending on schools is one step toward greater educational opportunity for low-income students, but many researchers now believe that programs to alleviate poverty and the social dysfunction that accompanies poverty are also needed to improve the academic performance of inner-city students.[7] Thus, we can say that fundamental changes in our nation's economy are necessary for achieving real reforms in our educational outcomes.

No Child Left Behind

In addition to charters and vouchers, President George W. Bush has touted the No Child Left Behind program. The new legislation, approved by Congress, embodies four key principles: (1) stronger accountability for results, (2) greater flexibility for states, schools districts, and schools in the use of federal funds, (3) more choices for parents of children from disadvantaged backgrounds, and (4) an emphasis on teaching methods that have been demonstrated to work. All students are required to take tests annually in reading and math in grades 3 and 8. These tests will allow the public to track the performance of every school in the country. Data will be disaggregated for students by income levels, race, ethnicities, disabilities, and limited English proficiencies to ensure that no child, regardless of background, is left behind. This disaggregation means that even if the school as a whole has good test results, it will also be evaluated on the test results of any minority or disadvantaged groups. The act also requires schools to report on safety issues and insists on English-language proficiency for non-English-speaking children. Schools that do poorly will be targeted for assistance and then be subject to corrective action and ultimately restructuring. Students in poor-quality schools will be given a new range of options, including a transfer to better public schools and additional educational services such as tutoring, after-school services, and summer school. This program is similar to the charters, magnets, and vouchers insofar as it seeks to enhance competition and accountability in education. If schools do poorly, the consequence is that students would go to alternative schools.

Final Words on Public K–12 Education

As a nation, we pride ourselves on the equal opportunity we offer our citizens. One of the most important means of ensuring equal opportunity is through our public school system. The public schools are meant to give all students the tools to survive and compete in our highly technological economy. If differences in spending per student are vast because of the way we finance our public schools, then we do not have equal educational opportunities. And, if we do nothing about the underlying poverty that affects student performance in our inner cities, then we still will not have equal educational outcomes.

HIGHER EDUCATION

At the present time, higher education is plagued by many economic problems. Costs have risen. State government support of public higher education has decreased, and as a result, tuition in public institutions has increased greatly. The recently poor economy, along with a decline in stock values, has reduced the endowments of private institutions. Financial aid rules have changed, and value of Pell grants (for low-income students) has declined. Colleges and universities have adopted various policies to cope with these problems, and students (especially, but not exclusively, students from low-income families) have had to cope with problems of access to our nation's public colleges.

Let's look at some issues related to higher education. First, we will consider the two types of higher education: public and private. Then, we will look at the notion of higher education as an investment in human capital. Next, we will examine who benefits from state government support of public universities. Fourth, we will consider the trend toward decreasing government support of higher education. Fifth, we will analyze the possible use of different tuition for different programs to increase the efficiency of our colleges. Sixth, we will look at financial aid programs, including the Pell grants intended to extend educational opportunity to poor students. And finally, we will consider affirmative action in higher education.

Public and Private Higher Education

U.S. postsecondary (higher) education consists of colleges, universities, community (junior) colleges, and technical-vocational schools. Some are private schools, not operated by the government. Many others are public schools run by the states and occasionally by municipalities. Virtually none of these schools, private or public, is free to the student, as is K–12 education. Costs to the students and their families vary widely, however. The estimated average tuition plus room and board paid by a student in 1998–1999 at a four-year private institution was $19,970; the estimated tuition plus room and board at a similar public institution that year was only $8,018. In other words, the average cost of a private institution is about 2½ times the average cost of a public institution. Note, however, that there is considerable variation around both averages.

Why are the costs of public institutions and those of private institutions so different? Is it simply because the cost of delivering education in private colleges is far greater than in public colleges? The answer is no. Expenses of similar types of private and public schools are not that different. Table 4-2 on page 94 shows educational and other expenses of public and private four-year colleges.

Note that both types of colleges spend about the same per student on instruction, whereas public institutions spend more on research and less on student services than

TABLE 4-2 Educational and General Expenditures of Public and Private Four-Year Colleges, 1993–1994, per Student

Expenditure on:	Public	Private
Instruction	5,486	5,593
Administration	2,638	3,481
Student services	780	1,512
Research	1,351	713
Libraries	389	475
Public service	619	655
Maintenance, etc.	1,170	1,395
Scholarships, etc.	727	3,032
Mandatory transfers	242	321
Total	13,403	17,177

*Source: U.S. Department of Education, **www.ed.gov**.*

FIGURE 4-3 Sources of Revenue for Public Institutions of Higher Education, 1995–1996

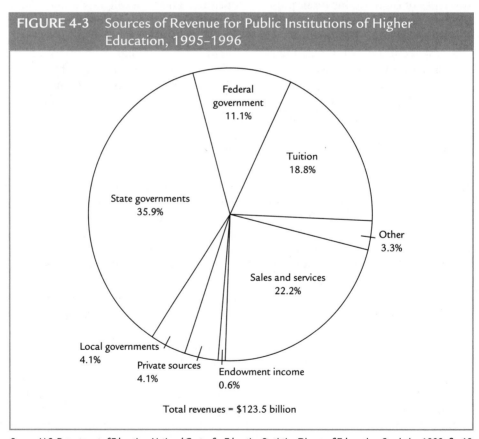

Federal government 11.1%

Tuition 18.8%

State governments 35.9%

Other 3.3%

Sales and services 22.2%

Local governments 4.1%

Private sources 4.1%

Endowment income 0.6%

Total revenues = $123.5 billion

Source: U.S. Department of Education, National Center for Education Statistics. Digest of Education Statistics 1999, fig. 18.

do private schools. Private schools spend more on administration and far more on scholarships to partially offset their higher tuition. But on average, total spending per student varies far less than tuition does. What, then, is the explanation for the great difference in average tuition?

The answer to this question lies in the funding of the two types of institutions. Private schools receive a large proportion of their income from tuition, whereas public schools receive a large proportion from state governments. Figure 4-3 shows funding sources for public institutions of higher education. In contrast, Figure 4-4 shows funding sources for private institutions. The figures are for all types of institutions: vocational-technical schools and community colleges, four-year colleges and universities, and doctoral-granting research-intensive schools.

Note that the single biggest source of revenue for public postsecondary schools is state governments, which contribute about 36 percent of revenue. Tuition contributes only about 19 percent of the income of the public higher education system. Clearly, tuition does not cover the full cost of education in the public institutions,

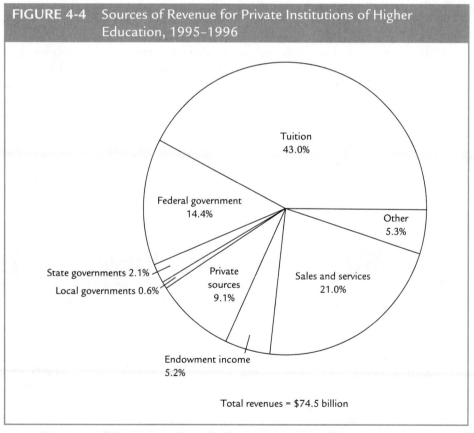

FIGURE 4-4 Sources of Revenue for Private Institutions of Higher Education, 1995–1996

Tuition
43.0%

Federal government
14.4%

Other
5.3%

State governments 2.1%

Local governments 0.6%

Private
sources
9.1%

Sales and services
21.0%

Endowment income
5.2%

Total revenues = $74.5 billion

Source: U.S. Department of Education, National Center for Education Statistics. Digest of Education Statistics 1999, *fig. 19.*

and states contribute a large share of those costs from tax revenues. Thus, the states heavily **subsidize** public education. We will look at who receives these subsidies later.

On the other hand, tuition is the major source of revenue for private schools, accounting for 43 percent of their income. These schools also receive some subsidies from government, but these payments account for a much smaller share of their revenues. Moreover, they have larger endowments than do public schools. **Endowments** are investments owned by the school that earn income for the school. Income from endowments accounts for more than 5 percent of revenues of private schools, but less than 1 percent of revenues of public schools. However, as already noted, endowments are falling now because of the poor economy and stock market. Private schools also receive greater income from private gifts, contracts, and grants than do public schools.

The single most striking difference in the funding of public and private schools is the share of costs covered by tuition. Given that education is highly subsidized by the states in public universities, it is not surprising that by far, most postsecondary students attend public institutions.

Higher Education as an Investment in Human Capital

Education, as well as other services (such as health care and job training), is often referred to as an investment in human capital. An **investment in human capital** is any spending designed to increase the productivity of people. Through education, students can improve their skills and productivity and thereby also increase their earnings. Government data show that earnings increase as education increases, regardless of the worker's race, ethnic group, or gender, although disparities in earnings among these groups persist. Table 4-3 shows median annual earnings for men and women age 25 or older who worked full-time, year-round in 1998. (The term **median** is different from **mean**, which means average. Median earnings refer to the earnings exactly in the middle of a list of all earnings levels, ranked from highest to lowest.) Note the systematic increase in median earnings for both gender groups as the level of education rises, as well as the lower earnings of women at all levels of education. We also note the differential earnings for people of various race and ethnicities in Chapter 5.

TABLE 4-3 Median Annual Earnings of Year-Round Full-Time Workers, 25 Years Old or Older, by Gender, 1998

Highest Educational Attainment	Male	Female
Not high school graduate	$21,699	$15,266
High school graduate	30,838	21,963
Bachelor's degree	49,982	35,408
Master's degree	60,168	42,002
Doctoral degree	69,188	52,167

Source: U.S. Department of Commerce, Bureau of the Census, **www.census.gov**.

Obtaining an education costs money, as you know. But having an education and the increased skills and knowledge acquired in the process of getting that education makes you a more valuable worker. Therefore, wages will increase as your level of education increases. The decision to bear the costs of obtaining your education is a decision to invest in your own skills and future as a worker, at least to some extent. Furthermore, students and their families consider many of the same variables that a business would consider if deciding whether to invest in new machinery or equipment.

In considering an educational investment, you analyze the expected benefits and costs. The benefits are increased earnings throughout your working life subsequent to your graduation. The costs are both direct and indirect. **Direct cost** refers to the tuition and fee payments, costs of books and supplies, and all the other expenditures you make to obtain a degree. **Indirect cost** is the opportunity cost of forgone earnings. (Recall from Chapter 1 that opportunity costs are forgone alternatives.) Because you are in school, you do not work—at least most of you do not work full-time—so you give up earnings. Like your tuition payments, these forgone earnings are a cost. You will theoretically make the investment only if the expected increased earnings justify the total direct and indirect costs.

Figure 4-5 on page 98 describes the decision variables. Pretend you are the decision maker. The horizontal axis represents your expected working life if you graduate from high school at the age of 18 and can expect to work until retirement at 65 years. We have assumed that you will either attend college full-time until the age of 22 and then graduate or not attend college at all. We further assume that you will not work while you are a college student, which is not the case for many students but which simplifies the discussion greatly. If you do not attend college, you will go to work in a relatively low-wage job after graduating from high school. Therefore, annual earnings will be relatively low and increase only modestly as you gain job experience throughout your working life. Some earnings will occur, however, during the four years subsequent to high school graduation.

If you attend college instead of working, those first four years' earnings will be given up, so they are part of your opportunity costs of obtaining a college education. The earnings given up to attend college are labeled Indirect cost in Figure 4-5. Direct costs will also be incurred. You (or your family) must pay tuition and fees, buy supplies and books, and pay board and room (or at least the amount in excess of what you would incur by living at home). The direct costs are shown by the area below the horizontal axis because they are negative amounts (money paid out).

After you graduate, you may go to work for only slightly higher earnings than you would receive had you simply worked since high school. But because you obtained your education, you will be more promotable. Employers put more-educated employees into positions of greater responsibility. Furthermore, employers invest in more on-the-job training for educated workers than they do for uneducated workers. On-the-job training makes you a more valuable employee. You can reasonably expect your earnings to increase substantially as you establish yourself in your field. The possibilities are much greater if you graduate from college than if you do not. Therefore, your annual earnings will be greater and the difference between what

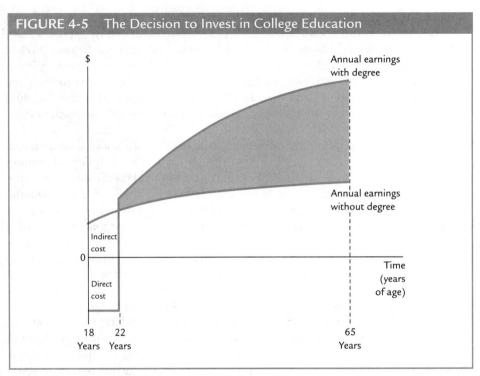

FIGURE 4-5   The Decision to Invest in College Education

$

Annual earnings
with degree

Annual earnings
without degree

Indirect
cost

0

Time
(years
of age)

Direct
cost

18   22
Years   Years

65
Years

The investment will be made only if the increase in lifetime earnings justifies the direct and indirect costs of education.

you earn and what you would have earned without the degree will increase over time. The total increased earnings over your working life are represented by the shaded area in Figure 4-5.

You compare the expected increased earnings to the costs of your college education. Alternatively, you may compare the increased earnings to other earnings that you might have accrued if you had invested your college costs in some other way, such as in an apprenticeship program or a vocational school. If you are a very sophisticated decision maker, you compute a rate of return on your investment, which is your net benefit (benefit minus cost), divided by the amount of your investment. Then you compare the **rate of return** on your college education to the rates of return on other investments you could have made.

The preceding discussion is based on the assumption that you are a traditional student who entered college right after high school. In fact, you may be a nontraditional, older student, and you may be a part-time rather than a full-time student. Almost half of all postsecondary students were age 25 years or older in recent years, and almost half attended college part-time. Clearly, U.S. colleges have diverse populations. For those of you over age 25, the decision may be more complex because you probably have greater responsibilities and greater indirect costs, but it will be made on much the same basis.

Rate of return
The "benefit rate," computed by dividing the net benefit by the amount invested.

Investment in human capital theory has been criticized for being overly simplistic and for its implicit assumption that the only reason we obtain an education is to increase our lifetime earnings. Many of us obtain an education because we simply like to learn. We know that our life will be fuller and more intellectually rewarding if we are educated. In some disciplines, we may not necessarily expect to earn a great deal more money with our degree, but we do hope to have a job that is more rewarding in its nonmonetary aspects. In short, our decisions have more dimensions than the theory incorporates.

Investment in human capital theory does have considerable explanatory power, however. It offers an explanation for the young age of most people in college. First, young people have many years to earn the higher salaries that result from their education. The increased earnings over their lifetimes are therefore greater. Second, young people will have smaller opportunity costs than older workers who have some labor market skills and who probably earn at least slightly higher wages.

This theory also helps us explain the effects of financial aid to students on enrollment in our colleges and universities. Financial aid decreases the students' direct costs, which makes the investment (and enrollment) more likely.

Who Benefits from State Government Support of Public Higher Education?

In most states, the public postsecondary education system consists of one major research institution (the flagship), a number of comprehensive (four-year) universities, and a number of community (junior) colleges. The flagship institution is a major, doctoral degree–granting institution, whereas the comprehensive schools are principally four year teaching institutions that may offer a few master's degree programs. The two-year community colleges offer associate's degree programs and serve as feeder institutions to the comprehensive schools. These two-year schools also offer remedial programs, and their cost is significantly lower than the cost of four-year schools. In most states, vocational and technical schools are financed separately and are governed by a different board than is the university and community college system.

As you will recall from Figure 4-3, state taxes are the major source of income for these public school systems. Because the states contribute to the cost of operating these schools, tuition is lower than the full cost of educating a student. In other words, education is subsidized by the state government. Historically, the subsidy has been justified with two reasons. First, the existence of spillover benefits to the state of having an educated citizenry means that higher education will be provided at less than efficient levels if government does not intervene. (Recall that in the case of positive externalities, too few resources are allocated to the good or service. Government subsidies will encourage a larger, more efficient outcome.) Our economic theory can therefore be used as a justification for government subsidies of higher education. Second, Americans believe in the concept of equal access to education. Although we don't necessarily believe that all people should receive equal benefits of a market economy, we do generally believe that all citizens should have an equal opportunity to be educated and thereby have a chance at higher incomes.

EconNews

"College: To Go or Not Go—That Is the Question"

Read why some question the value of college by visiting the Labor Markets category.

http://econapps. swlearning.com

Although, the first of these two justifications is warranted, the second one is not. This is because when we examine financial aid records, we learn that most of the students in our public colleges and universities come from high- or middle-income families. This means that if our purpose is to improve access to higher education by low-income students, our state subsidies are a very inefficient way to do it. We may still justify the government subsidy of education by its social spillover benefits, but we must recognize that most of the students we are subsidizing are not from poor families. We will revisit this issue shortly.[8]

Decreasing State Government Support for Public Higher Education

As we've already noted, state support of public higher education has been decreasing over time. Except for the brief increase in spending at the height of our growing economy at the turn of the twenty-first century, this trend has been occurring for some time. Indeed, the proportion of state spending that goes to postsecondary education has decreased almost every year since 1982.[9] This trend represents a change in social values and spending priorities. At the state level, higher education has been squeezed out by increased spending on prisons and health care, which are discussed further in Chapter 2 and Chapter 11, respectively.

As state spending on higher education has decreased, U.S. public universities and colleges have reacted in various ways. First, virtually all of our states have increased tuition significantly. Second, many schools have established enrollment caps. Let's look at each of these policies.

Raising Tuition

When state tax funds decrease, an obvious reaction is to increase the tuition charged to all students to make up the missing funds. Over time, tuition revenues must cover a larger share of the costs of the public institutions. As a result, tuition has increased substantially. Average public four-year in-state tuition has more than doubled since 1990.

Quite obviously, tuition levels affect access to the university system. Some students simply cannot afford the higher tuition unless they can obtain greater financial aid to offset their higher educational costs. Equally obviously, the students who feel the negative effects most are from low- and middle-income families.

Enrollment Caps

An **enrollment cap** is a maximum limit on the number of students allowed to enroll in a school. In order to maintain relatively low faculty/student ratios, reasonably small class sizes, and other widely accepted measures of quality in a time of declining state education budgets, many state college systems have instituted enrollment caps.

Once established, enrollment caps will generally decrease enrollment to some specified level over time, necessitating rationing of openings. A common way to accomplish this task is to increase admission standards. Raising the cutoff score on the American College Test (ACT) or the Standard Achievement Test (SAT) college entry

EconNews

"Education Pays, but Also Costs"

Read more under the Labor Markets category.

http://econapps. swlearning.com

Enrollment cap
A maximum limit on the number of students allowed to enroll in a school.

test or increasing the minimum high school class rank for entry into the college system will eliminate a number of students who would have been admitted in the past. This measure has the advantage of eliminating students who might have been poor risks for completion of college, rather than simply excluding students at random. On the other hand, it might eliminate "late bloomers," who achieve mature study habits in college instead of in high school. At any rate, enrollment caps serve to reduce access of the general public to publicly supported education.

As more students graduate from high schools and seek to enter the public university system, there is pressure on the system to become more efficient and to move students speedily through the educational pipeline. In some schools, this pressure is contributing to new policies that raise tuition for students who have already achieved some number of credits. Students would be charged normal tuition rates for some maximum number of credits, and then charged higher rates for credits taken beyond the acceptable norm. There is also pressure on specific popular programs. After a certain level of class overcrowding in these programs is reached, schools tend also to limit entry into these particular programs because they simply do not have the resources to allow students into them. They might also charge differential tuition rates for different programs, as we will consider now.

Different Tuition for Different Programs

There are tremendous pressures on U.S. universities and colleges to become more efficient. Greater efficiency would enable schools to meet student needs at lower cost and therefore hold down tuition to an affordable level. One suggestion has been to charge different tuition for different programs to increase efficiency.

One problem that universities face is that they are slow to react to changing demands for programs. To attract quality faculty to the university, the institution has made a commitment to tenured faculty in particular disciplines. The school has acquired physical facilities that are needed for a particular program and may be inappropriate for most other uses. Yet demand for particular programs varies over time. Schools' adjustments to these changes in demand take time, and while the adjustment is taking place, efficiency decreases. There may be either surpluses or shortages of class sections in particular majors.

A number of years ago, there was a great deal of discussion in higher education about charging higher tuition for very popular, growing majors and lower tuition for declining majors. You will probably recognize this discussion as an exercise in demand and supply analysis, and you are right. Consider the following situation. A school has a pre-law program, which is growing rapidly. Influenced by the popular television show *The Practice,* many freshmen are declaring pre-law majors. At the same time, interest in the school's philosophy major is declining. Tuition and fees are the same whether you major in pre-law or philosophy. Figure 4-6 on page 102 illustrates this situation.

Assume that the school's tuition is $3,000 and that the school would supply classes for 300 majors in either program at that tuition (price). But the number of students demanding the pre-law major (quantity demanded) at that tuition is 600. So, there is a shortage of 300 slots for pre-law majors at the $3,000 tuition. In fact, the

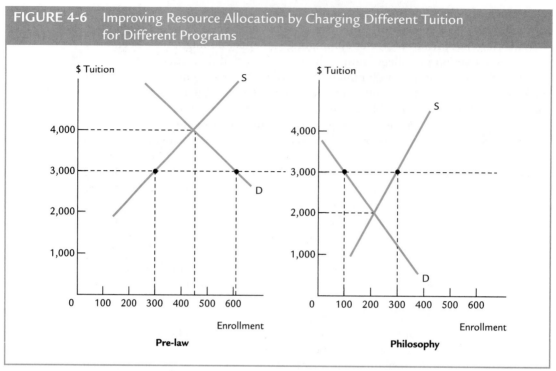

FIGURE 4-6　Improving Resource Allocation by Charging Different Tuition for Different Programs

At uniform tuition ($3,000), there will be a shortage for pre-law students and a surplus for philosophy students. Different tuition ($4,000 and $2,000) eliminates the shortage and surplus and improves resource allocation.

shortage is not so obvious, but it is felt in greatly increased class size in the pre-law major. It is observed in closed classes and bottlenecks in students' programs. Students cannot graduate in four years, because they cannot get the classes they need. The demand is simply beyond the school's capacity to meet it.

Now look at the graph for the philosophy program. Here again, the school will supply classes for 300 students at the uniform $3,000 tuition. But demand is so low that only 100 philosophy students enroll. There is a surplus of philosophy classes available. This surplus will be felt in very small classes and inefficient use of university resources. To help alleviate the problem, some philosophy professors may become part-time administrators or participate in a program to advise students who have not yet decided on majors.

Now assume that the school increases the tuition in the pre-law program to $4,000, the equilibrium price. The shortage will be eliminated, and the school will have an equilibrium number of 450 pre-law majors. Because the school receives extra tuition, it can hire part-time faculty to teach more sections of pre-law courses, and pre-law students will encounter fewer bottlenecks.

Simultaneously, the school lowers the tuition to $2,000 for philosophy majors. At $2,000, philosophy attracts 200 majors (quantity demanded), and the surplus is eliminated. Classes are a reasonable size, and resources are used more efficiently. Differential tuition has greatly decreased the school's resource allocation problems.

You may be somewhat skeptical. You might wonder why a student would change majors just because the tuition was lower. Or you might think it is unfair to charge different tuition for different programs. You might not believe that schools could adjust tuition precisely enough to achieve a really efficient allocation of resources. And, indeed, the educational community has had the same reservations, so there has been little experimentation with different tuition for different programs.

There has been some experimentation with user fees, however. As state funding has decreased, schools have instituted various fees in an attempt to increase their revenues. Some fees are, in fact, surcharges designed to discourage students from entering overcrowded majors or to cover the costs of providing majors that require expensive supplies and equipment. Science and art are two areas in which this might occur.

Financial Aid: What About Low-Income Students?

In addition to state support for public higher education, financial aid is available through many sources to help low-, middle-, and upper-income students bear the costs of education. Some aid comes directly from the federal government, some from states, and some from the college or university directly. This aid comes in many forms: scholarships and fellowships, employer assistance, veterans' assistance, college work study, loans, and Pell grants.

The program that is the foundation of the financial aid package for students from low-income families is the Pell grant. Targeted to poor students, this grant is not received by high- and middle-income students. Although the Pell grant program was targeted to students from the lowest-income families when the first grants were awarded in 1974, eligibility criteria have been liberalized over the years, so now students from less-poor families receive some grants. The Pell grant has never covered all costs for poor students. Other forms of aid have been added to financial aid packages to help the neediest students meet educational costs. Now the most common aid package for those students is a Pell grant and a loan. More important, the Pell grant has lost considerable purchasing power in the last 20 years or so. In 1979, the maximum possible Pell grant was $1,800, which covered 77 percent of the average costs at a public four-year college. In 1998, the maximum Pell grant had risen to $2,700, but that $2,700 covered less than 40 percent of costs at such a school.[10] To meet the remainder of the costs, students must take out correspondingly larger loans. The Pell grant program appears to have veered from its original focus. It is available to a wider range of students than originally intended, but its value to these students is significantly less.

A new element in aid for higher education was added during the Clinton administration. Families with incomes as high as $100,000 could qualify for the credits, which are not refundable. That means that families so poor that they do not pay income taxes receive no tax credit. Thus, these tax credits are not a vehicle for financing the education of very low-income students.

Tuition subsidies of our state universities and financial aid packages help students meet the direct costs of higher education. But these policies do not address the indirect cost of education in the form of forgone earnings from work. Low- to middle-income students may not be able to afford the opportunity cost of these forgone earnings, because they and their families count on this income for survival.

All this means is that not all students have equal access to our institutions of higher education. First, you need to graduate from high school before attending college, and not all Americans have an equal chance to graduate from high school. Income is the major factor in determining who goes to a good high school with a high graduation rate, and low-income students are more likely to attend poor high schools with high dropout rates. Second, the state subsidizes tuition by financing a large share of the construction and operation of public postsecondary schools, but this benefits all students who attend public postsecondary schools, most of whom are not students from low-income families. Third, the value of Pell grants to really poor students has declined over time, and financial aid is not adequate to enable students from very low-income families to afford college. Finally, the opportunity cost of education in the form of forgone earnings while attending school prevents many low-income persons from obtaining higher education.

Affirmative Action: What about Underrepresented Groups?

Although our discussion of low-income student access to higher education has ended on a negative note, this is not the case with access by racial and ethnic minorities. As we see in Chapter 5, the United States Supreme Court recently ruled that affirmative action is constitutional in the case of graduate admissions to the law

VIEWPOINT: CONSERVATIVE VERSUS LIBERAL

Conservatives favor policies to increase competition in our public K–12 system, whereas liberals emphasize tax reform and the redistribution of tax dollars from rich to poor districts to equalize educational opportunities. Therefore, conservatives favor school voucher systems to give parents and students more choices of schools and curricula. Liberals, on the other hand, fear that widespread use of school vouchers would endanger our public school system by transferring funds away from the poor schools that need them most.

Both liberals and conservatives usually believe that providing universal education in K–12 level is a legitimate government role, given basic education's demonstrated spillover benefits to society. Conservatives do not, in general, favor extensive tuition subsidies or financial aid for students in *higher education*, however, unless spillover benefits can be shown to result from this postsecondary education. Liberals are more likely to favor expanded financial aid to low-income students, as well as tax credits for educational purposes. Conservatives are more likely to favor general tax cuts instead of tax credits for specific purposes.

school at the University of Michigan. The Court stated that race *can* be used as a factor in university admission decisions, and that indeed "a diverse student body has its own benefits." Still, the issue of affirmative action is controversial. President George W. Bush opposed the University of Michigan affirmative action program, whereas other members of his administration supported it.

As the diversity of our population continues to increase, we must continually seek broader exposure to other cultures. As such, the movement toward multiculturalism in our schools and colleges is a positive one. Beyond merely spreading greater knowledge of other cultures, our multicultural educational opportunities will spread greater tolerance of people different than ourselves.

SUMMARY

Funding our public elementary and high schools primarily from local property taxes results in extremely unequal spending per student. As a result, underfunded schools have inadequate facilities, high student/teacher ratios, unstaffed classrooms, and various other inadequacies. Underfunded high schools have very high dropout rates, and their graduates receive a poor education. A number of proposals have been put forth to improve our public schools. These include efforts to increase competition in education through charter schools, magnet schools, and vouchers. Others prefer to equalize education between poor and rich school districts through state or federal funding or through property tax reform. We also know that increasing funding to schools in areas of concentrated high poverty will not be effective in itself in improving student outcomes. It is also necessary to alleviate poverty in these areas.

Our postsecondary school system consists of vocational-technical schools, community colleges, four-year colleges, and universities, both public and private. Public schools have lower tuition than private schools, because the states subsidize them. By far, most American postsecondary students attend public institutions. Our public higher education system benefits mainly upper- and middle-income families, not low-income families. Decreasing state support, rising tuition, and the decreasing value of Pell grants have worsened problems of access to higher education for both low- and middle-income students.

NOTES

1. U.S. Department of Education, **www.ed.gov**. Unless otherwise noted, all data in this chapter are from this source.

2. Much of this discussion is taken from Jonathan Kozol, *Savage Inequalities: Children in America's Schools* (New York: HarperCollins, 1992). See specifically pages 58–59, 69, and 225.

3. Margaret E. Goertz, "The Finances of Poor School Districts," *Clearing House* (November–December 1994): 74–77.

4. U.S. Department of Education, **www.ed.gov**. The data show that in 1999 the number of elementary school pupils per teacher was 14.5 in Austria, 13.9 in Belgium, 10.6 in Denmark, 11.3

in Italy, 12.6 in Norway, and 13.3 in Sweden. Countries with significantly higher numbers than the United States were Australia, Canada, France, Germany, Ireland, Japan, New Zealand, Spain, Turkey, and the United Kingdom.

5. The U.S. Charter Schools Organization, **www. uscharterschools.org**.

6. The principal source for the material in this section is the *Chicago Fed Letter* (Chicago: Federal Reserve Bank of Chicago, May 1994).

7. See Traub, "What No School Can Do," and Denise C. Morgan, "The Less Polite Questions:

Race, Place, Poverty and Public Education," in the *Annual Survey of American Law* (New York: New York University School of Law, 1998).

8. Thomas G. Mortenson, ed., *Postsecondary Education Opportunity* (March 1994): 3–8.

9. Mary McKeown-Moak, Financing Higher Education: An Annual Report from the States (**www. sheeo.org/Other/finance99.htm**).

10. Thomas G. Mortenson, ed., *Postsecondary Education Opportunity* (January 1998): 11.

DISCUSSION QUESTIONS

1. How do spillover benefits distort the allocation of resources to education? Can you think of other examples of goods with spillover benefits?

2. Draw a graph indicating how negative externalities (spillover costs) would (1) result in a lower price of a good when its production creates the spillovers, and (2) cause overallocation of resources. (*Hint:* Refer to Chapter 3.)

3. How does property-tax funding of K–12 education create inequality? Consider your response in terms of both the tax rate and the tax base. What can be done to create greater equality?

4. What could be done to help inner-city schools other than providing them with more funding?

5. What do you think of the No Child Left Behind Act, especially its requirements that schools test their students annually? Do you think these tests are accurate indicators of school quality? Do you see any problems associated with the testing programs?

6. What do you hope to gain by your attendance at institutions of higher education? Is it primarily a higher income, as suggested by human capital theory, or do you have other objectives in mind?

7. How would charging different tuition for different majors improve the allocation of a school's resources? Do you think this measure would be a good one? Can you think of any problems that might arise?

8. Who benefits from public higher education? Why do middle- and low-income students encounter problems as they seek access to higher education?

9. Consider the following. Joe is deciding whether to go to college full-time. If he does not attend college, he will continue to work at his present job. Joe earns $14,000 annually. He estimates that tuition and fees at the local public college will be about $10,000 per year and that he can graduate in four years if he does not work. The starting salary in the field he hopes to enter is about $30,000, and he estimates that he will earn about $600,000 more in his working lifetime with a college degree than without one. What will be Joe's opportunity cost of four years of college? What will be his net benefits (benefits minus costs)? Should he make the investment in education?

10. Do you think you received a good quality K–12 education? Why or why not?

11. Go to the Census Bureau Web site (**www.census.gov**). Click E for *education* in the A–Z option. Find the latest data for the percentage of the population that has a high school degree only and the percentage of the population with a bachelor's degree.

12. Go to the Department of Education's home page at **www.ed.gov** and seek out information about your possible eligibility for financial aid.

13. Check out the Cato Institute Web site at **www.cato.org**. This research institute has a reputation of supporting conservative causes. What examples can you find at this Web site for conservative opinions on issues such as school vouchers, No Child Left Behind, or other educational issues? Why would you say these are conservative?

14. Go to the home page of the Brookings Institution at **www.brook.edu**. This research institute has a reputation of supporting liberal causes. Can you find examples of liberal opinions on issues such as school vouchers, No Child Left Behind, or other educational issues? Why would you describe these as liberal?

15. Supporters of charter schools have a Web site at **www.uscharterschools.org**. This Web site seeks to support families choosing charter schools for their children by providing information about charter school startup and assistance, resources, calendars of events, and other topics pertaining to charter schools. Can you use the Web site to find out whether there are any charter schools in your geographical area?

16. Go to the White House Web site at **www.whitehouse.gov** and search for recent speeches given by President George W. Bush about education in the United States.

CHAPTER 5 ROADMAP

Chapter 6
U.S. Poverty
Discrimination is one cause of poverty in the United States

Chapter 10
Housing
Residential housing segregation concentrates poverty and leads to discrimination in education and employment

Public housing also concentrates poverty and leads to discriminatory outcomes

Chapter 4
Education
Property tax funding results in underfunded inner-city public schools that are attended by minority children

Human capital discrimination causes disparities in earnings and income

Chapter 5
Discrimination

Chapter 11
Health Care
Minorities are more likely to be uninsured than are whites

Infant mortality rates are higher for minorities than for whites

Chapter 14
Unemployment and Inflation
U.S. minorities have higher unemployment rates than do whites

Discrimination results in unemployment and inefficient use of labor, moving our economy from a point on the production possibilities curve to a point below the curve

THE ECONOMIC TOOLBOX

- diversity
- discrimination
- earnings differentials
- occupational crowding
- rational choice
- affirmative action

DISCRIMINATION

Our nation is moving toward two societies, one black, one white—separate and unequal.
—Report of the President's National Advisory Commission on Civil Disorders (the Kerner Commission), March 1, 1968

Over four decades have passed since Dr. Martin Luther King Jr. delivered his celebrated "I Have a Dream" speech at the foot of the Lincoln Memorial, climaxing the historic August 1963 March on Washington for Civil Rights. And more than three decades have elapsed since President Lyndon Johnson's Kerner Commission submitted its shocking 1968 report blaming racism and discrimination, poverty, and unemployment for the riots that had besieged the nation's central cities during the 1960s.

Still, it was late 2002 when Majority Leader of the Senate Trent Lott, Republican from Mississippi, stated publicly at a Senate party for Senator Strom Thurmond, "I want to say this about my state: When Strom Thurmond ran for president, we voted for him. We're proud of it. And if the rest of the country had followed our lead, we wouldn't have had all these problems over all these years, either." As your author read this quotation to a class of students similar to you, there was an audible gasp, as these students and the rest of the American public knew that in 1948, when Thurmond ran for president, he was running as the nominee of the Dixiecrats, a racist renegade party organized for only one purpose: to oppose civil rights for black Americans. During that campaign, Thurmond stated, "All the laws of Washington and all the bayonets of the Army cannot force the Negro into our homes, our schools, our churches." Lott subsequently apologized and resigned as majority leader, but his comments make us wonder if much has changed since the Dixiecrats, since Dr. King, or since the Kerner report.

We have opened this chapter with the Kerner Commission's dire prediction. Was it accurate? The ensuing years have been years of controversy and change. Have we come any closer to realizing Dr. King's dream? Have African Americans and other ethnic and racial minorities in America attained equal access to the prerequisites of our affluent society? Or are doors still closed to some people on arbitrary bases such as race, ethnicity, and gender?

The answers to these questions are not easy. Let us begin by looking at the composition of the U.S. population according to the last complete census in the year 2000. (A complete census is conducted by the U.S. Census Bureau every 10 years.) Then we will look at the sociological meaning of the word *minority* and discuss the concept of discrimination. We will also examine the available data on the socioeconomic position of our minorities. Finally, we will discuss the various policies with which we try to eliminate prejudice and discrimination.

THE DIVERSITY OF THE U.S. POPULATION

Our national heritage is one of diversity of race and ethnicity. The Native American Indian population had developed a rich and varied culture before the first nonnative populations journeyed to this country. In the fifteenth and sixteenth centuries, white European settlers began arriving in the United States. They came in search of freedom and a better way of life. More recent immigrants have come for the same reasons. The preponderance of the most recent waves of immigrants has been from Asia and Latin America, but immigrants come from everywhere on the globe.

The data in Table 5-1 illustrate some of this rich diversity. Numbers of people belonging to various racial and ethnic groups, as well as their percentage of the total population, are shown for 1990 and 2000. The largest group of people is white, rep-

TABLE 5-1	Resident Population, by Race and Hispanic Origin, 1990 and 2000 (Numbers in millions; % refers to percentage of total U.S. residents)			
	1990		**2000**	
	Number	**Percentage**	**Number**	**Percentage**
Total	248.7	100%[a]	281.4	100%[a]
White	199.7	80.3%	211.5	75.1%
Hispanic[b]	22.4	9.0%	35.3	12.5%
Black	30.0	12.1%	34.7	12.3%
Asian or Pacific Islander	7.3	2.9%	10.6	3.7%
American Indian, Eskimo, or Aleut	2.0	0.8%	2.5	0.9%
Some other race	9.8	3.9%	15.4	5.5%
Two or more races	na	na	6.8	2.4%

[a]Numbers and percentages do not add up to 100 because of rounding and the inclusion of Hispanics.

[b]Persons of Hispanic origin may be of any race.

Source: U.S. Department of Commerce, Census Bureau, **www.census.gov**.

resenting 75 percent of the population in 2000. The percentage of whites decreased during the 1990s, indicating growing diversity in the population.

Hispanics

By 2000, the Hispanic population became the largest nonwhite group shown in Table 5-1. Hispanic people may be of any race, although about 95 percent are white. Hispanics are persons with origins in one of the Latin American countries. (Many prefer the term *Latino* or *Latina* instead of *Hispanic*. Nearly two-thirds of U.S. Hispanics are from Mexico or descended from Mexican immigrants. Significant numbers also have roots in Puerto Rico, Central and South America, and Cuba. The percentage of the U.S. population that is Hispanic increased from 9 percent in 1990 to over 12 percent in 2000. The Hispanic population is highly concentrated in the southwestern states, with approximately half of all Hispanics living in Texas and California alone. Other states with high concentrations of Hispanic people include New Mexico, Arizona, New York, and Florida.[1]

African Americans

African Americans, still referred to as blacks by the Bureau of the Census, are one of the largest nonwhite groups in the United States. They represent over 12 percent of our population, just slightly behind the population share of Hispanics. (Until recently, African Americans were the largest nonwhite U.S. minority.) According to the Census Bureau, blacks are largely concentrated in the South and in central cities throughout the United States.

Asian or Pacific Islanders

Asian and Pacific Islanders represent almost 4 percent of the population. People in this group have origins in Japan, China, Taiwan, the Philippines, and Korea, and more recently in the Southeast Asian nations of Laos, Vietnam, Thailand, and others. Sixty percent of Asian Americans are foreign-born and 44 percent are naturalized citizens. Fifty-three percent of Asians and Pacific Islanders live in the western United States and 96 percent live in metropolitan areas.

American Indians, Eskimos, and Aleutian Islanders

The group of American Indians, Eskimos, and Aleutian Islanders makes up the smallest share of any single race or ethnic group in Table 5-1, just under 1 percent of our nation's population. This group comprises the native populations of the United States and consists primarily of Native American Indians. Slightly more than one half live outside metropolitan areas, and nearly one-half live in western states.

Trends in Population Growth

It is clear from Table 5-1 that population growth varies for different racial and ethnic groups. Figure 5-1 on page 112 shows the percentage of the U.S. population that was white, Hispanic, black, Asian American, and Native in 1990 and 2000. The Census Bureau has also projected that the percentage of the population that is white is

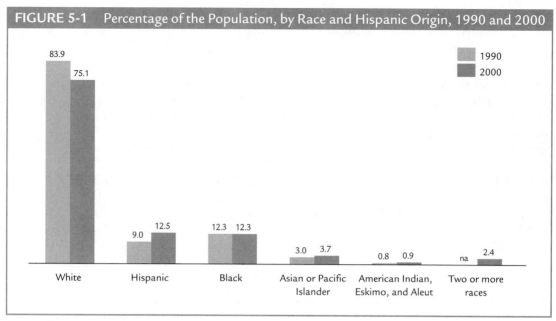

FIGURE 5-1 Percentage of the Population, by Race and Hispanic Origin, 1990 and 2000

- White: 83.9 (1990), 75.1 (2000)
- Hispanic: 9.0 (1990), 12.5 (2000)
- Black: 12.3 (1990), 12.3 (2000)
- Asian or Pacific Islander: 3.0 (1990), 3.7 (2000)
- American Indian, Eskimo, and Aleut: 0.8 (1990), 0.9 (2000)
- Two or more races: na (1990), 2.4 (2000)

Source: Table 5-1

expected to continue to decrease, and that Hispanics will continue to grow as our largest minority by a considerable margin. What causes a group's population to increase? The principal causes are natural increase and net immigration. *Natural increase* is births minus deaths; *net immigration* is immigration minus emigration.

The rate of population growth from natural increase is lower for whites than for any of the other groups. This lower population growth is primarily caused by the lower birthrate of whites. Blacks and Hispanics have shorter life expectancies (greater death rates), but their higher birthrates have more than offset these expectancies so that they have greater population growth from natural increase.

Net immigration is a major source of population growth for Asian and Pacific Islanders and Hispanics. Wars, political repression, and lack of economic opportunity have recently led large numbers of Southeast Asians and Latin Americans to seek asylum and a better life in the United States.

WHAT IS A MINORITY?

Minority
A group with lesser access to higher positions in society.

Quite obviously, we are a racially and ethnically diverse population, even though white people outnumber any other group. Indeed, they outnumber all other groups added together. Numerically, nonwhite groups are minorities. But when we are speaking of racism, prejudice, and discrimination, it is perhaps wiser to use the sociological definition of the word *minority*, because we are speaking of a phenomenon that is central to that discipline. A **minority** is a group that has lesser access to positions of power, prestige, and status in a society. The term has little to do with numbers and everything to do with power. From this perspective, women, who outnumbered men by over 5 million in 2000, are a minority because they do not have equal access to positions of power.

Let us define a few other terms before we go on. **Prejudice** is the prejudgment of individuals or groups on the basis of stereotypes and hearsay, plus the refusal to acknowledge evidence that conflicts with such prejudgment. Prejudiced people might believe, for example, that all Hispanics are lazy, and even though they may meet Latinos who are ambitious and conscientious workers, they hold fast to that belief by rationalizing that these ambitious people are the exceptions.

Prejudice is an internal attitude, but discrimination involves actions. **Discrimination** means treating people differently for arbitrary, often prejudicial, reasons. We discriminate if we do not rent to a Hmong family because they are Asian immigrants. We discriminate if we refuse to hire a qualified woman to fill a job formerly held by a man. Sociologists and psychologists have much to say about the types of prejudice and discrimination that exist in our world. They can explain the many causes of prejudice to us. We recommend that you take their courses to learn about these things. But some of the causes and many of the effects of discrimination are economic. Lower incomes, inferior education, higher rates of unemployment, poorer housing, and inadequate medical care may be consequences of discrimination. These are the things we wish to examine in this chapter.

Prejudice
A prejudgment on the basis of stereotypes and hearsay, plus the refusal to consider evidence that conflicts with the prejudgment.

Discrimination
Action that treats individuals differently on the basis of some arbitrary characteristic.

EARNINGS AND INCOME

Earnings and income are two different concepts. **Earnings** refer to income received in the form of wages and salaries from labor market activities (that is, from working). **Income**, on the other hand, is money received from all sources. It includes not only earnings, but also interest on savings accounts, dividends received on stock shares, rents received from ownership of property and land, welfare cash benefits, and so forth. About 80 percent of total income in the United States is in the form of wages and salaries, and earnings are the principal source of income for most American families. We will focus our attention on earnings in the pages that follow. But let us first note that families and individuals with high earnings are more likely to save and make investments that will provide other forms of income than are low-earnings workers. In other words, high-income people are more likely than low-income people to receive income in other forms besides earnings from working.

Earnings
Money received from labor market activities.

Income
Money received from all sources.

Types of Earnings Discrimination

Earnings from labor markets depend on both the wage rate that the worker receives and the number of hours that the worker works. Your earnings are your wage rate times the hours you work. If your family (household) has two, or even three, persons working full time, you will have more earnings than a family with only one person working full time at the same wage rate. So, let us look at the earnings of full-time workers to eliminate both the effect of part-time workers and the effect of different numbers of workers in the household. Table 5-2 on page 114

TABLE 5-2 Median Weekly Earnings of Full-Time Workers by Race, Hispanic Origin, and Gender, 2001

	Male	Female	Female as a Percentage of Male
All[a]	$672	$511	76%
White	$694	$521	75%
Black	$518	$451	87%
Hispanic	$438	$385	88%
Black as a percentage of White	80%		
Hispanic as a percentage of White	68%		

[a]*Includes other racial and ethnic minorities that are not shown.*

*Source: U.S. Census Bureau, Statistical Abstract of the U.S.: 2002, **www.census.gov**.*

Wage discrimination
Paying equally productive workers different wages on the basis of some arbitrary characteristic.

Employment discrimination
Not hiring certain workers on the basis of some arbitrary characteristic.

Occupational discrimination
Not hiring some groups of workers for particular jobs, resulting, for example, in men's jobs and women's jobs or minority jobs and white jobs.

compares the median weekly earnings of full-time workers. (*Median* means middle, so that if we have a list of people's earnings from highest to lowest, median earnings are right in the middle of the list.) Note that white women working full-time earn about three-fourths of what white men working full-time earn, and that minorities working full-time earn less than whites. The earnings differences are not proof of discrimination, although the pattern certainly makes one wonder what the causes of such large differences are.

Several types of discrimination can affect labor market activities. Technically, labor market discrimination occurs when *like* workers are treated unequally on the basis of some arbitrary characteristic such as race, gender, or ethnicity. In the context of the labor market, *like* means "equally productive." It is not discrimination when college graduates earn more than high school graduates if the college graduates are more productive because they have developed job-related abilities to a greater extent than the high school graduates. It is not discrimination if a concert violinist has greater innate ability than the rest of us, and the labor market compensates her by paying her a premium for her talent. It *is* discrimination if two equally productive workers are treated differently because one is black and the other white or because one is female and the other male.

Workers can be treated differently in at least four ways that may affect their earnings. First, they may be paid different wage rates solely on the basis of some arbitrary characteristic. This practice is called **wage discrimination**. Second, they may be last hired and first fired in an economic downturn; hence, they will be unemployed more than other groups. This practice is called **employment discrimination**. Third, they may be prevented, or at least discouraged, from working in some fields and encouraged to work in others, resulting in separate white and nonwhite occupations and/or separate men's and women's occupations. This practice is called **occupational discrimination**. All of these types of discrimination directly affect earnings, and they all occur after the worker has entered the labor market. (One enters the labor market as soon as he or she begins to actively seek employment.)

The fourth type of discrimination is more indirect. It occurs before the worker's entry into the labor market, but it certainly influences how he or she fares in the labor market. This discrimination is **human capital discrimination**, or discrimination with respect to education or training. If some groups receive more education or better quality education than do others, members of these groups will be rewarded by the labor market for the skills and abilities that they have developed through education and they will have higher earnings than workers who are less educated.

Human capital discrimination Anything that prevents certain groups from acquiring the level or quality of education or training to which other groups have access.

Earnings and Education

Let us pose a related question. To what extent do earnings differences reflect differences in education? The Census Bureau studied this issue in 1998, and some of the results are shown in Table 5-3. The conclusions will most likely be alarming for women and minorities in your classroom. The data reveal a pattern of higher median earnings for men than women, and for whites than minorities, even when we control for education. In other words, women with the same level of education as men earn less than men do, and minorities with the same level of education as whites earn less than whites do, on average. Earnings increase as education increases for all groups of workers, but the earnings differentials remain. And while earnings differences for whites, blacks, and Hispanics are considerable, the differences between

TABLE 5-3 Median Annual Earnings of Year-Round Full-Time Workers, 25 Years Old or Older, by Gender, Race, and Hispanic Origin, 1998

Highest Educational Attainment	Male	Female	Female as a Percentage of Male
Not high school graduate	$21,699	$15,266	70%
High school graduate	30,838	21,963	71%
Bachelor's degree	49,982	35,408	71%
Master's degree	60,168	42,002	70%
Doctoral degree	69,188	52,167	75%

	White	Black	Hispanic	Black as a Percentage of White	Hispanic as a Percentage of White
Not high school graduate	$19,576	$18,206	$16,525	93%	84%
High school graduate	27,303	22,369	23,154	82%	85%
Bachelor's degree	42,412	37,339	35,691	88%	84%
Master's degree	50,693	41,426	49,226	82%	97%
Doctoral degree	66,987	b	b		

b = Sample too small to calculate.

Source: U.S. Department of Commerce, Bureau of the Census, Educational Attainment, table 9 (**www.census.gov/population/socdemo/education/p20–528/tab09.txt**).

men's and women's earnings are even more pronounced. Notice that the earnings of women with doctoral degrees are not much higher than the median earnings of men with *bachelor's* degrees.

Earnings and Unemployment

Your earnings will be lower if you have frequent periods of involuntary unemployment than if you are employed continually. To be considered unemployed, a person must be actively looking for work. The government then calculates the unemployment rate, which is the number of unemployed people as a percentage of the number of people who are either working or actively seeking employment. Let us look at unemployment rates for blacks, Hispanics, and whites and for men and women. Table 5-4 shows these data. Unemployment rates for men and women are similar. But note that both blacks and Hispanics experience far higher rates of unemployment than do whites. Year after year, the black unemployment rate is at least twice the white unemployment rate, and the Hispanic rate falls somewhere between the other two.

Earnings and Experience

More difficult to assess is the effect of experience on earnings. For example, even if we compare the earnings of full-time year-round working women and men with identical levels of education, it is likely that women will on average have less experience in the labor market. This is because women are more likely to take time off from work to care for infants and young children. As a result, they may receive lower earnings than men.

SOME EXPLANATIONS OF DISCRIMINATION

Some discrimination may be the result of prejudice, but it is also possible for some labor market discrimination to occur without any prejudice in the personal, malicious sense. Let us look at the issues of statistical discrimination and occupational crowding.

TABLE 5-4	Unemployment Rates by Race, Hispanic Origin, and Gender, Selected Years				
	1985 (%)	1990 (%)	1995 (%)	1998 (%)	2002 (%)
Total population	7.2	5.5	5.6	4.5	5.8
Male	7.0	5.6	5.6	4.4	5.9
Female	7.4	5.4	5.6	4.6	5.6
White	6.2	4.7	4.9	3.9	5.1
Black	15.1	11.3	10.4	8.9	10.2
Hispanic	10.5	8.0	9.3	7.2	7.5
Asian American	na	na	na	na	5.9

Source: U.S. Department of Commerce, Bureau of Labor Statistics, **www.bls.gov**.

Statistical Discrimination

If an employer judges a prospective employee on the basis of the characteristics of the group she belongs to rather than on her own characteristics, the employer is practicing **statistical discrimination**. You will recognize this to be an example of employment discrimination as was just defined. For example, the employer might believe that a young woman is more likely to take a parental leave than a man is. Or the employer might believe that married women with children are absent more often than men because they will be the ones to stay home with sick children who cannot be taken to day care. He might believe that women are more likely than men to quit their jobs because their spouses are being transferred. And he might be right on average. He would not be right in each case, however, because individuals do not fit the characteristics of their group in every way. Many men take time off work to care for young children, and they often quit jobs to accompany wives who have been transferred.

But if the employer hires only men, he will on average avoid the characteristics to which he objects in the group. He will save money in the hiring process because screening individual applicants is expensive. So, he may see it as simply a good business decision to hire men for the position. Indeed, if the perceived differences between men and women are accurate, the discriminator's costs will be lower than a non-discriminator's. Young women who would have been equally productive, or even more productive, than the men who are hired in the job are therefore discriminated against. The discriminating employer may pass over extremely productive women workers. Furthermore, if the average labor market characteristics of men and women converge over time, the cost savings from statistical discrimination will disappear.

Can you think of other examples of statistical discrimination? One example on the minds of young adults is the fact that many auto insurance companies charge higher premiums for young men than young women, and for students will lower grade point averages than students with higher ones. This is because young men and students with lower grades can be shown statistically to have more automobile accidents. Nevertheless, the situation doesn't seem fair to you if you are a perfectly responsible and careful young man who receives poorer grades. And it isn't, but it still persists. Even though this isn't an example of job-related discrimination, it does demonstrate the idea of statistical discrimination.

> **Statistical discrimination**
> Judging an individual on the average characteristics of his or her group.

Occupational Crowding

Occupational crowding occurs when there are white people's jobs and nonwhite people's jobs, or men's jobs and women's jobs in the economy. Refer again to Table 5-3. As we've noted, the data for men and women are perhaps even more striking than those for whites and nonwhites. Why do women college graduates have earnings of 71 percent of those of their male counterparts? Why do women with master's degrees have earnings of 70 percent of those of similarly educated men? The answer to these questions is, at least in part, that in the U.S. economy, some occupations are dominated by men and other occupations are dominated by women, and that men's occupations are more highly paid than women's. Although this is slowly changing,

> **Occupational crowding**
> Crowding some groups of workers into a limited number of jobs.

women are crowded into relatively few occupations, whereas men have more occupational choices. Women are a high percentage of our elementary schoolteachers and our registered nurses. They are our college-educated social workers. They dominate retail sales and the clerical fields. The reasons for this occupational segregation are complex. Some women are in so-called women's fields because they have made a rational choice to take these jobs. It's what they have always wanted to do. Others are in such occupations because these traditional women's fields are the only ones they ever really considered working in or the only ones they have been encouraged to enter. Still others wind up in these fields because of discrimination against them in the fields in which they would rather work or because they lack the education to enter other vocations that they would prefer.

Figure 5-2 illustrates the effects of occupational crowding. Each graph represents a labor market that is similar to other markets we have examined. Instead of the quantity of tutors or drugs or education, the horizontal axis shows the quantity of labor (number of workers). The vertical axis shows the price of labor (the wage rate). The supply of labor shows the number of workers willing to work at various wage rates. The demand for labor shows the number of workers that employers are willing to hire at various wage rates.

Assume that there are 30 million workers in the economy and that one-half are men and one-half are women. Furthermore, there are three occupations at which the workers may work. Two of the occupations are traditionally men's jobs; one is traditionally a women's job. If there is equal demand for workers in all three occupations, the demand curves will look like the demand curves in Figure 5-2. Assume that Occupations 1 and 2 are the men's jobs, and that Occupation 3 is the women's job. In the top panel (A) of Figure 5-2, we have occupational crowding, and all the women are crammed into Occupation 3, whereas the men are divided between Occupations 1 and 2. As a result, men earn higher wages than women. In the bottom panel (B) of the figure, occupational crowding has been eliminated, and there are no men's or women's jobs. The 30 million workers are randomly distributed throughout the labor markets, and because there is equal demand, there will be equal numbers in each of them. The wage rates will be equal.

EFFECTS OF LABOR MARKET DISCRIMINATION

Some of the effects of discrimination are obvious; others are not. With discrimination there are always gainers and losers. The groups with higher employment and higher earnings (whites and males) are obvious gainers. The groups with lower employment and earnings (minorities, including women) are losers. But there is another, less obvious loser, and that is our economy as a whole.

FIGURE 5-2   Labor Markets with and Without Occupational Crowding

A. With Occupational Crowding

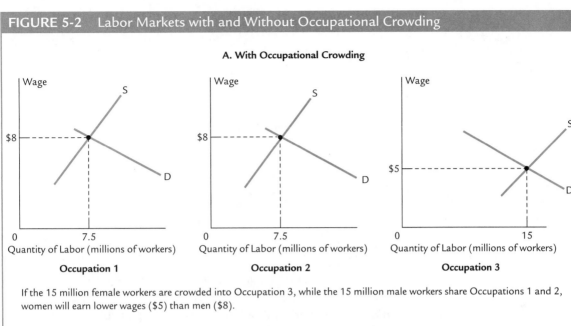

If the 15 million female workers are crowded into Occupation 3, while the 15 million male workers share Occupations 1 and 2, women will earn lower wages ($5) than men ($8).

B. Without Occupational Crowding

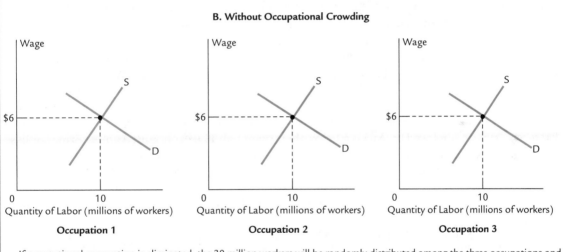

If occupational segregation is eliminated, the 30 million workers will be randomly distributed among the three occupations and they will earn the same wage ($6).

Effects on the Economy

Our national output will be reduced because we are not using our labor force in the most efficient way possible. Hiring on the basis of arbitrary characteristics does not achieve maximum productivity. Figure 5-3 on page 120 illustrates this concept using a production possibilities curve.

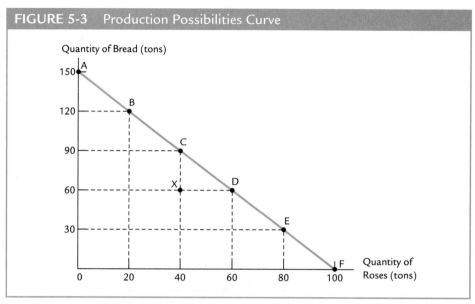

FIGURE 5-3 Production Possibilities Curve

Quantity of Bread (tons)

Quantity of Roses (tons)

With discrimination, labor is not utilized as efficiently as possible, and the nation's output of bread and roses is at point X, below the production possibilities curve.

As we discussed in Chapter 1, we are on the production possibilities curve only if we have full and efficient employment of society's resources. With discrimination, we are at some point such as X below the production possibilities curve. We are not achieving our maximum potential national output of capital and consumer goods, because we are inefficiently utilizing the labor of the economy. Qualified workers are unemployed or working below their potential. The economist Andrew Brimmer has estimated that eliminating discrimination against African Americans so that they could make full use of their education would have increased the gross domestic product, our national output, by $137 billion, or 2.15 percent.[2] Thus, discrimination hurts our society as well as individuals within it.

Effects on Individuals

The effects of labor market discrimination on the employment and earnings of women and other minorities can be extensive. For example, if we look at various measures of socioeconomic well-being, we can see that the same groups that are discriminated against in labor markets occupy an inferior position with respect to other aspects of their lives. For example, racial and ethnic minorities and families headed by women have much higher poverty rates than nonminorities. As we will see in Chapter 6, blacks and Hispanics have a poverty rate almost three times that of the white non-Hispanic population, and single-female-headed families have a poverty rate two times the poverty rate for single-male-headed families. We will also see that minority groups of people face restricted home ownership and poorer quality of housing (Chapter 10) and less access to adequate health care (Chapter 11). As a re-

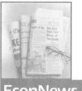

sult, African Americans, Hispanics, and Native Americans have higher infant and maternal death rates and lower life expectancies than whites. These are the very warnings expressed in the 1968 Kerner report.

PROBLEMS IN MEASURING DISCRIMINATION

Such systematic patterns as those revealed by the statistics presented earlier certainly raise questions about the presence of discrimination on the basis of gender, race, and ethnicity. But some of the disparities may be attributed to alternative factors. Some economists argue that many of the differences are the result of rational choice, not discrimination. Let us look at this viewpoint before we go on.

Rational Individual Choice

What if the difference between men's and women's earnings results from women choosing to work fewer hours than men on average? The data on men's and women's weekly earnings presented in Table 5-2 are for full-time workers, but the Bureau of Labor Statistics considers 39 hours weekly to be full-time employment. If men, on average, work more than 40 hours, while full-time female employees, on average, work only 40 hours, it might explain a large part of the difference in earnings. Because women are often still the primary caregivers of children and the chief housekeepers in most marriages, it makes sense that they might limit their time working outside the home. To the extent that this is true, their lower incomes are the result of rational choices on their parts.

Furthermore, some economists and sociologists argue that women choose the so-called women's occupations because these are complementary to their primary roles as mothers and wives. The skills learned to teach other people's children to read can be utilized within one's own family. The same is true of nursing skills. Therefore, the selection of a traditional women's occupation may be the result of rational choice, not discrimination.

Moreover, the decision not to finish high school may consign a minority worker to low-wage, dead-end jobs throughout his or her life, but it can be argued that this decision was a conscious choice that he or she made. Lower earnings caused by unfortunate past choices cannot be categorized as discrimination. In all of these cases, it is difficult, if not impossible, to determine how much of the earnings differentials is the result of rational choices and how much is due to discrimination.

Choice, Discrimination, and Culture Intermingled

Other people question whether either women or minorities make truly independent choices. Culture and tradition play a large part in our lives. We give little girls dolls and dollhouses, but we give boys building sets. Children still appear to leave elementary school believing that boys are good at math and girls are good at English. How much truly individual choice do young women have?

Furthermore, discrimination may be a cause of decisions that, having been made, affect earnings and incomes. If a minority youth sees that his older relatives who finished high school are frequently unemployed and appear to find jobs only near the minimum wage, he will have less incentive to finish high school. If a young woman believes that she will be discriminated against if she trains for the sciences, she will be far more likely to train as an elementary schoolteacher. In short, discrimination can be both a cause and an effect.

Individual choice, discrimination, and culture are intermingled to produce the results we have discussed. All the disparities are not attributable to discrimination, but some portion of them is. The controversy revolves around how large this portion is.

POLICIES TO ELIMINATE DISCRIMINATION

The government can, and does, act to reduce discrimination. Some policies involve direct intervention in markets, whereas others involve indirect intervention. Let us begin with direct labor market policies. Many such policies are a legacy of the civil rights movement of the 1960s. Among these are the following.

The Equal Pay Act of 1963

This landmark antidiscrimination law made it illegal for an employer to pay men and women different wage rates for doing the same job. The law was therefore an important policy against gender discrimination. Prior to its passing, the practice of paying women less than men who did the same job was common; it was justified on the traditional basis that men were the breadwinners of families, whereas women were mainly secondary earners in the family.

Although this important piece of legislation ended the practice of unequal pay, it clearly did not end all gender discrimination. It certainly had no impact on the occupational segregation that persists in the United States. As long as a hospital pays all its licensed practical nurses, male and female, the same wage rate for doing the same job, it is behaving in a lawful manner. But if employees in this traditionally female occupation are poorly paid in comparison to automobile mechanics, the Equal Pay Act will not address that issue.

The Civil Rights Act of 1964

This law is the most important antidiscrimination statute we have. It not only makes discriminatory compensation (including fringe benefits) illegal, but also forbids discrimination in hiring, promoting, and firing. Furthermore, it is broader in coverage than the Equal Pay Act. It forbids discrimination on the basis of race, gender, color, religion, or national origin. The law applies to all employers with 15 or more workers engaged in interstate commerce, to all labor unions with 15 or more members, and to all workers employed by educational institutions and by state, local, and federal government. The Civil Rights Act created the Equal Employment Opportunity Commission (EEOC), which administers it.

Executive Orders

In 1965 and 1968, executive orders intended to stop discrimination by firms that do business with the federal government were issued. These orders require that all federal contractors whose contracts total $50,000 or more develop **affirmative action** programs. The term implies that firms should be able to demonstrate that they are not discriminating. If, on examination, it is found that a firm underemploys women and minorities, numerical goals to increase the representation of these groups must

Affirmative action
Efforts to provide equal opportunities in terms of employment and education to underrepresented groups of people.

be established. The objective is for the firm's workforce to reflect the demographics of the available labor force. If the firm is a law practice and 25 percent of the lawyers in the area are women, the firm should strive to hire so that eventually 25 percent of its lawyers are female.

Affirmative action programs have been controversial since their inception. Critics argue that they have resulted in **quotas**, or rigid numerical proportions of jobs held for minorities and women. These jobs, they argue, are filled with little regard for the workers' qualifications. Still others argue that affirmative action has resulted in **tokenism**, or the hiring of certain workers solely to demonstrate an attempt to comply with the law. These critics regard affirmative action as a system of preferences that results in **reverse discrimination** against white males. And they maintain that affirmative action programs do not benefit disadvantaged minority workers as much as they benefit middle-class minority workers.

On the other hand, affirmative action proponents argue that affirmative action is the only way to end historical patterns of discrimination, and that it is justifiable to give preference now to groups that have historically been discriminated against. They point out the disparities in earnings of various ethnic, racial, and gender groups and maintain that affirmative action is necessary to narrow these gaps over time.

As you undoubtedly know, the Supreme Court interprets our laws. All laws must conform to the U.S. Constitution. The Supreme Court upheld the constitutionality of job-related affirmative action programs in a series of important decisions in the mid-1980s. More recently, however, Supreme Court decisions have seemed to chip away at affirmative action. The Court declared illegal a program to set aside a portion of the construction work of the city of Richmond, Virginia, for minority-owned firms. It also permitted certain public employees to challenge existing affirmative action programs on the basis of reverse discrimination. Affirmative action appears to be under legal attack as we write.

Some economists argue that direct government intervention in labor markets, such as affirmative action, is unnecessary, or even harmful. Nobel laureates Milton Friedman and Gary Becker have both argued that the employer who hires on any basis other than efficiency, which means finding the most productive worker for the job, will be at a competitive disadvantage compared with other employers. They argue that discriminating employers have higher costs than nondiscriminators, so eventually they will be driven from the market. Direct intervention in labor markets, they argue, is therefore unnecessary.

Thomas Sowell, a conservative African American economist, goes still further. He argues that government intervention in favor of disadvantaged groups actually hurts these groups. He cites as an example the Native American. Sowell states that Native Americans have the longest relationship (as a ward of the state) with the federal government of any of our minorities, and Native Americans are consistently at the very bottom of our economic ladder. Sowell argues that minorities such as Japanese Americans, who were not favored by the government, have succeeded far better than the recipients of the government's largesse.

Other economists argue that labor markets clearly have neither solved the problem of discrimination nor, for that matter, even made substantial progress toward eliminating discrimination. Nor do they believe that discriminators are necessarily at a cost disadvantage. Instead, they note that statistical discrimination probably

Quotas
Rigid numerical requirements in hiring.

Tokenism
Hiring minorities to comply with law, not for their abilities.

Reverse discrimination
Discrimination against white males.

results in short-run cost savings. Therefore, they argue that we need programs such as affirmative action. They propose that programs directed at the supply side of the labor market are especially needed. Affirmative action is now directed at the demand side of the market, or at the business firm that hires and promotes. Supply-side efforts would attempt to supply these employers with workers who have the proper education and skills for the positions available. What, they ask, is the advantage of an employer's willingness to hire female auditors if none are available? Therefore, training women and minorities so that they can supply the needed skills is important. They argue, for example, that we need more women accounting majors to fill the auditing positions and that we should be concerned about women's access to such training.

Affirmative action is the subject of extensive political debate. The state of California has passed a law to eliminate affirmative action considerations in hiring by the state and in admission to state universities. (We discuss affirmative action in education momentarily.) Opponents argue that a "system of preferences" is no longer necessary because our national values, as well as our laws, have changed so as to prevent discrimination from occurring. Others feel that affirmative action programs should be targeted more carefully toward disadvantaged groups. It is quite likely that the debate over affirmative action programs will continue well into the future.

Indirect Labor Market Policies

The government can also work in less direct ways to reduce labor market discrimination. For example, improving educational opportunities for racial and ethnic minorities and women will put them in a better position vis-à-vis the labor market. We will discuss this momentarily. Furthermore, many low-income workers with families have child-care problems, which can be alleviated by subsidized day care programs. Many families also lack reliable transportation, and mass transit is often inconvenient or unavailable. Since many jobs have shifted from central cities to the suburbs, central-city residents without adequate transportation may remain unemployed as a result. Indeed, Dr. Martin Luther King Jr. maintained that public transportation was a civil rights issue.

Maintaining a healthy economy through appropriate fiscal and monetary policies also can be construed as an antidiscrimination policy. A healthy economy implies job opportunities. If there is a relative surplus of job openings compared to workers, employers cannot afford to discriminate. The truly tight labor markets during World War II opened windows of opportunity for many female and minority workers.

Finally, other government policies can indirectly affect labor markets. For example, recent welfare reform that focuses on work requirements has made it extremely difficult for low-income single mothers to acquire college degrees. This often means that these women will remain in low skilled, low wage occupations indefinitely.

OTHER FORMS OF DISCRIMINATION

Although our discussion has focused primarily on labor market discrimination and its effects, there are certainly other forms of discrimination that are equally onerous and are, in fact, linked to labor market discrimination. These forms of discrimination include residential and educational segregation.

Recall from Chapter 4 that the quality of public schools varies considerably, in large part because of the way that public education is financed in our country. In short, low-income residential areas often end up with poorer-quality schools. Insofar as these schools are typically located in racially segregated central-city neighborhoods, minority children often receive a poorer-quality education than nonminority children. Thus, residential and educational segregation lead to lower-wage-paying jobs, higher unemployment rates, and unequal opportunities for minorities. Some children bear additional problems linked to education and residence, and sometimes to poverty. These include children of immigrants, children of migrant farm workers, children in homeless families, and children in violent situations. The instability in these families makes education difficult, at best.

Residential Segregation

Residential segregation institutionalizes discrimination. As nonminority populations have fled to the suburbs, minority residents often remain trapped in central cities. Still, many large urban areas of the South have had metropolitan-wide desegregation plans since the early 1970s. For example, two Supreme Court orders in the 1970s created mandatory desegregation across the entire metropolitan areas of Wilmington, Delaware, and Louisville, Kentucky. These orders have produced much higher levels of integration throughout the two states.

In contrast, the Supreme Court's 1974 Detroit decision in *Milliken v. Bradley* blocked desegregation across Detroit's metropolitan population. The central city was to desegregate separately from the suburban fringe. The ruling prevented effective desegregation, and Detroit is now one of the nation's most segregated metropolitan areas. With a high concentration of racial minorities within many of our country's central cities, and a high concentration of whites in the suburbs, desegregation must be carried out at the metropolitan level. As a result of the precedent set, as well as a failure of leadership on the issue, there has been little or no progress toward residential desegregation since 1974.

A Harvard study based on the 2000 census indicates that people still live in largely segregated neighborhoods. The researchers found that between 1990 and 2000, whites, blacks, Asians, and Hispanics still tend to live apart. In particular, the average white person living in a metropolitan area (including central cities and suburbs) lives in a neighborhood that is about 80 percent white.[3] Recent Census Bureau data indicate that the most segregated metropolitan areas for blacks and whites are Milwaukee, Detroit, Cleveland, St. Louis, and Newark, New Jersey. The most segregated metropolitan areas for Hispanics and whites are New York; Newark, New Jersey; Los Angeles; Chicago; and Philadelphia. One factor that may help to reduce segregation is the recent renovation of some central cities, which is expected to draw more white people into the inner cities.

Educational Segregation

It has been about 50 years since the United States Supreme Court struck down the "separate but equal" doctrine in *Brown v. Topeka Board of Education* (1954). In that case, the Court ruled that segregated schools were in fact unequal and did irreparable harm to minority children. Since then, our country has proceeded to integrate its schools at a pace that varies by state and region.

Evidence indicates that large-scale school desegregation works not only to improve objective measures of achievement such as test scores but also to increase the probability of college attendance. It also positively affects type of college, college major, and types of employment as an adult. Research by the University of Chicago's Metropolitan Opportunity Project, however, shows an extremely strong pattern of continued educational segregation for blacks and increasing segregation for Hispanics in our central cities. Furthermore, minority high schools in almost all cases have large numbers of low-income students. There are strong positive correlations between predominantly minority schools, high proportions of poor children, and low educational achievement. Far too many black and Hispanic students are trapped in schools where dropout rates are high and opportunities for success minimal.[4]

The Harvard study that revealed high residential segregation also demonstrates that educational segregation is increasing. Using data from 1980 to 1998, the study shows that white students, in particular, are the most segregated from racial and ethnic minorities. White students were found to attend schools in which more than 80 percent of the student body was white and less than 20 percent of the students were from nonwhite groups. Minnesota was found to have the highest incidence of educational segregation.

Certainly, residential and educational segregation are linked. People living in segregated neighborhoods are likely to attend segregated neighborhood schools. In turn, students who attend poor-quality segregated schools are more likely to eventually receive lower wages and experience higher unemployment rates. Furthermore, these people are more likely to live in poverty. What this all means is that equal opportunity in education is essential for overcoming decades of disadvantage. As discussed in Chapter 4, a better way of financing our nation's public primary and secondary education must be found, and segregation must be eliminated. In addition, the issue of affirmative action in higher education must be addressed.

AFFIRMATIVE ACTION IN EDUCATION

The issue of affirmative action in college and university admissions has been a politically volatile one, particularly during the administration of President George W. Bush. Early in 2003, President Bush argued in a brief to the Supreme Court that the University of Michigan gives unconstitutional preferences to black, Hispanic, and Native American applicants. He argued, "At the core, the Michigan policies amount to a quota system that unfairly rewards or penalized prospective students based solely on their race." Bush's statement drew immediate criticism from higher education officials and civil rights leaders. Even Bush's Secretary of State, Colin Powell, disagreed with President Bush on the matter. Dozens of large Fortune 500 businesses, including Microsoft, Intel, American Airlines and Proctor & Gamble, also disagreed with the president. According to James Hackett, chief executive officer of Steelcase Corporation, "If you're going to be a global company and you're going to attract and retain the best people, then the mirror you have to present is that you're a very diverse company."

In mid-2003, the United States Supreme Court ruled simultaneously on two University of Michigan cases, one for graduate admissions (the law school) and the other for undergraduate admissions. In the case of the law school, the Supreme Court stated that race *can* be used as a factor in university admission decisions, and that indeed "a diverse student body has its own benefits." However, the Court also ruled that in the undergraduate case, a more rigid system relying on specific points given to students based on their race and ethnicity is not constitutional. The University of Michigan cases were the first tests of affirmative action in college admissions since the famous 1978 *Bakke* decision, which invalidated racial quotas.

As the diversity of our population increases, we will naturally turn our faces toward a broader exposure to other cultures. The movement toward multiculturalism in our schools and colleges reflects the changes in our broader society. Schools attempt to reflect the diversity of the population in their faculty and students. The purpose of the multicultural teaching methods and materials is to spread greater knowledge of other cultures and to foster tolerance. An important objective of multiculturalism is to increase the respect with which we treat people of all races, genders, and ethnicities.

VIEWPOINT: CONSERVATIVE VERSUS LIBERAL

Many conservatives argue that remaining disparities between the earnings of minorities and whites and between those of women and men are the result of rational choice, not discrimination. They point out that gaps between these groups have narrowed somewhat since the 1960s. Conservatives oppose government intervention in markets, including labor markets. They see affirmative action as misguided and a source of great inefficiency. They believe that changing social values and the passage of antidiscrimination laws have alleviated the problem of discrimination and that affirmative action is no longer needed.

Liberals believe that government programs have done some good but that they have not completely solved the problem of discrimination. Therefore, they see a need to continue affirmative action programs. They see great value in diversity of the workplace and educational institutions, and they are committed to overcoming the results of decades of unequal treatment of minorities. In addition, they often propose alternatives to property-tax financing of public education, which creates inequality in education and thereby denies equal opportunity to all residents of our nation.

SUMMARY

The United States has a rich diversity of people of different races and ethnicities, including those who are Hispanic, African American, Asian American, and Native American. This diversity will continue to grow in the near future. The quality of life for people of minority races, however, may be substantially below that of white Americans. Furthermore, women are in a position similar to racial and ethnic minorities. All face lower earnings and greater likelihood of poverty, with all the implications that lower income and poverty have for health, housing, and education.

Labor market discrimination consists of wage discrimination, employment discrimination, occupational discrimination, and human capital discrimination. All of these can result in earnings differentials between minority and non-minority groups, even when educational levels are constant. Some of the wage differentials may be caused by statistical discrimination and occupational choice. Besides labor market discrimination, discrimination exists in the form of residential and educational segregation. Affirmative action has become an important though controversial tool to reduce labor market and educational discrimination.

The past 40 years have seen changes in our legal environment. Many overtly discriminatory practices are now illegal. But the relative positions of minorities and whites are still greatly unequal. Reduced discrimination and segregation in our society would increase our economy's efficiency and benefit us all. Multiculturalism enhances the richness of our society and experience.

NOTES

1. All data in this section are from the U.S. Department of Commerce, Bureau of the Census, **www.census.gov**.

2. Andrew F. Brimmer, "The Economic Cost of Discrimination Against Black Americans," in *Economic Perspectives on Affirmative Action*, ed. Margaret C. Simms (Washington, D.C.: Joint Center for Political and Economic Studies, 1995), p. 19.

3. The Civil Rights Project, Harvard University, **www.law.harvard.edu/groups/civilrights/**.

4. Much of this material is taken from Gary Orfield, "Have the Kerner Warnings Come True?" in *Quiet Riots*, ed. Fred R. Harris and Roger W. Wilkins (New York: Pantheon, 1988); and "Education in the Twenty-First Century," Christian Science Monitor Service (**www.nabe.org/press/ reprint 99050 4b.htm**).

DISCUSSION QUESTIONS

1. Go to the Census Bureau Web site and look up more recent data on the diversity of the U.S. population. Have the statistics for minority shares of the total population changed much since the text was revised? (*Hint:* Go to **www.census.gov** and click Population.)

2. Is it possible to be a member of a minority when, in fact, your group has greater numbers than another group? Can you think of any examples besides the one from the text?

3. What factors explain the disparities in earnings between men and women? Minorities and whites? Are the factors different for race and gender?

4. What is the relationship between education and earnings? Does this relationship explain all the earnings differences among various groups? Why or why not?

5. Explain statistical discrimination. Do you think such discrimination is widespread? Can you think of any examples besides the ones mentioned in the text?

6. Do you think occupational crowding is widespread? Is the pressure for young women to enter traditional women's fields as great as it used to be? If you are a young woman, will you be entering a traditional women's field when you graduate? Did your mother work in a traditional field?

7. Affirmative action began in the late 1960s. It has been accused of amounting to reverse discrimination. Do the data in the chapter support this view?

8. Do you believe in affirmative action? Can you support your opinion with rational analysis and explanation?

9. In the nineteenth century, secretaries were generally male, and the occupation was prestigious and well paid. Is this true today? Can you explain the change in attitudes?

10. Why is measuring the extent of discrimination in our culture so difficult?

11. Visit the Web site for the Bureau of Labor statistics at **www.bls.gov**. How do the statistics on unemployment rates vary for people of different gender, race, and ethnicity? What are some reasons for the differences? Is it possible that some of the unemployed people who are classified as unemployed are simply too lazy to search for a job? (*Hint:* Keep in mind how the Bureau of Labor defines unemployment.)

12. Check out the Equal Employment Opportunity Commission home page at **www.eeoc.gov**. Does this Web site provide information on how to charge an employer with violation of equal opportunities laws? Do you think you were ever discriminated against with in the labor market? If yes, what is the basis for your view (age, gender, etc.)?

13. Can you find information on the 2003 United States Supreme Court decisions about affirmative action on the Web site entitled **www.affirmativeaction.org**? How do the rulings distinguish between the University of Michigan Law School and its undergraduate program?

CHAPTER 6 ROADMAP

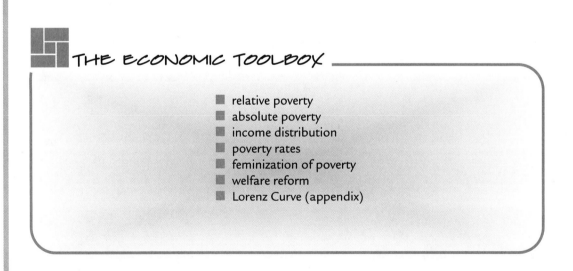

**Chapter 7
World Poverty**
The poor in the United States and in the rest of the world face some similar problems

**Chapter 11
Health Care**
The poor are more likely to lack health care and to experience poor health

**Chapter 5
Discrimination**
People of racial, ethnic, and gender groups that are subject to discrimination face higher poverty rates

**Chapter 6
U.S. Poverty**

**Chapter 4
Education**
The financing of elementary and secondary education results in less access to and poorer quality of education for the poor

**Chapter 14
Unemployment and Inflation**
Those groups with higher unemployment rates are more likely to be poor

**Chapter 10
Housing**
The poor are more likely to be homeless or live in substandard overcrowded housing

THE ECONOMIC TOOLBOX

- relative poverty
- absolute poverty
- income distribution
- poverty rates
- feminization of poverty
- welfare reform
- Lorenz Curve (appendix)

U.S. POVERTY

I went to college so that I can earn a living wage for my children and me. I want my children to play safely and have an opportunity to be educated. I want to raise socially responsible, morally responsible and psychologically sound children who are capable of coping and dealing with society and its ills. They must have a mother who isn't totally stressed out over every penny so that when clothes are accidentally ruined I don't flip out over how I am going to provide for that expense and rip unjustly on the unfortunate child. This comes with a livable income.

—From *In Our Own Words: Mothers' Perspectives on Welfare Reform*[1]

Most of us are concerned about the poor, but we tend to think that poverty is not a problem that will ever affect us personally. We picture the poor as people in central cities, possibly women with too many children or people whose families have always been dependent on welfare. The poor live on the reservations or in the hills of Appalachia or on the urban streets. We imagine that the poor are drug addicts or alcoholics. They are mentally or physically ill or disabled. They are the very old or the very young. But they are never ourselves.

These stereotypes are misleading. Many poor adults are people much like us. They are people who never imagined they would someday be poor. They are people like the single mother in the chapter introduction. They are people who have become poor as a result of some life crisis: the loss of a job, the death or desertion of a spouse, an unplanned pregnancy, or an unexpected illness. These are normal events that could alter the lives of any of us.

As of 2001, 32.9 million Americans, representing 11.7 percent of the total U.S. population, were poor by government definition.[2] This means that they lived in a household with total cash income falling below some level that is considered necessary to satisfy their basic needs. Poverty in the midst of plenty is an issue of equity. Recall from Chapter 1 that our market-based economy tends to be efficient, though not necessarily equitable. The poverty statistics appear large for one of the richest

Relative poverty

A situation in which people are poor in comparison to other people.

countries of the world. But what do the numbers mean? Who are these poor? And what can be done about the problem of poverty in the United States?

There are two ways to look at poverty. One is by considering **relative poverty**—a situation in which people are poor in comparison to other people. The other is by considering **absolute poverty**—a situation in which people experience actual hardship according to some objective criterion. We will consider both of these in turn, beginning with relative poverty.

RELATIVE POVERTY

Absolute poverty

A situation in which people experience the hardship of poverty according to some objective criterion.

Because relative poverty focuses on comparisons among people in different income classes, the standard measure of relative poverty is the income distribution.

Measuring Relative Poverty

Income distribution

The division of total income in an economy among people of different income groups.

The **income distribution** refers to the division of total income in the economy among different income groups. Statistics on the income distribution are based on the U.S. Census Bureau concept of **money income**: that is, all household income received from working, interest, rent, dividends, or any other source before payment of taxes. Included as money income is any government **income transfer** such as Social Security payments, veterans' cash benefits, and unemployment compensation. Not counted as part of money income, however, are **in-kind transfers**, which are government transfers of goods or services (or direct access to these goods or services) such as food stamps, health care, housing assistance, and free legal aid.

Money income

All household income from any source, including income transfers, calculated before taxes.

For the purpose of analyzing the income distribution, the total population of the country is ranked according to income and then divided into fifths. That is, the percentage of total money income going to the poorest 20 percent of the population is determined, as well as that going to the second-poorest 20 percent of the population, and so on. If income was distributed perfectly equally, each 20 percent of the population would receive 20 percent of total money income. Table 6-1 indicates that the income distribution in the United States is far from equal, with the richest one-fifth of the American population receiving about as much money income in 2002 as the 4 other groups combined. The poorest group receives only 3.4 percent of the total. The income distribution is also displayed for the year 1981.

Trend in the U.S. Distribution of Income

Income transfer

A cash transfer from the government to an individual for which no good or service is provided to the government in return.

The U.S. income distribution is becoming increasingly unequal. Comparisons between 1981 and 2002 in Table 6-1 indicate that the poorest four-fifths of the population have seen their share of total money income decrease, whereas the richest one-fifth has enjoyed an increased income share. In a relative sense, the rich are becoming richer, while the poor are becoming poorer.

It is important to point out that a perfectly equal income distribution is not necessarily the ideal. Most people, economists included, argue that some degree of income inequality is essential to preserve incentives. If you didn't think you would eventually have a higher income, you might have no incentive to work hard, study well, invest wisely, take necessary risks in business, and so on. Productivity and economic efficiency would suffer. On the other hand, many people also argue that the

TABLE 6-1 Distribution of Total Money Income in the United States by Fifths of the Total Population: 1981 and 2002

Fraction of Total Families	Percentage of Total Money Income Received	
	1981	2002
Poorest fifth	5.0	3.4
Second fifth	11.3	8.8
Third fifth	17.4	14.9
Fourth fifth	24.4	23.2
Richest fifth	41.9	49.6

Source: U.S. Department of Commerce, Census Bureau, Current Population Reports, Money Income in the U.S., 2002 (**www.census.gov/prod/2002pubs/**).

income distribution can be too unequal. Poor people may have very little incentive to try when income is so low and the odds of reaching the top of the ladder are so poor. Poverty also results in poor health and nutrition, which may sap energy and harm labor productivity. Finally, the argument goes, inequality of income to the degree experienced in the United States is hardly necessary to provide adequate incentives to work and produce.

As we begin to think of the reasons why the income distribution has become less equal over the 1980s and 1990s, we need to recognize that certain factors *have not* played a role. Important changes in our nation's tax system since 1981, for example, served to place more income into the hands of upper-income people. These changes in the nation's tax system do not directly affect the Census Bureau statistics on the income distribution, however, because these statistics are based on money income before taxes. The same is true of President George W. Bush's tax cuts that favor the rich. Similarly, changes in certain government in-kind transfers since 1981 do not alter statistics on the income distribution because the benefits of these transfers are also excluded from the calculation of money income. Thus, although changes in taxes and government in-kind transfers to the poor will indeed alter the well-being of people, they will not directly affect the statistics on the income distribution.

Other factors must account for the changes in the income distribution observed in these data. One of these factors would be the indirect effect of tax cuts for the rich. While the higher after-tax income that results from the tax cuts does not show up in the income statistics, certainly higher incomes permit greater financial investment by the rich, thereby indirectly raising their future incomes. One other obvious factor affecting the changes in the income distribution is structural change in the economy. The loss of blue-collar manufacturing jobs and the creation of low-wage service-sector jobs characterize such change. We will consider these matters shortly when we turn to the topic of absolute poverty. But first let's compare the income distributions across different countries.

In-kind transfers Transfers of goods or services (or access to goods or services) from the government to an individual for which no good or service is provided to the government in return.

International Comparisons

It is interesting to compare statistics on income distributions across different countries. The task is complicated, however, by the fact that data are not always accurate or comparable. Furthermore, statistics on the income distribution for other countries of the world are generally not calculated as frequently as for the United States. Nevertheless, the World Bank does provide some such information. These numbers suggest that the United States has the least equal income distribution of all the Western industrialized nations for which data are available. (Of the remaining nations, including the less-developed countries, slightly more than one-half have greater equality and slightly less than one-half have less equality of income distribution than the United States.)[3]

Finally, graphs can be used to compare the income distribution in one country over different time periods or to compare the income distributions of two countries. These graphs are discussed in the appendix to this chapter.

ABSOLUTE POVERTY

Because the poor are on the lower rungs of the income distribution ladder, the concepts of relative poverty and absolute poverty are intricately linked. Recall that absolute poverty refers to a situation in which people experience actual hardship according to some objective criterion.

Measuring Absolute Poverty in the United States

Poverty line
A level of income below which a household is considered poor.

The **poverty line** is the official criterion for determining absolute poverty. The poverty line is simply a level of household income that delineates an amount considered adequate to cover basic needs for survival: food, clothing, housing, and so on. The concept of money income that was used in the statistics on the income distribution is used in calculating poverty statistics as well. The poverty line is adjusted for family size. Larger families have a higher poverty line. If household money income falls below the poverty line, all members of the household are considered poor.

Origins of the Poverty Line

The poverty line was initially based on the Department of Agriculture's 1961 "Economy Food Plan," later refined and renamed the "Thrifty Food Plan." A minimum food budget was determined and multiplied by three, because the cost of food was considered to represent about one-third of consumer expenditures, according to studies of consumer spending patterns in the 1950s. In each subsequent year, the poverty line has been adjusted upward to reflect inflation, which is a rise in the average price level.

Meaning of the Poverty Line

It is important to realize that the concept of official poverty is not a measure of those who would be poor in the absence of government income transfers, because money income *does* include these cash transfers. Rather, the official poverty statistics include all of those people who are poor *despite* these transfers. It is equally important to realize that official poverty does not necessarily confer eligibility for government programs, either now or in the past. States may require that families have income much lower than the federal poverty line to qualify for certain welfare programs. Official poverty reflects a statistical measure only.

Measurement Problems with the Poverty Line

This measure of official poverty has been the target of much controversy. Some economists and politicians have argued that this indicator exaggerates the true extent of poverty in the country because it ignores the receipt of in-kind transfers. Because these benefits are ignored in calculating a family's money income, the family may be classified as officially poor, even though its actual well-being is enhanced by transfers such as food stamps and Medicaid health coverage.

Another problem arises when adjusting the poverty line for inflation. Many economists believe that the Consumer Price Index, which is used to measure inflation, actually overstates the extent of inflation. (This issue is discussed in Chapter 14.) In this case, inflation adjustments would result in an artificially high poverty line and an overstatement of the extent of poverty.

Others have argued that official poverty statistics do not exaggerate the actual extent of poverty in this country, but rather underestimate it. They argue that the concept of household income used to measure poverty ought to be after-tax income because this is the income that can actually be used by households for their personal needs. (As a case in point, the poor pay a very large share of their income in the form of Social Security taxes.) They also argue that the poverty line is inadequate. The threshold was established when food expenses actually were one-third of a consumer's budget; since then, increases in fuel, housing, and health care costs have increased the importance of these items relative to food expenditures in a typical budget. Recent studies indicate that U.S. families spend closer to one-fifth rather than one-third of their incomes on food. This statistic would suggest that food expenses perhaps ought to be multiplied by some number larger than three (such as five) to arrive at an official poverty line. Furthermore, the Department of Agriculture's minimum food budget was never intended to represent a long-term adequate diet.

EconDebate

"What Accounts for the Recent Increases in Income Inequality?"

Over 20 years, the gap between the rich and the poor has increased. Read more by navigating to the Income, Distribution, and Poverty category.

http://econapps. swlearning.com

Life at the Poverty Line

Consider the implications of life at the poverty line. Imagine that you live in a family of four, and household money income is at the 2002 poverty line of $18,244. Assuming that your family spends one-fifth of its income on food, your family would have $3,649 for food and the remaining $14,595 for all other expenditures for the year. Each person would have an average of $17.54 per week, or $2.51 per day for food. Have you tried to live on that? The family as a whole would have $1,216 per month to cover rent, fuel, utilities, insurance, transportation (including auto maintenance), clothing, medical and dental needs, educational expenses, entertainment, and taxes. Existence at the poverty line is frugal, to say the least.

Trends in Poverty Statistics

Poverty rate
The percentage of the population that is poor.

A comparison of poverty statistics over recent years shows fairly dramatic trends. When measuring the number of poor people as a percentage of the total population, poverty was very extensive up until 1960, when the **poverty rate** was 22.2 percent (see

TABLE 6-2	Poverty Rates: The Percentage of the Population Living below the Poverty Line, Selected Years 1960–2002		
Date	**Poverty Rate (%)**	**Date**	**Poverty Rate (%)**
1960	22.2	1995	13.8
1970	12.6	1996	13.7
1973	11.1	1997	13.3
1980	13.0	1998	12.7
1983	15.2	1999	11.8
1990	13.5	2000	11.3
1993	15.1	2001	11.7
1994	14.5	2002	12.1

Source: U.S. Department of Commerce, Census Bureau, 2000 (www.census.gov).

EconNews

"Poverty Persists"

Children live in poverty because of high costs of living and low wages. Go to Income Distribution and Poverty for more information.

http://econapps. swlearning.com

Incidence of poverty
The distribution of poverty within the country.

Composition of poverty
The number of poor people in each group of the population as a share of the number of poor in the nation.

Table 6-2). (Certainly, the nostalgia that many people have for the 1950s is misguided. The "wonder years" were not so wonderful for the fifth of our population that was poor.) However, this poverty rate declined substantially throughout the 1960s and the early 1970s with the economic prosperity of the period, as well as the antipoverty programs that began with the Johnson administration. The national poverty rate reached a low of 11.1 percent of the total population in 1973, and then climbed to 13.0 percent in 1980. The poverty rate rose to 15.2 percent by 1983, reflecting the poor economy of the early 1980s and Reagan-era budget cuts. Poverty rates recovered, then rose again in the early 1990s, again reflecting poor economy (this will be explained shortly). Poverty rates declined steadily during the 1993–2000 period, reaching a recent low of 11.3 percent in 2000. The latter period corresponds to one of the longest periods of steady economic growth in U.S. history. Unfortunately, as a result of the poor economy and various policies, the U.S. poverty rate increased to 12.1 percent in 2002. A national poverty rate of 12 percent is certainly very troublesome.

The Incidence of Poverty

Equally important to consider is the **incidence of poverty**. That is, what is the distribution of poverty within the country? There are two ways to look at statistics describing the poor. Both are correct, but they reflect very different perceptions of the poverty problem. We can examine who the poor are (telling us what share of our nation's poor are represented by various groups of people), or we can look at the share of each group of people that is poor (telling us the likelihood that someone within each group will be poor). The former is referred to as the **composition of poverty**, and the latter refers to poverty rates. We shall consider both approaches to the statistics and analyze their implications.

Who Are the Poor?

First, let's consider the total number of people who are considered officially poor in the United States and see who belongs to this group. Table 6-3 breaks down the population of the poor into groups based on race and ethnicity, age, residence, and family type.

TABLE 6-3   The Composition of Poverty: Who Were the Poor in 2002?

Group	Number of Poor in Each Group (millions)	Number of Poor in Each Group as a Share of the Number of Poor in the Nation (%)
Persons	34.6	100[a]
Race and Ethnicity		
White	23.5	68
Non-Hispanic white	15.6	45
Black	8.6	25
Hispanic[b]	8.6	25
Asian and Pacific Islander	1.3	4
Age		
Age under 18	12.1	35
Age 18–64	18.9	55
Age 65 and over	3.6	10
Residence		
Inside metropolitan areas	27.1	78
Inside central cities	13.8	40
Outside central cities	13.3	38
Outside metropolitan areas	7.5	22
Families	7.2	100[a]
Married couple	3.1	43
Female householder, no spouse present	3.6	50
Male householder, no spouse present	0.6	8

Source: Based on information from the U.S. Department of Commerce, Census Bureau (**www.census.gov**).

[a]Numbers do not add to 100 because of rounding errors, as well as indicated in following note.

[b]Hispanics may be of any race. This means that figures do not add up to 100 percent.

Of a total of 34.6 million poor persons in the United States in 2002, the majority were white (68 percent) and over one-third were children (35 percent). (Keep in mind that children are considered poor if they live in a household with income below the poverty line.) The largest percentage of the poor lived in central cities (40 percent). Additional statistics on poor families, as opposed to poor persons, indicate that half of poor families had a female householder (with no spouse present). (*Householder* refers to the person filling out the census form for the family.)

Although statistics such as these show who the poor are in the United States, they do not adequately show which groups bear a disproportionate burden of the nation's poverty. To identify these groups, we must approach the statistics from the

TABLE 6-4 Poverty Status of Persons and Families, 2002, by Race and Ethnicity, Age, Residence, and Type of Family

Characteristic	Poverty Rate (share of each group that is poor, %)
Persons	12.1
Race and Ethnicity	
White	10.2
Non-Hispanic white	8.0
Black	24.1
Hispanic[a]	21.8
Asian and Pacific Islander	10.3
Age	
Age under 18	16.7
Age 18–64	10.6
Age 65 and over	10.4
Residence	
Inside metropolitan areas	11.6
Inside central cities	16.7
Outside central cities	8.9
Outside metropolitan areas	14.2
Families	9.6
Married couple	5.3
Female householder, no spouse present	26.5
Male householder, no spouse present	12.1

Source: U.S. Department of Commerce, Census Bureau (**www.census.gov**).

[a]Hispanics may be of any race.

other perspective of poverty; that is, we must analyze which groups in the United States have higher poverty rates.

Which Groups Have Higher Poverty Rates?

The proportion of all persons in the United States who are poor is 12.1 percent (see Table 6-4). However, if we make comparisons among different racial and ethnic groups, we see enormous disparity. At 10.2 percent, the poverty rate for white people is well below the national average. Perhaps more significantly, the poverty rate for non-Hispanic whites (Hispanics may be of any race) is only 8.0 percent. The poverty rate for black people is three times this rate, at 24.1 percent. The poverty rate for Hispanics is just slightly lower than that for blacks, at 21.8 percent. Asian and Pacific Islanders have a relatively low poverty rate of 10.3 percent. Thus, although most of the poor in the United States are white, a black or Hispanic person has a far greater likelihood of being poor than does a white person.

What is surprising to many is that older people (age 65 and over) have a poverty rate of 10.1 percent, which is below the national average. This relatively low rate is caused in large part by the Social Security program, which is discussed in Chapter 13. The war on poverty among older people has not been won, however. According to earlier evidence from the Department of Commerce, poverty among elderly women is far more prevalent than poverty among elderly men.

Equally disconcerting is the fact that children have a greater likelihood of being poor than any other age group in the United States. Children under the age of 18 have a poverty rate of almost 17 percent. That is, about one of every six children in America suffers from poverty. Consider the words of one woman in poverty:

> [I am concerned] that my children will be strong healthy people, and not have to go through what I have; my daughter to be able to think clearly about things; my son to never abuse any woman in his life. For me—just to provide what my kids and I need and a little extra to survive; that I finish school someday—to be able to work where I want to work—because the way that I see it is if you're not happy doing what you're doing, it won't last long. I hope my kids will not inherit my poverty; they deserve much more.[4]

Poverty rates also vary by residence. People living in our central cities have a poverty rate of 16.7 percent. The poverty rate for people living outside metropolitan areas is 14.2 percent. The likelihood of poverty is lowest for people living in metropolitan areas but outside the central cities. In other words, the likelihood of poverty is lowest for people living in the suburbs (8.9 percent). Because blacks and other ethnic minorities are likely to live in the central cities and whites in the suburbs, these figures are consistent with the previous figures on race and ethnicity. The concentration of poverty from residential segregation is discussed in more detail in Chapter 5, and the effect of residential segregation on public education is discussed in Chapter 4.

Finally, families with a female householder and no spouse present have over a 26 percent chance of being poor. In contrast, families with a male householder and no spouse present have only about a 12 percent chance of being poor (less than one-half the likelihood of the female-headed families). All of these statistics imply quite clearly that poverty in our country is a children's issue; it is also a women's issue, and it is a racial and ethnic issue.

The Implications of Poverty

It has been said that poverty statistics are just people with the tears washed off. What is the real meaning of poverty as it affects people's lives? Certainly, hunger is a problem for the poor. Bread for the World, a national citizens' lobby on hunger issues, recently reported that of 270 million Americans, 31 million are hungry or at risk of hunger. Among these people, 12 million are children. This means that these children have to skip meals, rely on emergency food, eat less, or eat less-nutritional food because their families cannot buy the food they need.[5]

Homelessness is also an implication of poverty, and families with children represent the fastest-growing group among the homeless. Homelessness is discussed in more detail in Chapter 10. In addition, adequate health care is often not available to our nation's poor. As we will see in Chapter 11, many of the poor are not covered by **Medicaid** (the government medical program for low-income Americans). Also, despite the presence of **Medicare** (the government medical program for the elderly), many poor older people find themselves unable to afford the costs of medications, Medicare premiums and deductibles, and uncovered medical expenses.

Medicaid
A government program providing medical coverage for eligible low-income people.

Medicare
A government program providing medical coverage largely to elderly people.

The Feminization of Poverty

The statistics show that women bear the greatest burden of poverty. Many have suggested possible reasons for this feminization of poverty.[6] Historical reasons include the growth in the number of female-headed households, discrimination in the labor market, and domestic violence toward women. Racial and age discrimination may exacerbate the gender discrimination faced by these women. In particular, teenage girls who drop out of school for the birth and care of a child find it difficult to complete their education and eventually find remunerative employment. For those who do manage, additional factors may complicate their lives. For example: "I think I did things right even at the time I was only sixteen, . . . I married, finished high school, went on to college, and worked, got divorced . . . but haven't received one child support payment."[7]

Insufficient child care, inadequate educational and training programs, limited assistance, and insufficient or nonexistent child support prevent many single mothers, and especially teenage mothers, from participating successfully in our economy and achieving independence from the forces of poverty. Other women have forgone educational and career opportunities to remain at home to care for children and family. They frequently find themselves in poverty if their husbands die or desert them. Finally, recent research suggests that 20 to 30 percent of all welfare recipients are current victims of domestic violence. This threat to safety and well-being can prevent many women from entering the labor force, retaining jobs, and supporting their families.[8]

CAUSES OF POVERTY

As already indicated, the national poverty rate rose substantially during the 1980s and again during the early 1990s. If the economy continues to perform poorly in the mid-2000s, we can expect rising poverty rates in this decade as well. Analysis of these and other trends can help uncover some of the causes of poverty.

Recession
A decline in a nation's gross domestic product (output) associated with a rise in unemployment.

Recession

Rising poverty rates were just discussed as outcomes of a poor economy. What we really mean is that recession was an important factor in the high poverty rates of the early 1980s, the early 1990s, and the first years of the new millennium. A **recession** is a reduction in our nation's output. When businesses are producing lower output levels, the need to hire workers lessens, and lower employment levels result. (Recession is discussed in more detail in Chapter 15, which examines macro policy.)

With almost 10 percent of the labor force unemployed in 1982 and 1983, more than 7 percent unemployed in 1992, and almost 6 percent in 2002, one would expect a higher incidence of poverty as income decreased for laid-off workers and as new entrants to the labor force were unable to find jobs. Furthermore, many employed workers find their hours of employment reduced during a recession. However, national unemployment rates are only part of the explanation of poverty.

Subsequent to the recessions of the early 1980s and 1990s, poverty rates did not fall to the degree one might expect in a recovery. Other factors must be considered. These factors include labor productivity, structural changes in our economy, personal factors, demographic trends, and budget cuts for antipoverty programs.

Labor Productivity

People with few skills, limited experience, and little education often have a difficult time finding employment at a satisfactory wage because their labor productivity is considered to be low. As a result, these people are more likely to be poor than are those who are better trained and educated. Many of you are still in school because you expect that your higher education will enhance your productivity and therefore your future income. Low labor productivity also ties in closely with structural changes in the economy as a cause of poverty.

Structural Changes in Our Economy

Changes in the structure of our economy contribute to unemployment and poverty. Technological change (such as robotics in the automobile industry) has enabled machines to replace workers. Furthermore, the lower-wage service sector (child care, restaurant service, and so on) has grown at the expense of the higher-wage manufacturing sector. Finally, the flight of businesses and jobs to the suburbs has left poverty-stricken inner cities in its wake.

These structural changes relate directly to the issue of labor productivity. The point is that the number of good, high-wage, blue-collar jobs has decreased greatly, and the economic gap between high school graduates and workers with higher education has widened. There are simply few well-paying jobs with stable employment left for relatively unskilled and uneducated people.

Personal Factors

People without adequate skills and education are more likely to be poor. But these are not the only factors constraining their incomes. Many individuals lack what we refer to as "job readiness," or the capacity to show up ready to work, on time, on a daily basis. This lack of readiness may be caused by mental disability, inexperience, immaturity, or other factors. Many families, especially single-parent families, lack adequate child care that would enable parents to work. If parents do work, they must miss work when their child is sick, their child-care provider is on vacation, or other circumstances exist that make for spotty attendance at work. Still other workers lack adequate transportation to their job sites. Poorer individuals tend to have less-reliable cars, and when their cars break down, they may not be able to afford repairs. At the same time, public

EconDebate

"Do Technological Advances Result in Higher Unemployment?"

Read the full debate under the Productivity and Growth category.

http://econapps. swlearning.com

transportation may be time-consuming or unavailable in the locations where workers need to travel to work and to take their children to child care. Many poor families experience all of these difficulties. Clearly, the oft-quoted query, "Why don't they just get a job?" reflects a vast oversimplification of the problem.

Demographic Trends

Demographic statistics indicate that the percentage of births to all unmarried mothers increased steadily from 1990 to 2000, as revealed in Table 6-5, following a trend since the early 1960s. The increased percentage of births to unmarried mothers also holds for subgroups of unmarried mothers who are white, black, Hispanic, and Native (though statistics for the latter three groups fluctuate a bit within the time period). The increasing percentages of births to unmarried mothers certainly represent one factor that may contribute to poverty.

Furthermore, Table 6-6 shows that the percentage of all births to teenage mothers increased from 1990 to 1995. Just as the term *feminization of poverty* suggests, it is especially difficult for young single mothers to provide adequate incomes for their families when they lack access to good jobs and education, and quality child care is unavailable or unaffordable. The high unemployment rate faced by young unskilled fathers is a contributing factor in their absence from the family and their lack of support.

However, there are now some signs for optimism. Table 6-5 reveals that although the percentage of all births to unmarried mothers increased slowly but steadily over the time period, the percentage declined over the shorter time period of 1995 to 2000 for black and Asian women, specifically. Perhaps more important, Table 6-6 shows that the percentage of all births to teenage mothers declined steadily each year over this shorter period of 1995 to 2000 for teenage mothers as a whole and for teenagers in each racial and ethnic group. If these trends continue, we can perhaps expect falling poverty rates as a result.

TABLE 6-5 Percentage of All Births to Unmarried Mothers							
Mothers	**1990**	**1995**	**1996**	**1997**	**1998**	**1999**	**2000**
All Unmarried Mothers	26.6	32.2	32.4	32.4	32.8	33.0	33.2
White	16.9	25.3	25.7	25.8	26.3	26.8	27.1
Black	66.7	69.9	69.8	69.2	69.1	68.9	68.5
Native	53.6	57.2	58.0	58.7	59.3	58.9	58.4
Hispanic[a]	36.7	40.8	40.7	40.9	41.6	42.2	42.7
Asian[b]	na	16.3	16.7	15.6	15.6	15.4	14.8

*Source: U.S. Department of Commerce, Census Bureau (**www.census.gov**).*

na = not available.

[a]Hispanics may be of any race.

[b]Includes other races not shown separately.

Mothers	1990	1995	1996	1997	1998	1999	2000
All Teenage Mothers	12.8	13.1	12.9	12.7	12.5	12.3	11.8
White	10.9	11.5	11.3	11.2	11.1	10.9	10.6
Black	23.1	23.1	22.8	22.2	21.5	20.7	19.7
Native	19.5	21.4	20.9	20.8	20.9	20.2	19.7
Hispanic[a]	16.8	17.9	17.4	17.0	16.9	16.7	16.2
Asian[b]	5.7	5.6	5.3	5.2	5.4	5.1	4.5

TABLE 6-6 Percentage of All Births to Teenage Mothers

Source: U.S. Department of Commerce, Census Bureau (www.census.gov).

[a]*Hispanics may be of any race.*

[b]*Includes other races not shown separately.*

Budget Cuts

Many people mistakenly believe that our government spends an enormous amount of money on programs designed to improve conditions for the poor. Many others believe that these programs are ineffective, at best. As a result of these attitudes, support for cuts in government programs for the poor has been widespread since the early 1980s. The budget cuts that took place early in the Reagan administration (1981–1983) were a case in point and were particularly harmful to the poor. Many families, particularly those headed by single mothers, lost eligibility for or received lower benefits from government cash assistance programs. Their children also lost food stamps, access to Medicaid health coverage, eligibility for government school lunch and breakfast programs, and the benefits of a host of other services. Bear in mind that these expenditure cuts occurred during a period when unemployment and poverty rates in the country were high and increasing.

Controversy over government programs continued throughout the 1980s and 1990s, as rising concern over government budget deficits created pressure for reduced government spending on social programs. We will return to this issue later in the chapter with the topic of welfare reform. We will see that there are those who believe that government programs effectively decrease poverty and those who feel that government poverty programs are wasteful and even contribute to the poverty problem.

Additional Causes of Poverty

Additional causes of poverty are related to specific aspects of the labor market within our economy. Having a job does not necessarily preclude poverty. A person working for the federal minimum wage of $5.15 per hour for 40 hours per week and 52 weeks per year will earn only $10,712 annually, well below the $16,895 poverty line for a family of four, as noted earlier. A minimum-wage job clearly does not pull these families out of poverty! We also know that women, on average, earn far less than men do, at least in part because of labor market discrimination. This topic is discussed more extensively in Chapter 5. Racial and age discrimination also serve to lower the earnings of various

EconDebate

"Does an Increase in the Minimum Wage Result in a Higher Unemployment Rate?"

For more information, go to Income Distribution and Poverty.

http://econapps. swlearning.com

minority groups, older people, and teenagers. In addition, poverty-stricken individuals include those who for various reasons could not work even if adequately paying jobs were available.

SOLUTIONS TO POVERTY

Solutions to poverty are subject to considerable controversy: witness the continual stream of editorials and letters to the editor in your daily newspaper concerning welfare reform, welfare abuse, government spending, and the like. Let us analyze various solutions that might be used to confront the problem of poverty.

Macroeconomic Policies to Relieve National Unemployment

Given that recession was seen to be a cause of poverty, it is useful to know that the government and Federal Reserve System can undertake various fiscal and monetary policies designed to increase national employment. These policies are discussed more fully in Chapter 15. For the moment, it should suffice to say that although national economic prosperity cannot alleviate all poverty, it can work hand in hand with other poverty reduction programs. Certainly, it makes little sense to train, educate, and provide work-support services to the hard-core poor and unemployed in an attempt to help them obtain gainful employment, only to find that national unemployment rates dictate that jobs will be unavailable. *Requiring* the poor to work when jobs do not exist makes even less sense!

Microeconomic Policies to Improve Labor Productivity

We can address the problems of poverty associated with low labor productivity, structural changes in the economy, and some of the personal factors mentioned previously by investing in people. We often think about business firms investing in various forms of capital, such as factories and machinery. We can also talk about investment in human capital. An **investment in human capital** is any spending that improves the productivity of people. Obviously, spending on education and job training can improve the skills and abilities of people and make them more productive, enhancing their ability to get jobs and their likelihood of receiving higher incomes.

In addition to job training and education, various programs can improve the job readiness of workers who have difficulty finding or keeping jobs. Transportation and child care needs must also be addressed. During recent periods of low unemployment rates, many businesses were desperate to hire workers. As a result, these businesses began to recognize the need to provide training, child care, and transportation for their workers. Unfortunately, when the economy shifts to a position of scarcity of jobs rather than scarcity of workers, as exists in the early 2000s, businesses tend to cut back any responsibility for providing these services.

Investment in human capital Spending that is designed to improve the productivity of people.

Universal Entitlements

Many of those concerned about poverty have called for expanded systems of **universal entitlements**. These types of programs are not necessarily directed toward the poor. They are targeted to all people who meet various types of criteria. All school-

Universal entitlements Payments (or programs) to which eligible citizens have a right by law.

age children in our country, for example, are entitled to a public education. Thus, certain standards of education are ensured for all children, regardless of income. Many would expand these types of provisions and guarantees to other areas of importance: child care, medical coverage, maternity and paternity leaves, and child or family allowances. These types of programs are taken for granted in many other Western industrialized countries, and they certainly would address some of the problems associated with the feminization of poverty.

The arguments against universal entitlements center on their expense and their potential for disincentives. Opponents ask, for example, why the government should fund child care for all, rather than just for low-income families in need. And if child allowances provide cash income based on the number of children per family, won't the allowances cause the birthrate to increase?

Proponents reject these claims. They argue that the political likelihood of enacting and maintaining programs and policies is much greater if such programs benefit all, rather than just the poor. Furthermore, only if programs providing benefits such as medical care and child care are targeted to all will quality be ensured; programs for only the poor have often been of substandard quality. Finally, universal entitlements would avoid the stigmatizing of the poor and the pitting of various groups of citizens against one another in their quest for important services.

A Negative Income Tax

A **negative income tax** has been proposed by politicians and economists in a variety of forms but would typically tax income earners at various positive rates as long as income lies above some guaranteed level—for example, the poverty line. At this specified level, income would not be taxed. Below this level, people would actually receive payments from the government, amounting to a negative tax. Actual payments could be automatic, could work through our current income tax system, and could depend on family size.

Proposals vary considerably as to the size of payments as well as the overall intent of the program. For some proponents, the negative income tax would entirely replace all current government programs, including farm price supports, student loans, Social Security, and so on. For others, it would replace only government poverty programs; other programs would remain intact. Milton Friedman, an early advocate of the negative income tax, believed that it should replace a large number of government programs. Other proponents have suggested that the tax be used in conjunction with various other government poverty programs; indeed, they suggest that the beauty of the negative income tax is that it would free up funds and personnel currently involved in the bureaucracy of our cash assistance programs. These resources could be put to work meeting the various social needs of low-income clients.

The proposal has a number of other attractive elements. It is simple and probably efficient. It could be designed to cover the cash needs of all Americans, not just those in specific categories. There would be no incentive for family breakup. And, if properly run, it could minimize disincentives for work effort. As long as individuals receive at least some substantial portion of each additional work dollar and always are better off working than not, the incentive to work will remain. The actual feasibility and desirability of any such negative income tax proposal will depend on actual payment levels,

Negative income tax
A taxation system that taxes people with incomes above a certain level and pays people with incomes below that level.

Earned Income Credit (EIC)
A federal tax credit for low-income workers and families. The credit is available whether or not the worker pays federal personal income taxes.

the types of government programs that complement it, and the minimization of any potential work disincentives.

Despite the many positive aspects of the negative income tax, few politicians have been willing to consider it seriously. However, the 1986 tax reform took some steps toward the goals envisioned in the negative income tax plan. Various exemptions, deductions, and credits have virtually eliminated the obligation of very-low-income families to pay federal income taxes. Furthermore, increases in the federal **Earned Income Credit (EIC)**, a tax credit originally geared to low-income working families with children, has reduced the tax burden of these poor families. The EIC is actually a limited form of the negative income tax insofar as it returns money to low-income families even if they paid no federal income taxes. President Bill Clinton increased the EIC and expanded it to low-income single individuals and couples without children in 1993. As of 2003, workers who raise more than one child in their home and have a family income of less than $33,178 ($34,178 for married workers) can get a tax credit of up to $4,140. Workers with one or no children receive a smaller amount. If they paid no income taxes, they would simply receive a check from the government. If they have already paid taxes, they would be reimbursed by this amount and would potentially receive greater payment. However, they must first file a federal personal income tax form to be eligible.[9]

Because the Earned Income Credit works so well to help low-income working families without diminishing their incentive to work, many people have argued for expanded use of the credit at both the federal and the state government levels.

Miscellaneous Solutions

Public assistance
Any government program that is targeted to aid low-income people.

Because discrimination plays a role in poverty, it is important that our nation strive to provide equal opportunities to all people in the areas of education, housing, and employment. Equal opportunity legislation and affirmative action are discussed in more detail in Chapter 5. In addition, the financing of public education must be addressed to ensure quality schools for all children. This issue is discussed in more detail in Chapter 4. Our nation's housing programs and health care system must also address the needs of the poor, as we will see in Chapters 10 and 11. Finally, we need to consider an increase in the minimum wage. Because there are costs and benefits associated with the minimum wage, we need to consider carefully the issues that are discussed in Chapter 14 on unemployment and inflation.

Social Security
A federal program that provides income transfers to retired workers, the survivors of deceased workers, and disabled workers.

Welfare and Other Government Programs

Several government programs are designed to help the poor. These programs include food stamps; general assistance; Medicaid; the State Children's Health Insurance Program; Supplemental Security Income; the Special Supplemental Nutrition Program for Women, Infants, and Children; the Earned Income Credit; and Temporary Assistance for Needy Families. These programs are described as **public assistance** programs in Table 6-7.

Social insurance
Any government program funded by payroll taxes of employers, employees, or both and is targeted to aid certain eligible groups of people. A person need not have low income to qualify.

Although **Social Security** has removed many people from poverty, it is not considered an antipoverty program because it is available to all who are eligible, regardless of income. Social Security is an example of a **social insurance** program, into which workers pay while they work and from which they receive benefits when they become eligible. Thus, the public assistance programs in Table 6-7 are targeted to

TABLE 6-7   Explanation of Government Programs

Program	Explanation
Public Assistance Programs	
Food Stamps	Federal government program providing vouchers (coupons) to low-income people, which are accepted as payment by stores for food.
General Assistance	Local government assistance designed to meet local needs and fill gaps in state and federal government programs.
Medicaid	Combined federal and state government program providing medical coverage for eligible low-income people.
State Children's Health Insurance Program (SCHIP)	Combined federal and state government program providing medical coverage for eligible low-income children.
Supplemental Security Income (SSI)	Combined federal and state government program providing cash income to low-income aged, blind, and disabled people.
Special Supplemental Nutrition Program for Women, Infants, and Children (WIC)	Federal government program providing nutritious food to needy pregnant women and young children when special health needs exist.
Earned Income Credit (EIC)	Federal tax credit for low-income working people.
Temporary Assistance for Needy Families (TANF)	Block grants from the federal government to state governments for use in state welfare programs that comply with the Personal Responsibility and Work Opportunity Reconciliation Act.
Social Insurance Programs	
Social Security	Federal government program providing cash benefits to retired workers, survivors of deceased workers, and the disabled.
Unemployment Compensation	Combined federal and state government program providing benefits to eligible unemployed workers.
Medicare	Federal government program providing medical coverage largely to elderly people.

EconDebate

"Will Social Security Survive into the Twenty-First Century?"

To read the full debate go to Income Distribution and Poverty.

http://econapps. swlearning.com

low-income people, whereas social insurance programs are not. Other social insurance programs include Medicare and unemployment compensation.

Temporary Assistance for Needy Families (TANF) is a **block grant** from the federal government to state governments for use in state welfare programs. (TANF is pronounced TAN-EF.) It is the public assistance program that we will consider in detail momentarily. It replaces **Aid to Families with Dependent Children (AFDC)**, which was our nation's most important public assistance program for many years. The AFDC program provided cash assistance to poor families with children. This program generated controversy in the United States for decades and was revised many times. The controversy culminated in the passage of legislation that eliminated AFDC and replaced it with work programs. The issues that motivated this action are discussed in the next section.

WELFARE REFORM

Temporary Assistance for Needy Families (TANF)
A block grant from the federal government to state governments to be used in state welfare programs in compliance with federal guidelines. (Pronounced TAN-EF.)

Both conservatives and moderates agreed on the need for welfare reform, as was evident in the Republican "Contract with America" (the 1990s blueprint guiding conservative proposals for our nation's economy) and in President Clinton's election promise to "end welfare as we know it." Dialogue culminated in the passage of the welfare reform bill called the **Personal Responsibility and Work Opportunity Reconciliation Act (PRA) of 1996**. This legislation, signed into law by President Clinton in October 1996, called for the phaseout of the AFDC program and the phase in of the new TANF program. It is useful to examine the controversy that created the call for welfare reform.

Controversy over Welfare

Disincentives

Block grant
A lump sum of money given by the federal government to state governments to use as they wish within broad federal guidelines to develop programs to meet a broad category of need.

Many people were concerned about possible disincentives built into the AFDC program. Although individual state programs varied, the federal program was such that if a recipient (usually a mother) took a job and began earning income, she lost AFDC benefits dollar for dollar of the income earned. Although she may have received benefits to cover the additional costs of working (transportation, child care, and so on), often these were inadequate. If income rose and Medicaid benefits were lost (as well as eligibility for child nutrition programs and other services), the family may well have been placed in a far more precarious situation than before the mother went to work. Thus, economic disincentives were said to exist for work effort. Furthermore, severe restrictions on benefits had often been placed on families with a father present in the home. In many cases, these restrictions may have encouraged the father to leave the family so that the mother and children could receive benefits. Others argued that the program encouraged illegitimacy. Thus, disincentives were said to exist for family stability.

Welfare Dependency

Another concern was that government programs encouraged people to develop long-term dependence on welfare. Research results on this issue are mixed. Various studies reported different percentages of families remaining dependent on welfare.

Despite the discrepancies in findings, the data suggested that most people did not become persistently dependent on welfare but used such assistance to get through a difficult financial period resulting from a divorce, an unplanned birth, an illness or death, a lost job, or other factors. Even though the percentage of families persistently dependent on welfare may have been small, it was significant. The dependent recipient was the stereotype in the minds of people as they railed against AFDC.

Welfare Expense

Finally, people were concerned about the expense of welfare programs. Here, it is important to maintain a correct perspective. Census Bureau data reveal that in the last several years of the AFDC program, federal spending on this program represented only about 1 percent of the federal budget. (Food stamps and other nutrition programs combined represented only about 2 percent.) Although it is always important to use funds wisely, many people held the mistaken opinion that welfare was draining the federal budget.

The Personal Responsibility and Work Opportunity Reconciliation Act (PRA)

The 1996 PRA phased out the AFDC program and replaced it with Temporary Assistance for Needy Families block grants to individual states for use in their welfare programs. States were given until July 1997 to develop these welfare programs. The PRA allows the states wide discretion in determining their programs, eligibility standards, and benefit levels. States must comply, however, with some broad federal guidelines. These guidelines specify that (1) states must contribute matching money to their welfare programs, (2) adults must cease to receive benefits if they fail to work within two years of joining the welfare rolls, and (3) states may not use federal money to provide assistance to adults for more than five years in their lifetimes (although 20 percent of each state's welfare recipients can be exempted from this requirement).

In addition to these restrictions, states may add their own stipulations. They may require, for example, that minor, unmarried parents live with an adult and attend school in order to be eligible for benefits. They may deny additional assistance to children born to mothers already receiving benefits. They may also provide lower benefits to people moving to their state if the previous state's benefits were lower.

In addition to eliminating the AFDC program, the PRA eliminated many benefits for legal immigrants who are not citizens and have not already worked in the United States for 10 years. (Illegal immigrants were already ineligible for most programs.) Some, but not all, of these benefits have since been restored for some, but not all, poor immigrants. According to the Center on Budget and Policy Priorities, the 1996 welfare law substantially reduced the receipt of Medicaid, food stamps, TANF, and Supplemental Security Income (SSI) by noncitizens who were lawfully admitted to the United States.[10] The PRA also eliminated low-income entitlement to child care, tightened eligibility for benefits to disabled children, and allowed states to deny Medicaid to adults who lose cash assistance for failure to comply with work requirements.

Partly as a result of the new PRA legislation, welfare caseloads have fallen dramatically in almost every state since the early 1990s. The average state caseload reduction was almost 60 percent by the early 2000s.[11] The reduction in caseloads has

Aid to Families with Dependent Children (AFDC) Our nation's former welfare program that provided cash assistance to eligible low-income families with children.

Personal Responsibility and Work Opportunity Reconciliation Act (PRA) of 1996 Legislation that eliminated AFDC and replaced it with state programs that require work. It also tightened eligibility for and reduced the benefits offered by other social assistance programs.

been touted as a sign of the program's success, but many people are concerned about what has become of the former clients. Have they become employed with adequate wages? Have they dropped out of the system, overwhelmed by requirements and restrictions, or are they simply unwilling to work?

Various sources suggest varying outcomes. According to Bread for the World, two-thirds of welfare leavers lack full-time employment and 18 percent lack any employment once they leave the TANF program. About 40 percent of the women who have gone off welfare have neither a job nor cash assistance. In addition to these statistics, research shows that former welfare recipients' wages are low, averaging $6.00 to $7.50 an hour, or $12,000 to $15,000 per year. According to the Center on Budget and Policy Priorities, most people leaving welfare for work earn too little to adequately support their families. Their jobs are typically short-lived, low-wage jobs that lack health or other benefits and offer little room for advancement or wage growth. Other families have left or been dropped from the welfare rolls without work, and many of the people remaining on welfare have very serious unmet needs.[12] In another study by the Urban Institute, 86 percent of recipients in Washington, D.C., remained poor, and one third remained very poor (with income less than 50 percent of the poverty line).[13] Circumstances have worsened in the new millennium because of the unemployment and poverty created by the recession and slower economic growth that has characterized the early 2000s.

Although many of these results to date are discouraging, there was some initial optimism about the capacity of states to improve their programs. Within the context of the broad federal guidelines, states have had considerable discretion, flexibility, and financing for developing their own welfare programs. In an ideal situation, each state would take into account the complexity of poverty among its citizens and seek to provide solutions that incorporate training and education, child care, health care, nutrition, transportation, counseling, and other forms of assistance. They might also provide state earned income credits and subsidies to employers to cover the costs of hiring welfare clients. In other situations, unfortunately, states put forth only the minimal effort needed to comply with federal law. Furthermore, the fiscal crises of many state governments in the early 2000s have made it very difficult for states to improve their programs. According to the Center on Budget and Policy Priorities, more than 35 states have recently made cuts in programs funded with TANF and other funds, including some combination of substantial cuts in child care programs for low-income working families, work programs designed to help TANF recipients find jobs, services and supports for very disadvantaged families, cash assistance for low-income working families, and programs such as pregnancy prevention.[14]

EconDebate

"Is Workfare Working?"

An alternative to welfare is workfare, but is it really helping those in poverty? Read the full debate under the Labor Markets category.

http://econapps. swlearning.com

An Example of a TANF Program: Wisconsin Works

Wisconsin has long been a leader in welfare reform and boasts of having caseloads decline by 82 percent from January 1995 to January 2001. Wisconsin was one of the first states to implement its TANF program in September 1997. This new program is entitled Wisconsin Works (W-2), and it provides various forms of assistance to needy families with children, along with job preparation and job support services for needy parents. Wisconsin is more generous in providing various supports for the transition from welfare to work than are most states. Nevertheless, W-2 requires that all participating parents be placed in one of four tiers of "work" as soon as they are able to work and it restricts participants to 24 months in a single employment position category. (A single parent caring for a child who is less than 12 weeks old is exempt from the work requirement.) These four tiers of work extend from unsubsidized employment at the top (the program goal) to a "transition" tier at the bottom. This lower tier is for individuals with severe barriers to employment and provides a monthly grant of $628 for up to 28 hours per week of participation in work training or other employment-related activities, and up to 12 hours per week in education and training. This work training and education may consist of high school completion, technical courses, English as a Second Language, parenting and life skills, mental health counseling, caring for an incapacitated family member, and volunteer activity. Indeed, part of the success of the Wisconsin program is that the state provides these lowest-tier "jobs" for those who cannot be successful in higher-tiered jobs.

Currently, the maximum monthly TANF cash benefit for a family of three with no income is $673. The benefit is reduced by $5.15 for each hour that the participant fails without good cause to participate in assigned activities. An individual is eligible for income from any of the three tiers of work activity (excluding unsubsidized employment) for a period up to 24 months, with possible extensions.[15] Just as at the federal level, W-2 participants are limited to five years' lifetime participation in the program, though some may be eligible for extensions. Despite early optimism regarding job availability for TANF participants, the recession and slower growth of the early 2000's now has people concerned about job availability for participants.

The Wisconsin program emphasizes community involvement in the program and includes subsidies to employers who hire W-2 participants. The program also emphasizes pregnancy prevention and includes childcare and transportation assistance, food stamps, Medicaid, and emergency assistance for those who are eligible. Minor parents are not eligible for cash assistance but may receive case management services, cash assistance for childcare, and health care. Minors without a high school diploma must attend school to receive childcare assistance. W-2 payments are not adjusted for the number of children in a family, and W-2 participants receive health benefits in the form of a new insurance plan using health maintenance organizations. Wisconsin also has a state earned income credit and extends food stamps and W-2 services to eligible legal immigrants.

Many people living in and outside Wisconsin are watching the Wisconsin program carefully. Since its caseload reduction is among the highest of all states, a major question concerns the status of people who have ceased to participate in the W-2 program. In response, the Wisconsin Department of Workforce Development commissioned a study to examine the status of every participant who left the program between September 1997 and September 1999. The results of this study indicate that among participants who had not reentered the program by September 1999, approximately 76 percent had left the program because they had obtained household income through employment, other government cash assistance, child support, or some combination of these. Other participants left the program because they either chose not to enroll or to have eligibility review (9 percent), they chose not to meet program requirements (8 percent), they no longer met other eligibility requirements (4 percent), or they chose options other than receiving assistance (3 percent). The study was also able to obtain monthly earnings statements for 13,428 of the families that left the program after becoming employed. Of these, approximately 11 percent earned less than $800, 10 percent earned $800 to $899, 11 percent earned $900 to $999, 22 percent earned $1,000 to $1,199, 26 percent earned $1,200 to $1,499, 13 percent earned $1,500 to $1,999, and 8 percent earned more than $2,000.[16] The majority of these incomes are at or below poverty levels. A more recent study was conducted in 2001, and it showed that 38 percent of all welfare leavers reported no income at all.[17]

Concerns about the TANF Program

There are many controversial issues surrounding the PRA and the TANF program. A major issue is the level of federal funding. In his TANF reauthorization proposal in January 2003, President Bush proposed that PRA funding for basic assistance, welfare-to-work programs, and child care be frozen for the next five years and not even be adjusted upward to compensate for inflation. Many people are concerned that at a time when state governments are in their own fiscal crises of reduced tax revenue and reduced assistance from the federal government, the frozen federal funds will result in a reduction in job training, child care, and other services. They are also frustrated by the president's proposals for billions of dollars of tax cuts for high-income individuals, while they fail to provide adequate funding for the poor.

Another controversial element of welfare reform is whether mothers of young children should be required to work outside of the home. Many feel that work is better for mother and child. Others fear that child care for infants will be inadequate, and they believe that the choice to work should reside with the mother, as it does for higher-income families. Another issue is that when funds are inadequate for child care, children may be poorly cared for by an older sibling or by a neighbor or relative already overworked with children of their own.

Wisconsin Governor Jim Doyle recently proposed that the state's W-2 program allow women to stay home with their newborn infants for six months instead of just 12 weeks and still receive benefits. This proposal was blocked by the Wisconsin legislature. Regardless of viewpoints on the issue of mothers staying home with their infants, child care should be perceived as a valuable form of work in our society.

A third issue involves the importance of training and educational opportunities that would ultimately give a client access to jobs providing adequate wages and benefits. According to federal law, participation in vocational education can count toward a state's work participation requirement for up to 12 months for any individual, but for no more than 30 percent of the state's welfare recipients.

In his 2002 and 2003 budget proposals, President Bush sought to toughen the work requirements. Many people feel that the guidelines are already very restrictive because each client needs to meet specific work requirements, and any education and training beyond the minimal amount supported by the program must come out of the client's free time. There is little if any free time for a single parent of young children who is working full-time. As one single woman explained at the beginning of the program:

> I will complete the higher education degree I am currently seeking. . . . I am told that as of next semester, I will no longer be eligible for childcare assistance and will also be forced to work a minimum of thirty hours per week. School will no longer be a consideration in my case. My sons are three and one-half, and four and one-half, and will need to be in daycare for another year and a half at least. I

am eligible for student loans, which will cover the cost. However, my main concern is the work requirement. It will be extremely difficult to keep up a good grade point, work, and still be able to be a mother to my children. This will mean that we will be together as a family less than we are now. That's what frightens me.[18]

Another serious problem of a welfare system centered on work responsibility concerns business cycles. Our economy alternates between periods of growth and decline in GDP, or in other words, between expansions and recessions. Our new welfare system was initiated during a period of steady economic growth and prosperity, and optimism was high for the success of the program. The problem is what happens to the program when recession hits, as it has in the early 2000s. It is one thing to require people to work; it is another thing to require them to work when jobs do not exist.

One final controversy centers on the transfer of responsibility for welfare programs from the federal government to the states. Many have long contended that individual states know and understand their welfare needs better than does the federal government, which is perceived as distant and bureaucratic. President Bush has steadily sought to transfer more control over many social services to the states and to allow them more authority over not just the TANF program, but also housing subsidies, unemployment benefits, health insurance, and preschool for children from disadvantaged families. Indeed, his efforts to shift federal responsibility to states in a large number of areas are a major shift in U.S. policy.

Others believe that federal responsibility is essential to provide consistent benefits to all citizens. Affluent states can provide additional funding for generous benefits and eligibility, but poorer states with high unemployment rates and low property values find it difficult to raise additional tax revenue to meet the needs of their distressed population. Some people also question why poor citizens should be treated better in some states than others. As of July 1999, the disparity between states was striking: for example, the maximum cash benefit for a family of three with no income in the highest-benefit state (Alaska) was $923 per month, whereas the comparable benefit in the lowest-benefit state (Alabama) was $164. These differences exceed by far any possible disparity in the cost of living in these states. Last, state flexibility always raises the issue of whether people will migrate to other states in order to receive higher benefits there.

THE ROLE OF ECONOMIC GROWTH VERSUS GOVERNMENT PROGRAMS

Because recession—which is a decline in national output—causes unemployment rates to go up, we might expect that economic growth—which is an increase in national output—would cause unemployment rates to go down. Higher output levels mean more people working, which mean fewer people in poverty. This is, in fact, the essence of **trickle-down philosophy**: the benefits of economic growth and prosperity eventually trickle down to all. Support for this view has been a hallmark of both the Ronald Reagan and George W. Bush administrations.

Certainly, greater national prosperity does reduce poverty and is one reason for the falling poverty rates we observed during the 1990s. However, there are three particular problems with the trickle-down philosophy. First, some of the policies that are designed to generate economic growth may directly increase absolute and relative

Trickle-down philosophy
The view that the benefits of economic growth and prosperity will "trickle down" to all.

poverty, as well as worsen the standards of living of the poor. This phenomenon is discussed in greater length in the section on supply-side policy in Chapter 15, which describes the issues of cuts in government programs that affect low-income people and cuts in taxes that primarily affect higher-income people. Second, the newly created jobs that result from economic growth benefit those who are hired into these jobs. Remember that many others are left behind in the labor market, including those who are ill or disabled, the elderly, the young, those who face labor market discrimination, and single parents of young children, as well as people without adequate job skills, education, experience, and transportation. The benefits of economic growth fail to trickle down to these people. Finally, a job does not guarantee a living wage. Recall that the minimum wage may well leave a family below the poverty line. One final issue involves greater reliance on private charities to deal with the problems of poverty. Indeed, a hallmark of President Bush's administration is the creation of "faith-based initiatives." Others recognize that although the use of faith-based initiatives may help alleviate the poverty problem, the ability of private charities in funding antipoverty programs will be inadequate (especially in times of recession when charitable contributions fall off). Government programs will always be necessary to help those who cannot achieve success through economic growth alone.

VIEWPOINT: CONSERVATIVE VERSUS LIBERAL

People generally adopt either a liberal or a conservative approach to the poverty issue. Liberals are more inclined to stress the need for government involvement in antipoverty efforts; they believe there are equity issues that are not dealt with by the market economy. Conservatives are much more leery of government involvement and are concerned that too many programs or too much assistance creates inefficiencies and disincentives for work effort. Liberals tend to prefer extensive federal involvement in poverty programs, whereas conservatives prefer greater responsibility by private charities and by state governments (as with the 1996 welfare reform bill and with President George W. Bush's proposals). Liberals favor a direct approach to dealing with the problem of poverty; conservatives often favor an indirect, trickle-down approach.

On the other hand, many economists believe that solutions to poverty should not be viewed as alternative courses of action. Indeed, an effective solution might combine elements of each alternative. A prosperous economy with high employment is an important—but only a partial—solution. Universal entitlements may ensure more adequate standards for many, as would a negative income tax (or expansion of the earned income credit). Efforts to improve the productivity and job readiness of workers are lauded by liberals and conservatives alike. Given the complexity of poverty and the individual needs of people, many economists believe that solutions to poverty must be varied and individualized.

COMPLEXITY OF POVERTY

The problem of poverty is very complex and without simple solutions. If there were only one cause and one type of poverty, solutions would be readily found. Instead, there is a variety of circumstances affecting different individuals. The solutions to poverty among elderly women will be far different from the solutions to poverty among unskilled and uneducated 18-year-olds. The needs of single women with children will be far different from the needs of the disabled. The problems of poverty in inner-city ghettoes are far different from the problems in the suburbs and the countryside.

Many students who work hard to finance their education find it difficult to be sympathetic to the poor. They work hard, so why don't the poor? We must remember that it is one thing to be successful at work, but it is another thing to be successful at work while caring for young children, coping with a disability, or lacking transportation or opportunities for employment. Some Americans have adopted a punitive attitude toward the poor, but many others are sincere in their concern for the poor, though they have different views about how to approach the issue of poverty. What we must do is try to understand the complexities of poverty and avoid stigmatizing and stereotyping the poor. At the same time, we must seek common ground for solutions to poverty that work. We cannot expect these solutions to be simple.

SUMMARY

Relative poverty is a situation in which people are poor in comparison with other people. Relative poverty is measured by the distribution of total money income to different income groups. Recent U.S. statistics on the income distribution indicate that the poorest fifth of the population receives less than 4 percent of total income, whereas the richest fifth of the population receives about 50 percent. The income distribution in the United States has become less equal since 1981. The United States has the least-equal income distribution of all the Western industrialized nations.

Absolute poverty is defined through the use of the poverty line. If a family's money income falls below the poverty line, all members of that family are defined by the government as being poor. The poverty line varies depending on family size and is adjusted annually for inflation. The 2002 poverty line for a family of four is $18,244.

The U.S. poverty rate exceeded 20 percent in 1960. This rate fell dramatically during the 1960s and 1970s, reaching a low of approximately 11 percent in 1973. Poverty rates increased once again in the early 1980s, the early 1990s, and the early 2000s. Although most poor people in the United States are white, blacks and Hispanics have considerably higher poverty rates. Households with single female parents have higher poverty rates than other households, and children have the highest poverty rate of all age groups. The implications of poverty include hunger, homelessness, and poor health.

Causes of poverty include recession, low labor productivity, structural changes in our economy, personal factors, demographic trends (such as numbers of female-headed households), and cuts in government programs that assist the poor. Proposals to reduce poverty have taken a variety of approaches and include macroeconomic policies to reduce national unemployment, microeconomic policies to improve worker productivity, a system of universal entitlements, a negative income tax and the earned income credit, antidiscrimination policies, the minimum wage, and welfare. The debate over welfare reform culminated in the passage of the Personal Responsibility and Work Opportunity Reconciliation Act (PRA) of 1996, which eliminated Aid to Families with Dependent Children (AFDC) and replaced it with Temporary Assistance for Needy Families (TANF). The new program emphasizes work and time limits for assistance.

NOTES

1. These words, and the words of other women throughout the text, are actual quotations of women who were involved in a project of the Women and Poverty Public Education Initiative, funded by the Charles Stewart Mott Foundation. The source is *In Our Own Words: Mothers' Perspectives on Welfare Reform*, the Women and Poverty Public Education Initiative, 1997 Women's Studies Consortium Outreach Program, University of Wisconsin-Parkside, Kenosha, WI. Major portions of the report were prepared by Laura Wittmann, Anne Statham, and Katherine Rhoades, as well as Loretta Williams, Jean Verber, Julie Elliott, Selina Vasquez, Kathe Johnson, Nancy Bayne, Ethel Quisler, May Kay Schleiter, Diana Garcia, Iredia Seiler, Mary Ellen Lemke, Michelle Graf, Bets Reedy, Jean Radtke, Kim Noyd, Susan Taylor Campbell, and Davida Alperin. (Quotations may contain slight grammatical alterations made by the authors.)

2. U.S. Department of Commerce, Census Bureau (**www.census.gov**).

3. World Bank, *World Development Report 2003* (New York: Oxford University Press, 2003), pp. 236–237. Comparisons are based on the Gini coefficient, a measure of distribution of income or consumption expenditures, for the most recent year available (generally in the 1990s).

4. Laura Wittmann et al., *In Our Own Words*.

5. Bread for the World, *A Future with Hope* (Washington D.C.: Bread for the World Institute, 2001).

6. The phrase *feminization of poverty* was first used by sociologist Diana Pearce, "The Feminization of Poverty: Women, Work, and Welfare," *Urban and Social Change Review* (February 1978). It also appears, along with an extensive discussion of the feminization of poverty and its causes in Ruth Sidel, *Women and Children Last: The Plight of Poor Women in Affluent America* (New York: Viking, 1986). In her book, Sidel emphasizes the point made in the introduction to this book—namely, that women are often just one normal life crisis away from poverty. She also makes the arguments in favor of universal entitlements that are discussed subsequently under the section in this chapter entitled "Solutions to Poverty."

7. Laura Wittmann et al., *In Our Own Words*.

8. Center on Budget and Policy Priorities, "Windows of Opportunity: Strategies to Support Low-Income Families in the Next State of Welfare Reform" (**www.cbpp.org/3-30-00wel.htm**).

9. More information is available in the document "Facts about the Earned Income Credit" on the Center on Budget and Policy Priorities' Web site at **www.cbpp.org**.

10. Center on Budget and Policy Priorities, "Immigrant's Use of Public Benefits has Declined Substantially Since 1996," March 26, 2003 (**www.cbpp.org/3-26-03imm-pr.htm**).

11. Bread for the World Institute, *A Future with Hope*. This and other information in this section are based on studies reported by this source, unless otherwise mentioned.

12. Center on Budget and Policy Priorities, "States Have Substantial Unspent Welfare Funds, but Low-Income Families Continue to Need Key Supports," January 12, 2000 (**www.cbpp.org/1-12-00wel-pr.htm**).

13. The Urban Institute, Gregory Als and Pamela Loprest, October 2003 (**www.urban.org**).

14. Center on Budget and Policy Priorities, Sharon Parrott, and Nina Wu, "States Are Cut-

ting TANF and Childcare Programs," June 4, 2003 (**www.cbpp.org/6-3-03tanf.htm**).

15. Information in this and the next paragraph is from the Wisconsin Department of Workforce Development, "Wisconsin State Plan for the Administration of the Block Grant to States for Temporary Assistance for Needy Families," June 1, 2000 (**www.dwd.state.wi.us/dws/w2/tanf96.htm**) and from Bread for the World, *A Future with Hope.*

16. Department of Workforce Development, "Welfare Closure Study: A Study of All AFDC and W-2 Closures (September 1997 through September 1999)," March 2000 (**www.dwd.state.wi.us/dws/w2/w2closure/transmittal.htm**). Note that some of the participants in the study had started with AFDC funds and transitioned into W-2. Separate data are available for participants who left W-2 and were subsequently reinstated. The earnings data cited for participants who left because of subsequent employment do not include other forms of government cash assistance or child support.

17. Bread for the World, *A Future with Hope.*

18. Laura Wittmann et al., *In Our Own Words.*

DISCUSSION QUESTIONS

1. Should incomes in the United States be distributed equally? If not, should there be at least a greater degree of equality than we presently have? What are the advantages and disadvantages of greater equality? How might greater equality be achieved?

2. Is the official government definition of poverty an adequate one? Does it understate the true extent of poverty? Does it overstate it? How might the measure of poverty be improved? The Census Bureau (**www.census.gov**) has begun recording poverty statistics with alternative definitions of poverty. Check the Web site.

3. Many people would be surprised by the information on declining teenage birthrates. Does this information surprise you? Does it mean than young people are less likely to become pregnant, or does it mean that abortion rates are increasing? Look up the reasons for lower birthrates in the health statistics of the Center for Disease Control, (**www.cdc.gov**).

4. Are you eligible for the Earned Income Credit? Find out if you're eligible by reading about the Earned Income Credit on the Web site for the Center on Budget and Policy Priorities (**www.cbpp.org**). If you find yourself eligible, be sure to file your income tax returns even if you are not required to do so because of low earnings. Otherwise, you will not benefit from the EIC.

5. Should mothers of young children be required to work in return for government assistance? Does the age of the child make a difference? What about the number of children? What are the issues involved?

6. Should states or the federal government be given more responsibility for poverty programs? What are the implications of placing greater responsibility for these programs on the states? Think about the financing of programs, the extent of poverty in different states, and problems relating to different eligibility criteria and benefit levels across different states.

7. Which do you feel is more effective in reducing poverty: government poverty programs or economic growth of the nation? How do private charities fit in? Are you conservative or liberal when it comes to addressing poverty?

8. This textbook uses 2002 statistics for poverty rates and income distribution. Update these figures by using the Census Bureau Web site (**www.census.gov**). Search under Income and Poverty.

9. Check the Web site of the Wisconsin Department of Workforce Development (**www.dwd.**

state.wi.us) for information regarding Wisconsin participants that have been terminated because of the five-year time limit.

10. Check the Web site for the Center on Budget and Policy Priorities (**www.cbpp.org**) to discover a wealth of information on government programs and their effects on people. What are some of the topics that are of interest to you?

11. Go to **www.cbpp.org/3-30-00wel.htm** to see the many suggestions by the Center on Budget and Policy Priorities about how state governments can improve their welfare programs. How do these suggestions address poverty-related issues, such as housing, health care, and nutrition?

12. Browse through the Web site for the Center on Budget and Policy Priorities once again at **www.cbpp.org**. Do you think this is a liberal or a conservative research institute? Why?

13. Browse through the Web site of the Heritage Foundation at **www.heritage.org**. Do you think this is a liberal or a conservative research institute? Why?

14. The Center for Disease Control explores many health topics and issues, mostly discussed from a noneconomic perspective. Check out the Web site at **www.cdc.gov** to discover health care problems associated with poverty.

15. Are you concerned about the problem of poverty in the United States? If so, there are many organizations such as Bread for the World that lobby our government on behalf of the poor in the U.S. and the rest of the world. The Web site at **www.bread.org** can fill you in on current legislative issues involving the poor and provides web links to other organizations concerned about similar issues. What legislative issues involving poverty are currently being discussed in Congress?

CHAPTER 6 APPENDIX: GRAPHING THE DATA ON THE INCOME DISTRIBUTION

I t is useful to have a "picture" of the income distribution that can readily be used to compare different time periods or countries. In other words, we need to be able to graph the data on the income distribution.

Lorenz curve
A graphical technique that exhibits the income distribution.

In Figure 6-1, information from the 2002 statistical table (Table 6-1 in the text) is presented graphically in a **Lorenz curve**. In a graph with the percentage of population on the horizontal axis and the percentage of total money income on the vertical axis, the 45-degree diagonal line would indicate perfect equality of income among the various income groups. For example, the poorest 20 percent of the population would receive 20 percent of total money income; the next 20 percent of the population would receive 20 percent of total money income, and so on. This 45-degree line is useful as a reference line.

The Lorenz curve shows the actual income distribution. Note that the Lorenz curve is based on cumulative distributions derived from numbers in Table 6-1. First, the poorest 20 percent of the population received 3.4 percent of total money income. The poorest 40 percent of the population (the two bottom income groups) received 12.2 percent of total money income (3.4 percent to the poorest 20 percent of the population plus 8.8 percent to the next poorest 20 percent of the population). The poorest 60 percent of the population (the three bottom income groups) received 27.1 percent of total money income (3.4 percent plus 8.8 percent plus 14.9 percent). Continuing this process completes the Lorenz curve.

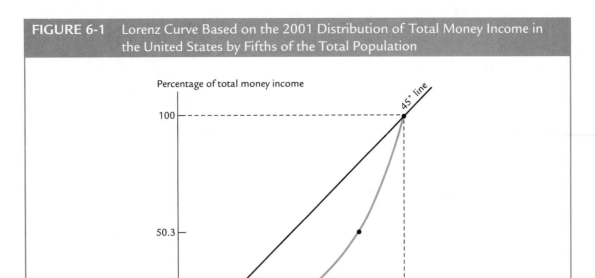

FIGURE 6-1 Lorenz Curve Based on the 2001 Distribution of Total Money Income in the United States by Fifths of the Total Population

The Lorenz curve displays the distribution of total money income among fifths of the total population. According to this curve, the poorest 20 percent of the population received 3.4 percent of total money income in 2002 (see Table 6-1). Because the second poorest 20 percent of the population received 8.8 percent of total money income, the poorest 40 percent of the population received 12.2 percent of total income (3.4 percent plus 8.8 percent). Additional points on the Lorenz curve are calculated similarly. The 45-degree line represents perfect income equality. The larger the area between the actual Lorenz curve and the 45-degree line, the less equally is income distributed.

Source: Based on information presented in Table 6-1.

The larger the area between the actual Lorenz curve and the diagonal, the less equally is income distributed (since a Lorenz curve directly on the diagonal would mean perfectly equal income distribution). One nice feature of the Lorenz curve is that it can visually represent differences in the income distribution among different time periods or different countries, allowing easy comparisons.

For example, the Lorenz curves in Figure 6-2 show the increasing inequality of the income distribution in the United States. The 2002 graph shows a larger area between the 45-degree line and the Lorenz curve than the 1981 graph. (Both graphs are based on information in Table 6-1 of the text.)

As another example, compare the graphs of the Lorenz curves for the United States and Canada in Figure 6-3. (To maintain comparability, 1994 data are used for both countries.) Clearly, Canada has a more equal income distribution than the United States.

1981

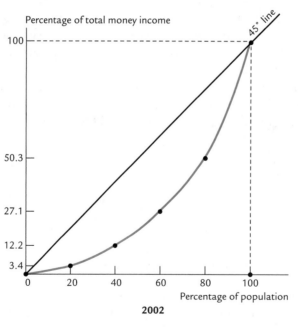

2002

Source: Based on information presented in Table 6-1.

United States

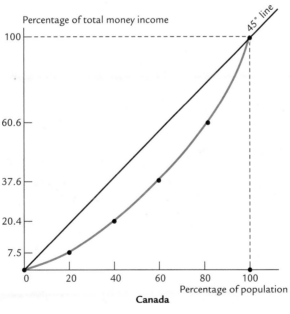

Canada

*To maintain comparability, both graphs are based on 1994 data.

Source: Based on data from the World Bank, World Development Report 1999/2000 (New York: Oxford University Press, 2000), p.238.

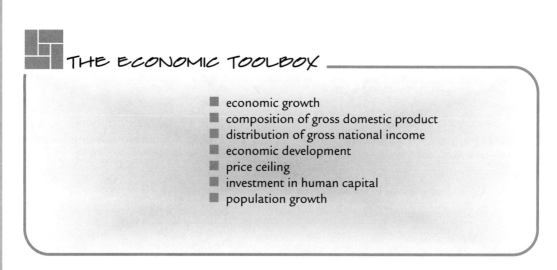

**Chapter 12
Agriculture**
Agricultural development is important in poor countries
Poor country commodity markets are similar to U.S. agricultural markets

**Chapter 3
The Environment**
Many environmental issues are global and some apply specifically to poor countries

**Chapter 14
Unemployment
and Inflation**
These are two frequent problems in poor countries

**Chapter 7
World Poverty**

**Chapter 9
International Trade**
Some aspects of trade have severe impacts on poor countries

**Chapter 17
Globally Free
Markets for the
Twenty-First
Century?**
International debt is the source of much poverty in poor countries

**Chapter 6
U.S. Poverty**
There are some similarities between poverty and income distribution in the U.S. and poor countries

THE ECONOMIC TOOLBOX

- economic growth
- composition of gross domestic product
- distribution of gross national income
- economic development
- price ceiling
- investment in human capital
- population growth

WORLD POVERTY

Yesterday I ate that macaroni from the garbage with fear of death, because (I remembered the) little black boy. . . .
Someone had thrown meat into the garbage, and he was picking out the pieces. He told me "Take some, Carolina.
It's still fit to eat." He gave me some, and so as not to hurt his feelings, I accepted. I tried to convince him not to
eat that meat, or the hard bread gnawed by the rats. He told me no, because it was two days since he had eaten.
He made a fire, and roasted the meat. His hunger was so great that he couldn't wait for the meat to cook. He heated
it and ate. So as not to remember that scene, I left thinking: I'm going to pretend I wasn't there. This can't be real
in a rich country like mine. . . . The next day I found that little black boy dead. His toes were spread apart. The space
must have been eight inches between them. He had blown up as if made out of rubber. His toes looked like a fan.
He had no documents. He was buried like any other "Joe." Nobody tried to find out his name. The marginal people
don't have names.

—Carolina Maria de Jesus, in *Child of the Dark*[1]

n Chapter 6, we considered the problem of poverty in the United States. Although U.S. poverty is a very serious matter, we must remember that the problem of poverty is far more serious for the "marginal people" in many other parts of our globe. Consider the boy in the Brazilian *favela* (slum) described in the quotation that opens this chapter. The poor countries of the world go by a variety of terms: developing countries, less-developed countries (LDCs), low-income countries, and Third World countries are but a few. Throughout this discussion, these terms will be used interchangeably.

The less-developed countries are located in three geographical regions of the world: Latin America, Africa, and Asia. Table 7-1 on page 164 lists most of the less-developed countries by region. As the name of a country appears in our discussion, you should reinforce your knowledge of geography by checking the region to which it belongs.

TABLE 7-1 The Less-Developed Countries of the World, by Region

Latin America and the Caribbean	Africa		Asia
Argentina	Algeria	Liberia	Afghanistan
Barbados	Angola	Libyan Arab	Bahrain
Belize	Benin	Jamahiriya	Bangladesh
Bolivia	Botswana	Madagascar	Bhutan
Brazil	Burkina Faso	Malawi	Cambodia
Chile	Burundi	Mali	China
Colombia	Cameroon	Mauritania	India
Costa Rica	Central African	Mauritius	Indonesia
Cuba	Republic	Morocco	Iran
Dominican Republic	Cape Verde	Mozambique	Iraq
Ecuador	Chad	Namibia	Jordan
El Salvador	Comoros	Niger	Korea, Dem. Rep. of
Grenada	Congo, Dem. Rep. of	Nigeria	Korea, Rep. of
Guadeloupe	Congo, Rep. of	Rwanda	Kuwait
Guatemala	Côte d'Ivoire	Senegal	Laos
Guyana	Djibouti	Sierra Leone	Lebanon
Haiti	Egypt	Somalia	Malaysia
Honduras	Equatorial Guinea	South Africa	Mongolia
Jamaica	Eritrea	Sudan	Myanmar
Mexico	Ethiopia	Swaziland	Nepal
Nicaragua	Gabon	Tanzania	Oman
Panama	Gambia	Togo	Pakistan
Paraguay	Ghana	Tunisia	Papua New Guinea
Peru	Guinea	Uganda	Philippines
Suriname	Guinea-Bissau	Zambia	Qatar
Uruguay	Kenya	Zimbabwe	Saudi Arabia
Venezuela	Lesotho		Singapore
			Sri Lanka
			Syrian Arab Republic
			Thailand
			United Arab Emirates
			Vietnam
			West Bank and Gaza
			Yemen

Source: United Nations Development Program, Human Development Report 2002 *(New York: Oxford University Press, 2002).*

The World Bank recently published statistics indicating the enormous poverty of many people around the world.[2] In the poorest countries of the world (those with an average income of less than $746 per person in 2001), more than 11 of every 100 children born will die before reaching the age of five. Life expectancy is 59 years, and 46 percent of females age 15 years or older cannot read and write. For many countries, the statistics have worsened over the last few years.

GNI PER CAPITA

Economists have traditionally measured the prosperity of a country according to its gross domestic product (GDP) or gross national product (GNP), where both of these terms vary slightly in their measurement of production in a country. More recently, the World Bank has begun reporting data for **gross national income (GNI)**. GNI is identical to GNP in value and can be thought of as the income generated from the production of the nation's output. Gross national income is the broadest of all income concepts and allows us to focus on the more concrete idea of people's incomes rather than a nation's production.

The phrase *per capita* simply means "per person." Thus, **GNI per capita** means gross national income per person on average, and it is calculated as follows:

$$\text{GNI per Capita} = \frac{\text{Total GNI}}{\text{Total Population}}$$

Thus, GNI per capita can be thought of as income per person on average. The phrase *on average* is important. It refers to the typical person in the country, if (and this is a big if) this income is distributed to all people equally. As we will see, equal distribution is not an appropriate assumption.

If GNI per capita is used to measure the prosperity of a country, then it is interesting to compare the prosperity of different countries throughout the world. In doing so, we are struck by the enormous differences and the incredible poverty of the least prosperous ones. Table 7-2 shows comparisons of GNI per capita for the richest and poorest countries of the world and for a few countries in between.

Notice that Switzerland has the highest GNI per capita of nearly $37,000. The United States ranks fourth in the world, with GNI per capita equal to almost $35,000. With GNI per capita relatively low, but still much higher than the very poorest countries, are countries such as Mexico and Brazil, with figures of $5,540 and $3,060, respectively. The 10 poorest countries of the world are listed at the bottom. Ethiopia and Burundi are the world's poorest country with GNI per capita of $100.

As you examine the 10 poorest countries on the list, refer back to Table 7-1 to identify the regional location of each. You will discover that almost all of these countries are located in Africa. Nevertheless, most of the world's poor live in Asia, because of the huge numbers of poor people living in Asian countries such as China, India, Indonesia, and Pakistan.

Gross national income (GNI)
The income generated from the production of a nation's output. Gross national income is the broadest of all income concepts.

GNI per capita
Gross national income per person on average. Calculated by dividing total gross national income by total population.

TABLE 7-2	2001 GNI per Capita in U.S. Dollars for Richest, Poorest, and Select Countries	
	Country	**GNI per Capita ($)**
	Switzerland	36,970
	Japan	35,990
	Norway	35,530
	United States	34,870
	Argentina	6,960
	Mexico	5,540
	Costa Rica	3,950
	Botswana	3,630
	Brazil	3,060
	Russia	1,750
	China	890
	Zimbabwe	480
	Vietnam	410
	Laos	310
	Mali	210
	Mozambique	210
	Burkina Faso	210
	Chad	200
	Eritrea	190
	Tajikistan	170
	Niger	170
	Malawi	170
	Burundi	100
	Ethiopia	100

Source: World Bank, World Development Report 2003 *(New York: Oxford University Press, 2003).*

ECONOMIC GROWTH

Even though economists look at GNI per capita as a measure of a country's prosperity, they often look at the growth in real GDP per capita as a measure of economic growth. Economic growth will be discussed in more detail in Chapter 17. For now, merely recognize that **economic growth** is calculated as the difference between the average annual growth in GDP over some time period and the average annual population growth over the same time period. Economic growth rates for select countries for the period 1990 to 2001 are listed in the last column of Table 7-3. These growth rates are expressed as average annual growth rates, meaning that they represent growth rates *per year, averaged* over the 11 years of the time period. The first two columns remind us that economic growth is calculated as the average annual growth rate of GDP minus the average annual population growth rate.

TABLE 7-3 Average Annual Growth Rates, Select Countries, 1990–2001, with Economic Growth Calculated as Column 1 Minus Column 2

Country	Column 1: Average Annual Growth of GDP (%)		Column 2: Average Annual Growth of Population (%)		Column 3: Economic Growth (%)
China	10.0	–	1.0	=	9.0
Vietnam	7.6	–	1.7	=	5.9
Chile	6.4	–	1.5	=	4.9
Honduras	3.1	–	2.7	=	0.4
Central African Republic	2.1	–	2.2	=	-0.1
Burundi	-2.2	–	2.2	=	-4.4
Sierra Leone	-2.8	–	2.3	=	-5.1
Congo, Dem. Rep. of	-5.1	–	3.2	=	-8.3

Source: World Bank, World Development Report 2003 *(New York: Oxford University Press, 2003).*

Notice that economic growth rates may be positive, approximately zero, or negative, ranging from a high of 9 percent in the table to a low of under negative 8 percent. The growth rates of China, Vietnam, and Chile are extremely high, because of high GDP growth rates and relatively low population growth rates. The approximately zero economic growth rates for the Honduras and the Central African Republic (CAF) are caused by growth in GDP that is cancelled out almost precisely by growth in population. The negative growth rates for Burundi, Sierra Leone, and Congo are caused by negative growth in GDP coupled with rapid population growth. The table demonstrates that any discussion of economic growth must encompass the issues of population growth as well as GDP growth.

Economic growth
Growth in GDP per capita over time, usually several years. Calculated as the average annual growth in GDP minus the average annual population growth, over some time period.

Negative growth rates sound abominable, and positive growth rates sound so good. And they are! But before we can address the problem of poverty in less-developed countries, we must ask an important question. Economists have traditionally viewed the per capita income or output of a country as an indicator of poverty versus prosperity, and they have viewed economic growth as an indication that matters are improving. But we must ask whether these income and output statistics are adequate measures of the economic well-being of people. As we shall see, they are not!

Problems in Measuring Well-Being

One problem with the use of GNI and GDP data is that they ignore the issue of the **composition of GDP**. That is, of what does gross domestic product actually consist? Certainly, it makes a great deal of difference whether a country produces quality health care, education, housing, and food for its people or whether it produces large amounts of military hardware for regional warfare, nonessential luxury goods for a few, and grandiose skyscrapers and structures that fail to serve the needs of most. Compare Costa Rica and Argentina. The 2001 GNI per capita for Argentina is $6,960, well above the GNI per capita of $3,950 for Costa Rica, yet Argentina has

Composition of GDP
The items of production of which GDP consists.

Average life expectancy
The age to which a baby born in a particular year can be expected to live.

Infant mortality rate
The number of babies who die within their first year of life per 1,000 live births.

Distribution of GNI
The distribution of income between different income groups.

a lower average life expectancy and a much higher infant mortality rate. **Average life expectancy** is the age to which a baby born in a particular year can be expected to live. The **infant mortality rate** is the number of infants who die within their first year of life, per 1,000 live births. The average life expectancy in Argentina is 74 years, whereas the average life expectancy in Costa Rica is 77 years. The infant mortality rate in Argentina is 18, whereas the infant mortality rate in Costa Rica is only 9. A likely explanation for these differences is that 7 percent of GDP is devoted to health care in Costa Rica, whereas only 4 percent of GDP is devoted to health care in Argentina. Costa Rica does not have an army and diverts 0.6 percent of GNP to military expenses. (Its constitution prohibits any armed forces.) Contrast this military expense with that of Argentina, which devotes 1.2 percent of GNP to the military. (This is not a very high percentage when compared with the rest of the world. Nevertheless, it is twice as high as Costa Rica's.) Life expectancies and infant mortality rates in Costa Rica are similar to those of much more prosperous countries because Costa Rica chooses to produce more goods and services that benefit its people.

An even more serious problem concerns the **distribution of GNI**, the distribution of the income generated from the production of output. Recall that this issue was discussed in the previous chapter on U.S. poverty. Remember that GNI per capita tells us the average income per person, assuming that this income is distributed equally to all. We know, in fact, that neither in prosperous countries, such as the United States, nor in poor countries, such as Ethiopia, is income distributed equally. To the extent that a small, well-to-do elite of any particular country may receive the bulk of the nation's income, the masses of people may live very poorly indeed. A high value of GNI per capita really tells us nothing about the standard of living of most of the country's residents, because it tells us nothing about the distribution of this income.

Income Distribution

One way of examining the income distribution is with the Lorenz curve introduced in the appendix to Chapter 6. You may recall that this curve is based on data showing the share of total income in a country that goes to each fifth of the population. Another measure of income distribution is the share of total income that goes to the poorest 20 percent of the population. We can say that those countries with the largest share of income going to the poorest 20 percent of the people have the greatest equality of income distribution, and those countries with the smallest share going to the poorest 20 percent have the least equality of income distribution. Statistics for selected countries are presented in Table 7-4. Even though differences may appear small, they have a great impact on the income distribution. Note that many of the lowest-income countries—Pakistan and Rwanda, for example—have more equitable income distributions than do higher income countries such as Venezuela and Brazil. (Recall that in Chapter 6, we observed that the share of income that goes to the poorest 20 percent in the United States is 3.4 percent, meaning that the poorest 20 percent of people in countries such as Bangladesh and Vietnam receive a higher *share* of total income than the poorest 20 percent in the United States.)

TABLE 7-4 Share of Total Income Going to the Poorest 20 Percent of the Population, Select Countries

Country	Share (%)	Country	Share (%)
Paraguay	1.9	Trinidad and Tobago	5.5
South Africa	2.0	Ghana	5.6
Brazil	2.2	Tunisia	5.7
Nicaragua	2.3	China	5.9
Venezuela	3.0	Thailand	6.1
Colombia	3.0	Jamaica	6.7
Chile	3.2	Cambodia	6.9
El Salvador	3.3	Algeria	7.0
Mexico	3.4	Uganda	7.1
Panama	3.6	Jordan	7.6
Bolivia	4.0	Nepal	7.6
Malaysia	4.4	Laos	7.6
Peru	4.4	Sri Lanka	8.0
Nigeria	4.4	Vietnam	8.0
Costa Rica	4.5	India	8.1
Uruguay	4.5	Indonesia	8.4
Zimbabwe	4.6	Egypt	8.6
Dominican Republic	5.1	Pakistan	8.8
Ecuador	5.4	Bangladesh	9.0
Philippines	5.4	Rwanda	9.7

Note: Based on studies in various years, mostly in the 1990s and 2000s. Data may represent distribution of income or distribution of consumption expenditures, depending on availability.

Source: United Nations Development Program, Human Development Report 2003 *(New York: Oxford University Press, 2003).*

Brazil provides a good example of a relatively prosperous country with an income distribution that is severely distorted in favor of the rich. According to Table 7-4, just over 2 percent of total income is distributed to the poorest 20 percent of the Brazilian population. Despite a per capita GNI of $3,060, Brazil has an average life expectancy of 68 years and an infant mortality rate of 31. The fact that much poorer countries are superior in these measures attests to the significance of income distribution. Contrast Brazil with Vietnam, which has a per capita GNI of only $410 (less than $\frac{1}{7}$ of Brazil's), but a life expectancy of 69 years and an infant mortality rate of 30. Table 7-4 shows that the poorest 20 percent of people in Vietnam receive 8.0 percent of total income, explaining the higher standards of living in poverty-stricken Vietnam than in Brazil.

Mechanisms to improve the equality of the income distribution are almost always controversial, at least in the short run, because some individuals must lose while other individuals gain. Policy measures might include the elimination of price distortions to ensure that certain groups of people receive more adequate incomes.

Assets
Property that
is owned, such
as land.

EconNews

"How Do Some
Spell Relief? Lower
Debt"

Some countries are
heavily in debt, but
if the money were
freed, it could be
spent on educa-
tion, sanitation,
and health care.
Get more informa-
tion by navigating
to Developing and
Transitional
Economies.

http://econapps.
swlearning.com

Indigenous
People who are
of native-born
ancestry in a
country.

The raising of agricultural prices would lead to higher incomes for low-income farm-ers, for example. (This measure will be discussed in greater detail shortly.) Higher taxes on the wealth and income of high-income people might also be imposed, and the government might use this revenue to improve basic services to the poor. Gov-ernment provision of adequate nutrition, health care, and education could go a long way to improve the well-being of the poor. Finally, government policies might in-clude a redistribution of **assets** (the most notable of which is land), because greater equality in ownership of income-earning assets is often fundamental to ensuring greater equality of incomes.

One of the problems facing many countries with an **indigenous** population is the loss of ownership of native-owned land. The situation in Chiapas State in Mexico is a case in point. The 1990s brought forth a series of changes designed to move the Mexican economy toward a more market-based economy. One of these changes was an alteration of the Mexican constitution to allow commercial sales of indigenous land. The native Indian people traditionally maintained communal ownership of their land, and rights to use the land were allocated to individual people and fami-lies within the community. As more and more indigenous land is now being sold, In-dian farmers are losing their livelihoods, as well as their cultural ties to the land. This and other issues culminated in January 1, 1994, when the people of Chiapas rose up in demonstration against the Mexican government. The Mexican army responded by destroying farms, killing livestock, confiscating property, and taking the lives of many Chiapas residents. The January date of the uprising corresponded with the date that the North American Free Trade Agreement (NAFTA) was implemented. This treaty is discussed in Chapter 9.

The issue of land ownership has come to a controversial test in the eastern cen-tral African nation of Zimbabwe, which is one of the poorest countries and has one of the most unequal income distributions in the world. The cause of the unequal in-come distribution is the fact that a tiny white minority owns about one-third of the productive land in the country, leaving very little remaining for each of the vast ma-jority of black farmers. In the year 2000, squatters began occupying white-owned farms with the support of President Robert Mugabe, who called the occupation a le-gitimate protest against unfair ownership. Legitimate or not, some of the occupa-tions have become violent, and some people have been killed. With government plans to confiscate more than half of white-owned farming land becoming increas-ingly controversial at the international level, it remains to be seen whether there will be a stable and peaceful reform in Zimbabwe's land distribution. At the present time, the occupations have devastated the agricultural production of the country, which is now suffering from extensive hunger as a result.

ECONOMIC DEVELOPMENT AND STANDARDS OF LIVING

Largely because of the issue of distribution, we cannot say that growth in GDP per capita is synonymous with economic development. This notion bears repeating: eco-nomic development is not the same as economic growth. Indeed, we can define **economic development** as a multifaceted process that improves the living conditions of the masses. It entails improvements in standards of living and reductions in poverty, as well as growth in GDP per capita. Economic development also incorporates the idea of liberation from any economic or political oppression. Although growth in GDP per capita is one element of the definition of economic development, it is clearly not the whole story.

Many economists use measures that directly indicate the actual well-being of people of less-developed countries rather than rely on income or output data alone. Some of the best indicators of living standards are the average life expectancies and infant mortality rates already mentioned. These measures avoid the distribution problem mentioned previously with respect to income per capita. Although life expectancies tend to be higher for the very elite of a country, they will not differ by multiples of hundreds and thousands, as income levels often do. A high-income person may have an income of 1,000 times the income of a low-income person, but the rich person's life expectancy will not be 1,000 times the life expectancy of the poor person.

Moreover, indicators such as life expectancies and mortality rates avoid the measurement problems inherent in income and output statistics. Life expectancies, for example, do not need to be adjusted for inflation, exchange rates, market prices, and so on. These measurement problems sometimes distort comparisons of income and output between different countries.

In addition, life expectancies and mortality rates measure end results of government programs and the state of the economy. Other measures sometimes used to reflect standards of living, such as calories per capita, number of doctors per person, or school enrollment figures actually measure inputs into the development process. They do not tell us the quality of calories, health care, or education; and they do not tell us the outcome of these measures. Life expectancies and mortality rates, on the other hand, measure the impact of all such policies and programs. Finally, life expectancies and mortality rates are easily conceptualized by policymakers and the populace alike.

Life expectancies range from a low in Sierra Leone and Botswana of 39 years to a high in Japan of 81 years. The United States has an average life expectancy of 77 years. It is important to realize that a life expectancy of 39 in Sierra Leone, for example, does not mean that a typical person will die at age 39. What it means is that a very large number of babies and children die, bringing down the average life expectancy for the country as a whole.

Worldwide statistics for infant mortality rates range from a high of 182 in Sierra Leone (meaning that 182 of every 1,000 babies, or roughly 18 of every 100, will die before their first birthdays) to a low of 3 in Japan. The United States has an infant mortality rate of 7. Life expectancies and infant mortality rates are shown for select LDCs in Table 7-5 on page 172. Countries are listed in order of their GNI per capita, from highest to lowest.

All of these statistics suggest both enormous divergence of the standards of living in poor countries and those in prosperous countries and the appallingly miserable conditions in the very poorest countries. With this understanding of standards of living in mind, as well as the definitions of economic growth and development, we need to address the most important question of all: how can economic development

Economic development
A multifaceted process that involves improvements in standards of living, reductions in poverty, and growth in GDP per capita.

TABLE 7-5 Life Expectancies and Infant Mortality Rates for Select Countries, 2001

Country[a]	Life Expectancy (years)	Infant Mortality Rate[b]
Argentina	74	18
Mexico	73	24
Costa Rica	77	9
Botswana	39	80
Brazil	68	31
China	70	31
Zimbabwe	40	76
Vietnam	69	30
Sierra Leone	39	182
Ethiopia	42	116

Note: Some data are for 2000.

[a]*Countries are listed in order of their GNI per capita, from highest to lowest.*

[b]*Number of infant deaths per 1,000 live births.*

Source: Data from **www.wto.org** *and World Bank,* World Development Report 2003 *(New York: Oxford University Press 2003).*

and economic growth be achieved to improve the economic well-being of all? The sections that follow will address this issue.

GROWTH AND DEVELOPMENT

Newly industrializing countries (NICs)
Singapore, South Korea, Taiwan, and other countries achieving rapid growth through industrialization.

Development economists and Third World governments have traditionally favored development theories and practices patterned after the Western industrialized world. This preference has led to policies directed toward the urban and industrial sectors. This strategy has proved successful for countries such as Singapore, South Korea, Taiwan, and Hong Kong (as of 1997, Hong Kong is no longer considered a separate country from China). These countries are classified as **newly industrializing countries**, or NICs. They had many characteristics contributing to the success of their industrialization strategies, including a well-educated labor force; a fairly homogeneous, entrepreneurial culture; and international conditions conducive to their success at the time of their early development. Nevertheless, industrialization strategies failed to produce the same results in many other countries. One major reason is that industrialization emphasized **capital-intensive technology** (technology utilizing large amounts of physical capital), as well as mechanisms to squeeze savings for investment from low-income residents. Agriculture was viewed only as a means of acquiring cheap food and tax revenue with which to develop the industrial sector and support the urban population. Only more recently have economists and policymakers begun to see that other policies may be more appropriate for many developing countries. We are discovering that the key to development often lies in the agricultural sector. We are recognizing the importance of **labor-intensive technology** (as opposed to capital-intensive technology), which can utilize large numbers of people who would otherwise be unemployed. At the same time, we are beginning to acknowledge the important role of women—indeed, all people—in development.

Agricultural Development

The specter of famine was rising on the horizon. . . . The rice drooped, then wilted, and finally died. . . . He saw tears on his mother's cheeks. His father came and put an arm around his wife's shoulders. "Mother of my sons," he said, "we shall both go without food for ourselves so that the rice lasts longer. The children must not suffer." The summer passed almost without a single downpour and once again it was time for the winter sowing. Without water, however, there would be no winter sowing. . . . It was then that he realized that all the livestock was going to perish. November went by. The departure of the cattle had cut off the peasants' only fuel supply. . . . Gone was the sound of the children's laughter. Their small stomachs swelled up like balloons and several of them died, the victims of worms, diarrhea, and fever—yet in reality victims of hunger. . . . the women wept in silence.[3]

Development of the agricultural sector in most less-developed countries is now recognized as extremely important for several reasons. First, most of the world's poor live in the agricultural sector; hence, efforts to benefit this sector will most directly benefit the needy as well. Second, the agricultural sector typically offers the greatest potential for development. In a society with scarce technology and capital, the fruits of investment come most easily from agriculture. Techniques also tend to be far more labor-intensive in agriculture than in modern industry, thereby offering employment for larger numbers of people. And finally, the agricultural sector most directly addresses the most vital need of all people, that of food security. With careful planning and policy, the Indian famine described in the preceding passage needn't occur.

Access to Inputs, Extension, and Markets

For agricultural development to occur and food security to be achieved, both the government of the developing country and the international community must fulfill important roles. The local government must recognize that although appropriate policies can dramatically improve agricultural productivity and the lives of the poor, inappropriate agricultural policy can do far more harm than good. Policies aimed at land reform are often vital. In many countries (especially throughout Asia and Latin America), a select few control large landholdings, resulting in severely distorted income distributions, as well as inefficiencies in agricultural production. Land must be redistributed in a manner that allows more appropriate income distribution and maximum incentives for agricultural production. In addition to land, other agricultural inputs are important. Farmers must have access to the necessary seeds, fertilizer, irrigation, animals, structures, and vehicles. Perhaps the most important input is agricultural credit; unless financing can be arranged for the masses of poor farmers, access to the other inputs will probably also be denied.

Capital-intensive technology Technology utilizing large amounts of capital.

Labor-intensive technology Technology utilizing large amounts of labor.

Adequate inputs are not enough. Farmers will require extension services if they are to use increasingly complex but more productive farming techniques and inputs. They will also require reliable transport and market facilities. Poor farmers frequently must travel long distances over poor-quality roads, and without any form of transport other than their own labor, to reach areas to market their products. Even when transport vehicles are available, there may be serious problems. Consider this Kenyan farmer's story:

> One Friday afternoon, Mwangi Muchai, 50, . . . climbed into his Toyota pick-up bound for Nairobi, 100 kilometers away. He had loaded over a ton of cabbages from his farm onto the pick-up, hoping to sell them in the capital's . . . wholesale market. "I never made it to Nairobi," he says sadly. "I was barely 15 minutes on my way when it started raining and the earth road became slippery." . . . The pick-up skidded into a ditch, and that was the end of his journey. Mr. Muchai says he and some neighbors tried to push the vehicle out of the ditch, but it proved too heavy. . . . In any case, the road was altogether too slippery to drive on even if the pick-up had been rescued. "As I walked back to my house and abandoned the pick-up," Mr. Muchai remembers, "I felt the greatest disappointment of my life and, for a while, regretted ever becoming a farmer. I felt anxious about facing my wives and telling them that a whole season's sweat for the family would go down the drain as the vegetables rotted in that ditch." Before the time the rains ended, Mr. Muchai had lost his entire load of cabbages.[4]

Infrastructure
Social overhead capital, including facilities for transportation, communication, marketing, and extension services.

Economists recognize that governments must take responsibility for providing adequate **infrastructure**, such as the extension services, roads, and market facilities just discussed, lest agricultural productivity break down at any of these points. This undertaking is difficult for governments strapped for financial resources.

Agricultural Prices

Price ceilings
Legalized maximum prices for goods or services.

Beyond ensuring access to inputs, extension, and markets, government policy must focus on appropriate agricultural prices. Economists and international agencies have recently promoted market-based prices to revitalize the agricultural sector. Far too often LDC governments have established **price ceilings** in order to maintain low food prices and placate the end consumer, who is typically a resident of an urban area. One goal of price ceilings is to keep prices of basic necessities low for poor consumers. Although many urban people may be poor, urban dwellers tend to have higher incomes than rural residents do. In the process of holding down prices for this better-off—but politically more vocal—group, the government also keeps low the agricultural prices received by farmers. This practice results in two serious problems. First, rural incomes fall and poor farmers become poorer. Second, incentives for agricultural production are reduced; those with other options will seek to produce in sectors where the incentives are greater. These problems are illustrated in Figure 7-1, using the market for rice as an example. A similar example, using the market for rental housing, is discussed in Chapter 10 on housing.

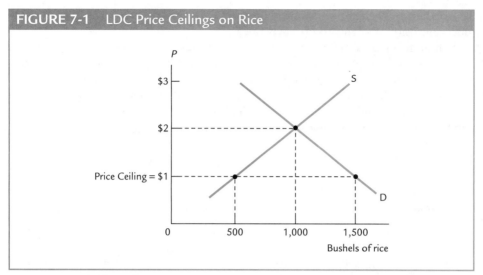

FIGURE 7-1   LDC Price Ceilings on Rice

At the market equilibrium price of $2 per bushel, quantity demanded equals quantity supplied at 1,000 bushels of rice. When a price ceiling of $1 per bushel is imposed, quantity demanded increases to 1,500 bushels, while quantity supplied falls to 500 bushels. A shortage of rice results, and the producer incomes fall.

The demand for rice is indicated by D. The supply curve is indicated by S. If the market operates freely, an equilibrium will occur at the point at which the price of rice is $2 per bushel and the quantity is 1,000 bushels. If the government places a price ceiling on rice, however, the price may be held down at a level such as $1 per bushel (representing the price ceiling). The rice cannot legally be sold at a price above this price ceiling. The artificially low price causes consumers to move down along their demand curve, as they try to buy larger quantities of rice at the attractive low price. Consumers will wish to purchase 1,500 bushels (quantity demanded). Suppliers, on the other hand, will have less incentive to produce and sell rice. They will move down along their supply curve, reducing the quantity supplied to 500 bushels (they may produce other products instead). Quantity demanded exceeds quantity supplied. A shortage of rice is the result. Consumers have been encouraged to "overconsume." Suppliers have been encouraged to "undersupply." Despite the lower prices, many consumers have become worse off, particularly those who are unable to buy the rice. Incomes to many poor agricultural workers have fallen as well.

Many less-developed countries have adopted market-determined agricultural prices, including the communist country of Vietnam. As part of the economic reforms designed to move the Vietnamese economy closer to a market-based economy, the government of Vietnam has raised rice prices to market-determined levels. Previously, as in many other countries, the government had kept the price of staple food artificially low to please urban consumers. As a result of the price decontrol, Vietnam's status has changed in just a few short years from a rice importer to one of the world's largest rice exporters. Rising incomes in the rural sector have come far in reducing previously high rural poverty rates.

Although agricultural prices are often found to be too low, care must be taken as governments promote market-based prices. Poor urban residents, who must purchase their food, will suffer from higher prices. We are also becoming aware that even rural residents are often net buyers of food, selling their agricultural produce at harvest and buying food and other agricultural products throughout the year. Rising food prices will hurt these farmers as well. In the face of rising agricultural prices, government assistance must be targeted directly to low-income purchasers of food. In addition, poor farmers may require special assistance to ensure their access to inputs, infrastructure, credit, and markets. The benefits that result from this assistance, productivity improvements and rising incomes, would outweigh the increased prices that farmers would pay for their purchases.

Export Cropping

Export cropping
Agricultural production for export, rather than production of food for local consumption.

In relation to food security, the issue of export cropping must also be addressed. **Export cropping** refers to a pattern of agricultural production for export, rather than production of food for local consumption. Many countries choose to produce products such as coffee, tea, rubber, and cocoa to export and thereby obtain foreign currency. Although the theory of international trade tells us that a country should specialize in products it is "good at," as we will see in Chapter 9, it is also true that export cropping can trigger food insecurity and inequality in the income distribution in low-income countries. We will see in Chapter 17 that the international debt crisis has increased LDC dependence on export cropping, as Third World governments are forced to earn foreign currency to pay off their debts. This practice has often been at the expense of the food security needs of local residents.

International Role

Buffer stock
A mechanism for stabilizing agricultural prices, whereby an agricultural product is purchased and placed in storage during years of high production and released from storage and sold during years of low production.

The international community must assist low-income countries to meet their agricultural development and food security needs. We must develop systems to ensure that adequate and timely food aid will be available to countries in emergency situations. At the same time, we must be cautious about continuing to provide food aid in nonemergency situations, a practice that can often do more harm than good. As will be discussed in Chapter 12 on agriculture, ongoing food aid leads to dependence by less-developed countries and pushes down food prices, thereby lowering incentives for local food production. Nevertheless, it is vital that food aid be available in emergency situations and other times when it is appropriate.

The international community might also enact measures to ensure the greater stability of world food prices. One suggested measure is the establishment of an international **buffer stock** of cereal grains, whereby managers can buy up grain in years of high production (thereby pushing up low market prices) and sell off grain in years of low production (thereby pushing down high market prices). In this manner, prices are stabilized within a medium range rather than allowed to fluctuate wildly. Greater price stability would ensure that low-income food-importing countries are not left unable to buy when world shortage conditions would normally send prices skyrocketing.

We must also undertake efforts to ensure that the bottlenecks of inadequate transport, shipping, ports, and storage facilities are resolved. We can offer technical assistance in terms of better seed varieties, improved production methods, and agricultural extension services. Most important, we must recognize that hunger is caused by poverty. If we assist agricultural development and help alleviate rural poverty, we will go a long way toward reducing the travesty of hunger in a world of plenty.

Human and Natural Resource Development

Regardless of emphasis on industrial or agricultural development, investment must also be made in each nation's most precious resource: people. Economists sometimes refer to this as an **investment in human capital**, likening it to an investment in physical capital. This concept is discussed in Chapter 6 on U.S. poverty and Chapter 4 on education. Human investment programs have not only an immediate benefit, namely, the improved standard of living of the beneficiary, but also a long-term payoff, just as other forms of investment do. The long-term benefit is the development of a more productive labor force and a better-educated citizenry.

Investment in human capital Spending that is designed to improve the productivity of people.

Human investment programs include those designed to improve health, sanitation, education, and skills. Again, it is important that we abandon some of our Western notions about the form of these programs. Most poor Third World countries can derive far more benefit from village-level health practitioners providing basic health care, immunizations, and prenatal care than from expensive high-tech hospitals located in capital cities, out of reach of the masses of people. Most countries will benefit more from the spread of primary education to school-age children and basic literacy training to adults than from several expensive doctoral universities located in major cities. Just as with income distribution, benefits that spread to large masses of people rather than to an elite few are most likely to foster positive development.

Education probably holds the greatest promise. Numerous studies have linked education (primarily of women) to widespread benefits: reduced infant mortality rates, improved child nutrition, later age at marriage, lower birthrates, and greater likelihood that their children will be educated. The cycle is thus self-perpetuating.

Increasingly, development economists are also recognizing the need for a safe and convenient water supply. Many women and children have the task of spending several hours every day walking long distances to retrieve water, carrying it home in the exhausting fashion of headloading. Often the water carries bacteria and waterborne diseases. Fresh wells located in villages would improve the health of the people and free the time of women and children for other activities.

Deforestation The clearing of forested areas in an unmanaged fashion.

Women also spend considerable time gathering firewood, especially as wood becomes increasingly scarce. Wood is the primary source of fuel, and cooking is its primary use, especially in Africa. The clearing of forests for expansion of farming and commercial timber operations is causing a serious problem of **deforestation** in many countries. As trees are depleted, soil and wind erosion increase. **Desertification** may follow, as desert areas are left with no natural barriers to their continual

Desertification The encroachment of desert on previously fertile land.

encroachment on cropland. The ultimate effect is the depletion of soil fertility. Villages and organizations have begun the search for solutions to this problem, ranging from the production of wood lots for village fuel use to the invention of simple, fuel-efficient cooking stoves. Natural resource development as such should improve the well-being of people and at the same time preserve the environment.

Women's Role in Development

In the workplace, women are at the bottom of the pyramid inside the country. They are also the poorest people in the country. They are the people who lose their jobs first. They're the people who are taken off of agricultural farms when these farms are turned into cash crop farms. They ultimately decide whether or not a child is fed. They cry when their boys or husbands are detained, arrested, or made refugees, or die.[5]

As the previous discussion suggests, women play an important role in economic development. And in the words of the South African woman quoted here by lobbying group Bread for the World, we see that women face the greatest obstacles. For a long time, government and international policies alike have neglected women in developing countries. Women have therefore been treated unfairly. Third World women also have lower standards of living than their male counterparts. Women typically have **literacy rates** far below those of men. In Niger, for example, only 9 percent of women can read and write, whereas 21 percent of men are literate. In Nepal, the literacy rate is 60 percent for men, but only 24 percent for women. The reason for this disparity in many less-developed countries is simply that fewer girls go to school than do boys, often for cultural reasons and because girls are needed to help their mothers on their farms. Furthermore, because families often must pay expensive school fees, they choose to invest in the boy child instead of the girl child. The boy will often remain responsible for his family of origin, whereas the girl will go to live with the family of her husband. Where adult education programs exist, women are frequently unable to participate for the same types of reasons that girls don't participate. Child care, farmwork, and homemaking leave little time for the "extravagance" of education.

Since society receives so many benefits from the primary education of its citizens, and especially the education of girls, creative ideas should be used by governments and international agencies to promote the primary education of all children. Aside from eliminating school fees, one policy measure might be to reward the child's family by providing free breakfast and lunch for the child at school and sending home additional food or small amounts of money for the family of the child in school.

High maternal mortality rates are another serious problem. The **maternal mortality rate** is the number of deaths of women for pregnancy-related reasons per 100,000 live births. In Eritrea, for example, the rate of 1,100 tells us that 1,100 of every 100,000, or just over 1 of every 100, live births are associated with the death of the mother. Because women in Eritrea have an average of six children in their lifetime, the average Eritrean woman has a 6 percent chance of dying for pregnancy-

Literacy rates
The percentages of populations that can read and write.

Maternal mortality rate
The number of deaths of women for pregnancy-related reasons per 100,000 live births.

related reasons (1 × 6). These statistics are alarming, especially when we consider the children left behind when their mothers die.

The problems of women in developing countries go far beyond unfairness, however. Although women are primarily responsible for producing most **subsistence food crops** in much of the Third World, and although they produce and market many other agricultural crops and processed items, they are least likely to receive agricultural extension services, agricultural credit, and access to agricultural inputs such as quality land. Women also tend to be primarily responsible for food preparation and homemaking; fuel and water acquisition; safeguarding of the family's nutrition, hygiene, and health care; and oversight of the children's education. As long as policy measures that provide education, credit, agricultural extension, technology, and agricultural inputs are targeted toward men, neither the agricultural productivity of the country nor the well-being of the family will be adequately served.

Subsistence food crops Crops grown primarily as food for the family. A small amount may be marketed.

POPULATION GROWTH

The preceding discussion of the role of women in developing countries returns us to the issue of population growth. Many people believe that high population growth is a problem in many low income countries because more people means more sharing of already limited resources. Other people, including many in the less-developed countries, do not believe that population growth is a problem. If we consider population to be a problem only relative to resources, then we must consider that the 15 percent of the world's population in the developed world consumes three fifths of the world's total production of goods and services.[6] The residents of LDCs consume very little. One could argue further that the problem is not so much too many people in the developed world, but rather our highly consumption-oriented lifestyles.

To the extent that rapid population growth is a problem in the Third World, intense controversy attends possible solutions. One thing we know: merely passing out contraceptives to the world's low-income women is ineffective. This simple strategy does not address cultural and religious factors, nor does it get at the issue of the motivation to have children. Clearly, people have important reasons for having the children that they do. In agricultural societies, children are necessary to provide labor on the farm and assist their mothers in gathering water and fuel. Because poor countries lack formal social security systems, and because poor people are often unable to accumulate savings, then having children is usually the only means that parents have to ensure that they will be cared for in their old age. And finally, as long as women expect that a certain number of their children will die (recall the high infant mortality rates), they will have "extra" children to ensure the survival of a certain number. Consider the words of a woman farmer in Africa: "My first child died at the age of two," says Hamza Amadou, a farmer in Niger who wants to have at least eight children. "The second caught malaria and died at the age of seven. At this rate, how can I think of practicing contraception? If I don't have any children, who will help me to produce food and feed my family, and who will take over when I die?"[7]

EconLinks

World Factbook (CIA)

One of the best sources for general economic information on all the countries of the world. A great resource.

http://econapps. swlearning.com

On a more optimistic note, we also know that as development proceeds, population growth rates naturally tend to fall because women become motivated to have fewer children, and they gain a greater sense of control over their lives. As women receive greater income-earning alternatives to the bearing of children, as they have greater expectations that their children will survive, as agricultural productivity improves, and as schools and better futures become available to their children, women naturally tend to have fewer children and are better able to provide for the ones they do have. An important element in all of this change is a sense of empowerment. Once women are able to ensure their children's survival as well as control the economic aspects of their family's well-being, they have a greater sense of control over their entire lives and take a more active role in structuring them. To talk about limiting births to the Nigerian woman whose first two children died is to ignore the root of her problems.

If we view development as a process of liberation from oppression, population policy must not be oppressive. Any policies to limit births must take into account the religious and cultural values of the people involved. In an area of devout Roman Catholics, for example, research on and promotion of effective natural family-planning techniques would perhaps be appropriate. Policies that intrude on the morals and human rights of individuals, particularly policies that are coercive, are not elements of true development.

It is also important to keep in mind that real development is necessary for birthrates to fall. That is, a rise in GDP per capita alone may not achieve the desired results. The benefits of economic development must accrue to the masses of people, including women, before a substantial impact on birthrates can be expected. The fundamental problem underlying rapid population growth is poverty. The fundamental solution is economic development. A narrow focus on birthrates alone will not be effective.

URBANIZATION AND RURAL–URBAN MIGRATION

The problem of highly concentrated population is particularly evident in many Third World cities. In fact, 7 of the 10 largest metropolitan areas of the world are in developing countries. Five of the 10 cities are in Asia, 2 are in Latin America, and 1 is in Africa. See Table 7-6.

Along with high concentrations of people is the concentration of poverty in many Third World cities. More than one-third of the entire Third World metropolitan population lives in slums or shantytowns. In some cities, such as Mexico City (Mexico), Kolkata (India), and Casablanca (Morocco), the proportion of people dwelling in slums is very high. Most of these slum dwellers lack adequate water supplies, sewerage, plumbing, electricity, and even shelter. Many inhabitants are forced to live in makeshift shacks of cardboard, tin, or plastic sheeting; many simply live on the sidewalk.

Under-employment
A situation in which people work limited hours or with low productivity.

One of the causes of urban poverty is a high level of unemployment and **underemployment**. Underemployment refers to situations in which people work limited hours or with low productivity. Much underemployment occurs in the urban **informal employment sector**. The informal sector consists primarily of service occupations: shoe shining, drug dealing, prostitution, collection of paper and metal scraps

TABLE 7-6 Population of the World's 10 Largest Metropolitan Areas, 2000 Estimates

Cities in Order of Population Size	Population (in millions)
1. Tokyo-Yokohama, Japan	33.1
2. New York, United States	20.3
3. Seoul-Inchon, Korea	19.9
4. Mexico City, Mexico	19.6
5. São Paulo, Brazil	17.7
6. Mumbai (Bombay), India	17.6
7. Los Angeles, United States	16.2
8. Manila, Philippines	14.1
9. Cairo, Egypt	14.0
10. Kolkata (Calcutta), India	13.9

*Source: Demographia (**www.demographia.com/db-world-metro2000city.htm**).*

Informal employment sector
An employment sector consisting primarily of service occupations in an unofficial setting.

for sale, bicycle transportation, and street sales. The latter include the sale of virtually everything: cigarettes, used clothing, charcoal, blood, sticks for starting fires, food, and so on. Low productivity, low incomes, irregular work hours, and no benefits characterize many of these services. They do, however, provide work and income for people who might otherwise remain unemployed. Furthermore, some of these informal occupations provide important services to the community, such as carpentry, bricklaying, and sewing.

Rural–urban migration
The movement of people from the rural sector to the urban sector, often in search of better living conditions.

Although natural population increases can sometimes explain high urban population density, the other important factor is migration. **Rural–urban migration** brings in countless people from the countryside to the cities each day. These people are searching for better jobs, higher incomes, and the "glamour" of the city life. Thousands of migrants arrive daily in the cities listed in Table 7-6. Even on the African continent, several million migrants come to the cities each year.

An interesting problem may emerge when policymakers attempt to reduce the poverty and misery in many Third World cities. As better housing and services are provided and better employment opportunities are created, even larger numbers of migrants may be attracted to the cities. As migrant numbers swell, even more people may become homeless and unemployed. Efforts to reduce urban problems may turn out to be counterproductive!

This consideration returns us to our earlier focus on agricultural development. Along with any policy efforts to improve urban standards of living must be policy measures to improve the well-being of people in the countryside. Only then can the incentives for rural–urban migration be reduced and the flow of urban migrants tempered. Policy measures must focus on improving agricultural productivity and incomes. Health care, educational programs, infrastructure, and services must be provided in the rural sector as well as the urban sector. Price incentives for agricultural production and opportunities for small-scale, labor-intensive industries in rural areas must exist. Only then will the rural–urban balance be improved and urban problems reduced.

AIDS

One final challenge of many less-developed countries is that of AIDS (Acquired Immune Deficiency Syndrome). AIDS is a serious problem in many countries around the world, but it has reached epidemic proportions in many countries of Africa. According to the United Nations, AIDS has replaced malaria as the leading cause of death in Africa. Of the estimated total of 3.1 million AIDS-related deaths around the world in 2002, 2.4 million were in sub-Saharan Africa. An additional 29.4 million Africans are currently living with AIDS or are infected with HIV, the virus that leads to the development of AIDS. Women represent more than half of the African adults with AIDS/HIV, and more than 12 million African children have been orphaned from the disease. In many African countries, the share of infected adults is astounding, as high as 31 percent in Lesotho, 34 percent in Zimbabwe, 33 percent in Swaziland, and 39 percent in Botswana.[8] Many children are dying

VIEWPOINT: CONSERVATIVE VERSUS LIBERAL

Different economists have different views about how economic development should take place. Conservative economists prefer a growth-oriented strategy that focuses on increasing GDP per capita. The assumption is that all people will eventually benefit from the growing prosperity of the country. Issues such as income distribution and poverty do not receive primary attention because it is assumed that the incomes of all people will rise as economic growth proceeds. Indeed, conservative economists may argue in favor of an unequal income distribution on the grounds that high-income people save more than low-income people do. (Low-income people need to spend all of their income on food and consumer goods.) By placing more income in the hands of the rich, savings will increase, thereby enabling greater investment and ultimately increased national productivity and growth.

Liberal economists feel that economic growth by itself is not the panacea for underdevelopment. They note that although some people benefit from economic growth, notably the owners of large landholdings and businesses and those able-bodied and fortunate enough to take newly created jobs, many others do not benefit. In particular, workers with few skills and little education, those who are physically disabled, the very young and the very old, and farmers who grow crops on too little land with too few inputs will not be able to take advantage of benefits of economic growth. Strategies must be designed to focus on poverty and income distribution. Otherwise, it is argued, high-income groups will only become richer, while low-income people become poorer.

as well, acquiring AIDS from their mothers at birth. Aside from the direct impact of AIDS, the health systems of poor countries are overwhelmed in the face of the epidemic. Efforts to assist AIDS patients reduce the systems' capacity to deal with other important health problems, including preventative and primary care. We are seeing the stark effects of AIDS as life expectancies drop in afflicted countries. The life expectancy in Botswana, for example, has fallen from 47 years in 1997 to 38 years in 2001.

A PEOPLE-ORIENTED STRATEGY

Many issues of development have been addressed. As we consider each issue, as well as any strategy to invoke change, we must be mindful of the needs and participation of Third World people. Empowerment not only of women but of all residents of low-income countries is important. Poverty and lack of opportunity undermine power, preventing people from taking control of their lives and, in the process, improving their lives. This consideration suggests that development efforts must ultimately meet the needs of the masses of people if they are to be successful.

SUMMARY

Economists define economic growth as the increase in real gross domestic product per capita. GNI per capita reflects income accruing to each individual person, on average. In 2001, GNI per capita ranged from a high in Switzerland of almost $37,000 to a low in Ethiopia of $100. Other measures, such as infant mortality rates and life expectancies, are usually better indicators of standards of living, particularly because income and output per capita do not address the issues of the composition and distribution.

Economic development is a multifaceted process involving growth in GDP per capita, improvement in standards of living, and reduction of poverty. Economic development must take into account the needs of agricultural development and food security, human and natural resource development, and the role of women and all residents of low-income countries, as well as the issues of population growth, AIDS, and rural–urban migration. Appropriate policies at the domestic and international levels are vital to the development needs of low-income countries.

NOTES

1. From *Child of the Dark,* by Carolina Maria de Jesus, translated by David St. Clair, translation copyright (c) 1962 by E. P. Dutton & Co., Inc., New York, and Souvenir Press, Ltd., London. Used by permission of Dutton, a division of Penguin Putnam, Inc. The words are those of a woman (the author) living in a *favela* (slum) of São Paulo, Brazil.

2. **www.worldbank.org**, or the World Bank, *World Development Report 2003* (New York: Oxford University Press, 2003), or earlier editions. Unless otherwise indicated, all data in this chapter are from these World Bank sources.

3. Dominique Lapierre, *The City of Joy* (New York: Warner Books, 1985), pp. 15–21. These words describe the despair of a family in famine-struck India.

4. John Araka, Wilfred Machua, Wainaina Bidan, Fanwell Zulu, Colleen Lowe Morna, Ben Ephson, Abdou Gninguc, Methaetsile Leepile, "Getting Produce to Market," in *African Farmer* (New York: The Hunger Project, December 1989).

5. Sharon Pauling, "She Speaks with Wisdom," in *BREAD* (Washington, D.C.: Bread for the World, Spring 1988).

6. Calculation based on data in World Bank, *World Development Report 2000/2001* (New York: Oxford University Press, 2001).

7. Souleymane Anza, Shadrack Amokaye, Colleen Lowe Morna, Pierre Pradervand, "Farmers and Family Planning," in *African Farmer* (New York: The Hunger Project, December 1989).

8. United Nations AIDS Program, "Report on the Global HIV/AIDS Epidemic," June 2003 (**www.unaids.org**). Adults are defined as persons age 15 to 49 years.

DISCUSSION QUESTIONS

1. Is GNI per capita an adequate indicator of the well-being of people in less-developed countries? Why or why not? Are there better indicators?

2. Consider the countries listed in Table 7-1, and choose one that interests you. Go to the World Bank Web site at **www.worldbank.org**, and choose the country from the country listing. What is the country's current GNI per capita and life expectancy? How do these statistics compare with those of other countries mentioned in this chapter? Is the life expectancy what you would expect, based on the level of GNI per capita?

3. Now choose the same or a different country, and look it up on the CIA Web site (**www.odci. gov/cia/publications/factbook**). After locating the country, click People, and find statistics relating to standards of living. What is the infant mortality rate? Compare the statistics that are available for males and females. How do their life expectancies compare? How do their literacy rates compare?

4. Refer to the information in Chapter 6 on the U.S. income distribution. How does the United States compare with the countries listed in Table 7-4 with respect to its share of income to the poorest 20 percent of the population? Does the comparison surprise you? Prosperous countries have greater means to ensure equitable income distribution, but this greater capacity does not mean that they choose to do so.

5. Why does hunger persist in a world of plenty? Is the problem one of underproduction, overpopulation, distribution of income, overconsumption, or all of these factors? Explain.

6. How might land reform be achieved in developing countries? What issues are involved? What are the political and ethical implications?

7. Agricultural development has garnered much attention. Equally important is the development of human capital—that is, improvement in the most important economic resource: people. How can better education, housing, health, hygiene, and nutrition develop human capital—and thereby develop the country as well?

8. Why must women be targeted for assistance in the development process? Why is it important that all beneficiaries of development policies and programs be active participants in the design and operation of these programs?

9. What are some of the means used to control population growth in various parts of the world? Are these effective? Are they appropriate? Are they ethical? Do the ends justify the means?

10. How can efforts to reduce unemployment and misery in Third World cities be counter-productive and actually increase urban problems? What are some alternative solutions?

11. What is the role of the developed countries in promoting development policies in the less-developed countries? What are the ways that we as individuals can become involved?

12. Would you like to be able to make a difference in the lives of people in the less-developed world? One source of information is the organization *Bread for the World*. This national citizens' lobby has a Web site at **www.bread.org** and it contains information on current U.S. legislation involving world hunger and poverty, as well as contact information for U.S. legislators so that interested citizens can contact them. This Web site also provides links to other similar organizations.

13. Go to the Web site of the United Nations AIDS Program at **www.unaids.org**. Choose a country and look up the prevalence of AIDS/HIV in that country. How does the country compare with other countries in the world?

CHAPTER 8 ROADMAP

**Chapter 1
Introduction**
The pure competition assumed in the tutoring example contrasts with the market power discussed in Chapter 8

**Chapter 9
International Trade**
Imports decrease domestic market power

As European markets become more free, U.S. antitrust agencies will cooperate more with their European counterparts

**Chapter 12
Agriculture**
Concentration is increasing in the agricultural sector

**Chapter 8
Market Power**

**Chapter 7
World Poverty**
Higher prices due to market power contribute to declining terms of trade and international debt in LDCs

THE ECONOMIC TOOLBOX

- competition
- market power
- monopoly
- oligopoly
- barriers to entry
- antitrust system

MARKET POWER

The monopolists, by keeping the market constantly under stocked, by never fully supplying the effectual demand, sell their commodities much above the natural price.

—Adam Smith, *The Wealth of Nations*, 1776

Do you ever worry about the effects of powerful firms? Have you ever written your senator about the high price of automobiles or even the high price of gasoline? Have you ever protested the operating practices of the one cable television system in your area? Have you ever questioned how the electric company is regulated? Have you ever demonstrated against additional fees you've had to pay when you buy tickets for a rock concert?

Our guess is that you probably have not. Perhaps you haven't realized that the way markets are structured has serious implications for prices, output levels, efficiency, income distribution, and political influence. Much of the American public seems uninterested in, or at least unaware of, the effects of market power in the United States. Some people naively assume that because we have antitrust laws and economic regulation of some monopolies, we do not have a problem. Others argue that regulation decreases business efficiency and should be eliminated. But consumer advocate and Green Party presidential candidate Ralph Nader has noted that the general public views antitrust matters as "too complex, too abstract, and supremely dull."

In this chapter, we will look at the effects of market power on the American economy. The implications for consumers are significant. We hope we can do this in a way that is neither complex, abstract, nor dull. To gain an understanding of the problem of market power, you must learn something about three market structures: competition, monopoly, and oligopoly.

COMPETITION

Market power
The ability of an individual firm to influence the market price of its product.

Recall that the markets in Chapter 1 were described as competitive. Because there were many small buyers and sellers, no one producer could influence the "going market price" of its product. Another way of saying this is that no individual supplier had any **market power**. The examples suggested that if one tutor out of many identical tutors decided to charge an exorbitant price, consumers would simply buy the services of other competing suppliers. Thus, competition protected consumers from potentially unreasonable prices.

A market structure in which the seller cannot influence price is what economists call **competition**. A competitive market has three characteristics:

Competition
A market in which many small producers sell a standardized product to many small buyers.

1. There are many small buyers and sellers
2. There is a standardized product
3. There are no barriers to entry or exit

Let's consider each of these characteristics separately. As we've just noted, the first characteristic has bearing on the going market price. Because many small buyers constitute the total demand in the market, no individual buyer is powerful enough to extract a lower price on the product. Because there are so many small firms selling the product, no one supplier can charge a higher price for the product. If it has occurred to you that the terms small buyers and small sellers are not very specific, you are correct. Firms can be large in absolute terms and do many million dollars of business annually, but by perfect competition, we mean they are small relative to the entire market. Agricultural markets are often viewed as competitive. We have many small suppliers of corn, for example. Even the largest corn producer in the country produces only a very small share of the entire supply of corn in the country.

Second, in a competitive market, the products of all producers are standardized or roughly identical. Most agricultural products, if we carefully specify the grade, are standardized. So are the markets for standard-sized rubber bands, pencils, and floppy disks. See if you can think of other standardized products. The importance of this standardization is that the buyer will not care which seller she buys from, because the products are roughly the same. Therefore, she will not be willing to pay a higher price for one firm's product since that firm's product is no better than any other firm's product.

Barrier to entry
A market characteristic that prevents new firms from entering the market.

Third, there are no barriers to entry into the competitive market. A **barrier to entry** is some condition that makes it difficult or expensive for a new producer to enter the market. Perhaps start-up costs are so huge that a great deal of capital must be raised before a new firm begins operations. Or the government may require a firm to obtain a license before it can sell its good or service. Or the products of existing firms may be protected by patents, so that production of a similar product carries the risk of a patent infringement lawsuit. These barriers to entry are not present in a competitive market. If they were present, there would not be "many small sellers."

Price taker
A firm that is unable to influence the market price of its product.

An important implication of these characteristics is that the competitive firm will be a **price taker**. That is, it will take the market price as given and will not (by itself) have any influence over this market price. Any level of output that it could possibly produce is too small to affect the market price. Consider Figure 8-1, which shows the

FIGURE 8-1   A Competitive Market for Fresh Fish

Price, $

S

120 - - - - - - - - -

D

0   7,000   Quantity (100 lb.)

Market for Fish

The competitive market determines the price per unit of fish. Equilibrium price is $120 per unit (hundredweight), and equilibrium quantity is 7,000 units.

market for fresh fish offered for sale in one week by fishing boat operators in a north-western U.S. port.

The market price of $120 per hundredweight (100 pounds) is established by the interaction of total market demand and supply. At this price 7,000 hundredweight of fish will be sold in the port's commercial fish market. Let's assume that Mr. Diaz can offer for sale any quantity between 0 and 50 hundredweight this week, but any of these quantities is too small to influence the market price. Therefore, Mr. Diaz offers his desired quantity of fish to the market and charges the market price of $120 per hundredweight. He takes this market price as given.

Why doesn't Mr. Diaz charge a price higher than $120? The answer is simple. If he does, his customers will buy from other producers. His fish are no different from fish caught by other fishing boat captains. If he tries to get a higher price, he will lose all his business.

Perhaps Mr. Diaz believes that if he lowers his price, he can sell more fish and increase his revenue. However, he is pretty much guaranteed that he can sell all of his fish at the going market price, so that lowering the price would merely reduce his revenue. (The intersection of market demand and supply means that quantity demanded will equal quantity supplied at the market price.)

The competitive market price is a reasonable one; the market demand curve reflects the value of fish to all the buyers in the market, and the market supply curve reflects the costs of production incurred by producers in this market. (Recall from Chapter 1 that costs of production is one of the most important factors that influence supply.) Mr. Diaz (and all other fish suppliers in this market) will be prohibited from charging a price higher than the market price. This is not a legal or even a spoken prohibition; it is just the way that perfect competition works to assure that consumers are not charged exorbitant prices. This outcome is one of the great advantages of competitive markets.

MONOPOLY AND OLIGOPOLY

Monopoly
A market in which only one firm produces a product with no close substitutes.

Monopolist
The single firm in a monopoly market.

Price maker
A firm that is able to influence the market price of its product.

The opposite of a competitive market is a monopoly. A **monopoly** is a market with only one seller of the product. We can also refer to this single seller as a **monopolist**. The product produced by the monopolist has no close substitutes, so if buyers want the product, they have no choice but to buy it from the monopolist. The monopolist is not a price taker but a **price maker**. Another way of saying this is that the monopolist has market power. Again, market power is defined as the ability of an individual firm to influence the market price of its product. This ability does not mean that the firm will simply set the highest possible price; it means that the firm can raise its price by decreasing the quantity that it supplies. Unlike the competitive firm (which accepts the market price as given), the monopolist knows that its output level will help determine its price. The monopolist faces the entire downward-sloping market demand curve (since it is the only supplier in the market). When it offers for sale a particular quantity, it is establishing where along the market demand curve the market equilibrium quantity is located. This simultaneously establishes the market price.

Consider Figure 8-2, which shows a market demand for cable television service. The price is the monthly fee for basic cable services, and the quantities are the numbers of subscribers in the area in the month. There is only one cable supplier in the area. Note that if the cable television company sells 25,000 units, it can get a price of $15, but if it decides to sell only 20,000 units, it can charge a price of $20. The way that the firm influences its price is by controlling its quantity. By selling fewer units, it can charge a significantly higher price for those units that it does sell. Also note that its revenue will be greater if it sells only 20,000 units. A firm's total revenue is always the product price times the quantity sold. If the cable television company sells 20,000 units at $20 each, its revenue will be $400,000. But if it sells 25,000 units at $15, its revenue will be only $375,000. (For more information about the elasticity conditions that are necessary for the monopolist to reduce output and increase revenue, please see the appendix to this chapter.)

When a monopoly dominates the market, the competitive supply curve based on the costs of production of many small producers simply no longer exists. Instead, the monopolist will choose to supply a lesser amount of the product to get a higher price and receive a larger profit. So, compared with a competitive market, a monopoly with the same production costs will produce less, charge a higher price, and receive larger profits. Keep in mind that while the monopolist controls its supply, it does not control its demand. The demand curve faced by the monopoly firm is controlled by consumers of the product.

There are few true monopolies in the United States. Most of the monopolies that do exist are regulated by some agency of the government (we will look at the controversy over regulation later). Historic examples are long-distance phone service and the post office. AT&T once was a monopoly supplier of long-distance phone service until

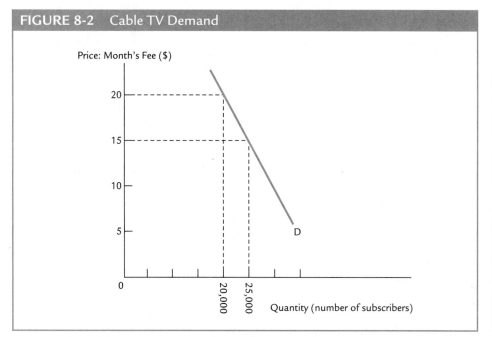

FIGURE 8-2 Cable TV Demand

Because the cable TV company's demand curve is downward sloping, the company simultaneously establishes a price when it supplies a certain quantity.

EconDebate

"Is Microsoft a Monopoly?"

Decide which argument you agree with by checking this debate under the Monopoly heading.

http://econapps. swlearning.com

the government broke up this monopoly and more providers of long-distance phone service entered the scene. Similarly, the U.S. post office was once a monopoly supplier of letter delivery. (United Parcel Service, or UPS, delivered only packages.) Now, other suppliers of letter delivery include UPS, Federal Express, and other companies. In addition to these, local areas often have monopoly suppliers of services to the locality. These might include the provision of electricity, water, sewage, garbage pickup, bus service, and others. At least at the local level, these would be considered monopolies. To summarize, let's note that a monopoly has the following characteristics:

EconNews

"Steel Supply Strategies"

Read more on the U.S. steel industry by navigating to the Oligopoly heading.

http://econapps. swlearning.com

1. It is a single firm.
2. It offers for sale a unique product with no close substitutes.
3. Its market has strong barriers to entry.

In addition to these limited numbers of monopolies, our nation faces market power in another type of market structure, referred to as oligopoly. An **oligopoly** is a market in which only a few large firms dominate the market. The individual firms in these markets are referred to as **oligopolists**. These firms produce a large enough share of the total market supply of their product so that each of these large firms can influence the market price. When we speak of the "big three" automobile companies or the "big four" ready-to-eat cereal companies, we are referring to oligopolies. All of these companies have market power. In addition, if oligopoly firms agree to get together and cooperate on their output levels, they can set a price as high as if they were a monopoly.

Oligopoly
A market in which only a few large firms dominate.

Oligopolists
Individual firms in an oligopoly market.

MEASURING BIGNESS AND CONCENTRATION

The American economy contains some extremely large firms. One interesting way to consider the size of these large firms is to compare their sales (income) with the gross domestic product (income) of various nations around the world. Table 8-1 makes this comparison for the largest U.S. firms and for several countries. We can see from this table that large firms such as General Motors and Wal-Mart sell more output than many countries produce, even though the examples in the table are mostly industrialized countries. Certainly, sales by General Motors and Wal-Mart far surpass the gross domestic product of most of the developing countries of the world. These data suggest that a great deal of economic and political clout is held by large industrial firms.

Another, and perhaps better, way to look at bigness is to measure the level of concentration within a particular market. When there are only a few relatively large firms in a market, we say that the market is concentrated. Concentration implies the existence of market power. We often measure concentration by means of the **concentration ratio**, which is usually defined as the percentage of output produced by the four largest firms in the industry. The higher the concentration ratio, the greater is the concentration in the industry. If there are four or fewer firms in the industry, the concentration ratio will be 100. That is, the four largest firms produce 100 percent of the output. If the industry contains many small firms, the concentration ratio will be very low. A concentration ratio of 10 would mean that the four largest firms produce only 10 percent of the output and that the industry probably contains many competing firms. Table 8-2 shows the concentration ratios for a number of U.S. industries.

Concentra-tion ratio
The percentage of output produced by the four largest firms in an industry.

TABLE 8-1   Sales (Income) and GDP (Income) of the Largest U.S. Firms and Selected Countries in Billions of Dollars, 1998

Firm or Country	Sales or GDP
General Motors	161.3
Poland	158.6
Norway	145.9
Ford Motor Company	144.4
Wal-Mart	139.2
South Africa	133.5
Saudi Arabia	128.9
Exxon	100.7
New Zealand	52.8

Source: Data from Fortune, April 26, 1999, and **world bank.org/data.countrydata**.

Note: Sales and GDP are not directly comparable, since GDP is tabulated as "value added," whereas sales includes the value of the final product sold by the companies. Firms are listed in boldface.

TABLE 8-2 Concentration Ratios for Selected Manufacturing Industries, 1997

Industry	Concentration Ratio
Cigarettes	99
Light truck and utility vehicles	99
Breweries	90
Aircraft	85
Breakfast cereal	83
Automobiles	80
Soap and detergent	66
Cookies and crackers	60
Coffee and tea	53
Butter	52
Soft drinks	47
Roasted nuts and peanut butter	38
Computers and equipment	37
Musical instruments	34
Pharmaceuticals and medicine	32
Ice cream and frozen dessert	32
Audio and visual equipment	30
Office furniture	29
Footwear	28
Paper	19
Textiles	14
Chemicals	12

Source: U.S. Department of Commerce, Census Bureau, 1997 Census of Manufactures: Concentration Ratios in Manufacturing, **www.census.gov/mcd/mancen/download/ mn92cr.sum**.

Note: Calculations based on the share of the value of shipments.

Most economists consider a concentration ratio above 60 to indicate a tight oligopoly in which firms have significant market power. A concentration ratio of 40 or less would indicate less market power. Approximately 60 percent of U.S. manufacturing is done in industries in which concentration ratios exceed 60.

But when using concentration ratios, we must be careful. Although they are useful indicators of possible market power, they are not perfect measures of market power. Some cautions are therefore in order.

First, concentration ratios are based only on domestic (U.S.) production and exclude foreign competition. Some industries face significant competition from imports. The American automobile industry is a case in point. Although there are only three major domestic car manufacturers, imports account for more than 30 percent of U.S. sales. American automobile markets are therefore more competitive than the concentration ratio implies. As U.S. industries face increasingly more global competition, U.S. concentration ratios tend to overstate their market power.

Second, the concentration ratios in Table 8-2 are calculated for the entire nation, yet many markets are in fact regional. Take ice cream and frozen desserts, for example. The concentration ratio of 32 understates the market power in individual localities where most people buy their ice cream. (Of course, we may be more than happy to pay high prices for Bridgeman's Raspberry Fudge Torte Ice Cream and not view it as a serious problem.) The problem is more significant with other products, such as newspapers. Even though market power at the national level is very low for newspapers, most cities have only one or two local newspapers. These smaller newspapers may have significantly more market power than the concentration suggests, especially in shaping opinions about current issues.

These problems do not mean that concentration ratios are useless as approximations of market power. They do mean, however, that concentration ratios are not perfect measures of market power. They should be used carefully and adjusted when necessary to conform to the realities of the market. At the same time, keep in mind that a more broadly defined product (such as food) will have less concentration than a narrowly defined product (such as ice cream). This is because there are many businesses that produce food, but there are fewer businesses that produce ice cream.

BARRIERS TO ENTRY

The principal reason that some markets are dominated by only a few large firms is that there are barriers to entry into these markets, just as there are in the case of monopoly. New firms therefore find it difficult, if not impossible, to begin operations. Barriers to entry are the source of the existing firms' market power and the reason that concentrated markets remain concentrated year after year.

Let's consider seven of the most commonly encountered barriers to entry.

Economies of Scale

Economies of scale
A situation whereby a large amount of a product can be produced at a lower cost per unit than a small amount of the product.

First, some markets are characterized by **economies of scale**. This means that a large amount of the product can be produced at a lower cost per unit than a small amount of the product. For example, a bakery may be able to produce 100 loaves of bread at a cost of $1.00 per loaf, or 1,000 loaves of bread at a cost of $0.50 per loaf. Economies of scale arise from the technology used in manufacturing the product, as well as the organization of labor and any discounts that a producer may receive on large purchases of inputs. In the case of the bakery, perhaps the company can purchase 100-pound bags of flour (when producing large quantities of bread) at a much lower price per pound than if it purchases only 10-pound bags of flour (sufficient for producing the small quantities of bread). Similarly, the bakery may organize its workers into an assembly-line production process which is more efficient than having each worker produce entire loaves of bread, but which is only feasible for large quantities of bread. For example, a bakery producing large quantities of bread may have one worker mix the dough, another worker bake the bread, and another worker slice and package the loaf. The smaller bakery may be unable to efficiently use more than one worker at a time.

Although the bakery demonstrates the idea of economies of scale, the issue really becomes quite significant when we consider industries such as automobiles, steel, aluminum, or aircraft. An automaker may be able to keep the cost of producing each car relatively low only if it produces on a very large scale. The cost of producing each car may be extremely high if the company produces relatively few cars. In this type of market, it is impossible to start small and grow. If a new firm enters the market and produces a small number of cars, it will not be able to compete with established large firms that are already producing large numbers of cars. Starting small eventually leads to failure, not growth. This lesson was learned by a number of firms that have tried to enter the automobile industry during the past 45 years. Consider the entry of the Bricklin and the DeLorean into the sports-car market. Although both were exciting vehicles, their producers eventually failed because they could not match the low per-unit costs of the comparable cars produced by established firms.

Exclusive Franchises

A second barrier to entry occurs when the government becomes involved and permits a single firm to monopolize the market. This is often the case when there is a **natural monopoly**, which occurs when economies of scale are extensive. In these circumstances, the government may step in and issue an exclusive franchise to one producer. An **exclusive franchise** gives the firm the sole right to conduct business in a particular geographic area. Because the exclusive franchise is granted to the firm, the firm is usually regulated by an agency of the government to ensure that consumers receive some of the benefits of large-scale production. Examples of regulated natural monopolies are your local telephone company, natural gas company, and electric company. If economies of scale are truly significant in these markets, the granting of an exclusive franchise simply recognizes the inevitable. The market will be concentrated with or without the government's action, but at least regulation will help protect the consumer. However, the exclusive franchise acts as a barrier to entry into the market, because new firms cannot legally enter the market. A problem arises when natural monopoly-type regulation is imposed on sectors that are potentially competitive. In this situation, regulation is the source of monopoly power within the industry, and the outcome is much inferior to that in a competitive market.

Natural monopoly
A market with significant economies of scale.

Exclusive franchise
Permission by the government (often a local government) for a monopoly firm to exist. (It is normally accompanied by government regulation.)

Control of Essential Raw Materials

Third, a firm's control of essential raw materials to manufacture a product will serve as a barrier to entry into the market because new firms will not be able to obtain the raw materials to begin operations. Consider, for example, the aluminum industry. The essential ingredient in the production of aluminum is bauxite. When aluminum was first produced, the Aluminum Company of America (Alcoa) cornered the market on bauxite and for many years had a monopoly on the production of aluminum.

Patents

Fourth, some products are protected by patents, which serve as barriers to entry. **Patents** are limited-term monopoly grants from the government to the inventor of the product. Our government gives patents for new products and new processes to encourage innovation and invention. After all, firms incur costs in developing new

Patents
Legal protections that allow the inventor of a product to be the sole provider of the product for a period of time.

products. If a firm is not guaranteed the benefits of its new inventions because its competitors begin selling the new product shortly after it does, how can we expect the firm to put money into research and development? When a firm has a patent on a product, it can protect itself by bringing a patent infringement suit against any new firm that tries to produce a similar product. Although patents do encourage invention, they also encourage the development of market power in three respects: (1) The holder of the patent will be the sole producer of the product for many years. The patent will enable the firm to establish itself in the minds of consumers as the preeminent seller of the product, giving the firm a competitive advantage even after the patent has expired and other firms can legally begin production of the product. (2) Patents can be misused. Established firms sometimes "blanket" the patent by seeking and obtaining patents that they have no intention of using. In other words, they obtain patents on many more variants of the product than they will actually produce simply to prevent other firms from producing a similar product. Only about one-half of the patents granted are actually used. (3) The common practice of aggressively defending patents with patent infringement lawsuits discourages would-be competitors from producing close substitutes.

Product Differentiation

Product differentiation
The creation of the image that one firm's product is different from or somehow superior to other similar products.

Fifth, products are frequently differentiated, and product differentiation acts as a barrier to the entry of new firms. **Product differentiation** is any characteristic that makes the product of one firm different from another firm's in the eyes of the buyer. The difference may be real (style, quality, color, or taste) or it may be entirely artificial (created solely by labeling and advertising). A good example of a differentiated product is household laundry bleach, which is simply a solution of sodium hypochlorite. Despite the uniformity of the product, Clorox has dominated the bleach market for many years, commanding a higher price than other brands because many consumers are convinced that Clorox is a better product than the other brands on the market. Product differentiation acts as a barrier to entry because new firms must spend a great deal of money on advertising their product in an effort to compete against the established brand name of the firm already in the market. The expenditures are too high for a business firm just starting up production of the product. Some differentiated products are film, breakfast cereals, and automobiles.

Licensing

License
A permit to operate in a trade or profession.

Sixth, the government requires new entrants to obtain a **license** before beginning operation in many professions and trades. We license doctors, dentists, lawyers, beauticians, barbers, and undertakers, among others. The reason for licensing is fairly obvious. We accompany the granting of the license with the passing of an examination to ensure some minimum level of competency. But licensing also restricts entry into fields.

Behavior of Established Firms

Seventh, the actions of established firms can also deter entry into the market. For example, these firms may occasionally lower the prices for their products so that new firms wanting to enter the market would have to match these low prices in order to compete with the existing firms. Although the established firms can afford temporarily low profits arising from the price cuts, newer entrants into the industry cannot. This type of price-cutting by established firms can drive new firms out of business or prevent firms from entering the industry in the first place.

A good example of this type of behavior comes from the cigarette industry, which was dominated by three large firms back in the 1930s. These firms sold established brands of cigarettes nationally and accounted for about 90 percent of cigarette sales. There were many small local tobacco companies that sold only in limited geographic regions. When one of the small firms would increase its sales, the big three would retaliate by introducing "fighting brands," which were off-label cigarettes sold at below cost. A market with a history of such predatory competition is not an attractive market for new firms to enter. Can you think of other examples in which firms temporarily lower their prices in order to drive out or prevent competition? (For example, have you ever noticed "gasoline price wars," where all gas stations within a locality temporarily lower their prices? Do you think they were successful at eliminating some of their competition?)

These seven examples of barriers to entry keep markets concentrated over time. Because the firms in the industry will be relatively few and rather large, they will be able to control the supply in the market and to charge a price higher than the competitive market price. They will possess market power.

EFFECTS OF MARKET POWER

We have already discussed some of the effects of market power. The firms will charge a higher price, produce a smaller quantity, and receive higher revenue than would competitive producers. Figure 8-3 compares the price, output, and revenue levels under conditions of competition versus monopoly. Assume first of all that there are many firms of relatively equal size so that the market is competitive. The supply curve labeled S_C is the total supply curve under competition and is made up of all of the supply curves of all the individual firms that provide long-distance phone service totaled together. The intersection of demand and supply indicates that the price will be $1.50 per long-distance call and the quantity will be 1,200 calls under competition. (We are assuming, for simplicity, that all calls are charged the same amount.) Alternatively, assume that there is only one firm that supplies long-distance telephone service. We don't actually draw a supply curve in the case of monopoly, but we just indicate some point along the demand curve to show the quantity that the monopolist intends to supply. For example, this quantity might be 1,000 phone calls, with a corresponding price equal to $2.00 per call.

Notice that the total revenue to all the firms combined in the competitive alternative will equal price multiplied by quantity, or 1,200 × $1.50, which equals $1,800. On the other hand, the revenue to the monopoly firm will be 1,000 × $2.00, or $2,000. And since the monopoly produces a smaller quantity, its costs are lower than they are for the competitive firms, indicating that the profits will be higher in the monopoly market than in the competitive. (Once again, see this chapter's appendix for elasticity conditions.)

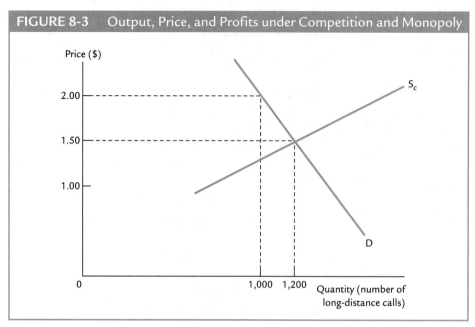

FIGURE 8-3 Output, Price, and Profits under Competition and Monopoly

Note that output is lower and that price and profits are higher under a monopoly than they would be under competition.

In addition to affecting price, output, and profits, market concentration often leads to collusion, inefficiency, and price discrimination. Let's discuss these phenomena one at a time.

Collusion

Collusion
Price-fixing.

Collusion is better known as price-fixing. It occurs when firms cooperate to restrict the total market output and thereby obtain a higher price. For collusion to be successful, all the firms in the market must cooperate. If some firms collude to charge a higher price, while others do not, consumers will simply buy from the noncolluders at a lower price. Collusion is therefore more likely in markets with relatively few firms and substantial entry barriers.

Cartel
A group of producers that explicitly engages in price-fixing.

There are two types of collusion: cartel agreements and price leadership. A **cartel** is a group of producers that has an explicit agreement among them to limit output and charge a price higher than the competitive price. Cartels with which you might be familiar are the Organization of Petroleum Exporting Countries (OPEC), an organization of 13 of the world's largest oil-producing nations, and the DeBeers diamond cartel, which controls the world's supply of diamonds. A colorful and illegal cartel known as the "electrical equipment conspiracy" existed for many years in the United States. It included 29 electrical equipment companies headed by industry giants General Electric (GE) and Westinghouse. When the conspiracy was uncovered, GE, Westinghouse, and 44 of their executives were charged with conspiring to fix prices over a 25-year period by rigging bids in the sale of billions of dollars worth of heavy electrical equipment. The firms took turns offering the low bid. This low bid had previously been agreed on by the cartel and was actually at a high level. The colluders had devised ingenious schemes to coordinate their bidding. A firm would know whether to bid high or low, for example, by the phase of the moon.

Price leadership is a more subtle form of collusion. It occurs in markets in which firms never *explicitly* agree to collude, but instead somehow come to the realization that it is in their best interests to charge similar prices and to restrict output to maintain these higher prices. When this happens, one of the firms emerges as price leader and the other firms adjust their price whenever the leader changes its price. American Tobacco was long the price leader in the cigarette industry, Kellogg in the cereal industry, Campbell in the canned soup industry, and General Motors in the automobile industry. (Incidentally, the long-established practice of price leadership in the American automobile industry collapsed in the early 1980s when the industry began contending with substantial competition from imports.)

Price leadership
A form of collusion in which firms follow the price increases of a leading firm.

As you perhaps know, collusion is illegal under our antitrust laws. And indeed, firms that form cartels are subject to severe penalties should they be caught. Our antitrust system has been quite effective against cartels. The sad truth, however, is that the system is ineffective against price leadership. Without convincing evidence that firms have formally met and agreed to collude, proving that they are guilty of price-fixing is nearly impossible.

Inefficiency

A second problem with concentration is that firms in concentrated markets have less incentive to be efficient than do firms in competitive markets. A competitive firm must minimize the cost of its product in order to survive. But the firm in a concentrated market, protected by entry barriers, has no such incentive. Security breeds laxness, and costs rise. The *Wall Street Journal* and other business publications abound with examples of dominant firms that, suddenly faced with competition, cut costs substantially. Caterpillar Tractor Company, long the leading U.S. producer of construction equipment, found it possible to cut costs by more than 20 percent when suddenly besieged by Japanese competition in the early 1980s. When the American automobile industry was hit hard by foreign competition in the late 1970s, General Motors, Ford, and Chrysler were able to reduce their costs by 20 to 30 percent. When the Harley-Davidson motorcycle company lost its market dominance to Japanese competitors in the 1960s, it first sought protection in the form of import tariffs on motorcycles, which were in place during much of the 1980s but slated to end in 1988. By 1988, Harley-Davidson had cut its inventory by two-thirds, improved productivity by 50 percent, and reduced its rate of defects by 70 percent. As you may have realized as you read these examples, the business publications reported the successful cost cutting measures, lauding the "lean and mean" American firms. But the firms had substantial excess costs to cut, and it was competition that forced them to do so.[1] Competition, whether domestic or international, promotes efficiency and benefits consumers.

There are also other sources of inefficiency in concentrated markets that are related to the product differentiation that these firms engage in. In order to attract consumers, oligopolists, for example, spend huge amounts of money on marketing and advertising their products. Frequently this includes prime time television commercials and color glossy ads in national magazines. In addition, firms in the auto industry spend enormous amounts of money on the annual style changes of their automobiles. Firms in the breakfast cereal industry spend large amounts of money on the packaging of their products so that they appeal to children, often with games on the back of the packages and prizes within the box. When marketing activities serve to inform customers about the product, then the money spent on marketing may be useful to consumers. Unfortunately, much of the marketing efforts are designed more to manipulate consumers than to inform them. These are the wasteful expenses of product differentiation and they represent a significant drain on society's scarce resources.

Price Discrimination

Another consequence of market power is **price discrimination**, or charging different prices to different groups of customers when the price differentials are not justified by differences in costs. Firms charge "what the market will bear," and different market segments will bear substantially different prices. Price discrimination is profitable for the discriminators, but it is only possible when firms have significant price-making power. Price discrimination is extremely common in the United States.

Let's consider some examples, beginning with the automobile industry, which has a rich history of price discrimination. As you undoubtedly know, American car manufacturers produce a variety of vehicles, ranging from small economy cars to luxury models. The markup over cost varies substantially with the model. Because purchasers of small economy cars tend to be more price conscious than purchasers of Cadillacs and Lincolns, firms take a smaller markup over cost on the economy models. The price differences reflect not only cost differences but also differences in what the market will bear.

Another way that automobile companies discriminate is illustrated in the area of replacement parts and optional equipment. The markup is much higher on parts and options than on the car itself. If your car is not running because it needs a new part, you are not particularly price conscious about the part. You may be horrified when you see the repair bill, but if you consider the car worth keeping, you have little choice other than to pay it. Also, the high markup on options explains why the salesperson pressures you so much to buy many options when you shop for a new car (one of the most frustrating events in American life). The auto industry is, by the way, not the only industry that discriminates in the sale of replacement parts. The practice is exceedingly common. If you don't believe this, price a replacement plate for your microwave oven.

The drug industry, the products of which are usually protected by patents, uses extensive and systematic price discrimination. Drugs that will ultimately be consumed by hospital patients are often priced higher than drugs that will be consumed by retail buyers. Large buyers such as the Veterans Administration can obtain drugs at far lower prices than can retail druggists. The drug industry claims that the huge price differences are the result of differences in the cost of packaging and selling drugs to different groups, but such differences are small, and Senate testimony in the 1970s revealed that druggists often paid prices more than three times that paid by the Veterans Administration for the same patented drug. Can you think of other examples of price discrimination?

FORCES THAT DECREASE MARKET POWER

It is obvious that market power produces some undesirable consequences that harm the consumer, whereas competition benefits the consumer. Let us now consider the forces that decrease market power. These forces are (1) technological change, (2) antitrust activity, (3) deregulation of unwisely regulated sectors, and (4) import competition.

Technological Change

Technology is a major force on market structure in the economy. Economies of scale, which characterize natural monopolies, are often eroded by the forces of technological change. Take, for example, the telephone industry. When phone messages were carried on wire cables, the industry was characterized by extensive economies of scale. Fiber-optic and microwave transmission of phone messages, however, involve lesser economies of scale, and long-distance telephone service, which was once a natural monopoly, is now potentially competitive. Since the divestiture of AT&T, consumers in most localities have had a choice of long-distance carriers, and competition has decreased the price of long-distance calls. Now, additional competition is coming from cell phones, a still newer innovation.

Consider next the railroads, which had significant market power during the late 1800s and the early part of the twentieth century. Technological change since then has resulted in new competitors for the railroads. The invention of the internal combustion engine and the subsequent development of cars, trucks, and airplanes led to a significant level of interindustry competition for the railroads. Once the dominant force in American transportation, railroads are now a slowly declining industry.

The U.S. Antitrust System

Our **antitrust** system is a set of weapons designed to combat market power. It consists of laws passed by Congress, agencies empowered to administer these laws, and a court system to try cases under the laws. The first federal antitrust law (*trust* is simply an old-fashioned word for monopoly) was the Sherman Act, which was enacted in 1890. The Sherman Act's provisions made illegal monopolization and conspiracies in restraint of trade. The law was quite generally written. Congress made known its intent and left it up to the Justice Department and the courts to apply the law to specific cases. As time passed, it became evident that the courts and agencies had difficulty interpreting the law, and another more specifically written law was passed. This was the Clayton Act of 1914. The Clayton Act contains many provisions that make it illegal to engage in actions that would "substantially lessen competition." The Clayton Act has been amended several times, most notably in 1950, when the passage of the Celler-Kefauver Act strengthened the law against **mergers** that would adversely affect competition.

The principal agencies charged with administering the law are the Antitrust Division of the Justice Department and the Federal Trade Commission (FTC). The FTC is also the federal agency with jurisdiction over trade practices such as deceptive advertising, so its resources—not great to begin with—are split between its two functions. The Antitrust Division is staffed at its lower levels with people who make a

Antitrust
Our laws, agencies, and court system established to control market power in the United States.

Mergers
The combining of two firms into one.

career of enforcing the antitrust laws, but its head is a political appointee, as is the attorney general to whom the chief antitrust officer reports. The vigor of antitrust prosecution therefore varies with the presidential administration, not only because the people at the head of the agency set its goals but also because the agency's budget is politically controlled. This is not to say that antitrust is ever abandoned. Every administration prosecutes price-fixers when they are apprehended. But prosecution of other antitrust cases, especially mergers, waxes and wanes.

The position of the Reagan administration (1981–1988) was that the economy is in fact more competitive than simple examination of concentration ratios would indicate. The administration argued that even markets with high concentration ratios seldom have barriers to entry so high that they are not subject to the "potential competition" of new entrants. It was assumed that the threat of this potential competition constrains the behavior of the established firms and leads them to behave in a relatively competitive manner. Finally, it was argued that firms must be large and unconstrained in order to compete effectively internationally. These arguments were used to curb antitrust budgets and decrease antitrust activity. Government actions against mergers were virtually eliminated under the Reagan administration, and as a result one of the heaviest periods of merger activity in U.S. history began in the 1980s.

Both the Antitrust Division and the FTC have always been small when compared to their job. Their resources, however, grew until the 1980s, when the Reagan administration cut their budgets by about 30 percent in inflation-adjusted dollars. The number of attorneys employed by the Antitrust Division and the relevant section of the FTC declined from 435 to 221 in the period from 1980 to 1989.[2]

Both the George H. W. Bush and Clinton administrations were somewhat more activist with regard to antitrust. The budgets and staff of antitrust agencies were increased. A price-fixing case against Archer Daniels Midland Company and the corn-processing industry was brought and won by the government. Proposed mergers were examined more closely. The only two acute-care hospitals in Dubuque, Iowa, were prevented from merging. However, the 1997 merger between McDonnell Douglas and Boeing, which left the United States with one civilian aircraft manufacturer, was allowed because international competition in aircraft manufacturing is substantial. But the proposed merger in 2000 of Sprint and WorldCom, two large telecommunications firms, was blocked by the U.S. Antitrust Division and its European counterparts. The telecommunications market is global, and the merger would have significantly decreased competition in telecommunications throughout the world.

The most recent, newsworthy antitrust action undoubtedly was the 2000 decision of District Court Judge Thomas Penfield Jackson that Microsoft Corporation was a monopoly that should be broken up. The case was filed in 1998. The government accused Microsoft of monopolizing the market for computer operating platforms with its 90 percent Windows market share. Furthermore, the government charged that the company had used its monopoly power to stifle competition by bundling its Internet Explorer Web browser into the Windows operation system, polluting Sun Microsystems's Java programming language to diminish its competitive threat to Windows, and threatening IBM and Compaq. As a result, innovations that would benefit consumers were never developed. The decision has, of course, been appealed.

Microsoft and its defenders argued that breaking up the firm would result in slower technological progress in the software industry. Furthermore, they argued that Microsoft's product is admired and used by millions of consumers. Microsoft subsequently settled with the Bush administration and most of the 19 states that had signed onto the government case. Among other things, Microsoft agreed to reduce the price it charges its competitors that want to use Microsoft's operating system in their software. As of 2003, Microsoft has begun to comply with the terms of the settlement.

A question facing U.S. antitrust authorities is how and to what extent they should cooperate with similar agencies in the European Union. As European countries have realized that they must protect competition within their economies, they have established agencies similar to our antitrust agencies. Furthermore, technological advances in communications have resulted in more markets that are truly global. International cooperation is necessary to protect competition in such markets.

Although antitrust laws do not eliminate all market power, they do constrain the activities of dominant firms. It can be argued that the antitrust system thus confers important benefits to consumers.

Regulation and Deregulation

Natural monopolies that exhibit substantial economies of scale are generally regulated by state or federal government agencies such as your state public service commission. Regulation involves limitation of market entry by the granting of exclusive franchises to firms. As we have already discussed, these franchises eliminate any real or potential competition. The natural monopoly is then regulated with respect to rates charged and level of service offered. Rates (prices) are set after hearings in which firms present data on their costs, and citizens' groups present testimony about the probable adverse effects of rate increases. The accounting data presented by the firm are scrutinized by the professional staff of the regulatory agency. The result is a compromise between the interests of the firm and those of its customers. Because markets with substantial economies of scale tend to be highly concentrated anyway, regulation can greatly improve the outcome.

The major problem with regulation occurs when a public utility-type of regulation is imposed on industries that are not natural monopolies because they do not have substantial economies of scale. When this happens, regulation shelters the firms from competition and actually causes inefficiency. In markets in which competition is possible, it should be encouraged. Regulation tends to be less flexible than competitive market forces, which would lead to a better outcome in terms of prices, services, and level of output.

Consider, for example, the trucking industry, which is not subject to economies of scale. Small and large trucking firms can compete on a relatively equal basis. However, interstate trucking was regulated by the federal government in 1935 and continued to be strictly regulated until 1980. Firms could not begin operating on particular routes without obtaining licenses to do so from the Interstate Commerce Commission (ICC), the agency given jurisdiction over highway carriers. The ICC limited entry into the industry to protect existing carriers, eliminating potential competition. Many trucking firms' licenses were for specific commodities, so all firms could not carry all commodities. If these firms could not obtain a load of

EconNews

"Peak Power Prices"

Read how the federal government regulates power costs under the Market Failure, Regulation, and Public Choice category.

http://econapps. swlearning.com

their regulated commodity at the end of a trip, they simply traveled back to their terminal empty. This practice obviously created inefficiency. All similar carriers charged the same regulated price. Since they could not compete on the basis of price, they competed on the basis of frequency of service and therefore often hauled loads that were less than their vehicles' capacity. This too was inefficient. Trucking regulation did not benefit consumers. Shippers paid significantly higher rates because of the industry's inefficiency, and these higher rates were passed along to consumers in the form of higher prices. In 1980, the industry was substantially deregulated. Because regulation was unwise in this case, efficiency improved and consumers benefited.

Deregulation simply means lessening regulatory restrictions, either in part or in total. Many formerly regulated industries were deregulated in the late 1970s and the 1980s. Because these industries were quite competitive without regulation, deregulation was appropriate. Among the industries deregulated in this period were natural gas production, airlines, railroads (the monopoly position of which had been eroded by interindustry competition), and, of course, trucking.

The bottom line with regard to regulation is that it can improve the performance of natural monopolies but that it is inferior to competition when competition is possible.

Import Competition

 Finally, competition from imported products curbs the market power of domestic firms. The presence of Toyota, Nissan, and Volkswagen provides effective competition for the big three U.S. auto companies. The industry's abandonment of price leadership in the 1980s stemmed not from government action but from competition from abroad. Our domestic producers have been forced to improve efficiency to compete with Japanese firms. Ultimately, American consumers have benefited.

Import quotas and tariffs that limit competition from foreign imports are often called upon to protect American firms. The powerful firms that lobby Congress to limit imports are often in concentrated markets. Restricting imports protects the market power in these concentrated industries, but does not benefit the American worker or consumers. By protecting market power in these concentrated industries, we ultimately cause lower output levels, lower employment, and higher prices to consumers. For example, the American automobile industry has been quite successful in increasing restrictions on imports. At the same time, it is building assembly plants abroad, where labor is cheaper. American workers, who are also American consumers, benefit from low or nonexistent import restrictions. Neither the U.S. worker nor the U.S. consumer benefits from trade restrictions. We will examine this in more detail in Chapter 9.

EXTENT OF MARKET POWER

How serious is the problem of market power? The answer is not simple. Various researchers have tried to address the issue of whether concentration (and market power) has increased over time. A classic study was conducted by William Shepard for the time period 1939 to 1980. Shepard concluded that market power fell from 1939 to 1958, and fell again from 1958 to 1980. He believed that greater competition was achieved through increased international trade, reduced government regulations, and vigorous government antitrust activity.

The major issue is whether concentration and market power have fallen *since* 1980. Some factors have contributed to lower concentration, including international trade and the information revolution (consumers now have better information about products and prices nationally, which thereby diminishes the market power of local monopolies). On the other hand, public resources devoted to antitrust are now well below their level in the years prior to President Ronald Reagan. According to the American Antitrust Institute (AAI), "Antitrust budgets remain too low, staff is stretched too thin, and the agenda is haunted by a 'laissez faire mentality.' "[3] As a result, the AAI believes that large segments of our economy are becoming more concentrated. What is clear is that merger activity has increased since 1980 and that concentration ratios are quite high in many industries.

ONE FINAL COMMENT

Markets consisting of large and powerful firms may lobby our government for protection of their interests. Outcomes may be reduced regulations, limited antitrust activity, and trade restrictions. All of these may be conducive to greater market power

VIEWPOINT: CONSERVATIVE VERSUS LIBERAL

Conservative and liberal economists differ greatly in their attitudes toward market power, antitrust activities, and economic regulation. Conservatives, who believe in a limited government role in the economy, feel that market power is seldom a serious problem. They believe that barriers to entry are seldom so high as to eliminate the threat of competition from new firms entering the industry. Furthermore, technological change erodes established monopoly positions. Thus, conservatives seldom see a need for antitrust or economic regulation, and they believe that such policies usually create inefficiency.

One of the ways in which conservative and liberal economists differ most is in their attitudes toward mergers. Conservatives argue that any increased market power that is created when firms merge is controlled by potential competition from new entrants into the industry and by technological change. Liberals, on the other hand, generally feel that the antitrust system is needed to control excessive market power and that proposed mergers should be scrutinized closely before they are allowed to take place.

Liberals believe that public utilities should be regulated to protect the consumer from monopolistic excesses. Conservatives, however, argue that the government actually creates monopoly power by granting the utility companies exclusive franchises. They argue that the problem is the government monopoly grant, not the economies of scale that result in a natural monopoly. Thus, conservatives view economic regulation largely as a source of inefficiency and too much expansion of the government role.

within already concentrated industries. Trade restrictions, for example, may effectively limit the competition faced by U.S. firms, thereby serving as a barrier to entry and enhancing the market power already existing in the industry. Unfortunately, consumers do not have the same level of influence over government policy as large and powerful business firms operating in unison. To the extent that we believe in democracy, we like to think that one person's vote counts just as much as any other person's vote. This may not be the case when oligopoly firms (or other firms, for that matter) have greater political clout through their lobbies and their contributions to political campaigns. One area where this has recently become controversial is in what President Eisenhower referred to many years ago as the "military-industrial complex." In the context of war with Afghanistan and Iraq, no-bid contracts for reconstruction activities have been given to firms such as Halliburton and Bechtel, companies that have had strong ties to the defense industry.

The conclusion is that market power remains high in particular markets. Automobiles, canned soups, newspapers, and many other markets are not effectively competitive. The airlines, which were quite competitive when first deregulated, have engaged in a series of mergers that have created a tight oligopoly. Many economists argue that we still need to support policies that limit market power.

SUMMARY

Market power exists when there are only a few dominant firms in a market. These firms are sheltered from competition by barriers to entry. Barriers to entry can include economies of scale, exclusive franchises, control over essential raw materials, patents, product differentiation, licensing, and behavior of firms such as price-cutting. Firms in concentrated industries can significantly influence their own prices by restricting the quantity of their products. The adverse consequences of market power are often higher prices, higher profits, lower quantities of goods available, inefficiency, price discrimination, and collusion.

The major factors that can inhibit the development and abuse of market power are technological change, our antitrust system, economic regulation of natural monopolies, and import competition. There are several reasons to conclude that market power exists in many U.S. industries, as is evident by large mergers, high concentration ratios, and limited government antitrust activity.

NOTES

1. Much of the discussion of inefficiency is based on the work of William G. Shepherd. See, for example, *The Economics of Industrial Organization*, 4th ed. (Englewood Cliffs, N.J.: Prentice Hall, 1997).

2. William G. Shepherd, *Public Policy toward Business*, 8th ed. (Boston: Irwin, 1991), p. 191.

3. American Antitrust Institute (AAI) (**www. antitrustinstitute.org/about.cfm**).

DISCUSSION QUESTIONS

1. What characteristics are necessary for a market to be competitive? Are there many competitive markets in the real world?

2. What are the disadvantages of market power for society? (Hint: Discuss price, output, profits, price discrimination, etc.)

3. What are barriers to entry? Why must barriers to entry be present if market power is to exist in a particular market?

4. Discuss the following barriers to entry: (a) economies of scale, (b) exclusive franchises, (c) licenses, (d) patents, (e) product differentiation, and (f) price-cutting. Describe how each functions as a barrier to entry by new firms.

5. Can you think of any examples of price-cutting that may exist in your community? Are you aware of any such activity involving some of the products that you purchase?

6. What are some examples of product differentiation in industries other than those discussed in the text? Especially think in terms of some of the products that you purchase.

7. Can you think of other examples of price discrimination besides those mentioned in the text? What about the way that airlines charge their business clients one price (noting that businesspeople often purchase fares just before they travel and that they have little flexibility in when and whether they travel) versus fares charged to vacationers (who often have alternative means of travel and choices over the time of travel and who can often purchase fares in advance)? Can you explain the different fares charged by the airlines in terms of price discrimination?

8. Can you explain why adult and child moviegoers are often charged different amounts when going to the movie theater, keeping in mind that both an adult and a child each takes up an entire seat?

9. You are undoubtedly aware that most of the tickets that you purchase for rock concerts and other musical events go through Ticketmaster, and of course there is always a fee connected with this. Do you believe that Ticketmaster uses its market power to charge unnecessarily high fees for its service? Do consumers (and rock bands) have any alternative to using Ticketmaster? Are you aware of any bands that have chosen to supply their tickets without using Ticketmaster? If so, how successful have they been?

10. How do tariffs and import quotas harm the consumer? How do they harm the U.S. worker?

11. Open the Department of Justice's antitrust page (**www.usdoj.gov/atr**), and click What's New? List the new cases that have been initiated.

12. Are you a liberal or a conservative with respect to antitrust and economic regulation?

13. Go back to the Department of Justice Web site at **www.usdoj.gov/atr**. Find the page that explains how to report possible antitrust violations or potential anticompetitive activity. Read the confidentiality page with respect to reporting violations.

14. Check out the Census Bureau Web page that focuses on concentration ratios (**www.census.gov/epcd/www/concentration.html**). Can you find concentration ratios for markets that are not reported in this book? Find one market you are interested in and determine whether it is competitive or concentrated.

15. Go to the Web site of the American Antitrust Institute at **www.antitrustinstitute.org**. This institute is an independent Washington-based nonprofit organization dedicated to education, research, and advocacy to assure competition and challenge unduly concentrated power in the U.S. and world economy.

CHAPTER 8 APPENDIX: MARKET POWER AND ELASTICITY

L et's think a bit about the role of the elasticity of demand in relation to market power. There are two issues in particular that relate to elasticity.

ELASTICITY AND MONOPOLY PROFITS

First, since the monopolist supplies a unique product, it is likely that the demand for this product is inelastic (since the only alternatives that consumers have if the price rises too high are to pay the price or go without the product). Remember that there are no close substitutes for the monopolist's product. As discussed in Chapter 2, we know that when demand is inelastic, consumers do not alter the quantities that they purchase very much when the price of the product changes. Monopolists take advantage of this situation by recognizing that even a small reduction in the quantity supplied will be associated with a much higher price (because of the inelastic demand). This is reflected in the relatively steep demand curve in our earlier Figure 8-2. Since we calculate revenue as price times quantity, and since the price variable will be going up more in percentage terms than the quantity variable will be going down, the monopolist can increase its revenue by restricting output. And, since the monopolist is producing a smaller amount of output, its costs of production will be lower as well. The fact that costs fall and revenue rises means that the monopolist can increase its profits by restricting its output. If the demand for the monopolist's product was not inelastic, the monopolist would be unable to increase revenue by reducing its quantity.

ELASTICITY AND PRICE DISCRIMINATION

We can also consider the relation between the elasticity of demand and price discrimination. Recall that price discrimination occurs when a business firm charges different prices to different groups of consumers. Let's return to the example of long-distance telephone service, and let's simplify by assuming that there are only two different groups of consumers of long-distance phone service. One group of businesspeople often must phone their clients during business hours. They may have few alternatives to making the phone call. However, a different group of nonbusiness consumers is more flexible. These consumers of long-distance phone service can perhaps write a letter or an e-mail instead, and they can often make their phone calls during evenings or weekends. The differences between these two groups of consumers can be explained in terms of elasticity of demand.

The first group of businesspeople has an inelastic demand for long-distance phone service. The businesspeople are inflexible and unable to cut down much on their phone calls when the cost of making the calls goes up. The supplier of long-distance phone service can increase its revenue by raising its price (since it knows that this group of consumers will cut down on long-distance phone calls very little). Recalling that revenue equals price times quantity, we know that the price will increase proportionately more than the quantity will fall. As a result, the firm increases its revenue by raising its price. This is the example we referred to earlier in Figure 8-2.

But what about the flexible group of consumers? Since they have more alternatives to making their long-distance phone calls during business hours, they can manage to be price conscious and will reduce their phone calls considerably if prices rise. For this group of consumers, the firm will increase its revenue by *reducing* its price. This is because when demand is elastic, people will increase their number of phone calls proportionately more than the price falls. Since revenue equals price times quantity, the price reduction will be more than offset by an increase in quantity, and the revenue to the supplier of long-distance phone service will increase. By charging the different prices to the different groups of consumers, the firm can increase its revenue and profits.

Of course, the conditions that must be met for this type of price discrimination to take place include the existence of market power (otherwise, the firm could not alter its price) and the ability of the firm to segment consumers into different groups with different elasticities. The phone company does this by offering high rates during business hours and low rates during evenings and weekends.

There are many more examples of price discrimination. For example, can you explain the different fares charged by airlines for businesspeople versus vacationers? (Hint: Use the same type of reasoning as in the case of long-distance phone service.) What about different charges for adult and child moviegoers? In all of these and other cases, the firm with market power can increase its revenue by charging higher prices to the group with inelastic demand and by charging lower prices to the group with elastic demand. In such a fashion, the price-discriminating firm can increase its overall profits.

CHAPTER 9 ROADMAP

Chapter 12
Agriculture
Agricultural products are major U.S. exports

Inelastic demand and fluctuating supply characterize U.S. agriculture as well as commodity exports of poor countries

Chapter 14
Unemployment and Inflation
Americans worry about the effect of trade on U.S. jobs

Trade is linked to immigration, which is linked to U.S. employment issues

Chapter 3
The Environment
Environmental protection is an increasingly controversial aspect of trade

Chapter 9
International Trade

Chapter 15
Government Macroeconomic Policy
Exports minus imports is part of aggregate demand

Chapter 8
Market Power
Market power of U.S. firms is reduced by international trade

U.S. market power leads to problems of trade for poor nations

Chapter 7
World Poverty
World poverty is related to international trade relations

Chapter 17
Globally Free Markets for the Twenty-First Century?
What is the controversy over globalism and trade?

What is the global effect of trade?

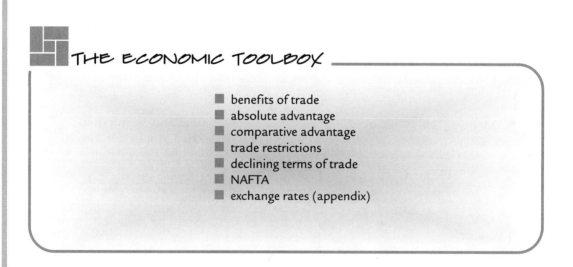

THE ECONOMIC TOOLBOX

- benefits of trade
- absolute advantage
- comparative advantage
- trade restrictions
- declining terms of trade
- NAFTA
- exchange rates (appendix)

INTERNATIONAL TRADE

For to what purpose is all the toil and bustle of this world?

—Adam Smith, *Theory of Moral Sentiments*, 1759

The year was 1999. The place was Seattle. Widespread protests broke out amid clouds of tear gas in the air and battalions of police in the streets. Environmentalists, human rights protesters, and labor activists were there. The target of the demonstrations? The World Trade Organization, on the occasion of its opening meeting to prepare for the policy discussions of the year.

The time, the place, and the setting were unusual. Now they have become commonplace. Rarely does a meeting of the World Bank, the International Monetary Fund (IMF), or the World Trade Organization (WTO) take place without their attendant protesters. Suddenly, demonstrations against these international organizations are on the nightly news, the daily newspapers, *Time* magazine, and the Internet. Demonstrators are protesting against sweatshops, environmental destruction, unsafe working conditions, child labor, unemployment, firm shutdowns, and a host of other problems perceived to be the result of the global economic system as "managed" by the international organizations responsible for the rules of the game across much of the globe.

We know that the world is becoming increasingly internationalized. As communications and transportation improve, we become more and more linked to other parts of the globe. Through imports, we consume products such as cocoa and bananas that we could never produce domestically. Through exports, we create jobs for our citizens. The World Bank, the IMF, and the WTO are now becoming household words. International investment takes place at a frantic pace. Multinational corporations

EconDebate

"Does the U.S. Economy Benefit from the WTO?"

Find out whether free international trade benefits or harms the U.S. economy by navigating to the International Trade category.

http://econapps. swlearning.com

locate subsidiaries in remote parts of the world. Chances are good that you will one day work for a company involved in international business. On your own computer, you can communicate around the globe by electronic mail in a matter of seconds. On your own campus, international faculty teach you and students from abroad share your classes. You are undoubtedly becoming more aware of international issues.

Yet many Americans seem reluctant to think "internationally." We see the world as complex and confusing, and sometimes refuse to think of matters beyond our own backyard. Why is international economics so intimidating? Is it because it's so foreign: foreign countries, foreign currency, and foreign terminology? It's a mistake for us to retreat to the familiar, for the world will march on without us, and international economics will grow increasingly important in our lives. And, as you will discover, international economics is not as complicated as you might think. The next several pages will convince you of that. Last, you'll find that by inserting phrases like "the dollar traded high today" into your everyday conversation, you'll soon be impressing your friends and relatives!

In this chapter, we'll focus on issues surrounding international trade. Along the way, we'll discover some of the trade issues that culminate in the controversy we've described. We'll also discover the importance of trade as an offset to the problem of market power discussed in Chapter 8. Finally, in the appendix, we'll discover the basics of international finance, which is the means of paying for internationally traded goods. So, let's begin.

THE IMPORTANCE OF TRADE

Exports
The value of goods and services sold to foreigners.

Imports
The value of goods and services purchased from foreigners.

Trade balance
The value of a nation's exports minus its imports.

Over time in the United States, we have seen the increasing importance of international trade in terms of the dollar size of our exports and imports. Our **exports** are the value of goods and services that we sell to foreigners, whereas our **imports** are the value of goods and services we buy from them. A good way to consider our exports and our imports is in terms of their share of gross domestic product (GDP). Recall that GDP is the value of our nation's production. As a share of GDP, our exports increased from 4 percent in 1960 to 11 percent in 2000, and then declined to 7 percent in 2001.[1] Our imports increased from 3 percent of gross domestic product in 1960 to 15 percent in 2000, and then declined to 12 percent in 2001. Our exports plus imports as a share of GDP are 19 percent. This number shows the importance of international trade in our economy. Our exports minus imports is our **trade balance**, valued at −5 percent of GDP ($7\% - 12\% = -5\%$). The negative number means that we have a **trade deficit** of 5 percent of GDP. If a country has more exports than imports, the trade balance is positive. We refer to this as a **trade surplus**. Table 9-1 displays data for a diverse group of countries around the world. We have not included a sufficient number of countries to discern any patterns, but column 4 reveals that international trade plays a very large role in some countries and a much smaller role in others. From the table, we can see that the importance of trade to the United States is much less than it is to many other countries. Column 5 shows that some countries have a trade deficit, whereas others have a trade surplus.

The statistics show that international trade is important for the United States, and increasingly so. But is this situation good or bad? To answer this question, we must consider the benefits of trade.

TABLE 9-1 Exports, Imports, Exports Plus Imports, and Trade Balance (Exports Minus Imports), as a Share of GDP, in Selected Countries, 2001

Country	Exports (% of GDP)	Imports (% of GDP)	Exports + Imports (% of GDP)	Exports − Imports (% of GDP)
Thailand	56	52	108	4
Ghana	32	57	89	−25
Canada	39	34	73	5
Nigeria	46	25	71	21
Saudi Arabia	39	19	58	20
Mexico	26	29	55	−3
France	25	25	50	0
Russia	32	17	49	15
Burkina Faso	9	23	32	−14
United States	7	12	19	−5
Argentina	10	8	18	2
Egypt	4	13	17	−9

Source: Data from World Bank, World Development Report 2003 *(New York: Oxford University Press, 2003).*

THE BENEFITS OF TRADE

Forget about the international environment for a moment, and think about yourself as a producer and consumer. Imagine: What would life be like if you tried to produce everything you need and want? You would grow your own food, build your own house, sew your own clothes, and teach yourself economics! Or you could try to specialize in something you're particularly good at, maybe accounting or computer programming, and then earn a living at this task. You could use your income to purchase all of the other things that you need and want.

Most of us would agree pretty quickly that we are better off specializing in what we are good at and exchanging our income for the things that we want to consume. Why? Because we are simply not very good at producing everything that we need. Some of us would spend so much time figuring out how to bake bread or fix the plumbing that we would never get around to any other activities. Far more efficient for me to teach economics, hire a plumber, and stop at the bakery!

This way of thinking is an appropriate analogy for individual countries trying to determine whether to engage in international trade. A country might try to be self-sufficient; that is, to produce everything that its people need and want. Indeed, politicians in many countries have advocated this goal from time to time. It sounds so strong and independent! But like an individual, a country can specialize in the production of a limited number of products that it is especially good at producing. It can then export these products and use the resulting income to import the other things that its people desire. Just like the individual, the country will gain from specialization and exchange.

More specifically, what is the source of these benefits? You now have some idea, but we need to be more precise than simply saying we ought to specialize in the

Trade deficit
The amount by which a nation's trade balance is in deficit (imports exceed exports).

Trade surplus
The amount by which a nation's trade balance is in surplus (exports exceed imports).

activities at which we are good. Exactly what do we mean by being "good at it"? The answers lie in the concepts of absolute and comparative advantage.

Absolute Advantage

Absolute advantage is defined as a situation whereby a country can produce a good at a lower resource cost than another country. Resources include labor, land, capital, and so on. Note that we are comparing the resource cost of producing a good in one country with the resource cost of producing the good in another country. Consider the United States and Brazil as examples. Brazil has a climate and land type far more beneficial to the growing of coffee than does the United States. Someone might be able to devise a climate control system that would allow coffee to be produced in the United States, but it would be very difficult to do so, and it would entail a high resource cost. Brazil can produce coffee at a lower resource cost.

On the other hand, the United States is better suited for the growing of barley than is Brazil. Proper land, weather, machinery, and technology allow the United States to produce barley at a lower resource cost than Brazil. We say that Brazil has an absolute advantage in coffee production (compared with the United States), whereas the United States has an absolute advantage in barley production (compared with Brazil). It would be far more reasonable for the United States to devote its resources to barley production (rather than to produce both barley and coffee) and then exchange with Brazil to acquire coffee. With the United States specializing in barley and Brazil specializing in coffee, both countries are producing more total output than if each country tried to produce both goods. Larger total output means larger total consumption: each country could benefit from specialization and trade.

Comparative Advantage

The situation we just described presents a fairly obvious example of the benefits of trade. A country need not possess absolute advantage as described previously to garner these benefits, however. Consider a situation in which one country enjoys an absolute advantage in the production of two goods, and another country possesses an absolute advantage in none. Suppose, for example, that the United States can produce both floppy disks and shoes at a lower resource cost than Greenland. Should the United States produce both floppy disks and shoes or specialize in production of one good and trade with Greenland for the other good? To answer this question, we need to consider the concept of comparative advantage.

Comparative advantage is defined as a situation whereby a country can produce a good at a lower opportunity cost than another country. Notice the similarity to absolute advantage. We are comparing two countries and two goods. However, the term *resource cost* is replaced with *opportunity cost*. This difference is important. Recall from Chapter 1 that opportunity cost refers to that which you give up in order to get something else. That is, to produce some amount of one good, a country must give up the opportunity for some production of another good. Resources are limited; when they are put into one use, they cannot be put into another. Let's be more specific.

Suppose that labor is the only resource used in producing floppy disks and shoes and that workers receive identical daily wages (two simplifying assumptions). Let's

TABLE 9-2 United States and Greenland Production of Floppy Disks or Shoes per Day, per Worker

Country	Floppy Disk Production	Shoe Production (pairs)
United States	8	4
Greenland	2	2

According to the table, each worker in the United States can produce either eight floppy disks or four pairs of shoes per day. Each worker in Greenland can produce either two floppy disks or two pairs of shoes per day. This means that, compared with Greenland, the United States has an absolute advantage in the production of both floppy disks and shoes.

assume that each worker in the United States can produce either eight floppy disks or four pairs of shoes per day (or some combination in between), and that each worker in Greenland can produce either two floppy disks or two pairs of shoes per day (or some combination in between). This information is displayed in Table 9-2.

Clearly, the United States has an absolute advantage in the production of both floppy disks and shoes. Because each worker in the United States can produce more floppies and more shoes than each worker in Greenland, the resource cost of producing both of these goods will be lowest in the United States.

But let's think in terms of comparative advantage. The opportunity cost of producing eight floppy disks in the United States is the four pairs of shoes that will not be produced. Or put another way, the opportunity cost of producing each two floppies in the United States is one pair of shoes (a 2:1 ratio). On the other hand, the opportunity cost of producing two floppy disks in Greenland is the two pairs of shoes that will not be produced (a 1:1 ratio). In terms of forgone shoe production, the United States has a lower opportunity cost than Greenland for floppy disk production. One floppy disk requires that we give up only one-half pair of shoes, whereas Greenland gives up a whole pair of shoes for each floppy disk. Because the United States gives up fewer shoes when producing floppy disks, it has the comparative advantage in floppy disk production.

Now consider the production of shoes. The opportunity cost of producing four pairs of shoes in the United States is the eight floppy disks that will not be produced. Put another way, the opportunity cost of producing two pairs of shoes is four floppy disks (a 1:2 ratio). On the other hand, the opportunity cost of producing two pairs of shoes in Greenland is only two floppy disks (a 1:1 ratio). In terms of forgone floppy disk production, Greenland has the lower opportunity cost for shoe production. That is, Greenland has the comparative advantage in shoe production.

What this means is that if the United States specializes in floppy disk production, and Greenland specializes in shoe production, the two countries will be able to come up with a rate of exchange in trade that will be mutually beneficial. The rate of four floppy disks in exchange for three pairs of shoes would benefit both countries, for example. Greenland could receive four floppy disks from the United States by selling three pairs of shoes in exchange. This is a more effective strategy than Greenland trying to produce the four floppy disks, for it would then have to give up four pairs of shoes in production (the 1:1 ratio). The United States could receive three pairs of shoes from Greenland by selling the four floppy disks in exchange. This is a

Absolute advantage A situation whereby a country can produce a good at a lower resource cost than another country.

Comparative advantage A situation whereby a country can produce a good at a lower opportunity cost than another country.

more effective strategy than the United States trying to produce the three pairs of shoes, for it would then have to give up six floppy disks in production (the 1:2 ratio). Each country can trade at a rate of exchange that is superior to the opportunity costs associated with domestic production. (Notice that this discussion is theoretical, since Greenland can only produce two of either goods in one year. It is realistic if we extend the time period to more than one year or consider more than two countries.)

Why shouldn't the United States produce both floppy disks and shoes? After all, it can produce both goods at a lower resource cost than Greenland. But by specializing in floppy disk production, the United States can obtain more floppy disks and shoes than if it tried to produce them both. This outcome can be easily illustrated by the production possibilities curve, a technique with which you are already familiar.

Recall from Chapter 1 that the production possibilities curve shows alternative combinations of the maximum amounts of two different products that can be produced by one economy, during a particular time period when resources are fully and efficiently utilized. Notice that the production possibilities curve in Figure 9-1 shows that each worker in the United States can produce either eight floppy disks or four pairs of shoes (or some combination in between) per day. (We could multiply these numbers by the number of workers in the United States to obtain the total number of floppy disks and shoes that the United States could produce, and end up with a

FIGURE 9-1 Production Possibilities for Each U.S. Worker per Day, No Trade

The production possibilities curve shows alternative combinations of the maximum amounts of two products that can be produced by one country (or one worker in a country) during a particular time period. This graph shows that each U.S. worker can produce either 8 floppy disks or 4 pairs of shoes (or some combination in between) per day.

more conventional production possibilities curve.) In the absence of trade, the United States cannot consume more floppy disks and shoes than it produces.

Now let us introduce the possibility of trade. Suppose the United States decides to specialize in floppy disk production because this is where it has its comparative advantage. Further, suppose that the United States agrees with Greenland to trade at the rate of exchange of four floppy disks for three pairs of shoes. Again, this trade ratio is arbitrary but is chosen as representative of a ratio that will benefit each country. This situation is displayed in Figure 9-2, with the production possibilities curve of Figure 9-1 repeated for convenience. Note that if the United States produces at point A (reflecting specialization in the production of eight floppy disks), it can move to alternative points along a new curve, which we might call a **consumption possibilities curve** with trade.

The United States, for example, may decide to sell four floppy disks to Greenland (back up four floppy disks from point A to A′) in exchange for three pairs of shoes (move up three pairs of shoes from A′), moving its consumption point back up along the consumption possibilities curve to point B (at which the United States ends up with four floppy disks and three pairs of shoes). Alternatively, the United States might sell another four floppy disks (back up four more floppy disks from point B

Consumption possibilities curve
A curve that shows alternative combinations of the maximum amounts of two products that can be consumed within a country during a particular time period.

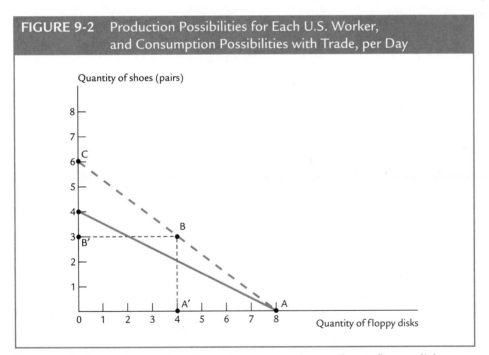

FIGURE 9-2   Production Possibilities for Each U.S. Worker, and Consumption Possibilities with Trade, per Day

This graph shows that each U.S. worker can produce either 8 floppy disks or 4 pairs of shoes (or some combination in between) per day. With no trade, the United States would be restricted to consuming amounts indicated along the production possibilities curve. With trade, and a trade ratio of 4 floppy disks for 3 pairs of shoes, the United States can consume along the higher consumption possibilities curve.

to B′) in exchange for another three pairs of shoes (move up three more pairs of shoes from B′), moving its consumption point back up along the curve to point C (at which the United States ends up with no floppy disks and six pairs of shoes). With the exception of point A, the United States is better off at all points along the dashed consumption possibilities curve made possible through specialization and trade than along the production possibilities curve in the absence of trade. We could draw a similar graph for Greenland, indicating the same types of benefits through specialization in shoe production and trade with the United States for floppies.

The Basis for Advantage

Why is one country better at producing a good than another country? Whether we're thinking in terms of absolute or comparative advantage, there are some basic reasons why one country will have the advantage. Some obvious factors are weather and climate. Sometimes weather and climate can be overcome (through the use of greenhouses to produce tomatoes, for example), but extraordinary efforts to overcome natural factors may entail a high resource cost. This high cost will give the advantage to the country with the more favorable natural conditions.

Labor is another important factor in determining advantage. A country with higher labor productivity might have an advantage in producing goods that require a large amount of labor input. Factors that contribute to labor productivity include the obvious ones, such as labor training and education, but other factors may be even more important. Sophisticated capital equipment and technology used in conjunction with labor will greatly enhance labor productivity. U.S. workers tend to be very productive because they are well trained and educated *and* because they often work with modern capital and technology.

When considering labor costs, both productivity and wages are important. Suppose that one worker in Gambia is paid the equivalent of $5 per hour and can produce 5 baskets per hour. Suppose that one worker in the United States is paid twice the wage rate, or $10 per hour, but can produce twice the baskets, or 10 baskets per hour. Which country has the higher labor cost? Neither! The labor cost of producing each basket is identical in each country ($1 per basket). Labor costs in the United States and Gambia are identical because the U.S. worker receives twice the wage but is also twice as productive. This productivity factor is important to keep in mind when there is talk about cheap foreign labor. It is cheap only if productivity is high and wages remain low. People often complain about U.S. workers losing jobs to cheap foreign labor. Do you see now how this may be untrue?

Other factors determining advantage include the quality and availability of land, capital equipment, technology, and other resource inputs. Singapore, for example, has scarce land, hence extremely high land costs. Such a country would not have an advantage in the production of most agricultural products.

All of the Benefits of Trade

Whew! The most basic benefits of trade are the gains from specialization according to absolute or comparative advantage that we have just discussed. Such specialization leads to greater output from limited resources and to benefits to each trading nation and the world as a whole. Some additional benefits are also important. Consumers receive a greater diversity of products and more choice among competing brands than they would if purchasing only domestic goods. We know you are choosy among brands when buying your compact disc player or your personal computer and that your choices include foreign products!

Furthermore, the increased competition among firms made possible by trade will reduce the likelihood and degree of market power, benefiting society. Recall from the previous chapter that concentration and market power within an industry result in lower output levels (and lower employment), less efficient production, and higher prices to consumers. Increased international competition reduces the probability of these negative outcomes by reducing concentration within the industry. Instead of only three major automakers, many automobile companies sell to the U.S. market. Larger numbers of firms have less ability to raise prices and restrict output.[2]

THE DISTRIBUTION OF BENEFITS

Economic theory clearly indicates that individual nations benefit from trade as they specialize according to their advantage, but we must realize that not all people within the country benefit from trade. Although the country as a whole becomes better off, there will be some gainers and some losers within the country. That is, the benefits of trade will not be distributed equally. This unequal distribution is one of the concerns about free trade.

We can see the distribution of benefits from trade if we consider a simple graph for a country as it moves from a no-trade situation to a situation in which it begins to import a product (the free trade situation). Let's consider the United States and the market for cotton cloth. The only assumptions we need to make to keep the analysis simple are that (1) all cotton cloth is identical whether produced in the United States or elsewhere, and (2) the United States is a large producer of cotton cloth. Consider Figure 9-3, in which D and S represent the hypothetical domestic demand and supply curves, respectively, for cotton cloth in the United States. Equilibrium at point E (with the corresponding price of $1 per yard and the quantity of 1,000 yards) reflects the situation in which the United States engages in no international trade of cotton cloth.

Now suppose the United States begins importing cotton cloth into the country. D will continue to represent the domestic demand (that is, the demand for cotton cloth by U.S. consumers) and S will continue to represent the domestic supply (that is, the supply of cotton cloth by U.S. producers). But note the new supply curve S^T as well. S^T represents the total free trade supply curve for cotton cloth. It includes all of the supply represented by the domestic supply curve S, plus additional supply by foreign countries. (Hence, the curve is drawn by simply shifting the domestic supply curve forward; that is, by increasing it.) The new supply curve S^T now becomes the relevant curve for determining equilibrium price and quantity consumed under the free trade situation. At the new equilibrium point E^T, determined by the intersection of D and S^T, the new free trade price is $0.75 per yard, and the quantity consumed is 1,500 yards. This new price is lower, representing an improved situation for U.S. consumers of cotton cloth. The new quantity consumed is higher, indicating

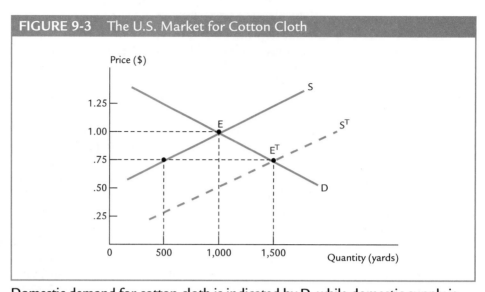

FIGURE 9-3   The U.S. Market for Cotton Cloth

Domestic demand for cotton cloth is indicated by D, while domestic supply is indicated by S. In the absence of trade, equilibrium is at point E, with the corresponding price of $1 per yard and quantity of 1,000 yards. As the United States begins to import cotton cloth, D continues to represent domestic demand, white S^T represents the total free trade supply curve. The new equilibrium is E^T. Equilibrium price falls to $0.75 per yard, quantity consumed increases to 1,500 yards, and quantity produced domestically falls to 500 yards.

EconNews

"A Tariff-ic Proposal?"

The World Bank and International Monetary Fund are trying to allow some of the poorest African and Latin American nations to sell their goods in the United States and other Western industrialized nations without tariffs or quotas. Why is the U.S. administration against this opportunity for economic growth? Find out by clicking the International Trade link.

http://econapps. swlearning.com

that consumers are now purchasing larger quantities of cloth. Clearly, consumers of cotton cloth gain from trade.

Consider U.S. producers of cotton cloth, however. Although the new supply curve S^T is the relevant curve for determining equilibrium price and quantity consumed under free trade, the old supply curve S is still the relevant curve for representing the supply decisions of domestic suppliers. At the new lower price of $0.75, domestic suppliers reduce the quantity they produce to 500 yards (the new domestic quantity supplied). Note that U.S. consumers are buying a quantity of 1,500 yards and U.S. suppliers are selling a quantity of 500 yards; the difference between them is made up by imports of cotton cloth into the country. U.S. producers of cotton cloth are harmed by free trade: they receive a lower price for their product, and they now sell a smaller quantity. Both the individual cloth companies and the workers for these companies (who may experience layoffs) lose as a result of trade.

Even though the benefits of trade accrue to the United States as a whole and to U.S. consumers of cotton cloth in particular, U.S. producers of cotton cloth are harmed. The effects of free trade are summarized in Table 9-3. It is the U.S. producers of cotton cloth (firms and workers) who will argue most vehemently in favor of trade restrictions. To the extent that these producers are politically powerful (typically more powerful than unorganized consumers), the U.S. government may respond to their appeals with a variety of trade restrictions.

TABLE 9-3	The Effects of Free Trade in Cotton Cloth Imports into the United States	
Effects of Free Trade on:	**Effect**	**Reason**
The United States as a whole	Gain	Efficiency through specialization and exchange according to comparative advantage, greater diversity of product, reduced market power
U.S. consumers of cotton cloth	Gain	Lower price and increased quantity consumed
U.S. firms producing cotton cloth	Lose	Lower price and decreased quantity supplied
U.S. workers producing cotton cloth	Lose	Jobs lost as cotton cloth production decreases

RESTRICTIONS TO FREE TRADE

Two common types of trade restrictions are quotas and tariffs. A **quota** is a restriction on the quantity of an imported good. A quota on sugar, for example, means that only a limited amount of sugar from other countries will be allowed to enter the United States. Once this quota is met, Americans will be forced to buy U.S.-produced sugar, or to go without. A **tariff** does not limit the quantity of an imported good but is simply a tax imposed on the imported product. A tariff on Canadian whiskey coming into the United States would serve to raise the price of the product (in this case, the Canadian whiskey) to American consumers, making them more likely to purchase American whiskey.

Quota
A restriction on the quantity of an imported good.

Tariff
A tax on an imported good.

The purpose of most U.S. trade restrictions is to force or encourage American consumers to buy more American-made products and fewer foreign counterparts. They are thus designed to protect American producers, despite the fact that the resulting trade barriers reduce the benefits of free trade that would otherwise accrue to our country. Trade restrictions on cotton cloth imports cause the price of cotton cloth to rise, thereby benefiting U.S. cloth producers (firms and workers) and hurting U.S. cloth consumers. (In the extreme case of a trade restriction that would totally prohibit imports of cotton cloth into the United States, we would revert back to the original demand and supply curves in Figure 9-3, a situation in which prices to consumers increase, smaller quantities are consumed, and larger quantities are supplied domestically.) The fact that we have many trade restrictions means either that American producers are more powerful in protecting their interests than American consumers, or that American consumers do not understand the consequences of trade restrictions for their own well-being. Both of these situations probably exist.

Trade restrictions have powerful effects beyond the ones discussed previously with respect to producers and consumers. The nation as a whole will lose the benefits of specialization and exchange according to advantage. Competition within protected industries will decrease because foreign competition among producers is lessened. Consequently, domestic producers will have more market power. (As we know, increased market power may cause output within the concentrated industry to fall. If firms produce less output, they may hire fewer workers, suggesting that workers

TABLE 9-4	Effects of Trade Restrictions on Imports of Cotton Cloth into the United States	
Effects of Trade Restrictions on:	**Effect**	**Reason**
The United States as a whole	Lose	Loss of efficiency through specialization and exchange according to comparative advantage, less diversity of product, greater market power
U.S. consumers of cotton cloth	Lose	Higher price and decreased quantity consumed
U.S. firms producing cotton cloth	Gain	Higher price and increased quantity supplied
U.S. workers producing cotton cloth	Gain	Jobs gained as cotton cloth production increases
U.S. producers of export goods	Lose	Loss of export sales

within concentrated U.S. industries, such as the American automobile industry, may falsely have been convinced that trade restrictions would protect their jobs. A graph like that of the cotton cloth industry may not accurately reflect workers' interests in the case of a concentrated industry with market power.)

And finally, producers within other industries, in particular our export industries, will likely suffer as a result of trade restrictions. If the United States imposes quotas on imports of cotton cloth, U.S. producers of wheat and corn for export may see their foreign sales decline. This sales drop may occur for a variety of reasons. First, other countries may respond to U.S. trade restrictions with restrictions of their own. This action is called **retaliation**. If the United States limits imports of cotton cloth, Sri Lanka, for example, may limit imports of U.S. corn. Moreover, incomes of foreign producers of cotton cloth may fall as the United States restricts its purchases. As the incomes of Sri Lankans fall, they will be less able to purchase U.S. corn. And finally, U.S. trade restrictions will affect the value of the U.S. dollar relative to foreign currencies. The change in this value will likely reduce U.S. exports, as indicated in the appendix to this chapter. Table 9-4 summarizes the effects of U.S. trade restrictions on cotton cloth imports.

Because U.S. producers (workers and firms) of cotton cloth are the only beneficiaries of trade restrictions and because the rest of the United States suffers, perhaps we should seek better ways to deal with the hardships suffered by these producers when we freely import cotton cloth. If other countries have the advantage in cotton cloth production, encouraging continued production by U.S. firms means supporting relatively inefficient industries. The United States does not really benefit in the long run. But, rather than leaving these U.S. firms and workers to suffer their losses through trade, we might seek solutions that improve the efficiency of U.S. industry (for example, through subsidies for research and development) or that retrain workers for and redirect firms into production of more advantageous goods. The latter solution is pursued under the North American Free Trade Agreement, which is discussed shortly. Do keep in mind the main point, however, that the United States as a whole benefits when importing products in which it does not have a comparative advantage. If a reason for the lack of comparative advantage is cheap foreign labor, then the United States as a whole benefits from cheap foreign labor.

Retaliation
A situation in which one country responds to the trade restrictions of another country by imposing trade restrictions of its own.

EconNews

"Going Bananas over Steel"

Read more about quotas, tariffs, and trade restrictions by navigating to International Trade.

http://econapps. swlearning.com

THE REST OF THE CONTROVERSY

U.S. job and business loss was one of the concerns underlying the Seattle and subsequent protests. It was not the only concern, however. Many of the issues are much broader and involve economic justice throughout the world. These global issues involve trade in less-developed countries, the politics of trade, and international trade agreements.

Less-Developed Countries

People of less-developed countries (LDCs) are among those who are sometimes hurt by trade. These poor countries of the world have experienced problems with trade, even when carefully following the economic theory of specialization according to comparative advantage. One problem is related to the lack of diversity in exports. Costa Rica, for example, relies on coffee exports for a large share of its export earnings. Yet, if bad weather significantly harms the coffee crop, or if international prices of coffee fall dramatically, the Costa Rican economy could be devastated. It would be better not to specialize so completely. Greater diversity of exports would provide some insurance against problems that might beset one particular product. In the meantime, however, poor countries are vulnerable to national and international circumstances that are largely beyond their control.

Another closely related problem concerns the reliance of many LDCs on primary commodities for export. **Primary commodities** are unprocessed raw materials or agricultural products, such as coffee, sugar, tea, cocoa, and rubber.

These types of products have experienced a problem known as **declining terms of trade**. Over time, the prices of poor-country exports (especially primary commodities) have declined relative to the prices of poor-country imports. Declining terms of trade is a long-term phenomenon, whereas price fluctuation is a problem in the short term. Demand for poor-country exports has tapered off (and therefore price of the exports has decreased), in part because of the development of synthetics and developed-country trade restrictions. At the same time, the prices of manufactured goods and petroleum products imported into poor countries have generally increased (because of market power in developed-country industry and the market power of the Organization of Petroleum Exporting Countries). As a result, poor-country export earnings have declined relative to poor-country expenditures for imports. This situation has undermined poor developing countries' attempts to import needed products and repay international debt, as discussed in Chapter 17. It has also made it necessary for LDCs to exploit natural resources, such as timber, as a source of export earnings. This practice has led to environmental degradation.

Another problem related to primary commodities is their instability. Prices for these types of products are often very unstable. This instability is related to two common characteristics of primary commodity markets. Consider the hypothetical market for coffee depicted in Figure 9-4. The demand curve is drawn fairly steep, suggesting that demand is inelastic. Recall from Chapter 2 that **inelastic demand** exists when consumers are relatively unresponsive to changes in price. That is, they do not alter the quantity they purchase very much when there is a price change. A steep demand curve reflects this small change in quantity relative to price. Compare the percentage change in quantity demanded between points A and B, for example, with the larger percentage change in price

Primary commodities
Unprocessed raw material and agricultural products.

Declining terms of trade
A situation in which the price of a country's exports declines relative to the price of its imports.

Inelastic demand
Demand in which buyers are relatively unresponsive to changes in price.

FIGURE 9-4 The Demand for Coffee

Price ($)

Quantity (thousands of pounds)

In the coffee market, the demand curve D is drawn relatively steep. This reflects an inelastic demand for coffee. Notice that a large increase in price from $1 to $2 (a 100 percent increase) is associated with just a small decrease in quantity demanded from 5,000 to 4,000 pounds (a 20 percent decrease).

between these two points. Quantity demanded falls from 5,000 pounds to 4,000 pounds (a 20 percent reduction) when price rises from $1 to $2 per pound (a 100 percent increase).

Inelastic demand characterizes the markets for many primary commodities. It makes sense in the coffee market, for when coffee prices rise, the coffee drinkers among us will be reluctant to reduce our consumption of coffee by very much. We are creatures of habit, especially when it comes to our caffeine consumption. The same is true for other commodities, such as tea and tobacco.

Another characteristic of markets for primary commodities is a fluctuating supply. The supply of many primary commodities is heavily dependent on weather, and weather tends to fluctuate a lot.

The combination of fluctuating supply and inelastic demand results in a large fluctuation in price, as is evident in Figure 9-5. (Experiment a little: redraw the graph with a relatively flat demand curve, yet identical fluctuation in supply. You will see that the price will no longer fluctuate as much.) Price fluctuation is a short-term phenomenon. That is, prices fluctuate from year to year, just as weather fluctuates from year to year. (We will revisit this issue in Chapter 12 when we consider the markets for U.S. agricultural products.)

This fluctuation in price can be very detrimental for countries producing primary commodities for export. Although prices may average to an acceptable medium, the fluctuation is hard to deal with. A producer might go out of business entirely, and a country may have its export earnings plummet in a particularly bad year. These potential outcomes have led to some developing countries' attempts to join together in commodity agreements that seek to stabilize commodity prices. These agreements have met with mixed success.

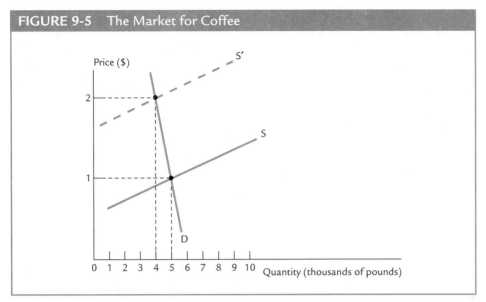

FIGURE 9-5   The Market for Coffee

The demand for coffee D is inelastic, while supply fluctuates from S to S'
from one year to the next. The combination of inelastic demand and
fluctuating supply results in large fluctuations in price, from $1 to $2 per
pound (a 100 percent increase).

An additional trade problem for poor countries is the possibility of overreliance on important imports from other countries. According to the theory of comparative advantage, a country is better off importing a good in which it lacks an advantage, but what if the importation of an essential product becomes unreliable? When international food prices skyrocketed in the early 1970s, developing countries dependent on food imports found themselves priced out of the market. Hundreds of thousands of people starved to death throughout the less-developed world. When international oil prices quadrupled during the 1970s, many poor oil-importing countries could no longer afford basic energy inputs. Often, imports may become unreliable for other than economic reasons: supplies may be cut off for political reasons, or shipping and transportation systems may be disrupted because of adverse weather, civil unrest, and war. We have repeatedly observed this dynamic in many African countries.

Finally, globalization has created opportunities for local and foreign companies to exploit local workers, including children, in the production of goods for export in many LDCs. This practice has especially been publicized in the garment and carpet industries. Most recently, the issue of "cocoa slavery" has arisen in the west African country of Côte D'Ivoire, where adults and children are in effect forced into slavery in the production of cocoa. Many of us are now becoming aware of our role as consumers, when we purchase items produced in so-called sweatshops and slave conditions. Our buying decisions may indeed affect the practices of international companies.[3]

All of these issues suggest that poor nations must be very careful as they plan their development strategies. Comparative advantage ought to be an important element of such strategies, but attention must also be directed to proper diversification and processing of commodity exports because processed goods are less vulnerable to trade restrictions and declining terms of trade. Wealthier countries must ensure that trade is fair and that their own trade restrictions on poor countries are reduced. In addition, wealthy countries and companies must accept their share of responsibility when their policies and profits encourage environmental degradation and unjust labor conditions.

Politics and Trade

Although international trade is an economic issue, it has often become politicized. The United States became the victim of politics during the Arab Oil Embargo in 1974 and the Iranian Oil Embargo of 1979. In each case, oil was cut off from the United States, causing an energy crisis in our nation.

Sometimes the United States restricts trade to bring about political goals. It commonly restricts trade with communist countries. Cuba is a case in point. In 1959, the Cuban revolution created a socialist economy headed by Fidel Castro, who initiated the nationalization (government confiscation) of U.S. property in Cuba. The United States responded with a **trade embargo**, as well as subsequent policies to "punish" some of the countries that trade with Cuba. The embargo has severely harmed the well-being of the Cuban nation and its people. Many people in the United States are opposed to Cuba's socialist economic system and communist political system, and they charge the Castro government with violating the human rights of Cuban people. Many others feel that far from violating human rights, Cuba has provided high-quality health care and education to all of its residents, despite the severe poverty of the country.

Efforts have been under way in the United States to reduce the trade restrictions of the embargo. In June 2000, the U.S. House of Representatives struck a deal to allow the sale of food and medicine to Cuba (under highly restricted conditions) for the first time in four decades. President Bill Clinton signed this bill a few months later. The agreement allows U.S. exports of similar goods to four other countries under embargo by the U.S. government: Iran, Sudan, Libya, and North Korea. In the case of North Korea, the embargo had been in effect since the early days of the Korean War in 1950. The new plan allowed U.S. firms to sell goods, especially farm products, to North Korea and allowed that nation to sell raw materials and finished goods to the United States. More recently, under the George W. Bush administration, the efforts to improve trade relations with these countries have tapered off or halted entirely.

China and Vietnam are two other countries whose trade relations with the United States have been improving. Both countries have socialist economies in partial transition to capitalism. Vietnam, like Cuba, provides its entire people with health care and education. Yet, both Vietnam and China have communist political systems that are opposed by the United States. China has a long history of human rights violations, which angers many U.S. citizens and makes them hostile toward the easing of trade restrictions. Many feel that maintaining trade restrictions is the only leverage that the United States has for improving human rights in China. Others argue that only through normalized relations will improvements be generated. They argue that free trade would benefit both the United States and China.

Those in the latter camp believe that free trade will improve not only trade relations but also other relations between the United States and foreign countries. Op-

Trade embargo
Restrictions on trade with another country for political reasons.

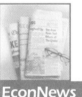

EconNews

"A Supersized NAFTA"

Opposition of free trade echoes debates over NAFTA, loss of jobs, and low-income industries. Why oppose free trade? Read more under the International Trade category.

http://econapps.swlearning.com

portunities for foreign investment may open up. In addition, travel restrictions may fade. Fewer restrictions on immigration may encourage greater intercountry mobility of workers, raising some issues addressed in Chapter 14 on unemployment. All of these topics arise in the debates and protests over globalization.

One final example of politically motivated trade relations involves the disagreement of France over the U.S. position on war in Iraq. Members of the U.S. Congress changed the name of "French fries" to "freedom fries" and many Americans began to boycott French wine, cheese, and other products. Although this response was temporary and limited, it does indeed show the impact of consumers on our trade relations.

International Trade Agreements

The world has been moving in the direction of far-reaching trade agreements. One of the more prominent is the **North American Free Trade Agreement (NAFTA)**. This agreement between the United States, Canada, and Mexico went into effect on January 1, 1994. NAFTA allows each of the three trading countries more equal access to one another's markets, along with reductions in trade restrictions. Congress passed the NAFTA Transitional Adjustment Assistance program to provide worker retraining and assistance to American workers displaced from jobs as a result of NAFTA. As we've already discovered, the United States benefits when importing a product from a country with lower labor costs. Indeed, most economists see benefits to all three of the countries. Nevertheless, there have been some concerns.

A major issue is that some of the lower production costs in Mexico are caused by unfair circumstances. Mexico has less restrictive controls on pollution, minimum wages, child labor, and working conditions in its factories. To deal with these circumstances, so-called side agreements were added to NAFTA, whereby businesses in Mexico are required to comply with child labor laws and laws requiring environmental protection, minimum wages, and safe working conditions. Many people believe that these requirements are inadequate and have been widely ignored,[4] thereby harming the Mexican worker and the Mexican environment. It also leads to concerns about unfair production cost differentials between the United States and Mexico that may be forcing U.S. firms to go out of business or to relocate in Mexico. Ross Perot, a former U.S. presidential candidate, once referred to the potential job loss associated with NAFTA as a "giant sucking sound."

In fact, economists believe that very few U.S. workers have lost jobs and that others have found jobs in our export industries as a result of NAFTA. The Mexican share of U.S. imports did increase, but the Mexican share of U.S. exports increased as well. Ross Perot's "giant sucking sound" seems more like a moderate whisper.

Nevertheless, the problems of pollution and poor working conditions continue in Mexico. These issues of sweatshop labor and environmental destruction are raised in protests against globalization.

The European Union (EU) has continued to reduce trade barriers and other economic restrictions between member countries in Europe, resulting in more open economic relations among them. One of the major recent achievements of the European Union was the adoption of a new common currency, called the **euro**.

In addition to these regional trade agreements, there have also been movements under way to extend the NAFTA accord to Chile and to the United Kingdom and to

North American Free Trade Agreement (NAFTA) An agreement between the United States, Canada, and Mexico allowing more equal access to one another's markets. The agreement went into effect on January 1, 1994.

Euro The common currency of the European Union.

General Agreement on Tariffs and Trade (GATT) An international trade agreement, first negotiated in 1947, that has included efforts to reduce tariff barriers among member countries of the world. It is now replaced by the World Trade Organization.

expand NAFTA into a larger Free Trade Agreement of the Americas. These efforts have not yet been successful. There are a number of other world trade agreements as well, including Mercosur (a trade agreement between Argentina, Brazil, Paraguay, and Uruguay), the Andean Community (a trade agreement between Bolivia, Colombia, Ecuador, Peru, and Venezuela), and ASEAN (a trade agreement between Brunei, Indonesia, Malaysia, Philippines, Singapore, and Thailand).

World Trade Organization (WTO)
The organization that replaced GATT in 1995 and continues to pursue GATT's agenda to reduce barriers to trade among member countries.

Finally, the **General Agreement on Tariffs and Trade (GATT)** was an international trade agreement in effect since World War II. GATT was replaced by the **World Trade Organization (WTO)** in 1995. Several rounds of discussions have taken place within the context of GATT, including the Kennedy Round completed in 1967, the Tokyo Round completed in 1979, and the Uruguay Round completed in 1993. These rounds have been remarkably successful in reducing tariff barriers among member countries of GATT. The average tariff on manufactured goods decreased from 40 percent in 1947 to 5 percent in 1992. The Uruguay Round reduced tariffs still further. The WTO, as the introduction to the chapter indicates, has recently evolved as a target of the Seattle and other protesters.

VIEWPOINT: CONSERVATIVE VERSUS LIBERAL

Historically, the lines have been drawn fairly clearly between traditional conservative and liberal views when it comes to the international economy, particularly in discussions of international trade. Economic conservatives within the United States have generally favored free trade. They have felt that free trade results in the efficiencies that arise in general from free markets. Economic liberals, on the other hand, have been concerned about the effects of free trade on U.S. workers and businesses. They have argued that government intervention in the form of quotas and tariffs is necessary to protect U.S. citizens from "unfair" trade practices in foreign countries. If, for example, foreign businesses keep labor costs artificially low by subjecting their workers to unsafe conditions, they have an unfair cost advantage relative to U.S. businesses. Labor in both the United States and the foreign country suffers.

The line between conservatives and liberals is no longer drawn so clearly. There appears to be much greater consensus that free trade will generally benefit the United States. NAFTA is a case in point. The Clinton administration lobbied hard for the passage of NAFTA, and the legislation received conservative and liberal support. Liberals are probably a bit more concerned about the effect of the trade agreement on U.S. labor and the environment than conservatives.

Development economists and policymakers have traditionally held the same types of views when it comes to the trade relations affecting poor countries. Liberals have feared the problems facing LDC exports, including many of the economic justice issues that have been raised. Conservatives have traditionally focused more on the inefficiencies associated with trade restrictions. They have promoted freer markets for international trade. Liberals and conservatives have generally come together in their attention to market forces and the promotion of exports.

SUMMARY

International trade and finance are becoming increasingly important for the United States, as well as for the rest of the world. Our imports provide important products for U.S. consumers, and our exports provide jobs for our workers. Residents of other countries around the globe benefit from trade in this manner as well. Indeed, as long as countries specialize along the lines of comparative advantage and exchange through trade, the world as a whole produces more output, providing higher total consumption levels for all trading countries.

The benefits of free trade are not equally distributed within a trading country. Although consumers and exporters gain from free trade, companies and workers displaced by imports lose. The plight of the latter parties triggers arguments for trade restrictions. Two common restrictions are quotas and tariffs, which both reduce the economic benefits of trade. As an alternative to trade restrictions, governments might provide direct assistance to and retraining programs for displaced workers and companies.

The theory of specialization and exchange sometimes breaks down in practice, especially in the case of many poor countries. Among the problems that these countries frequently encounter is a lack of diversity of exports, reliance on primary commodities with unstable prices, declining terms of trade, overreliance on essential imports, and economic injustice.

Some trade issues are political, as well as economic, such as politically motivated trade embargoes. Yet, throughout the world, countries have been moving toward far-reaching regional trade agreements, including the North American Free Trade Agreement. This agreement and the General Agreement on Tariffs and Trade (now the World Trade Organization) are aimed at reducing trade restrictions among member countries.

NOTES

1. World Bank, *World Development Report 2000/ 2001* (New York: Oxford University Press, 2001), and previous issues.

2. If the number of mergers of international corporations located in different countries continues to increase, international trade may become less effective in terms of reducing market power.

3. More information on sweatshop labor and slavery in the cocoa trade is available on the Web site of CorpWatch (**www.corpwatch.org**), an educational and activist organization that seeks to "foster democratic control" over global corporations, especially in the areas of human rights, labor rights, and environmental justice.

4. Jacqueline Brux, "Neo-Liberalism in Mexico," 2000.

DISCUSSION QUESTIONS

1. How does international economics affect you directly as a consumer and as a future worker? How do international events and circumstances touch you as a student in a U.S. university or college?

2. Find out about the World Trade Organization by checking out its home page (**www.wto. org/**). Click The WTO (in the menu that runs along the top of the page); then click What is the WTO? Check out the 10 benefits of the

WTO trading system, 10 common misunderstandings about the WTO, and frequently asked questions.

3. Have you ever considered trying to become self-sufficient, producing for yourself all the things that you need and want? What would be the benefits of this attempt? What would be the drawbacks?

4. Look up information about the trade situation of some of the countries listed in Table 9-1 in the CIA World Factbook Web site (**www.odci. gov/cia/publications/factbook**). Select a country, then click the link to the economy, read the Economy Overview, and scroll to the trade statistics. Discover the major exports and imports of the country, along with its trading partners. Is the country in deficit or surplus? What is the effect of warfare in some of the countries? Are there any reasons that statistics may be underreported? Remember this CIA Web site because it will provide you a wealth of information about any specific country that you may research in the future.

5. What are some goods in which you think the United States has an absolute advantage in production? What about low-wage countries such as Thailand and Pakistan? What about tropical countries such as Costa Rica and Cuba?

6. Based on the information in Table 9-2, and assuming a trade ratio of four floppy disks for three pairs of shoes, what would the production possibilities curve (without trade) and the consumption possibilities curve (with trade) look like for Greenland? Does Greenland benefit from specialization and trade?

7. Suppose that the U.S. Congress passes trade restrictions on imports of French wine into the United States. What will be the effect of these restrictions on (a) U.S. consumers of wine, (b) U.S. producers of wine, (c) French producers of wine, (d) U.S. farmers producing agricultural goods for export, and (e) the United States as a whole?

8. Why do U.S. companies and workers within particular industries that are harmed by trade tend to have more political influence than the consumers who benefit from this trade? Do U.S. consumers have a good understanding of how they benefit from trade? Are they a cohesive political lobby?

9. Suppose a concentrated U.S. industry, such as the aluminum industry, is successful in getting trade restrictions on aluminum imports passed through Congress. Because these restrictions will reduce the foreign competition faced by the American aluminum industry, they will also enhance the market power of American firms within this industry. What then is a possible impact of the trade restrictions on U.S. employment within this concentrated industry?

10. What are some of the problems of international trade that are faced by less-developed countries? What suggestions would you have for the government of a less-developed country as it plans its trade strategy?

11. Draw a graph of the market for a product, such as cocoa, but assume that demand for this product does not have inelastic demand (draw the demand curve relatively flat). Now draw in a supply curve that fluctuates from year to year (try to shift the supply curve forward and backward about the same distance as in Figure 9-5). Is the price fluctuation larger or smaller than that depicted in Figure 9-5? What does the answer tell us about less-developed country commodity exports for which demand generally is inelastic?

12. Navigate to the U.S. Department of Labor Web site (**www.dol.gov**), go to the A–Z index, and click Sweatshops. Do you believe that this is an impartial source of information on sweatshop labor? What are some things that you as a consumer can do about sweatshop labor?

13. Read the home page of the Anti-Slavery Organization (**www.antislavery.org**) to find information on the issue of cocoa slavery. What can you as a consumer do about cocoa slavery?

14. Go to the Global March Web site (**global march.org/index.php**), and read about child labor in the world. How extensive is the problem of child labor? How do you think child labor affects the child's daily life? How does it affect the child's future? What about the child's family? How can the use of child labor harm labor markets in both the less-developed countries and the United States? What do you think of an idea of a project that might provide food and even small amounts of money to the families of children who go to school (instead of the job market)?

15. What benefits do you think the United States receives from the North American Free Trade Agreement? What problems do you think the United States experiences as a result of NAFTA? How do you think the United States can benefit from the economic growth of Mexico, which is an expected result of the agreement?

16. (Refer to the appendix to answer this question.) Why would Japanese residents demand U.S. dollars? Why would U.S. residents demand Japanese yen?

CHAPTER 9 APPENDIX: INTERNATIONAL FINANCE

When residents of two countries engage in trade or when they transfer funds for other purposes, they must deal with the matter of foreign currency. If a product is worth $500 in U.S. currency, how much is it worth in terms of Mexican pesos? If I wish to invest my $1,000 in a Japanese company, how many yen does this amount represent? To answer these questions, we need to understand the concept of exchange rates and how these rates are determined.

EXCHANGE RATE DETERMINATION

An **exchange rate** is simply the price of one country's currency in terms of another country's currency. We can say, for example, that 1 U.S. dollar is worth 10.5 Mexican pesos. This is the exchange rate between dollars and pesos.[1] Alternatively, we can say that 1 Mexican peso is worth $0.11 (11 U.S. cents). (This exchange rate is calculated by taking the equation $1 = 10.5 pesos and dividing each side by 10.5. We end up with $1/10.5 = 7 pesos/7; or $0.09 = 1 peso.) The two expressions are identical: we can talk in terms of 10.5 pesos per dollar or 9 cents per peso. Note, however, that an exchange rate always expresses the value of one currency in terms of another. There is no such thing as an absolute value for a currency; exchange rates are always relative.

> **Exchange rate**
> The price of one country's currency in terms of another country's currency.

Most of the industrialized world uses a **flexible (floating) exchange rate system**, in effect since 1973. Under this system, exchange rates are determined on the basis of demand and supply. Using simple techniques with which you are already familiar, we can see how the exchange rate between the dollar and peso is determined.

To simplify matters, pretend that there are only two countries in the world, the United States and Mexico. This oversimplification enables us to use a graph and does not detract from the analysis. Let's consider the market for the dollar and determine the value of the dollar in terms of the Mexican peso. This market is portrayed in Figure 9-6 on page 232.

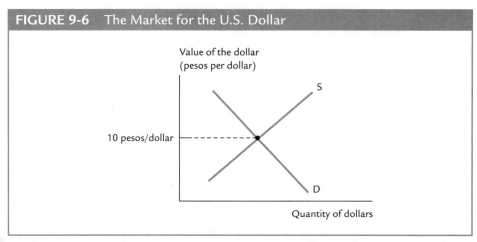

FIGURE 9-6 The Market for the U.S. Dollar

Value of the dollar
(pesos per dollar)

S

10 pesos/dollar

D

Quantity of dollars

Flexible (floating) exchange rate system
A system whereby exchange rates are determined on the basis of international demand and supply for a currency.

The demand curve D represents the demand for U.S. dollars by Mexican residents. The supply curve S represents the supply of U.S. dollars by U.S. residents, which is synonymous with the demand for Mexican pesos by U.S. citizens. The intersection determines the equilibrium price, or exchange rate, between the U.S. dollar and the Mexican peso. This exchange rate is 10 pesos per dollar.

Note the demand curve D is the demand for dollars by Mexico's residents. (Remember that there are only two countries in the world.) Why would Mexico's residents demand dollars? There are a number of reasons. An obvious one is that Mexican people may wish to travel in the United States. They will need to pay their hotel bill and taxi fare in dollars; hence, they first need to exchange their pesos for dollars. This process of acquiring dollars represents a demand for dollars.

There are more important reasons for demanding dollars, however. Suppose a Mexican resident wishes to purchase a General Motors car. GM wants to be paid in dollars. Although the Mexican customer won't need to come up with dollars, the Mexican company that imports the GM vehicle into Mexico will. The process of exchanging pesos in order to acquire dollars with which to purchase the vehicle represents a demand for dollars. Suppose another Mexican resident wishes to invest his savings in a U.S. financial market, perhaps by purchasing a U.S. government or corporate bond. He will have to first acquire dollars with which to pay for the bond; this transaction also represents a demand for dollars. Suppose a Mexican company wishes to buy and operate a plant in the United States. The owner will have to purchase the plant and pay the workers with dollars, thereby first exchanging pesos for dollars. This transaction again represents a demand for dollars. Although there are other reasons to acquire dollars, these are four important ones: to travel in the United States, to purchase U.S. goods and services, to invest in U.S. financial markets, and to buy and operate plants in the United States.[2]

Now consider the supply curve S in Figure 9-6. This curve represents the supply of U.S. dollars by American residents. Why would U.S. citizens wish to supply dollars? The answer to this question is very easy if we recognize that the process of U.S.

EconNews

"Talking Down the Yen"

The Japanese yen has risen against other world currencies, making Japanese goods more expensive to the rest of the world. Will a weaker yen help Japan?

http://econapps.
swlearning.com

residents supplying dollars is the same as the process of U.S. residents demanding pesos. In a two-country world, our process of acquiring one currency is the same as our process of supplying the other: we exchange our dollars for pesos. Consequently, the supply of U.S. dollars by U.S. residents can be simultaneously viewed as the demand for Mexican pesos by U.S. residents.

Why do U.S. residents demand pesos? For the same reasons that Mexican residents demand dollars! Many of us wish to travel to Mexico City, or purchase Mexican clothing, or invest in the Mexican stock market. Many of our companies want to buy and operate plants in Mexico. All these desires create a U.S. demand for Mexican pesos. And this makes our picture complete. We have a demand for dollars and a supply of dollars (demand for pesos). The intersection of the demand and supply of U.S. dollars determines the equilibrium exchange rate between the dollar and peso. This intersection occurs at the exchange rate of about 10 pesos per U.S. dollar in Figure 9-6.

We can extend this analysis by recognizing that either the demand or supply curve of Figure 9-6 can shift in response to changing economic conditions. The demand for U.S. dollars by Mexico's residents will increase if advertising of U.S. products increases in Mexico. This relationship is demonstrated in Figure 9-7. Note that the equilibrium exchange rate will change to 12 pesos per dollar, representing an increase in the value of the dollar relative to the peso (just what we would expect when the demand for dollars increases). Another way of saying this is that the dollar has **appreciated** (increased in value) relative to the peso. Because the value of one currency is always expressed relative to the other, we can also say that the peso has **depreciated** (decreased in value) relative to the dollar.

Is a higher value of the dollar good or bad? You may be used to this answer by now: it depends! In particular, it depends on who you are. For a U.S. consumer of Mexican clothing imported into the United States, a high dollar is good. It means that the peso is low, so that fewer dollars are needed to pay for the clothing denominated

Appreciate
The value of one country's currency increases relative to another country's currency.

Depreciate
The value of one country's currency decreases relative to another country's currency.

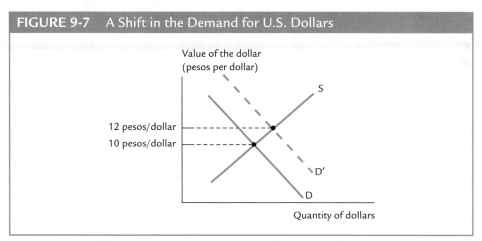

FIGURE 9-7   A Shift in the Demand for U.S. Dollars

Value of the dollar (pesos per dollar)

S

12 pesos/dollar

10 pesos/dollar

D′

D

Quantity of dollars

Increased advertising of U.S. products in Mexico will probably increase the demand for U.S. products by Mexican residents. This will cause Mexican residents to increase their demand for U.S. dollars with which to pay for the U.S. products, causing the demand for dollars to increase from D to D′. The new equilibrium exchange rate is 12 pesos per U.S. dollar.

in pesos. That is, Mexican products become cheaper for the U.S. consumer. On the other hand, a high dollar is not so good for a U.S. exporter. When the dollar is high, more pesos are needed to pay for U.S. automobiles denominated in dollars. That is, the U.S. automobiles have become more expensive for Mexican residents, who may now be less likely to make the purchase. U.S. exports may fall.

ECONOMIC POLICY

Group of Eight (G-8)
A group of eight countries (the United States, Canada, Britain, France, Italy, Germany, Japan, and Russia) that coordinate policies in an effort to influence exchange rates.

Economic policy in the United States (or any other country) can have an impact on exchange rates. Recall the earlier discussion of U.S. trade restrictions imposed on imports of cotton cloth. These restrictions reduce U.S. purchases of foreign cotton cloth. If our purchases of foreign cloth decline, so too does our demand for foreign currency with which to pay for the cloth. As our demand for a foreign currency falls, the value of that currency decreases (and the relative value of the dollar increases). A rising value of the dollar makes our exports more expensive to foreign consumers, who will likely purchase fewer of them. Now, we see the harm to U.S. producers of export goods when we impose trade restrictions designed to protect our cotton cloth industry. We may help one sector of the U.S. economy, but hurt another.

Six Markets Group (Asian G-6)
A group of six (original) countries (the United States, Japan, China, Singapore, Australia, and Hong Kong) that coordinate financial policies.

Consider another example of economic policy. Suppose policymakers decide to raise U.S. interest rates. A rise in U.S. interest rates relative to interest rates in other countries of the world means that U.S. financial markets now become more attractive to foreign investors. Why should a British citizen deposit her savings in a British financial institution when she can receive higher interest earnings by depositing the savings in a U.S. financial institution? Of course, she would first have to exchange her British pounds (the British currency) for U.S. dollars (thereby creating a demand for dollars). This increase in the demand for dollars with which to make the deposit pushes up the value of the U.S. dollar. Indeed, one of the most important factors affecting the value of a currency is the relative interest rate in different countries.

If nothing else, this discussion should make it clear to you that the world is indeed interdependent. An action by one country has an impact felt around the world. An action by a country as important as the United States can have an especially large impact. It has been said that when the United States sneezes, the rest of the world catches pneumonia. The ripple effects are often particularly significant for the smaller, poorer countries of the world.

INTERNATIONAL MANAGEMENT OF EXCHANGE RATES

Although much of the industrialized world uses flexible (floating) exchange rates, the real world system is not based entirely on the market forces of demand and supply. Individual countries may intervene, buying and selling currencies, to influence exchange rates. This action is sometimes referred to as a "dirty float." Since 1986, an entire group of countries has coordinated their policies in an effort to influence exchange rates. These countries are now referred to as the **Group of Eight (G-8)**. These countries are the United States, Canada, Britain, France, Italy, Germany, Japan, and Russia. A major goal of G-8 is to stabilize exchange rates of major world currencies within an acceptable range of one another. It is felt that all member countries benefit from greater stability among these rates.

Six Markets Group, also called **Asian G-6**, was formed in early 1997. This group is made up of the United States, Japan, China, Singapore, Australia, and Hong Kong (now part of China). Some expect that the group will extend to additional Asian countries and will evolve into an Asian counterpart to the Group of Eight. Trade groups are also developing in the Americas and other places.

NOTES

1. The actual exchange rate between the U.S. dollar and the Mexican peso was 1 U.S. dollar per 10.4811 Mexican pesos on July 29, 2003 (**www.imf.org**).

2. There is one additional reason why residents of many countries wish to acquire U.S. dollars. This is because the dollar is a relatively stable currency, whereas the currencies of many other countries fluctuate. People who fear the decline in the value of their own currency may acquire (demand) dollars in order to protect against this risk.

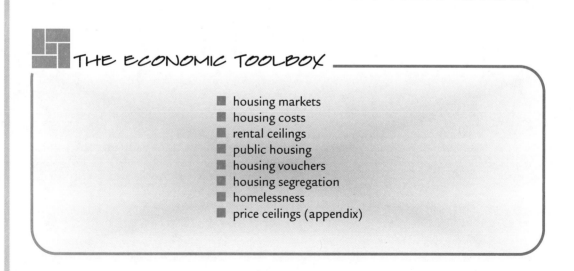

**Chapter 6
U.S. Poverty**
Public housing concentrates poverty
Residential segregation concentrates poverty

**Chapter 4
Education**
Property tax funding and residential segregation contribute to low-quality inner-city schools

**Chapter 5
Discrimination**
Residential segregation still exists

**Chapter 10
Housing**

**Chapter 7
World Poverty**
Price ceilings in poor countries work similarly to rental ceilings

**Chapter 16
Taxes, Borrowing, and the National Debt**
Tax breaks for homeowners and property taxes on home values are significant elements of our tax system

**Chapter 2
Crime and Drugs**
Public housing concentrates poverty and its dysfunctions

THE ECONOMIC TOOLBOX

- housing markets
- housing costs
- rental ceilings
- public housing
- housing vouchers
- housing segregation
- homelessness
- price ceilings (appendix)

HOUSING

I have to make the choice of whether to have a house with no gas or light, or have gas and lights . . . with no home to live in.
—From *In Our Own Words: Mothers' Perspectives on Welfare Reform*[1]

Housing, like food, is a commodity that has special connotations for many of us. Shelter from the elements is a basic biological need, and most of us see adequate housing (however defined) as a basic right. We are concerned, and often confused, about the homeless. We worry that low-income families (such as the family headed by the woman in the preceding quote) cannot afford to rent houses or apartments in our cities. We realize that the single largest investment most U.S. families make is the purchase of their home. And we regard home ownership as an essential part of the American dream. We wonder if young families just starting out will be able to afford to buy a home. We know that the federal and many state governments have developed policies to promote home ownership and access to adequate housing, but we often do not know details about these policies. In this chapter, we will look at the housing market in the United States.

We will begin by looking at issues involving home ownership, affordability, and government policy with regard to ownership. We will then turn our attention to low-income housing and measures that are intended to ensure that poor families have access to adequate housing. We look at the economic consequences of housing segregation. Finally, we will discuss the problem of the homeless among us.

HOUSING MARKETS: IS HOME OWNERSHIP WITHIN OUR REACH?

Although we speak of the housing market in the United States, there exist a great many markets for housing within our country. There are markets for single-family dwellings, duplexes, and multifamily dwellings such as cooperatives and condominiums. If you live in a college dormitory, that building is part of the broader housing market. Market conditions vary greatly with geography and the socio-economic characteristics of different locations. These markets are subject to the forces of supply and

FIGURE 10-1   Regional Differences in the Price of Housing

Detroit

Atlanta

The decreased demand for housing over time in Detroit will cause the price of housing to fall, whereas the increased demand in Atlanta will cause housing prices to rise.

demand, as are other markets. Thus, the price of the average residence, as well as its size and other characteristics, varies with the location of the house. Homes in areas with healthy economies and growing populations tend to gain in value over time, whereas the value of houses in depressed regions with declining populations goes down.

Figure 10-1 illustrates this concept. Assume that the two graphs are for houses with the same size and quality characteristics in two cities, Detroit and Atlanta. Detroit, part of the so-called Rust Belt, is a city in decline. Factories and jobs have moved out of Detroit to other cities and other countries. Unemployment is high, and many workers have left the area. Atlanta, on the other hand, is enjoying a boom. Companies are locating in this Sun Belt city, and workers are moving in as jobs are created. The declining population in Detroit results in a decreasing demand for housing in Detroit, whereas the growing population in Atlanta causes an increased demand for housing in Atlanta. Thus, the two cities will be subject to opposite shifts in the demand for housing, as shown in each graph as a shift from D to D′. As a result of the demand shifts, the equilibrium market price of housing will change to P′ in each of the diagrams. The price of housing in Detroit will be lower than in Atlanta.

Really large differentials in housing prices can occur as the result of long-term economic growth trends in particular areas. The economy and the population of the southern California region grew rapidly in the period following World War II, creating an increase in the demand for housing there. Housing prices escalated until, in the 1980s, houses in southern California cost three or four times as much as similar houses in the Midwest. With the post–Cold War defense cuts of the early 1990s, which threw the California economy into a severe recession, the regional

EconNews

"Home, Expensive Home"

The cost of owning a house is steadily rising. Want to know why? Go to the Supply and Demand category to find out.

http://econapps. swlearning.com

housing demand slackened and housing prices began to decline. With the more recent economic recovery and then recession, these prices have risen and fallen again.

Trends in Housing

When the U.S. Census Bureau first surveyed housing in the United States in 1940, 44 percent of housing units were occupied by their owners and 56 percent were occupied by renters. By 1999, 67 percent of housing units were occupied by their owners, and this number increased to 68 percent by 2001. We clearly saw a big jump in owner-occupied housing from 1940 to 1999, but a much smaller increase from 1999 to 2001.[2]

In terms of the cost of housing, we can compare the median values of owner-occupied housing and median rent. (Recall that the term *median* means middle. If we had a list of housing values, for example, from highest to lowest, the median value would be the one in the middle of the list.) In 1940, the median value of nonfarm owner-occupied homes was $2,938 and the median rent was $27 per month.[3] In 1999, the median value of existing U.S. housing units was $133,100 and the median rent was $785 monthly. Obviously, the 1940 and the 1999 figures are not directly comparable. If, however, we adjust the 1940 figures to account for inflation between 1940 and 1999, we will have comparable figures. When recalculated in terms of 1999 prices, the 1940 median value of homes would be $35,319 and the median rent would be $328. In real terms, the value of the average U.S. home has increased fourfold over this 59-year time period, and rent has more than doubled!

The U.S. Census Bureau has also noted that in the 50 years between 1940 and 1990, the U.S. housing inventory grew from 37 million units to 107 million units, more than doubling. By 2001, the housing stock remained almost the same as in 1990, at 106 million. Furthermore, the major housing problem in 1940 was the poor condition of our housing stock: 31 percent of units had no running water, 18 percent needed major repairs, 44 percent had neither a bathtub nor a shower, and 35 percent had no flush toilet in the structure. These deficiencies no longer exist; by 1990, 99 percent of all housing units had hot and cold running water, toilets, and a bathtub or shower. Our major concern now is the affordability of housing and the effects on people when affordable housing is not available.

If we focus on only the past quarter century, we see that the price of new housing has risen more rapidly than household income. Table 10-1 contains data on the median price of new houses in the United States, as well as median household income.

TABLE 10-1	Median Sales Price of New Housing Units and Median Household Income, 1970 and 1998		
Year	**Median Sales Price of New Housing Unit**	**Median Household Income**	**Housing Price/ Income Ratio**
1970	$ 23,400	$ 8,734	2.68
1998	$151,300	$38,885	3.89

*Source: U.S. Department of Commerce, Census Bureau, 1999 (**www.census.gov**).*

The last column of the table shows the ratio of the housing sales price to household income. In 1970, the median price of new housing units was only 2.68 times the median household income, whereas in 1998, it was 3.89 times the median household income. On average, households must spend almost an entire year's additional income to buy a new house now than they did 30 years ago. This statistic leads us to question whether the average American family can now afford a single-family home.

It should be noted, however, that houses being built now are not only larger than those built in 1970 but are also different in other ways. They are nearly three times as likely to have two stories as the homes built in 1970. They are more than twice as likely to be air-conditioned and nearly twice as likely to have fireplaces. Table 10-2 summarizes these changes.

Indeed, quality changes between the houses built in 1970 and those being built today are significant. Many of these new structures may have been built for middle-aged baby boomers who are "stepping up" to larger, more prestigious dwellings, selling their former residences to younger, less-affluent families.

Factors Influencing the Affordability of Housing

Down payment
The amount of a home buyer's own money required by the lender for the purchase of a home.

Will you be able to afford a house when you are ready to buy one? What factors determine the family's monthly house payments if they do buy a house? The elements that must be considered in analyzing the affordability of home ownership are (1) the down payment, (2) the monthly mortgage payments, and (3) the buyer's income and debt. Let us look at each of these elements.

The Down Payment and Other Expenses at the Time of Purchase

The **down payment** is the amount of the buyer's own money that must be paid at the time of the purchase. A standard mortgage often requires a 20 percent down payment, which means that the buyer must "put down" 20 percent of the purchase price

TABLE 10-2	Characteristics of New Privately Owned One-Family Homes Completed, 1970 and 1998	
Characteristic	**1970**	**1998**
Size (floor area)		
<1,200 square feet	36%	7%
>2,100 square feet	21%	50%
Average square feet	1,500	2,190
Number of stories		
One	74%	48%
Two or more	17%	50%
Split-level	10%	2%
With central air conditioning	34%	83%
With one or more fireplaces	35%	61%

*Source: U.S. Department of Commerce, Census Bureau (**www.census.gov**).*

at the time of the purchase. For those eligible, a housing loan from the Federal Housing Administration requires only a 10 percent down payment. Finally, some new houses are sold with only 5 percent down payments. These homes are seen as good investments, and the lender assumes that they can easily be resold if it is necessary to foreclose on the loan. Older housing usually is sold with traditional mortgages that require the higher down payments. As a general rule, lenders require buyers who pay less than 20 percent down to purchase mortgage insurance. **Mortgage insurance** protects the lender if the buyer defaults on the loan.

In addition to the down payment, the buyer must make other payments at the time of purchase. These payments include mortgage **points**, which are fees charged by lenders at the time they grant mortgages. Points are like interest in that they are a charge for borrowing money. One point equals 1 percent of the amount borrowed, so if you were to pay one point on $100,000, you would pay $1,000.

Lenders typically use both the interest rate and points to establish their charges for lending you money. Lenders might be willing to give you a lower interest rate if you pay more points, or they might charge more points if you make a smaller down payment. In some localities, laws have been passed that establish a legal maximum interest rate above which the financial institution is legally prohibited from charging. These laws are called **usury laws** and are discussed in more detail in the appendix to this chapter. In these localities, points are often used to offset the low interest rates that can legally be charged.

Closing costs refer to the total expenses, including points, that buyers pay at the time that the loan is finalized and the title to the property is conveyed to them. The closing cost is money you must come up with if you are to buy a house. Closing costs include loan application fees, points, title search fees, title insurance, attorneys' fees, appraisal fees, and other miscellaneous charges.

Mortgage insurance
Insurance that pays off a mortgage if the borrower defaults.

Points
Fees charged by a lender at the time it grants a mortgage.

Usury laws
Laws establishing a maximum legal interest rate.

Closing costs
Expenses paid at the time that a loan is finalized and the title is conveyed to the buyer.

Monthly Mortgage Payments

The monthly mortgage payment is made up of payments on the principal (unpaid balance) of the loan plus interest payments. For most of the life of the loan, more of the monthly payment goes to pay interest charges than to repay principal. The amount of interest paid over the life of the loan is extremely sensitive to the length of the loan. Table 10-3 illustrates this fact. The table shows the monthly payments for an 8 percent conventional mortgage loan of $50,000 to be paid over 10 years,

TABLE 10-3	Monthly Payments on a $50,000 Mortgage, Various Lengths of Loan			
Loan Terms	**10 Years**	**15 Years**	**20 Years**	**30 Years**
Monthly payment	$606.65	$472.85	$ 418.25	$ 384.50
Number of payments	120	180	240	360
Total paid	$72,798	$86,013	$100,380	$138,420
Principal	$50,000	$50,000	$ 50,000	$ 50,000
Interest paid	$22,798	$36,013	$ 50,380	$ 88,420

**Variable
rate
mortgages**
Mortgage
loans on which
interest rates
are periodically
adjusted.

15 years, 20 years, and 30 years. The borrower will pay 8 percent annually on the unpaid balance of the loan and the amount by which the unpaid balance is reduced is
much smaller if the payments are stretched out over a longer period of time. The
monthly payment is the amount that the buyer must pay if the $50,000, plus 8 per-
cent interest, is to be paid in the stated number of years. The total paid is the monthly
payment multiplied by the number of payments, and the interest paid is the difference between the total payments and the $50,000. Note that a 30-year conventional
mortgage involves the payment of nearly four times as much interest as a 10-year conventional mortgage.

The mortgage payment increases with the amount borrowed and with the interest rate charged by the lender. Therefore, an increase in the average price of housing units or in the interest rates charged by lenders will increase the home buyer's
monthly payments.

In the late 1970s, we experienced an extremely high rate of inflation, which is a
rise in the average level of prices in our economy. Both housing prices and the interest rates charged by lenders for long-term loans increased markedly. The housing
market was stifled by the high interest rates. Many potential buyers could not afford
the monthly payments at the high rates of interest. Lenders did not want to tie up
funds for 30 years because the interest rate they could receive on other loans or investments might increase significantly in that time period. Lenders therefore began
issuing **variable rate mortgages**, which are still used quite widely. On a variable rate
mortgage loan, a rate is established for a period of time, such as two or four years.
When the time is up, the buyer can either renew the mortgage at the currently existing market interest rate or pay off the remainder of the loan.

Property taxes and home owner's insurance are sometimes part of the monthly
payment of the borrower. **Property taxes** are levied by local governments to fund services such as education and police protection. These taxes are generally a given percentage of the approximate market value of property (land and buildings) within
the community, so more expensive houses will bear more property taxes. **Home
owner's insurance**, which covers the replacement cost of the house and its contents,
may be required by the lender to protect itself in the event of natural disaster.
Monthly payments toward insurance and property taxes are sometimes required by
the lender. These payments are placed in a temporary escrow account from which
insurance and taxes are paid when due.

The Income and Debt of the Buyer

Most lenders require that prospective borrowers satisfy affordability guidelines. The
most common affordability criterion is that monthly mortgage payments not exceed
25 to 30 percent of the borrower's before-tax income. Furthermore, total monthly in-
stallment payments—including, for example, auto loans and charge card payments—
cannot exceed 33 to 38 percent of before-tax income. The prospective home buyer's
monthly income is therefore an important factor in determining whether the family
can afford to buy a particular home.

In addition to income, debt is an important factor in a family's ability to purchase
a house. Credit cards "maxed out" or other consumer debts may prevent a buyer
from meeting mortgage lenders' guidelines.

Who Can Afford to Buy a House?

The Census Bureau periodically issues reports on the affordability of homes in the United States. It considers that three factors may prevent a household's affording a home: (1) insufficient cash for the down payment and closing costs, (2) insufficient income to afford the monthly mortgage payments, or (3) too much debt to qualify for a mortgage.

A 1995 Census Bureau report revealed that 44 percent of American households could not afford to buy a modestly priced home (defined as a house priced higher than 25 percent but lower than 75 percent of the houses in the same area). The most common reason that current home owners could not qualify for a mortgage on a modestly priced home was that their debt was too high. Renters usually did not qualify because of more than one of the three preceding reasons. The report found that houses are most affordable in the Midwest and least affordable in the West. Far more whites can afford the modestly priced home than can racial and ethnic minorities. More than 75 percent of single-parent families with children under age 18 cannot afford to buy the modestly priced home. Not surprisingly, the same groups that are overrepresented in the poverty statistics discussed in Chapter 6 are less likely to be able to afford home ownership than other groups. The Census study implies that it is not a foregone conclusion that American families can afford the single-family dwelling that is part of the American Dream.

It should be noted that neither the material discussed here nor the Census Bureau study considers alternative types of housing such as mobile homes and condominiums, both of which have increased as a percentage of our housing stock. In 1990, 7 percent of all U.S. housing units were mobile homes. Both the average income and the average age of mobile home owners were lower than the average income and average age of the population at large. The obvious inference is that some young families are buying mobile homes as starter homes.

Property taxes
Taxes levied by local governments to fund services such as education and police protection.

Home owner's insurance
Insurance that covers the replacement cost of a house and its contents.

Government Policy Toward Home Ownership

A number of state and federal policies promote home ownership. The Federal Housing Administration (FHA) insures home loans that allow mortgage applicants to spend a higher percentage of their income on housing and debt payments than conventional mortgage guidelines require. In addition, applicants can finance part of the closing costs, including points and the mortgage insurance premium, which otherwise is not permitted. Use of FHA-insured loan guidelines rather than conventional mortgage guidelines reduces the percentage of Americans who cannot afford to buy a house. These mortgages, therefore, benefit lower-income applicants. In practice, however, a smaller percentage of new homes are now financed with FHA-insured mortgages than in the past. In 1970, 30 percent of new homes were financed by FHA-insured loans. In 1998, the figure had decreased to 8 percent. In part, this change is caused by the FHA's raising of standards for homes of acceptable quality. Realtors have described the agency as "nitpicking," and many realtors steer buyers away if possible.

Far more important, the federal personal income tax code promotes home ownership by permitting the deduction of mortgage interest payments from income before personal income taxes are calculated. This deduction benefits mainly middle- and higher-income households, however, because higher-income households, on average, buy more expensive homes and also pay personal income taxes at higher tax rates. On the other hand, low-income households buy less expensive homes and are far more likely to rent than to own, in which case they receive no interest deduction on their federal income taxes.

The income tax deduction is a housing subsidy for middle- and upper-income classes, not for the poor. The value of the mortgage interest deduction was $51.7 billion in 1998. To put this figure into some sort of perspective, the government spent $28.7 billion on housing assistance for low-income families that same year. According to a 1996 study cited by the National Coalition for the Homeless, for every $1 spent on low-income housing programs, the government lost $4 in housing-related tax benefits, and 75 percent of these benefits went to households in the top 20 percent of the income distribution. Furthermore, in 2001, 59 percent of mortgage interest deduction tax savings went to households with incomes of $100,000 or more, while homeowners with incomes of $20,000 to $30,000 received 0.5 percent of the benefits. And, of course, renters received no federal tax benefit.[4]

HOUSING FOR LOW-INCOME FAMILIES

Some families cannot afford, or may not want, to buy a house. The availability of low-cost, adequate quality rental housing for low-income families is therefore important. Since 1970, the percentage of income that renters spend on housing has increased, as rental prices have increased far more rapidly than wages and other income. A study by the U.S. Department of Housing and Urban Development (HUD) indicates that in 1997 and 1998, rents *increased* at twice the rate of general inflation, while the number of affordable rental units *decreased* by 372,000 units between 1991 and 1997.[5]

The high price of rental housing results from the interaction of demand and supply. Figure 10-2 shows the changes that have taken place over time in the market for relatively low cost rental housing. The shift of supply from S to S′ is a decrease in supply. Some people trace the decrease in the supply of affordable housing units to the development of superhighways and urban renewal in the 1950s. Both of these programs destroyed thousands of low- and moderate-cost rental units in the name of urban development. Indeed, some pundits renamed the phenomenon of urban renewal "urban removal," because the poor tenants who had formerly lived in the "renewed" areas could no longer afford to live there. More recently, the process of **gentrification** has further reduced the supply of low-cost housing as traditional low-cost rental units have been restored and converted into middle- and upper-middle-class properties. The conversion of apartment buildings into condominiums throughout our cities has further decreased the supply of rental housing. In addition, some of our cities are experiencing a process of disintegration. Housing units have been abandoned and vandalized. Public housing stands vacant because of a lack of funds for upkeep and modernization. All of these factors have reduced the supply of adequate, low-cost housing.

The demand for low-cost rental housing has also increased over time. Part of the increase is the result of population growth. Part results from the growth in the number of poor and near-poor families as the income distribution has become more unequal, as we discussed in Chapter 6. Both the increase in demand and the decrease in supply have caused the price of so-called low-cost housing to increase, as is shown in Figure 10-2. The final result is a housing affordability crisis for poor families—a crisis that is worse in some regions than in others.

EconLinks

Panel Study of Income Dynamics (University of Michigan)

psidonline.isr. umich.edu

http://econapps. swlearning.com

Gentrification
The conversion of low-cost apartments into middle- and upper-middle-class housing.

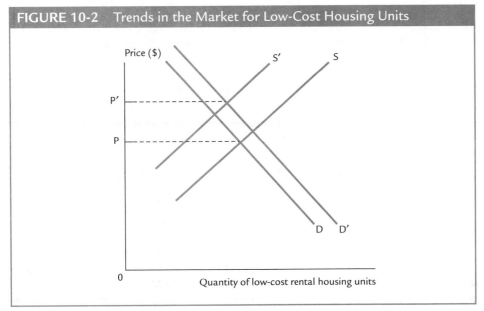

FIGURE 10-2 Trends in the Market for Low-Cost Housing Units

The reduced supply of low-cost housing and increased demand for it have resulted in higher-priced and less-affordable housing for low-income families.

The search for affordable rental housing has become more difficult for poor families. The high rental prices obviously harm the well-being of low-income families, because when families spend a large percentage of their incomes on housing, little remains for food, clothing, and other necessities. One result is that low-income families are often crowded into older housing units that have physical problems. Another result is an increase in homelessness.

One measure used to assist low-income households is **rental ceilings** (also called rent controls), by which the government establishes a maximum rent for certain housing units. Other programs to help the poor obtain affordable rental housing can be divided into programs to increase the supply of low-cost housing and programs to increase the demand for housing by enabling poor tenants to acquire (demand) adequate housing. Let us look at all three options individually.

> **Rental ceilings (rent controls)** Legally set maximum rents on apartments.

Rental Ceilings

During World War II, we had a national system of rental ceilings. After the war, only New York City retained its rental ceilings, but during the 1970s, a number of other cities, many of them "university towns," adopted such measures. Some cities considered, but did not adopt, rental ceilings.

Suppose that your school is located in College Town, which has adopted rental ceilings. Most college students are low-income people, and there is often a great demand in college towns for reasonably priced off-campus student housing of acceptable quality. At the same time, towns dominated by colleges often have landlords who buy up old houses and rent them to groups of college students, charging exorbitant rents. Therefore, you might initially be much in favor of controlling the rents that landlords could charge you. But let us consider the consequences of rental ceilings.

Rental ceilings are a specific example of price ceilings, which are legally imposed maximum prices (rents) of a good or service. Price ceilings are discussed in Chapter 7 in the context of food price ceilings in less-developed countries. (Other examples of price ceilings are discussed in the appendix to this chapter.) To be effective (which means to have an effect on the market), price ceilings must be below market equilibrium prices. Because prices are not free to rise above some specified maximum, price ceilings interfere with the rationing function of price. As we discussed in Chapter 1, markets tend to clear at an equilibrium price and quantity, and in the process, shortages and surpluses are rationed away. This is the rationing function of price in a competitive market. Because rent prices cannot rise above the rental ceiling to the equilibrium price, they cannot perform a rationing function. Therefore, they actually create a shortage.

Figure 10-3 shows the effects of the rental ceiling on the hypothetical rental market in College Town. Before the rent controls are imposed, the equilibrium rental market price is $500 per month and the equilibrium quantity of apartments is 1,000. The local government establishes a rental ceiling of $400 to help poor tenants, including struggling students. Initially, nothing much happens except that tenants pay lower rents and landlords receive lower rents. But as time passes, both prospective tenants and landlords adjust to the rental ceiling. Because they are receiving lower rents, landlords have less incentive to provide rental housing, and they move down their supply curve until they are supplying only 800 units at the rental rate of $400. They do this by abandoning units that need repairs, demolishing some units so the land can be used for commercial purposes, and converting some units to other uses such as condominiums. Meanwhile, the quantity demanded of these apartments increases to 1,200, because at the low rent, more people desire to live in rental housing. Young adults may move out of their parents' houses, students may move off

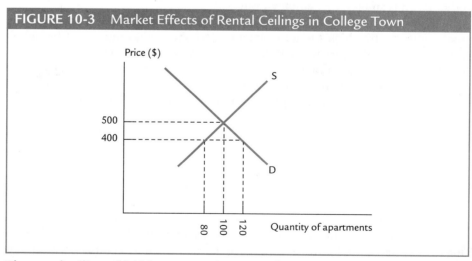

FIGURE 10-3 Market Effects of Rental Ceilings in College Town

The rental ceiling of $400 creates a shortage of 40 apartments in College Town.

campus, and people living with roommates may seek their own apartments. There is a shortage of 400 rental units in College Town. And it is a shortage that the market cannot ration away, because the rental price cannot rise above $400 to reach the market equilibrium.

Rental ceilings produce some gainers and some losers. Obviously, the original tenants in the rent-controlled units gain. They stay there and pay lower rents. Those who move into rent-controlled units also gain, because their rents are lower than they would be without the controls. But people that cannot find an apartment in College Town because of the rental ceilings lose. And the landlords lose in two ways. They receive lower-than-market equilibrium rents; and if they sell their buildings, they will receive lower prices, reflecting the lower income generated by the properties.

Over time, rental ceilings have other effects. Landlords do less routine maintenance, and the properties deteriorate more rapidly. In effect, landlords let the apartments deteriorate until they are worth only the lower rent. Because of the housing shortage, landlords also can afford to be choosy about who they accept as tenants. Therefore, they may refuse to rent to college students, pet owners, families with children, or racial minorities.

The rent-controlled units that are in good repair are a real bargain, encouraging development of illegal markets. Units might be subleased at rates higher than the rental ceilings. Alternatively, landlords may require large payments, perhaps in the form of huge damage (security) deposits, before they rent out their property. Both the subleasers and the prospective tenants who make upfront payments to obtain the rent-controlled apartments are usually middle-class families, rather than the poor. A program to help low-income households afford decent rental housing has become a program that subsidizes the middle class.

Rental ceilings are generally intended to help the poor, which certainly include many college students. In the end, however, the poor are probably the group harmed the most by rent controls. They have fewer choices. They cannot afford to buy homes. They cannot afford to move out to the suburbs. They cannot afford the huge security deposits needed to move into a rent-controlled apartment in good repair. They are likely to be crowded into substandard, overpriced housing or to become part of our nation's homeless.

Rental ceilings are attractive on the surface, but they cause shortages and a deteriorating stock of affordable housing. Because these rental ceilings do not benefit the poor households for which they were intended, but instead benefit higher-income people, rental ceilings are a very inefficient method for providing affordable rental housing to low-income families.

Programs to Increase Supply

Public Housing

The oldest and perhaps best-known program to supply low-income housing is called **public housing**, which began in 1937. Constructing public housing was justified initially as a means to create employment during the Great Depression of the 1930s. Public housing units are owned and operated by a local public housing authority, but the units are federally subsidized and often federally regulated. The federal government establishes the eligibility requirements for tenants and the ratio of rent

Public housing
Housing units owned and operated by a local public housing authority but federally subsidized and often federally regulated.

relative to income that will determine what the individual tenant will pay for housing. The current rent/income ratio is .30, which means that the tenant will pay 30 percent of his or her monthly income as rent.

Currently, about 1.3 million Americans live in public housing, but the public housing program is criticized because it tends to concentrate poor and distressed populations in particular areas. It may also segregate people both racially and by income level. Thus, life in the "projects" has become synonymous with poverty, social dysfunction, and high crime rates.

Much of the political support for public housing over the years has come from the construction industry. Indeed, the whole program was terminated under President Richard Nixon's administration in 1973, which was a boom year in the construction industry. The program was then reactivated in 1976, when the bottom had fallen out of the construction market. Moreover, several studies have shown that public housing is an expensive method to house the poor. Public housing units cost more than either new private housing units or used low-income housing. Therefore, the availability of public housing is limited. Many eligible families remain on waiting lists for years.

Furthermore, some economists argue that public housing displaces private housing, causing the latter to be abandoned or converted to other purposes because the supply of public housing units causes the market price of available private housing units to fall. The private landlords then either retire some of their units or use them for other purposes. Public housing is an increasingly controversial policy, so let us look at other methods to house the poor.

Subsidies to Developers

Subsidies to developers
Government payments to landlords who build housing for the poor.

Fair market rent
An amount determined by HUD to be reasonable rent for low-income housing.

One alternative method is the provision of **subsidies to developers** to encourage them to build or convert other property to low-income housing units. The major federal program of this type is the Section 8 project-based program that began in 1975. This program pays landlords the difference between the rental payments received from tenants and the market rent that the landlord would otherwise receive. A **fair market rent** for each unit is established and guaranteed to the landlord. The fair market rent is an amount determined by the Department of Housing and Urban Development to be a reasonable rent for low-income housing in a given area. The eligible tenant's rent is then set at 30 percent of the tenant's income. The government pays a subsidy equal to the difference between the fair market rent and the actual rent paid by the tenant to the landlord. Thus, if an eligible low-income family has income of $600 per month, it could rent an apartment in the Section 8 building at $180 per month (30 percent of $600). If the fair market rent for the apartment is $500, the government will pay an additional $320 to the landlord as a subsidy. Initially, landlords were required to sign 20-year contracts to provide Section 8 housing. Now, many of the original contracts are expiring, and HUD is signing contracts for a shorter duration. A current concern is that many of the original 20-year contracts will not be renewed and that these nonrenewals will decrease the supply of affordable housing for the poor. The Section 8 program has led to the construction of moderately priced housing. Studies of both public housing and subsidies to developers, however, indicate that one of the biggest gainers is the construction industry, rather than the poor. As with public housing, waiting lists for these housing units are often long.

Programs that Affect Demand

Supply-side policies help the poor by providing more low-income housing in the rental market. Another way to help low-income households would be to give them subsidies (vouchers) and to let them choose their own housing. These subsidies increase the poor families' ability to express their demand for housing in the private housing market.

Housing (Rent) Vouchers

The principal demand-side housing program is the **housing vouchers** program, which is also part of the Section 8 housing program. Most housing vouchers go to very poor families. Recipients must occupy a dwelling that meets minimum government standards. The housing vouchers are based on the difference between the fair market rent for the locality and 30 percent of the tenant's income. If the fair market rent for an apartment is $450 and the family's income is $700, the voucher will be in the amount of $240 ($450 minus 30 percent of $700). The family will receive this housing voucher based on its income even if it rents an apartment with a lower actual rent. If the family moves, it takes the voucher with it. The number of Section 8 housing vouchers was frozen between 1995 and 1998 but then began rising. Unfortunately, the Bush administration's 2003 request to Congress for funding this program in 2004 underestimated the need for the program and is $1.2 billion below what is needed to maintain the current level of assistance. According to the Center on Budget and Policy Priorities, 184,000 or more households will lose their vouchers and this will be the first time in the program's 30-year history that fewer households will be served than the year before. Most of the households that would lose their vouchers are working families, the elderly, and the disabled, who together make up about 70 percent of those served by the program. As it is now, the program serves only a modest fraction of eligible households because of its underfunding. There are long waiting lists for voucher assistance and they will grow longer unless additional dollars are appropriated. The prospective loss of vouchers comes at a bad time, when the poor economy is causing greater need for housing assistance.

> **Housing voucher**
> Housing subsidies in the amount of the difference between the fair market rent and 30 percent of a poor family's income.

In terms of economics, demand-side housing subsidies initially cause the price of low-cost housing to increase, because the demand for such housing increases. However, over time, we can expect landlords to supply more units. They increase maintenance on their dwellings and upgrade lower-quality housing to participate in this housing submarket.

Many economists prefer demand-side subsidies to the supply-side methods of aiding low-income families to obtain housing. Demand-side subsidies actually increase the private supply of low-cost housing units, whereas public housing appears to decrease that supply. The demand-side subsidies are paid directly to low income households rather than to developers or construction firms, and some argue that the benefits thus are more certain to go to the intended group, our low-income families.

Adequacy of Current Programs and New Directions for Policy

Although three million U.S. families are helped by one or the other Section 8 program, housing activists maintain, and government officials acknowledge, that there is simply not enough money available to provide adequate housing for all our ill-housed poor and near-poor families. Many families eligible for housing assistance receive no aid, because budget constraints do not permit assistance for all qualifying families. Fiscal appropriations for assisted housing decreased throughout most of the 1990s as we strove to balance the budget, and appropriations only began to increase again after 1998. As we've noted, more recent appropriations have been insufficient.

Henry Cisneros, HUD secretary in the first Clinton administration, vowed to replace money, which is simply not available, with innovation. He therefore initiated many small and inexpensive programs, most on an experimental basis. One of the more promising was the conversion of some of the hundreds of thousands of housing units owned by the government to low-income housing. The government acquired many of these units as the result of foreclosures in federal insurance and loan programs, such as the Federal Housing Administration's. HUD's goal was to make these units available to families of low and modest means.

HUD also expanded a program to sell property obtained by the government in the savings and loan crises of the late 1980s. Since 1990, HUD has sold more than 20,000 single-family homes obtained from the Resolution Trust Corporation (RTC) to families of modest means. RTC is the agency responsible for selling off the assets of failed savings and loan institutions. Approximately 600 apartment buildings from the RTC have been sold to public agencies, nonprofit organizations, and other owners that agree to rent at least 35 percent of the units to low- and very-low-income families.

The problem with these creative attempts to provide affordable housing to the poor is that the RTC and other government-owned housing units are often not located where the need for such housing is greatest. Furthermore, even though rents on RTC apartments are usually set quite low, they are still too expensive for the very poor in high-cost municipalities such as New York, Boston, and San Francisco.

Many regard the RTC program as a model program, but HUD is also guilty of great waste and inefficiency. Probably the most obvious example was its role in promoting so-called welfare hotels for the homeless, which we discuss shortly in the section on homelessness.

HOUSING SEGREGATION

The problem of racial segregation in housing in the United States is serious. The year 2000 census data reveal that 55 percent of blacks and 48 percent of Hispanics live in our central cities. Blacks make up 23 percent of the central-city population in the United States but only about 8 percent of the population in the suburban areas surrounding these cities. Hispanics represent 18 percent of the central-city population but only 10 percent of the population of the suburban ring. Many metropolitan areas that have countywide desegregation plans, especially in the South, have slowly become more racially integrated. But inner cities that are heavily populated by minorities and surrounded by a ring of white suburbs display persistent racial segregation.

Index of dissimilarity
A measure of segregation.

Segregation occurs not only between the central city and its suburbs, but within central cities as well. Several indexes have been developed to measure the extent of segregation within central cities. The one most commonly used is the **index of dissimilarity**. This index is calculated by adding together the differences between the percentage of blacks and the percentage of whites living within each district of the city and dividing this sum by two. The reason we divide by two is that if segregation were to be reduced, a two-way move would have to take place. A white person would have to move into a black area, replacing a black person who would move into a white district.

To illustrate the calculation of the index of dissimilarity, assume that a city consists of two equal-size districts. In District 1 live 80 percent of all blacks and 20 percent of all whites. The difference in the district is 60 percent, or 60. In District 2 live 20 percent of all blacks and 80 percent of all whites. Again the difference is 60. To calculate the index, add together the differences and divide by two, as follows:

$$\text{Difference in District } 1 = 60$$
$$\text{Difference in District } 2 = 60$$
$$\text{Sum of Differences} = 120$$
$$120 \text{ divided by } 2 = 60$$

If there were no segregation, 50 percent of both blacks and whites would live in District 1, so its difference would be 0. The same would be true of District 2, in which the remaining 50 percent of each race would live. The index of dissimilarity would therefore be 0. On the other hand, if we had total segregation, with 100 percent of blacks in District 1 and 100 percent of whites in District 2, the index would be 100. The index of dissimilarity will vary between 0 and 100, and the higher it is, the greater is residential segregation.

Table 10-4 displays the weighted average index of dissimilarity for all U.S. metropolitan areas in 1980, 1990, and 2000. As we can see, the index has fallen over time, revealing less segregation. However, the decline is not very large. In addition, these calculations are made for whites and blacks only and do not measure segregation with respect to Hispanics, Asian Americans, Native Americans, and so on. Finally, the index for U.S. metropolitan areas overall disguises the high degree of segregation that occurs in certain metropolitan areas. For example, Detroit, Milwaukee, and Cleveland are examples of metropolitan areas that have had much higher than average levels of segregation.

Housing segregation, in combination with the labor market discrimination discussed in Chapter 5 serves to isolate minorities, especially African Americans, who are among the most strictly segregated of all minorities. Isolation puts blacks at an

---

TABLE 10-4 Weighted-Average Index of Dissimilarity for African Americans for All U.S. Metropolitan Areas in 1980, 1990, and 2000

Year	Index of Dissimilarity
1980	0.727
1990	0.678
2000	0.640

The index of dissimilarity shows the degree of segregation between white Caucasians and African Americans. The larger the number, the more segregation exits.

Source: U.S. Department of Commerce, Census Bureau (**www.census.gov/ hhes/www/housing**).

economic disadvantage. They live in the ghetto, and the jobs are usually in the suburbs. They have neither information about who is hiring nor easy access to work sites by means of public transportation. We have seen that African American poverty rates are significantly higher than the poverty rates of whites. Therefore, poverty is concentrated in the ghetto. These circumstances guarantee that poor blacks have a markedly inferior economic environment than do poor whites. Concentrated poverty often leads to family instability, crime, welfare dependency, housing abandonment, and low educational attainment. The housing stock of the inner cities deteriorates. The public schools are seriously underfunded, as explained in Chapter 4, and the quality of public education is exceedingly poor. In short, segregation contributes to the isolation and impoverishment of U.S. minorities. An underclass is created in this fashion.

HOMELESSNESS IN THE UNITED STATES

By the very nature of homelessness, the homeless are difficult to count, so estimates of their number vary widely. Traditional methodology for counting the homeless has been to count the people who are in shelters or on the streets. This approach may be useful for determining how many people need services such as shelter and soup kitchens. However, these counts often fail to find the "hidden" homeless, those who sleep in automobiles, campgrounds, boxes, caves, or boxcars. These counts also ignore other people in "homeless situations" who are forced to live with relatives and friends in overcrowded or substandard temporary conditions.

Despite the difficulties in counting the homeless, the National Coalition for the Homeless, an advocacy group for the homeless, estimated in 2002 that as many as 3.5 million people may have been homeless in the United States, and that 39 percent of these are children. Focusing on the adequacy of emergency shelters, a recent study of 27 U.S. cities found that in 2001, 37 percent of all requests for emergency shelter went unmet because of a lack of available resources. This is a 13 percent increase over the year 2000. The statistics are even worse for families, for whom 52 percent of emergency shelter requests went unmet. This is a 22 percent increase over the previous year. Finally, a review of homelessness in 50 U.S. cities found that in virtually every city, the official estimated number of homeless people greatly exceeded the number of emergency shelter and transitional housing spaces. Despite the inadequacy of these services, President Bush proposed no increases in host homeless assistance programs in his budget request for 2004.[6]

The homeless population is diverse. Some homeless people are women and children fleeing abusive relationships. Some homeless people are teenagers running away from dysfunctional families. But families with children are among the fastest-growing group of people without homes and are thought to represent about 40 percent of the homeless. The homeless include entire families, single parents with children, single men and women, and children (usually teenagers) living alone.

The most common stereotypes suggest that many homeless persons are alcoholics, drug addicts, or persons with mental illness. Some of the homeless do fit into these categories, but many others are people very much like us, only poorer. Many of the homeless work at the minimum wage, providing incomes inadequate to pay rents. Furthermore, many of our nation's families are just one or two paychecks away from homelessness. If an emergency (such as the loss of a job, death or desertion of a spouse, or serious illness) occurs, their savings may not be adequate to pay the rent or the mortgage. These situations are far more dire in our current economy with low wages and high unemployment.

Our government policy since the 1970s has been to deinstitutionalize mental health care. So, we have released many patients with mental illness from public mental hospitals. At the same time, government has not allocated adequate funds needed to support community-based mental health services such as halfway houses. Many deinstitutionalized patients have joined the ranks of the homeless. Others come to be homeless because their substance abuse is so severe that they simply cannot hold a job or pay rent on an apartment.

Still others are homeless simply because they cannot afford housing in the area in which they live. As low-quality housing is renovated to rent to middle-class tenants, the very poor are often displaced. Their former residence may have been substandard housing and a blight on the city, but it was housing they could afford. Its renovation decreases the housing stock available to the poor.

Unemployment may be a consequence of homelessness. Holding down a job when you are primarily concerned about where you and your family will sleep is difficult. Wages in today's economy are often far too low to enable rent of an apartment. Homelessness may also be a consequence of unemployment. Losing a job and the income it represents can cause a poverty-level family to lose housing because it can no longer pay the rent.

Probably the most desirable way of leaving the ranks of the homeless is to find a job that pays enough for rent on a housing unit. But searching for employment is difficult, if not impossible, for homeless people. It is hard to present yourself well if you do not have bathroom facilities available to you, let alone washing machines and ironing boards. The homeless also have neither an address nor a phone by which prospective employers can contact them.

Homelessness compounds the problems of poverty. Homeless children often do not attend school, or they attend school sporadically. Homeless parents have difficulty keeping their children clean and appropriately dressed for school. The children are often malnourished as well as homeless, and malnourishment leads to difficulty in learning. Studying and doing homework while homeless are obviously far more difficult than studying and doing homework in a supportive environment. Thus, homeless children face great burdens that keep many from succeeding in school, a prerequisite to rising out of poverty as an adult.

Government Policy Concerning the Homeless

Homeless advocates argue that we have no coherent, long-run policy concerning the homeless. Instead, we react in an ad hoc way to emergencies. When the temperature drops in our northern cities, we worry that the homeless will die of exposure. If a tragedy occurs, such as the 1993 death of a homeless woman in a bus-stop shelter across the street from the Washington headquarters of HUD, we initiate emergency programs designed to put the homeless in shelters run mainly by private charities or into controversial and expensive welfare hotels.

Housing advocates, and some economists, argue that the country needs a comprehensive housing policy that includes both emergency shelters and permanent low-cost housing. They argue that our reactive policies, such as the welfare hotel strategy, are both inadequate and wasteful. They believe that we must devise policies to prevent homelessness, rather than using so-called Band-Aid treatments once the problem occurs.

Housing policy is one area in which the conservative and liberal viewpoints are quite clearly delineated. The conservative position is that government participation in housing markets should be eliminated, or at least minimized. Thus, conservatives would encourage the transfer of public housing units to the private sector (private tenants or landlords) and eliminate subsidies to the construction industry. Consistently, conservative economists would also eliminate the mortgage interest deduction, although many conservative politicians regard this deduction as the equivalent of a sacred cow. (Politicians who argue for the repeal of cherished middle- and upper-class tax breaks seldom get reelected.) If it is necessary to aid poor families to obtain shelter, conservatives favor such measures as rent vouchers, which allow poor families to afford housing in the private sector. Their principal argument is that the market is more efficient in solving housing problems than is the government.

Like conservatives, many liberals favor rent certificates and rent vouchers to help the poor. Unlike conservatives, however, liberals are more likely to stress government's role in solving housing problems. They see homelessness as a problem that government should treat by building public housing and temporary shelters. Liberals are not unconcerned with efficiency, but they stress that government's involvement in housing markets may be necessary to increase poor people's access to housing.

SUMMARY

The housing market is in fact many markets, which differ by region, type of housing, and other characteristics. The cost of the median single-family dwelling has increased more rapidly than average family income over the past 25 years, leading to concern about the affordability of housing. Census data indicate that many American households cannot afford the modestly priced single family homes in their area. Whites and two-parent families are more likely to be able to afford the median-priced home than are minorities and single-parent families.

Policies to aid low-income households in obtaining shelter included rental ceilings, supply-side policies such as public housing and subsidies to developers, and demand-side policies such as rent certificates and housing vouchers. Rental ceilings create shortages of housing. Supply-side policies benefit both the construction industry and low-income households. Demand-side policies appear to benefit low-income families and to encourage the provision of low-cost and moderate-cost housing units by the private sector.

Residential segregation remains a problem in the United States. It leads to a disadvantaged economic environment for minorities in this country. In addition, the problem of homelessness is complex and only partially related to a scarcity of low-cost housing. Housing advocates argue that we need a cohesive, long-run strategy to attack the problem, instead of the reactive strategies we now have.

NOTES

1. These words, and the words of other women throughout the text, are actual quotations of women who were involved in a project of the Women and Poverty Public Education Initiative, funded by the Charles Stewart Mott Foundation. The source is *In Our Own Words: Mothers' Perspectives on Welfare Reform*, the Women and Poverty Public Education Initiative, 1997. Major portions of the report were prepared by Laura Wittmann, Anne Statham, and Katherine Rhoades, as well as Loretta Williams, Jean Verber, Julie Elliott, Selina Vasquez, Kathe Johnson, Nancy Bayne, Ethel Quisler, May Kay Schleiter, Diana Garcia, Iredia Seiler, Mary Ellen Lemke, Michelle Graf, Bets Reedy, Jean Radtke, Kim Noyd, Susan Taylor Campbell, and Davida Alperin. (Quotations may contain slight grammatical alterations made by the authors.)

2. U.S. Department of Commerce, Census Bureau, **www.census.gov/hhes/housing/**. Unless otherwise noted, the Census Bureau is the source of all housing statistics in this chapter.

3. Nancy E. Schwenk, "Trends in Housing," *Family Economics Review* (March 1991): 14.

4. The National Coalition for the Homeless (**www.nationalhomeless.org**), citing in part N. Dolbeare, Cushing and Jim Baumohl, ed. "Housing Policy: A General Consideration," in *Homelessness in America,* (Greenwood Publishing Group, Inc., Westport, Connecticut, 1996).

5. Department of Housing and Urban Development, "The Widening Gap: New Findings on Housing Affordability in America" (**www.hud.gov**).

6. Most of the information in this section is from the National Coalition for the Homeless, **www.nationalhomeless.org**. Its citations also include the U.S. Conference of Mayors and the Urban Institute.

DISCUSSION QUESTIONS

1. What are the factors that affect a family's ability to afford housing? According to the Census Bureau study cited in this chapter, what was the major factor that made American households unable to afford the modestly priced homes in their area in 1995?

2. Describe the effects of rental ceilings. Who benefits from rental ceilings? What are the long-run effects of rental ceilings? How can landlords and tenants cheat on rental ceilings? Do you think that rental ceilings might lead to more discrimination against certain groups?

3. What is the housing situation in your college town? Do you believe that rents are unjustly too high? What is the quality of housing? Are you aware of situations in which students were discriminated against or students were unfairly denied the recovery of their security deposits?

4. Which two groups are the primary beneficiaries of public housing and subsidies to developers?

5. How are rent certificates and rent vouchers different? If we had only so much money for housing assistance, would we be able to help more families with a program of rent certificates or a program of vouchers?

6. Should we subsidize housing for each of the following groups?
   a. Homeless families
   b. Low-income families
   c. Middle- and upper-income families
Do we subsidize these groups? How so?

7. Do you take the conservative or the liberal position on the issue of housing?

8. How many paychecks away from homelessness is your household? What would you do if

disaster struck and you (or your family) lost your income? Would you rely on savings, relatives, or friends? What if none of these resources were available to you?

9. Go to the Web site of the National Association of Realtors (**www.realtor.com**) and find the most recent value of the average existing home.

10. Check out the Web site of the National coalition for the Homeless, **www.nationalhomeless.org**. Do you think this is a liberal or conservative organization? What kinds of policies does it promote?

11. Go to the following Web site: **www.hud.gov/ news.html**. This Department of Housing and Urban Development Web page provides links to other research and sources of data on housing of low-income families and on welfare reform. How does this Web site compare with the Web site of the National Coalition for the Homeless in terms of liberal versus conservative? Why do you feel this way?

CHAPTER 10 APPENDIX: PRICE CEILINGS

You may never have lived in rent-controlled housing, but some real-world examples of price ceilings have almost certainly affected you and your family. Let's consider some of these price ceilings.

A PRICE CEILING ON FOOTBALL TICKETS

Your school probably has a football (or basketball, hockey, or baseball) team that you, your fellow students, and even college alumni follow. Imagine that your team is having an exceptional year. All seating is filled to capacity. In fact, many fans who want to attend games cannot get tickets. To obtain tickets, you either have to stand in line for hours or have some "connection" allowing you to receive preferential treatment.

Such a situation is shown in Figure 10-4. Note first that the supply curve is vertical (perfectly inelastic). There are 20,000 seats in the football stadium, so regardless of the price of football tickets, there will be just 20,000 tickets available. Quantity will not change, no matter what happens to price. The demand curve for tickets, however, has the usual downward slope, implying that more people are willing and able to buy tickets if the price is lower. If the market were allowed to operate by itself, an equilibrium would occur at a price of $9 and the quantity 20,000. There would be no shortage of football tickets.

But let's assume that the school administration sets a price for football tickets of $5, which administrators believe to be a fair and appropriate price for sports tickets. After all, the administrators do not want to unduly burden students and alumni with high ticket prices. They want only to bring in enough ticket revenue to cover the team's costs.

The $5 price operates like a price ceiling, because the price is set below the equilibrium level. Thirty thousand fans demand the $5 tickets. But there are only 20,000 seats available, so only 20,000 fans will be able to obtain tickets. There is a shortage of 10,000 tickets in the market.

Without intending to do so, the school administration created an inefficient market. Fans were given an overincentive to buy a football ticket, and a shortage was the natural result. In addition, people wasted hours standing in line. If the price of tickets were allowed to rise to the $9 level, these conditions could have been avoided.

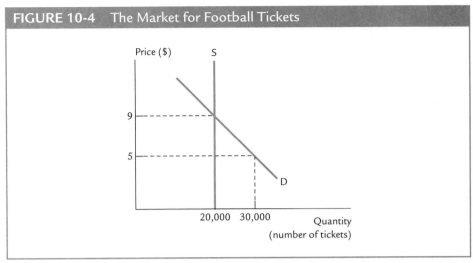

FIGURE 10-4　The Market for Football Tickets

Price ($)

S

9

5

D

20,000　30,000

Quantity
(number of tickets)

The $5 price ceiling for football tickets results in a shortage of 10,000 tickets.

A PRICE CEILING ON GASOLINE

If you did not drive in the 1970s, ask your parents (or grandparents?) about the gasoline shortage that occurred. They will undoubtedly tell you about long lines of cars trying to reach gas pumps and about gas stations closing early because they had sold all their gasoline. Some gas stations sold only to their established customers and turned away strangers. Many customers were unable to purchase gasoline. Other customers continually "topped off" their almost-full tanks whenever they had a chance. We got up early to wait in line, spent a lot of time looking for gas, worried about shortages of gas, and were extremely frustrated by the situation. If ever a market were inefficient, it was the 1970s U.S. gasoline market.

Problems in the gasoline market were closely related to problems in the market for petroleum. In the early 1970s, many Arab governments initiated a boycott on petroleum products sold to the United States. This was known as the Arab Oil Embargo. It effectively reduced oil supplies headed toward the United States. At almost the same time, the 13-member Organization of Petroleum Exporting Countries (OPEC) flexed its economic muscles by reducing the world supply of crude oil. The natural result of these actions was a dramatic increase in the price of crude oil. Prices went from $2.50 per barrel in the fall of 1973 to $10.00 per barrel in the spring of 1974. Consequently, prices of petroleum products, including gasoline, also skyrocketed. Because oil-based inputs are central to many production processes, the higher prices for oil products caused the supplies of virtually all manufactured and agricultural products that use petroleum products in their production to decrease. These declining supplies caused prices in general to rise, resulting in inflation.

Again in 1979, oil supplies were reduced as Iran cut off its supplies to the United States. Petroleum prices jumped again, and gasoline prices rose as well. Gas shortages became acute. Once again, inflation was the political and economic problem of the day.

The restricted supplies and resulting high prices of petroleum did not cause the gasoline shortages. If price is free to increase, equilibrium will occur at the point at which quantity demanded equals quantity supplied, and there will be no shortage. A shortage will result only if price is

FIGURE 10-5 The Effect of a Gasoline Price Ceiling

Price ($)

S

P_C

D

0   Q^S   Q^D   Quantity
(gallons of gasoline)

The effective price ceiling on gasoline results in a shortage of gasoline.

prevented from rising to the equilibrium level. This phenomenon is exactly what occurred in 1973–1974 and again in 1979. Price ceilings on petroleum and petroleum products existed throughout this period. These ceilings became effective (that is, had an effect on the market), however, only when the market prices of petroleum products rose above them. (As long as the market price remains below a price ceiling, the government prohibition against charging prices too high cannot have an impact. Price simply remains at the equilibrium level.) When gasoline prices skyrocketed in 1973–1974 and again in 1979, the price ceilings became effective and encouraged suppliers to undersupply at the same time they encouraged consumers to overdemand. The shortage depicted in Figure 10-5 was the result.

Would it have been better to simply allow the higher gasoline prices to exist? Certainly, the market would have been more efficient; quantity demanded would have equaled quantity supplied, and no shortages would have been created. But the high gasoline prices might have created problems for low-income consumers. Gasoline is a necessity to those who must drive to work. Can you think of any better ways to ensure that low-income commuters had the necessary gasoline?

A PRICE CEILING ON INTEREST RATES

Do you recall the mention of usury laws near the beginning of this chapter? Usury laws are price ceilings on interest rates (that is, interest rate ceilings). Often governments put these interest rate ceilings into effect in order to prevent interest rates from rising too high. The outcome is the same as the other price ceilings that we've considered. The graph is shown in Figure 10-6, with the quantity of loanable funds on the quantity axis (the amount of funds to be borrowed and lent) and the price of loanable funds (the interest rate) on the vertical axis. The demand for loanable funds represents all people who would like to borrow money. The supply of loanable funds represents all people who would like to lend money. Lenders are also often savers: if you place your money in a savings account, you are lending your money to the bank, which is lending the money to other borrowers. Equilibrium would exist at point E, with an equilibrium quantity of $3 million and an equilibrium interest rate of 8 percent. If, however, the government places an interest rate ceiling at 6 percent, we can see that the quantity demanded of loanable funds will be $4 million and the quantity supplied will be $2 million. A shortage of $2 million is created.

OTHER EXAMPLES

In Chapter 7, we considered price ceilings on foods, such as corn or wheat, in less-developed countries (LDCs). Even though farmers in the rural sector tend to be poorer than consumers in the urban sector, LDC governments often impose price ceilings on staple foods (such as cereal grains) in order to keep urban residents happy. As is often the case, people riot in the cities when food prices rise too high, creating political instability for governments. The price ceilings create the typical problem of food shortages, as well as artificially low prices received by farmers, who in turn face lower incomes and less incentive to produce food. Partly because of pressure from international organizations, many LDCs are now removing their price ceilings. Similar price ceilings have existed in socialist countries such as the former Soviet Union. As these countries are now engaged in economic reforms, they are decontrolling these prices. The trade-off: consumers now pay high prices for food, but there are no shortages. Governments are wise to use market prices in order to provide appropriate incentives, but they still must find programs that directly assist low-income farmers and consumers.

One more example: we discuss pharmaceutical prices in the next chapter on health care. Because pharmaceutical prices are often very high and rapidly rising, many people are calling for price ceilings on these medications in order to keep their prices more affordable. Like housing and food, health care is a "special market" that often calls for government involvement. The outcomes of price ceilings would be typical, however: lower prices but at the cost of creating shortages. Do you have any ideas about better ways to deal with the fact that many people cannot afford pharmaceutical drugs?

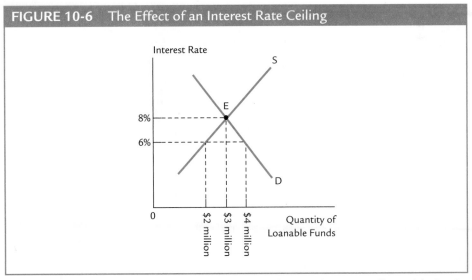

FIGURE 10-6 The Effect of an Interest Rate Ceiling

The effective interest rate on loanable funds results in a shortage of loanable funds.

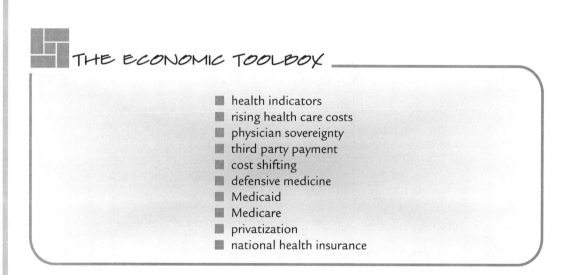

**Chapter 6
U.S. Poverty**
Poor people often lack access to quality health care
Medicaid is subsidized health care for low-income people
Poverty can lead to poor health

**Chapter 7
World Poverty**
Poverty in poor countries leads to poor standards of health

**Chapter 5
Discrimination**
Minorities are more likely to be uninsured than are whites
Minorities have lower life expectancies and higher infant mortality rates

**Chapter 11
Health Care**

**Chapter 10
Housing**
Residential segregation concentrates poverty and contributes to lack of access to quality health care

**Chapter 13
Social Security**
Medicare provides health insurance for most elderly Social Security recipients
Social Security provides income for disabled workers

**Chapter 14
Unemployment and Inflation**
Health coverage is often dependent on having a full-time job

THE ECONOMIC TOOLBOX

- health indicators
- rising health care costs
- physician sovereignty
- third party payment
- cost shifting
- defensive medicine
- Medicaid
- Medicare
- privatization
- national health insurance

HEALTH CARE

Our . . . goal is high quality, affordable health care for all Americans. The American system of medicine is a model of skill and innovation, with a pace of discovery that is adding good years to our lives. Yet for many people, medical care costs too much—and many have no coverage at all. These problems will not be solved with a nationalized health care system that dictates coverage and rations care.

—President George W. Bush, State of the Union Address, January 2003

These few lines from President Bush's 2003 State of the Union Address encompass three very important notions. The first is that the U.S. health care system is considered to be of high quality and a model for the rest of the world. The second is that medical care costs too much and that many people do not have access to health care. And last, the president shows his conservative approach by opposing a nationalized health care system. These are the types of issues we consider in this chapter.

What do you think of the health care that you and your family receive? Do you worry about your grandmother's ability to afford prescription drugs? Do you have good health insurance that is tied to a family member's job? Do you ever worry about losing your health insurance if that person loses that job? Do you have to remain a full-time student to be covered by your parents' medical insurance? What will happen to your health insurance after you graduate? Has your insurance plan changed to a health maintenance organization (HMO) from a more traditional plan?

Ask Americans what they think of health care in the United States, and most of them will respond that U.S. health care is the best in the world. After some thought, a few might qualify that response by noting that medical care is certainly expensive. Still others might express concern for people who cannot afford health insurance or who cannot buy health insurance because they have a pre-existing illness. In an era of organ transplants, nuclear medicine, and technological innovations in pharmaceuticals, many of our medical concerns involve the economics of medical care. Our

TABLE 11-1 National Health Expenditures, Selected Years, 1960–2000 (current dollar amounts in billions)

Year	1960	1965	1970	1975	1980	1985	1990	1995	2000
Expenditures	$27	$41	$73	$130	$246	$427	$696	$990	$1,300

Change from 1960 to 2000: 4,715%
Average annual change from 1960 to 2000: 118%

Source: U.S. Department of Commerce, Census Bureau, Statistical Abstract of the United States (**www.census.gov**).

medical delivery system has been characterized by escalating costs, inadequate access to quality medical care, and waste and inefficiency.

In this chapter, we examine data on health care in the United States. We look at our expenditures and examine where we rank relative to other countries in terms of these expenditures and the quality of our health. We then look at the unique characteristics of health care that contribute to a quality of health that is lower than we would like. Finally, we look at proposals for reform of our health care system. Let us begin by looking at health care expenditures in the United States.

U.S. HEALTH CARE EXPENDITURES

Total health care expenditures in the United States are shown in Table 11-1 for the time period 1960 to 2000. We see that total health care expenditures in the United States reached $1,300 billion in the year 2000, an increase of a whopping 4,715 percent over the 40-year time period. This represents an average *annual* change of 118 percent per year over the time period. Although these expenditures are not adjusted for **inflation**, they have clearly increased far more rapidly than the average level of prices in our economy.

Inflation
An increase in the average price level.

Furthermore, Table 11-2 shows how the United States compares with other Western industrialized countries in terms of health care expenditure as a share of **gross domestic product (GDP)**. Of the 11 countries listed, the United States clearly ranks the highest. The table shows that the United States spends 13.0 percent of GDP on health care.

Regardless of how you put it, we are spending a large percentage of GDP on health care, and these health care expenditures have risen enormously over time. Simply put, we are spending much more on health care, as a society and as individuals, than we have in previous years.

Gross domestic product (GDP)
A measure of the total output (and income) produced in a nation in one year.

Social Significance of Increased Expenditures

Financial costs are a claim on the nation's resources. When health care expenditure as a percentage of our national output increases, it means that we are allocating more of our resources to health care. Therefore, we are giving up other goods and services to acquire medical care. Recall the production possibilities curve from Chapter 1. Over any given time period, assuming full employment and a fixed quan-

TABLE 11-2 National Health Expenditures as a Percentage of GDP of 11 Western Industrialized Countries with Population over 10 Million, 1998 (in order of highest to lowest)

Country	Percentage	Country	Percentage
United States	13.0	Greece	8.3
Germany	10.6	Portugal	7.8
France	9.6	Japan	7.6
Canada	9.5	Spain	7.1
Netherlands	8.6	United Kingdom	6.7
Italy	8.4		

*Source: Centers for Disease Control (**www.cdc.gov**).*

tity and quality of resources and technology, our nation is capable of producing only a limited amount of goods and services. If we choose to have more of one good, such as health care, we must necessarily produce less of something else. Figure 11-1 shows a production possibilities curve for medical care and all other goods and services. We have moved from point A in 1960 to point B today. As a result, we are sacrificing the production of other goods. (Figure 11-1 is not drawn to scale.)

FIGURE 11-1 Production Possibilities Curve for Health Care

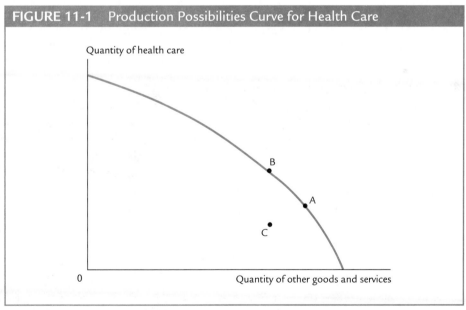

As we have moved from point A to point B, we have obtained more health care, but we have given up other goods and services. At point C, we are using our resources inefficiently.

Outcomes of Health Expenditures

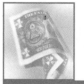
Since we are spending so much on health care, we want to know whether these expenditures are resulting in a high standard of health for our nation's citizens. The two most commonly used health care indicators are life expectancy at birth and infant mortality rates. **Life expectancy** is the average number of years that a child born in a particular year is expected to live. The **infant mortality rate** measures the number of infant deaths (deaths of children under one year of age) per 1,000 live births. These measures are shown in Table 11-3 for the United States and for the other countries we considered in Table 11-2.

Note that the United States ranks 10th among the 11 countries for life expectancy, and it has the worst infant mortality rate among the 11 countries. Furthermore, nations that spend less than the United States on health care as a share of GDP perform better than the United States on these two health indicators. Although there are certainly other factors affecting the health indicators, as we'll discuss momentarily, the data displayed in this table show cause for concern.

Furthermore, statistics reveal that the quality of health care in the United States varies enormously among racial and ethnic groups. Table 11-4 shows the differences in the United States by race and ethnicity with respect to infant mortality rates. Using the infant mortality rate for the United States as a whole (6.8) as a baseline national average, we can see whether a particular group of people has a higher- or lower- than average infant mortality rate. The differences are enormous. First, the statistics show that the Caucasian (white) group has an infant mortality rate (5.7) well below the national average. The African American group has an astounding infant mortality rate that is more than twice the Caucasian rate. The Native American group also has infant mortality rates well above the national average. In addition, infant mortality rates vary among states in our nation, ranging from a low of 4.8 in Maine and Utah,

Life expectancy
The age to which a baby born in a particular year can be expected to live on average.

TABLE 11-3 Life Expectancy at Birth and Infant Mortality Rate (per 1,000 live births) of 11 Western Industrialized Countries with Population over 10 Million, 2001 (in order of highest life expectancy to lowest)

Country	Life Expectancy (years)	Infant Mortality Rate	Country	Life Expectancy (years)	Infant Mortality Rate
Japan	80.8	3.9	Netherlands	78.4	4.4
Canada	79.6	5.0	United Kingdom	77.8	5.5
Italy	79.1	5.8	Germany	77.6	4.7
France	78.9	4.5	United States	77.3	6.8
Spain	78.9	4.9	Portugal	75.9	5.9
Greece	78.6	6.4			

*Source: U.S. Department of Commerce, Census Bureau, Statistical Abstract of the U.S., 2002 (**www.census.gov**).*

TABLE 11-4 A Comparison of Infant Mortality Rates in the United States, by Race and Ethnicity, 2000

Group	Infant Mortality Rate
Total United States	6.8
Caucasian	5.7
African American	13.7
Native American	9.7
Hispanic	5.4
Asian American	4.7

Source: Centers for Disease Control (**www.cdc.gov**).

to a high of 15.0 in Washington, D.C. The high infant mortality rates for these racial and ethnic groups and for cities, such as our nation's capital, are on par with many less-developed countries.

Infant mortality rate The number of infants who die before their first birthday per every 1,000 live births.

Although nutritional, cultural, and other lifestyle characteristics influence these statistics, the statistics also depend on income and discrimination. We noted in the poverty statistics in Chapter 6 that African American people have poverty rates much higher than Caucasians. The same is true of Native Americans. These groups are also more likely to experience discrimination, as we discussed in Chapter 5. At the same time, the unequal *quality* of health care and the unequal access to health care are certainly important factors. Pregnant women with limited *access* to quality prenatal care, for example, are more likely to die from complications of pregnancy and delivery, and their babies are more likely to be premature or in poor health. As the director of the World Health Organization recently stated, there are three Americas. There is high-quality health care for the rich and mediocre health care for the middle-income class. However, he notes that "it's the bottom 5 percent or 10 percent, made up of Native Americans living on reservations, the inner city poor, rural blacks and Appalachia that is a third America. They have health conditions as bad as those in sub-Saharan Africa."[1]

In summary, we have seen high and increasing health care expenditures in the United States, and yet our health indicators are below those of other Western industrialized countries. We've also seen that health indicators vary enormously by race and ethnicity within our country. What are the reasons for these outcomes? *Why do we spend so much on health care, yet we have relatively poor outcomes?* Let's explore two reasons for this inconsistency in the next section on health care problems. These problems include rising health care costs and a lack of access to health care.

U.S. HEALTH CARE PROBLEMS

Escalating Health Care Costs

The reasons why we as a nation spend so much on health care are twofold: (1) we consume a growing amount of health care, and (2) the price of this health care is rising. Both of these factors have to do with unique characteristics of the health care market, a market that is quite unlike the market for hamburgers, pajamas, or mystery novels. Let's consider a number of these characteristics.

Physician Sovereignty

Physician sovereignty
A medical doctor's control over the demand for medical procedures.

Physician sovereignty means that it is the doctor (or other health care professional) that controls the demand for medical care. We do not shop around for the most appropriate medical care, comparing price and quality characteristics of numerous models, as we would if we went to the hardware store to buy a hammer. Instead, we accept that we need the tests, drugs, and treatments that the doctor prescribes. Medical care requires expert knowledge; we are not capable of making sophisticated diagnoses on our own. Instead, we rely on the physician. The doctor may take cost considerations into account, but they are clearly secondary. Decisions are made on the basis of accepted medical practice and the assurance of good medical care. The normal frugality of a shopper who compares prices carefully and budgets wisely is not present in medical care. Furthermore, under traditional **fee-for-service** insurance, the more services that are recommended mean the more income the medical clinic receives. This situation may lead to unneeded services with benefits that are not worth their costs. Indeed, there may even be a tendency to overprescribe, overtest, and overservice, especially if this overcare reduces the likelihood of costly medical malpractice suits. Physician sovereignty thus leads to a higher demand for medical care, waste, and higher medical costs.

Fee-for-service
The charging of a specific fee for provision of a specific health care service.

Third-Party Payment

Third-party payment
A health care payment made by someone other than the patient or the patient's family.

Third-party payment means that most medical expenditures are paid for by either government programs or private insurance. This phenomenon makes patients less cost conscious than they would be if they had to pay directly for medical services themselves. The indirect link between insurance premiums and our medical costs is tenuous—our insurance premiums do not appear to us to be directly linked to the number of visits we make to the doctor's office or to the number of trips we make to the hospital emergency room. When a third party pays for our medical care, we are more willing and able to ask for additional medical services. Like physician sovereignty, third-party payment increases the demand for medical care and therefore its price.

Rapid Technological Change

Kidney dialysis machines, magnetic resonance imaging, transplant techniques, nuclear medicine, high-dosage chemotherapy, and Viagra are some medicine-related technological advances in recent years. When hospitals invest in highly specialized equipment, hospital costs, which have been the most rapidly escalating element of health care costs in the past 30 years, must then increase.

Medical experts and their patients judge hospitals by the quality of physicians who are on their staffs. Reputable medical doctors choose to practice at hospitals that have all the latest technology available, so that every hospital competing for first-class medical specialists must have it all. Thus, expensive machinery is duplicated in the several hospitals of our cities. Doctors must use the technology to justify its installation. The number of expensive tests and treatments increases, representing a rise in demand for health care. Many experts believe that expensive and rapidly changing technology is the major force driving hospital costs.

In the last half of the 1990s, one of the fastest-growing elements in health technology spending was prescription drugs. New pharmaceutical products can increase the quality and length of life. Many of these new drugs are very expensive, and they may bring new patients into the health care system. (Experts estimate that a large portion of Viagra sales was to men who had not previously been treated for impotence.) Thus, spending on prescription drugs has increased rapidly.

Inadequate Cost Containment

Responsibility for containing the costs of medical treatment is so diffused that keeping these costs down is very difficult. Third-party payment makes the patient and the patient's family less concerned about costs. Hospital administrators find it relatively easy to pass along cost increases for needed treatments. Furthermore, hospitals and physicians routinely engage in **cost shifting**, which is the transfer of the unpaid costs of some patients to well-insured patients through the raising of fees. The hospital reimbursement procedures of Medicaid and Medicare often leave a portion of a patient's costs uncovered, and hospitals treat very urgent cases even if payment is unlikely. They then cover these uncompensated costs by raising their rates and collecting more from insurance companies for the treatment of patients who have good insurance (or from affluent patients with no insurance). Cost shifting distorts decisions made about health care and makes calculation of the costs of a given treatment difficult.

Cost shifting
The practice of recovering the unpaid costs of some patients by charging higher prices to other patients.

Attitudes of Patients

Americans' attitudes toward medical care affect our health care system in several ways. First, we believe in our high-tech medical system. We hear on the television and radio about new treatments and studies, and we believe that virtually any treatment should be available to us. We believe that more tests are better than less, that aggressive medical treatment can cure virtually anything, and that we do not need to take much responsibility for our own health. This belief leads us to demand excessive care without much regard for cost.

Second, we are a litigious society; if we suspect a physician of an error, we sue for malpractice. As a result, doctors take out **malpractice insurance**. Malpractice insurance pays the settlement if a physician is found guilty of a mistake that harms a patient. As malpractice case settlements have increased over the years, malpractice insurance premiums have increased, and higher insurance costs have driven up medical fees. In addition, doctors have sought to protect themselves by practicing **defensive medicine**, which also drives up medical costs. Rather than be found guilty of carelessness, doctors prescribe tests that are virtually certain to be unnecessary. It has been estimated that one-half of the cesarean-section deliveries performed in the United States each year are unnecessary, but malpractice awards are so large when babies are injured in the birth process that cesareans are done at the first sign of any irregularity, despite their high cost. (Cesarean operations cost about twice what vaginal deliveries cost.) Such defensive medicine also implies an increased demand for medical services.

Malpractice insurance
Insurance carried by health care professionals to protect themselves from large malpractice damage awards.

Defensive medicine
The ordering of unnecessary tests and services by health care professionals solely to protect themselves from charges of malpractice.

Defensive medicine distorts medical care markets in other ways also. Many clinics carry obstetric malpractice insurance on only a few physicians, for example, and many family practice doctors therefore no longer deliver babies. Consequently, some areas of our country suffer a shortage of obstetricians.

Consequences of These Characteristics

These characteristics of the market for medical care have caused medical costs to skyrocket over time as shown in Figure 11-2. Physician sovereignty, third-party payment, and the increase in tests and treatments caused by rapid technological change and defensive medicine all imply increases in the demand for health care. Our attitudes as patients also create larger demands for medical care. On the other hand, the installation of new technology and the continual replacement of "old" technology, as well as expansion of the number of hospital beds and doctors, represent an increase in the supply of health care. Since 1960, therefore, both the demand for and the supply of medical care have increased, but demand has increased by a much greater amount than supply. We now consume more medical care at higher prices.

In addition, consumer advocates maintain that much of our health care expenditures are wasted. These wasted dollars represent the unnecessary tests and medical procedures already discussed and unnecessary surgeries and drugs. Expensive technologies, such as magnetic resonance imaging (MRI), are overused. As noted, many hospitals each operate extremely expensive equipment instead of sharing identical million-dollar machines. This duplication leads to both higher costs and more unnecessary tests, because use justifies the investment in the machines in the first place.

FIGURE 11-2   Increased Demand and Supply of Medical Care

Because demand has increased more than supply since 1960, medical care prices have risen as we have consumed a greater quantity of health care.

Finally, paperwork costs are tremendous. Every private insurance company and the government have their own forms to be filled out. If you have a friend who works for a physician or hospital, ask about the paper maze. The paperwork adds greatly to health care costs.

Refer again to Figure 11-1 on page 263. In terms of the production possibilities curve, we are probably neither at point A nor at point B, but at a point such as point C, inside the curve. By cutting some of the waste and inefficiency now present in U.S. medical care, we could move toward the curve and clearly be better off.

Lack of Access to Health Care

A second reason for our relatively poor health outcomes is the lack of access of many people to health care. Unless we have unlimited wealth, we all depend on some form of health insurance or program. This may be either private insurance that is purchased privately or provided by our employers or public health programs that are provided by the government. As shown in Table 11-5, 14 percent of our nation's population is without any health coverage. We also note that coverage varies considerably among different groups of people in the United States. Poor people and people of racial or ethnic minority are more likely to be without any health coverage.

Other statistics reveal that most people who have private insurance acquire it as a fringe benefit from employment. Employees of large firms are much more likely to have such a fringe benefit than are employees of small firms. Only 69 percent of workers in firms with fewer than 10 employees are insured, compared with 91 percent of workers in firms employing more than 1,000 workers.[2]

TABLE 11-5	Percentage of Persons with Health Coverage by Characteristics of the Population and by Type of Health Coverage, 2000		
	Type of Coverage		
Group	**Private**	**Government**	**None**
All Persons	72.4	13.6	14.0
Children[a]	70.6	17.8	11.6
Male	72.8	12.3	14.9
Female	72.1	14.8	13.1
Caucasian	75.0	12.1	12.9
African American	58.9	22.6	18.5
Hispanic	47.9	21.1	32.0
Asian American	69.9	12.1	18.0
Persons below the poverty line	27.8	42.6	29.6

*Source: U.S. Department of Commerce, Census Bureau, Statistical Abstract of the United States, 2002 (**www.census.gov**).*

Note: Numbers do not add to 100 percent because of rounding and because some recipients carry two types of insurance.

[a]Children are defined here as people under age 18 years.

Medicaid
A government program providing medical coverage for eligible low-income people.

Medicare
A government program providing medical coverage largely to elderly people.

Premium
A payment to purchase and keep in force an insurance policy.

Deductible
A payment on an annual or per-service basis that must be made by the insured person before the insurance company's payments begin.

Coinsurance payment
A percentage of medical expenses that the insured person must pay over and above the deductible.

Thus, we see that financial access to medical care depends on health insurance coverage or eligibility for government health programs, such as Medicaid or Medicare. **Medicaid** is subsidized health care for poor people and the medically indigent, and **Medicare** is a system of subsidized health insurance for the aged. Let's consider each of these programs separately.

Private Insurance

With private insurance, the patient pays a portion of the cost through an array of premiums, deductibles, and coinsurance payments. A **premium** is a payment (usually made on a monthly basis) to own an insurance policy and to be eligible for its benefits. A **deductible** is an amount of health care charges that the patient must pay before receiving insurance payments on the remainder of health care charges. It is usually a given amount specified for a time period or on a per-service basis. A **coinsurance payment** is some percentage of medical care charges over and above the deductible that the subscriber must pay.

If your insurance company requires a $200 deductible annually and 10 percent coinsurance, and your yearly covered medical expenses are $1,000, you will pay the $200 deductible plus 10 percent of the remaining $800 ($80) for a total of $280. The insurance company will pay the remaining $720. Most health care policies have maximum amounts that they will cover as well. In addition to the $280 that you must pay, you will pay a premium (unless it is paid by your employer) and you will be responsible for any expenses that go beyond the maximum amount covered by your insurance program. So, even if you have health insurance, your out-of-pocket expenses may still be high.

Deductibles and coinsurance keep costs to the insurer down, as well as discourage excessive use of medical services. If subscribers are required to pay some amount per service, they will be less inclined to use unnecessary services frivolously. On the other hand, the expense to the subscribers may actually deter them from seeking important services. Furthermore, the financing, including premiums, becomes regressive for subscribers. Even if a low-income and a high-income family pay the same dollar payments of premiums, deductibles, and coinsurance, the low-income family is paying a larger percentage of its income in these payments. Thus, the poorer family has a greater burden in paying these expenses. This **regressivity** could be eliminated if premiums and other payments were tied to income.

Our current Medicare system has the regressivity mentioned here. Some low-income elderly people refrain from using medical services because they cannot afford the deductible. Some cannot afford the optional portion of Medicare, because they cannot afford the monthly premiums. And, as discussed previously, some important medical services and supplies are not covered at all. The lack of prescription drug coverage is one of the major Medicare issues today.

Medicaid

One of the keys to understanding why large percentages of the poor are without health coverage has to do with the way that Medicaid is administered. Medicaid (as opposed to Medicare) is a program designed to pay for medical services for the nation's poor families and for medically indigent persons. (Medically indigent people have such high medical expenses that, whatever their income, they cannot afford their medical care.) Since eligibility depends on the family's income, we say that Medicaid is **means-tested**.

Although Medicaid is national in scope, it is administered by the individual states, and states are free to establish their own eligibility requirements and benefit levels within certain federal guidelines. This type of flexibility has been increasing over time and was greatly expanded as a result of the 1996 welfare reform. Individual states also have the option of supplementing federal financing with state revenues. As a result, Medicaid varies considerably by state. In 1995, fewer than half the families with income below the poverty line received medical assistance.[3] In many states, the family must not only be poor, it must be extremely poor before it receives health assistance. Typically, an eligible family must also include children. As a result, poor single individuals and couples, including the working poor, are often ineligible for Medicaid. One of the consequences of the recent reform of our welfare laws was that nearly a million poor parents lost Medicaid coverage when they went off welfare and began working at low-wage jobs. Furthermore, eligibility for Medicaid does not guarantee access to quality medical care. Medicaid recipients may find it hard to find physicians who will treat Medicaid patients, because the government reimburses only about one-half the average physician's fee, and doctors are prohibited from passing the remainder on to the Medicaid patient.

More than one-half of Medicaid payments are for nursing home care of people over the age of 65 years. Medicare (discussed later) does not cover nursing home care. It is quite common for middle-class couples to use up their assets keeping one or the other in a nursing home. When their assets are exhausted, they are considered medically indigent, and Medicaid pays the nursing home.

Regressivity A situation in which a larger percentage of income is taken from low-income people than high-income people.

Means-tested A way of determining who is eligible for a program, based on the person's low-income status and/or low asset ownership.

Medicare

The Medicare program was established in 1965 when it became evident that many aged Americans could not afford the health care that they needed. Medicare is an insurance program sponsored by the federal government. Medicare hospital insurance is financed by required payroll taxes on workers and employers. Optional Medicare medical insurance for physicians' services, medical equipment, certain treatments, and other medical services is financed through monthly premiums paid by the insured person. Because these premiums never cover the full amount of the covered services received by Medicare patients, the federal government finances the difference each year. Almost all elderly persons over the age of 65 years are covered, as well as disabled people who are eligible for Medicare benefits. Medicare is not means-tested—that is, benefits do not depend on a person's having few assets and low income. Both rich and poor are covered alike.

Because of both rising medical costs and the increasing proportion of elderly people in our population, Medicare has become an increasingly expensive program. As costs have increased, the burden of taxes on workers and employers has increased, until each is now responsible for taxes equaling 1.45 percent of all wages earned. As a result of the program's expense, efforts have been made to cut government costs.

EconDebate

"Should Medicare Provide Prescription Drug Coverage?"

What do you think? Check out Scarcity, Choice, and Opportunity Cost to read the full debate.

http://econapps. swlearning.com

Premiums paid by recipients have increased, deductibles have increased, and certain benefits have been cut. The elderly are being encouraged to enroll in managed care health delivery organizations. (These terms are discussed shortly.) As a consequence of these austerity measures, Medicare recipients are now paying larger out-of-pocket amounts of their health care costs than they formerly did.

Diagnosis-related groups (DRGs)
Approximately 500 categories into which a medical diagnosis might fall. The DRG determines the prospective payment made by Medicare.

In 1983, **diagnosis-related groups (DRGs)** were established for the Medicare program. This change was made in an attempt to contain runaway program costs. When admitted to a hospital, a Medicare patient is given a diagnosis that will fall into a particular diagnosis-related group. A **prospective payment** is the total reimbursement to the hospital for treatment of the patient; its amount depends on the diagnosis-related group into which the patient falls. This prospective payment is determined before any health care is provided. No matter what the actual cost of the patient's treatment is, the hospital is paid the prospective payment. If the hospital can treat the patient for less, it keeps the difference. If the patient's treatment costs the hospital more than the prospective payment, the hospital is out these costs (they cannot be passed along to the patient). Prospective payment provides an incentive for hospitals to curtail lengths of stay in their facilities, to avoid unnecessary treatments, and generally to promote efficiency. Critics argue that Medicare patients may be discharged before they are recovered sufficiently, but it is not clear whether this is true.

Prospective payment
A flat rate paid a hospital by Medicare to treat a particular patient having a given diagnosis.

Medicare does not cover all of older people's medical care. It covers only 80 percent of most hospital bills. Many older Americans therefore carry expensive "Medigap" insurance, which covers the medical expenses not covered by Medicare. Medicare also severely limits covered nursing home care and does not cover prescription drugs.

Many issues with Medicare are similar to the issues of medical care in general. High and escalating costs, affordability of care, and access to care (because clinics and hospitals do not have to accept Medicare patients) concern the elderly who rely on this program. One particular topic that has become a political and an economic issue is expansion of Medicare coverage to include prescription drugs. Many older Americans take a number of expensive pharmaceuticals that did not exist at the time Medicare was created. In December 2003, President Bush signed new legislation that would include prescription drug benefits in the Medicare program, as well as increase the role of private insurers in the system. These moves will undoubtedly be controversial (and expensive) over the next 10 years as the program begins implementation.

To summarize this section, we see that the lack of access to health care coverage, whether it be private or governmental, is a problem for many people. And, even when people *do* have access, they may still face restricted coverage and incur high out-of-pocket expenses, or they may go without health care as a result. The high cost of health care is certainly a problem for many people without adequate health care coverage.

THE RATIONING OF HEALTH CARE

Most people do not like rationing systems. Especially in the area of health care, we do not like to exclude certain people or exclude certain medical services. Nevertheless, we *do* ration health care on the basis of income and health insurance. Is there a better way?

Any health care system that does not offer comprehensive (complete) coverage of virtually all medical expenses must deal with the issue of what medical services will be covered. This issue faces Medicaid, Medicare, private insurance, and any proposed national health program. It is a form of rationing on the basis of which procedures will be covered. It has been suggested that because most people can afford to pay for routine care, such as checkups, immunizations, and prenatal visits, programs ought to address themselves to catastrophic coverage for serious and expensive medical conditions. After all, treatment of these conditions is beyond the means of all but the wealthiest Americans. Incurring some of these expenses could wipe out the savings and assets of even middle-income families. Indeed, health care problems are implicated in 50 percent of the consumer bankruptcy filings in the United States.[4]

On the other hand, others argue that this type of focus is not cost-effective and it certainly ignores the basic needs of the poor. Low-income people must make huge sacrifices in their choices between health care, food, and housing; and even low costs are large burdens that prevent their access to health measures. Furthermore, many of the low-cost items are preventative in nature. Assuring that all people have access to preventative measures such as prenatal visits, well-baby visits, pharmaceuticals, and immunizations will prevent other expensive outcomes from occurring. Certainly, it is cheaper to receive a meningitis vaccine than to experience (and possibly die from) meningitis. Similarly, ensuring that poor women get quality prenatal care is cheaper than treating low-birth-weight premature infants in neonatal intensive-care nurseries. If patients must pay for preventive care out-of-pocket, then many will be forced to go without that care and society may bear greater expenses in the long run. Preventive medicine is cost-effective, and according to many, it is equitable. (The cost-effectiveness of prescription drugs is only one of the many issues surrounding these drugs. Other issues involve their expense, their inclusion in health insurance programs, patent infringement regarding African AIDS treatment, the overseas sale of U.S. medicines that the Federal Drug Administration deems too dangerous for the United States, and the purchase of the same but cheaper drugs from Canada and Mexico by Americans.)

Another issue is the choice to finance educational and lifestyle programs (such as stop-smoking clinics and nutritional counseling) or to finance curative programs (such as surgeries and organ transplants). Any time that we do not provide all types of health care to all people, some form of rationing of health interventions must take place. Some people believe that it is better to spend money on the masses of people than to spend the same amount on just a few. Thus, the issue of rationing also has to do with determining who will receive health care. Should we attempt to focus our health care dollars on expensive treatments of elderly people who will likely die shortly regardless of care, or should we focus on health care for large numbers of people. Once again, we do not like to make these choices, but they become imperative when we do not provide total health care to all people.

As the production possibilities curve shows, we must make choices between medical care and other goods and services. We must also make choices such as: Who gets health care? How much health care do they get? What kind of health care? Who provides the health care? The list is endless. Some of these choices are made in the marketplace; some are made by the government. Regardless of who makes the decisions, we must realize that they *are* being made. We *do* ration health care in our country. Within our society, decisions are made about what share of GDP will be allocated to medical care. Within the field of health care, decisions are made about what types of health care will be funded and who will receive this health care. We do not like to make choices concerning health care. We do not want to choose between treatment of a heart transplant patient or a person on kidney dialysis. We do not want to choose between spending money on prenatal care for poor pregnant women or surgery for a wealthier man with lung cancer.

Even though we don't like to make such choices, they *are* being made, in part on the basis of income and ability to pay, and in part on the basis of eligibility for private or public health programs. At times, decisions appear to be made by default. The wisdom of our choices is difficult to assess because of cost shifting, which distorts the market. But many of us are upset by the continually increasing costs of health care, or the problem of access, or simply the waste. If we wish to change the distribution of medical benefits or the types of medical services available, we as a nation certainly have that power. What then are the possible alternatives for health care in the United States?

ALTERNATIVES FOR HEALTH CARE IN THE UNITED STATES

Given the many problems in U.S. health care, there have been many proposals for alternative programs. Some of these alternatives move in the direction of a more market-based (conservative) approach; other alternatives rely on greater government involvement in the health care industry, a liberal approach.

EconDebate

"Should There Be a Market for Human Organs?"

View the full debate by going to the Scarcity, Choice, and Opportunity Cost category.

http://econapps. swlearning.com

Privatization
The transfer of government-owned enterprises or responsibilities to the private sector.

Privatization and Increased Competition in Health Care

Some economists and political scientists argue that the government has too big of an influence on health care in this country. They desire the elimination or a sharp reduction in the government's participation in the health care market. Similarly, they want the **privatization** of publicly owned hospitals. Recall that the strength of free markets is their efficiency in equating private demand and supply, as long as there are competitive markets. This consideration fosters arguments in favor of a return to free markets on both the demand and the supply side of the health care market.

Curtailment or Elimination of Medicare and Medicaid

It has been noted that rising health care costs are at least partly the result of demand that is not tempered by the usual norms of frugality and concern for price. Certainly, the existence of Medicare and Medicaid is of prime consideration here. Without these programs, many people who could otherwise not afford medical care presumably would not receive such care, or at least not the type of care that they now receive. Because a high level of care for these people is reflected in the total demand for medical care, demand would decrease without these programs, and health care prices would go down. This withdrawal of medical care from the poor and the elderly would, however, be deemed unfair by others in society. A fairly significant portion of Americans view basic medical care as a fundamental right.

Medical Savings Accounts

A related proposal would replace current health insurance with the **medical savings account**. Some proponents of this proposal view it as a possible way to eventually reform Medicare. The medical savings account is a type of insurance. The purchaser—whether employer, government, or insured—makes regular payments into a medical expenses account, which the insured can draw against if he or she becomes ill. Catastrophic-care insurance to take care of very high medical bills is usually included in the proposal. The insured party controls how the funds in the account are spent: what tests are performed, what procedures are done, and by whom they are done. Monies not spent for medical care are returned to the insured person, giving him or her a stake in minimizing the costs of treatment. Proponents of medical savings accounts believe that the accounts would eliminate the perverse incentives built into other third-party payment systems (incentives that increase demand). Critics believe that they would benefit only relatively healthy people, who would save money on health care. Seriously ill people, they argue, would find that their insurance was inadequate for any high level of sophisticated care.

> **Medical savings account**
> A type of insurance in which the purchaser makes payments into an account that can be drawn against in times of illness.

Privatization of the Supply of Medical Services

Elements on the supply side of health care contribute to high medical costs as well. Many argue that a more privatized, competitive supply of health care services would result in lower costs. First, most hospitals are not run on a "for-profit" basis; other goals, such as offering quality overall care, utilizing the most advanced technology, or specializing in particular services, are paramount. Critics argue that the way we finance health care allows hospitals to pursue these goals by allowing them to shift uncompensated costs to well-insured patients. The privatization of government-owned and government-run hospitals and other reforms to increase competition among hospitals, it is argued, would force them to pay more attention to the bottom line, thus eliminating a great deal of inefficiency. On the other hand, supporters of public hospitals argue that some existing for-profit hospitals have increasingly come under attack for their "bottom line" mentality: their specialization in high-profit services, their neglect of other less profitable but important services, their cost-cutting measures (which dangerously decrease the quality and safety of patient care), and their highly publicized turning away of uninsured and low-income patients.

Second, advertising within the health care industry, especially the type of price advertising in which we see optical companies engaging, was long considered unethical. Since optical firms have begun to advertise, we have seen lower prices for glasses and contact lenses. If prices charged by physicians, clinics, and hospitals were advertised, as well as the prices of various services and medications, perhaps competitiveness among suppliers would increase, keeping prices lower. It should be noted, however, that the sort of nonprice television and magazine advertising in which the large pharmaceutical firms are now engaging will not make prices lower. Advertising of Zocor and Lipitor is aimed at increasing patient demand, increasing both price and quantity. And, of course, the advertising campaigns drive up the drug companies' costs, putting even more upward pressure on prices.

Group Practices and Managed Care

Various forms of group practices may increase efficiency and lower costs. For example, physicians operating in a clinic may have lower costs per service than a doctor in solo practice. Expensive technology and equipment can be more efficiently utilized, and physicians can specialize in various fields. Specific forms of group practices may yield additional efficiencies. **Health maintenance organizations (HMOs)** utilize the services of group physicians either working within or for the organization. The organization contracts with insurance companies to care for the insured person's medical need for a given rate. A patient's care is coordinated by a medical clinic or primary care physician. The patient needs a referral from the primary care physician to be treated by a doctor who is not in the organization. A similar form of group practice is the **preferred provider organization (PPO)**, which contracts with health insurance companies to provide health services at a reduced rate. Together, these organizations are what is meant by "managed care."

Managed care is rapidly replacing traditional fee-for-service insurance in the United States. The major reason is the high cost of providing fee-for-service coverage. Managed care is simply a less expensive way of obtaining medical care. As medical care costs rise, driving up the cost of standard fee-for-service insurance, many people are electing to become members of managed care organizations, and these organizations are becoming larger. The growth of managed care and the evolving competition among managed care organizations are generally credited with slowing the growth of U.S. health care expenditures in the 1990s and early 2000s. It is worth noting that fee-for-service insurance and other characteristics of our health care system, especially when combined with physician sovereignty, provide an incentive to give more medical care, whereas managed care provides an incentive to give less.

As with the Medicare program of prospective payment, there is an incentive for the managed care provider to be cost-efficient in its provision of medical services. Service costs that "go over contract" would be costly to an HMO. Costs below the contracted price would benefit the HMO. As a result, services that cut costs in the long run, such as health screening, nutrition and exercise classes, and smoking cessation clinics are often provided by HMOs. There is a healthy emphasis on preventive medicine. Still, some people complain that they cannot get a referral for coverage of a visit to an outside specialist, and others worry about the quality of care when the emphasis is on cost control. There is some evidence that HMOs' pressure on rates for medical reimbursement is slowing the pace at which some geographic areas adopt new technology. Many states, therefore, have passed laws regulating HMOs, while Congress has considered a "Patient's Bill of Rights."

National Health Insurance

National health insurance represents the opposite alternative to privatized market-based care. National health insurance of one kind or another is common throughout the Western industrialized world. Indeed, we are in a minority by having no national health insurance. Of all the industrialized countries of the world, only the United States and South Africa lack such a program. Furthermore, the United States covers a lower percentage of its expenditures (through Medicare and Medicaid)

Health maintenance organizations (HMOs)
Health insurance plans under which the covered care is limited to designated providers and the use of services is coordinated by a patient's primary care physician. HMOs often encourage preventative care.

Preferred provider organization (PPO)
A health insurance plan under which a group of medical providers contract to provide the insured patient's medical care at discounted rates.

than any other country in the list in Table 11-2. The goal of national health insurance is universal coverage. Under such coverage, everyone would have health insurance; people would not fall between the cracks, as they do in our present health care delivery system.

Canada has a system of national health insurance. The Canadian system stands midway between the United States' free enterprise system and Britain's socialized medicine, in which doctors are salaried government employees. Like U.S. physicians, Canadian doctors can practice wherever they want and charge whatever they like. Most doctors choose to practice within the Canadian insurance program. They are paid by the government according to a negotiated schedule of fees for services. The tax-supported Canadian program pays all hospital and medical bills. The system is thus an example of a single-payer health insurance system, and the single payer is the government. A single-payer system is much less expensive to administer than is a multipayer system. And, all people, whether rich or poor, employed or unemployed, have access to medical services.

The system is not perfect, however, and its costs are rising as new technologies are adopted. Although most Canadian citizens and physicians are happy (on balance) with the system, a common criticism is that elective surgeries are often postponed (and sometimes more critical interventions are delayed) because of shortages of health care. Indeed, one way the Canadian system contains costs is the deliberate slowdown of the adoption of new technologies. Many U.S. citizens are uncomfortable with the overt rationing of medical services under the Canadian system.

A very different proposal for national health insurance was made by the Clinton administration in 1993 and was defeated in Congress. The proposal would have stressed managed care to contain costs and would have required employers to purchase health insurance for their employees, while the government would have provided insurance for the unemployed. It was an extremely complex proposal that was opposed by the small business lobby, which argued that the increased costs to businesses would lead to loss of jobs, and by the insurance lobby, which argued that patient choice would be constrained. Discussion of alternative ways to improve access and cut costs in U.S. health care continues.

National health insurance A government program ensuring universal and comprehensive coverage of the population.

RECENT POLICY AND PROPOSALS

Recent Policy Change

Before considering recent (and controversial) proposals for altering our health care system, let's consider some of the recent policies that have already been placed into effect. The Kennedy–Kasselbaum Health Care Reform Bill, passed in 1996, requires insurers to continue to offer policies to workers who change jobs or lose their jobs. It makes health insurance easier to purchase by workers with preexisting chronic health problems.

In 1997, a federal plan to expand health care coverage for children in low-income working families was passed. Under the **State Child Health Insurance Program (SCHIP)**, states could expand Medicaid or begin a new program to provide health care to children in families whose income was too high for the children to qualify

State Child Health Insurance Program (SCHIP) A federal program providing health care coverage for children in low-income working families.

for Medicaid, but too low for the family to afford private insurance. Congress appropriated $40 billion to help the states improve insurance coverage for children during the first 10 years of SCHIP.

Although poor children are more likely to have insurance coverage now than in the early 1990s, their parents often remain uninsured. A particular problem with the 1996 reform of welfare is that many families went off welfare and into very-low-paying jobs. When they left welfare, they lost Medicaid, but they did not obtain a job that provided medical insurance and they cannot afford to purchase health insurance. The 1996 welfare reform law did give the states the flexibility to expand Medicaid coverage to people at whatever income level they determine is appropriate. Some states have extended Medicaid coverage to all families below the poverty line, and a few states now cover families whose income is above the poverty line. In addition, state plans to increase coverage for low-income pregnant women have become more common. Although no national health plan has been adopted, incremental changes have been made to improve access.

A few states have capped the amount of damages that can be awarded in a malpractice lawsuit. Juries have made truly huge malpractice awards, which both drive up malpractice insurance premiums and lead physicians to practice defensive medicine. Caps, it is argued, will decrease health care costs by decreasing the unnecessary tests doctors order solely to protect themselves.

Recent Proposals

President Bush, in his 2003 State of the Union Address, called for increased government spending on the Medicare program. At the same time, he promised our seniors the option of purchasing an insurance program with prescription drug coverage. Privatization of health care has become a controversial issue and will continue to be so during the campaigns for the 2004 presidential election.

In terms of the Medicaid program, state government budgets have recently suffered greatly as a result of the poor economy and restricted revenues from the federal government. The Bush administration has proposed a choice for state governments to deal with their difficulty in financing Medicaid. Under the proposal, states could choose between receiving some modest funding from the federal government to get them through their current fiscal crises, or they could choose to operate their Medicaid programs without any financial relief from the federal government. According to the Center on Budget and Policy Priorities, both of these choices would substantially weaken health coverage for low-income children, parents, and elderly and disabled people.[5] In the former alternative, states must agree to convert much of their Medicaid program into a block grant, under which federal funding doesn't automatically rise to meet any increased need for health care in the state. States electing this option would have to pay back the additional funding by the end of the decade. Under the latter approach, the likely consequence would be immediate cutbacks now in the number of low-income people whom Medicaid insures or in the medical services that Medicaid covers. Many people are concerned that both of these choices will eliminate benefits at a time when so many people need assistance.

Compromise?

Aside from the issue of prescription drug coverage, we obviously recognize that if we wish to extend health coverage to all people, our desire to cut health care costs will not be possible. On the other hand, not all people need to be covered by government programs, such as with national health insurance. A national health plan might cover only those without access to health care, and high-income and employed individuals might continue to be covered by private insurance. In addition, the national plan might pick up catastrophic coverage for individuals with exorbitant medical costs when their private benefits run out.

The benefits of this option are reduced costs to taxpayers. Government financing would cover only those who could not privately finance their health care. One concern, however, is that physicians and other health providers might prefer to treat private patients, especially if government payments are not as high as private ones. The result might be a two-tiered system of health care: one for the rich and one for the poor. Another concern is that, as is the case with Medicare and Medicaid now, health care providers would shift uncompensated costs to private insurance companies. Another problem is that patients may continue to pay rising out-of-pocket expenses on health care premiums, deductibles, and coinsurance.

Similar changes could be made in Medicare. Medicare currently covers all elderly retired people, whatever their income or assets. Some have suggested, however, that eligibility should be tied to income. Elderly people who can afford to purchase private insurance should be required to do so, or they would receive lower Medicare benefits. Those with lower incomes should receive full Medicare coverage. As we debate the addition of prescription drug benefits to Medicare, one option to stem the rising tide of Medicare costs would be to extend such benefits only to lower-income elderly people.

VIEWPOINT: CONSERVATIVE VERSUS LIBERAL

Conservatives, who believe in limited government, strongly oppose national health programs on the basis that such programs signify an expansion of the government's role. They favor privatization, the trimming of Medicare and Medicaid, the development of medical saving accounts, and a stronger role for the unregulated market. President Bush is on record for strongly pushing for greater privatization of our health care system.

Liberals, on the other hand, believe that the market has done a poor job of allocating medical care. They argue that the special characteristics of health care make it unlikely that the market will ever reach a fair and equitable solution. They therefore favor policy ranging from bolstering Medicaid and Medicare to developing national health programs on the order of those in other industrialized countries.

SUMMARY

The United States spends large and increasing amounts of money on health care, both in absolute dollars and as a percentage of gross domestic product. Despite these expenditures, the United States does not have the world's highest life expectancies or lowest infant mortality rates. Furthermore, the racial and ethnic differences in these statistics are pronounced.

The market for health care is different from other markets in ways that cause demand to be inflated and costs to be poorly constrained. As a result, we face escalating health care costs, inefficiency and waste, and unequal access to health care. Public and private health insurance leave 14 percent of Americans uncovered.

Alternative proposals for health care in the United States include an increase in privatization and competition, expansion of managed care practices, development of national health insurance, the revision of laws governing malpractice suit damages, and the revision of the existing Medicaid and Medicare programs. The choice among these programs is controversial, as is the direction of new policy proposals by the president and Congress.

NOTES

1. Chris Murray, *St. Paul Pioneer Press*, June 21, 2000, p. 1A.

2. Committee on Ways and Means, U.S. House of Representatives, *1998 Green Book* (Washington, D.C.: U.S. Government Printing Office, 1999).

3. U.S. Department of Commerce, Census Bureau, *Statistical Abstract of the United States*, 1999 (**www.census.gov**). Unless otherwise noted, all statistics in this chapter are from the Census Bureau.

4. Melissa B. Jacoby, Teresa A. Sullivan, and Elizabeth Warren, "Medical Problems and Bankruptcy Filings," *Norton Bankruptcy Law Adviser* (May 2000): 2.

5. Center on Budget and Policy Priorities, January 31, 2003 (**www.cbpp.org**).

DISCUSSION QUESTIONS

1. Go to the Organization for Economic Cooperation and Development Web site (**www.oecd. org**), and find the latest figures on health care expenditures for industrialized countries. How does the United States compare with other countries in the latest year?

2. How do the health expenditures of the United States compare with those of other countries?

3. How do life expectancies and infant mortality rates in the United States compare with those of other industrialized countries? How do they compare with the less-developed countries discussed in Chapter 7?

4. Which other factors besides health care enter into the statistics on life expectancy and infant mortality rates?

5. Define each of the following terms and explain how each affects the demand for medical care: (1) physician sovereignty, (2) third-party payment, (3) defensive medicine, and (4) attitudes of patients.

6. Do you agree that it is possible to overallocate resources to health care, or do you believe that the reasons for a high demand for health care (mentioned in question 5) are appropriate?

7. How does cost shifting make the calculation of the cost of particular medical treatments difficult?

8. Go to the Centers for Medicare and Medicaid Services at the Department of Health and Human Services Web site at **www.cms.hhs.gov**. Use the information on this Web site to understand the differences between Medicare and Medicaid.

9. Go to the White House Web site (**www.whitehouse.gov**), and click speeches given by President Bush on the Medicare program. Do you agree with his statements?

10. How does managed care result in a decrease of health care costs?

11. Do you believe that basic medical care is a right of citizenship? What features do you think a national health plan should have? (This does not necessarily mean national health insurance.)

12. What is the conservative position on national health insurance? What is the liberal position? What is your view toward national health insurance? Justify your answer. Visit the Web site of the Physicians for a National Health Program (**www.pnhp.org**) for more information on national health insurance.

13. Check out the Web site of the World Health Organization (WHO) at **www.who.int**, and find and read about a global health issue that is interesting to you.

14. Go to the Census Bureau at **www.census.gov**. Click H for *health* in the A–Z option, and see what types of U.S. statistics are available at this site.

Chapter 5
Discrimination
Immigrant farm workers and Native American populations work for low wages and/or lose their agricultural land

Chapter 8
Market Power
Concentration is increasing in farming

Chapter 3
The Environment
Certain farming practices are a source of pollution

Policies such as removing highly erodible land from cultivation satisfy both environmental and agricultural policy goals

Chapter 12
Agriculture

Chapter 9
International Trade
Agricultural products are a major U.S. export

Government policy toward U.S. agriculture affects our competitiveness in world markets

Less-developed countries producing and exporting primary commodities face problems similar to those faced by U.S. agriculture

Chapter 7
World Poverty
U.S. agricultural subsidy and export policies harm less-developed country farmers

Agricultural development is essential to economic development in poor countries

THE ECONOMIC TOOLBOX

- agricultural markets
- inelastic demand
- immobile resources
- price supports (floors)
- dumping
- biotechnology
- U.N. World Food Summit
- target prices and deficiency payments (appendix)

AGRICULTURE

When the farmer comes to town with his wagon broken down,
Oh, the farmer is the man who feeds them all.
If you'll only look and see, I am sure you will agree
That the farmer is the man who feeds them all.
The farmer is the man lives on credit till the fall.
With the interest rate so high, it's a wonder he don't die,
For the mortgage man's the man who gets it all.
When the banker says he's broke, and the merchant's up in smoke,
They forget that it's the farmer feeds them all.
It would put them to the test if the farmer took a rest,
Then they'd know that it's the farmer feeds them all.

—American folk song, from Alan Lomax, *Folk Songs of North America*, Doubleday, 1960

Indeed, as the folk song says, the farmer is the one who feeds them all. And in the United States, a relatively small body of farmers (men as well as women) feeds a multitude of nonfarmers. One person engaged in agriculture feeds about 130 nonfarmers. Less than 2 percent of the country's population is engaged in farming, but the country is well fed. Yet one hears of small farmers going bankrupt and farming towns losing residents.

So, what's happening in agriculture? How does agricultural policy affect our farmers? How does it affect consumers? And how does it affect producers and consumers around the globe? In this chapter, we will discuss the unique characteristics of American agriculture, the history and effects of government policy toward agriculture, and the politics and outlook for agriculture in the future.

CHARACTERISTICS OF AGRICULTURE

Certain characteristics of agriculture distinguish the farm sector from the remainder of the economy. Some of this discussion involves the short run (one year to the next) and some involves the long run (over several years). The characteristics are as follows:

1. An inelastic demand for farm products in the short run
2. Extensive technological change in the past half century
3. Immobile resources

Let's see how these characteristics affect farmers.

Inelastic Demand for Farm Products in the Short Run

Inelastic demand
Demand in which buyers are relatively unresponsive to changes in price.

Recall our discussion of inelastic demand when we considered the market for addictive drugs in Chapter 2. When we say that a product has **inelastic demand**, we mean that its buyers are relatively unresponsive to changes in its price. This means that buyers show little variation in the quantity they buy when the price changes. This is the case for most farm commodities, as well as the many commodity exports from less-developed countries that we discussed in Chapter 9. As discussed in previous chapters, we represent inelastic demand with a relatively steep demand curve. And, as we shall see, the inelasticity of demand has considerable significance for farm prices and farmers' incomes.

Price Instability

Let's begin by looking at the significance of the inelastic demand for farm products on the stability of farm prices in the short run. If demand is inelastic, the small fluctuations in supply that might result from either exceptionally good or exceptionally bad weather will have a resounding effect on the prices that farmers receive for their products. Figure 12-1 illustrates this effect. The demand curve is shown to be relatively steep, reflecting the fact that any small percentage change on the horizontal axis (quantity) is associated with a large percentage change on the vertical axis (price).

The graph in the figure shows a hypothetical demand curve for corn with an initial equilibrium price of $3 per bushel and an initial equilibrium quantity of 5 million bushels. Now consider an increase in supply from S to S′ caused by exceptionally good weather. The equilibrium quantity increases to 6 million bushels, which is a relatively small percentage increase (20 percent). Now consider the price change. Because of the inelastic demand, the effect of the supply shift on the market price is very large. The increase in supply causes the price to fall all the way to $2 per bushel (a relatively large decrease of 50 percent). Similarly, a relatively small decrease in supply caused by poor weather (from S to S″) would cause a relatively large increase in price up to $4 per bushel (a 50 percent increase). The combination of short-run weather-related supply fluctuations and inelastic demand results in large fluctuations in agricultural prices in the short run. To convince yourself of the outcomes of inelastic demand, try drawing the same graph but with a flatter demand curve. When

FIGURE 12-1   The Effect of Inelasticity on Price and Farm Incomes

Quantity (millions of bushels)

Because the demand for farm products is inelastic, an increase in supply from S to S′ will cause a sharp decrease in price, as well as a decrease in farmers' incomes. Note that price falls from $3 to $2, while incomes decrease from $15 million to $12 million. Conversely, a decrease in supply to S″ will increase price to $4 and increase total farm incomes to $16 million.

demand is not inelastic, identical fluctuations in supply will cause much less price variation than when demand is inelastic.

Farm Income

Now let's consider how farmers' incomes are affected by this inelastic demand in the short run. If good weather causes an increase in supply (a **bumper crop**), which causes price to decrease, then overall farm income will also fall. This is because income from a corn crop is equal to the number of units sold times the price at which they are sold. Refer again to Figure 12-1. At the initial price of $3, farmers sold 5 million bushels, earning income of $15 million from their corn crop. (Five million bushels times $3 per bushel is $15 million.) After the increase in supply, farmers sold 6 million bushels at a price of $2 per bushel. They earned only $12 million for their corn crop. Because consumers have an inelastic demand for agricultural products, a short-run decrease in price results in a short-run decrease in farm income. Similarly, a short-run increase in price (from bad weather) results in a short-run increase in farm income. (For a more mathematical discussion of the effects of elasticity on prices and income, see Appendix 1 of this chapter.)

EconLinks

White House Economics Statistics briefing room.

See what the president has to say about his views on agriculture and the economy at **www.whitehouse.gov/news/releases/2001/07/20010727-2.html.**

Bumper crop
An unexpectedly large crop resulting from good growing conditions.

Note that these counterintuitive results are true for total farm income, not the income of an individual farmer. The farmer who has lost an entire crop will certainly not have higher income in the bad-weather year. Also note that these were short-run results. Demand is inelastic in the short run; and supply, price, and income fluctuate in the short run. These refer to year-to-year situations, as opposed to changes that occur over a long period of time. We now consider this long-run time period.

Extensive Technological Change in the Past Half Century

Real price
Price as adjusted for the effects of inflation. We do this when we consider price changes over time.

In the long run, technological change and slow growth in demand have caused the real prices of farm products to fall. (When we say **real price**, we mean the price as adjusted for inflation.) Commercial farmers have not only adopted new techniques, but also use new, efficient (and expensive) machinery. New high-yield crop varieties exist. Intensive use of fertilizers and pesticides increases yield per acre. Artificial insemination and other improved breeding techniques have resulted in more reliable growth in cattle herds. Center-pivot irrigation systems dot the Great Plains. And, as we discuss shortly, biotechnology is rapidly gaining supporters and opponents. The results of all of these technological changes are a trend toward capital-intensive and chemical-intensive agriculture, a movement toward large-scale farming enterprises, and a pronounced increase in the supply of farm products. Although the number of Americans engaged in agriculture is much smaller than a half century ago, the supply of farm products has increased markedly.

Compared with the large increase in supply, the increase in Americans' demand for food over time has been relatively small. That increase is attributable mainly to an increase in our population. We have grown more affluent over time, but we have spent our additional income on things other than food. As a people we have been well fed for a great many years.

The combined effects of this large long-run increase in supply and the modest increase in demand have greatly decreased the real price of farm products. This change is not a year-to-year price fluctuation of the sort caused by agriculture's inelastic demand, but a long-run trend instead. This is shown in Figure 12-2, where we see that the equilibrium quantity of agricultural products is larger but that the real price has decreased.

Immobile Farm Resources

The principal resource used in farming is, of course, land. With the exception of land near rapidly growing cities, which can be developed, there are few alternative uses for most farmland. So, although one farmer may leave farming and find a job in the city, land tends to remain in agriculture. Some other farmer buys the land and continues to farm it. If real prices fell as precipitously in other sectors as they have in farming, people and resources would rapidly flow out of these markets into other markets that are believed to be more profitable. But land is not removed from agriculture. Either farmland lies fallow or someone farms it. Agriculture's main resource is slow to respond to adverse industry conditions.

FIGURE 12-2 Effects of a Large Increase in Supply and a Smaller Increase in Demand on the Market for Farm Commodities in the Long Run

The larger increase in supply, coupled with the relatively small increase in demand, has caused the real prices of agricultural commodities to fall in the past 68 years.

Although the limited use to which farmland can be put undoubtedly contributes to this resource immobility, it can also be argued that the government's agricultural policies have kept agricultural resources *in* agriculture when they perhaps should have been transferred to other lines of production. Let's consider this policy.

GOVERNMENT POLICY TOWARD AGRICULTURE

The U.S. government has been extensively involved in agriculture since the Great Depression of the 1930s. The entire country (indeed, much of the world) was in distress during the 1930s, but agriculture suffered more than other sectors. Real farm prices fell, and farm income and profits plummeted. Furthermore, the prices that farmers received for their crops decreased more than the prices that they paid for their inputs.

Because the price of farm products was too low to cover farmers' costs, the government initiated a variety of policies to assist farmers. Congress passed the

Agricultural Adjustment Act in 1933 to restore the standing of farm incomes relative to incomes in the rest of the economy. This was one of the first pieces of Franklin D. Roosevelt's New Deal legislation to be enacted. The government has been extensively involved in agriculture ever since.

The objectives of farm policy have been to stabilize conditions in farming and to increase real farm incomes. Accordingly, programs were devised to affect the supply of agricultural products, the demand for agricultural products, and the price received by farmers. Two policy instruments were used early on. These were price supports and programs to restrict supply. As time passed, price supports became less important policy instruments, and target prices and deficiency payments became more important. Our government has also attempted to increase the demand for agricultural products in order to raise prices. We now discuss the price supports, programs to restrict supply, and policies to increase demand, and we leave the discussion of target prices and deficiency payments for Appendix 2 of this chapter.

Price Supports

Price supports are examples of **price floors**, which are government-imposed minimum prices for a good or service. These minimum prices set a "floor" below which the market price is not permitted to fall. To be effective, which means to have an effect on the market, these price floors must be above the market equilibrium price. (A price floor set below the market equilibrium would not have an effect on the market, since the market-determined price would take over. There is no law that says the prices cannot go *above* a certain level.) Agricultural prices are thereby prevented from falling below the price floor. As we discussed in Chapter 1, markets tend to clear at an equilibrium price and quantity. In the process, shortages and surpluses are rationed away. This is the rationing function of price in a competitive market. When agricultural prices are kept artificially high, they cannot perform the rationing function. Let's look at this problem through a hypothetical example of the U.S. wheat market in Table 12-1.

The equilibrium price is $3.50, at which both quantity demanded and quantity supplied equal 2,500 million bushels of wheat. At this equilibrium price, 2,500 million bushels will be exchanged and the market will clear. If price is temporarily above

EconNews

"Chiquita Going Bananas over Quotas"

Go to the International Trade category, and read more on the tariffs and trade restrictions.

http://econapps. swlearning.com

Price supports
Legally imposed minimum prices of goods or services. Price supports are specific examples of price floors.

Price floors
Legally imposed minimum prices of a good or service.

Quantity Demanded (millions of bushels)	Price ($)	Quantity Supplied (millions of bushels)
1,500	4.50	4,500
2,000	4.00	3,500
2,500	3.50	2,500
3,000	3.00	1,500
3,500	2.50	500

TABLE 12-1 Demand and Supply of Wheat (hypothetical data)

equilibrium, at $4.00, a surplus will exist in the market. Figure 12-3 shows the supply and demand data graphically, indicating the surplus at $4.00.

At the price of $4.00, farmers produce and offer 3,500 million bushels for sale, but consumers are willing to buy only 2,000 million, so only 2,000 million bushels are exchanged. The remaining 1,500 million bushels are an unsold surplus in the market. If the price is free to fall, the surplus will cause it to decrease. It will fall as long as there is a surplus to push it down. As price falls, a message is sent to buyers: increase the amount you demand, because price is falling. An opposite message is sent to sellers: decrease the amount you supply, because price is falling. Buyers and sellers each move down their respective demand or supply curve. When the equilibrium price ($3.50) is reached, quantity supplied equals quantity demanded, and there is no more surplus to drive the price down further. The falling price has rationed away the surplus. This process is what economists mean when they refer to the **rationing function of price**, which makes markets efficient means to allocate goods and services.

Now assume that the government had set the legal minimum price at $4.00, so that price could not fall in response to the surplus. The surplus would not be rationed away. Instead, the market would have a persistent surplus of wheat. And that is what happens when the government supports the prices of farm commodities. The price supports actually create surpluses.

Rationing function of price
The ability of a flexible market price to clear the market of shortages and surpluses.

FIGURE 12-3 Wheat Market with Price Support

When a price support keeps the price of wheat from falling below $4.00, a surplus of 1,500 million bushels of wheat is created.

The method by which some U.S. farm prices are supported is indirect, but the result is the same as the price floor. Prices are supported by granting farmers loans on their stored commodities through the Commodity Credit Corporation (CCC), which was established in 1933 for this purpose. Farmers can get loans on the value of their commodities at a rate established by the government (such as $4 per bushel). They put up their commodities as collateral. If the market price is above the loan rate, the farmer can withdraw the commodity from storage, sell the commodity, repay the loan, and keep the profits. On the other hand, if the market price is below the support price, the farmer simply surrenders the commodity to the government instead of repaying the loan. The loan rate is therefore the effective price support. The government is the buyer of the surplus, and it is the government (and taxpayers) that bear the losses.

By means of price supports, income is redistributed to the farm sector from taxpayers in general. Whenever income is redistributed, some groups gain and others lose. Let's look at the losers and the gainers. Taxpayers, who are also consumers, are obvious losers. Their taxes are used to buy and store the surplus at artificially high prices, and the higher prices lead to at least slightly higher food prices. (We say "slightly" because most of the price you pay for food results from the costs of processing and distributing the food, not from the cost of the farm products.) Unless our government also subsidizes our agricultural exports, the support price makes U.S. farm commodities more expensive on world markets, so our farm sector is less competitive internationally. This comparative lack of competitiveness undoubtedly decreased our exports in the years when we had many high price supports.

Let's summarize the results of the agricultural price floors. Agricultural prices are held artificially high, which encourages excess production. Surplus crops result, which are costly for the government and taxpayers. At the same time that surplus crops are produced, both U.S. consumers and foreign consumers are discouraged from purchasing the crops because of the artificially high prices. Our agricultural system is inefficient and it transfers benefits to our farm sector.

The farm sector is the gainer, but in a manner that many taxpayers do not understand. The lion's share of the support goes to large farmers, because the subsidy is paid on a per-unit-of-output basis. Large-scale farmers produce more bushels (units of output), so they receive bigger subsidy payments from the government. This reality undoubtedly conflicts with our vision of government farm programs as helping small, struggling American farmers. Most of us picture small-scale production on the "family farm" when we think of farmers. Agricultural economists Willard W. Cochrane and C. Ford Runge refer to the average citizen's false image of agriculture as the "Little House on the Prairie" image.[1] The average voter is far more likely to support farm programs that he or she believes guarantee a decent living to the hard-pressed, hardworking small farmer than to support programs that offer huge subsidies to large farms. We shall return to this topic shortly. Consider the following words of a farmer: "Nostalgically, many remember when farming was considered a comfortable, laid back, safe and healthy way of life. The farm was a 'good place to raise kids.' The hard work of farming was offset by a sense of independence, the joy of being your own boss."[2]

Programs to Restrict Supply

Price supports have been combined with **programs to reduce supply**. Refer again to Figure 12-3 on page 289. Assume that government analysts believe that a "fair" price for farm commodities is $4. This price would cover the costs of production, including some level of wages for the average farmer. One way to ensure that farmers receive $4 per bushel is to support the price at $4 and create a surplus in the process, as we've just discussed. Another method would be to shift the supply curve back to the point at which supply intersects demand at $4. The effects of this method are shown in Figure 12-4.

> **Programs to reduce supply** Policies to decrease the amount produced and offered for sale.

After the decrease in supply, the equilibrium price is $4, and the market clears with 2,000 million bushels of wheat being exchanged. There is no surplus for which the government is the buyer of last resort. There are no storage charges. There is no loss of the stored grain from rodents or simple deterioration with age. Programs to reduce the supply of farm products appeared preferable to rigid price supports in the 1930s, and these programs remain preferable today.

Accordingly, the history of farm policy in the United States is filled with efforts to reduce supply. Early efforts were voluntary and often involved land rent payments on acres taken out of the production of specific crops coupled with support prices on crops grown on the individual farmer's remaining land. Despite these attempts to control supply, the surpluses grew. Commercial warehouses were filled. Abandoned schoolhouses and (in some cases) churches were used for storage. Consequently, efforts to restrict supply became more formal and far-reaching.

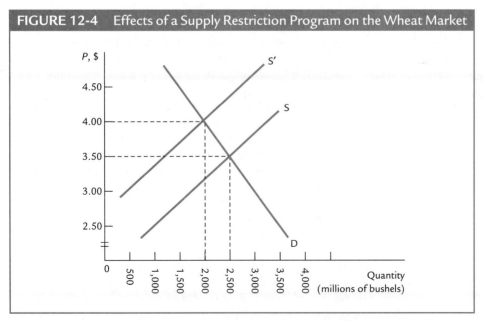

FIGURE 12-4   Effects of a Supply Restriction Program on the Wheat Market

If the supply of wheat can be decreased from S to S' by a government program, the market price will increase from $3.50 to $4.00.

In 1956, the Soil Bank was instituted. It encouraged the long-term withdrawal of farmland from production of any crops and stricter compliance with acreage controls on specific crops. Farmers were paid for not farming. In subsequent legislation, supply restriction programs were continued under other names: the Set-Aside program, the Payment-in-Kind (PIK) program, and the "10-year plan," which encourages farmers to put highly erodible acres in a long-term supply restriction program. Under the Set-Aside program, farmers were paid for setting aside and not farming a proportion of their total acres. They were guaranteed support prices on crops grown on their remaining acreage. Under the PIK program, they were given surplus commodities from the government's storehouses instead of cash, but PIK resembled the Set-Aside program in other respects. The ten-year plan (CRP) required a longer commitment of farmers not to farm their entire acreage and it restricted alternative uses of land by more than the two prior programs, but otherwise the programs were similar.

These supply restriction programs have not worked. Acres were taken out of cultivation, but supply continued to increase, pushing down market prices. Why? Put yourself in the place of the American farmer. Would you put your best or your worst land in the Set-Aside program? Of course you would put aside those swampy, poorly drained acres on which you get your tractor stuck every spring! You would be foolish to set aside well-drained, fertile acres in favor of your less productive land. And that is what farmers have done: they have put their poorest land into supply restriction programs and then farmed the remaining acres more intensively. If rows of corn are planted closer together, and irrigation and fertilization of the crop is increased, the supply of corn increases despite acreage reduction programs. Simply by behaving in an economically rational way, the farmer dooms supply restriction programs to failure.

Like price supports, supply restriction programs favor large farms over small farms. The more acres put into the supply restriction program, the larger will be the payment to the farmer. And like price supports, supply restriction programs represent a redistribution of income from taxpayers at large to the agricultural sector.

The failures of price support and supply restriction policies are evident in the large stockpiles of agricultural products in the United States. The problem is perhaps most evident in the case of powdered milk. As of August 2003, the U.S. government was storing mountains of powdered milk that taxpayers were paying for. The dry milk stockpile hit a record 1.28 billion pounds and was growing. Every pound of nonfat dry milk in storage costs taxpayers $.80 to buy it, so it is a $1 billion mountain. These costs don't include the cost of storing the milk.

U.S. agricultural surpluses have pushed our government to experiment with demand-side programs in addition to supply restriction programs.

Efforts to Increase Demand

Efforts to decrease supply have been accompanied by various efforts to increase domestic and international demand for U.S. agricultural products. You are undoubtedly familiar with some of the programs used in an attempt to increase domestic demand. Surplus commodities are distributed to the public school system for use in the school lunch program. (This practice explains some of the strange menus you encountered as an elementary school student.) Food stamps are distributed to poor families so that they can purchase more food. Surplus commodities such as cheese and milk powder have been distributed directly to the poor through various welfare agencies and food banks. The objectives of these programs are both humanitarian and pragmatic. Feeding the poor and seeing that schoolchildren receive a free or subsidized lunch are worthy humanitarian aims, and the pragmatic purposes of these programs are to increase the demand for agricultural products and to get rid of our surpluses.

Foreign demand for U.S. farm commodities has been affected by two types of programs: foreign food assistance programs (such as Food for Peace) and export subsidies. The foreign food assistance programs have been a means of disposing of surplus commodities abroad. When U.S. surpluses accumulate, we distribute more food abroad. When our surpluses are smaller, we send less humanitarian food aid to less-developed countries. In postwar Iraq, surplus milk powder was made available to citizens of that country. In the world food crisis of the early 1970s, millions died of famine while the United States cut off food aid because our surpluses were relatively low. In many cases, our food aid programs have done more harm than good to Third World residents, as we will see shortly.

The U.S. government also pays export subsidies (government financial assistance) to U.S. agricultural exporters, as well as the assistance to U.S. farmers that we've discussed. These serve to make our agricultural exports "more competitive" (cheaper) to foreign consumers. This serves to increase the foreign demand for U.S. agricultural products because U.S. prices will be lower than those of other countries. Indeed, we have lowered the world price of some commodities so much that we have been accused of **dumping**, or selling our farm products abroad at prices well below cost. These types of subsidies have also been used to a large extent in much of western Europe. The decrease in the price of U.S. and European commodities has greatly upset the other grain-producing and grain-exporting countries of the world, such as Canada. They also have negative effects on less-developed countries, as we shall see.

Efforts to increase the price of farm products by increasing demand have not been very effective. In most cases, we have merely disposed of accumulated surpluses. There is, however, some evidence that some of the domestic programs meet their humanitarian objectives. For instance, the Food Stamp program increases poor families' access to food.

Recent Agricultural Policy

In recent years, the United States has attempted to coordinate and reevaluate these various farm programs. In 1990, for example, farmers were first required to put some of their acreage in a supply restriction program if they were to participate in the deficiency payments program. Attempts were made to decrease farmers' incentives to continuously increase yields. Then, in 1996, Congress passed the so-called Freedom to Farm Bill, which eliminated the target prices and deficiency payments on some crops such as feed grains and wheat. It provided income support payments based on acreage. Restrictions on what farmers could plant and remain eligible for

EconNews

"Farmers Dump on Canada for Dumping"

Get more information on this news story by clicking Perfect Competition.

http://econapps. swlearning.com

Dumping
Exporting goods at low prices, even below the cost of production.

government farm programs were virtually eliminated, an action that was viewed as a major step toward "getting the government out of farming." The income support payments were scheduled to last for seven years until passage of the new farm bill.

The effects of the Freedom to Farm Act have been what you probably would have predicted from reading the previous sections. At first farmers were delighted to have less government interference with their decisions about what (and how much) to plant. But the supplies of grains and other crops affected by the act have increased markedly, causing the market prices of corn and many other commodities to fall to historically low levels. Many farmers' incomes have not covered their costs. More farmers have left agriculture. And in response to a number of natural disasters, such as floods and droughts, as well as the adverse market conditions just mentioned, Congress passed emergency farm aid measures in 1998, 1999, and 2000.

Most recently, President George W. Bush signed a new farm bill in May 2002, after it passed the U.S. Senate and House of Representatives. This farm bill is entitled the Farm Security and Rural Investment Act, and it covers the time period from 2002 to 2007. However, the nearly $180 billion budget for the bill will be expended over 10 years. Once again, the benefits of the farm bill are heavily targeted to large U.S. agribusinesses. Little is done to alter the price distortions and commodity overproduction that have resulted from previous farm bills. The new farm bill also eliminates many provisions that would have targeted assistance to small and medium-size farms. While it does expand programs for farmland conservation and rural development, it fails to address concentration in the U.S. farm industry and it fails to strengthen competition in rural America. Instead, this bill (along with the crop insurance bill) will provide $191 billion in direct subsidies to farmers over the next decade, and it will cost U.S. consumers an additional $271 billion in the form of higher food prices, bringing the total to $462 billion over the 10-year time period. This expenditure is more than what Congress expects to spend on K–12 education and environmental protection combined over the next 10 years. Amazingly, *almost 60 percent of all of the farm payments will go to the largest 10 percent of farm producers.*[3]

AN EVALUATION OF U.S. FARM POLICY

For 29 years, my family has made its living growing corn and soybeans in Mazon, Illinois—population 764. Most of my neighbors live on or near farms; they always have. Many of the people I worship with every Sunday at Mazon Congregational Church still work on farms, though they're not sure how long they'll keep going. Still, the personal satisfaction—the sense of fulfillment—that we all used to experience from working hard and bringing in a harvest has dwindled, and for some, disappeared. My first year in farming was 1973, and that year we sold corn for $3.90 per bushel; I was able to buy a new tractor for $12,500. Last year I sold corn for $1.90, and a similar new tractor cost $100,000.[4]

As is obvious to the farmer quoted here, government policies have not solved the core farm problem of declining real incomes to small and medium-sized farmers, and they have had some unforeseen side effects. By treating a symptom rather than a cause, they have contributed to an increasingly concentrated agricultural sector and promoted productive techniques that have harmful environmental consequences. Additional issues involve farmworkers and Native Americans, and the existence of biotechnology is just one more example of technical advance with questionable effects.

Treating a Symptom

The low price of farm products is a symptom of a resource allocation problem in the economy. We simply produce too many farm products in comparison with other goods. The solution to the problem is to decrease the resources devoted to farming. As long as prices are supported artificially, there will be an incentive to continue to overproduce. Indeed, government policies are a part of the farm problem because they encourage the retention in agriculture of resources that would otherwise leave farming and be used for other purposes.

Increasing Concentration in Agriculture

A market is said to be concentrated if it contains a relatively few large firms. There is a trend toward greater **concentration** in agriculture. As we discussed previously, the "Little House on the Prairie" image of American agriculture is a false one today, but it was a more accurate image in the 1930s, when government involvement in agriculture began. The average farm was much smaller, and 25 percent of the population resided on farms.[5] Now, less than 2 percent of the population is engaged in farming, and the average size of farms has greatly increased. The organization Bread for the World examined the change in U.S. farm size over the time period 1993 to 1999. The number of large farms with sales of $500,000 or more increased by 38 percent and the number of moderately large farms with sales of $250,000 to $499,999 increased by 14 percent. However, smaller farms with sales of $100,000 to $249,999 decreased by 11 percent and the smallest farms with sales of $50,000 to $99,999 decreased by 22 percent.[6] This growing concentration of sales by the largest farms raises concern over potential market power among these farms. The effects of concentration are discussed in more detail in Chapter 8.

Concentration
The domination of a market by a few large firms.

Harmful Environmental Effects

Another false image of American agriculture noted by Cochrane and Runge is that farmers are "stewards of the land" or protectors of the land and environment.[7] Farming is viewed as a healthy, wholesome way of life. In fact, modern farming has been reliant on chemical fertilizers to increase yield per acre to thereby obtain more government payments. It relies on pesticides to decrease insect damage and maximize yield. It creates nitrate pollution of water wells in farm states and other environmental problems. Despite this background, the Environmental Working Group criticizes the new farm bill for cutting farmland conservation and for funding controversial and environment-threatening operations.[8]

As people have left farming, they have been replaced by machines that are both expensive and dangerous. Farming is now one of the most dangerous sectors of the economy as measured by workplace accidents and deaths. Irrigation in the lower Midwest has damaged aquifers (underground water supplies serving large areas) but increased bushels per acre on which deficiency payments are earned. Commodity programs have encouraged the production of crops that are particularly likely to cause erosion, because these crops often have had high target prices. Farm life is neither particularly healthy nor environmentally benign. And our government programs have contributed to these adverse effects.

Some economists argue that the increasing concentration of agriculture worsens the environmental problems associated with large-scale production. Huge cattle feedlots, factory hog farms, and dairies with 1,200 cows on relatively few acres create significant problems of odor and waste disposal. Realistically, we will never return to the idealized nation of small family farms. We can, however, preserve the 500,000 or so medium-sized farms that remain if we adjust our national farm policy so that it no longer favors the largest producers. Policies that promote the greatest possible yield have proved self-defeating because they worsen the resource allocation problem and, in the process, they increase concentration. Policies that promote a more diverse and less chemical-dependent agriculture appear to make more sense.

Farmworkers and Native Americans

A particular group of at-risk populations in rural farm areas includes farmworkers (often migrants from within the United States or across national borders) and the original inhabitants of the land, Native Americans. Wages to farmworkers are often very low and their housing and living conditions are often very poor. In addition, it is ironic that Native Americans, the original inhabitants of the land, experience high rates of poverty and hunger. Nearly one-third of Native Americans live in poverty, and nearly a fourth of all Native households are considered food insecure.[9] The 2002 Farm Bill includes provisions to promote greater equity and nondiscrimination among farmers and farmworkers.

Biotechnology

Production of genetically modified organisms (GMOs) has increased greatly over recent years. By 2001, GMOs represented 62 percent of soybeans, 21 percent of corn, 12 percent of cotton, and smaller amounts of other products.[10] U.S. agricultural companies have taken the lead in developing biotechnology, in which seed varieties are genetically altered in order to increase yields. Farmers use the GMOs as a means of preventing crop disease and reducing pesticide use. Some people have characterized biotechnology as the means to solve the ever present problem of world hunger, much as the Green Revolution was expected to relieve famine in earlier decades. Opponents maintain that there are severe environmental and health risks of biotechnology and that the technology will do little to help with world hunger reduction. They argue that the development of GMOs will benefit large multinational corporations, and not the smaller farmers or consumers of agricultural products. European countries have banned the importation of GMOs because of health and environmental concerns. Leaders in these countries state that they merely want GMO food crops to be advertised as such, so that European consumers will know what they are eating. President George W. Bush has responded by saying that the European health and environmental concerns are groundless and that the European response will prolong famine in Africa. In August 2003, the United States, Canada, and Argentina formally filed papers asking the World Trade Organization to outlaw a European Union prohibition of importing GMOs. The debate over GMOs is expected to continue for some time and to create controversy between leaders of various governments. The effect of biotechnology, for better or worse, is probably most pronounced for less-developed countries.

AGRICULTURE AND LESS-DEVELOPED COUNTRIES

Some economists argue that our heavily subsidized agricultural sector produces commodities that compete unfairly with those of less-developed countries (LDCs). The LDCs often rely on their own agricultural exports for much-needed foreign currency. If, for example, the price of rice produced in Arkansas is artificially low because of U.S. government subsidies, Thailand's rice exports to the United States and our number of trading partners will be diminished. This is an especially serious problem because European countries, another major market for Third World agricultural exports, have policies similar to our own.

The U.N. World Food Summit of June 2002 was dominated by the issues of U.S. and European farm subsidies and the use of biotechnology. Since both of these serve to increase food production, it is natural to assume that they will reduce world hunger and famine. Let's try to understand why this is probably not the case.

First, there is currently a lot of food produced in the world. Except for the world food crisis years of the early 1970s, our world has been characterized as having abundant supplies and indeed surplus stocks of agricultural products that are never even consumed. The problem of world hunger has far less to do with global food production and a lot more to do with how this produce is distributed. Food, as well as other production, is distributed to people who have the incomes to buy it. Low-income people in poor countries cannot afford to buy enough food for themselves and their families. Thus, hunger is a problem of poverty, not production. In addition, civil war, political instability, bad weather, poor transportation, and lack of storage facilities can exacerbate problems of hunger.

Second, we must remember that most of the residents of less-developed countries live in the rural sector and earn their incomes through food production. When U.S. and European subsidized agricultural products flood the world markets, causing very low agricultural prices, poor farmers in less-developed countries earn very little income from the production of food and they have very little incentive to produce food. They may seek employment in sectors that can more reliably provide for the needs of their families. Or they may swarm to cities in hopes of higher incomes, but in reality become unemployed and live in squalid conditions. Although famine conditions require emergency food aid, prolonged food aid and dumping of agricultural products actually exacerbate the problem of world hunger.

A third reason that LDCs are disadvantaged has to do with the trade restrictions imposed by the wealthy countries to prevent the agricultural commodities produced by LDCs from entering the United States and other prosperous countries. Oxfam, a nongovernmental organization concerned with world hunger, estimates that rich-country governments receive $43 billion from these trade barriers and that the barriers cost less-developed countries about $100 billion in sales annually. (This is double the amount of development assistance offered by rich countries to poor countries.)

And finally, the patents owned by U.S. multinational corporations and agribusinesses prevent outsiders from producing genetically modified food and allow these large U.S. corporations to flood the world market with their agricultural products. Just as Green Revolution technology wasn't made available to many poor farmers in low-income countries in the past, the new biotechnology will not be available to poor farmers throughout the world today. In addition to health and environmental concerns about biotechnology, the most likely economic effects will be large increases in world food production, causing lower prices of agricultural products and preventing poor farmers from succeeding in agriculture. And it is the latter outcome that may serve to increase, rather than decrease, world hunger.

THE POLITICS OF U.S. AGRICULTURAL POLICY

We've already noted that the benefits of government agricultural programs have mostly gone to large farms because subsidies have been designed to be paid on output or acres. In fact, by far, most of the benefits go to large farms and agribusinesses that earn more than $250,000 per year. According to the Environmental Working Group, beneficiaries include 15 Fortune 500 companies and celebrities such as Sam Donaldson and Ted Turner. Payments to some of the Fortune 500 companies include $375,000 to International Paper Corporation, $269,000 to Westvaco Corporation, $260,000 to Chevron, and $189,000 to John Hancock Mutual Life Insurance. This compares with the average payment of $6,000 to the bottom 80 percent of farm subsidy recipients.[11] It is no wonder that some people ask why our taxpayers, many of whom have low or medium incomes, should shift their earnings to higher-income farms. And why do farm payments dwarf expenditures for other programs that we've discussed in this text, including programs for education, environmental protection, poverty reduction, health care, and housing? And finally, why should high-income farmers receive government benefits when smaller farmers and other small business owners receive little, if any? What are the politics behind all this, and how could our policy be improved?

If most Americans are concerned about small to medium-sized family farmers, then most farm payments should not go to the wealthiest farmers. The fact that they do is the effect of politics and economics. How many consumer groups band together and advocate against farm policy that raises the price of food purchased in supermarkets? If you said none, you are probably right. And how many citizens of less-developed countries group together and request a reduction in U.S. trade restrictions and agricultural subsidies that create hunger abroad? Again, the answer is probably none. *But*—how do you think the U.S. farm lobby compares with these diffuse and uninformed consumer groups? There are farm lobbying groups in virtually every state in our nation. These groups are well financed by the large commercial farmers who use their vast financial resources to seek not just beneficial agricultural policies, but policies that particularly benefit them as opposed to smaller farmers. Unfortunately, the smaller farmers that need the government benefits are neither informed about the effect of policies nor powerful as a lobbying group.

In addition, almost all members of the U.S. House of Representatives have at least one crop in their states whose producers vote pro-farmer. Senators are overrepresented by rural populations that vote pro-farmer as well. It is difficult to be reelected when ignoring this group of farmers. Typically, the lobbying and voting does not emphasize the need to target benefits to the poorest farmers.

Can our agricultural policy be improved? Certainly! Politicians and the news media need to deflate the myths of the "Little House on the Prairie" farmer, as well as the myth that needy farmers benefit from our agricultural programs. And, as is often the case, economists generally prefer programs that directly target needy groups, rather than policies that distort market prices and create poor incentives and disincentives. One alternative is to untie the amount of food production to the

VIEWPOINT: CONSERVATIVE VERSUS LIBERAL

Conservatives have argued for a long time that price supports, target prices, and supply restriction programs have contributed to our farm problem instead of solving it. Because of these programs, our country simply allocates too many resources to agriculture. Theoretically, conservatives would end virtually all farm programs and let market forces determine the outcomes for farmers. Also, by encouraging less government antitrust activity and fewer government environmental regulations (so that there is less government involvement in agricultural markets), the outcomes of conservative policy might be greater concentration in agricultural markets and unchecked environmental harm.

These conservative policies and outcomes might not actually take place, however. This is because politicians on both the left (liberal) and the right (conservative) face strong lobbying activity in favor of government programs that benefit farmers in their state. For example, conservative southern senators and representatives to Congress are under a great deal of pressure to support farm programs that benefit tobacco producers. There are other examples in almost every other state. And since large agribusinesses have more political power than do smaller farmers, the unequal distribution of the benefits of our farm programs has been accepted by many conservatives as a natural phenomenon.

Liberal politicians, on the other hand, are more comfortable supporting agricultural programs both within and outside their states. Liberals do not wholeheartedly endorse the programs, however, and many believe that they should be gradually phased out. Their major objection to the programs is that the bulk of government payments go to large farms rather than small family farms. They would also like government efforts to reduce concentration in agricultural markets and to ensure environmental protection.

amount of government benefit. Instead, the government might simply assure all farmers an adequate income, perhaps at twice the poverty line. If income for a farmer falls below this, the government writes a check. If income for a farmer rises above this, the farmer receives no check. And, rather than distorting markets with artificial prices, the government can work on providing appropriate incentives (subsidies) to farmers who engage in environmental protection and appropriate disincentives (taxes) to farmers who do not engage in environmentally sound practices. This direct approach to incomes and the use of market incentives and disincentives for environmental protection would help to reduce the concentration in agricultural markets as well. Finally, the problem of world hunger will not be solved until the problem of poverty is addressed. In this area, the world's wealthy countries have been called on by the Food and Agriculture Organization and others to provide real development assistance rather than just food aid.

SUMMARY

Agriculture is characterized by inelastic demand in the short run, fluctuations in short-run supply, immobile resources, and such rapid technological change that supply has increased far more rapidly than demand. Thus, agriculture has long been a troubled sector of the U.S. economy. Since the 1930s, government policies aimed at the farm problem have promoted the overallocation of resources to the agricultural sector. Furthermore, despite these policies, the proportion of our population engaged in farming has shrunk to less than 2 percent. Supply restriction programs, price supports, and target prices have not saved the small American farm but instead have con-

tributed to the farm problem. Concentration has increased in agriculture, in part because of our farm policies. Policies that promote the greatest possible yield have proved self-defeating because they worsen the resource allocation problem and in the process increase concentration.

Finally, our farm policies affect the rest of the world. The policies of such a large and prosperous country can either help or hinder the development efforts of less-developed countries. Food aid, development assistance, and biotechnology all become possible solutions or contributors to the problem of world hunger.

NOTES

1. Willard W. Cochrane and C. Ford Runge, *Reforming Farm Policy* (Ames: Iowa State University Press, 1992), p. 21.

2. Jon Evert quoted in *Agriculture in the Global Economy: Hunger 2003* (Washington, D.C.: Bread for the World Institute, 2003), p. 44.

3. The Environmental Working Group, 2003 (**www.ewg.org/farm/farmbill**).

4. Doug Harford quoted in *Agricultural in the Global Economy: Hunger 2003* (Washington, D.C.: Bread for the World Institute, 2003), p. 38.

5. Cochrane and Runge, *Reforming Farm Policy,* p. 22.

6. Bread for the World, *Agriculture in the Global Economy,* p. 51.

7. Cochrane and Runge, *Reforming Farm Policy,* p. 24.

8. The Environmental Working Group, 2003 (**www.ewg.org/farm/farmbill**).

9. Bread for the World, *Agriculture in the Global Economy,* p. 46.

10. International Service for the Acquisition of Agri-Biotech Applications, as reported by Amy Becker and Lee Egerstrom, "International Food Fight," *St. Paul Pioneer Press,* August 24, 2003, 1D, 5D.

11. The Environmental Working Group, 2003 (**www.ewg.org/farm/farmbill**).

DISCUSSION QUESTIONS

1. How does demand inelasticity affect farm prices and farmers' incomes? How does this issue compare between agricultural production in the United States and primary commodity production in less-developed countries (as discussed in Chapter 9 on international trade)?

2. What is the direction of the trend in concentration in farming? How have government programs contributed to this trend?

3. How do price floors interfere with the rationing function of price? Use price supports as an example. Can you think of any other examples of price floors in our economy? (Hint: Remember that there are markets for goods as well as for *services!*)

4. Why don't supply restriction programs work well in increasing farm prices and incomes?

5. Do you believe that the government should be involved in agriculture? What kinds of policies would you suggest? Do you think that direct benefits to low-income farmers might be a possible solution?

6. Go to the Census Bureau Web site (**www.census. gov**). Click A for *agriculture* in the A–Z option. Go to the Agricultural Census. Look under "farm count" for the number of farms in your state.

7. Visit the official Web site of the Department of Agriculture at **www.usda.gov**. What information can you find about current agricultural policy? What other type of material is available there?

8. Check out the statistical arm of the Department of Agriculture at **www.nass.usda.gov**. This site contains the latest of the agricultural censuses.

9. Go to the Web site of the Farm Services Agency at **www.fsa/isda/gpv/pas/farmbill/fbfaqhome. asp**. Read more about the 2002 Farm Bill, including the answers to frequently asked questions.

10. The Web site of the Food and Agriculture Organization of the United Nations (FAO) provides information about U.S. farm subsidies and how they affect the rest of the world. Go to the Web site at **www.fao.org**, and investigate the effects of U.S. agricultural subsidies on the less-developed countries of the world. This site contains information about biotechnology, farm conservation, hazardous pesticides, and more.

11. Go to **www.ewg.org** to see the home page of the Environmental Working Group. This nonprofit organization has assembled the records of farm benefits that have been paid out from

1996 to 2000 as well as other types of information. Do you think this is a liberal or conservative Web site?

12. For which nonfarm products is demand likely to be inelastic? Why is this the case? For which types of products is demand more likely to be elastic? (This topic is discussed in Appendix 1 of this chapter.)

13. How do target prices differ from price supports? Do different groups win or lose from these programs? (This topic is discussed in Appendix 2 of this chapter.)

CHAPTER 12 APPENDIX 1: INELASTIC DEMAND

The graph in Figure 12-5 shows the same hypothetical demand curve for corn that we discussed previously. The graph shows an initial equilibrium price of $3 per bushel and an initial equilibrium quantity of 5 million bushels. Now consider an increase in supply from S to S' caused by exceptionally good weather. The equilibrium quantity increases to 6 million bushels,

FIGURE 12-5   The Effect of Inelasticity on Price and Farm Incomes

Because the demand for farm products is inelastic, an increase in supply from S to S' will cause a sharp decrease in price, as well as a decrease in farmers' incomes. Note that price falls from $3 to $2, while incomes decrease from $15 million to $12 million. Conversely, a decrease in supply to S' will increase price to $4 and increase total farm incomes to $16 million.

which is a relatively small increase of 20 percent. We calculate this increase in quantity by taking the 6 million bushels minus the 5 million bushels, giving us 1 million bushels. To express this in percentage terms, we take the 1 million bushels and divide by the original 5 million bushels, giving us a 20 percent reduction in quantity. This is shown in the following two steps:

1. 6 million bushels − 5 million bushels = 1 million bushels

2. $\dfrac{1 \text{ million bushels}}{5 \text{ million bushels}} = \dfrac{1}{5} = 0.20 = 20\%$

Recall that to transform a decimal (such as 0.20) into a percentage (such as 20%), all you do is move the decimal two spaces to the right and add a percentage sign.

Now consider the price change. Because of the inelastic demand, the effect of the supply shift on market price is great. The increase in supply causes the price to fall all the way to $2 per bushel, a decline of 50 percent. We calculate the 50 percent decline by taking the prices $3 per bushel minus $2 per bushel, giving us $1 per bushel price. To express this as a percentage, we take the $1 and divide it by $2, giving us a 50 percent decrease in price. This is shown in the following two steps:

1. $3 per bushel − $2 per bushel = $1 per bushel

2. $\dfrac{\$1 \text{ per bushel}}{\$2 \text{ per bushel}} = \dfrac{1}{2} = 0.50 = 50\%$

Alternatively, a relatively small decrease in supply caused by poor weather (from S to S″) would cause a large increase in price of 50 percent (up to $4 per bushel). We summarize by stating that the combination of weather-related supply fluctuations and inelastic demand results in large fluctuations in agricultural prices in the short run.

Now let's generalize the effects of an inelastic demand on farmers' *incomes* in the short run. We've already noted that if good weather causes an increase in supply, which causes price to decrease, then overall farm income will also fall. This is because income from a corn crop is equal to the number of units sold times the price at which they are sold. Refer again to Figure 12-5. At the initial price of $3, farmers sold 5 million bushels, earning income of $15 million from their corn crop. (Five million bushels times $3 per bushel is $15 million.) After the increase in supply, farmers sold 6 million bushels at a price of $2 per bushel. They earned only $12 million for their corn crop. Because the farmers face an inelastic demand, a short-run decrease in price results in a short-run decrease in farm income. Similarly, a short-run increase in price (from bad weather) results in a short-run increase in farm income. These outcomes, as well as the outcomes in situations in which demand is elastic (instead of inelastic), are shown in Table 12-2.

TABLE 12-2	The Effects of Elastic and Inelastic Demand on Total Income	
When demand is:	Then a decrease in price will cause:	And an increase in price will cause:
Inelastic	Farm income to fall	Farm income to rise
Inelastic	Farm income to rise	Farm income to fall

CHAPTER 12 APPENDIX 2: TARGET PRICES WITH DEFICIENCY PAYMENTS

By the 1960s, the government had acquired huge surpluses under the price support program. Something had to be done. In many commodity markets, rigid price supports were replaced by flexible price supports based on past market prices. These price supports (loan rates) were markedly lower than those used previously. They became a less important instrument of farm policy for most commodities, whereas **target prices** became a more important instrument. Under target pricing, farmers received direct payments. These payments are called **deficiency payments**. They cover the gap between the target price and the actual market price.

> **Target prices**
> A program in which farmers are paid the difference between the target price and the market price.

Figure 12-6 illustrates how target pricing works. Suppose that policymakers determine that a $4.00 target price is justified by the costs of producing wheat, but the market price is below $4.00. They establish $4.00 as the target price for wheat. At a target price of $4.00, farmers will offer 3,500 million bushels (quantity supplied) of wheat for sale.

Follow the arrow in the graph. The price at which buyers are willing to buy (quantity demanded) 3,500 million bushels is $2.50. So, the price will fall to $2.50, and the entire quantity supplied by farmers will be purchased. Farmers will receive $2.50 from the market for a bushel of wheat, but

FIGURE 12-6   Effects of Target Pricing on the Wheat Market

With target prices, price is allowed to fall to the level that clears the market ($2.50); farmers receive deficiency payments for the difference between the target price ($4.00) and the market price ($2.50).

the government will send them a check for the difference between the target price ($4.00) and the market price ($2.50). So, for each bushel sold, the farmer will receive a government deficiency payment of $1.50. A farmer selling 10,000 bushels will receive a check for $15,000.

Deficiency payments The target price minus the market price, multiplied by the number of units sold.

Target prices differ from the previously discussed price supports in a number of important ways. First, because the market price is much lower than the target price, the cost of farm commodities does not drive up the cost of food. Indeed, because target prices drive down the market price for farm products to below the free-market equilibrium, food is made cheaper for buyers. Second, because prices are lower for consumers whether they are in the U.S. or the export market, American farm products are more competitive on world markets at the lower prices. Of course, this causes the same international problems that we've already discussed. Third, the market is less distorted by target prices than by price supports, because no surplus is created. Finally, the costs to taxpayers of target prices and deficiency payments are easier to count because the costs associated with surpluses are not incurred.

There are, of course, some similarities between price supports, target prices, and supply restriction programs. They all result in a transfer of income from taxpayers to farmers. They all favor large-scale farmers over small farmers. And they all harm the exports of other nations, including the less-developed countries of the world.

**Chapter 6
U.S. Poverty**
Social Security can be credited with preventing many elderly and disabled people from being in poverty

**Chapter 13
Social Security**

**Chapter 16
Taxes, Borrowing, and the National Debt**
Social Security is financed by payroll taxes

**Chapter 5
Discrimination**
Elderly women are more likely to be poor than elderly men and many women receive lower Social Security benefits than men

THE ECONOMIC TOOLBOX

- social insurance
- pay-as-you-go
- social adequacy
- regressive versus progressive taxes
- adverse selection
- widows' income gap
- privatization

SOCIAL SECURITY

As we continue to work together to keep Social Security strong and reliable, we must offer younger workers a chance to invest in retirement accounts that they will control and they will own.

—President George W. Bush, Statement by the President on the 2003 Report
of the Social Security Trustees, www.whitehouse.gov

Hmmm . . . the president raises two issues. On the one hand, he wants to assure us that Social Security will remain strong and reliable (even though many people, especially those of college age now, are concerned that Social Security benefits will not be there when they retire). But second, the president voices his view that the program will not remain strong unless we offer some degree of privatization of the system.

As we shall discover again in Chapter 17, **privatization** means the transfer of assets or responsibility from the government to the private sector of the economy. In the case of Social Security, the president wishes to offer young workers the possibility of investing in private retirement accounts.

> **Privatization**
> The transfer of government enterprises or responsibilities to the private sector.

As you probably know, the U.S. Social Security system, and the associated Medicare health insurance system, affect us all. If we work, we pay Social Security and Medicare taxes. If we become disabled, we will be able to collect benefits from the Social Security Administration. If our spouse dies, we may be able to receive benefits for ourselves and our surviving children from the Social Security Administration. When we retire, we will collect retirement benefits from Social Security. Retirement probably seems impossibly far away for most of you, but you undoubtedly have relatives who are retired, and they receive Social Security checks on the third of each month (unless their Social Security is automatically deposited to their bank account). You may sometimes worry about the future of the Social Security system, and you may worry whether it will be there for you when you finally retire.

A Social Security payment is an **entitlement**, or a payment to which eligible citizens have a right to receive based on U.S. law. Entitlements are a huge share of the federal budget, and because these payments are mandated by law, they are outside the discretionary control of Congress. The only way payments can be decreased is to change the law that entitles citizens to them. In the current political atmosphere, in which cutting federal government expenditures appears to be of paramount importance, discussion of entitlements and the laws that govern entitlements is both loud and emotional. Social Security and Medicare are therefore controversial. And, they are expensive. The Social Security Administration paid benefits to more than 50 million people in 2002, including Social Security benefits to over 4 million people. Social Security provided at least half of the income for 65 percent of the aged population. In 2002, Social Security revenue was $540 billion, and payments were $394 billion.[1] Expenditures for Medicare also continue to climb. Because Social Security receives so much media coverage, it is one of those programs about which most of us have an opinion but little knowledge to back it up.

In this chapter, we describe the Social Security program as it now exists and look at some of the problems and controversial issues that surround it. We also discuss the probable future for the program.

SOCIAL SECURITY: A SOCIAL INSURANCE PROGRAM

The Social Security Act of 1935 established the Social Security program. Widespread unemployment, hunger, poverty, and wasted human resources during the Great Depression of the 1930s had focused the nation's attention on the economic insecurity that resulted. The Social Security Act was seen as a solution to these problems. The original law provided only retirement benefits at age 65 for most workers in industry and commerce. Since then, the law has been amended many times. Social Security now has provisions for disabled workers and their dependents and for survivors of deceased workers. It covers virtually the entire working population, including the self-employed, and benefits are tied to the consumer price index so that they increase automatically with inflation in the economy. Therefore, the purchasing power of retirees' benefits remains the same even when the average price level goes up. (You often hear about older people living on a "fixed income," meaning that income does not adjust for inflation. In fact, older people are in the age group that is *least likely* to be living on a fixed income, because of Social Security!) Medicare, which provides highly subsidized medical insurance for aged and disabled Social Security beneficiaries, was established in 1965.

Social Security is a good example of **social insurance**. A social insurance program is like a private insurance program, except that benefits are provided by the government instead of by private companies. Like your private life or health insurance, the purpose of social insurance programs is to pool risk of losses from such occurrences as death or illness. This means that combining high-risk and low-risk individuals enables us to manage the consequences better. Because the concept of social insurance is sophisticated and difficult to explain by itself, we are going to contrast social insurance to two other types of programs that contribute to the economic security of the population. These are private insurance and social (public) assistance.

Private insurance is provided by for-profit insurance companies, not the government. Its purpose is like that of social insurance, the pooling of risk of losses. Table 13-1 compares social insurance with private insurance programs.

Although the basic purpose of the two kinds of insurance is the same, they differ in most other characteristics. Social insurance is compulsory, whereas private insurance is voluntary. If you are a covered worker, you must pay Social Security taxes and participate in the program, whereas no one requires that you purchase a private insurance policy. The reason that social insurance is compulsory is obvious. Many people might choose to postpone participation until they neared retirement or choose not to participate at all if the decision were left up to them. Then the cost of the program for other covered workers would increase.

The private insurance industry is composed of a large number of competing firms, although it is dominated by a much smaller number of large firms. The Social Security Administration is the sole provider of this social insurance, and it is therefore a government monopoly.

Revenue for social insurance programs is provided by taxes that are earmarked for providing benefits to those who qualify. Since the funds are taken directly from your paycheck, they are referred to as **payroll taxes**. In the case of Social Security and Medicare, the payroll tax is a matching tax with equal amounts paid by employees and their employers. This financing mechanism contrasts with private insurance, in which funds are generated from premium payments made by policyholders.

By law, private insurers must operate on a **fully funded** basis—that is, they must have reserves sufficient to pay all the claims likely to be made on them. Social insurance, such as Social Security, is not fully funded. Instead it is a **pay-as-you-go system**. The taxes collected from current workers and employers are used to pay benefits to current retirees and other current beneficiaries. The decision to make Social Security a pay-as-you-go program, rather than a fully funded one, came about in the 1930s. It was reasoned that there would always be new workers coming into the compulsory program to pay taxes to support beneficiaries, so a fully funded program was unnecessary. Contingency funds intended to cover six months' to one year's benefits were established, but the program's current taxes were intended to pay current benefits.

Private insurance
A private program provided by for-profit insurance companies and funded by premiums. Its purpose is the pooling of risk of losses.

Payroll taxes
Taxes based on earnings from work, usually deducted directly from workers' paychecks.

Fully funded
Having sufficient reserves to pay all expected liabilities; it is a legal requirement of private insurance.

Pay-as-you-go system
A program in which current taxes pay current benefits.

Statutory right
A right that is specified by law.

Your right to benefits under Social Security is a **statutory right**—that is, this right is defined by the current Social Security law. If Congress changes the law to make benefits either more or less generous, your right to benefits will change with the law. On the other hand, you have a **contractual right** to payments as specified in a policy purchased from a private insurer. The company cannot unilaterally change the terms of your policy.

Contractual right
A right that is specified in contract between parties.

Finally, private insurance is based on the principle of **individual equity**. You get back benefits proportional to what you paid in. If you purchased a larger policy, paying more premiums to do so, you will get back larger payments (or your heirs will). Social insurance is based on the principles of individual equity and social adequacy, or the need to provide a minimum floor of economic security to the population as a whole. Furthermore, the emphasis of the program is more on **social adequacy** than individual equity. Low-wage workers will therefore receive benefits that are proportionately larger in comparison to the taxes they paid in than will high-wage workers.

Individual equity
The principle that benefits received are proportional to amounts paid in.

Social insurance shares some characteristics with private insurance, but it shares other characteristics with social assistance. **Public assistance** programs are needs-based welfare programs of the government. Table 13-2 contrasts social insurance with public assistance programs.

Social adequacy
The principle that benefits are sufficient to provide a minimum level of economic security to the population as a whole.

We said that public assistance programs are needs-based. This means that to receive benefits from these welfare programs, a person must demonstrate that he or she is poor or that assets and income are below a certain level. Benefits are paid not from earmarked taxes, but from the government's general revenues. There is no relationship between taxes paid in, currently or in the past, and the benefits received by recipients. Public assistance programs are pure welfare programs. Because every worker is eligible for Social Security and Medicare, but only the poor receive welfare, a stigma is attached to welfare that is not present for social insurance programs.

SOCIAL SECURITY TAXES AND BENEFITS

Public assistance
Any government program that is targeted to aid low-income people.

Social Security and Medicare taxes account for more than one-third of federal taxes collected. Moreover, Social Security's share of the budget has increased greatly over time. Let's first discuss taxes and benefits separately; then we will look at the total program.

Social Security Taxes

The Social Security tax you pay is determined by the tax base and the tax rate. The **tax base** is the maximum amount of an individual worker's earnings that is subject to the tax. The **tax rate** is the percentage of the tax base that will be collected for Social Security.

As of 2003, the tax rate is 6.2 percent for Social Security and 1.45 percent for Medicare, so we often speak of a total payroll tax rate of 7.65 percent. Because employees and employers pay equal amounts of these payroll taxes, the combined tax rate of both workers and employers for both taxes is 15.3 percent. Self-employed per-

TABLE 13-2	Characteristics of Social Insurance and Public Assistance

Social Insurance	Public Assistance
1. Covers entire population	1. Covers needy
2. Financed by earmarked payroll taxes	2. Financed from general government revenues
3. Operates under principles of social adequacy and individual equity	3. Operates under principle of social adequacy
4. No stigma attached to receipt of benefits	4. Stigma attached to receipt of benefits

Tax base
Income, earnings, sales, property, or other valued items that have a tax rate applied to them. In the case of the Social Security tax, the tax base is earnings subject to payroll taxes.

Tax rate
The percentage of the tax base that must be paid to the government as tax.

Regressive taxes
Taxes that take a larger percentage of income from low-income people than from high-income people.

Progressive taxes
Taxes that take a larger percentage of income from high-income people than from low-income people.

Proportional taxes
Taxes that take the same percentage of income from people at all income levels.

sons pay the entire 15.3 percent after some adjustments have been made to their earned income. The Social Security and Medicare tax bases are also different. As of 2003, the Social Security tax base was only the first $87,000 of each worker's annual earnings, whereas all of the worker's earnings were taxable for Medicare.

Let's examine how the tax has increased during the life of the Social Security program. In 1937, the tax base was $3,000, and the tax rate was 1 percent. (At that time, the program only covered retirement benefits for those over 65 years of age.) Even if we adjust for inflation, the average worker pays a much larger share of his or her earnings in Social Security taxes now than at the inception of the program.

The Social Security tax is often criticized because it is regressive. Taxes may be regressive, proportional, or progressive. **Regressive taxes** take a larger percentage of income from low-income people than from high-income people, whereas **progressive taxes** take a larger percentage of income from high-income people than from low-income people. **Proportional taxes** take the same percentage of income from all people. There is certainly room for discussion about whether proportional or progressive taxes are fairer, but not very many people would argue that regressive taxes are equitable. This issue is discussed in greater detail in Chapter 16.

The Social Security tax is regressive for two reasons. First, only the tax base is taxed in any given year. So, in 2003, only the first $87,000 earned by each worker was taxable. Therefore, the entire wages and salaries of most workers were subject to the tax, but only a portion of the earnings of workers who earned more than $87,000 was taxable. So, low-earnings workers paid Social Security taxes equal to 6.2 percent of their total earnings, and high-earnings workers paid a lower percentage of taxes on their total earnings. (Think how much of Julia Roberts's earnings was exempt from the Social Security tax!)

Second, only earnings from working are taxable for Social Security and Medicare. Other forms of income, such as rents, interest, capital gains, and stock dividends, are not subject to these taxes. Because higher-income people have more income from sources other than wages and salaries, they also have more income that is not taxable for these social insurance programs. Thus, Social Security and Medicare taxes are rightly characterized as regressive, with their greatest burden on low-income people. We shall see shortly, however, that the progressivity of benefits offsets the regressivity of taxes.

Social Security Benefits

Social Security benefits are mainly in the form of checks mailed by the U.S. Treasury to beneficiaries on the first of each month. Most recipients receive their checks on the third of the month if the benefits are not automatically deposited into their bank account. Medicare benefits are in the form of payments to hospitals and doctors for medical care. Medicare's effects on our health care system are discussed in Chapter 11. Here, we concentrate on the discussion of Social Security retirement benefits.

To qualify for Social Security benefits, the recipient must be a fully insured worker or the dependent of a fully insured worker. That is, the worker must have paid Social Security taxes on a minimum amount of earnings for 40 quarters (10 years).

Benefit amounts are based on the retired worker's prior Social Security tax contributions. A complex formula that takes into account the worker's entire earnings and Social Security tax history, rather than a small number of years, such as private pensions often use, determines the amount of the worker's monthly check. The benefits are progressive in the sense that low-earnings workers will receive a higher replacement rate than high-earnings workers do. The **replacement rate** is the percentage of the final working year's earnings that is replaced by Social Security benefits. Table 13-3 contains data from a Social Security Administration study showing the relationship between earnings, benefits, and the replacement rate.

Replacement rate The percentage of the worker's last working year's earnings that is replaced by Social Security retirement benefits.

The Social Security Administration estimated that in the year 2000, workers who retired the previous year at 65 years of age, and who earned $13,100 in the previous year, would receive $6,943 in Social Security benefits. This would replace 53 percent of the previous year's earnings. On the other hand, maximum-earner workers, whose earnings were equal to the tax base of $72,600 (in 2000), would receive a larger benefit ($17,424), but only 24 percent of their previous year's earnings would be replaced.

As we see, the progressivity of Social Security benefits offsets the regressive effects of Social Security taxes.

TABLE 13-3	Preretirement Earnings, Social Security Benefits, and the Replacement Rate for Workers Retiring in 1999		
	Earnings ($)	Benefits ($)	Replacement Rate (%)
Low earner	13,100	6,943	53
Average earner	46,663	14,932	32
Maximum earner	72,600	17,424	24

Source: Social Security Administration Office of Policy, "Is Social Security All I Need for Retirement Income," April 8, 1999.

PROBLEMS AND ISSUES

Let us discuss some of the many problems and issues connected with this social insurance program. First, we examine U.S. demographics, which is the system's long-run problem as the nation ages, and possible solutions to this problem. Second, we discuss the issue of making the Social Security system voluntary rather than compulsory. Third, we analyze whether Social Security is a "bad buy" for younger workers. Fourth, we look at the system's treatment of women workers. Finally, we discuss the controversy over Social Security's effect on private savings.

The Long-Run Problem: An Aging Population

The long-term problem of Social Security is demographics. The average age of the U.S. population is increasing, which implies that we have fewer workers paying taxes and more retirees receiving benefits. In addition, more workers are retiring at earlier ages, and early retirements imply longer periods of retirement during which workers do not pay Social Security taxes but do receive benefits. Moreover, the baby boomers, that post–World War II demographic bubble, are expected to begin retiring in the first decade of the twenty-first century. This group will swell the ranks of the retired still more.

Because Social Security is a pay-as-you-go system, it is sensitive to such demographic changes. In 1960, 5.1 workers paid taxes for every Social Security beneficiary. Since then, fewer and fewer workers paid taxes for every beneficiary, and this number is expected to continue to fall. The implications of this for taxpayers, retirees, and the financial viability of the system are substantial. Let us look at these implications.

First, if fewer taxpayers are going to provide the same benefits to Social Security retirees on a pay-as-you-go basis, then these taxpayers individually must pay higher taxes. On the other hand, if more taxes are not collected per worker, then benefits must be cut or a source of funding other than the payroll tax must be found. If nothing is done, the financial viability of the system is in doubt.

Congress first wrestled with this problem in the early 1980s, and the result was an amendment to the Social Security Act in 1983. Major provisions of the amendment are (1) to raise the normal retirement age, (2) to begin building up trust fund accounts to take care of the increase in benefits expected when the baby boomers retire, and (3) to begin to tax a portion of Social Security retirement benefits for income tax purposes. Let's consider these in turn.

Increasing the Normal Retirement Age

The **normal retirement age** is the minimum age at which covered workers can retire and still receive full benefits from Social Security. For the first 60 years of the program, the normal retirement age was 65 years. Workers can also retire at 62 years of age, but their retirement benefits are proportionally reduced if they do so. At the present time, many workers choose to retire earlier and receive smaller benefits.

Life expectancy in the United States has increased since the beginning of the Social Security program. In 1940, the life expectancy at birth of a male was 61 years; in 2003, it was estimated to be 74 years. The increase in life expectancy for females

EconNews

"Oldies Are Seen as Golden"

Read why older workers are being discouraged from retiring by going to the Labor Markets category.

http://econapps. swlearning.com

Normal retirement age
The minimum age at which workers can retire with full Social Security benefits.

during this period was even more pronounced. In 1940, a female's life expectancy at birth was 66 years; in 2003, it was 80 years.[2] The percentage of the population that is over 65 years of age is increasing. Increased life expectancy means that there will be more older people collecting retirement benefits.

Note that life expectancies represent average life spans for males and females. But keep in mind that the increase in male and female life expectancies of 13 and 14 years, respectively, does not mean that men and women will live 13 and 14 years longer on average. Instead, it means that child and infant deaths are falling, thereby raising the average life expectancy for the population as a whole. Thus, beneficiaries will receive benefits for somewhat longer periods of time, but they will not receive benefits for the full 13 to 14 years longer that is indicated by the changes in life expectancies. A larger fraction of infants now born will live to collect Social Security benefits, however.

However we interpret it, the increase in life expectancy is one factor that has decreased the worker/beneficiary ratio. Some way had to be found to offset the effects of this change. The 1983 amendment to the Social Security Act gradually raises the normal retirement age to 67 years of age by the year 2022. Workers will still be able to retire at age 62 if they are willing to accept lower monthly benefits for the remainder of their lives. The closer to the normal retirement age that they are when they retire, the smaller the reduction in benefits that they will incur.

The increase in the normal retirement age means that many workers will pay taxes for two years longer, and they will collect retirement benefits for two years fewer. Because we are living longer on average, working longer on average may make sense.

Building Up Trust Fund Balances for Baby Boomer Benefits

The other change begun in 1983 was a partial departure from the pay-as-you-go philosophy of Social Security. Tax levels were set to increase **trust fund** balances to pay benefits to baby boomers. The baby boomers were born between the end of World War II and about 1965, a period during which the economy was booming and the birthrate increased. As this exceptionally large cohort of similarly aged Americans has advanced through life, they have made a difference. When they began school, they overcrowded the nation's schools and put stress on our public education system. When they reached maturity, they began families of their own and strained the nation's housing resources. They will begin retiring in about 2010, stressing the Social Security system.

To accommodate the baby boomers, trust fund balances are being built up. That is, the government is now collecting more taxes than are needed to pay benefits to current retirees. The surplus taxes are invested in U.S. government securities and therefore earn interest that is also credited to the trust funds. The intention is to have the funds available to pay benefits to baby boomers. As more and more baby boomers retire, the trust fund balances will be drawn down, because more benefits will be paid out than will be collected in taxes. Eventually, the trust fund balances will be virtually exhausted, and the system will revert to a strictly pay-as-you-go system.

Taxing Social Security Retirement Benefits

Originally, Social Security retirement benefits were exempt from income taxation. In 1984, retirees first began to pay federal income tax on a part of their Social Security benefits. The taxes paid are credited to Social Security trust funds and invested

Trust fund
Taxes collected and invested specifically to pay future Social Security benefits.

in U.S. securities. This taxation is somewhat controversial and is discussed in more detail later, but let us point out here that the taxation of benefits has resulted in substantial revenues and contributed to the financial viability of the system.

Long-Run Financial Viability of Social Security

The board of trustees of the Social Security program must file periodic reports about the long-range (75-year) financial outlook of the program. In preparing these reports, analysts make assumptions about growth in the economy, growth in the workforce, number of retirees, and length of time that retirees collect benefits, as well as other economic variables. They use different sets of assumptions, ranging from rosy to bleak outlooks about projected variables affecting the program in the future. A study by the Social Security Administration projected that trust funds would continue to be built up over the next 15 years and then begin to be drawn down but that they would not be exhausted until 2037.[3] After the trust funds are exhausted, the system will return to a pay-as-you-go system. Given the increasing proportion of older people in the population, this change could lead to either higher Social Security taxes or decreased retirement benefits. If no changes are made to the program, the Social Security Administration estimates that retirees after 2037 will receive benefits equal to 72 percent of the benefits of today's retirees. In the short term, the program is solvent, but in the long run, the program is not expected to be financially sound. Although more steps will be needed to ensure the financial viability of the Social Security retirement system in the future, it is currently not in any danger of collapsing.

The same cannot be said of Medicare. This social health insurance system reflects the problems of all health care in the United States. Outlays on a per-patient basis are rising rapidly. The outlays on current beneficiaries are increasing more rapidly than are the payroll taxes collected to fund Part A, the compulsory portion of the Medicare program. Part B, voluntary supplemental Medicare coverage, is financed by premiums paid by beneficiaries and by the general revenues of the federal government. Each year premiums are inadequate to cover increasing costs, and the government contributes from its revenues to cover the program's shortfall.

Should Social Security Be Made Voluntary?

U.S. citizens are independent souls, and they tend to dislike being forced to do anything. The compulsory nature of Social Security therefore has been controversial since the program's beginnings. Many conservatives argue that Social Security should be made voluntary, rather than compulsory. Their arguments are based on principles of greater economic freedom and limitation of the role of government in our lives. A related question concerns the fairness of the Social Security system to younger workers (a complex issue we examine in detail in the next section).

A voluntary system implies that individuals would have the option of participating or not participating in Social Security. If they choose not to participate, they could buy private insurance to satisfy their needs for economic security, they could choose to provide for their needs through other means, or they could decide not to provide for these needs at all.

The arguments for a compulsory Social Security program are (1) that a voluntary program would make provision of a minimum level of economic security to the entire population more difficult, (2) that the poor could not afford to purchase private insurance or save to provide for their own economic security, and (3) that a voluntary system would be subject to greater adverse selection. Let us look at these arguments more closely.

First, social insurance is intended to provide a minimum level of income to the entire population. Carrying out this intention through a voluntary program would be far more difficult. Some people simply would choose not to participate in any program and not to provide for their retirement. Others might purchase retirement income insurance through private firms but let the insurance lapse if they encounter hard times. Because society does not want our elderly population to starve or go homeless, we might find ourselves taking care of these individuals through welfare programs instead of social insurance.

Second, low-income workers who work at or near the minimum wage simply may not be able to afford to buy private insurance that provides benefits that are similar to those provided by Social Security. Remember that lower-income workers have a higher replacement rate (benefits as a percentage of earnings) than higher-income workers. Premiums necessary to purchase similar coverage from private insurers would be beyond the financial capability of this group. Nor would these low-earnings workers be able to save enough to provide for their families' economic security.

Finally, a voluntary system would increase the probability of adverse selection. **Adverse selection** is a problem for both social and private insurance. Adverse selection is any process by which the choices made by insured persons lead to higher-than-average loss levels for the program. (If healthy people do not purchase health insurance but sick people do, for example, the insurance companies will have higher average loss ratios and receive fewer premium payments.) Remember that the benefits of social insurance are based more on social adequacy than on individual equity. Therefore, some workers receive a higher return on their tax contributions than do others. If the program were made voluntary, the workers receiving the lower returns (younger workers, healthier workers, and workers with fewer dependents) might well decide to withdraw from the program and purchase private insurance in which the returns are based only on the principle of individual equity. If they were to withdraw from the Social Security program, the program would cover a greater proportion of high-risk people (workers slated to retire soon and workers likely to become disabled) and a smaller proportion of low-risk people. Loss levels and the cost per covered worker of the program would rise. Taxes for those who chose to participate would need to be increased, and more workers would find private insurance a desirable option. Social Security might eventually be reduced to an expensive program covering mainly those who are poor risks.

During the congressional debate that led to the passage of the Social Security Act of 1935, an alternative proposal for a voluntary system was made. It was not adopted, because the arguments for a compulsory system were more compelling. As we have seen, the issue is controversial to this day.

Adverse selection
A process by which insured people's choices lead to higher-than-average loss levels for the program's sponsor.

The "Bad Buy" Issue: Is Social Security Unfair to Younger Workers?

One of the concerns you may have about Social Security is its fairness to you and your generation. Social Security is quite generous to current retirees. But will it be as generous to you? Would you be able to provide better for your old age if you could just use your current Social Security taxes to invest any way you want? Is Social Security a bad buy for young workers?

One of the most complex issues involved in the Social Security program is whether young workers will receive their money's worth from Social Security. These workers pay Social Security taxes to support currently retired persons, survivors, and disabled persons. The value of the taxes paid by younger workers and their employers exceeds the value of the benefits that they can expect to receive. Thus, some critics of Social Security argue that younger workers are being cheated and that they should be allowed to opt out of Social Security and purchase private insurance protection. They argue that young people will get a fairer deal from buying private insurance than they get from Social Security. This is, of course, an argument for a voluntary Social Security program. Let us look at the bad buy argument carefully.

Most of the studies indicating that the young worker is cheated under Social Security make the assumption that the individual employee is entitled to all of his or her employer's tax contribution. This assumption is based on the belief that firms pay lower wages to their workers in order to compensate themselves for the Social Security taxes they pay on behalf of their employees. If this assumption is not valid, and workers *do not* receive lower wages because of their employers' Social Security contributions, then the belief that the system is unfair to younger workers is not justified. It all depends on how much money we assume the worker places into an alternative program. The alternative program looks good if we assume the worker puts in the entire amount otherwise paid by employer and employee into Social Security; the alternative program does not look so good if the worker only puts in the amount paid by the worker into Social Security.

The employer's matching half of the Social Security tax was never intended to be credited to an individual worker's account. Its purpose is to benefit all covered persons rather than a specific person. At the beginning of the program, it was necessary to provide benefits to many workers who worked a relatively few years in employment that was covered by Social Security. When they retired and began collecting Social Security benefits, the employer's portion of the tax was intended to make that possible. Moreover, the employer's contributions make redistribution of income from high-income to low-income workers possible. The employer's share of the tax provides for social adequacy, not individual equity.

In addition, many of the studies supporting the bad buy argument consider only survivor and retirement benefits. Researchers make the assumption that if the individual worker were given the taxes paid by both the employer and the employee, the worker could purchase life insurance and a retirement annuity more cheaply than he or she could acquire the same coverage through the Social Security program. This assumption does not account for all the benefits provided by Social Security.

Social Security is a unique social insurance program that also provides disability coverage and medical insurance through Medicare. If we adjust for these benefits by removing taxes paid to support them, the results of the studies change greatly. It is far less clear that Social Security is a bad buy for younger workers when these benefits are taken into consideration.

Social Security's Treatment of Women

Social Security is meant to be gender-neutral; it is supposed to treat men and women equally. But, largely because our society and culture do not treat the sexes equally, men and women are not treated equally under Social Security. We discuss two of the women's issues in Social Security. They are the widow's income gap and the possibly unfair treatment of working wives under the program.

The Widow's Income Gap

Widows (or widowers) of covered workers can collect monthly survivorship benefits based on the earnings record of the deceased spouse. Surviving children are also entitled to benefits until they reach the age of 18. The surviving spouse's benefits are paid only until the youngest child reaches the age of 16. Then, at the age of 60, the surviving spouse can again collect benefits on the earnings record of the deceased worker. The benefits will be lost if the surviving spouse remarries before reaching the age of 60.

Consider the following case. Tom and Mandy are a young couple with three small children. Mandy worked before their second child was born but hasn't worked outside the home since that time. Tom suddenly dies. Mandy is 28 years old. Her youngest child is 3 years old. Mandy can receive survivorship benefits, as can the three children. Her benefits will end, however, when the 3-year-old reaches 16 years of age. Mandy will be only 41 years old. She cannot again collect benefits on Tom's earnings record until she reaches the age of 60. If she has stayed home with the children, she will probably have few marketable skills with which to support herself.

Mandy will face a gap in survivor's benefits of 19 years. So will many middle-aged widows (women) who are under 60 years of age but who have grown children when their husbands die. It should be noted that widowers (men) face the same problem as widows. If the wife was the primary (or even an equal) wage earner in the marriage, a surviving widower will face the same situation. Given, however, that there are still a great many so-called traditional marriages in the United States and that men on average earn more than women, the coverage gap is primarily a women's issue.

Unfair Treatment of Working Wives

A wife can receive retirement benefits based on her own earnings record, or she can receive retirement benefits based on her husband's record as his spouse. As a matter of course, the Social Security Administration will pay her the highest retirement benefits after calculating the benefits using her own record and her husband's. Usually, her spousal benefits will be one-half of what her husband receives. Wives who have never worked outside the home, or who did not work enough to be fully covered for retirement benefits, are entitled to the same spousal benefits as are wives who worked throughout their married lives.

Many wives, on applying for Social Security retirement benefits, discover that they are entitled to larger spousal benefits than they would be entitled to if they were to receive benefits based on their own earnings record. It therefore appears as if their tax contributions are lost, and, at least for Social Security retirement purposes, that their years of working do not matter.

Why is this the case? Remember from Chapter 5 that women make significantly less on average than do men. If the couple is typical in this way, the man will have compiled a larger earnings record. Furthermore, women are in and out of the labor market because of family responsibilities more than men are. This too will contribute to a lower earnings record. Thus, the one-half of her husband's retirement benefit is more than the benefits based on her own earnings. It appears as if her years of working and paying payroll taxes are wasted.

Again, it should be noted that husbands might find themselves in the same situation if their earnings record is much smaller than their wives'. They might find that their spousal benefits are larger than benefits paid on their own records. The Social Security law treats spouses of either gender the same. But the labor market institutions of the United States treat men and women differently, and this differential treatment is reflected in treatment for Social Security.

Does Social Security Decrease Savings?

Critics of the Social Security program argue that it has decreased private savings in the United States. They argue that the need to save for retirement privately is decreased because the Social Security program exists. This phenomenon is called the **Social Security wealth effect**. The wealth effect causes us to spend more during our working years on consumer goods, because we do not feel the need to save. Indeed, the United States has one of the developed world's lowest private savings rates, as we shall see in Chapter 17.

Others argue that Social Security actually increases private savings by encouraging earlier retirements. This effect is called the **early retirement effect**. Workers who retire earlier must provide for a longer period of retirement and therefore must save more during their working years. If the wealth effect is greater than the early retirement effect, then Social Security decreases private savings. If the early retirement effect exceeds the wealth effect, then Social Security increases private savings.

Social Security's effect on private savings is an issue for empirical research, and many studies have been done on the issue. Trying to measure the portion of savings that is affected by Social Security as opposed to the portion of savings that is not affected by Social Security is difficult, and the results of the studies are inconclusive. Most of the studies do not take into account that workers may save for purposes other than retirement. For example, many workers save for vacations, down payments on houses, their children's education, or other purposes. Nor do the studies consider that children might have to support their aged parents if Social Security did not exist. The question is truly complex, and we simply do not know the effect of Social Security on savings.

Social Security wealth effect
The tendency of the population to substitute Social Security for private saving, thus decreasing private saving.

Early retirement effect
Social Security's effect of increasing private savings by encouraging earlier retirements.

COMMON MISCONCEPTIONS ABOUT SOCIAL SECURITY

Let's examine some common misconceptions about the Social Security system and its finances. Some people argue that the trust funds are fictitious, because the government securities held by the trust funds are merely IOUs owed by one branch of the government to another. This conception is incorrect. The trust funds are real. The collected taxes are invested in U.S. securities so that the money earns interest instead of just sitting in a non-interest-bearing account. The government securities, also called government bonds, are issued by government agencies to borrow money from the public. They are similar to the government savings bonds you may have received from your Aunt Gertrude. The government bonds held by the trust contribute interest to the Social Security program and can be redeemed whenever the trust fund managers decide to redeem them. Government bonds are one of the safest possible investments that the trust funds could make, because the bonds are backed by the full faith and credit of the United States.

Others argue that the trust funds increase the national debt when Social Security taxes are invested in government securities. This conception also is incorrect. The national debt increases when the government decides to spend more money than it collects in tax revenues in any particular year. This results in a budget deficit, which is discussed in more detail in Chapter 16. When the government has a budget deficit, it sells newly issued government securities, which are really just pieces of paper saying that the government owes the purchaser the money it has borrowed. The government decides, on the basis of its desire to borrow, how many government securities to issue. It doesn't matter after that whether a government agency, a bank, or a private citizen buys these securities. The purchase of new securities by the Social Security trust funds has no more effect on the national debt than does your Aunt Gertrude's purchasing a new Series EE savings bond. In fact, the two transactions are alike from the perspective of financing the government.

WHAT DOES THE FUTURE HOLD FOR THE SOCIAL SECURITY SYSTEM?

When we talk to our students, they express doubt that Social Security will be there for them. You probably have the same worries. If you are working, you know that a large chunk of your earnings is taken for Social Security taxes. You know you must continue to pay Social Security taxes—but what, if any, benefits can you expect to receive?

Americans have long been skeptical about the promise of Social Security. Each generation has applauded the system's support of their parents and grandparents but has doubted that Social Security will "be there for them." Each generation fears the collapse of the system before that generation reaches retirement. In opinion poll after opinion poll, Americans express their uneasiness. This skepticism was only briefly allayed by the changes made by Congress in 1983.

In part, workers' renewed doubts are the result of Social Security's worsening financial position. It is now obvious that trust fund balances will be drawn down more rapidly than was predicted in the early 1980s. But part of the skepticism arises because most Americans simply do not understand the system. And inaccurate reporting in the media contributes to both their uneasiness and their lack of understanding. When, for example, the Social Security board of trustees reported in 1999 that the retirement trust fund balances were to be exhausted by 2037, newspaper headlines throughout the country read "Social Security Bankrupt by 2037." Although the exhaustion of trust fund balances is not exactly good news, the return to a pay-as-you-go system is not the same as bankruptcy. After 2037, the system will continue to pay benefits at a level of about 72 percent of today's benefit level, even without our making changes to increase its financial stability. But benefits will have to be paid from current tax collections after that date.

Nevertheless, issues of financing and financial soundness remain. Trust fund balances are now predicted to be drawn down more rapidly than previously expected. The Medicare hospital insurance trust fund is in really poor condition. There is some cause for concern, and proposals to amend the system have been made in the past few years. Without doubt, changes will be made to the Social Security system. Because the system offers a measure of economic security to us all, we should be concerned about whether these changes reflect the underlying principles and values of the social insurance system. If we allow the system to deteriorate until it reaches a crisis situation, changes made at that point may not be consistent with these values. Let's look at some of the changes that might be made in the future.

Altering the Social Security Tax

Some are concerned about the heavy burden of Social Security taxes on low-income workers in our economy. We have noted that the tax is highly regressive and that this regressive tax has increased in size over time. There has been little outcry about the regressivity of this tax, perhaps because most people do not fully understand its implications. On the other hand, recent cuts in capital gains taxes, dividend taxes, and personal income taxes have primarily benefited high-income people. We address the issue of the effects of taxes on income distribution in greater detail in Chapter 16.

For now, let's just think about how we might reduce the regressivity of the Social Security tax. It may not be as hard as we think. Instead of placing a ceiling on the amount of our earnings that is taxed each year (currently $76,200), we might put a floor in place instead. That is, we might say something along the lines that your earnings below $76,200 are not taxed but your earnings above this level are. In this way, very-high-income earners would be taxed more heavily than low-income earners.

Cutting Current Social Security Benefits

Various proposals have been made to cut current Social Security benefits, either across the board or for high-income recipients. Some proposals would tinker with the benefits formula to decrease the benefits of particular earnings classes. Others would eliminate adjustments for inflation, either temporarily or permanently. Eliminating such cost-of-living adjustments is, in fact, a form of benefits reduction. Obviously, cutting current benefits would make the trust funds last longer.

A proposal introduced in Congress in 1999 would have cut current benefits. The proposal was to revise the cost-of-living adjustment (COLA) of current Social Security recipients. Social Security benefits are adjusted each January to cover the inflation that occurred in the preceding year. The inflation is measured using the consumer price index (CPI). Economists generally agree that the CPI somewhat overstates inflation but they disagree about how much. (This issue is discussed in Chapter 14.) The legislative proposal would have adjusted the COLA and decreased the annual increase in benefits of current beneficiaries. The proposal was defeated in Congress.

Proponents of cutting the benefits specifically of high-earner retirees point out that not all Social Security recipients are poor. People who earned more while working are also more likely to have received private pensions and have investment income than low earners. In other words, they do not need the Social Security check as much as lower earners. Eliminating or cutting their benefits would make the system more progressive, keep a minimum floor of income under the lower and average earners, and cut the costs of the Social Security program.

On the other hand, cutting the benefits of high earners might threaten the individual equity principle that makes Social Security a social insurance program instead of a welfare program. As a social insurance program, Social Security has enjoyed widespread acceptance and a lack of stigma. As a wise person once said, "Programs for the poor tend to be poor programs." Social Security has always been perceived as a program for everyone. Eliminating the benefits of high earners might lead people to view Social Security as a welfare program, and welfare programs are more vulnerable to political maneuvering than are social insurance programs.

Taxing All Social Security Benefits

A proposal that is highly likely to be adopted in the future is taxation of all Social Security benefits as though they are any other sort of income. This proposal does not mean that income taxes would be paid on every dollar of Social Security benefits. Our income tax system is progressive, and people with very little income pay little or no taxes. So, the individual who was paid at near the minimum wage for all the years he or she worked, and whose total income is in the form of Social Security, would probably not pay tax on those benefits. But people with other sources of income or very high Social Security benefits would pay taxes on Social Security benefits just as they do on income from investments.

Increasing Retirement Ages

As we mentioned previously, the so-called normal retirement age will increase over time to 67 years under our current law. But the earliest age at which workers can retire with reduced benefits remains 62 years under current law. Another suggestion to strengthen the system is to raise both the normal retirement age *and* the early retirement age.

Proponents of an additional increase in the normal retirement age point out that the U.S. economy is evolving from a manufacturing economy to a service and information economy. Jobs are therefore less physically demanding, on average. Furthermore, advances in health care have made U.S. workers healthier in their fifties and sixties. Therefore, they argue, it will not be a disservice to increase the normal retirement age further.

Over time, U.S. workers have retired at younger ages. Many argue that Social Security has contributed to this trend. Currently, a worker can retire at age 62 and receive 80 percent of the monthly Social Security benefits that he or she would have received at age 65. When the normal retirement age increases to 67 years, the worker will still be able to retire at age 62 and receive 70 percent of the monthly benefits that he or she would have received at the normal retirement age. Those who propose an increase in the earliest age that a worker can retire and still receive Social Security benefits argue that workers who choose early retirement at reduced benefits often do so without realizing how long they will need to provide for themselves in retirement. As their other assets are exhausted, their reduced Social Security benefits may not be adequate to provide for their needs, or certainly not enough to keep them comfortably. Raising the early retirement age would encourage workers to continue working—and paying Social Security taxes—longer. Because their monthly benefits would be greater when they retire, they would be better off, and so would the Social Security system.

Investing Social Security Taxes in the Stock Market

Recall that the Social Security trust funds are invested to earn interest until they are needed to pay benefits. The trust funds must, by law, be invested only in government securities, which are the safest possible investment because the full faith and credit of the federal government stands behind them. But stocks in America's corporations often pay investors far higher rates of return than do government bonds. Many critics of the system argue that allowing the managers of the Social Security trust funds to invest a portion of the tax revenue in the stock market would greatly increase the investment earnings of the funds. Others point out that investment in the stock market is more risky than investing in government securities, as we've seen in the early 2000s. Nevertheless, a portion of the trust funds will probably be invested in stocks at some point in the future.

Partial Privatization

As we have noted, President Bush continues to propose that portions of the Social Security program be privatized. His original proposal was that 2 percent of a worker's earnings be put into investment accounts selected by the worker. The Social Security tax rate would be reduced by the same amount. Thus, instead of the Social Security Administration investing all Social Security tax revenue in government securities, the individual worker would direct a portion to be invested in stocks or mutual funds. The worker would then retain control over this portion of his or her retirement funds. Allowing workers to direct the investment of tax contributions is quite different from simply allowing the managers of the Social Security trust funds to invest in corporate stocks. Critics argue that high-wage earners will receive more sophisticated investment advice than will low-income workers. Thus, they argue, the proposal would increase the retirement income of high earners and decrease the retirement income of low-income earners.

Whether this change in the Social Security system takes place remains to be seen. In the current environment of corporate scandals and public mistrust of these institutions, it seems unlikely that the system will change greatly in the very near future.

Social Security has been called the "third rail" of American politics. It represents economic security to some people and an undue tax burden to others. One thing is certain: Social Security will change over time. And it is highly unlikely that the system will be as generous to us as it is to today's retirees. What does this mean to you as you begin your careers? It means that you should save and invest for your retirement to maintain your living standard. Social Security may supplement your savings, but you should not expect to be able to retire comfortably on Social Security benefits alone.

VIEWPOINT: CONSERVATIVE VERSUS LIBERAL

Conservatives believe that Social Security represents big government. They argue that we would be better off if we did not have to pay Social Security taxes but were encouraged by some measure, such as a tax break, to provide for ourselves in retirement or disability through private investments. Many conservatives therefore favor partial or total privatization of the system. They also, of course, would favor making Social Security voluntary.

Liberals, on the other hand, tend to support the principle of social, not private, insurance to provide a minimum floor of income support under the total population. Liberals worry about the regressivity of the Social Security payroll tax and want to make changes to ensure the continued financial viability of the system. They do not worry about the size of the system. Nor do they worry that the system represents big government.

SUMMARY

Social Security is a social insurance system. Although Social Security taxes are regressive, the program's benefits are progressive. The purpose of the system is to provide a minimum floor of economic security to U.S. workers. The size and tax burden of the system have increased over time.

Social Security is controversial. Its long-run problem is that fewer workers pay taxes to support each recipient as time passes. Trust fund balances are now being built up to pay benefits to the baby boomers. Other issues include the system's fairness to women and to younger workers, the effect of Social Security on private savings, the desirability of making the system voluntary, and the long-run financial viability of the system. Changes likely in the future are a decrease in benefits, an increase in the normal and early retirement ages, and the full income taxation of benefits.

NOTES

1. The Social Security Administration, Facts and Figures About Social Security (**www.ssa.gov/ policy/docs/chartbooks/fast_facts/2003**).

2. The CIA *World Factbook* (**www.cia.gov/cia/ publications/factbook/**). Aug. 1, 2003 and earlier. 2003 numbers are estimates.

3. Social Security Administration, *2000 OASDI Trustees Report* (**www.ssa.gov**).

DISCUSSION QUESTIONS

1. Do you believe that Social Security is unfair to women? to younger workers? Why or why not? If you think that Social Security is unfair, what could be done to make it more fair? What other problems might these measures cause?

2. Explain how Social Security taxes are regressive. Remember that regressivity does not mean that the low-income person pays more actual tax, but that he or she pays more tax as a percentage of his or her income. How could the tax be made less regressive?

3. Compare and contrast social insurance with private insurance. Can you think of other examples of social insurance programs?

4. Compare and contrast social insurance programs with public assistance programs. Can you think of other examples of public assistance programs?

5. Do you believe that Social Security should be made fully funded? What would the advantages and disadvantages be?

6. What changes do you feel are likely to be made in Social Security in the next 15 to 20 years? Why? Go to the Social Security Administration Web site at **www.ssa.gov**. Click About Social Security's Future to see some frequently asked questions about the future of Social Security, as well as the answers supplied by the Social Security Administration.

7. Again, go to the home page of the Social Security Administration at **www.ssa.gov** and notice many other links, both serious and light-hearted. For example, click Most Popular Baby Names.

8. What is the long-run problem with Social Security? Do you feel that steps taken in 1983 to solve the problem were adequate?

9. For a conservative view of the Social Security system, go to **www.cato.org**, the home page of the Cato Institute, a conservative research institute. The site has links to papers arguing for privatization of Social Security.

10. For a more liberal view of the Social Security system, go to the Center for Budget and Policy Priorities at **www.cbpp.org**, and look for recent discussions of voluntary Social Security accounts and/or privatization of Social Security. What is the difference between the liberal and conservative views?

11. Go to the White House Web site at **www.whitehouse.gov** to find information about a variety of policies and reports, including many speeches by the president. Search for speeches that include comments about Social Security.

CHAPTER 14 ROADMAP

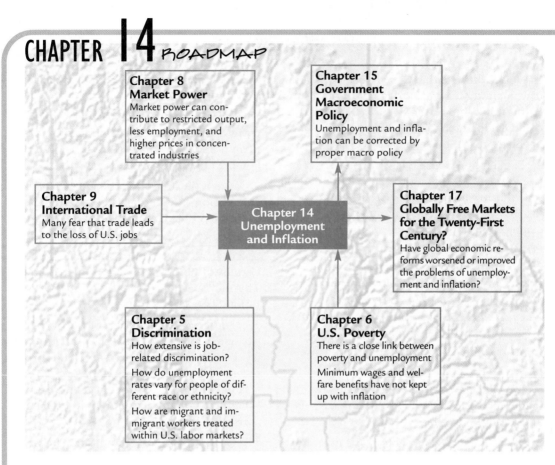

**Chapter 8
Market Power**
Market power can contribute to restricted output, less employment, and higher prices in concentrated industries

**Chapter 15
Government Macroeconomic Policy**
Unemployment and inflation can be corrected by proper macro policy

**Chapter 9
International Trade**
Many fear that trade leads to the loss of U.S. jobs

**Chapter 14
Unemployment and Inflation**

**Chapter 17
Globally Free Markets for the Twenty-First Century?**
Have global economic reforms worsened or improved the problems of unemployment and inflation?

**Chapter 5
Discrimination**
How extensive is job-related discrimination?

How do unemployment rates vary for people of different race or ethnicity?

How are migrant and immigrant workers treated within U.S. labor markets?

**Chapter 6
U.S. Poverty**
There is a close link between poverty and unemployment

Minimum wages and welfare benefits have not kept up with inflation

THE ECONOMIC TOOLBOX

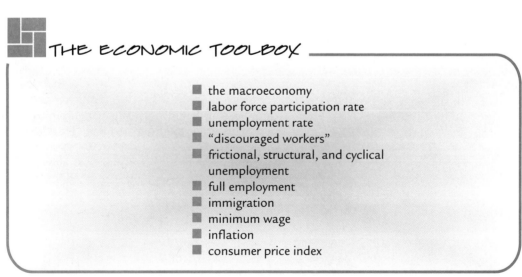

- the macroeconomy
- labor force participation rate
- unemployment rate
- "discouraged workers"
- frictional, structural, and cyclical unemployment
- full employment
- immigration
- minimum wage
- inflation
- consumer price index

UNEMPLOYMENT AND INFLATION

We are fortunate to be alive at this moment in history. Never before has our nation enjoyed, at once, so much prosperity and social progress with so little internal crisis.

—President William Jefferson Clinton, State of the Union Address, 2000

Our first goal is clear: We must have an economy that grows fast enough to employ every man and woman who seeks a job. After recession, terrorist attacks, corporate scandals and stock market declines, our economy is recovering—yet it's not growing fast enough, or strongly enough. With unemployment rising, our nation needs more small businesses to open, more companies to invest and expand, more employers to put up the sign that says, "Help Wanted."

—President George W. Bush, State of the Union Address, 2003

How quickly things change! Just three years after President Clinton's quotation demonstrated unbridled optimism about our economy, the Bush quotation reveals deep concern about the economy and related issues. We entered the new millennium in a position of macroeconomic health after a decade of economic growth and expansion. Unemployment and inflation rates were the lowest in decades. The unanswered question then was, "How long can this state of affairs last?"

We now know that it didn't last long. If you are a traditional student in your late teens or early twenties, you have only been familiar with a healthy economy until recently. The stories of job layoffs and unemployment lines were just that—stories from years gone by. Perhaps your grandparents lived during the Great Depression of the 1930s. Ask them to tell you about the one of four people who couldn't find work, the bread lines, and the frugality of the era. Perhaps your grandparents still won't throw anything away, despite being comfortably well off. The lessons of hard times are difficult to erase.

Maybe your parents remember the inflation of the 1970s, with skyrocketing energy prices and long lines for gasoline, or the recession of 1981–1982, when President Ronald Reagan and the Federal Reserve brought inflation under control but ushered in the highest unemployment rates since the Great

Depression. Perhaps you even remember talk of higher-than-normal unemployment at the beginning of the 1990s, when jobs were more scarce and the job search more lengthy.

Although our current economy is not as bad as the years of the Great Depression, it is clear that the rosy economic picture of President Clinton is now behind us. We are now experiencing poor macroeconomic health. What does this mean for us? What does it mean for you as you look to your job horizon and to your spending habits as an American consumer? And more important, how long will it be before the health of our economy improves?

THE MACROECONOMY

Macro-economy
The total economy.

Macro-economics
The study of the total economy.

Micro-economics
The study of individual aspects within the total economy.

Gross domestic product (GDP)
Total output in an economy.

As you recall from Chapter 1, when we study unemployment and inflation and the policies designed to control them, we are focusing on the **macroeconomy**. Indeed, **macroeconomics** is the study of the overall economy. In previous chapters, we've considered individual markets such as the markets for health care, housing, and agricultural products. The study of individual markets within the economy is part of the study of **microeconomics**. Some economists refer to microeconomics as the study of the trees, whereas macroeconomics is the study of the forest. We're looking at the same economy, but contrasting the individual parts with the overall picture.

Recall our study of agricultural markets in Chapter 12. We were interested in the output of corn or wheat and how the prices of these agricultural goods were changing. In macroeconomics, we are concerned instead with the quantity of total output in our economy (which we call **gross domestic product**, or **GDP**) and how the average price level for all of this output is changing. An increase in the average price level is what we mean by inflation. And although employment within any individual market is closely related to output in that market, in macroeconomics we are more concerned with employment for the country as a whole, which is closely related to total production.

Also notice that President Bush used the term *recession* in his words that open this chapter. This term will be used occasionally throughout this chapter and discussed in more detail in the next chapter. For now, just realize that a **recession** is simply defined as a decline in a nation's output, which results in a decline in the number of people hired to produce this output.

UNEMPLOYMENT

Recession
A decline in a nation's gross domestic product (output) associated with a rise in unemployment.

We began the new century with over 20 million new jobs, the fastest economic growth in more than 30 years, and the lowest unemployment rate in 30 years. Now our economic growth has slowed and our unemployment rate is high. So, let's begin our study of macroeconomics with topics related to unemployment. To do so, we need to understand what is meant by the concepts of the labor force and the labor force participation rate.

The Labor Force Participation Rate

The **labor force** refers to all people age 16 and older who are working for pay plus all people in this age range who are actively seeking employment. Think about this definition for a moment. Clearly, the concept of the labor force goes beyond just those people who are working. It also includes those who would like to be working and who are looking for a job. We sometimes refer to the labor force as the work-force. It refers to those actively interested in working.

Who is not included in the labor force? Obviously, not children. But neither are retired people, full-time homemakers who do not desire a job outside of the home, full-time students who do not wish to work for pay along with their studies, people in institutions such as prisons and mental hospitals, nor anyone else who is not actively seeking a job. The labor force is clearly a subset of the entire population.

Why is this concept of the labor force important? First, it demonstrates the quantity of our labor resource available for the production of national output. It also reflects societal trends and attitudes. In the 1950s and 1960s, for example, many women did not work outside of the home. Indeed, many in society believed that women's place was in the home, and not in the labor force. This attitude was not prevalent during earlier wartimes or in recent years. Attitudes have changed about the work habits of teenagers, single mothers, and even fathers of newborns; and financial necessity has increased the likelihood that many college students support themselves with part-time work.

The phenomenon of working mothers is very interesting. In the early 1960s, only about one-fourth of married mothers worked outside the home, whereas more than one-half of single mothers did. Over the next few decades, the share of working married mothers increased dramatically, but the share of working single mothers remained stable. By the mid-1980s, the share of working married mothers exceeded that of single mothers, and by the late 1990s, almost two-thirds of married mothers worked.[1] What do you think are the reasons for these trends?

The **labor force participation rate** is the share of the population age 16 and older that is in the labor force. It is calculated as the number of people in the labor force divided by the total number of people age 16 and older. We can think of the labor force participation rate as the percentage of all adults who are actively interested in working. Table 14-1 shows the U.S. labor force participation rate for males and females, individually and combined, in 1964 and 2002. Overall, the labor force participation rate has increased since 1964. Notice, however, that the participation rate of men has decreased substantially, whereas the participation rate of women has increased dramatically. The rate remains much higher for men than women though.

To compare the labor force participation rate of one country with that of another country, we must adjust our definition of that rate. Because child labor is much more extensive in other countries, particularly in less-developed ones, we must take a broader view of the labor force. World Bank data indicate, for example, that more

Labor force
All people age 16 and older who are working for pay or actively seeking employment.

EconNews
"Child Labor"

Read how U.K. parents support their children at their own cost by going to the Labor Market category.

http://econapps. swlearning.com

Labor force participation rate
The ratio of the number of people in the labor force to the number of people age 16 or older in the population.

TABLE 14-1	U.S. Labor Force Participation Rates for Men and Women, Individually and Combined, 1964 and 2002		
Year	Men (%)	Women (%)	Men and Women (%)
1964	81.0	38.7	58.7
2002	74.1	59.6	66.6

*Source: U.S. Department of Commerce, Bureau of Labor Statistics (**www.bls.gov**).*

than 52 percent and 47 percent of children ages 10 through 14 years are part of the labor force in the west African countries of Mali and Burkina Faso, respectively. In other parts of the world, 43 percent of children in this age group in Nepal and 29 percent in Bangladesh belong to the labor force. In the United States, of course, the official percentage is zero.

We can use complete population data and statistics on all people in the labor force, regardless of age, to calculate an adjusted labor force participation rate. A sampling of countries is shown in Table 14-2. Because the countries chosen are not necessarily representative of the various regions of the world, we cannot use this sample to make generalizations about the regions. In addition, we must be cautious about our interpretation of the data, because many people in less-developed countries work in informal labor markets and are not always counted as among the officially employed. We do see a wide variation in the participation rates, however, ranging from 39 percent in Argentina to 60 percent in China.

The Unemployment Rate

Ask your friends how they think the unemployment rate is calculated. Unless they've had an economics course, they will probably stammer a little and then make some vague statements about people without jobs. Unfortunately, this answer is not adequate for economic analysis.

TABLE 14-2 Adjusted Labor Force Participation Rates (inclusive of children) for Select Countries, 1999

Continent	Country 1	Country 2	Country 3
Africa	Mali 46%	Ethiopia 43%	Nigeria 40%
Asia	China 60%	Japan 54%	Bangladesh 52%
Latin America	Brazil 46%	Argentina 39%	Colombia 44%
Western Europe	France 44%	Britain 51%	Italy 43%
Eastern Europe	Russia 53%	Poland 51%	Ukraine 50%
North America	United States 51%	Canada 55%	Mexico 40%

Source: Data from World Bank, World Development Report 2000/2001 *(New York: Oxford University Press, 2001).*

Note: The calculations are made by dividing the entire labor force, inclusive of children, by the entire population in each country.

The **unemployment rate** is defined as the percentage of the labor force that is unemployed. The unemployment rate is calculated as follows:

$$\text{Unemployment Rate} = \frac{\text{Number of Unemployed People}}{\text{Number of People in the Labor Force}}$$

To qualify as an **unemployed person**, a person must be in the labor force. As you already know, the U.S. concept of the labor force refers to all people age 16 and older who are working for pay plus all people age 16 and older who are not employed but who are actively seeking employment. The latter are considered unemployed.

Think about this definition for a moment. Some people are not counted in either the numerator or the denominator. The only people who are classified as unemployed are those who are actively looking for jobs. That is, they must be answering want ads, sending out vitae, engaging in job interviews, or doing whatever is necessary to find a job. Therefore, full-time homemakers and students who are not seeking employment for pay are not categorized as unemployed. (Neither are children, retired people, volunteer workers, people in prison or mental hospitals, or those who would simply rather not work.)

Because the labor force consists of people who are either employed or unemployed, it may sound as though the labor force and the total population are the same. This is not the case! Remember that all of the homemakers, students, retired people, children, and so on that were excluded from the numerator of the unemployment rate are excluded from the denominator as well. Your great-grandmother and your next-door "stay at home" mother of four are not unemployed, nor are they part of the labor force. Nor are you and other students, if you are not working or seeking a job for pay.

The Data

What is the national unemployment rate? We already know that the current rate is relatively high. Just what is considered low and what is high? How do current rates compare with those of the recent past? Do all groups of people within our economy face the same probability of becoming unemployed? What are your chances of becoming unemployed?

The National Unemployment Rate

Let us begin to answer these questions by looking at the annual unemployment rates for our nation in recent years. Table 14-3 on page 332 displays these data.

Notice that the year 2000 unemployment rate was extremely low by historical standards. This all-time recent low was lower than imaginable even in the prosperous years of the 1960s, not to mention the economic slowdowns of 1975, 1981–1983, and 1992. The relatively low unemployment rate in the year 2000 had a lot to do with the steady expansion of our economy since 1992. The higher, more recent unemployment rates reveal that our economy is not growing as we would like it to. We discuss these situations more carefully in the next chapter. Nevertheless, it is clear that the unemployment rate in 2002 was the highest since 1992. The unemployment rates since 1992 are shown more visibly in Figure 14-1. Notice the precipitous decline until 2001 and 2002!

TABLE 14-3	U.S. Unemployment Rates, Select Years from 1960 to 2002		
Year	**Unemployment Rate (%)**	**Year**	**Unemployment Rate (%)**
1960	5.5	1993	6.8
1965	4.5	1994	6.1
1970	4.9	1995	5.6
1975	8.5	1996	5.4
1980	7.1	1997	4.9
1981	7.6	1998	4.5
1982	9.7	1999	4.2
1983	9.6	2000	4.0
1985	7.2	2001	4.7
1991	6.7	2002	5.8
1992	7.4		

*Source: U.S. Department of Commerce, Bureau of Labor Statistics (**www.bls.gov**).*

FIGURE 14-1 Change in Unemployment Rates Since 1992 (based on the data in Table 14-3)

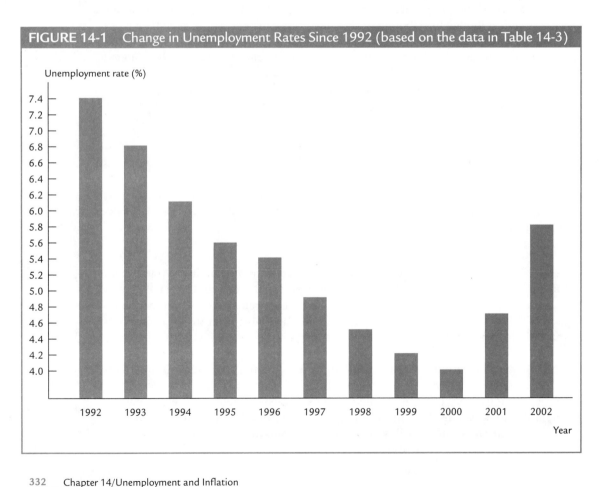

Unemployment Rates for Selected Groups of People

Like the national unemployment rates indicated in Table 14-3, the relative unemployment rates of certain groups of people are important for national policy. Table 14-4 displays these data for the month of June 2003. The national average unemployment rate for this month was 6.5 percent. We can use this number as a benchmark for comparing the unemployment rates of individual groups of people.

Notice first of all that the unemployment rate for men is slightly higher than that for women. This is not always the case. In fact, some economists believe that unemployment rates for women are lower than those of men during and immediately after recessions. They explain this in terms of "discouraged workers," which is described momentarily. In any event, in any one year the unemployment rate may be a little higher for men, whereas in the next year it may be a little higher for women. Keep in mind that to be classified as unemployed, a person must be actively seeking employment. Therefore, any full-time homemakers who are not seeking outside employment are not included in the unemployment statistics.

Second, notice the very high unemployment rate for teenagers, more than three times the national average. This group of young people has the highest unemployment rate of any age group, year after year. Part of the difficulty for our teenagers is that they lack the education, skills, and experience that are often required by employers.

Finally, notice that the unemployment rate for white people is well below the national average and far below the rates for blacks and Hispanics. The unemployment rate for blacks is more than twice that for whites, and the unemployment rate for Hispanics is usually between the rates for blacks and whites. The unemployment rate for Asian Americans is the lowest among the minority groups. Again, we are referring only to people who are actively seeking employment. Clearly, the burden of unemployment is not borne equally by all groups. Although there are many reasons for the differing unemployment rates for people of differing race and ethnicity, the numbers suggest that the equal opportunity and affirmative action policies discussed in Chapter 5 continue to be very important.

TABLE 14-4 U.S. Unemployment Rates for Select Groups, June 2003	
Group	Unemployment Rate (%)
Nation	6.5
Men	6.7
Women	6.4
Youth ages 16–19	22.3
Whites	5.6
Blacks	12.0
Hispanics	8.2
Asians	7.8

Source: U.S. Department of Commerce, Bureau of Labor Statistics (**www.bls.gov**).

Problems in Measuring Unemployment

The official unemployment rate gives us a rough idea of how the economy is doing. We believe the economy is doing better if this rate falls. But measurement problems may cause the official statistics to understate the economic hardship of unemployment.

Many economists believe that the unemployment rate understates the true extent of economic hardship from unemployment in our country for two reasons. First, anyone working at least part-time for pay is considered to be employed. Although many people prefer part-time work, many others prefer full-time employment and need full-time work to support their families. When these people can find only part-time jobs, they experience economic hardship even though they are officially classified as being employed.

Discouraged workers
People who would like to work, but have become so discouraged in the job search that they have stopped actively seeking employment.

Second, some people who would like to work and who have actively sought employment have become so discouraged in their search that they have given up looking for jobs. In many ways, these **discouraged workers** are perhaps the ones most severely affected by unemployment, yet they cease to be tallied in the unemployment statistics as soon as they cease their active job search. When the economy is depressed, the number of discouraged workers increases, and the understating of unemployment becomes more severe. During the Great Depression of the 1930s, the official unemployment rate rose to 24.9 percent. Most economists believe that if all the discouraged workers had been counted, the unemployment rate would have been much higher.

We've just noted that unemployment rates for women are often lower than unemployment rates for men during and immediately after recessions. This may be the case if more women become "discouraged" and drop out of the labor market in times of limited employment. This means that even though women may face more difficulty in the labor market, their actual unemployment rates may be lower than those of men.

Economists believe that mismeasurement of the unemployment rate can have serious ramifications. First, many of our macroeconomic policies are based on the unemployment rate, and if unemployment is understated, policymakers may not take the problem seriously enough. Second, changes in our economy can have a misleading impact on official unemployment rates. When the economy is in a downturn, for example, many people who are unable to find employment give up their job search. At that point, they fall out of the unemployment statistics entirely, because they are no longer classified as being unemployed. Thus, simply because these workers are now ignored in the statistics, the official unemployment rate may be decreasing as the economy is worsening!

The Effects of Unemployment

Personal Effects

The effects of unemployment on individual workers and their families are obvious. Clearly, the income of the family will fall when the breadwinner loses a job. Many people are unaware that most unemployed people do not receive unemployment compensation. Unemployment compensation is an income transfer from the government to the eligible unemployed person. To be eligible, one must first have had a job. Even when eligible, unemployed people receive benefits well below their former income and for only a limited period of time.

Beyond the income loss, the unemployed person suffers other tangible losses. One such loss might be employment-related health benefits, thereby harming the health of the family. Another loss is on-the-job experience, which might reduce the unemployed person's productivity and marketability.

Unemployment causes a variety of problems, not just strictly economic ones. Researchers at Johns Hopkins University and other organizations have noted a high correlation between unemployment rates and a variety of social ills. When unemployment rates go up, we typically see an increase in domestic violence, divorce, alcoholism, child abuse, and suicide.

Macroeconomic Effects

The problem posed by unemployment to the macroeconomy is quite different from the problems it posed to individuals. Recall the production possibilities curve of Chapter 1. This graph is repeated in Figure 14-2.

Recall that when we use society's resources and technology to their fullest, the economy is represented somewhere along the production possibilities curve. The economy may choose to produce at a point such as point C, with production of 90 tons of bread and 40 tons of roses. However, if some of our resources sit idle, we will not be able to produce to our full potential. With unemployed workers, we may instead be at a point such as point U, perhaps producing only 60 tons of bread and 40 tons of roses. The macroeconomic problem of unemployment is the reduction in our nation's output that it causes. As long as there is scarcity in our world, we must be concerned when we are not producing to our full potential.

Types of Unemployment

There are three basic types of unemployment: frictional, structural, and cyclical unemployment.

FIGURE 14-2 Production Possibilities Curve

Frictional Unemployment

Do you remember looking for your first part-time job? Did you expect to apply, interview, be hired, and begin work the moment you began your job search? Of course not! Similarly, when you graduate from college with your degree in hand, you should not be surprised when it takes time to find that long-awaited "real" job. There is a normal time delay before finding a job—or, for that matter, when changing jobs or reentering the labor force after a period of absence. This is an expected situation and is referred to as **frictional unemployment**. The name reflects the "friction" present in the labor market—that is, our imperfect information about job vacancies and business firms' imperfect information about job seekers. It takes time for employer and employee to get together, to discover their compatibility, and to move through the red tape that is necessary before the job vacancy is filled.

Frictional unemployment
Temporary unemployment caused by a normal time delay when a person seeks a first job, changes jobs, or reenters the labor force after an absence.

Because frictional unemployment is very normal and is assumed, by definition, to be temporary, it is not generally considered to be a serious form of unemployment. In fact, many consider some frictional unemployment to be necessary for a healthy economy. We need to have people move to better jobs to maintain an efficient economy. Of course, the longer the job search, the more serious the situation becomes. Hence, we are interested in programs that can improve job information for employers and job seekers. Your college career services office, state job service office, and local employment agency provide this type of service. At the national level, computerized job searches can minimize the time spent seeking information and ultimately bring together employer and employee.

Structural Unemployment

Now consider a more serious problem than the time delay in finding your first post-college job. Suppose you are majoring in elementary education, with the hope of teaching at the primary level. Perhaps the demand for elementary teachers was very high at the time you planned your career and you have been intently preparing yourself since then. Now, suppose a shift is taking place in our economy. The number of schoolchildren may be decreasing, thereby reducing the overall demand for elementary teachers. At the same time, the demand for more specialized schoolteachers may be increasing, as more school districts seek to meet the needs of children with emotional or learning disabilities. There may be unfilled vacancies for specialized teachers at the same time that many nonspecialized teachers remain unemployed. This situation is an example of structural unemployment.

Structural unemployment
Unemployment that results from structural changes in our economy, such as changes in demand or technology.

As the name suggests, **structural unemployment** is caused by structural shifts within our economy. Consider, for example, how the structure of demand has changed within our economy over the last several decades. Consumer demand is on the increase for a variety of services such as health care and child care, whereas in previous years, demand was higher for manufactured goods. As a result, job opportunities have opened up in the health and child care fields, whereas jobs have been lost in the manufacturing sector.

Technological advance is another example of structural change within our economy. Robotics in the auto industry has enabled machines to replace welders, creating job loss in the auto industry, at least in the short run. At the same time, jobs have opened up as a result of other forms of technological advance—in the computer industry, for example. The welders who lost their jobs in the auto plant, however, probably do not have the skills to take the jobs in the computer industry. In addition, circumstances change. For example, the sunny years of the technology industry have suddenly disappeared. Instead, we are now experiencing unemployment in the information technology and telecommunications industries, though there may be openings in other areas, such as nursing.

The point is that with structural unemployment, a job vacancy may exist for each unemployed worker, but because of structural circumstances within the economy, the unemployed worker is not suited to the particular job. The laid-off welder is available, but lacks the skills for the computer industry. The laid-off steelworker lacks the education necessary for a job in the health care field.

Other structural factors that prevent people from taking available jobs may be present. Some workers may lack necessary child-care facilities, or may face discrimination, or may live in an inner city or a part of the country where jobs are scarce. The fact that jobs are available in Florida's service sector means very little to the unemployed person on the Minnesota Iron Range, who is unable to participate in that job market.

Many people believe that structural unemployment is serious enough for the government to take action. Job training and education programs are obviously important. So, too, are the provision of child-care facilities and the enforcement of anti-discrimination policies. Mass transit may be helpful to inner-city commuters, and relocation assistance may be needed for workers who must move to find jobs. And finally, the unemployed schoolteacher may need help to return to school to learn specializations that make him or her more employable. These interventions represent microeconomic policies by nature.

Cyclical Unemployment

Cyclical unemployment is the type of unemployment most closely linked to the macroeconomy and to macroeconomic policy. Hence, it is the type of unemployment with which we are primarily concerned in this chapter and the two chapters that follow.

Cyclical unemployment is defined as unemployment that results from a drop in economic activity in our economy as a whole. Whereas structural unemployment has to do with changes in sectors within the economy, cyclical unemployment has to do with the macroeconomy in total. When our economy is expanding and producing larger levels of output, the number of jobs expands as well, for we need workers to produce higher levels of output. On the other hand, when our economy contracts and produces lower levels of output, the number of jobs will contract as well. Many people lose their jobs in a downturn of the economy, and many are unable to find first-time jobs.

Notice that only with cyclical unemployment do we assume that the economy has an insufficient number of jobs. With frictional unemployment, a job is available for the job seeker. He or she simply hasn't found it yet! With structural unemployment, there are job losses in one sector or geographical area of the economy, but there are job vacancies in others. There is simply a mismatch between available jobs and workers, who lack the skills, education, location, or other forms of access to these jobs. Only with cyclical unemployment is the number of jobs insufficient. Macroeconomic policy is necessary to expand the economy and create new employment opportunities.

Cyclical unemployment
Unemployment that results from a drop in economic activity in our economy as a whole.

Full Employment

Have you ever heard the term *full employment?* It's natural to assume that full employment means a job for everyone who wants one, but this is not the definition of full employment. **Full employment** is defined as a situation in which there is no cyclical unemployment; that is, jobs are available for all who want to work. It doesn't mean that everyone is suited to a job that exists, or that everyone has actually found a job. What it means is that any unemployment that exists will be structural or frictional, not cyclical. An unemployment rate of 4 to 5 percent or slightly higher is often considered by economists to represent full employment.

Although it appears deliberately misleading, the full employment concept is in fact useful. When the economy achieves full employment, there may be a need to provide better information, training, education, or other services; but there is no need for macroeconomic policy to correct the economy. On the other hand, when the economy does not experience full employment, macro policies must come into play. These policies are discussed in the next chapter.

Employment Effects of Immigration

In the United States and abroad, immigration is a controversial issue. Some of the animosity toward immigrants stems from bigotry, and much stems from fear—fear that large-scale immigration will increase unemployment and cause wage rates to fall. The fact that significant numbers of immigrants enter the United States illegally only increases this fear.

The polar attitudes in the United States toward immigrant workers can be expressed by the following statements: (1) immigrants work for next to nothing and take jobs away from native-born Americans, or (2) immigrants work hard and only take jobs that native-born workers wouldn't want anyway. The truth, as is often the case, is somewhere between these two extremes.

Evidence of animosity toward immigrants permeates our public policy. Proposition 187 was a referendum, approved by California voters by a 3-to-2 margin, preventing illegal immigrants from receiving state education, welfare, and nonemergency medical benefits. Legal immigrants in the United States have seen their eligibility for welfare benefits cut. They have also faced new requirements that recipients of welfare and applicants for citizenship use English on their forms and exams. This requirement is especially onerous for elderly immigrants who have difficulty learning a new language. And although activists for economic justice have attempted to restore benefits and to permit citizenship exams to be offered in foreign languages, the economic fears that foster the anti-immigration sentiment persist. Therefore, let's consider the economic implications of immigration for U.S. labor markets.

In the short run, large-scale immigration increases the supply of low-skilled workers, lowering the wage rate for these workers. The graph of the low-skill labor market is shown in Figure 14-3. This graph is similar to all of the demand and supply graphs we have considered for various goods and services. But instead of the quantity of a product (such as bushels of corn), we have the quantity of labor (such as the number of workers) on the horizontal axis. The vertical axis represents the price of labor, which is the wage rate. The demand curve D is the demand for low-skilled

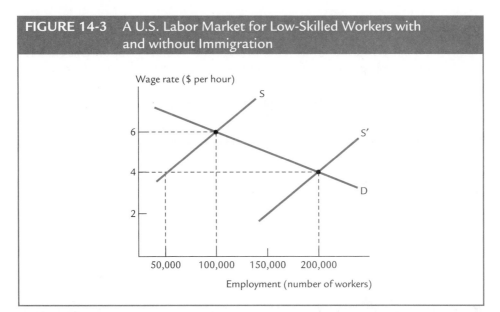

FIGURE 14-3 A U.S. Labor Market for Low-Skilled Workers with and without Immigration

The quantity of labor (the number of workers) is shown along the horizontal axis and the price of labor (the wage rate) is shown along the vertical axis. The demand curve D is the demand for low-skilled workers and S is the supply of native-born U.S. workers who offer their labor services to the low-skill labor market. The equilibrium wage rate is $6 per hour and the equilibrium number of U.S. workers is 100,000. The immigration of low-skilled workers increases the supply of labor to S', thereby lowering the wage rate to $4 per hour. As a result, the number of native-born workers is just 50,000 workers, while the total number of workers is 200,000.

workers by business firms (and anyone else who hires low-skilled workers). S is the supply of native-born U.S. workers who offer their labor services to the low-skill labor market. The equilibrium wage rate is $6 per hour, and the equilibrium number of U.S. workers is 100,000.

Now let's show the effects of large-scale immigration. With such immigration, the supply of low-skilled workers increases to S', which includes both U.S.-born and immigrant workers. The increase in supply causes the equilibrium wage rate to fall to $4 per hour. Employment increases to 200,000 workers. But notice that the number of employees supplied by the U.S. native-born labor force is now only 50,000. The remaining jobs are worked by immigrant workers. So, we could summarize the labor-market effects of large-scale immigration by saying that large-scale immigration increases the supply of low-skilled labor, thereby decreasing the wage rate in low-skilled labor markets. At the lower wage rate, fewer U.S. workers will take the low-skill jobs, and immigrants will fill more of these jobs. Other specific low-skill labor markets, such as the markets for domestic workers and for seasonal agricultural labor, are also affected in this way by large-scale immigration.

In the longer run, the effects of immigration are less clear. Lower wages decrease business firms' costs of production, thereby increasing their profits. This situation may encourage businesses to expand. American consumers can purchase a larger array of consumer goods and services at lower prices. A larger labor force encourages expanded productivity and economic growth. In addition, research shows that immigrants, as a group, are entrepreneurial and that they are more likely to start up businesses than are native-born citizens.

Last, we must keep in mind that many immigrants to the United States are indeed highly skilled and educated. Because of our immigration law, they are often permitted to immigrate to meet the needs of U.S. businesses that cannot find adequate numbers of U.S. workers with the same qualifications. And from a noneconomic perspective, we benefit from greater cultural diversity. After all, we are a nation of immigrants.

The Minimum Wage

Another issue concerning unemployment and labor markets is the implications of the **minimum wage**. As of the year 2003, the federal minimum wage rate was, with a few exceptions, $5.15 per hour. Several proposals to increase the minimum wage, which has not kept up with the rate of inflation, have been made.

To analyze the effects of the minimum wage, we can return to the type of graph of the low-skill labor market that we examined in the discussion of immigration. In Figure 14-4, the horizontal axis shows the quantity of labor (number of workers), the vertical axis shows the wage rate, D represents the demand for low-skilled labor, and S represents the supply of low-skilled labor. In this example, we'll assume that the equilibrium wage rate is $4.50 per hour and that the equilibrium quantity of labor is 100,000 workers.

Suppose that the government decides that a wage rate of $4.50 per hour is too low. People may argue that this wage is a poverty wage, and that it doesn't compensate the worker for the value of a hard day's work. The wage is considered to be inequitable. As a result, the government decides to establish a minimum wage at $5.15 per hour. A minimum wage is similar to the price floors discussed in Chapter 12 on agriculture. The minimum wage is just one example of a **price floor**. Price floors are intended to help the supplier, whether it is a supplier of corn or a supplier of labor. The price floor makes it illegal to pay a price (wage) below the established price floor. Therefore, it represents a minimum price (or wage).

The minimum wage of $5.15 is indicated in Figure 14-4. Notice that the minimum wage is above the equilibrium wage in this market for low-skilled labor. If the minimum wage is not set above the equilibrium wage, it will have absolutely no effect on the market. Recall that the minimum wage merely prohibits payment of a wage rate below the minimum. It doesn't prevent payment of wages above the minimum. If the minimum wage is below the market equilibrium, the normal equilibrium wage rate will take over.

We can see the effects of the minimum wage in the graph by extending this wage rate to the demand and supply curves for low-skilled labor. We hit the demand for labor curve at a relatively low point on the demand curve, a point corresponding to a quantity of labor demanded of 90,000 workers. This quantity demanded is reasonable, because business firms will try to cut back on the quantity of labor they hire when labor becomes more expensive. We hit the supply of labor curve at a relatively high point on

Minimum wage
A legally imposed minimum price (wage) for labor.

Price floor
A legally imposed minimum price for a good or service.

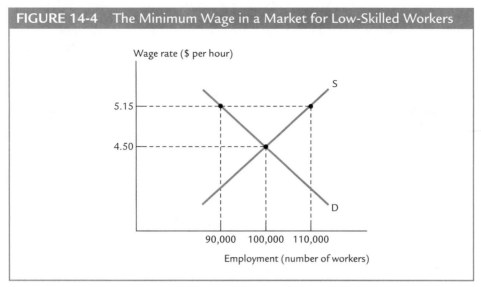

FIGURE 14-4 The Minimum Wage in a Market for Low-Skilled Workers

The quantity of labor (the number of workers) is shown along the horizontal axis. The demand curve D is the demand for low-skilled labor and the supply curve S is the supply of low-skilled labor. The equilibrium wage rate is $4.50 per hour, and the number of workers is 100,000. A minimum wage of $5.15 results in a quantity of labor supplied of 110,000 workers and a quantity of labor demanded of 90,000 workers. The result is a surplus of 20,000 workers.

the curve, a point corresponding to a quantity of labor supplied by 110,000 workers. This quantity supplied is also reasonable, because more people may be willing to work when wages are higher. The result is a disequilibrium situation in which the quantity of labor supplied (110,000 workers) is greater than the quantity of labor demanded (90,000 workers). A surplus of labor exists, which is another way of saying that the minimum wage has created some unemployment. Although the minimum wage has benefited some workers (those who are able to find jobs and receive the higher wage), it has harmed other workers (those who become unemployed). Business firms also lose as they are forced to pay higher wages. Thus, the results are mixed.

Although our graphical representation of the minimum wage may be appropriate for many low-skilled professions, it is not appropriate for most occupations in our country. Certainly, the minimum wage is below the equilibrium wage rates in these higher-wage-paying professions, and therefore the minimum wage becomes ineffective in these professions. It does not raise wages, and it does not create unemployment. The analysis is valid therefore for only the low-skill occupations we've discussed.

Is there a better way to ensure adequate incomes for hard-working individuals other than the minimum wage, since the minimum wage creates problems (unemployment) as well as benefits (higher wages)? Most economists dislike artificial prices, whether they are price ceilings or price floors. They oppose these measures because they create disequilibrium situations (shortages and surpluses) and distort incentives in markets. Therefore, direct assistance to targeted groups of people is often preferable. If our concern is for workers who receive poverty wages, a direct solution would be for the government to simply pay the worker the difference between his or her market wage and the wage necessary for an adequate income. Many people are averse to this type of solution because it appears to amount to a hand-out, but it avoids the market distortions caused by the minimum wage. Indeed, we do have an example of the alternative solution in the form of the Earned Income Credit, which was discussed in detail in Chapter 6 on U.S. poverty. This **Earned Income Credit (EIC)** reduces the taxes owed by (or provides a payment to) workers with incomes below a certain level. It has certainly helped low-income working people, and expansions of the tax credit have been proposed.

Earned Income Credit (EIC)
A federal income tax credit for low-income workers and families.

INFLATION

We must double our fight against the persistent inflation that has wracked our country for more than a decade. We know that inflation is a burden for all Americans, but it's a disaster for the poor, the sick, and the old. No American family should be forced to choose among food, warmth, health care, or decent housing because the cost of any of these basic necessities has climbed out of reach.

—President Jimmy Carter, State of the Union Address, 1979

Inflation threatens to put an end to everything we believe in and to our dreams for the future.

—President Ronald Reagan, State of the Union Address, 1981

Inflation, that thief. . . .

—President George H. W. Bush, State of the Union Address, 1992

Just like unemployment, it would seem "that thief," inflation, threatens the American dream, at least if the words of the three U.S. presidents in office before Clinton provide a clue. But note that finding the word *inflation* in any of the speeches by President Clinton or President George W. Bush during their years of office is virtually impossible. Does the recent lack of reference to inflation mean that this phenomenon is no longer perceived as an economic threat? Or has the recent state of our economy eliminated, for the time being, the problem of inflation?

We have mentioned elsewhere in this text that **inflation** is a rise in the average price level. As you might expect, therefore, **deflation** is a decrease in the average price level. Most of our recent experience is with inflation, so this is the topic that will concern us. Note, however, that for the first time in many years, some people are now concerned with deflation. But first, to learn how economists calculate the inflation rate, we need to review the **consumer price index (CPI)**.

The consumer price index is what we usually mean when referring to the cost of living. It is defined as a weighted average of the prices of a fixed basket of goods and services purchased by a typical urban household. In the early 1980s, studies were done to determine which goods and services, and which quantities of these items, were purchased by American households. The average, or typical, urban household is then determined. The basket of goods and services purchased by this typical household is assumed to remain fixed over time, until a new survey is done. The prices of items within this fixed basket are based on prices in a variety of urban stores; a weighted av-

Inflation
A rise in the average price level.

Deflation
A decrease in the average price level.

erage of these prices is calculated by weighting the prices of large-quantity items more heavily than low-quantity items in the basket. That is, if the typical household purchases 10 pairs of jeans and 1 movie video, the price of jeans receives a weight 10 times the weight of the video when calculating the average price of this basket.

Because the CPI is an index, the weighted-average price of this basket of consumer goods and services is manipulated further. We leave the actual construction of the consumer price index for the appendix to this chapter. Keep in mind, though, that the resulting CPI does not actually tell us the prices that exist in a particular year. It tells us only how prices in one year compare with those in another year.

Using the consumer price index to calculate the inflation rate is easy. We subtract the CPI for one year from the CPI for the prior year, and then divide the answer by the CPI for the earlier year. For example, if the CPI is 180 in 2002 and the CPI is 177 in 2001, we can calculate the 2002 inflation rate as follows:

$$\text{2002 Inflation Rate} = \frac{(\text{2002 CPI} - \text{2001 CPI})}{\text{2001 CPI}}$$

$$= \frac{(180 - 177)}{177}$$

$$= \frac{3}{177}$$

$$= 0.017, \text{ or } 1.7\%$$

In this example, the 2002 rate of inflation is 1.7 percent. (Notice that a decimal, such as 0.017 here, can be translated into a percentage by moving the decimal point to the right by two spaces and adding a percentage sign. That is, 0.017 becomes 1.7%.)

Inaccuracy of the Inflation Rate

We noted earlier that the unemployment rate tends to understate the true problem of unemployment. We will see that the consumer price index tends to systematically overstate the true problem of inflation for two reasons, both of which have to do with the notion of the fixed basket of consumer goods and services.

The basket of goods and services purchased by a typical household is deliberately assumed to remain fixed for several years so that changes in the prices of the basket reflect changes in prices only, not changes in the quantities of the goods and services themselves. When we ignore quantity changes, we are ignoring the fact that consumers tend to conserve on items for which price is increasing. During a period of rising energy prices, for example, such as we began experiencing in 2000 and 2001, consumers may reduce the amount of energy they consume. They may insulate their homes, drive more fuel-efficient cars, turn down their thermostats and air conditioners, and so on. When we assume a fixed basket of consumer goods, we ignore the fact that consumers are reducing the amount of energy they consume, thereby reducing the price of their actual basket of consumer items below the price of the fixed basket. Hence, the inflation rate, based on the assumption of a fixed basket, is overstated.

Similarly, some quality changes within the basket of consumer items are taken into account, but many other quality changes go unrecorded. A price increase may be recorded for a particular item, such as a personal computer, without taking into account some of the quality improvements of this computer. We think of an increase in price as an indicator of inflation, whereas at least some of the price increase may be caused by a change in the nature of the product (its quality). In this fashion, the consumer price index again overstates the problem of inflation.

The issue of the accuracy of the inflation rate is not entirely academic. Certainly, if policymakers are to design appropriate policy, they must know with accuracy how serious the problem is. If the problem of inflation is overstated, policies designed to reduce inflation may at times be inappropriate. Other practical issues involve the **cost-of-living adjustment (COLA)** that is made in wage contracts, Social Security benefits, and other payments that are adjusted for inflation. As was mentioned in the Social Security chapter, politicians have sought to reduce Social Security benefits by offering a revised (lower) estimate of inflation than that provided by the consumer price index, thereby making a more modest inflation adjustment to Social Security benefits. This unpopular measure was never enacted.

Cost-of-living adjustment (COLA)
An adjustment that automatically increases incomes or benefits when the average price level rises.

The Data

Despite problems with the consumer price index, economists and policymakers continue to use it. Table 14-5 shows inflation rates based on the consumer price index for select years between 1970 and 2002. We can see the reason for the lack of concern regarding inflation during the 1993–2000 Clinton administration and the early years of the George W. Bush administration.

Hyperinflation

We in the United States consider any inflation rate above 10 percent to be very high. But many countries of the world experience inflation rates far above this. Many Latin American countries, for example, commonly experience annual inflation rates in the range of several hundred, or even several thousand, percent. Recent examples include Brazil (2,739 percent), Argentina (3,080 percent), Peru (7,650 percent), and Nicaragua (14,316 percent). Many eastern European countries are experienc-

TABLE 14-5	U.S. Inflation Rates, Select Years 1970–2002, Based on CPI with Base Year 1982–1984		
Year	**Inflation Rate (%)**	**Year**	**Inflation Rate (%)**
1970	5.8	1996	3.0
1980	13.5	1997	2.3
1990	5.4	1998	1.6
1991	4.2	1999	2.2
1992	3.0	2000	3.4
1993	3.0	2001	2.8
1994	2.6	2002	1.6
1995	2.8		

*Source: U.S. Department of Commerce, Census Bureau (**www.census.gov**).*

ing extremely high inflation rates during their transition to market-based economies with market-based prices. The inflation rate in Russia, for example, was 1,353 percent for the year 1992.[2] In the context of these extremely high inflation rates, money becomes almost worthless. No one is willing to save, because the value of savings decreases rapidly as the average price level rises. The smart course of action appears to be to spend your money as soon as you get it, because things hold value, whereas money does not! On a recent trip to an African country, your author changed a $10 bill to buy souvenirs. Because of inflation, she ended up carrying a bag full of 20,000 small units of the African currency. In other countries, people literally go shopping with wheelbarrows or baby buggies filled with money.

Even with wheelbarrows and armloads of money, the prices of groceries in an economy hit by severe inflation may be rising before the customer can leave the store. Theater prices may increase while you're watching the movie! Motel prices may double while you are sleeping! (Indeed, your same author had this experience while peacefully sleeping in a motel in Russia!) In any of these cases, even a cart full of money may not be enough to pay the bill. In such situations, people may resort to **barter**, because their money is worth nothing. Inflation this severe is what we mean by **hyperinflation**.

Many people fear inflation because they believe it will lead to hyperinflation, but hyperinflation almost always occurs in countries experiencing war, revolution, or other severe disruptions of their economies. Hyperinflation should not be a concern for the United States—even if severe economic disruptions were to occur, the policies of the Federal Reserve System and the government could mitigate their impact on inflation rates. We examine these policies in the next chapter.

The Effects of Inflation

Inflation is generally not as serious a problem as you might think, at least not in the ways you might expect. Most people assume that a rise in the average price level means that we as a nation cannot afford to buy as many goods and services—that is, inflation harms our **purchasing power**. In fact, a period of inflation in and of itself does not have that effect because our purchasing power depends on both the price level and our incomes. If the average price level rises by 10 percent at the same time that our incomes rise by 10 percent, our purchasing power is not altered. Unless some other factors are present, the income for the country as a whole does rise along with the price level during a period of inflation. Therefore, the purchasing power of our nation is not harmed.

There are, however, other problems associated with inflation. They can be categorized as problems of redistribution, uncertainty, menu costs, and international effects.

Redistribution

Even though the purchasing power of the nation is not harmed by inflation, certainly some people in the country will gain and some people will lose. The economic situation of others will remain unchanged.

Consider Social Security recipients as an example. Because the Social Security program has an automatic cost of living adjuster built into it, Social Security benefits will rise at the rate of inflation. If the rate of inflation in any given year is 4 percent, for example, Social Security benefits will also rise by 4 percent. In this way,

Barter
The direct exchange of goods and services for other goods and services rather than for money.

Hyperinflation
Extremely high inflation, whereby money becomes almost worthless.

Purchasing power
The ability to buy goods and services.

the purchasing power of Social Security recipients is unchanged during a period of inflation.

On the other hand, the purchasing power of other people will suffer if their incomes do not increase as rapidly as the price level. Retirees receiving private pensions (not Social Security), workers who have signed a long-term labor contract, and welfare recipients may all experience a decrease in their purchasing power. Civil servants, including professors at public colleges and universities, may also experience such a decrease. The negative effects of inflation on these people will be offset by the positive effects on others who see their incomes rise more rapidly than the average price level (such as workers protected by powerful unions). Although these various groups of people will offset one another so that the purchasing power of the nation is unchanged, it is clear that some people within the country benefit while others lose during a period of inflation. This redistribution of purchasing power means that President Carter (in his statement quoted earlier in this chapter) was wrong, both about old people and about all Americans!

Borrowers are said to gain during a period of inflation, whereas lenders are said to lose. Imagine that you lend $100 to your best friend and agree to charge an interest rate of 3 percent. One year from now, you expect to receive your $100 back, plus $3 to compensate yourself for the year you went without your $100. Imagine, however, that the rate of inflation over the year is 7 percent. Your $103 at the end of the year will not buy as much as the $100 when you lent it to your friend. You lose, but your best friend (still your best friend?) gains.

Realize, however, that most lenders will recognize the significance of inflation when entering into a lending contract. If a bank wishes to charge an interest rate of 10 percent and anticipates an inflation rate of 5 percent, it will charge an interest rate of 15 percent (10 percent plus 5 percent) when it makes a loan. In this way, the bank protects itself from the harmful effects of inflation. Borrowers gain and lenders lose during inflation only if inflation is unanticipated. When inflation is highly variable, borrowers and lenders may be less willing to engage in loan contracts because of uncertainty, resulting in slowdowns in economic activity.

Uncertainty: Inefficiency and Risk Aversion

Another problem with inflation is the inefficiency that may result from uncertainty about prices. Suppose that the rate of inflation has been 3 percent per year for the past 20 years. In this case, we have good, reliable information on which to base our economic decisions. But suppose, instead, that the inflation rate has varied considerably from year to year, and no one can reliably predict what the rate of inflation will be over the next few years. You will not know now whether you can afford your tuition four years from now. Others will not know whether it's to their advantage to buy a car or a house in a few years when their finances are in better shape, or whether to buy it now before the prices go up too much. Businesspeople will not be able to predict their costs of production, or their revenues, or their rates of return over the next few years and will not know whether they should pursue a particular investment project. Our collective decisions may be incorrect in the face of uncertainty about inflation. Furthermore, if we are all risk-averse, meaning that we prefer not to undertake risks, we may all choose to do nothing rather than risk doing the wrong thing. You may decide not to go to college, others may decide not to buy the house or the car, and the business may decide to forgo productive investment. As we slow down our economic activities, we slow the growth of our economy. People and businesses are unwilling to engage in long-term contracts and activities. The uncertainty effects of inflation are most severe when inflation rates are extremely high or volatile.

Menu Costs

When inflation is 2 percent per year, the owner of a restaurant will likely reprint its menu with higher prices at the end of the year. If inflation is 15 percent per year, however, the restaurant owner will likely redo its menu every month or two. The costs associated with making adjustments due to inflation are what is meant by the **menu costs** of inflation. However, these menu costs are not restricted to the restaurant example. They apply whenever the prices on gasoline pumps must be raised, whenever airlines and bus lines must revise their price schedules, and whenever vending machines and pay phones must have their prices and coin slots altered. These costs are not usually considered too serious, but they (like the uncertainty effects of inflation) tend to be more problematic when inflation rates are high or fluctuating rapidly. Pay telephones in Russia are the greatest bargain around simply because officials have not been able to change the sizes of the coin slots as rapidly as inflation has made this procedure necessary!

International Effects

Finally, another problem of inflation in any country is that it makes the prices in that country higher than those in other countries. If the United States has an inflation rate of 4 percent and Japan has an inflation rate of 1 percent, the prices of Ford vehicles are probably rising more rapidly than the prices of Toyotas. American and Japanese consumers alike will be encouraged to buy Toyotas rather than Fords, thus increasing our imports while reducing our exports. However, as the world becomes increasingly interdependent, inflation in one industrialized country can sometimes spread to other industrialized countries as well. It may therefore become less likely that only the United States will experience inflation and not our trade and financial partners.

Types of Inflation

Different types of inflation are identified according to the conditions that lead to them. We introduce these types now so that they are familiar to you in the next chapter, in which we see how inflation is caused in the context of the macroeconomy. First, **demand-pull inflation** is caused when any sectors of the economy (consumers, businesses, or government) increase their demand for goods and services. **Cost-push inflation** occurs when there are increases in costs of production, such as rising energy prices or wages. (Cost-push inflation is the type of inflation that occurred when energy prices were increasing in the 1970s. Rising energy prices again threaten to create the same problem, though of a smaller magnitude.) Finally, **profit-push inflation** occurs when, as a result of market power, business firms deliberately restrict output to drive up prices and profits.

Menu costs
The costs associated with reprinting menus, revising cost schedules, adjusting telephones and vending machines, and so on, when inflation occurs.

Demand-pull inflation
Inflation that occurs when any sectors of the economy increase their demand for goods and services.

Cost-push inflation
Inflation that occurs as a result of increases in the costs of production.

Profit-push inflation
Inflation that occurs when businesses use market power to restrict output in order to push up prices and profits.

WHICH PROBLEM IS MORE SERIOUS: UNEMPLOYMENT OR INFLATION?

Policymakers are often faced with the question: which is more serious, unemployment or inflation? It's an important question. As we shall see in the next chapter, policy designed to cure one of the two problems will often trigger the other problem. The answer to the question depends largely on who has been asked the question. An unemployed person will naturally feel that unemployment is the more serious problem. Yet the effects of unemployment on the individual can be alleviated somewhat with government transfers. Thus, unemployment in a country such as the United States will be less problematic for the individual than will unemployment in a country such as Mexico, for example, which lacks an adequate safety net for its unemployed. Unemployment will nevertheless be very serious for most people in the United States. Furthermore, the effects of unemployment on our nation's output cannot be modified. Output that is forgone today as a result of resources sitting idle will never be available for consumption tomorrow.

A person living on a fixed income will consider inflation the more serious problem. It is indeed a serious problem for individuals whose incomes do not rise as rapidly as the

VIEWPOINT: CONSERVATIVE VERSUS LIBERAL

It is difficult to place the issues of unemployment and inflation into the traditional framework of conservative versus liberal. Certainly, both conservatives and liberals alike prefer to see lower rates of unemployment and inflation. Some specific policy actions may correspond more with one philosophical viewpoint than the other, however. For example, the federal government could become more involved in offering computerized national job search programs in an effort to minimize frictional unemployment. More important, liberals may wish to see the government heavily involved in reducing certain types of structural unemployment. For example, they may want to see government provision or subsidies for child-care services and greater government enforcement of affirmative action and equal opportunity legislation. Both efforts would remove some constraints that prevent groups of people from obtaining available jobs. Another government role could be in expanding training and education opportunities, thereby qualifying more people for available jobs. The government might offer retraining, relocation, and retooling assistance to people laid off and businesses shut down as a result of technological change or international trade. All of these government efforts may be viewed cautiously by those conservatives who are reluctant to see an expanded role of government in the economy and who have more confidence in the private sector to solve our economic problems. More often than not, however, both liberals and conservatives see the value of programs such as these.

As we look at macro policies designed to reduce cyclical unemployment and inflation in the next chapter, we see that conservatives as well as liberals are concerned with these problems. But they support very different types of macro policies, depending on their general view toward government involvement in our economy.

price level. Many have suggested that incorporating a cost of living adjuster into all economic contracts can minimize this problem. Thus, all wage contracts, pension plans, lending and rental agreements, welfare programs, and the minimum wage would provide incomes or benefits that rise along with the average price level, just as Social Security benefits do. Although this measure would eliminate some inequity, uncertainty, and inefficiency, it would not rectify the problems of menu costs and international effects.

Policymakers must face the world as it is and make difficult decisions about the outcomes of policy on unemployment and inflation. As we see in the next chapter, there is often a trade-off in the sense that one policy will reduce unemployment while increasing inflation, and vice versa. If we are combating unemployment, we want to stimulate the economy, which may cause inflation. If we are concerned about inflation, we try to contract the economy, which increases unemployment.

Last, recall that we questioned how long it will be before the health of our economy improves. As we've looked at the data, we've noted that although our economy is prosperous one year, it can be problematic the next. Our recent history is dotted with serious problems of unemployment and inflation. Although our policymakers today have the wherewithal to prevent Great Depression types of situations, certainly less serious levels of unemployment can resume at any time. Nevertheless, you, as an aspiring college graduate, are at much less risk than the overall population.

SUMMARY

Unemployment and inflation are two important topics in the context of the macroeconomy. A person is considered to be unemployed when he or she is actively seeking employment but is unable to find a job. Inflation is defined as a rise in the average price level. The national unemployment rate has been high recently, and certain age groups and racial and ethnic groups are more likely than others to experience unemployment. The inflation rate has recently been very low, hovering below 2 percent.

Unemployment is categorized as frictional, structural, or cyclical. Inflation is classified as ei-

ther demand pull, cost push, or profit push. Both unemployment and inflation can cause serious problems in our economy. Unemployment creates both monetary and nonmonetary problems for the unemployed person and reduces output for our nation as a whole. Inflation, especially when severe, creates problems of redistribution, uncertainty and inefficiency, menu costs, and international effects. Policies to correct these problems are an important consideration in the next chapter on government macro policy.

NOTES

1. David T. Ellwood, "Anti-Poverty Policy for Families in the Next Century: From Welfare to Work—and Worries," *Journal of Economic Perspectives* 14, no. 1 (Winter 2000): 187–198.

2. International Monetary Fund, *World Economic Outlook* (Washington, D.C.: International Monetary Fund, May 1995). The years for the inflation rates are 1992 for Russia, 1990 for Brazil, 1989 for Argentina, 1990 for Peru, and 1988 for Nicaragua.

1. What does it mean when we say that macroeconomics is the forest, whereas microeconomics is the trees? Which topics are important in macroeconomics? Which topics are important in microeconomics?

2. Why do you think the labor force participation rate of men is higher than that of women in the United States? Why has the labor force participation rate of women been increasing so dramatically? What are some of the reasons for variation in labor force participation rates of different countries?

3. Have you ever been unemployed? (Remember the technical definition of unemployment.) If so, which type of unemployment did you experience?

4. Ask your friends or family how the unemployment rate is calculated. Are they able to give the proper technical procedure?

5. Check the Bureau of Labor Statistics Web site (**www.bls.gov**) to find out the current unemployment rate. Would you say that our economy is currently experiencing full employment?

6. Can you explain why it is sometimes the case that unemployment rates increase while additional jobs are being created in our economy? And why is it sometimes the case that unemployment rates decrease while jobs are being lost in our economy? (Hint: Think in terms of discouraged workers.)

7. What are the effects of unemployment on the individual unemployed person? What are the effects on the economy? Which effects are more serious?

8. What are some policies that can be used to reduce structural unemployment? Try to come up with some of your own ideas.

9. In June 2000, 58 illegal Chinese immigrants were found dead in a sealed area of a truck, smothered by heat and lack of air during a five-hour journey to Britain. It was said that the victims had died "a most terrible death." Similar situations occur frequently as illegal Mexicans cross the U.S. border, often locked in small, airless vehicles, and as Cubans traverse stormy waters in poorly equipped boats. Who do you think is to blame for these situations? Is it the desperate immigrants, crime syndicates that provide the transportation, a rigid immigration system, a public attitude of hostility toward immigration, or a global economic system that permits poverty in one country alongside prosperity in another? Defend your answer.

10. Why is the understatement of unemployment statistics a problem? Why is overstatement of inflation statistics a problem?

11. Look up the Census Bureau Web site (**www.census.gov**), and click Prices to find the current and last year's consumer price index. Use these numbers to calculate the current inflation rate.

12. Go to the Census Bureau Web site (**www.census.gov**), and find the most recent inflation rate for the United States. (Hint: Look under Prices.)

13. How are you affected by inflation? Think carefully about the effects discussed in this chapter. Are you a gainer or a loser?

14. Which problem do you believe is more serious: unemployment or inflation? Defend your answer.

CHAPTER 14 APPENDIX: CONSTRUCTION OF THE CONSUMER PRICE INDEX

An index is constructed first by choosing a base year, such as 1984.[1] We then calculate the 1984 consumer price index by dividing the actual weighted-average price of the fixed basket of consumer goods and services by the same value and multiplying the result by 100. Let's calculate the consumer price index for a small hypothetical country. If the 1984 weighted average of prices of the basket of consumer items is $4,000, we calculate the 1984 index as follows:

$$\text{1984 Consumer Price Index} = \frac{\$4,000}{\$4,000} \times 100$$
$$= 1 \times 100$$
$$= 100$$

The consumer price index for the base year will always be 100.

Now suppose that we want to calculate the consumer price index for the year 2004. Suppose the weighted-average price of the fixed basket of consumer items is $8,000 in 2004. We calculate the 2004 consumer price index by dividing the $8,000 by the weighted-average price for base year 1984, then multiplying by 100. That is, we calculate the 2004 price index as follows:

$$\text{2004 Consumer Price Index} = \frac{\$8,000}{\$4,000} \times 100$$
$$= 2 \times 100$$
$$= 200$$

Again, a consumer price index of 200 means nothing to us by itself. An index is not an average price of anything. We can use the CPI to compare prices in one year with those in another year. In our example, we can say that prices have doubled between 1984 (with a CPI of 100) and 2004 (with a CPI of 200).

NOTES

1. The base year currently used for the CPI is an average over the 1982–1984 time period.

CHAPTER 15 ROADMAP

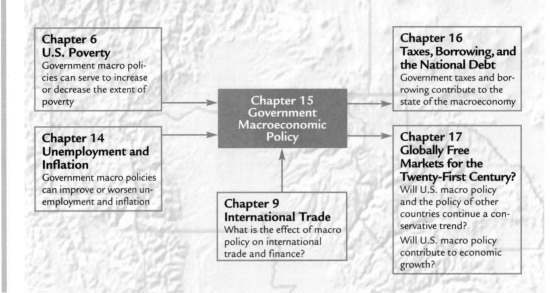

**Chapter 6
U.S. Poverty**
Government macro policies can serve to increase or decrease the extent of poverty

**Chapter 14
Unemployment and Inflation**
Government macro policies can improve or worsen unemployment and inflation

**Chapter 15
Government Macroeconomic Policy**

**Chapter 9
International Trade**
What is the effect of macro policy on international trade and finance?

**Chapter 16
Taxes, Borrowing, and the National Debt**
Government taxes and borrowing contribute to the state of the macroeconomy

**Chapter 17
Globally Free Markets for the Twenty-First Century?**
Will U.S. macro policy and the policy of other countries continue a conservative trend?

Will U.S. macro policy contribute to economic growth?

THE ECONOMIC TOOLBOX

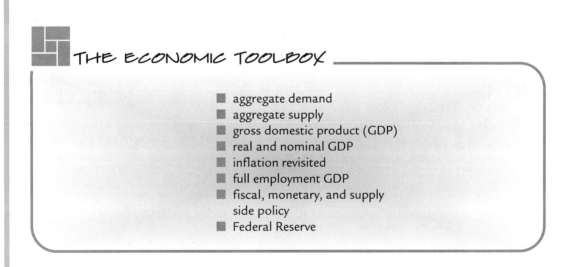

- aggregate demand
- aggregate supply
- gross domestic product (GDP)
- real and nominal GDP
- inflation revisited
- full employment GDP
- fiscal, monetary, and supply side policy
- Federal Reserve

GOVERNMENT MACROECONOMIC POLICY

In the long run, we are all dead.

—John Maynard Keynes

ow it is time to jump into a complete discussion of the macroeconomy. In doing so, you will find that you can more easily understand the issues of unemployment and inflation, as well as other important economic issues facing our nation today. You will also discover the meaning of government macro policies such as fiscal policy and monetary policy, terms that everyone has heard before but that few people really understand. Because you already understand demand and supply, you will have no difficulty understanding these macroeconomic topics.

GRAPHING THE MACROECONOMY

You undoubtedly remember that we promised to present only two basic types of graphs for most of the book. But also remember that we told you we could get a lot of mileage out of these graphs. In particular, we can revise our thinking about the demand and supply graphs of Chapter 1 and use the graphs to represent our economy as a whole.

Recall that each demand and supply graph in Chapter 1 was used to represent the market for a particular good or service, such as tutoring services. The graph representing the market for tutoring services is repeated in Figure 15-1 on page 354. Now let's transform this graph into one representing our economy as a whole. Let the P on the vertical axis no longer represent the price of tutoring services, but the average price level for the economy as a whole. That is, *P* in Figure 15-2 now represents the average price of all output produced in our economy. (For example, *P* could be measured by the consumer price index discussed in Chapter 14.)

Instead of the *Q* on the horizontal axis representing the quantity of tutoring services, let's use the symbol GDP to represent total output of all goods and services in our economy. Note that GDP stands for

FIGURE 15-1   The Market for Tutoring Services, One Week

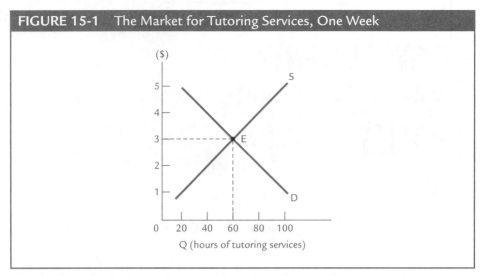

The market will clear at point E. At the price of $3 per hour, quantity demanded equals the quantity supplied (60 hours) of tutoring services.

FIGURE 15-2   The Macroeconomy

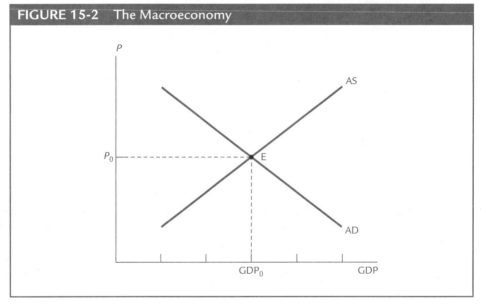

In the graph of the macroeconomy, *P* represents the average price level, GDP is total output, AD is aggregated demand, and AS is aggregate supply. At equilibrium E, the average price level is equal to P_0, and GDP is equal to GDP_0.

gross domestic product, which was introduced in Chapter 1 and is defined as our nation's total output. We discuss GDP in greater detail and define it more precisely shortly.

Now let's redefine the downward-sloping demand curve as AD rather than D, where AD stands for **aggregate demand** and is defined as the quantity of total output (GDP) demanded (purchased) at alternative price levels. This definition sounds very similar to the definition of demand, except that now we are looking at the total demand for GDP by all sectors of the economy. Keep in mind that aggregate demand refers to the "purchasing" side of our economy—that is, the quantity of GDP that will be purchased at various price levels. It represents all people in the world who purchase U.S. GDP.

Similarly, we will use the symbol AS for the supply curve, where AS stands for aggregate supply. **Aggregate supply** is defined as the quantity of total output (GDP) supplied (produced) at alternative price levels. Here, we are looking at the total supply of GDP by all producers in our economy. Keep in mind that aggregate supply refers to the "production" side of our economy—that is, the quantity of GDP that is produced. Aggregate supply represents all the people who produce U.S. GDP.

Notice in Figure 15-2 that aggregate demand is downward sloping (just like a normal demand curve), whereas aggregate supply is upward sloping (just like a normal supply curve). The reasons for the upward slope of aggregate supply are very similar to the reasons for the upward slope of a supply curve in an individual market. Higher prices for products give producers greater incentive to produce their products; hence, the quantity of output supplied increases when the prices of output increase.

The reasons for the downward-sloping aggregate demand curve are very different from the reasons for the downward-sloping demand curve in an individual market, however. In considering the market for oranges, for example, people are willing to buy more oranges when the price falls because they can more easily afford them. They also might substitute oranges for other types of fruit such as apples and bananas. This kind of substitution is not possible when we are considering aggregate demand, because we are looking at the total demand for all output, and substituting all output with something else is impossible. Similarly, realize that a decline in the average price level does not make GDP more affordable, since our purchasing power depends on both incomes and prices. We generally assume that overall income in the economy declines as the average price level declines, unless other factors are at work. This concept is discussed in more detail in Chapter 14 on inflation. These considerations suggest that there must be other reasons why the quantity of GDP demanded increases when the average price level falls. These reasons have to do with trade, assets, and interest rates and are discussed in detail in the appendix to this chapter.

Finally, notice that aggregate demand and aggregate supply intersect at point E in Figure 15-2. At this equilibrium point, we can see that the average price level is designated as P_0 and gross domestic product is equal to GDP_0.

Aggregate demand
The quantity of total output (GDP) demanded (purchased) at alternative average price levels.

Aggregate supply
The quantity of total output (GDP) supplied (produced) at alternative average price levels.

Gross domestic product (GDP)
The market value of all final goods and services produced *in* the economy in a given time period (usually one year).

GROSS DOMESTIC PRODUCT

A Definition of GDP

Gross domestic product (GDP) is defined as the market value of all final goods and services produced in the economy in a given time period, usually one year. We need to think about this definition in detail. First, realize that final goods and services include all products (for example, cars and dishwashers) as well as all services (for example, education and health care) that are purchased as final products. Suppose you buy a bag of flour from the supermarket. This bag of flour is a final product, because it will not be processed and resold later. (You may bake a cake and eat it, but you will not sell the cake.) However, suppose the bakery downtown purchases large bags of flour and uses the flour to produce doughnuts and cookies for sale. In this case, the flour is an intermediate product, and the doughnuts and cookies are the final products. Only the purchased product at the final stage of production is included in gross domestic product to avoid double counting. The value of the flour is incorporated into the price of the bakery's products; we do not want to count the flour twice.

Second, realize that all of the goods comprising GDP must be produced during the particular year. If, for example, you sell your 10-year-old home this year, the value of your home does not constitute part of this year's GDP. However, if you employ the current services of a realtor, the value of the realtor's services is included in this year's GDP because they are current services. Similarly, if a car is produced in one year but is held over as inventory to be sold in the following year, it is counted as part of GDP in the year that it is produced. We consider the car to have been "purchased," for the time being, by the producer, who holds it in the form of inventory.

Third, realize that it is necessary to define gross domestic product in value terms, specifically dollars in the United States. We could not add up all the apples, oranges, refrigerators, and television sets produced in our economy, nor could we determine whether GDP was higher in one year in which we produced lots of refrigerators than in another year in which we produced lots of television sets, because we can't compare refrigerators with televisions. And we could not compare the GDP of the United States—let's say it produces plenty of baseball cards, beer, and hot dogs—with that of Russia—let's say it produces large amounts of potatoes, vodka, and caviar—because we can't compare the quantities of these countries' respective products. We think you are getting the picture: we cannot add apples and oranges, nor can we compare them.

For these reasons, we must first attach value to the physical quantities of output produced; then we can add them up to tabulate total domestic product. We use market prices to value the physical quantities of output. **Market price** includes the retail price of the product plus any sales and excise taxes paid by the consumer. Once output is valued in dollars, we can simply add up the dollar values of output to tabulate total GDP. Money serves as a common denominator.

Finally, notice that the definition of gross domestic product refers to goods and services produced in the economy. This little word *in* is significant, because it distinguishes gross domestic product from gross national product.

Because some statistics rely on data for gross national product, abbreviated GNP, it is useful to define GNP as well. **Gross national product (GNP)** is defined as the market value of all final goods and services produced by the economy over a particular time period. The only difference between the two definitions are the words *in* and *by*!

When we refer to goods and services produced in the economy, we mean they are produced within the physical boundaries of the United States. If, for example, a Mexican citizen comes up to the United States during the summer to pick tomatoes, the value of these tomatoes would be included in U.S. gross domestic product, be-

EconNews

"Hot Gas Prices Cool the Economy"

Learn more by going to the Aggregate Supply/Aggregate Demand category.

http://econapps. swlearning.com

Market price
The retail price of a product plus any sales and excise taxes paid by the consumer.

Gross national product (GNP)
The market value of all final goods and services produced *by* the economy in a given time period (usually one year).

cause the tomatoes are produced within the physical boundaries of the United States. If, however, a U.S. citizen spends the summer making earrings in Mexico, the value of the earrings would not be part of U.S. GDP, because the earrings are not produced within the physical boundaries of the United States.

On the other hand, when we refer to goods and services produced by the economy, we mean by U.S.-owned factors of production (that is, by U.S. workers, business owners, and so on). Now, for example, if a U.S. citizen makes earrings in Mexico, the value of the earrings is counted as part of U.S. gross national product. It doesn't matter where the earrings are produced, as long as a U.S. citizen produces them. Handbags produced by a Canadian citizen in the United States would not be tabulated as part of U.S. GNP (because the producer is a foreign citizen), but would count as part of U.S. GDP (because they are produced in the United States).

Gross domestic product is the concept generally used by the U.S. government and generally used in this textbook. However, data for GDP are occasionally not available, and GNP is used instead. In either case, the concepts can be viewed as roughly identical for our purposes, both depicting our national production.

Real versus Nominal GDP

Whenever we use any variable expressed in value terms, including gross domestic product, we must be careful about comparing different time periods. Suppose GDP doubles over the time period 1990 to the year 2000. Does this increase mean that actual output doubles, that just the prices of this output double, or that both output and prices have risen? If we are interested only in whether actual output increases, we need to think in terms of real GDP, rather than nominal GDP.

Real GDP is defined as GDP calculated at constant prices. **Constant prices** refer to the prices that exist in a particular base year. If 1982 is the base year, for example, real GDP in 1990 is calculated by valuing the 1990 production of apples and oranges (and everything else) at the prices that existed in 1982. Similarly, real GDP in the year 2000 is calculated by valuing the year 2000's production of apples and oranges (and everything else) in the prices that existed in 1982. Then, when we compare real GDP in the year 2000 with that in the year 1990, any increase in real GDP will be caused by increased output, and not rising prices (because the prices are kept constant).

Nominal GDP is defined as GDP calculated at **current prices**, which are actual prices during a particular year. Nominal GDP for the year 2000 would include the production of all those apples, oranges, and everything else, valued at prices that exist in the year 2000; 1990 nominal GDP is valued at 1990 prices. Nominal GDP is the number we want to consider when we are trying to make sense of information for one year only. Real GDP is the number we want to use when we are comparing information over different time periods. Real GDP is adjusted for inflation; nominal GDP is not.

Flaws of GDP

Gross domestic product is typically used as an indicator of economic activity, as well as a measure of standards of living. When GDP is high, the assumption is that the economy is doing well and that standards of living are high. When GDP is growing over time, the assumption is that economic activity and standards of living are

EconNews

"Output, Income, and Price Level"

For more information on real GDP, including exercises, diagrams, and data, go to the Macroeconomics category.

http://econapps. swlearning.com

Real GDP
GDP calculated at constant prices.

Constant prices
Prices that exist in a base year.

Nominal GDP
GDP calculated at current prices.

Current prices
Actual prices of a particular year.

increasing. There are some flaws in these assumptions, however. Nonmarket activities, the underground economy, and the distribution and composition of national output make GDP an imperfect measure of economic activity and our standards of living.

Nonmarket Activities

Remember that GDP is defined as the market value of all goods and services produced in the economy. What if a good or service is produced but not marketed? What if you paint your own apartment, eat food from your own garden, or volunteer your services at the local hospital? Or perhaps more important, what if you provide homemaking services in your own home, preparing meals, caring for children, and cleaning the house? All of these activities are productive, but because they are not bought and sold in the marketplace, no market value is attached to them, and they are excluded from GDP statistics.

The exclusion of nonmarketed goods and services serves to understate the full value of productive activity in our economy. Many would argue it also undermines the value of homemaking services, traditionally the domain of women. Failure to fully value these important services may translate into failure to fully appreciate the contributions of women (and an increasing number of men) in our economy.

Exclusion of nonmarketed goods and services also distorts comparisons. During the 1950s, most women stayed home as full-time homemakers. By the 1990s, many women had entered the formal labor market, paying out money for services that they had previously provided themselves. As soon as a baby-sitter is hired, a housekeeper is paid, and fast food is purchased on the way home from work, these goods and services enter into GDP statistics. GDP is artificially higher in the 1990s and 2000s than it was in the 1950s in part because people are now being paid to provide the homemaking services that went unrecorded in the 1950s.

Comparisons of countries' GDPs are distorted as well. In many Third World countries, many families grow their own food, build their own homes, and gather their own water and fuel, and GDP statistics are very low in part because many of these nonmarketed activities go unreported. Once again, the services of many women (who perform many of these activities) go unrecorded and are undervalued.

Underground Activities

The underground economy involves economic activity that is never reported to the government, either because the activity is illegal or the participants wish to evade taxes. Such underground activity causes GDP to understate actual economic activity.

Suppose you are engaged in illegal activity such as gambling, prostitution, or the drug trade (we hope not!). You will naturally report your income from this activity to the government—not! For obvious reasons, illegal economic activity goes unrecorded in gross domestic product statistics. Although we do not know how much underground activity exists, we do know that for many countries it is sizable. In some Latin American countries, for example, a very large share of economic activity consists of illegal drug sales.

Similarly, any time a person engages in under-the-table exchange, usually to avoid payment of personal income taxes, the activity is not recorded and therefore doesn't enter GDP statistics. This type of exchange might include legal activity, such as haircuts or baby-sitting, but if payment for the service is unreported, it never enters the GDP statistics. People who underreport their tips distort the GDP statistics in a similar fashion. Again, the magnitude of such underground activity is unknown, but it is thought to be significant in the United States.

Composition and Distribution

There are two more important reasons why gross domestic product is not an adequate indicator of people's standards of living. These reasons are discussed at length in Chapter 7 on world poverty. For now, let it suffice for us to mention that the **composition of GDP** is as important as the total value of GDP. If a small country primarily produces armaments and other military hardware, for example, its people may not be achieving the same quality of life as those of another country that has a similar level of GDP but primarily produces health care, educational services, and other goods and services directly meeting the needs of people.

Composition of GDP
The goods and services of which GDP consists.

Also very important is the distribution of GDP, or more technically, the **distribution of income** generated from the production of GDP. It makes a great deal of difference whether a nation's income flows primarily to a small, select, elite group of people or is distributed more equally within the country. The masses of people will live much better in the latter situation. For this reason, standards of living are not adequately measured by the total value of gross domestic product.

Distribution of income
How national income is distributed within an economy.

One final note: suppose that the GDP of a country is growing very rapidly over time, but at the same time, the country experiences more and more pollution, congestion, and depletion of natural resources. Or what if the people of the country must work more and more hours each week in order to produce the high levels of output? Or what if the *Exxon Valdez* disaster, Midwest floods, and Hurricane Andrew all were associated with increased GDP in the clean-up phase? Can we really say that standards of living are improving? Even though we focus a great deal of attention on gross domestic product, be sure to tuck away somewhere in your mind that high GDP is not necessarily synonymous with high standards of living.

AGGREGATE DEMAND AND SUPPLY

Because aggregate demand refers to the quantities of U.S. gross domestic product demanded at alternative price levels, it is useful for us to think of the various sectors that purchase this GDP and that are represented along the aggregate demand curve. In doing so, we can also think through the factors that will shift aggregate demand. For simplicity, let's just think in terms of the factors that might increase aggregate demand. Aggregate demand will increase whenever any sectors of the economy increase their purchases. Let's consider each of these sectors in turn.

Durable goods
Products with a life of longer than one year.

What Sectors Are Represented by Aggregate Demand?

Consumers

Individual consumers such as you and I purchase U.S. durable and nondurable goods and services. **Durable goods** are products with a life of longer than one year, whereas **nondurable goods** are those that usually last less than one year. Durable goods include items such as appliances, furniture, and automobiles; food is a good

Nondurable goods
Products with a life of less than one year.

example of a nondurable good. Household purchases of services such as haircuts and doctor visits are included in the consumer category as well. Indeed, consumer purchases represent the largest component of aggregate demand. It is a relatively stable component as well, particularly the portion consisting of nondurable goods. Regardless of whether the economy is doing well or poorly, people tend to purchase products such as food on a steady basis. Durable goods are less stable; when the economy is doing poorly, many people are forced to reduce their purchases of large-ticket items such as automobiles and home entertainment centers. When the economy picks up, purchases of these items pick up as well.

Consumers will increase their purchases of goods and services as a result of a variety of factors. When consumer incomes rise, consumer purchases go up. When consumer expectations of the future improve, consumer purchases also go up. (If you expect a promotion in the near future, you may well go out and start celebrating now!)

Consumer incomes can be directly affected by government policies. Policies to reduce personal income taxes, for example, will serve to increase consumer incomes because what is left after paying their taxes will be higher. Similarly, government policies that increase government income transfers (welfare payments, Social Security payments, and so on) will also increase consumer incomes.

Consumers are also responsive to changes in interest rates. When interest rates fall, the cost of borrowing money declines. As a result, consumers are more willing to purchase expensive items that they must buy with borrowed money (houses, cars, and appliances). Finally, note that although U.S. consumers make purchases of foreign-produced goods (such as Toyotas and Acer computers), these purchases are not part of U.S. GDP. Therefore, these purchases of imports are not represented along the aggregate demand curve for U.S. GDP.

Businesses

Private business firms in our economy also purchase U.S. GDP. They buy a variety of equipment such as machinery, tools, and computers. They also purchase structures such as factories, office buildings, retail outlets, and restaurant buildings. Finally, businesses "purchase" changes in inventories, which were referred to earlier. A business normally holds a variety of **inventories**, which are unsold goods and materials. These inventories include the final product, the product in intermediate stages of production, and raw materials and component parts.

Business inventories may be held for a variety of reasons. An automobile company, for example, may hold huge inventories of finished cars because the managers anticipate a large demand for the cars in the near future or because demand for the cars has currently fallen off and the product remains unsold. Whatever the reason, increases or decreases in inventories are included in aggregate demand as business purchases. We can envision these inventories as though they are purchased by business firms, even though manufacturers do not actually purchase their unsold inventories.

Business purchases are a relatively small component of aggregate demand, but they tend to fluctuate a lot. When the economy is in a downturn, owners of businesses are reluctant to expand by purchasing new factories and equipment. When the economy improves, they are willing to increase factory and equipment purchases.

EconNews

"It's Supposed to Be a Two-Edged Sword"

Read one example of how a decrease in wealth did not decrease consumer spending under the Aggregate Supply/ Aggregate Demand category.

http://econapps. swlearning.com

Inventories Unsold goods and materials.

Business purchases are influenced by a variety of factors. Expectations of the future are an important factor. If the economy is improving and businesses expect their sales to boom, they may begin purchasing new factories and equipment now to meet the future consumer demand. Furthermore, businesses, like consumers, are influenced by interest rates. A decline in interest rates means that new factories and equipment are cheaper and easier for businesses to buy. Last, as with the consumer sector, we are including only business purchases of U.S. GDP and not foreign-produced imports.

Government

Government purchases of goods and services represent the third component of aggregate demand. The government purchases a variety of items, including food for government nutrition programs, office supplies for government administrators, and the university computer on which we are writing this book. The government also purchases services, including the services of police officers, firefighters, military personnel, and public teachers (including your author!). Last, the government purchases structures, such as prisons and school buildings. Again, only government purchases of U.S. GDP are represented along the aggregate demand curve.

Note that income transfers are not included in the category of government purchases of goods and services. An **income transfer**, as you may recall from Chapter 6 on U.S. poverty, is a cash transfer from the government to an individual for which no good or service is provided in return. Examples of income transfers include Social Security benefits, unemployment compensation, and veterans' cash benefits. These items are not included in the government purchases component of aggregate demand. (When the income transfers are eventually spent by the recipients, their expenditures are then included in the consumption component of aggregate demand.)

Income transfer A cash transfer from the government to an individual for which no good or service is provided to the government in return.

The decisions of government can have important impacts on aggregate demand. Because government purchases of goods and services are included as part of aggregate demand, an increase in government spending on national health care, the space program, public education, or any other program will directly increase aggregate demand. It doesn't matter whether the policy is deliberate or not, any increase in government purchases will increase aggregate demand. Thus, if the country goes to war, and the government purchases military hardware and the services of the armed forces, aggregate demand will increase just as if the government had chosen to expand any other program.

Keep in mind that government policies can also indirectly affect aggregate demand. The decrease in taxes or increase in income transfers mentioned previously will increase the incomes of consumers, which will cause their purchases to go up. These government policies influence the consumption component of aggregate demand. We examine these more carefully shortly.

Foreign Purchasers

As the final component of aggregate demand, we must recognize that foreigners purchase some of our production, ranging from around 8 to 12 percent of U.S. GDP in recent years. These foreigners include individual people, businesses, and governments of other countries, and we refer to their purchases as U.S. exports.

Anything that causes our exports to increase will result in an increase in aggregate demand. The size of our exports is largely determined by factors out of the control of the United States. Because foreigners are purchasing our exports, their purchases depend on variables such as foreign incomes.

Shifts in Aggregate Demand

An increase in aggregate demand caused by an increase in purchases by consumers, businesses, government, or foreigners is represented as a forward shift in aggregate demand. This shift is shown in Figure 15-3. Similarly, a decrease in purchases by any of the four sectors causes a backward shift in aggregate demand.

Shifts in Aggregate Supply

Aggregate supply can shift for the same kinds of reasons that the supply of tutors in Chapter 1 could shift. An increase in aggregate supply would occur if the costs of production (such as energy prices or wage costs) decrease. Aggregate supply would also increase if technological advance makes production of our nation's output cheaper and easier. In the case of agricultural production, aggregate supply would increase if the weather is good. Some economists and politicians believe that the government can use policies to influence a shift in the aggregate supply curve; this issue is discussed shortly.

An increase in aggregate supply for any of these reasons causes the aggregate supply to shift forward to the right, as shown in Figure 15-4.

We are now ready to translate this analysis into a discussion of inflation, unemployment, and government macro policy.

INFLATION REVISITED

In Chapter 14, we defined the three types of inflation and noted that these could be more easily understood in the context of the macroeconomy. Let's consider each type in terms of the graph of aggregate demand and aggregate supply, focusing on different periods of time in the U.S. economy.

FIGURE 15-3   An Increase in Aggregate Demand

When aggregate demand increases, it shifts forward from AD to AD′.

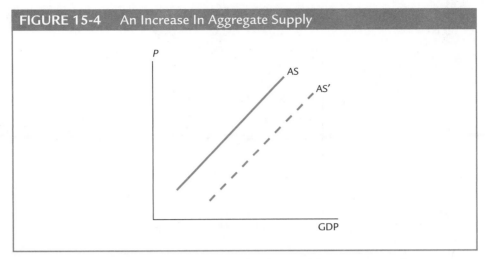

FIGURE 15-4   An Increase In Aggregate Supply

When aggregate supply increases, it shifts forward from AS to AS'.

Demand-Pull Inflation

Recall that demand-pull inflation is caused by an increase in aggregate demand. Consider the graph in Figure 15-5 on page 364. Initial gross domestic product is GDP_0, corresponding to an average price level of P_0. Now imagine some of the conditions that existed during the early 1960s. President John Kennedy had initiated a variety of social programs, which were expanded during the Great Society years of President Lyndon Johnson. All of these programs represented increases in government purchases of goods and services, as well as increases in government income transfers to low-income people. Personal income taxes were also cut in 1963, resulting in higher after-tax income, and consumers increased their purchases of goods and services as a result. Finally, the war in Vietnam consisted of a demand by the U.S. government for armaments and other military supplies, as well as the services of armed service personnel.

All of these factors caused an increase in aggregate demand. The aggregate demand curve shifted forward, as in Figure 15-5, resulting in an increase in gross domestic product to GDP', as well as an increase in the average price level from P_0 to P'. This rise in the average price level is what we mean by inflation; and in this case, it represents demand-pull inflation.

Cost-Push Inflation

Cost-push inflation was earlier defined as inflation caused by an increase in the costs of production. Recall that inflation rates were very high in the mid- and late 1970s. These rising prices can be explained as cost-push inflation.

In 1973–1974, oil supplies were cut off to the United States by Arab countries in response to U.S. support for Israel during the Arab–Israeli wars. Oil prices rose as a result. And in 1979, the Shah of Iran was overthrown, and Iranian oil was once again cut off to the United States. This time oil prices soared. All these events occurred in

FIGURE 15-5 Demand-Pull Inflation

An increase in aggregate demand from AD to AD′ results in a higher average price level (*P′*) and a higher level of gross domestic product (GDP′).

the context of increasing market power by OPEC, the Organization of Petroleum Exporting Countries. OPEC used its market power to initiate overall increases in the price of oil. Because oil and related energy products are important components of our overall purchases, the rise in oil prices directly caused an increase in the average price level. But beyond this, realize that energy is an important input in the production of most goods and services. Thus, rising energy prices represent an increased cost of production. An increase in the costs of production causes the aggregate supply curve to shift to the left, as shown in Figure 15-6.

In Figure 15-6, the backward shift in aggregate supply results in a decrease in gross domestic product to GDP′, as well as an increase in the average price level to P′. The rise in the average price level is the problem of inflation, whereas the decline in GDP is what we mean by **recession**, as defined in Chapter 14. During a recession, total production declines, and employment falls off as well. (Fewer workers are needed to produce lower levels of output.) Thus, the United States experienced the double whammy of simultaneous inflation and recession. This situation is referred to as **stagflation**. Despite the fact that these problems in the macroeconomy were caused by oil price increases, President Jimmy Carter was largely held accountable for them. Many believe that these problems are the reason that President Carter was voted out of office and President Ronald Reagan was voted in during the 1980 presidential election.

Recession
A decline in a nation's gross domestic product (output) associated with a rise in unemployment.

Stagflation
Simultaneous inflation and recession.

Profit-Push Inflation

This form of inflation results from the market power of various industries within the U.S. economy. When business firms use their market power, discussed in Chapter 8 as the ability to influence market prices, output is deliberately restricted to drive

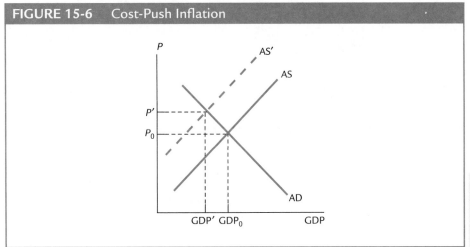

FIGURE 15-6   Cost-Push Inflation

A decrease in aggregate supply form AS to AS′ results in a higher average price level (P′) and a lower level of gross domestic product (GDP′).

up prices and profits. If market power is extensive, these conditions show up as a backward shift in the aggregate supply curve. The graph would look identical to Figure 15-6. Although many fail to recognize it, U.S. market power restricts output and employment in the United States and raises the prices of manufactured items, harming workers and consumers alike. The rising prices of manufactured products have also had negative implications for Third World countries that import these products, as will be discussed in Chapter 17.

GOVERNMENT MACRO POLICY

We are now in a position to analyze the policies available to the government to deal with the problems of unemployment and inflation. You have probably heard the terms *fiscal policy* and *monetary policy*. And beginning with President Reagan's first term of office, the nation became familiar with the term *supply-side policy*. Despite our familiarity with these terms, most Americans do not understand exactly what they mean. We consider each of them in turn.

Fiscal Policy

Fiscal policy is defined as the use of government spending and taxes to shift the aggregate demand curve. Fiscal policy can be either **expansionary** (shifting the aggregate demand curve to the right) or **contractionary** (shifting the aggregate demand curve to the left). John Maynard Keynes, who is quoted at the beginning of the chapter, was the economist who developed the idea that the government could use active fiscal policy to correct the economy. He felt that government should act while the problem was occurring, rather than wait for the long-run time period when "we are all dead."

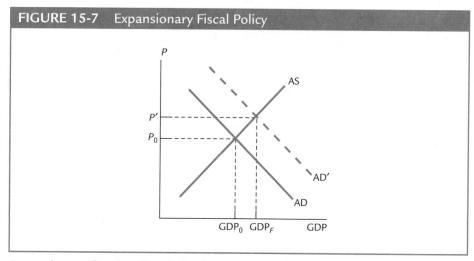

FIGURE 15-7 Expansionary Fiscal Policy

Expansionary fiscal policy shifts the aggregate demand curve forward, resulting in a higher level of gross domestic product (GDP_F) and a higher average price level (P').

Full-employment GDP

The level of gross domestic product associated with full employment of the labor force. (It is a hypothetical concept.)

The effects of expansionary policy are shown in Figure 15-7. Suppose that the economy is operating with gross domestic product at GDP_0, and the average price level at P_0. Let's assume that full employment GDP occurs at GDP_F. We define **full-employment GDP** as the level of gross domestic product associated with full employment of the labor force. At full-employment GDP, cyclical unemployment is zero.

If the government can successfully use fiscal policy, the aggregate demand curve will shift forward. Gross domestic product will rise to GDP_F, increasing employment in the country. The average price level will increase as well.

You already understand the tools that can be used by the government to cause the shifts in aggregate demand. They are government purchases of goods and services, government taxes, and government income transfers. Recall that government purchases of goods and services represents a component of aggregate demand. Thus, whenever the government increases its purchases, aggregate demand will shift forward. Alternatively, the government can reduce personal income taxes. The higher after-tax income of consumers encourages them to increase their purchases, thereby increasing the consumer component of aggregate demand. This higher after-tax income will also cause the aggregate demand curve to shift forward. Finally, an increase in government income transfers will serve to raise consumer incomes, again causing the aggregate demand curve to increase.

Any or all of these fiscal policy tools can be used independently. The government may increase its purchases while lowering taxes, for example, because there are other ways it can finance its purchases besides raising tax dollars. Therefore, when one of these policy tools is used, do not necessarily assume that another tool is used simultaneously.

When President Bill Clinton took office in 1993, the nation had been experiencing some difficulty with recession. Unemployment rates were higher than normal, and President Clinton was seeking ways to increase gross domestic product. That is, he was seeking some form of expansionary fiscal policy.

More recently, President George W. Bush faced a recession as well. And even once the recession ended in late 2001, it was still billed as a jobless recovery, since unemployment rates remained high. It is not clear which of President Bush's policies were designed to fix the economy, and which were initiated for other reasons. For example, President Bush was able to push large tax cuts through Congress. Ideally, these tax cuts would expand the economy, since lower taxes means more money in the hands of consumers, who in turn purchase more U.S. output. One of the problems with the tax cuts is that the largest benefits accrued to high-income consumers who are less likely than poorer people to use the tax cuts to increase spending. Other Bush administration policies, including the increased spending on the war with Iraq, the defense department, and homeland security, would theoretically increase aggregate demand, whether they were intended for this purpose or not. We consider the nature of Bush administration spending and tax policies in more detail in Chapter 16.

To summarize, expansionary fiscal policy consists of one or more of the following tools:

1. An increase in government purchases of goods and services
2. A reduction in taxes
3. An increase in income transfers

Similarly, contractionary fiscal policy consists of one or more of the following tools:

1. A decrease in government purchases of goods and services
2. An increase in taxes
3. A decrease in income transfers

Monetary Policy

Monetary policy is defined as changes that are made in the nation's money supply in order to shift aggregate demand. Whereas fiscal policy is under the control of the government (the president and Congress), monetary policy is under the control of the **Federal Reserve**. The Federal Reserve is our nation's central banking system. The seven members of the board of governors of the Federal Reserve are appointed by the president and approved by Congress. They serve staggered 14-year terms, such that a member is generally appointed every 2 years. Thus, although the membership of the board of governors is determined by the government, the role of any one presidential administration is limited. Therefore, the Federal Reserve is somewhat immune to politics.

Among other things under the control of the Federal Reserve is our nation's money supply. Changes in the nation's money supply will affect the interest rate. (Although economists refer to the interest rate, in fact there are many interest rates, depending on the type of loan or financial investment. These rates do tend to move up and down together, however.) Think of the interest rate as the price of money. An increase in the supply of money will cause a reduction in the interest rate (just as an

EconLinks
Find links to the Federal Reserve Banks under the Government category.

http://econapps. swlearning.com

Monetary policy
Changes made in the nation's money supply to shift the aggregate demand curve.

Federal Reserve
The U.S. central banking system.

increase in the supply of corn will cause a reduction in the price of corn). A decrease in the nation's money supply will cause an increase in the interest rate.

Monetary policy affects the economy through its effects on interest rates. A rise in the interest rate will cause a reduction in business purchases of factories and equipment, as well as a decrease in consumer purchases of cars, houses, appliances, and other expensive items. Businesses and consumers must borrow money to finance these major purchases, and rising interest rates raise the cost of borrowing. Many business firms and consumers decide that they cannot afford to purchase the items because of the high cost of borrowing money. Thus, a reduction in the nation's money supply will cause a rise in interest rates, causing a decrease in consumer and business purchases, and therefore a decrease in aggregate demand. A decrease in the nation's money supply reflects contractionary monetary policy (monetary policy that reduces aggregate demand, thereby contracting GDP). An increase in the nation's money supply will increase aggregate demand, and is therefore called expansionary monetary policy. It will expand GDP.

Thus, monetary policy, just like fiscal policy, is an aggregate demand–side policy. Students sometimes get confused when they think of the term *money supply* and assume it affects the supply side of the economy. Rather, monetary policy, just like fiscal policy, is designed to influence aggregate demand.[1]

The Federal Reserve may choose either **expansionary** or **contractionary monetary policy**, depending on the state of the economy. A good case in point is the situation encountered by newly elected President Reagan in 1981. As a result of the rise in oil prices already described, the president faced a serious problem of inflation. Although the president has no direct control over monetary policy, President Reagan did make a national plea to the Federal Reserve to engage in contractionary monetary policy to reduce aggregate demand. The Federal Reserve complied; the results are indicated in Figure 15-8.

As the Federal Reserve reduced the nation's money supply, interest rates soared. The construction industry and the automobile industry were particularly hard hit, as businesses and consumers were unable or unwilling to borrow at such high interest rates and were therefore unable to finance purchases of factories, houses, and automobiles. The reduction in aggregate demand reduced gross domestic product to the level depicted as GDP′ in Figure 15-8. The consequent recession resulted in the high unemployment rates of the early 1980s. Inflation was controlled, but at the serious cost of recession and unemployment. A similar monetary contraction occurred in the early 1990s, resulting in similar, though less intense, recession and unemployment.

A more recent example concerns the recession of the early years of the new millennium. The Federal Reserve enacted a series of increases in the nation's money supply in order to reduce interest rates. As a result, interest rates fell on several occasions, but it is not clear whether consumers and businesses responded by increasing their spending. Keep in mind that a consumer who is worried about losing his job, or a business-owner who is worried about losing her business, will not be inclined to borrow money for expensive purchases no matter how low the interest rates fall. Indeed, this is one problem with monetary policy. There is also a natural limit to how low interest rates can go.

Expansionary monetary policy
Monetary policy that increases aggregate demand, thereby expanding GDP.

Contractionary monetary policy
Monetary policy that decreases aggregate demand, thereby contracting GDP.

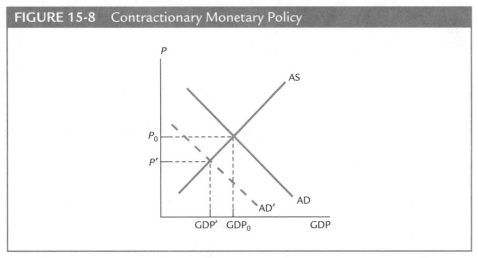

FIGURE 15-8   Contractionary Monetary Policy

Contractionary monetary policy shifts the aggregate demand curve backward, resulting in a lower level of gross domestic product (GDP′) and a lower average price level (P′).

These examples of fiscal and monetary policy demonstrate one shortcoming of policy that operates on the aggregate demand side of the economy. An increase in aggregate demand, as in the case of the expansionary fiscal policy in the early 1960s, results in an increase in GDP and employment, but at the cost of creating inflation (the rise in the average price level). A decrease in aggregate demand, as in the case of the contractionary monetary policy in the early 1980s, reduces the problem of inflation, but at the cost of creating recession and unemployment. Thus aggregate demand-side policy creates a trade-off between the problems of unemployment and inflation, at least in the short run. (This trade-off is modified somewhat in Appendix 2 with a bit more realistic view of the aggregate supply curve.)

Wouldn't it be nice to come up with a policy that would simultaneously reduce inflation and unemployment? This objective underlies supply-side policy and was the reason for its widespread welcome during the Reagan administration of 1981–1984.

Supply-Side Policy

Supply-side economics was a revolution in thought. Adopting a general philosophy that promoted less involvement of government in the economy, President Reagan undertook supply-side policies with the stated objective of increasing aggregate supply. The idea behind **supply-side policy** is that by increasing aggregate supply rather than aggregate demand, GDP and employment will rise, and the average price level will fall. This phenomenon is illustrated in Figure 15-9 on page 370.

The supply-side tools of President Reagan included cuts in personal income tax rates, cuts in government transfer programs, and cuts in government regulations. These policies are relevant today, because they are the same types of policies that

Supply-side economics
The view that conservative economic policies can be used to increase aggregate supply.

Supply-side policy
The use of various tools to improve the incentives for workers and businesses to produce more, thereby increasing aggregate supply and GDP.

FIGURE 15-9 Supply-Side Policy

Supply-side policy shifts the aggregate supply curve forward, resulting in a higher level of gross domestic product (GDP′) and a lower average price level (P′).

economic conservatives, including President George W. Bush, have been proposing. Each policy is considered in turn in the following sections.

Cuts in Personal Income Tax Rates

This policy tool is a little confusing, because fiscal policy as well as supply-side policy can utilize cuts in taxes. Recall that in terms of fiscal policy, a tax cut will place more income in the hands of consumers, who will increase their consumption purchases. This phenomenon is reflected in an increase in aggregate demand. The effects of the tax cut are very different from the perspective of a supply-side theorist, however. From this perspective, the tax cut must take the form of a reduction in tax *rates*, because it is assumed that tax rates influence our decisions about work effort. A reduction in tax rates is considered tantamount to an increase in hourly wages, and it is assumed that people will respond to the incentive of higher after-tax wages by increasing their work effort. That is, some people will take second jobs, others will accept overtime hours, and still others will take a job that they previously were unwilling to take. Supply-side policies typically center on incentives, and here the incentive is to increase work effort. If the nation's workers respond as desired, the increased work effort will result in expanded production, which will increase the supply side of the economy. Aggregate supply will shift forward, as in Figure 15-9, resulting in expanded GDP and a decreased price level.

In 1981, President Reagan proposed a series of large, three-year tax rate cuts. Although Congress scaled back the magnitude of the cuts somewhat, they were the largest tax cuts in our nation's history up to that time. The tax cuts were subsequently criticized, because high-income households received by far the largest tax reductions, whereas low-income households received very little benefit. More recently, President George W. Bush pushed through similar cuts in the federal income tax and worked for the reduction and elimination of other types of taxes. Although he stated that everyone who pays income taxes deserves a tax cut, in fact his tax proposals were designed once again to primarily benefit higher-income earners. Even though President Bush recognized the fiscal and supply-side nature of his proposed tax cuts, the conservative agenda of low taxes and less money in the hands of the government motivated his efforts, as was the case with President Reagan.

Cuts in Income Transfers

Like cuts in taxes, cuts in income transfers can be construed as part of fiscal policy and supply-side policy. In terms of fiscal policy, the cuts in income transfers would lower recipients' incomes, causing their consumption purchases to fall. This outcome would be reflected in a decrease in aggregate demand. In terms of supply-side policy, incentives again become important. Many conservatives argue that transfer programs provide incentives for people to be lazy, seeking handouts from the government instead of going to work. By reducing transfers, people are forced to seek employment. With more people working, production expands and aggregate supply increases.

President Reagan enacted large cuts in government income transfers, primarily Aid to Families with Dependent Children, as well as other programs for the poor. As discussed in Chapter 6, our recent welfare reform has gone beyond work incentives, instead requiring that participants work. Whether the issue is incentives or requirements, the intention is to increase work, thereby increasing production and increasing aggregate supply.

Deregulation

A third supply-side tool used by President Reagan was that of **deregulation** which is reductions in government regulations affecting American business. The largest cuts were made in the areas of environmental protection and worker safety. The Reagan administration argued that these regulations tie the hands of business and increase the costs of production. By reducing these regulations, President Reagan argued that businesses would expand production, thereby increasing the aggregate supply side of the economy. The current conservative agenda is really no different, and deregulation has been a goal of President Bush. Conservatives believe that reducing government regulations not only creates an incentive for businesses to expand production, but also restricts the role of government in the economy.

Deregulation
The reduction of government regulations.

Effects of Supply-Side Policy

Were the supply-side tools of the early 1980s successful in increasing GDP? Are the more recent conservative policies effective in expanding our economy? Answering these questions is difficult because supply-side policies do not operate in a vacuum. Implemented simultaneously with the supply-side policies of the early 1980s was the contractionary monetary policy already described. The effects of the monetary contraction by far dwarfed any supply-side effects that may have occurred. Similarly, the effects of supply-side policy in the early 2000s are probably much smaller than other forces that have served to increase aggregate demand. As is discussed in the next chapter, these forces include increased spending by the Bush administration on warfare, national defense, and homeland defense.

We have reasons to question supply-side effectiveness. Cuts in tax rates have a limited effect, if any, on work effort. Most people are unable to alter the number of hours they work each week, so increased incentives for work effort will not change the number of hours worked. Others may increase their work hours when their after-tax wages go up because the incentive to do so is now greater. Still others may decide to cut their work hours because tax-rate cuts allow them to maintain their desired level of income while working fewer hours. Labor economists believe that the overall impact of changes in after-tax wages is close to zero, meaning that overall work effort remains unchanged.

Many have argued that just like tax rate cuts, cuts in government transfers do not result in expanded work effort. After all, transfer programs such as Aid to Families with Dependent Children in the early 1980s were meant for women with small children and others who were unable to work. Furthermore, many participants in our current welfare system (TANF, as discussed in Chapter 6) will not be able to work unless child care, transportation, job training, and education are made available. Finally, given the possibility of recession at any time, jobs may simply be unavailable (as was the case in the early 1980s and in the early 2000s). Just because a person has an incentive to work does not mean that he or she will find a job. Clearly, jobs must exist if the incentives are to be effective in increasing aggregate supply.

Keep in mind that the supply-side policies of the early 1980s, as well as the conservative proposals of the early 2000s, all have as their objective a reduced role for government in the economy. Supply-siders would reduce government spending and involvement in social programs, would reduce taxes to increase the spending ability of the private sector, and would reduce government regulatory control over business. The conservative objective of reducing the government role in the economy is at the root of supply-side policies.

If we question the effectiveness of supply-side policy to create economic growth, then what are the factors that might be more successful? The forces that do serve to increase aggregate supply are discussed in Chapter 17, as we look at economic conditions in the twenty-first century.

Trickle-Down

Did President Reagan's willingness to reduce taxes largely for the rich and to reduce government spending largely for the poor mean that supply-siders are interested in benefiting the rich and hurting the poor? Does President George W. Bush's support for further reductions in taxes for the rich and for changes in welfare reform that emphasize work mean that he discards his father's notion of a kinder, gentler America? Supply-side economists and politicians would answer with a resounding no! Instead, they argue that these policies are necessary to generate economic growth (that is, a forward shift in aggregate supply that persists over time). They argue that economic growth will improve the prosperity of the nation, and eventually the benefits of this prosperity will trickle down to everyone, rich and poor alike. No wonder this approach to economics has been dubbed **trickle-down philosophy**! We'll leave it to you, the reader, to decide if this conservative approach to economics will indeed provide benefits to all, or whether the poor will continue to be left out of the prosperity of the nation. This issue is important because the conservative Republican agenda incorporates trickle-down philosophy today.

Economic Policy for the New Century

George W. Bush was elected to the nation's highest office in 2000, ending eight years of a Democratic presidency. Bush campaigned as a moderate conservative against the moderate liberal Al Gore. With a margin of just a few thousand votes separating the two candidates and the popular vote going to Gore, the American public was clearly divided. Congress was similarly divided. The unemployment rate was extremely low at 4.0 percent, and the inflation rate was relatively low at 3.4 percent. The government budget was in surplus, a conservative welfare system was in

VIEWPOINT: CONSERVATIVE VERSUS LIBERAL

Any one of the tools of fiscal policy or the use of monetary policy can successfully expand the economy. Theoretically, the use of supply-side policy can do the same. Even if all these expansionary policies are equally effective, people will disagree about the type of policy to be used. Liberals, you should note, would be in favor of fiscal policy that increases government purchases and transfers, especially if the government purchases are for domestic social programs.

Conservatives would prefer to see fiscal policy that reduces taxes and places more purchasing power in the private sector of the economy, though conservatives are often supportive of high levels of defense-related spending.

Conservatives would also prefer the use of monetary policy, which, by lowering interest rates, enables private consumers and businesses to increase their purchases. And, of course, conservatives are the ones who favor the use of supply-side policy.

Thus, although the various policies may be similar in terms of their impact on the macroeconomy, the philosophies underlying them vary greatly. And even though these policies may cause identical change in the size of our gross domestic product, the composition of GDP and the distribution of income will certainly be affected. We may have more national defense, but less national health care. We may have more money in the hands of the rich, but no change in the incomes of the poor. And we may have more purchases of homes and factories, but fewer purchases of public school buildings. Certainly, the composition of GDP and the distribution of income are as important as the size of GDP itself.

effect, and an eight-year stretch of economic growth had continued unmitigated. George Bush left no doubt about his intentions to reign in government spending, reduce government taxes, and privatize portions of Social Security, health care, and education.

As you now know, our economy changed dramatically in the few years since President Bush entered office. Our nation has experienced recession and the highest unemployment rates in a decade. Our country has experienced 9–11, a war with Afghanistan, and an invasion of Iraq. Despite high defense-related expenditures, unemployment remains high. Aside from these defense-related expenditures (which economic conservatives often have favored), taxes and domestic programs have been cut. In these ways, President Bush maintains a conservative agenda, similar to the conservative supply-side policy of the early 1980s. And except for defense, the conservative objective is once again to reduce the role of government in the economy.

SUMMARY

We can analyze the macroeconomy with a graph of aggregate demand and supply. Aggregate demand is the quantity of total output demanded at alternative price levels, whereas aggregate supply is the quantity of output produced at alternative price levels. The intersection of aggregate demand and supply determines the country's average price level and level of gross domestic product. Gross domestic product refers to the market value of all final goods and services produced in the economy, usually within a one-year time period. Aggregate demand consists of the purchases of consumers, businesses, government, and foreigners.

The government and the Federal Reserve can use policies to shift aggregate demand and sup-

ply in an effort to reduce inflation or unemployment. The two types of policies used to shift aggregate demand are fiscal policy and monetary policy. Fiscal policy includes changes in government spending and taxes, whereas monetary policy works by changing the nation's money supply to affect interest rates. Supply-side policies may be used in an effort to increase aggregate supply.

At the root of supply-side policies is the desire to reduce the government's role in the economy. In the process, the goal of these policies is to achieve economic prosperity, the benefits of which are to trickle down to all. Critics of supply-side policies maintain that these policies are ineffective and harm the poor.

NOTES

1. In the examples of fiscal monetary policy in this chapter, we are deliberately simplifying the effects of changes in purchases on aggregate demand by ignoring the "multiplier effect" of initial spending changes on larger ultimate spending changes in the economy. This simplification does not detract from the conclusions of this and the next chapter.

DISCUSSION QUESTIONS

1. Many have argued that the government should attach a value to homemaking services and include this value in gross domestic product statistics. Do you agree? Why?

2. Is gross domestic product an accurate measure of standards of living? Why or why not?

3. Describe the effect on gross domestic product, employment, and inflation of each of the following: (a) war, (b) elimination of environmental regulations, and (c) cuts in welfare benefits.

4. Look up the current level of GDP at the Census Bureau's Web site (**www.census.gov**). What is the value of nominal GDP? What is the value of real GDP? What is the base year(s) used in calculating real GDP?

5. Look up the current unemployment rate at the Bureau of Labor Statistics Web site (**www.bls.gov**). Would you say we currently have full employment?

6. Conservatives favor a lesser role for government in the economy, whereas liberals favor a greater role. How would each of these groups feel about a fiscal policy that increases government purchases and income transfers? fiscal policy that reduces taxes? monetary policy that reduces interest rates?

7. What is your opinion about the role that government should play in the economy?

8. Do you believe in the trickle-down philosophy?

9. Got to the Web site of the President (**www. whitehouse.gov**), and search for a recent speech by the President that focuses on government spending or tax policies. What type of macroeconomic policy is he promoting? Do you agree with him?

CHAPTER 15 APPENDIX: THE SLOPE OF THE AGGREGATE DEMAND CURVE

It was noted earlier that the aggregate demand curve slopes downward, as shown in Figure 15-10 on page 376. The downward slope indicates that the quantity of gross domestic product demanded increases when the average price level falls and that it decreases when the average price level rises. The relationship between the quantity of GDP demanded and the average price level is negative for three reasons.

First, let's consider the international trade effect of a rise in the average price level. If the average price level in the United States rises relative to the price levels in other countries, then American consumers will tend to buy more foreign goods and fewer American goods. The price of a Ford vehicle may rise, for example, in comparison with the price of a Toyota. U.S. consumers (as well as the consumers of other countries) will probably buy more Toyotas and fewer Fords. This reduction in U.S. GDP demanded occurs as a result of the rise in the U.S. average price level.

Second, a rise in the average price level reduces the value, or purchasing power, of assets. The money you have tucked away in a savings account (or under your mattress, for that matter), for example, is no longer worth as much when the average price level rises. That is, a fixed amount of money loses its purchasing power when the prices of purchased items increase. Less wealth means that people cut back their purchases (because they feel less wealthy). Thus, the quantity of GDP demanded falls when the average price level rises.

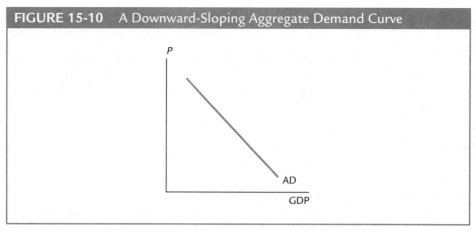

FIGURE 15-10 A Downward-Sloping Aggregate Demand Curve

P

AD

GDP

A downward-sloping aggregated demand curve means that the quantity of gross domestic product demanded increases when the average price level falls and decreases when the average price level rises.

Third, a rise in the average price level has implications for interest rates. When people experience a loss in the value of their assets, as we have described, they need to borrow more money from their banks. This increase in the demand for credit pushes up the price of credit—in other words, the interest rate. As interest rates rise, people and businesses reduce their purchases of big-ticket items such as cars, homes, and factories. Thus, the quantity of GDP demanded decreases as the average price level rises.

In all of these examples, we have considered why a rise in the average price level causes a reduction in the quantity of GDP demanded. Realize that a decrease in the average price level will cause the opposite effect that is, an increase in the quantity of GDP demanded.

Keep in mind the difference between factors that cause a movement along the aggregate demand curve and factors that cause a shift in the aggregate demand curve. Because the average price level is on the vertical axis of the graph of aggregate demand, any change in the average price level that causes changes in the quantity of GDP demanded is reflected as a movement along the demand curve, according to the curve's downward slope. On the other hand, changes not precipitated by a change in the average price level—such as changes in population size, consumer incomes, or government fiscal or monetary policy—will cause a shift in the entire aggregate demand curve.

THE SLOPE OF THE AGGREGATE SUPPLY CURVE

The actual slope of the aggregate supply curve is important when it comes to policy prescription. Throughout the chapter, we've used a simplified version of the aggregate supply curve, one with a straight-line upward-sloping shape, as is shown in Figure 15-11. This shape is responsible for one of our conclusions in this chapter: that aggregate demand-side policy creates a trade-off between unemployment and inflation. This trade-off is not quite so clear-cut if we look at the aggregate supply curve more carefully.

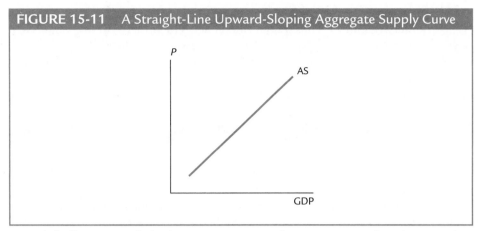

FIGURE 15-11   A Straight-Line Upward-Sloping Aggregate Supply Curve

A straight-line upward-sloping aggregate supply curve means that the quantity of gross domestic product supplied rises when the average price level rises and falls when the average price level falls.

Economists have come to various conclusions about the shape of the aggregate supply curve, depending on whether they consider the long run or the short run, as well as other assumptions. We can simplify, however, and draw an aggregate supply curve that incorporates many of these views. This supply curve is depicted in Figure 15-12.

FIGURE 15-12   An Aggregate Supply Curve with Three Distinct Ranges

The flat region (Range A) represents low output and employment, the upward-sloping region (Range B) represents a moderate level of output and employment, and the vertical region (Range C) represents high output and full employment.

Notice that the aggregate supply curve in Figure 15-12 has a flat range (Range A), an upward-sloping range (Range B), and a vertical range (Range C). The upward-sloping range corresponds to the aggregate supply in Figure 15-11 and can be viewed as reflecting a typical state of the economy—that is, one with moderate levels of GDP and employment. Any shift of aggregate demand within this range will create the trade-off between unemployment and inflation. (See the shift from AD_2 to AD_3 in Figure 15-13. GDP increases from GDP_2 to GDP_3, and the average price level increases from P_2 to P_3.)

The flat range of the aggregate supply curve is sometimes called the Keynesian range, because it is typical of the depression era when John Maynard Keynes developed his theory of the economy. Specifically, GDP was low and unemployment rates were extremely high, and workers were willing to work for whatever low wages were being offered at the time. Capital equipment (factories and machinery) was underutilized, operating perhaps only one shift per day instead of two or three. In this context, firms can easily expand production to meet expanded demand. Production costs per unit of output (per car, for example) will not rise because wages and capital prices will not be pushed upward. Without rising costs of production, firms have no reason to raise their prices to consumers. This means that within the flat Keynesian range of aggregate supply, any increase in aggregate demand will increase output and employment, without causing any attendant inflation. This situation is shown in Figure 15-13, where the shift in aggregate demand from AD_1 to AD_2 increases GDP from GDP_1 to GDP_2, but P_2 is equal to P_1.

FIGURE 15-13 Shifting Aggregate Demand in the Three Ranges of the Aggregate Supply Curve

An increase in aggregate demand in Range A increases output and employment without creating inflation; an increase in aggregate demand in Range B increases output and employment and also creates some inflation; and an increase in aggregate demand in Range C results in no increase in output and employment, but merely creates inflation.

Finally, the vertical range of aggregate supply corresponds to a situation of high GDP and a fully employed economy. Keeping in mind the definition of full employment from Chapter 14, expanding production beyond this level is very difficult. If aggregate demand increases, for example, and the manager of an automobile company wishes to expand production to match additional demand, the only way to hire additional workers will be to offer higher wages. Similarly, if capital is fully utilized, any expansion of car production will require additional capital. Both of these situations will create rising costs of production, which firms will try to pass on to consumers in the form of higher prices. Despite the inflation, however, overall GDP will not expand, because the only way to hire additional resources in a fully employed economy is to bid them away from other firms. The automobile company may be able to expand car production, but a refrigerator company, for example, may lose employees and end up reducing output. An increase in aggregate demand in this context will only create inflation, without creating any additional output or employment. This outcome is shown in Figure 15-13, where aggregate demand increases from AD_3 to AD_4. The average price level rises from P_3 to P_4, but GDP does not increase.

Although the economy is generally not in a state as extreme as Range A or Range C, we can understand that an increase in aggregate demand when employment is low will fairly easily result in expanded output and employment, without triggering much inflation. On the other hand, an increase in aggregate demand when employment is high will largely create inflation, without triggering much of an increase in production or employment.

**Chapter 2
Crime and Drugs**
Taxes could be used to discourage drug use if drugs became legal

**Chapter 3
The Environment**
Taxes can create incentives to protect the environment

**Chapter 13
Social Security**
Social Security taxes are among our most regressive taxes

**Chapter 9
International Trade**
Taxes (tariffs) are a form of trade restrictions

**Chapter 16
Taxes, Borrowing, and
the National Debt**

**Chapter 14
Unemployment and
Inflation**
These two macro problems are affected by government taxes

**Chapter 5
Discrimination**
Property-tax financing of public education leads to unequal educational opportunities for segregated minorities

**Chapter 6
U.S. Poverty**
Many of our taxes heavily burden the poor
The Earned Income Credit helps the working poor

**Chapter 17
Globally Free
Markets for the
Twenty-First
Century?**
Raising taxes as part of global economic reform stabilizes budgets but creates hardships for the poor

**Chapter 15
Government
Macroeconomic
Policy**
Taxes and borrowing enable government spending and affect the macroeconomy

THE ECONOMIC TOOLBOX

- tax base
- tax rate
- progressive, proportional, and regressive taxes
- Earned Income Credit
- tax burden
- loanable funds
- crowding out
- budget deficit
- national debt

TAXES, BORROWING, AND THE NATIONAL DEBT

In this world nothing can be said to be certain, except death and taxes.

—Benjamin Franklin (1706–1790), *Complete Works*, 1887–88

So far, we have considered a variety of government expenditures, including spending on social and poverty programs, expenditures to control pollution and big business, spending to ensure equal opportunity, expenditures on agriculture and the control of crime, and government spending to increase aggregate demand and stabilize the economy. Most recently, we have seen large spending increases for national defense and homeland defense. In particular, government spending has increased dramatically in relation to the U.S. wars in Afghanistan and Iraq. But we have not yet carefully addressed a critical question: how does the government come up with the money to finance these programs and policies?

One of the most obvious ways that the government acquires revenue is through taxes. By taxing the public (including individual income earners, property owners, businesses, and consumers), the government acquires a large portion of the expenditure dollars that it needs. The other means of financing government spending is by government borrowing. The government borrows when it issues **government securities**, which include government bonds, treasury notes, and treasury bills. A government security is really just an IOU: it is a piece of paper saying that the government has borrowed money and promises to repay it, plus interest, at some future point in time. The government sells these pieces of paper to banks, corporations, some foreigners, and a large number of ordinary American citizens. You may own some government savings bonds; if so, you are lending your money to the government. We will consider these two basic means of financing government spending in the sections that follow.

Government securities
Government bonds and treasury bills.

GOVERNMENT TAXES

As the quotation opening this chapter states, "In this world nothing can be said to be certain, except death and taxes." People who are civic-minded recognize that government programs require government revenue, so that taxes *are* a certainty. Still, people want these taxes to be fair and reasonable.

Government taxes come in various forms and are imposed by the federal government as well as by state and local governments. We will consider these various taxes and then analyze their impact on the macroeconomy, the distribution of income, and individual markets within the United States.

Federal Taxes

Figure 16-1 displays the principal federal taxes and the proportion of 2002 federal tax revenue accounted for by each type of tax.

We can see from Figure 16-1 that the federal personal income tax is the most important of the taxes levied by the federal government. The personal income tax brings in roughly 52 percent of total federal tax revenue. This tax is placed on most forms of individual income. A different **tax rate** is applied to different increments of income. In

Tax rate
The percentage of the tax base that must be paid to the government as tax.

Tax base
Income, earnings, sales, property, or other valued items that have a tax rate applied to them. In the case of the personal income tax, the tax base is incremental income.

Capital gains
The net income received when an asset is bought at a particular price and sold at a higher price.

Exemptions
Amounts of money for each household member that can be deducted from household income before personal income tax rates are applied.

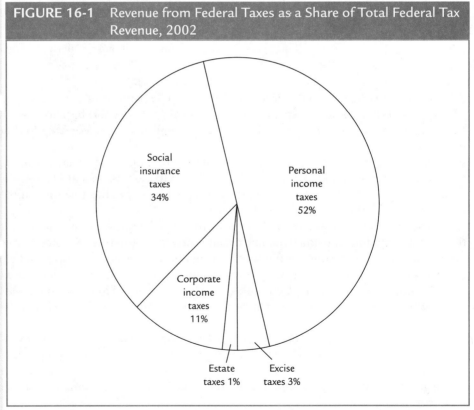

FIGURE 16-1 Revenue from Federal Taxes as a Share of Total Federal Tax Revenue, 2002

- Social insurance taxes 34%
- Personal income taxes 52%
- Corporate income taxes 11%
- Estate taxes 1%
- Excise taxes 3%

*Source: U.S. Internal Revenue Service (**www.irs.gov/taxstats**). Note taxes do not add to 100% because of rounding.*

this case, taxable income is called the **tax base**. The first portion of your income is covered by one tax bracket and a corresponding tax rate, the next portion of your income is in the next bracket and covered by a higher rate, and so on. Until 1986, there existed 14 different tax brackets. The portion of the income of highest-income individuals that was in the very highest bracket was taxed at the highest rate. This maximum tax rate was 90 percent until 1964, when it underwent the first of several reductions until reaching a low of 28 percent. In 1991, this maximum tax rate increased to 39.6 percent for a small number of high income Americans and there were four additional tax brackets with tax rates of 15 percent, 28 percent, 31 percent, and 36 percent.

One continual political issue is whether capital gains should be taxed in the same way as other forms of income. **Capital gains** refers to the net income received when an asset is bought at a particular price and subsequently sold at a higher price. For example, if I purchase a share of corporate stock for $100, but I sell it later for $150, I receive $50 worth of capital gains. It would be nice *for me* if there was a very low tax, or even no tax, on these capital gains. Since higher-income people tend to receive by far more capital gains than low-income people, cutting the capital gains tax would largely benefit high-income people.

Americans can take advantage of several tax breaks in the federal personal income tax. Households can claim **exemptions** for each family member. They can also deduct various expenditures (deductions) from their taxable income. One example of such a deduction is a household's mortgage interest payments. Alternatively, they may take the **standard deduction**, which is a fixed amount of income that taxpayers can deduct from their taxable income if no other deductions are claimed. Taxpayers might also be eligible for various **tax credits** that directly reduce their tax amount payable to the government.

Aside from reducing the number of tax brackets and reducing tax rates, the 1986 tax code eliminated many deductions, increased the standard deduction, and increased the Earned Income Credit. The **Earned Income Credit (EIC)** has increased in size over time and is available to eligible low-income workers. It is **refundable**, meaning that it provides a refund to eligible workers even if their earnings are too low to be taxed.

The federal personal income tax was the target of controversy during President Bill Clinton's Administration, and both Al Gore and George W. Bush promised changes in the tax code during the 2000 presidential campaign. Gore's plans went by the wayside, but President Bush's pledge to cut taxes had quite an impact. After pledging large tax cuts as a major focal point of his campaign promises, President Bush delivered on his promise in 2001 by pushing through Congress the largest tax cuts in our nation since 1981. This legislation, signed by President Bush, immediately created an additional tax bracket at the bottom of the income ladder with a tax rate of 10 percent. The 15 percent tax rate remained unchanged, and after implementation by the year 2006, the other five brackets will have new lower tax rates of 25 percent, 28 percent, 33 percent, and 35 percent. In addition to changes in the brackets and tax rates, the legislation makes adjustments for married couples (eliminating the so called "marriage tax"), increases the size of the standard deduction (described shortly), and doubles the child tax credit for families with children (regardless of income). In addition, heirs to very large estates (valued up to $3.5 million

Standard deduction
A fixed amount of money that taxpayers can deduct from their taxable income when calculating their personal income taxes, if other deductions are not claimed.

Tax credits
Amounts of money by which the income taxes payable to the government can be directly reduced. A person or business must meet certain criteria to be eligible for a credit.

Earned Income Credit (EIC)
A federal tax credit for eligible low-income working individuals and families. State governments may also utilize an EIC for their personal income taxes.

Refundable
A refund is available even if an income earner does not pay taxes, as long as he or she files a tax form.

are immediately exempt from paying estate ("death") taxes, and these taxes will be entirely eliminated on all estates by the year 2010. And, just as with the Earned Income Credit (EIC), the new tax cut is refundable to low income families that would otherwise not be required to file their taxes. Under the new law, these families can obtain a refund even if they have no tax liability. The total value of all of the tax cuts will be $1.35 trillion over 10 years.

The second-largest federal category of taxes is for social insurance. Taxes in this category are also called **payroll taxes**, because they are deducted directly from your paycheck or paid by your employer to fund various social insurance programs. The worker and the employer are taxed an equal amount for the two major social insurance programs, Social Security and Medicare. These two programs provide income to retired workers and their dependents, disabled workers, and survivors of deceased workers, as well as hospitalization and basic medical care for retired and disabled persons. All social insurance taxes together represent 34 percent of federal government tax revenue. They are discussed in greater detail in Chapter 13 on Social Security.

Payroll taxes
Taxes based on earnings from work and usually deducted directly from the paycheck.

Corporate profits are taxed according to the corporate income tax. The corporate income tax generates about 11 percent of federal tax revenue. Despite its name, the tax base for the corporate income tax is actually the profits of corporations and not their revenue (income). **Excise taxes**, operating like sales taxes but levied only on particular goods and services, bring in approximately 3 percent of federal tax revenue. Last, estate taxes bring in about 1 percent of the total.

Excise taxes
Taxes applied to the purchase of specific goods or services.

Even though estate taxes bring in a small share of total federal tax revenue, they deserve some additional mention. Until recently, estate taxes were levied only on highly valued estates that were passed on to others as an inheritance. (Estate taxes are also called inheritance taxes.) President George W. Bush proposed the elimination of the estate tax on highly valued property, thereby returning billions of dollars to the public. Because wealthy people own the bulk of taxable estates, most of the benefit goes to the nation's wealthiest individuals. It is interesting to note that President Bush, as well as other conservatives, often refers to the estate tax as a "death tax." Some commentators argue that this is done to confuse the voters, making them think that people are taxed just for dying. Regardless of politics, the opening quotation of this chapter links together the certainty of death and taxes. In the case of the death tax, we link the concepts of death and taxes even further!

EconLinks
Find links to look at your local tax rates by clicking the State and Local Government link under the Government category.

http://econapps. swlearning.com

State and Local Taxes

State and local governments also impose various taxes, and they each place different emphasis on one tax or another. Figure 16-2 displays the various state and local taxes, as well as the overall relative importance of each type of tax in 2002.

As revealed by Figure 16-2, sales and excise taxes bring in the second-largest share of state and local tax revenue (31 percent). Sales taxes are levied on goods and services sold within the state, locality, or both. Some states exempt certain items, such as medicine and food. Other states do not. Excise taxes are placed on the sale of goods such as cigarettes, gasoline, tobacco, and alcohol. (State and local excise taxes are often placed on the same products as are federal excise taxes.) In the case of sales and excise taxes, the tax base is the market value of the purchased items.

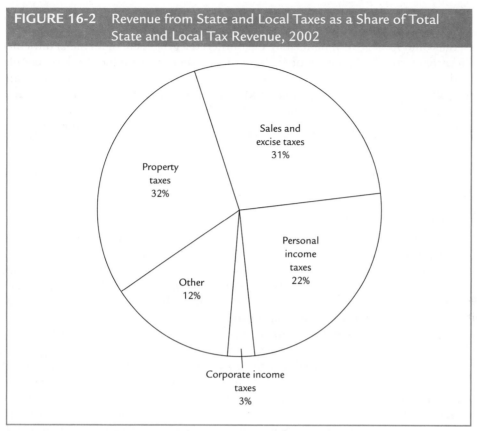

Source: U.S. Census Bureau (**www.census.gov/govs**).

Personal income taxes are also usually levied at the state (and sometimes local) level and bring in approximately 22 percent of total state and local tax revenue. In some states, there are different tax brackets and rates, as at the federal level. In other states, one tax rate applies to all people's taxable income. (The latter tax would be an example of what is often referred to as a *flat-rate tax*.) Note that various exemptions, deductions, and credits may apply to state personal income tax systems as well as those at the federal level. For example, some states have an EIC built into their state personal income taxes. Some states also have a corporate income tax, which brings in 3 percent of total state and local tax revenue.

Property taxes are levied by local governments and bring in the highest (32) percentage of *combined* state and local tax revenue. These taxes are levied directly on owners of houses and land and they depend on the value of this property. Economists usually assume that much of the property tax is passed from owner to renter (in the form of higher rents) in the case of rental housing. Property taxes are used to fund local public schools, as is discussed in greater detail in Chapters 4 and 5. Because property values are low in low-income school districts, educational opportunities are often poor in these areas.

The remaining portion of state and local taxes comes from various fees, licenses, and other miscellaneous collections, including state lotteries.

State and local governments have encountered a great deal of financial difficulty in recent years. The poor economy has reduced their tax revenue (because people with lower incomes and lower property values pay lower taxes, and these same people also purchase fewer taxable goods and services that create sales tax revenue). At the same time, transfers from the federal government to state and local governments have been restricted. Many also claim that the federal government places more mandates (rules) on state and local governments, but does not provide funding to meet these mandates. By 2003, many state and local governments were faced with the problem of scarcity and opportunity cost as they were forced to choose between the schools, prisons, and other programs that they wished to support.

Effects of Taxes on the Macroeconomy

Recall the aggregate demand curve of Chapter 15. Remember that aggregate demand is the total output (U.S. GDP) demanded by all sectors of the economy at alternative price levels. The sectors comprising aggregate demand include individual consumers, business firms, the U.S. government, and foreigners. Government taxes have an impact on the buying decisions of people within some of these groups. Let us consider the effect on individual consumers.

Suppose that the federal government increases spending on public parks by $1 million. As we know from Chapter 15, this greater spending will increase aggregate demand, as indicated by the arrow in Figure 16-3, panel A. Real GDP increases from GDP to GDP'. Now suppose that the government wishes to finance this $1 million expenditure through an increase in personal income taxes. Consider what happens when the government raises these taxes. As you and I pay more of our income to the government, we have less after-tax income to spend as we wish. As a result, our consumption spending goes down. As the consumption component of aggregate demand decreases, aggregate demand decreases as well, as shown by the lower arrow in panel B of Figure 16-3.

Even though aggregate demand falls, it will not fall as much as the increased government spending on public parks caused it to increase in the first place. The reason is that the $1 million spent on parks represents a direct component of aggregate demand, whereas the increase in taxes of $1 million causes a decrease in spending by consumers, but not by the full $1 million. The reason is that we rarely change our consumption spending by the full amount of an income change. If our income goes up by $100, we may go out and spend an additional $80. We will save the rest. When the income of consumers goes down by $1 million, they will reduce their spending by less than $1 million. Thus, spending may fall by $800,000 rather than the full $1 million.

The point of this discussion is that the rise in aggregate demand caused by increased government purchases (expenditures) will be substantially offset by the decline in aggregate demand through decreased consumer spending when taxes go up. This will not be a total offset. That is, the combined effect of the increase in government spending and taxes will be a small net increase in aggregate demand. A small expansion in the economy is represented by some small increase in GDP (from GDP to GDP″ in panel B).

The important point is as follows: *if the government finances its increased expenditures through increased taxes, a moderate expansion of the economy will occur.* A moderate ex-

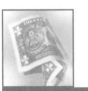

FIGURE 16-3 Increased Government Spending on Public Parks, Financed by Increased Taxes

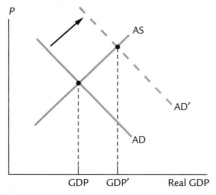

Panel A. Increased Government Spending on Parks.

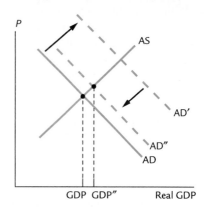

Panel B. Increased Government Spending on Parks, Financed by Increased Taxes.

Panel A shows the increase in aggregate demand that occurs as a result of the increased government spending on parks. A relatively large increase in GDP results. Panel B shows the impact of the increased government spending on parks, assuming that this spending is financed by increased government taxes. Aggregate demand increases as a result of the increased government spending, but it shifts back somewhat as a result of the increased taxes, which result in lower after-tax income for consumers, thereby reducing some of their consumption spending. The net increase in aggregate demand is very small, resulting in just a very small increase in GDP.

pansion may be appropriate if the economy is operating at a high level of capacity; too much expansion would put undesired upward pressure on the price level. On the other hand, if the goal of government is to substantially expand the economy, raising taxes to finance increased expenditures is not the most effective way to proceed. As we shall see shortly, it would be preferable to finance the increased expenditures by government borrowing.[1]

Effects of Taxes on the Income Distribution

In addition to their effect on the macroeconomy, taxes have an important impact on the distribution of income. Indeed, taxes can be designed specifically for this purpose. When economists consider the redistributive effect of taxes, they usually classify taxes according to three basic types: progressive taxes, proportional taxes, and regressive taxes. Each of these has a different impact on the income distribution.

As we noted in Chapter 13, a **progressive tax** is one that takes a larger percentage of income from high-income people than from low-income people. Note that the key phrase is *percentage of income*. We are not concerned here with absolute dollar amounts of taxes; we are concerned with the taxes that people pay *relative to their incomes*.

Progressive tax
A tax that takes a greater percentage of income from high-income people than from low-income people.

The prime example of a progressive tax is the rate structure of the federal personal income tax. Many state income taxes are progressive as well. A progressive tax rate structure relies on different income brackets. As we previously discussed, the first portion of a person's income goes into the first tax bracket and is taxed at a corresponding tax rate. The next portion of income goes into a higher tax bracket and is taxed at a higher tax rate. This procedure continues until the last increment of a person's income is placed into the highest appropriate tax bracket. Thus, the higher the person's income, the higher are the tax rates applied to increments of income. As a result, a higher-income individual pays a larger percentage of his or her income to the government; a lower-income individual pays a smaller percentage of his or her income. This type of tax places a greater burden on the higher-income individual, thereby redistributing income away from high-income households. Recall that the 1986 tax reform bill greatly reduced the progressivity of the income tax rate structure by reducing the number of brackets and by lowering the maximum tax rate. Subsequently, President George W. Bush signed legislation that further lowered these tax rates and the number of tax brackets. Also note that once various exemptions, deductions, and tax credits are taken into account, the actual income tax may be less progressive, or perhaps no longer progressive at all, because many of these tax breaks are targeted to the middle- and upper-income classes, not to the poor. (The deduction of mortgage interest, discussed in Chapter 10, is a case in point.)

Proportional tax
A tax that takes the same percentage of income from people of all income levels.

A **proportional tax** is one that takes the same percentage of income from people of all income levels. An example of this type of tax is the flat-rate personal income tax levied by various state governments. Some have proposed that a flat rate income tax be used at the federal level as well. Because a flat-rate tax takes the same percentage of income from people of all income levels, it does not redistribute income. Again, bear in mind that the proportionality of actual flat-rate taxes will depend on the existence of various exemptions, deductions, and credits combined with the taxes. The overall result may well be a regressive tax.

Regressive tax
A tax that takes a greater percentage of income from low-income people than from high-income people.

Finally, a **regressive tax** is one that takes a larger percentage of income from low-income households than from high-income ones. Most of the taxes in our country are regressive. Does this surprise you? Our regressive taxes include sales taxes, most excise taxes, property taxes, and the Social Security tax. Because some of these taxes are not levied directly on income, seeing why they are regressive is sometimes difficult. Let us consider a state sales tax as an example.

Suppose that a state levies a sales tax of 5 percent of the value of taxable goods purchased within the state. The 5 percent is the tax rate, whereas the value of taxable goods is the tax base. Actual percentage rates vary by state, as do the taxable goods covered by the tax. Let us consider two typical families, a high-income family with an annual income of $100,000, and a low-income family with an income of $10,000. The situations of these two families are outlined in Table 16-1.

Although the numbers chosen are made-up, they provide realistic results. Note that the high-income family spends $50,000 per year on taxable goods, whereas the low-income family spends only $8,000. A low-income family can be expected to have smaller consumption expenditures than a high-income family. But note that the low-income family spends a larger *percentage* of its income on taxable consumer goods. The reason is that low-income families must spend their income on necessi-

TABLE 16-1	Effects of the Sales Tax on Two Hypothetical High- and Low-Income Families in One Year	
	High-Income Family	**Low-Income Family**
Income	$100,000	$10,000
Purchases of taxable goods	$50,000	$8,000
Sales tax rate	5%	5%
Amount of sales tax paid	$2,500	$400
Amount of sales tax paid as a % of income	$\frac{\$2,500}{\$100,000} = 2.5\%$	$\frac{\$400}{\$10,000} = 4.0\%$

ties and they have little income left over for saving. Higher-income families, on the other hand, can afford to save a larger share of their income, thereby "consuming" a smaller share. Because the higher-income family does spend more money on taxable goods, in absolute terms, it will also spend more money on the state sales tax, again in absolute terms. When these tax amounts are expressed as percentages of family income, however, we see that the lower-income family pays a higher percentage of its income (4 percent) on the tax, whereas the higher-income family pays a smaller percentage (2.5 percent). The 5 percent sales tax results in the lower-income family paying a higher *percentage of its income* on the tax. Thus, the tax is regressive.

Property taxes and excise taxes are regressive for very similar reasons. Low-income families tend to spend a larger percentage of their income on goods covered by excise taxes and on housing (either owned housing or rental housing) than do higher-income families. Assuming that property taxes are passed on to renters in the form of higher rent, low-income families end up paying a larger percentage of their incomes on excise and property taxes than do higher-income families.

The Social Security tax is also highly regressive, but for different reasons. First, the Social Security tax is levied only on income earned by working: that is, on wages and salaries. Because lower-income families earn most of their income in the form of wages and salaries, all of this income is taxed. On the other hand, most of the income of high-income people may be in the form of interest, capital gains, dividends, and so on. Therefore, most of their income may not be taxed for Social Security purposes. The Social Security tax rate on eligible income is 6.2 percent. (Medicare is taxed separately.)

Social Security taxes also are regressive in that they are assessed on earnings only up to a certain limit. Beyond this limit, earnings are not taxed. This earnings limit has been $76,200 for recent years. Any income earned beyond this level is not taxed for Social Security purposes. Therefore, all of the income of low-income earners may be taxed, whereas some of the income of high-income earners may not be.

As a result of the earnings limit and the taxation of only work-earned income, low-income families pay a much larger share of their income on the Social Security tax than do high-income families. Remember that once Social Security benefits are taken into account, the overall Social Security system loses some (or all) of its regressivity. This situation is discussed more completely in Chapter 13.

EconLinks

Find links to look at the status of the economy under the General category.

http://econapps. swlearning.com

EconNews

"The Taxing Debate"

What is the appropriate distribution of taxes to help economic growth? Read this article under the Fiscal Policy category.

http://econapps. swlearning.com

Regressive taxes redistribute income in favor of the rich and to the detriment of the poor. Progressive taxes do the opposite. Over the course of the 1980s, 1990s, and early 2000s, a number of factors helped to make our overall tax system increasingly regressive. Large cuts made during the Reagan administration in personal and corporate income tax rates, our two most important progressive taxes, have reduced the significance of these two taxes as tax revenue sources. In addition, large increases in Social Security, excise, sales, and property taxes have occurred over the same time period. Thus, we are seeing less emphasis on progressive taxes and increasing emphasis on regressive ones. Changes proposed by President George W. Bush have also resulted in a more regressive tax system. Federal personal income tax rates have been cut, providing the greatest benefit to high-income individuals and further reducing the significance of this progressive tax in the overall tax system. President Bush has justified this tax cut for the rich, claiming that high-income people pay the most taxes, and should therefore receive the largest cuts. While this rationale may be valid in terms of the income tax, it is less applicable in the case of our *overall* tax system (where low-income people pay large amounts of social security, excise, sales, and property taxes). In other words, there is a move to reduce the taxes that burden the rich, but not to reduce the taxes that burden the poor. Furthermore, conservative support for the elimination of the estate tax on highly valued property, the elimination of the dividend tax, and the cut in the capital gains tax rate all benefit the rich instead of the poor. Finally, other proposals have been made by conservative politicians from time to time, including replacing the current federal personal income tax structure with a flat-rate tax, and replacing the federal personal income tax with a national sales tax. These would also make our overall tax structure far more regressive.

Effects of Taxes on the Microeconomy of Individual Markets

Excise and property taxes affect markets for specific goods. Consider an excise tax in a hypothetical local market for gasoline.

Demand and supply for gasoline are indicated by the curves D and S in Figure 16-4. Without any excise tax, equilibrium occurs at point E; equilibrium quantity equals 100 gallons, and equilibrium price equals $1.00 per gallon. Now consider the imposition of an excise tax of $0.50 per gallon. We can view this excise tax as an additional cost of production because the supplier of gasoline must actually hand the tax dollars to the government. Just as the supplier must pay wage costs, energy costs, rental costs, and so on, it now must pay an additional cost of $0.50 per gallon on each gallon of gasoline sold. Recall that any increase in the costs of production will cause supply to decrease. This is shown by the backward shift of the supply curve, as indicated by the arrow and the new supply curve S'.

With the imposition of the excise tax, a new equilibrium is established at point E'. Equilibrium quantity has fallen to 75 gallons, and the equilibrium price has risen to $1.25 per gallon. What has happened is that supply has decreased, causing gasoline prices to rise. In response to higher prices, consumers have moved back up along their demand curve, reducing the quantity they wish to buy. Both quantity demanded and quantity supplied are now at the lower level of 75 gallons.

FIGURE 16-4 Effects of an Excise Tax on a Hypothetical Market for Gasoline

A $0.50 per gallon excise tax will shift back the supply curve for gasoline. At the new equilibrium E′, the price is $1.25 per gallon and the quantity of gasoline is 75 gallons. The excise tax of $0.50 per gallon is paid by the suppliers of gasoline to the government. Because consumers pay more and suppliers keep less, both groups bear part of the burden of the excise tax.

Why has the price risen by $0.25 to $1.25, and not by the full $0.50 per gallon? The actual price increase is the result of demand and supply. Note that the vertical distance between the two supply curves (measured on the vertical axis) represents the $0.50 per gallon excise tax. The cost of supplying each gallon of gasoline has gone up by exactly this amount. But the market price of gasoline has risen by only a portion of this amount, in this case by $0.25 per gallon. The implication is that the **burden of the tax** has been borne by suppliers and consumers alike. Consumers bear a portion of the full burden of the tax in the form of the extra $0.25 they must pay for each gallon of gasoline they purchase. Suppliers bear a portion of the full burden in the form of lower profits; they now must pay an additional $0.50 for each gallon that they sell (the tax), but they receive only an additional $0.25 from consumers. The difference comes out of their pockets.

The results of this exercise are fairly typical. As a consequence of the imposition of the excise tax, a smaller quantity of the product is produced and sold, the price is higher, and both consumers and suppliers share the burden of the tax. Realize, however, that the burden need not be shared equally by these two groups. The price of a product upon which an excise tax is imposed could rise substantially, perhaps even

Burden of the tax The impact of the tax that is felt by producers and consumers. Consumers bear the burden in the form of higher prices paid for the product; producers bear the burden in the form of lower profits.

the full amount of the tax. In this case, consumers bear the entire brunt of the tax. Likewise, the price could rise only negligibly. In this event, suppliers bear the greater burden. The appendix to this chapter considers some of the circumstances that determine which group actually bears the greatest burden of any particular excise tax. Generally, consumers bear a large share of the burden of the gasoline excise tax.

Property taxes can operate in a similar way. Consider a local market for rental housing, depicted in Figure 16-5. Demand and supply determine an equilibrium quantity of housing of 1,000 units and a market rental price of $200 per unit per month. The $100 per month property tax can be viewed as an additional cost of supplying the housing, as property owners must hand the tax dollars to the government. The higher cost will be reflected in a backward shift of the supply curve to S'. A new equilibrium will be established at point E'. Quantity has decreased to 750 units, and the market rent has gone up to $250 per unit. Recall our earlier assumption that at least a portion of property taxes is passed along to renters. The analysis indicates how and why a portion of the burden is redirected. As mentioned in the appendix, the renter may indeed bear most of the burden of the tax.

GOVERNMENT BORROWING

Neither a lender nor a borrower be.

—Proverb

Despite this well-meaning advice, individual people and families do borrow money. In doing so, they go into debt. The debt may be good or bad for the family, depending on a number of factors. But what about the government? Is the country well served or poorly served when the government borrows money and in doing so goes into debt? The next several pages will help us answer this question.

Recall that the government can finance its expenditures not only through taxes but also by borrowing. The latter process occurs as the government issues securities. Anyone can purchase a government security: another level or agency of government, a bank or other financial institution, a corporation or other form of business, and individual people like us. When I purchase a government bond, I am lending my money to the government. At some specified point in the future, I will receive my money back, plus interest. Because no coercion is involved, presumably this deal is a good one for both the government and me. Is it a good deal for the economy?

To answer this question, we must consider the impact of government borrowing in a couple of respects. We will analyze the impact on the macroeconomy, on income distribution, on interest rates, and finally on the government budget and national debt in the following sections.

Effects on the Macroeconomy

Recall our earlier scenario in which the government wishes to increase spending on public parks by $1 million. As indicated before, the higher spending will cause aggregate demand to shift forward, as we see in panels A and B of Figure 16-3 on page 387. This time, taxes will not increase, since the government is financing its expenditures by borrowing. Thus, there is no reason for the aggregate demand curve to shift backward once again. The final impact of the transaction is indicated in panel A. A sig-

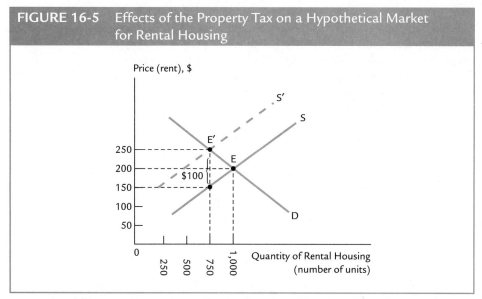

FIGURE 16-5 Effects of the Property Tax on a Hypothetical Market for Rental Housing

The property tax on rental housing will shift back the supply curve, resulting in a new equilibrium at E′. At the new equilibrium, the rental price of housing has increased from $200 to $250, but the landlord must pay $100 to the government in property tax. Because the tenant pays more and the landlord in effect receives less, both groups will bear part of the burden of the property tax. Note that the equilibrium quantity has decreased.

nificant economic expansion has occurred. Again, whether this result is desirable depends on the state of the economy. If the economy is operating at high capacity, the expansion is most likely to bring unwanted price rises in its wake. On the other hand, if the economy is operating well below capacity and perhaps is in recession, the expansion is exactly what the doctor ordered. *Government spending financed by borrowing expands the economy more than government spending financed through increased taxes.*

Effects on the Income Distribution

If I buy government bonds, I will benefit from this decision. The government will repay me at some future time, with interest to boot. Who will finance the interest payment? One possibility is that the government will merely borrow again to finance its interest expenditures. There is nothing wrong with this practice. Unlike you and me, the government can borrow indefinitely. Alternatively, the government may increase taxes to finance my interest payment. If you pay the additional tax and I receive the interest benefit, income is redistributed from you to me. I will be happy, but you will not.

The redistribution of income that occurs in this process may in fact cause greater income inequality in our country. Bond owners tend to be middle- to upper-income people; rarely do low-income people have the means to participate in this type of investment activity. On the other hand, we have seen that our tax system has become increasingly regressive. To the extent that low-income people bear a greater burden of tax payments, and high-income people receive a greater benefit from interest receipts, income redistribution occurs from the poor to the rich.

This redistribution does not mean that government borrowing is bad, per se. We can alter the impact of government borrowing on income distribution without reducing the government's borrowing ability. We can devise means to restructure government securities in ways that make them more accessible to low-income people. And of course, we can alter our national system of taxation to achieve greater progressivity, if we have the desire to do so. The negative impacts of government borrowing on the income distribution could be dealt with directly in this fashion. Finally, we know that both tax revenue and borrowed funds can be used by the government to finance policies and programs that foster greater or less equality, depending on the nature of the policies and programs.

Effects on Interest Rates

Interest rate
The percentage of borrowed funds that must be paid to the lender (or investor) for the privilege of using the funds.

Loanable funds
Money that is borrowed and lent.

We can analyze the impact of government borrowing on interest rates if we view market interest rates as simply the price of loanable funds. An **interest rate** is the percentage of borrowed funds that must be paid to the lender (or investor); **loanable funds** refers to money that is borrowed or lent. To see how interest rates are determined, we must consider the market for loanable funds. This task is not difficult because our demand and supply analysis works in the market for loanable funds just as easily as it does in the market for rental housing, pocket calculators, or corn.

Figure 16-6 shows the market for loanable funds. The quantity axis represents the quantity of loanable funds. The demand curve for loanable funds represents all who wish to borrow money: business firms, individuals like us, and, of course, our government. The curve is downward sloping, indicating that we are more willing and able to borrow money at low interest rates than at high interest rates. The supply curve for loanable funds represents all who wish to lend money, including commercial banks and credit unions. The supply of loanable funds also incorporates all individuals who place money in savings accounts (lending their money to banks) or who purchase government securities (lending their money to the government). The supply curve is upward sloping, indicating that we are more willing to lend as the interest rate that we can receive becomes higher. Note that we are simplifying by talking about "a market interest rate." In fact, there are many rates, depending on types of loans, their lengths of maturity, and whether you are borrowing or lending. We are ignoring these differences and perhaps looking at what might be an average market interest rate. Equilibrium will occur at point E, with quantity Q_0 being borrowed and lent and a market interest rate of 10 percent.

Now suppose the government wishes to finance its expenditures by issuing government securities—that is, by borrowing money. This is reflected in the increased demand for loanable funds, as shown by the new demand curve D′, which results in the new equilibrium E′. In this new equilibrium, the quantity of funds both borrowed and lent has increased to Q', and the market interest rate has risen to 12 percent. What has happened is simply that the demand for loanable funds has gone up, causing an increase in the "price" of loanable funds. Lenders have moved up along

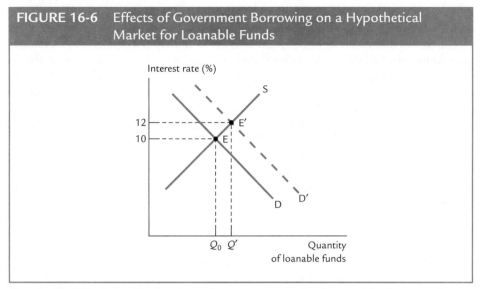

FIGURE 16-6 Effects of Government Borrowing on a Hypothetical Market for Loanable Funds

The demand for loanable funds curve D represents the demand for borrowed funds by consumers, businesses, and government. If the government wishes to increase its spending on goods and services and chooses to finance these expenditures by borrowing, the demand for loanable funds will increase to D'. This increase in demand will cause an increase in the interest rate from 10 percent to 12 percent and an increase in the amount of money borrowed and lent to Q'.

their supply curve, increasing the quantity they are willing to lend to match the increase in quantity demanded.

As a result of government borrowing, interest rates go up. The amount depends on the state of the economy and the market for loanable funds. The most serious concern about rising interest rates is their impact on business and consumer spending. As we've noted before, when interest rates are high, business firms are less likely to purchase factories and other capital equipment, and individuals are less likely to purchase big-ticket items such as cars, houses, and appliances. We simply are less willing and able to pay the higher costs of borrowing. Economists refer to this situation as **crowding out**. Government spending, financed by borrowing, has caused interest rates to rise. As a result, individuals and businesses in the private economy choose to borrow less and therefore spend less. Government spending has partially crowded out private spending. Those who wish to see a reduced role for government in our economy, and consequently an increased role for the private sector, are particularly concerned about crowding out.

Crowding out is certainly an issue, but we must keep it in perspective. First, crowding out is never complete, at least in the short run. Suppose that the government borrows and increases its spending by $1 million. This government borrowing of $1 million does not mean that there is $1 million less for the private sector to borrow and spend. Remember that the rising interest rates increase the willingness of people to lend; thus, more funds are available for everyone. Individual people and

Crowding out

A situation in which government spending, financed by borrowing, causes interest rates to rise, which results in less spending by the private economy.

businesses now borrow and spend less, but not by the full $1 million that government borrowing and spending increases. Second, rising interest rates need not occur. Recall that monetary policy can be used to control these rates. An increase in the money supply will cause interest rates to fall, offsetting the impact of the increased government borrowing on interest rates. Whether this policy is desirable again depends on the state of the economy. In an overheated economy, simultaneous fiscal and monetary expansion will probably cause an overexpansion of the economy and a serious threat of inflation. In a less-active economy, economic expansion may again be just what the doctor ordered. Economists, like politicians, are divided on the desirability of the various options. But understanding the impacts of the policy choices is important to forming an intelligent opinion.

Finally, note that a rise in interest rates, for any reason, will have some implications for international trade and finance. These implications are considered in Chapter 9.

Effects on the Government Budget and the National Debt

The federal government is too big and it spends too much money. [We need] a constitutional amendment that mandates a balanced budget.

—President Ronald Reagan, 1988

We must bring the federal budget into balance.

—President George H. W. Bush, 1989

We have an obligation to leave our children a legacy of opportunity, not debt.

—President Bill Clinton, 1996

My plan pays down an unprecedented amount of our national debt. And then, when money is still left over, my plan returns it to the people who earned it in the first place.

—President George W. Bush, 2001

EconDebate

"How Should the U.S. Budget Surplus Be Used?"

The full debate is available under the Fiscal Policy category.

http://econapps. swlearning.com

Budget deficit
The difference between federal government spending and federal government tax revenue in any one year.

Budget surplus
The difference between federal government tax revenue and federal government spending in any one year.

Every U.S. president in office during the lifetimes of most students has spoken out strongly against budget deficits. Indeed, one of the major issues of the new millennium is the government budget. Until the late 1990s, our national concern was how to manage government budget deficits. With the turn of the century, the issue became how to manage government budget surpluses. By 2002, our concern once again reverted to dealing with budget deficits, in this case, massive ones!

The **budget deficit** is simply the difference between federal government spending and federal government tax revenue in a particular year. If the government spends $1,500 billion and brings in tax revenue of $1,300 billion, we have a budget deficit of $200 billion. The deficit is the amount by which the government is currently in the red: that is, the amount that the government must borrow to make up the difference. The budget deficit is an annual concept; it represents the difference between spending and taxes over the course of any one year.

The opposite of a budget deficit is a **budget surplus**. If the government brings in tax revenue that is greater than government spending, we have a budget surplus. Thus, if the government spends $1,500 billion and brings in tax revenue of $1,700 billion, we have a budget surplus of $200 billion. Just like the budget deficit, the budget surplus is an annual concept.

In 1998, the last year of the string of federal budget deficits, the deficit was approximately $22 billion. By 1999, government tax revenue *exceeded* government spending by about $126 billion. The budget deficit had turned into a budget surplus. The year 2000 surplus was approximately $236 billion, and the surplus was $127 billion in 2001.[2] The surplus that existed during these early years of the new century ushered in vast disagreement over the best use of this money. There were those who urged the government to use the surplus to finance increased spending on social programs and transfers. Others argued that the surplus should be used to shore up the Social Security program. President George W. Bush argued that the bulk of the surplus should be used to finance tax relief. In the absence of deliberate decisions such as these, the surplus would automatically go toward reducing the national debt.

Unfortunately, the disagreement over the use of budget surpluses ended rather abruptly by 2002 and 2003, when spending for homeland defense, national defense, the fight against terrorism, and the wars in Afghanistan and Iraq caused government expenditures to spiral upward. At the same time, President Bush pushed forward the tax cuts that were discussed in the previous section. The results were ballooning budget deficits by 2002 and 2003 and projections of huge deficits in years to come. The Center for Budget and Policy Priorities reported in June 2003 that the budget deficit would be $455 billion for that year. The projections over the next 10 years are for deficits totaling $4.1 trillion if Bush is able to extend the tax cuts he initiated and follow through with some of his policy plans.[3]

The national debt is different but closely related to the budget. The **national debt** is the total amount of money owed by the federal government. It represents the accumulation of all funds borrowed by the federal government, up to the present, that have not yet been repaid. A budget deficit in any one year will increase the size of the national debt (whereas a budget surplus will decrease the national debt). Hence the concern over government borrowing. Is there anything wrong with the government running a budget deficit and incurring an increasing national debt? Most politicians say yes. Most citizens also say yes. People often make an analogy between government and individual households. They say that we ought to be responsible. We ought to spend within our means. We ought to repay prior debts before borrowing more. We cannot borrow forever. Eventually a day of reckoning will arrive; eventually there must be repayment or bankruptcy. If individual households must exhibit financial responsibility, certainly our government should do the same.

National debt
The total amount of money owed by the federal government. It represents the accumulation of all funds borrowed by the federal government that have not yet been repaid.

This analogy is not entirely appropriate, however. As we noted before, the government can continue to borrow indefinitely. Unlike individual households, the country does not have to answer to the frowning face of the bank loan officer. With no limit on borrowing, the government can continually "roll over" its debt; that is, it can continue to borrow money to repay previously borrowed money. No day of reckoning will arrive. There will be no day of bankruptcy. There will be no shortage of people and businesses willing to lend to the government.

Does this mean that the national debt causes no problems? Many of our politicians and many of our citizens believe that it does cause problems, though they often misunderstand the types of problems it creates. To complicate matters, economic conservatives have traditionally opposed a large national debt and the deficits that contribute to it, whereas economic liberals have typically been largely unconcerned. By the year 2003, however, these positions seem to have become reversed, for reasons discussed in the Viewpoint section of this chapter. To analyze the concerns about the national debt, we should begin by considering the actual size of the debt and the owners of the debt, and then we can examine the impact of the debt on our economy.

THE NATIONAL DEBT

The Size of the National Debt

Recall our discussion of gross domestic product (GDP) in Chapter 15. We recognized that any variable that is expressed in dollar terms and compared over different time periods must first be adjusted for inflation. Otherwise, increases in the value of the variable may simply express a rising average price level, not a rise in the real variable itself. The same care is necessary when considering the size of the budget deficit, as well as the size of the national debt. If we are comparing their size over time, we must adjust for inflation to eliminate the impact of rising prices. Often when the sizes of the budget deficit and the national debt are reported in newspapers and compared over different years, the writer neglects to adjust for inflation. This failure results in reporting of a grossly exaggerated increase in the size of the debt.

It is also important to use an appropriate benchmark when considering the size of the debt. Gross domestic product represents one such reference. A simple illustration should demonstrate why we should be interested in the size of the debt relative to GDP (which is really our capacity to produce and repay), and not just in the debt's size alone. Consider a simple economy with the following budget deficit in a particular year:

GDP   = $100,000
Government spending   = $20,000
Government tax revenue   = $18,000
Budget deficit   = $2,000
Budget deficit relative to GDP = $2,000/$100,000 = 2%

In this example, the budget deficit is $2,000. This deficit represents 2 percent of gross domestic product. This $2,000 is contributing to the size of the national debt. Now suppose the economy has doubled over time:

GDP   = $200,000
Government spending   = $40,000
Government tax revenue   = $36,000
Budget deficit   = $4,000
Budget deficit relative to GDP = $4,000/$200,000 = 2%

The size of the budget deficit has doubled, from $2,000 to $4,000. Yet nothing in this example should alarm us. As GDP doubles, it appears quite natural for government spending to double (as well as consumer and investment spending), for government tax revenue to double, and for the size of the deficit to double as well. Relative to GDP, however, the deficit has not grown; it remains at 2 percent. Although an enormous doubling of the budget deficit would appear to contribute to an enormously rising national debt, this example suggests no cause for concern. The national debt will grow, but we should be more interested in the size of the debt relative to GDP, just as we are interested in the size of the budget deficit relative to GDP.

TABLE 16-2	The Size of the National Debt Relative to Gross Domestic Product, Select Years, 1940 to 2001		
Year	National Debt/GDP (%)	Year	National Debt/GDP (%)
1940	53	1996	69
1946	122	1997	67
1960	56	1998	65
1970	38	1999	64
1980	33	2000	63
1990	56	2001	57
1995	68		

Source: U.S. Department of Commerce, Census Bureau, Statistical Abstract of the United States (**www.census.gov/statab**).

What it all means is this: if we wish to accurately consider the growing size of the budget deficit or the national debt, we must adjust the data for inflation. We also must consider the size of the variable relative to GDP. Our discussion of the increase in the size of the budget deficit since 2002 neglected an adjustment for inflation and GDP, but this is not a serious problem since the rise in the average price level was very low at this time and the size of GDP was not changing much over this short time period. However, since the data in Table 16-2 show the size of the national debt over a longer period of time, we must make the appropriate adjustments. The table presents the size of the national debt relative to GDP for the time period 1940 to 2001.[4]

We see from Table 16-2 that the size of the national debt relative to GDP was 53 percent in 1940, increasing to 122 percent in 1946. This dramatic increase in the national debt was caused by huge government spending during World War II. The debt relative to GDP was quite low in 1980, but it increased steadily, especially over the decade of the 1980s, until 1996. Recall that the 1980s was a time of tax cuts, but government spending on Social Security and national defense soared. The money had to be borrowed, thereby increasing the debt. For the time period of 1996 through 2001, the size of the debt relative to GDP steadily decreased, as government budget deficits fell and surpluses rose. Since then, the size of the national debt relative to GDP has risen dramatically. The recent large budget deficits similarly increase the size of the debt relative to GDP.

Who Owns the National Debt?

Recall that anyone can purchase government securities. Buyers of these securities are the owners of the national debt. Table 16-3 on page 400 indicates the percentage of the national debt that is owned by (owed to) various groups. Note that our government and government agencies own approximately 56 percent of the national debt (calculated by adding the first three items in Table 16-3). Thus, more than half of the federal debt represents transfers among different levels and agencies of government. Depository institutions (such as commercial banks) and insurance companies own 6 percent of the total, and U.S. savings bonds represent 3 percent.

TABLE 16-3 Who Owns the National Debt? (2nd quarter, 2000)	
Holder	Share of National Debt (%)
U.S. government and federal reserve banks	47
State and local governments	5
Pension funds owned by state and local governments	4
Pension funds owned privately	3
Depository institutions	4
Insurance companies	2
Mutual funds	6
U.S. savings bonds	3
Foreign and international owners	22
Other miscellaneous investors	4

Source: Based on data from the U.S. Treasury Department *Treasury Bulletin* (***www.fms.treas.gov/bulletin***).

Also note that a substantial, though relatively small, share is owed to foreigners. This group concerns some Americans the most. As interest payments are made to foreign owners of the national debt, a transfer of real resources out of the United States occurs. This circumstance is the only one in which such a transfer occurs in terms of the debt.

The Impact of the National Debt

EconNews

"Debt Has Its Virtue"

Read more under the Money and Financial System category.

http://econapps. swlearning.com

The implications of the national debt are really the implications of government borrowing that we have already considered. The negative effects of government borrowing involve an inequitable income redistribution and rising interest rates. As noted, the interest payments made to foreign people generate particular concern for some, because they represent a real transfer of income out of the United States. Some people are also concerned about a potential burden passed on to our children. This burden would take the form of taxes imposed on future generations to make interest payments to owners of government securities.

On the other hand, government borrowing has some positive consequences. It enables the government to expand the economy as needed and to make expenditures that can specifically benefit our society. Whether these are programs benefiting us directly in the present, such as Social Security and poverty reduction, or programs that invest in future generations, such as programs of health and education, the benefits accrue to our nation. These benefits must be considered whenever we concern ourselves with potential problems with the national debt.

PROPOSALS TO REQUIRE A BALANCED BUDGET

No discussion of budget deficits and the national debt is complete without a discussion of the many proposals that would require a balanced budget by the federal government. An annually balanced budget would mean no government borrowing, hence no addition to the national debt. It would mean that all government expenditures must be financed by tax revenue and that any government spending increase must be matched by an increase in tax revenue.

Unlike politicians, economists see many problems with a requirement that the federal government balance its budget. First, balancing the budget in any given year is extremely difficult. Too many variables are unknown. Suppose, for example, that the nation must deal with extensive flooding or tornado destruction. By declaring a national emergency, the federal government is committed to spending additional amounts to assist in the cleanup. Or even more to the point, suppose that the nation goes to war and increases its defense spending. These unplanned events would create a budget deficit. It's true that the government could change the tax code or establish additional taxes, but such measures would not be feasible on a regular basis. It's also true that the government could reduce its spending on other programs, but these funds may have already been committed. (Halting highway construction already under way, denying Social Security benefits already promised, or closing federal prisons just because the budget is headed into deficit would be inappropriate!)

Second, suppose that our nation is entering a recession. As you will recall from the discussion of fiscal policy in the previous chapter, the government would like to pull the nation out of the recession by increasing government spending or by reducing government taxes. In the context of a balanced budget requirement, the government can do neither because each would create a budget deficit. The government's hands are tied, as it can no longer use fiscal policy to correct the economy.

Now let's take this discussion one step further. During a recession, people lose their jobs. When people lose jobs, their incomes decline. When people's incomes decrease, they pay fewer taxes. They also are more likely to receive unemployment compensation and welfare assistance. For these reasons, an economy in recession creates an automatic decrease in government tax revenue and an automatic increase in government spending. Together, this revenue decrease and spending increase create an automatic increase in the budget deficit. (The opposite would be the case in an expansion of the economy.) Now, according to a balanced budget requirement, the government must eliminate the deficit by initiating either an increase in taxes, a decrease in government spending, or some combination of the two. Although difficult, carrying out these measures is possible. But they are exactly the *wrong* policy prescription for a nation in recession! What the government must do to correct the recession is increase its spending or decrease taxes. In other words, complying with the balanced budget amendment would exacerbate the recession and create even greater instability for the economy.

The proposals for a balanced budget requirement have come in the form of proposals for new legislation and proposals for a constitutional amendment. The proposals have varied somewhat; those that allow exceptions for periods of recession, and those that require the budget to be balanced over several years rather than in one year, mitigate some of the problems we have cited. We should keep in mind that philosophies about government spending and taxes have motivated proposals that require a balanced budget. These proposals reflect the conservative viewpoint that less government involvement in our economy is best.

As you might suspect, conservatives and liberals hold disparate views on the issues of government taxes and borrowing. Conservatives generally favor reductions in government taxes for several reasons. First, they prefer to see income remain in the hands of the private economy, rather than turned over to the government. And they prefer to see private-sector spending rather than public-sector spending. Second, they worry about the effect of various taxes on incentives. They believe that if personal income taxes are too high, people will work less. If business taxes are too high, businesses will produce less. If income from savings is taxed too much, people will save less. And the list goes on. On the other hand, liberals are more comfortable with government taxes and spending, as long as the taxes do not heavily burden the poor and the middle class. They also like to use tax credits to support what they consider worthwhile activity, such as spending on higher education or the care of elderly people.

High levels of government spending that are financed by government borrowing have historically been a real problem for conservatives. They have been concerned that attendant increases in interest rates will crowd out private spending, and they worry about the increased government spending that government borrowing permits. They have strongly and publicly argued in favor of legislation or a constitutional amendment that requires a balanced budget. Ironically, conservatives generally feel differently about government spending and budget deficits when it comes to expenditures for national defense. The huge budget deficits resulting from a combination of reduced taxes and increased defense and wartime expenditures in the last few years have not been a problem for many conservatives of the Bush administration. There is historical precedent for such a view. In the 1980s, another conservative president (Ronald Reagan) was unconcerned with the budget deficits that resulted from tax cuts and massive increases in national defense.

It is also ironic that current liberals are now expressing alarm over the recent buildup of the budget deficit. Although historically unconcerned with government borrowing, they are now worried about the rising budget deficits caused by the tax cuts and expanded defense spending. It would appear that, for both liberals and conservatives, the issue of government borrowing and budget deficits hinges on the purpose of government spending. Liberals prefer spending for domestic social programs and tend to be uncomfortable with government borrowing to support large defense spending and tax cuts. Conservatives are untroubled by budget deficits as long as they are caused by the same defense spending and tax cuts.

SUMMARY

The U.S. government has two means of acquiring financing for its expenditure programs: taxing and borrowing. The largest source of federal government tax revenue is the personal income tax. Other federal taxes include social insurance taxes, the corporate income tax, excise taxes, and estate taxes. Individual state and local governments commonly levy sales and excise taxes, personal income taxes, corporate income taxes, and property taxes. Government expenditure programs that are financed by taxes have a moderate impact on the macroeconomy in terms of expanding gross domestic product. In addition, taxes have important implications for income distribution, depending on whether they are progressive, proportional, or regressive. The federal personal income tax—and some state personal income taxes—have progressive rate structures. Sales and excise taxes, property taxes, and social insurance taxes are all regressive. Finally, excise and property taxes have an impact on the markets for specific goods such as gasoline, alcohol, cigarettes, and rental housing. They generally cause prices (and rents) to rise and quantity consumed to decrease.

Government borrowing occurs whenever the government issues government bonds and treasury bills. When you and I purchase a government bond, we are in effect lending our money to the government. Government expenditures, financed by borrowing, cause the greatest expansion of the macroeconomy in terms of increasing gross domestic product. Government borrowing also has an effect on income distribution in that it benefits higher-income owners of financial securities and harms lower-income taxpayers. Finally, government borrowing has the effect of raising interest rates, which may serve to reduce private investment expenditures within the economy. This process is referred to as crowding out.

The budget deficit is the difference between government spending and government tax revenue. The deficit is an annual concept; it represents the amount that the government borrows in a particular year. Similarly, the budget surplus is the difference between government tax revenue and government spending. When the budget is in deficit, politicians argue about how to reduce the deficit. When the budget is in surplus, politicians argue over how to spend the surplus. The national debt is the total amount of money owed by the government. A budget deficit in any one year will increase the size of the national debt.

The size of the national debt is exaggerated when we do not make adjustments for inflation and properly compare the debt with the nation's gross domestic product. Much of the national debt is owed to various levels and agencies of government; smaller shares are owed to businesses and financial institutions, individuals, and foreigners. Any negative effects of government borrowing and the national debt must be considered relative to the positive results of government borrowing. These results include expansion of our economy and spending on government programs that benefit our nation.

NOTES

1. In the macroeconomic examples in this chapter, we deliberately simplify the effects of changes in purchases (spending) by ignoring the multiplier effect. The *multiplier effect* is a "spiraling effect" of initial spending changes on larger ultimate spending changes in the economy. This simplification does not detract from the conclusions of this chapter.

2. U.S. Census Bureau (**www.census.gov**). These statistics include revenue through Social Security taxes.

3. Center on Budget and Policy Priorities (**www. centeronbudget.org**, July 15, 2003).

4. It is not necessary to adjust the size of the national debt for inflation when we are considering the debt as a share of GDP. This is because we would adjust both the numerator and denominator of the fraction and the inflation adjustment would cancel itself out.

DISCUSSION QUESTIONS

1. Consider the recent cuts in the federal personal income tax. What is the effect on the income distribution? Do you believe this is fair? Why or why not?

2. Consider other proposals to replace the federal income tax structure with a flat-rate tax structure or to replace the income tax with a national sales tax. How would these actions affect the income distribution? Do you agree with these proposals? Why or why not?

3. How do you feel about the elimination of the estate tax on extremely high values of inheritance? Why does the Bush administration refer to this tax as a "death tax"?

4. How do you feel about a reduction in the capital gains tax? an increase in the Earned Income Credit? What is the effect of these on the income distribution?

5. Should the Social Security tax be overhauled to reduce its regressivity? Why or why not? How might this be done?

6. Why does the government place excise taxes on goods such as cigarettes and alcohol? Is it because these products are "sinful"? (These taxes are often called "sin taxes.") Do you believe that we cut down on our consumption of these goods by very much as a result of excise taxes? What does our response imply for the amount of government excise tax revenue?

7. What sort of tax system do you feel is the fairest? What are the advantages and disadvantages of regressive, progressive, and proportional taxes?

8. During the 2001 presidential election campaign, Al Gore and other Democrats proposed the addition of tax credits for a variety of "worthwhile" activities, rather than lowering tax rates across the board. In other words, people who pay college tuition, families that care for elderly and disabled relatives, individuals who drive fuel-efficient vehicles, and those who save for retirement would receive new tax breaks. Gore also proposed a major increase in the standard deduction and in the EIC, increasing the latter by approximately $500 over 10 years. What do you think of these proposals? What do you think of the conservative argument that government should not be involved in creating incentives for various types of behavior?

9. Visit the Census Bureau Web site (**www. census.gov**) to find current information on federal government spending and tax revenue. What is the major spending category? What is the major tax revenue source?

10. Visit the Treasury Bulletin Web site (**www. fms.treas.gov/bulletin**) to determine the current size of the budget surplus and of the national debt. How have these figures changed, if at all, from the data in this textbook?

11. Do you believe that the current budget deficit should be reduced? If so, how should it be done? Should taxes be increased? Should government spending be reduced? If so, which specific programs should be reduced?

12. Are you concerned about the national debt? Why or why not? Has your opinion changed as a result of what you have learned in this chapter? Has your opinion changed as a result of the large buildup of expenditures related to national and homeland defense and the wars in Iraq and Afghanistan?

CHAPTER 16 APPENDIX: THE IMPACT OF EXCISE TAXES WITH PERFECTLY INELASTIC DEMAND AND SUPPLY

W e have already considered the impact of an excise tax on gasoline and the closely related case of a property tax on rental housing. Let us consider a few additional cases of excise taxes to further "observe" the workings of our economy. For more detailed information about elasticity, refer to the appendix of Chapter 2 on crime.

Consider a hypothetical market for cigarettes. In Figure 16-7, an extreme assumption is made. The supply curve is drawn with its usual shape, but the demand curve is perfectly vertical. Consider what this vertical demand curve means. Although price is free to move up and down, the quantity demanded will always remain fixed. That is, people wish to buy a particular quantity of cigarettes and refuse to adjust this quantity merely because of a price change. Economists refer to this lack of adjustment to price changes as a **perfectly inelastic demand**. Of course, perfectly inelastic demand isn't entirely realistic. Although many people are so addicted to cigarettes that they appear willing to pay almost any price for the product, at least some smokers (particularly teenagers) will adjust quantity demanded in response to price changes. But we'll ignore this possibility and assume for simplicity that cigarette smokers will pay any price, as long as they can get their desired quantity of cigarettes. Equilibrium occurs at point E, with a market price of $1.50 per pack, and an equilibrium quantity of 5,000 packs of cigarettes.

Perfectly inelastic demand
Demand in which buyers are completely unresponsive to changes in price.

FIGURE 16-7 Effects of an Excise Tax in a Hypothetical Market for Cigarettes with Perfectly Inelastic Demand

An excise tax of $0.50 per pack of cigarettes will cause a backward shift in the supply curve from S to S'. At the new equilibrium E', the price of cigarettes has increased from $1.50 to $2.00 per pack, the full amount of the tax. Consumers will bear the full burden of an excise tax when the demand curve is perfectly inelastic.

Now consider the imposition of a $0.50 per pack excise tax. As you know, this tax will result in a backward shift of the supply curve to S'. A new equilibrium results at E', at which point a higher price is charged for the cigarettes. Recall that the vertical distance between the two supply curves represents the amount of the tax. Note that the price has gone up by the full amount of the tax, from $1.50 to $2.00 per pack. Equally important, the quantity of cigarettes bought and sold has not changed at all.

What has happened is that supply has decreased, pushing up the market price of cigarettes. But consumers have *not* responded in the usual fashion; they have refused to cut down on their purchases of cigarettes. As a result of this inflexibility (inelasticity), they incur the full burden of the tax. They pay the full additional $0.50 in the form of a higher price; suppliers bear no burden whatsoever.

Although this case is an extreme and somewhat unrealistic one, it does demonstrate an important principle. As consumers are more unresponsive to price changes (that is, as they have a more inelastic demand), they will bear a larger burden of any excise tax. This is also true in the case of excise taxes on gasoline and alcohol and the similar case of property taxes on rental housing. It is also true of the highly addictive drugs mentioned in the appendix to Chapter 2. All of these products have an inelastic demand (though not perfectly vertical).

Now let's consider an opposite case, shown in Figure 16-8. Let's analyze the local farmers' market in your town, where local growers try to sell their tomatoes. On any given day, let's assume that

FIGURE 16-8   Effects of an Excise Tax in a Hypothetical Market for Tomatoes with Perfectly Inelastic Supply

An excise tax of $1 per pound of tomatoes would ordinarily be reflected in a backward shift of the supply curve. When supply is perfectly inelastic, we can express this shift as a vertical extension of the original supply curve. Equilibrium remains at point E, and the price remains at $2 per pound. Because the supplier must pay $1 per pound to the government, but receives no increase in the price paid by the consumer, the supplier bears the full burden of the excise tax when supply is perfectly inelastic.

growers have a fixed supply of tomatoes. This quantity is available for sale, regardless of the price it can command, because the tomatoes have already been picked. No others are available on this day, and those already picked cannot be saved for another day (let's assume they turn into mush on day 2). This kind of situation results in a market for tomatoes in which the demand curve has its normal slope, but the *supply curve* is now perfectly vertical. Equilibrium occurs at point E, with a market price of tomatoes of $2 per pound and an equilibrium quantity of 50 pounds of tomatoes.

Now consider an excise tax imposed by local authorities on the sale of tomatoes. Let's suppose this tax is $1 per pound. We would like to shift the supply curve by the vertical distance of the tax. There is no way to go but up, however. We cannot shift the curve in the usual fashion; we can indicate the shift merely as a vertical extension S'. The equilibrium remains at point E, with no change in quantity or price.

Why doesn't the price change? Why don't the growers say to heck with the market (or something similar) and raise their price by $1 anyway? Well, they're certainly free to do that. But look at the problem that would result. At a price of $3 per pound, quantity demanded falls to 25 pounds, but quantity supplied remains unchanged (as we know it must). A surplus of tomatoes is the result. The natural process we considered in Chapter 1 will result in a bidding down of the price as the only means of eliminating the surplus. Farmers are stuck with the realities of the market; their inability to alter their quantity supplied means they are stuck with the entire burden of the tax. They pay an extra $1 to the government, but they receive not one extra penny from consumers. This time, producers have the **perfectly inelastic supply**. This extreme example gives way to the more general result that the *more unresponsive suppliers are to price changes (that is, the more inelastic their supply), the greater the burden of the excise tax they will bear.*

The results of the cigarette and tomato cases can be generalized in a number of respects. *First, the group—be it consumers or producers—that is more unresponsive (inelastic) to price changes bears the greater burden of any excise tax. Second, this principle applies to any situation in which production costs increase,* whether because of excise taxes, government regulations for safety or pollution standards, increased energy prices, or whatever. When rising costs of production cause a decrease in supply, the price will rise by some amount that depends on the relative elasticity of demand and supply. The more inelastic the demand, the more the increased cost will be passed on to consumers in the form of increased prices. The more inelastic the supply, the more the cost will be borne by producers in the form of lower profits, and the less probable it is that prices will rise very much.

Perfectly inelastic supply
Supply in which producers are completely unresponsive to changes in price.

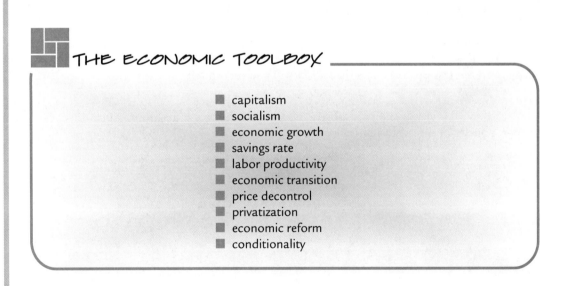

**Chapter 8
Market Power**
How does world-
wide market power
affect the less-
developed country
economies?

**Chapter 7
World Poverty**
Do the factors con-
tributing to world-
wide economic
growth increase or
reduce world
poverty?

**Chapter 15
Government
Macroeconomic
Policy**
What is the link between
supply-side macro policy
and economic growth?

**Chapter 3
The Environment**
How does environmental
protection affect economic
growth?

**Chapter 17
Globally Free Markets
for the Twenty-First
Century?**

**Chapter 9
International Trade**
How does international
trade affect worldwide
economic growth?

**Chapter 16
Taxes, Borrowing,
and the National
Debt**
How does tax policy and
government borrowing af-
fect economic growth?

**Chapter 6
U.S. Poverty**
Do the factors contributing to U.S. economic
growth increase or reduce U.S. poverty?

THE ECONOMIC TOOLBOX

- capitalism
- socialism
- economic growth
- savings rate
- labor productivity
- economic transition
- price decontrol
- privatization
- economic reform
- conditionality

GLOBALLY FREE MARKETS FOR THE TWENTY-FIRST CENTURY?

Year after year in Washington, . . . debates seem to come down to an old, tired argument: on one side, those who want more government regardless of the cost; on the other, those who want less government, regardless of the need. We should leave those arguments to the last century, and chart a different course.

—President George W. Bush, Address of the President to the Joint Session of Congress, February 27, 2001

More government or less government: that has been the debate throughout the last century, as well as throughout this textbook. As indicated in the quotation opening this chapter, President George W. Bush believes this is a "tired" debate, one that should be left behind. As we shall see, however, the world has recently embraced a direction decidedly in favor of globally free markets—markets characterized by minimal government involvement. But what about the future?

The title of this chapter ends with a question mark. Although the direction of change is clear, there is no reason to expect that free markets will work for all countries and all times. There is also no reason to assume that the transition to free markets will go smoothly for all nations or that a return to policies of the past will not occur.

MARKETS

Throughout this book, we have made repeated reference to demand and supply and the workings of markets in general. We also have made repeated reference to government intervention in the economy. The proper role for government versus the proper role for the marketplace has prompted heated discussion between economists and politicians for decades. The respective roles for government and market have been the focal point for the Viewpoint sections throughout this text. In terms of economic philosophy and in U.S. terminology, those who favor a limited role for government are generally referred to as conservatives, whereas those who favor a greater role for government are regarded as liberals. The conservative view maintains that free markets are

Capitalism
An economic system wherein the economic decisions are made by the private sector via the marketplace and the means of production are owned by the private sector.

Socialism
An economic system wherein the economic decisions are made by the public (government) sector and the means of production are owned by the public sector.

Western industrialized world
The industrialized capitalist countries of the world.

Formerly socialist industrialized world
The industrialized ex-socialist countries of eastern Europe.

Less-developed world
The less-developed countries of the world.

efficient and provide the proper incentives for economic prosperity and growth to occur. Government interference in properly functioning markets can only create inefficiencies and restrict growth; limiting the government role as much as possible is best.

This conservative view was evident in the discussion of supply-side policy in Chapter 15. Supply-side economists favor reductions in government regulations, taxes, programs, and transfers. Their view is that the marketplace works efficiently; we must untie the hands of businesses and consumers to enable them to make their own private decisions, and the economy will be better as a result.

Liberals, on the other hand, see the marketplace as imperfect. In their view, markets are not necessarily equitable, and sometimes not even efficient. Furthermore, society has goals, such as environmental protection, care for the poor and elderly, and economic stabilization, that cannot be met by the marketplace operating freely on its own. Liberals believe that the government must intervene in markets to achieve these goals.

Most economies have some combination of markets and government involvement. Some countries are more heavily capitalist, whereas some are predominantly socialist. Under **capitalism**, economic decisions are made by the private sector (individuals and private business) via the marketplace, and the means of production (factories, equipment, and land) are owned by this private sector. Under **socialism**, by contrast, economic decisions are made by the public sector (the government), and the means of production are owned or controlled by this public sector. Under capitalism, consumers and producers interact through the marketplace, responding to market-determined prices. Under socialism, the government has a more prominent role in determining which goods will be produced, how they will be produced, and what their prices will be.

Keep in mind that capitalism and socialism refer to economic systems. They imply nothing about political systems, such as democracy and communism. Certainly, a socialist economy may exist under either communism (Vietnam) or democracy (Chile); and a capitalist economy may exist under communism (Hong Kong) or democracy (the United States). In this text, we are focusing our attention on economic systems.

The movement toward free markets is a global phenomenon, the direction entailing different circumstances in different parts of the globe. We will consider each of the three major regions of the world in turn. We will define the **Western industrialized world** as the industrialized capitalist countries of the world, including the United States, Canada, most of western Europe, and other countries (including Japan) that have achieved high economic performance through predominantly stable market conditions. We will define the **formerly socialist industrialized world** as the industrialized ex-socialist countries of eastern Europe. These countries include the former Soviet Union and much of the rest of eastern Europe. Finally, the **less-developed world** encompasses all of the less-developed countries (LDCs), including most countries of Africa, Asia, and Latin America. These countries are often referred to as Third World countries.

One more term should be clarified. Economists often refer to the changes taking place in the formerly socialist and less-developed countries as **liberalism** (or sometimes neo-liberalism). This term is confusing, because it refers to a movement toward markets with less government intervention, rather than the traditional liberal philosophy we have described. Do not confuse the words *liberal* and *liberalism*. The first implies government involvement in the economy; the latter implies change toward free markets.

THE WESTERN INDUSTRIALIZED WORLD: ECONOMIC GROWTH

Conservative Republicans controlled the U.S. presidency for the 12 years from 1981 to 1992. And although a Democrat became president in 1993, conservative Republicans took control of both houses of Congress in 1994. A conservative Republican once again took the presidential office in 2001, with an administration that includes conservatives from prior Republican administrations. President George W. Bush's views toward tax policy, education, health care, the environment, and government regulation reflect the familiar undercurrent of supply-side economics and a philosophy of free markets with a minimal economic role for government.

Liberalism A movement toward freer markets.

This conservative framework has not been unique to the United States. In many of the larger democracies of the Western industrialized world, a conservative philosophy has resulted in restricted government involvement in their economics and more focus on free markets. Even the Social Democrats in Germany have moved to reduce transfer programs and the general role of government in the economy, although these efforts have run into significant resistance. Members of popular "populist" movements in the Scandinavian countries are demanding less government involvement, but they have not yet changed the overall role of government in these economies. Throughout western Europe, it is argued that markets create economic growth, whereas too much government interference stifles it. Economic growth drives the Western industrialized world in the new century.

Economic growth A sustained increase in production, represented by an outward shift of the production possibilities curve. An increase in GDP (or GDP per capita) over an extended time period.

Economic Growth Rates

Recall that **economic growth** is defined as a sustained increase in production. One standard measure of economic growth is the annual growth rate of GDP, averaged over a period of several years. (An alternative measure, the growth rate of GDP per capita, was used in Chapter 7.) Table 17-1 displays average annual GDP growth rates for selected Western industrialized nations for the time period 1990 to 2001. As revealed by the data, these growth rates generally range from about 1.0 to 4.0 percent

TABLE 17-1	Average Annual Economic Growth Rates, Select Western Industrialized Countries, 1990–2001		
Country	**Average Annual Growth of GDP (%)**	**Country**	**Average Annual Growth of GDP (%)**
Ireland	7.6	Belgium	2.1
Australia	4.0	Sweden	2.0
United States	3.5	France	1.8
Canada	3.0	Italy	1.6
Netherlands	2.8	Germany	1.5
Spain	2.6	Japan	1.3
United Kingdom	2.6	Switzerland	0.9

Source: Data from World Bank, World Development Report 2003 (New York: Oxford University Press, 2003).

FIGURE 17-1   Effects of Supply-Side Policy on the Macroeconomy

Supply-side policy is designed to cause an increase in aggregate supply, as shown by the shift of the aggregate supply curve AS to AS′. The result is an increase in GDP to GDP′ and a reduction in the average price level from P to P′.

per year (with the exception of more rapidly growing Ireland). The United States ranks at the high end, with an average growth rate of 3.5 percent per year.

The increase in GDP that underlies the growth rates in Table 17-1 can be discussed in the framework of aggregate supply (in the short run) and production possibilities (in the long run).

Aggregate Supply and Production Possibilities

Supply-side philosophies are based on the idea that reductions in government regulations, programs, taxes, and transfers create incentives for greater productivity, thereby increasing aggregate supply. This forward shift in the aggregate supply curve would be associated with an increase in gross domestic product. Figure 17-1 summarizes the desired effects of supply-side policy.

Supply-side policies are intended to increase GDP, but a sustained expansion of GDP requires additional policies that create long-term changes. These fundamental changes can be analyzed in the context of the production possibilities curve discussed in Chapter 1.

Recall that the production possibilities curve shows the alternative combinations of the maximum amounts of output that an economy can produce if all of its resources and technology are fully and efficiently utilized. The economy can achieve higher levels of production if the production possibilities curve shifts outward over time. We have defined economic growth as a sustained expansion of output. The factors that cause this outward shift in production possibilities include an increase in the quantity or quality of society's resources or an improvement in technology. These factors can generate a sustained expansion of output—that is, economic growth.

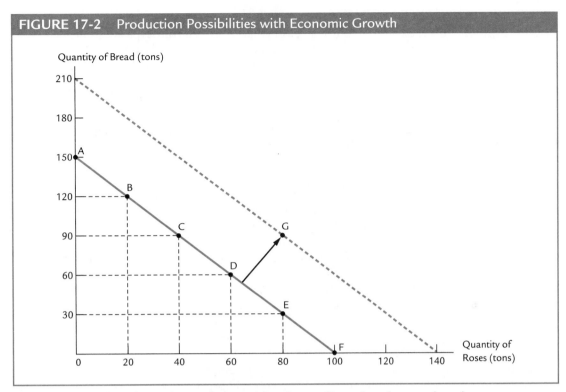

FIGURE 17-2 Production Possibilities with Economic Growth

Points A through F show alternative combinations of bread and roses that the economy can produce. More of both bread and roses can be produced when the production possibilities curve shifts outward as a result of economic growth.

Policies to Achieve Economic Growth

The production possibilities curve from Chapter 1 is repeated in Figure 17-2. Let us consider four factors contributing to economic growth. These factors are central to current discussions of economic growth; they are an increase in capital, an improvement in technology, an improvement in labor productivity, and a decrease in unnecessary regulation. As we examine these factors, we can consider government policy with respect to each of them.

An Increase in Capital

Economic growth can occur if there is a sustained increase in the quantity of physical capital: that is, an increase in our nation's stock of factories, equipment, machinery, and the like. This increase in capital is made possible by an increase in investment, and investment is made possible by saving—either private saving by households and businesses or public saving through government taxes.

Savings rate Total savings divided by gross domestic product.

   High investment activity necessitates a high **savings rate**, which is defined here as total savings divided by total GDP. The current U.S. savings rate is around 17 percent, up from 15 percent in 1990. The U.S. savings rate is among the lowest in the

Western industrialized world, along with that of Greece, Portugal, and the United Kingdom. Savings rates in the 20 to 29 percent range are typical for most countries in the Western industrialized world, but several countries (Ireland, Japan, and Norway) have even higher rates. The relatively low rate of the United States concerns many economists.[1]

Some expect the U.S. savings rate to increase in the twenty-first century as the baby-boomer generation grows older, enjoying higher incomes and finishing their payments for houses and education for their children. However, government savings and dissavings will play a role as well. When the government spends less than it brings in through tax revenue, it engages in saving. When it spends more than its tax revenue, it engages in dissaving. The recent spate of budget surpluses encouraged those who sought a higher U.S. savings rate. However, the more recent tax cuts of the Bush administration, coupled with increased expenditures on homeland security and national defense, imply continued government dissaving for the foreseeable future.

Numerous efforts and proposals have been made to increase the national savings rate through supply-side policy. These efforts and proposals have been aimed at increasing incentives for households and businesses to save and invest. The 1981 tax law accelerated tax write-offs for new investment by businesses, greatly reducing corporate income taxes. The 1981 and subsequent tax laws provided tax breaks to households placing income into individual retirement accounts (IRAs) and 401(k) accounts. There have also been repeated efforts to reduce the capital gains tax. As discussed in Chapter 16 on taxes, a **capital gain** is the net income earned when one sells an asset at a higher price than was paid for the asset. Proposals to cut the capital gains tax have been controversial because the majority of the tax benefits accrues to the wealthiest Americans, the ones who are more likely to receive capital gains.

Finally, there have been repeated proposals for a **consumption tax** to replace our current personal income tax. Like a national sales tax, a consumption tax taxes only the share of household income that is spent on consumer goods and services; it does not tax the portion of income that is saved. Although the goal is to provide greater incentives for saving, this tax would place the greatest burden on low-income individuals, who by necessity must spend virtually all of their incomes on consumption. This would represent a very regressive tax (recall the definition of a regressive tax in Chapter 16) unless deductions, credits, or a progressive rate structure were built in to relieve the poor.

If these types of policies prove successful in increasing savings, we would expect to see an expansion in investment in our nation's stock of physical capital. The expansion of our nation's factories, equipment, and machinery would result in an expansion of gross domestic product—that is, in economic growth.

Although most of the conservative emphasis has been on providing incentives for increased private saving and investment, liberal interest in increasing government investment should not be overlooked. The government can play an important role by investing in highways, mass transit, and airports, as well as schools and health care facilities. Since all of these forms of investment can improve the business environment, as well as the productivity of workers, they can enhance both the physical and human capital of our nation.

Capital gains
The net income received when an asset is bought at a particular price and sold at a higher price.

Consumption tax
A hypothetical tax on the portion of income that is spent on consumer goods and services, as opposed to income that goes into savings.

An Improvement in Technology

Technology can be thought of as ways of using available resources to produce output. Improvements in technology enable us to produce more output, given our limited resources. These improvements are embodied in new and more efficient machines, new products, and new methods of production.

Technological advance depends on research and development (R&D). Some 3,676 scientists and engineers are engaged in R&D per each million people in the United States, placing it second behind Japan (with 4,909 scientists per million people).[2]

Government policies can again be used to encourage research and development. The government can increase university funding available for research and offer tax breaks for businesses that engage in research and development. The government also can provide patent protection to developers of new products. A **patent** is a government grant of exclusive rights to use or sell a new technology for a period of time. Without patents, other businesses might copy the new technology or product, thereby creating profits for themselves at the expense of the developer. Without patents, businesses have little incentive to develop new products. Patents have been extremely important in areas such as pharmaceuticals, communications technology, and consumer goods. The United States ranks second only to Japan (again) in the number of patents applied for annually. Residents of Japan applied for 351,000 patents, whereas residents of the U.S. applied for 126,000.

Nowhere has technological advance been more prominent than in the area of computers. Indeed, investment in information technology, including computers, software, communications networks, and Internet infrastructure, has contributed to a large share of economic growth in recent years. The United States has the largest number of personal computers per 1,000 people in the world: 459. It also has the highest number of Internet hosts per 10,000 people (close to 2,000). Computer technology has enabled U.S. business to produce more and better products at the same or lower costs of production. It has also been a major factor in improving labor productivity.

> **Technology**
> Ways of using available resources to produce output.

> **Patent**
> A government grant of exclusive rights to use or sell a new technology or product for a period of time.

An Improvement in Labor Productivity

Labor productivity is defined as total output per average work hour, calculated as gross domestic product divided by the number of work hours performed in the economy. Annual U.S. labor productivity growth, which lagged in the 1970s and 1980s, has now soared to around 3 percent per year. Labor productivity hinges on the type and amount of capital and technology used in conjunction with labor, and these, of course, have improved in recent years. Keep in mind, however, that labor productivity also depends on human capital. Human capital includes the skills and abilities of people. Once again, government support for training programs, education, health, and nutrition all remain important for ensuring high levels of human capital.

> **Labor productivity**
> Total output per average work hour, calculated as GDP divided by the number of work hours.

A Decrease in Regulation

The government regulates business in a variety of ways, including protections for consumers of pharmaceuticals, food, and manufactured goods; safeguards for workers in industry; and protection of the environment. In light of recent deaths caused by unsafe tires and certain pharmaceutical drugs, the necessity for wisely developed government regulations is clear. On the other hand, unwise and unnecessary regulation merely increases business costs and decreases output. Therefore, cutting unwise regulation is a desirable policy and is conducive to economic growth. The problem, of course, is recognizing which regulations are harmful and which are beneficial.

Generally speaking, economic conservatives prefer less government regulation, whereas economic liberals prefer more. The supply-side policies since the early 1980s include widespread cuts in government regulations. Environmental protection is a good case in point. President Ronald Reagan and the first President George Bush greatly reduced government regulations in this area. Many of President Bill Clinton's proposed regulations met a hostile Congress and were not passed. President George W. Bush has continued the trend toward less environmental regulation and a more industry-friendly environmental policy. Although this policy may provide some short-run benefit to the economy through a reduction in the compliance costs of business and a resulting forward shift of aggregate supply, the long-run costs might outweigh this benefit. Just as an increase in productive resources will shift the production possibilities curve outward over time, a decrease in our natural resources caused by environmental damage and resource depletion will shift the curve inward. The capacity of our nation to produce and grow will be compromised, and the quality of life of our citizens will decline.

 As suggested in Chapter 3 on the environment, environmental protection is a global necessity. Deforestation and the burning of fossil fuels contribute to global warming and loss of precious biodiversity. Acid rain destroys crops, waterways, and capital structures across countries. Use of certain chemicals destroys the ozone layer. Air and water pollution know no boundaries.

In the final days of his administration, President Clinton considered but ultimately decided against an executive order that would have protected nearly 60 million acres of U.S. forested area by prohibiting oil exploration in Alaska's Arctic National Wildlife Refuge. President George W. Bush's plan for oil exploration in this refuge is a central part of his energy policy. Clearly, a battle looms between the president and environmental advocates in Congress. Similarly, an international battle hovers over the issue of global warming. President Bush opposes the 1997 Kyoto Accord, signed by President Clinton, which forces industrial nations to reduce greenhouse gases. This treaty is seen as critical to reducing the problem of global warming and is discussed in more detail in Chapter 3 on the environment. Other global environmental issues are discussed in that chapter as well.

Implications of Growth for the Twenty-First Century

The market-oriented growth policies of the Western industrialized world are likely to persist for at least the near future. However, there may be a cyclical movement of philosophy from a restricted government role to an expanded government role and back again, as dissatisfaction with the drawbacks of either extreme becomes evident. In the United States, post–World War II economic growth did little to mitigate extremely high poverty rates. The War on Poverty and the civil rights movement of the 1960s addressed the needs of the population to which the prosperity of the 1950s did not trickle down. Yet the policies of the 1960s and 1970s brought forth a conservative backlash as politicians in the 1980s and 1990s sought to reverse years of affirmative action and antipoverty policies. In the twenty-first century, concern for the

EconNews

"Working Longer and Harder"

Find out which country is the most productive by reading this article under the Labor Markets category.

http://econapps. swlearning.com

people left behind from the prosperity of worldwide economic growth may well again precipitate a greater call for government response.

THE FORMERLY SOCIALIST INDUSTRIALIZED WORLD: ECONOMIC TRANSITION

The recent changes in eastern Europe are nothing short of revolutionary. The Cold War has ended. Germany is reunified, and the Berlin Wall is down. The Soviet Union no longer exists; it has been divided into some 15 independent nations (the largest of which is Russia). And finally, the formerly socialist economies of eastern Europe are now undergoing an economic transition toward capitalism.

This transition has achieved varied levels of success, as evidenced by diverse economic growth rates. Table 17-2 displays the variation in growth rates for selected countries of the formerly socialist industrialized world over the period 1990 to 2001. More successful countries such as Poland and Albania have the highest average annual growth rates of 4.5 percent and 3.7 percent, respectively. Less successful countries such as Moldova and Ukraine have growth rates of −8.4 percent and −7.9 percent, respectively. Russia also has a negative average annual growth rate: −3.7 percent for the time period. A negative growth rate means that the production of goods and services is declining. The good news is that most of the growth rates in this region are now improving.

The most prominent elements of the transition to capitalism are the movement toward market-determined prices and the process of privatization, as well as the development of entrepreneurship. Russia has experienced some of the difficulties inherent in the transition process. Nevertheless, in terms of entrepreneurship, there is no question that everyday Russian citizens have embraced entrepreneurial activities; whether in the form of kiosks lining the streets of Moscow's famous Arbat and metro stops, babushkas selling homemade fast foods and household articles at every

TABLE 17-2	Average Annual Economic Growth, Select Formerly Socialist Industrialized Countries, 1990–2001		
Country	**Average Annual Growth of GDP (%)**	**Country**	**Average Annual Growth of GDP (%)**
Poland	4.5	Romania	−0.3
Albania	3.7	Armenia	−0.7
Slovenia	2.9	Belarus	−0.8
Slovak Republic	2.3	Bulgaria	−1.5
Czech Republic	1.1	Russia	−3.7
Croatia	1.1	Georgia	−5.6
Yugoslavia	0.7	Ukraine	−7.9
Estonia	0.2	Moldova	−8.4

Source: Data from World Bank, World Development Report 2003 *(New York: Oxford University Press, 2003).*

bus stop, teenagers selling gasoline along highways near the long lines at gas stations, professionals moonlighting as translators and drivers, and residents seeking Western partners in Russian joint ventures.[3] Problems in Russia are more evident in the area of prices and privatization.

Market-Determined Prices

Recall the efficiencies associated with market-determined prices. Demand and supply equate so that shortages and surpluses are eliminated. (It is when the government intervenes by setting rental ceilings in housing or price supports in agriculture, for example, that we end up with shortages or surpluses.) In a free market, the high prices of scarce goods encourage consumers to be frugal in their use of the goods and encourage suppliers to expand production of the goods. Shortages do not result. On the other hand, the low prices of plentiful goods encourage consumers to use the goods more extensively and encourage suppliers to produce fewer of these goods and shift production away from these goods and toward a greater number of goods more desirable to consumers. Surpluses are thus prevented.

Under socialism, the government sets the prices of goods and services. Prices have traditionally been set artificially low in the socialist economies of eastern Europe. For example, consumers have been able to afford to buy basic items of food, clothing, and gasoline. Artificially low prices operate like price ceilings, however, and shortages are the result. So, although people could afford to purchase needed items, these goods were often unavailable in stores. People would expend considerable time and energy standing in long lines and leaving their jobs to rush to stores whenever new supplies arrived.

These shortages are largely relics of the past. Prices of most items have been allowed to rise to market-determined levels in most eastern European countries. In other words, **decontrol of prices** has occurred. Government no longer sets the prices. Because wages have typically not risen as rapidly as prices, the purchasing power of consumers has declined. Supplies are now plentiful, but people cannot afford the goods.

Decontrol of prices
Removal of government controls on prices.

Price decontrol in Russia was abrupt. Within days, prices on 80 to 90 percent of wholesale and retail goods were decontrolled.[4] The rise in prices of so many goods and services naturally caused a sudden rise in the average price level. The inflation rate soared, peaking at approximately 1,353 percent per year at the height of price decontrol in 1992. Inflation has since subsided but is still considered to be a serious problem. (The average annual inflation rate over 1990 to 2001 was still a very high 140 percent.[5])

Privatization

Privatization refers to the sale of government enterprises to the private sector. Throughout eastern Europe, governments have owned everything from industry and businesses to agricultural land, energy facilities, agricultural marketing boards, and transportation networks. The process of privatization presumes that private ownership of the means of production enhances efficiency and growth.

Privatization
The transfer of government-owned enterprises or responsibilities to the private sector.

Once again, Russia presents an interesting example of this process of privatization. The Russian privatization program started in April 1992 with the sale of municipally owned shops. At the same time, the government began the process whereby state and collective farms would convert to private ownership. In June, the government began to convert large and medium-sized firms into shareholding companies (meaning that individuals may own shares in the company). Finally, in October the government began to issue to all Russian citizens a voucher that can be used to purchase shares in such companies.[6] (Your author even managed to purchase a voucher, a "piece of Russia," in a secondary market to a secondary market—that is, a hallway outside of an auction site.)

The Russian privatization program has not been without difficulty. First, different elements of the Russian government have disagreed greatly over the pace of privatization. Second, small businesses, mostly shops and services, have been sold off more rapidly than larger enterprises. The largest enterprises are far more difficult to privatize. Third, machinery and equipment in many Russian enterprises are outmoded and in poor repair. Productivity in these enterprises is very low. As privatized businesses have become more profit-oriented, and as government subsidies to these businesses have declined, many firms have gone bankrupt, resulting in worker layoffs. Fourth, Russian enterprises tend to be monopolies. Before the transition, Soviet planners had categorized industry into 7,664 "product groups." Of these product groups, 77 percent were produced by single firms.[7] Even as these government-owned monopolies become privatized, there remain the problems associated with monopoly that were discussed in Chapter 8. Finally, nearly 15 percent of Russia's industries were defense-related. Since the end of the Cold War, Russian demand for defense-related products has been low.[8] All of this suggests that Russia will face serious hurdles in the forms of privatization, demonopolization, and defense conversion.

Effects of the Transition

The objectives of the transition from socialism to capitalism throughout the formerly socialist industrialized world are greater efficiency and growth. But this transition has posed many problems for people. Inflation has made it difficult for consumers to afford basic necessities. Farmers have been hard hit by increases in the prices of inputs such as fertilizer, and the prices that they receive for their food products often still remain artificially low. Workers have been laid off in defense industries, government jobs, and privatized businesses. Other workers have received no paychecks for months. Corruption is often widespread, and organized crime is often rampant. Whereas most people have been struggling to make do in light of these difficulties, some have been profiting from liberalization. The masses of people are deeply troubled by this blatant inequality. Alcoholism and suicide rates in some countries have been rising, and life expectancies have even declined. A quotation from a young Russian woman studying in the United States summarizes some of these difficulties.

> The situation in Russia is very difficult for the ordinary citizen. My father recently lost his government job, though he was soon hired into a different job. My mother, who works at a bank, did not lose her job but she was not paid for seven months. Imagine, a bank with all that money, and my mother not being paid! Lost jobs and non-payment of wages are common. People get by by moonlighting. Old women

beg or sell homemade food, used clothing, or anything that anyone will buy. Pensions are often very small, as low as $30 per month (900 rubles) or less. This will buy maybe a loaf of bread and a bottle of milk each day, plus a little bit of meat each week. With wages falling behind prices, it now takes about seven days of work at a typical wage to purchase a tube of mascara, and two months of work to purchase a good pair of shoes. Twenty rubles will buy a bottle of bad vodka. Many people drink. In the meanwhile, middle-aged men flaunt their wealth and drive their Mercedes, Audis, and BMWs. It is easy to recognize the Mafia.[9]

The Twenty-First Century?

The twenty-first century is a question mark. Although policies of liberalization will undoubtedly continue, the struggles and dissatisfactions of ordinary people may slow down or change the nature of the transition. In some countries, the transition may even be reversed. In Russia, the rise in power of politicians who wish to return to the policies of the past exemplifies the dissatisfaction of people with the current political and economic situation. Opinion polls show that large shares of the population wish to return to the "old days," when they were provided with housing, jobs, child care, and health care. In other formerly socialist countries, such as Poland and Belarus, some policies of liberalization have been reversed and some socialist-leaning politicians have been elected. In other eastern European countries, significant minorities favor the return to socialist economies.

One of the critical issues in the transition to freer-market economies in eastern Europe is a safety net for people. Under socialism, governments had guaranteed jobs, housing, child care, and medical coverage for all citizens. As ordinary citizens now experience a loss of jobs and purchasing power, governments must ensure that people's basic needs are met. Otherwise, the transition will proceed neither smoothly nor successfully.

THE LESS-DEVELOPED WORLD: ECONOMIC REFORM

Economic reform
Change in policies and institutions that moves economies to freer (more capitalist) markets.

Much of the less-developed world is undergoing a process referred to as **economic reform**. This means that developing countries are adopting policies that move their economies toward freer markets. The economic growth rates reported in Chapter 7 indicate much variation in the success of less-developed countries in increasing GDP per capita. The economic reforms predominant in the 1990s and 2000s have their roots in the international debt crisis of the 1980s. And that crisis has its roots in the world economic conditions of the 1970s.

The 1970s: Oil Crisis

The most significant economic events of the 1970s began with the restriction of oil supplies by the Organization of Petroleum Exporting Countries (OPEC), the Arab oil embargo, and the quadrupling of oil prices between 1973 and 1974. The OPEC countries experienced massive increases in their export earnings, and the non-oil-exporting, less-developed countries suffered huge increases in their spending for oil imports. The effects of the oil shock were threefold. First, the OPEC nations began a process of "recycling" the revenue earned through their international sales of oil.

That is, they deposited much of their oil revenue in U.S. and European financial institutions. These **petrodollars** greatly enhanced the lending capacity of these commercial banks and other financial institutions. Second, the oil price increase caused a generalized inflation, and subsequent recession, throughout much of the world. Ultimately, the worldwide recession caused a decline in demand for exports from less-developed countries and a consequent decline in the export earnings of these countries. And finally, the combination of reduced export earnings and increased oil import expenditures forced the non-oil-exporting developing countries to borrow from the **International Monetary Fund (IMF)**, as well as from commercial banks. At the time, the cost of borrowing was low because of low real interest rates, and the lending capacity of Western financial institutions was large.

The next stage of the debt crisis began in 1979, when OPEC and the Iranian oil embargo again sent oil prices soaring. (This event was described as an example of cost-push inflation in Chapter 15.) Along with this second oil shock came another phase of petrodollar recycling. The commercial banks were now quite capable and willing to make even larger loans to developing countries. Many non-oil-exporting countries borrowed heavily to finance their oil imports. Several other oil-exporting developing countries, such as Mexico, borrowed to develop their oil sectors and diversify their economies. Most of these new loans came from private commercial banks, rather than the IMF, which by now was running low on lending funds. For a variety of reasons that we will discuss, this second phase of borrowing placed developing countries in a situation even more precarious than the first phase.

The Early 1980s: U.S. Reaction

The second phase of borrowing occurred at a time of great concern in the United States over the inflation that was partly generated by the escalating oil prices. High inflation rates persisted until the early 1980s, when the Federal Reserve engaged in **contractionary monetary policy** (recall the discussion in Chapter 15 on macro policy in the early 1980s). Inflation was brought under control, but at the expense of skyrocketing interest rates and consequent U.S. recession that later spread worldwide. An outcome of LDC borrowing from commercial banks, as opposed to the IMF, was that larger proportions of lending agreements then stipulated variable interest rates. This meant that as market interest rates rose, interest payments of LDC borrowers increased as well.

Rising interest rates in the United States had a secondary effect of pushing up the value of the dollar. The rising dollar made developing countries' payment for oil imports even more difficult because oil is valued in dollars. It also made repaying predominantly dollar-denominated debt more difficult for developing countries. Less-developed-country debt was now a full-blown crisis.

The 1980s: International Debt Crisis

By 1988, the less-developed countries had borrowed more than a trillion dollars, and the number was increasing. They borrowed for a variety of reasons, including those related to the oil market, which we noted earlier. Many less-developed countries borrowed for a variety of laudable purposes, including investment in infrastructure and industry and development of agricultural and export sectors.

Petrodollars
Money earned from the sale of petroleum. Petroleum prices are denominated in dollars.

International Monetary Fund (IMF)
An international organization, largely funded by Western industrialized countries, that provides conditional loans and financial assistance to needy countries.

Contractionary monetary policy
Reductions in the nation's money supply that serve to raise interest rates and reduce aggregate demand.

In other countries, borrowed funds were grossly misused. Countless stories tell of funds that were squandered on grandiose but inefficient government projects, on luxury goods for the rich, and on the coffers of wealthy businesspeople and government officials. For example, Tyler Bridges, then a writer for the *Washington Post*, examined Venezuela's use of borrowed funds in the mid-1980s. He wrote:

> I discovered that the government hadn't kept track of where the money had gone, though various sources indicated that only a portion of the money was invested in projects fostering long-term growth. [I found that Venezuela] borrowed heavily from abroad in the late 1970s to finance food imports and to subsidize domestic food prices. As food imports soared, however, local agriculture was neglected and production declined. Once self-sufficient, Venezuela today imports about fifty percent of Venezuela's food. . . . [In another example] thanks in part to a presidential decree requiring that every public bathroom and elevator have an attendant, public-sector employment tripled from 1974–1984.[10]

Capital flight
A process whereby less-developed (or other) countries invest funds in foreign countries.

Another problem was that of capital flight. **Capital flight** is a process whereby borrowed funds are reinvested in financial markets or real estate abroad. Corrupt government officials or businesspeople with access to borrowed funds often invested these funds overseas, rather than using them for local projects. Capital flowed outward, profits and interest earnings accrued to wealthy investors, and developing countries failed to benefit from the borrowed money. When governments fail to invest borrowed funds productively, this naturally hampers the ability of borrowing countries to repay their debt. The fault may lie with an inefficient or corrupt government, but it is the residents of the borrowing countries who then bear the burden of the debt.

The enormous burden of the debt becomes clear when one carefully considers the process by which a country tries to pay off its debt. First, the amount of money that must service the debt (interest payment plus repayment of principal) represents a large expenditure in any particular year, meaning that a significant proportion of the income generated from the production of goods and services (GDP) must be transferred out of the country. Recall that the gross domestic product of developing countries is typically small. Thus, the income generated from production of GDP is low as well. The demands on this limited income represent a bewildering array of choices in a typical low-income country trying desperately to develop. Large expenditures must go to satisfying the basic consumption needs of people: food, shelter, and medical care. Government expenditures are also necessary for a variety of social services, public education, and infrastructure. With a population at the margin of subsistence and with a driving need for development, any expenditures diverted toward repaying the debt will directly harm the well-being of people. This state of affairs explains a commonly made observation: "In poor countries, the debt crisis has a child's face." The reallocation of expenditure toward servicing of debt has harmed the well-being of people, the most vulnerable of whom are typically the very young.

In addition to the problem of allocating income for debt servicing, there is the problem of the form that this transfer must take. Debt repayment must be made in the form of the currency initially borrowed; thus, repayment must typically be in U.S. dollars or in the currency of major developed countries. We'll refer to this currency as foreign currency. Less-developed countries have very limited means of obtaining foreign currency with which to make their payments. They may earn foreign currency through their exports to other countries. Typically, these export earnings are very limited, and they declined for many LDCs over the 1980s as a consequence of the U.S. and worldwide recession. (Do you recall the problem of LDC declining terms of trade discussed in Chapter 7?) A country may also acquire foreign currency through foreign investment by other countries and through international assistance. A final option, and one that has been increasingly chosen by LDC governments, is to continually borrow to repay past debts. Obviously, the latter results in a vicious cycle of continuous borrowing in which LDCs have little hope of becoming debt free.

In a country with limited opportunity to earn foreign currency, such currency must be carefully spent. When that currency must be used for debt repayment, it cannot be used for other important activities such as the purchase of foreign capital or technology or the import of important food and energy products. Yet perhaps the most dire implications of debt servicing take place in the long term. Countries that are desperate for foreign currency earnings to service their debt will undertake overall development policies that are quite different from the ones they might normally undertake. Countries under pressure to acquire export earnings may feel forced to expand patterns of export cropping that worsen the income distribution, use up limited resources, and cause environmental problems. They may succumb to pressures to encourage indiscriminate foreign investment that may not be the most conducive to their overall development objectives. They may emphasize industrial over agricultural sector development. Under more ideal conditions, a country might well pursue very different, and more beneficial, paths to development.

The 1990s: Economic Reform

The final phase of the debt crisis occurred as many countries were forced by their inability to meet payment schedules to seek financial assistance from the International Monetary Fund. IMF assistance is helpful, but it has typically involved **conditionality**, forcing countries to undertake the economic reforms referred to earlier (often called "austerity measures") as a condition for assistance. These reforms include requirements that governments reduce their spending, reduce general inflation and wages, and privatize government enterprises. Governments are also required to allow food and other prices to rise to market levels and to reduce their controls on foreign trade and investment. In other words, they must move toward freer markets, reducing their role in the economy and allowing the market to determine prices. Some countries have voluntarily adopted economic reforms, but most others have had these reforms forced on them. Some of these reforms have run counter to development policies and have created tremendous hardship for governments and residents alike. One African leader expressed his frustration this way:

> You do not talk of "austerity" to a [person] who has not tasted food for days, who can conceive of no more ecstatic pleasure than to have a few drops of water to wet his [or her] lips and tongue. . . . Enforced increases in food prices are meaningless mutterings to the mother brushing the flies off her baby's eyes, watching [the child] starve to death by the minute because there is no food or milk or water.[11]

Conditionality
The obligation to meet certain requirements in exchange for financial assistance.

The Twenty-First Century?

Less-developed countries have had mixed reactions to economic reforms. In many countries, such as Nigeria and other African countries, privatization has resulted in massive layoffs of public-sector employees. The private sector has not yet been able to restore employment adequately in these countries. In other countries such as Kenya and Indonesia, rising food prices have been met with riots by urban consumers. In still other countries such as Chile, economic reforms have created rapid economic growth and national prosperity despite the fact that large segments of the population remain abysmally poor. (Chile has returned to more socialist policies with the recent election of socialist President Ricardo Lagos.) It is hoped that economic reform throughout the less-developed world will lead to economic growth and that the benefits of this growth will trickle down to the poor, but at least in the short term, the poor are the ones who suffer most. Once again, a critical issue is the existence of an adequate safety net for the poor.

It remains to be seen how the less-developed countries, like the formerly socialist industrialized countries, will respond to the effects of economic reform. Some will undoubtedly move forward; others will react like Chile has to the hardships borne by their people. They will seek policies to soften, or even nullify, the policies of economic reform.

VIEWPOINT: CONSERVATIVE VERSUS LIBERAL

This chapter has examined a conservative movement throughout the world toward capitalism and globally freer markets. Economists vary in their views of this movement. Market economies often lead to efficiency and growth, but issues of equity may be neglected. If this is the case, and if governments fail to provide adequate programs for the poor and the unemployed, the benefits of a market economy will fail to trickle down to the needy. In the new millennium, the disparity between the rich and the poor may become greater. Liberals tend to be more concerned than conservatives about this equity issue.

On the other hand, if government interventions go so far as to reduce the usefulness of the price system and the incentives of the marketplace, economies may stagnate and fail to grow. Conservatives tend to be more concerned than liberals about these issues of incentives and efficiency.

Where is the balance between the conservative and the liberal view? You have studied this contrast throughout the course, whether the issue is agriculture, housing, or environment. You now have the information and insight you need to analyze this issue by yourself and to come to the policy conclusions that make sense to you.

SUMMARY

The Western industrialized world, the formerly socialist industrialized world, and the less-developed world are all currently embarked on a movement toward freer markets for their economies. Much of the Western industrialized world has embraced conservative economic policies in the hope of generating economic growth. Most formerly socialist industrialized countries are experiencing a revolutionary transition from socialism to capitalism. And finally, large numbers of less-developed countries have adopted economic reform policies, voluntarily or involuntarily, that are designed to make their economies more market-oriented. The long-term success of these changes remains to be seen.

NOTES

1. Based on data from the World Bank, *World Development Report 2000/2001* (New York: Oxford University Press, 2001). Savings rates in other western European countries range from 12 percent in Greece to 17 percent in Portugal, 15 percent in the United Kingdom, 37 percent in Ireland, 30 percent in Japan, and 32 percent in Norway. Statistics are for 1999.

2. These and other statistics in this section are from the World Bank, *World Development Report 2000/2001* (New York: Oxford University Press, 2001). Statistics are for the most recent year available. Data on patents are originally from the World Intellectual Property Organization, *Industrial Property Statistics* Geneva, 1999. Data on personal computers are originally from the International Telecommunication Union's *World Telecommunication Development Report,* International Telecommunication Union, Geneva, 1999. Data on Internet hosts are originally from the Internet Software Consortium (**www.isc.org**), Internet Domain Survey, Jan. 2000.

3. Jacqueline Brux and Jacques Foust, "Doing Business in the Russian Economy in Transition" (paper presented at the Midwest Economic Association meetings, Chicago, Ill., March 1994).

4. U.S. Department of Commerce, Business Information Service for the Newly Independent States (BISNIS), International Trade Administration, *Commercial Overview of Russia,* Moscow, January 28, 1993.

5. These and other statistics in this section are from the World Bank, *World Development Report 2003* (New York: Oxford University Press, 2003).

6. "Russia Reborn," *The Economist,* December 5, 1992.

7. "Russia Reborn."

8. U.S. Department of Commerce, *Commercial Overview of Russia.*

9. Yana S. Yurgelyanis, in a conversation with the author.

10. Tyler Bridges, "Before Bailing Them Out, Plug the Leaks," *Washington Post National Weekly Edition,* March 22–April 7, 1989.

11. Bread for the World Institute, **www.bread. org**. *Africa: Crisis to Opportunity,* 1995.

DISCUSSION QUESTIONS

1. Are you an economic liberal or conservative? What is your view of government social programs, taxes, and regulation of business?

2. Consider the U.S. supply-side policies and proposals of the 2000s, such as proposals to reduce taxes and environmental regulations. Do you expect these policies to achieve efficiency and economic growth? Do you expect the benefits of these policies to trickle down to all?

3. What do you think about some of the specific conservative tax proposals, such as replacing the personal income tax with a consumption tax and reducing the capital gains tax? Do you think these would be effective in creating economic growth? How do you feel about the effect they would have on U.S. income distribution?

4. How might the U.S. government encourage greater research and development? How would R&D benefit the economy?

5. Suppose that the government of a formerly socialist country decontrols prices and permits them to rise to market levels. How can the government assist low-income consumers who might be unable to afford higher food and other prices?

6. Assume that the process of privatization continues successfully in Russia. Would all the problems of Russian industry by solved? What other policies may be necessary?

7. Use the Central Intelligence Agency (CIA) *World Factbook* at **www.odci.gov/cia/publications/factbook/docs/faqs.htm** to look up the current economic situation in any one of the formerly socialist industrialized countries. Has GDP been increasing or decreasing? How high is the inflation rate? How do some of the standards of living (life expectancy, infant mortality rate, and so on) compare with those presented in Chapter 7 for less-developed countries?

8. How have international conditions outside the control of less-developed countries exacerbated the problem of international debt? Do you believe it is right for the IMF to stipulate conditions when providing financial assistance to debt-ridden less-developed countries?

9. Go to the International Monetary Fund (IMF) Web site at **www.imfsite.org**. It provides links to countless statistics, reports, and other global information, including the transformation of countries to capitalism.

10. Go again to the International Monetary Fund (IMF) Web site (**www.imfsite.org**), and click Conditionality to learn more about the history, role, operation, and effectiveness of IMF conditionality (in the IMF view).

11. Use the World Bank Web site (**www.worldbank.org/data**) to look up debt information on a less-developed country of your choice. Look for the debt service ratio, which is the ratio between debt service (annual repayment of debt plus interest) and export earnings and which is written as Total Debt Service/Exports. This ratio is the best indicator of the debt burden of an individual country.

12. Go to the home page of the World Bank at **www.worldbank.org** to discover the wealth of information on worldwide economic and social indicators, including information on savings rates, standards of living, and international debt. To obtain data quickly, use the Country at a Glance tables.

13. What type of safety net is necessary for residents of formerly socialist and less-developed countries as they move toward market economies?

14. Do you believe that the global movement toward freer markets will continue well into the twenty-first century, or will it reverse itself? Why?

EPILOGUE
YOU AND THE WORLD
AROUND YOU

Now you have finished your study of economic issues in the world today. You have used economic tools to analyze a broad spectrum of social issues. And in the process you have learned techniques that you can use to analyze other issues. You have developed critical and analytical thinking skills that you can use all your life. You will be better able to understand how government policy affects you and your family. You have learned the vocabulary to understand what you read in the newspaper or see on the TV news. Indeed, you are now a better-educated citizen.

What does this mean? Are you a "better" person? Will you contribute to a more just society? Will you have a better quality of life? Will you make an impact on the world in which we live?

We hope your answer is yes to all of the questions above. Or at least we hope that you now have interest in improving the world around you. For all its imperfections, the United States is a rich, diverse country with one of the world's longest-lasting democratic governments. The U.S. gross national income per capita in 2001 was almost $35,000, among the highest in the world. You will be among the 25 percent of the age-25-or-older population in this land of opportunity who have a college degree. What all of this means is that you have both the ability to affect policy and the responsibility to do so. You can inform yourself about social issues, exercise your right to vote, and contact your legislators.[1] You can campaign for a candidate who reflects your views or run for public office yourself. You can exercise your right to free speech by writing a letter to the editor of your local paper. You can demonstrate and carry a poster supporting a cause about which you feel strongly. You can agree with government policy, and you can disagree. You can make a difference in our society! You are an educated citizen.

The issues we analyzed in this book will not go away. You will finish your formal education (no one ever finishes learning), and you will go on to your career. We hope some of you will take more economics courses and perhaps even become economists. But you will be workers of all sorts: social workers, biochemists, teachers, accountants, doctors, nurses, controllers, and production managers. You may work in prisons or in foreign countries. Your investment in your education will make you a more productive worker wherever you go to work. We hope you will remain concerned about issues of poverty and discrimination, pollution, and abuse of market power. The real world forces you to take ethical positions on these issues as they are related to your workplace and your life.

Finally, you are a part of a global economy. The events of 9-11 brought this home to us. In polls subsequent to September 11, 2001, Americans showed an alarming inability to locate Middle Eastern countries on a map, and a total misconception of which countries the perpetrators of 9-11 were from. Results of a National Geographic-Roper 2002 Global Geographic Literacy Survey that polled young adults age 18 to 24 revealed the following: Only 13 percent of those surveyed could locate Iraq or Iran, only 14 percent could pinpoint Israel, and only 17 percent could locate Afghanistan on a map. Fifty-eight percent of those polled could not locate Japan, 65 percent couldn't locate France, and 69 percent couldn't locate the United Kingdom on a map. And, unbelievably, about 11 percent of the young Americans polled couldn't even locate the United States on a map! In comparison, the survey found that young people in other countries, notably Sweden, Germany, Italy, France, Japan, Canada, and Great Britain scored above young people in the United States. Among the countries polled, only youth in Mexico scored below the United States.

What this means is that you must continue your education. In order to stay in tune with world-wide events and issues, you must become a life-long learner. Take international courses, and if your courses do not have international content, be sure to notify your teachers that you need an international education. And make sure you don't only learn about the Western industrialized countries. Some four-fifths of the world's population will soon reside in the less developed countries of Asia, Africa, and Latin America. Talk with international students and faculty. Read the newspapers and browse the Internet. When you come to articles about foreign countries, be sure to read them! When you read your first article about Burundi, you will wonder where this nation is located and why you should know about it. But the next time you read about Burundi, you will recognize it. Pretty soon you will know more, not just about Burundi, but about the entire global economy than any of your friends and family. You will truly be an educated citizen.

As a citizen of the world, you will increasingly be called on to understand international issues, to work in businesses with international linkages, and very likely to travel in foreign countries yourself. The world has indeed become a global village. And you are a resident of that village!

NOTE

1. You may contact your U.S. senators at the U.S. Senate Office Building, Washington, DC 20510, and your U.S. representatives at the U.S. House of Representatives, Washington, DC 20515. You may leave a telephone message for either at (202) 224-3121. You may write the president at The White House, Washington, DC 20500, or leave a message at (202) 456-1111. You may also send an e-mail to the president at President@Whitehouse.gov. Web sites and e-mail addresses of members of the U.S. Senate and House of Representatives are available at **www.senate.gov** and **www.house.gov**, respectively, as is information about schedules, bills, committees, and so on.

GLOSSARY

A

Absolute advantage A situation whereby a country can produce a good at a lower resource cost than another country.

Absolute poverty A situation in which people experience the hardship of poverty according to some objective criterion.

Adverse selection A process by which insured people's choices lead to higher-than-average loss levels for the program's sponsor.

Affirmative action Efforts to provide equal opportunities in terms of employment and education to underrepresented groups of people.

Aggregate demand The quantity of total output (GDP) demanded (purchased) at alternative average price levels.

Aggregate supply The quantity of total output (GDP) supplied (produced) at alternative average price levels.

Aid to Families with Dependent Children (AFDC) Our nation's former welfare program that provided cash assistance to eligible low-income families with children.

Antitrust Our laws, agencies, and court system established to control market power in the United States.

Appreciate An increase in the value of one country's currency relative to another country's currency.

Asset Property that is owned, such as land.

Average life expectancy The age to which a baby born in a particular year can be expected to live.

B

Barrier to entry A market characteristic that prevents new firms from entering the market.

Barter The direct exchange of goods and services for other goods and services rather than for money.

Block grant A lump sum of money given by the federal government to state governments to use as they wish within broad federal guidelines to develop programs to meet a broad category of need.

Budget deficit The difference between federal government spending and federal government tax revenue in any one year.

Budget surplus The difference between federal government tax revenue and federal government spending in any one year.

Buffer stock A mechanism for stabilizing agricultural prices, whereby an agricultural product is purchased and placed in storage during years of high production and released from storage and sold during years of low production.

Bumper crop An unexpectedly large crop resulting from good growing conditions.

Burden of the tax The impact of the tax that is felt by producers and consumers. Consumers bear the burden in the form of higher prices paid for the product; producers bear the burden in the form of lower profits.

C

Capital flight A process whereby less-developed (or other) countries invest funds in foreign countries.

Capital gains The net income received when an asset is bought at a particular price and sold at a higher price.

Capital goods Goods such as machinery and factories that are used to produce other goods.

Capital-intensive technology Technology utilizing large amounts of capital.

Capitalism An economic system wherein the economic decisions are made by the private sector via the marketplace and the means of production are owned by the private sector.

Cartel A group of producers that explicitly engages in price-fixing.

Closing costs Expenses paid at the time that a loan is finalized and the title is conveyed to the buyer.

Coinsurance payment A percentage of medical expenses that the insured person must pay over and above the deductible.

Collusion Price-fixing.

Comparative advantage A situation whereby a country can produce a good at a lower opportunity cost than another country.

Competition A market in which many small producers sell a standardized product to many small buyers.

Composition of GDP The goods and services of which GDP consists.

Composition of poverty The number of poor people in each group of the population as a share of the number of poor in the nation.

Concentration The domination of a market by a few large firms.

Concentration ratio The percentage of output produced by the four largest firms in an industry.

Conditionality The obligation to meet certain requirements in exchange for financial assistance.

Constant prices Prices that exist in a base year.

Consumer goods Goods that are consumed (used) by consumers.

Consumer price index (CPI) A weighted average of the prices of a fixed basket of goods and services purchased by a typical urban household.

Consumption possibilities curve A curve that shows alternative combinations of the maximum amounts of two products that can be consumed within a country during a particular time period.

Consumption tax A hypothetical tax on the portion of income that is spent on consumer goods and services, as opposed to income that goes into savings.

Contractionary fiscal policy Fiscal policy that decreases aggregate demand, thereby contracting GDP.

Contractionary monetary policy Monetary policy that decreases aggregate demand, thereby contracting GDP. This takes place through reductions in the nation's money supply that serve to raise interest rates and reduce the consumer and business portions of aggregate demand.

Contractual right A right that is specified in a contract between parties.

Cost of living adjustment (COLA) An adjustment that automatically increases incomes or benefits when the average price level rises.

Cost shifting The practice of recovering the unpaid costs of some patients by charging higher prices to other patients.

Cost-benefit analysis A study that compares the costs and benefits of a policy or program.

Cost-push inflation Inflation that occurs as a result of increases in the costs of production.

Crowding out A situation in which government spending, financed by borrowing, causes interest rates to rise, which results in less spending by the private economy.

Current prices Actual prices of a particular year.

Cyclical unemployment Unemployment that results from a drop in economic activity in our economy as a whole.

D

Declining terms of trade A situation in which the price of a country's exports declines relative to the price of its imports.

Decontrol of prices Removal of government controls on prices.

Deductible A payment on an annual or per-service basis that must be made by the insured person before the insurance company's payments begin.

Defensive medicine The ordering of unnecessary tests and services by health care professionals solely to protect themselves from charges of malpractice.

Deficiency payments The target price minus the market price, multiplied by the number of units sold.

Deflation A decrease in the average price level.

Deforestation The clearing of forested areas in an unmanaged fashion.

Demand curve A graph showing the quantities that consumers are willing to buy at alternative prices during a specified time period.

Demand schedule A table showing the quantities that consumers are willing to buy at alternative prices during a specified time period.

Demand-pull inflation Inflation that occurs when any sectors of the economy increase their demand for goods and services.

Depreciate A decrease in the value of one country's currency relative to another country's currency.

Deregulation The reduction of government regulations.

Desertification The encroachment of desert on previously fertile land.

Design standard A regulation that specifies both the required level of performance and the means of compliance.

Diagnosis-related groups (DRGs) Approximately 500 categories into which a medical diagnosis might fall. The DRG determines the prospective payment made by Medicare.

Direct cost Actual paid expenses.

Discouraged workers People who would like to work, but have become so discouraged in the job search that they have stopped actively seeking employment.

Discrimination Action that treats individuals differently on the basis of some arbitrary characteristic.

Distribution of GNI The distribution of income between different income groups.

Distribution of income How national income is distributed within an economy.

Down payment The amount of a home buyer's own money required by the lender for the purchase of a home.

Dumping Exporting goods at low prices, even below the cost of production.

Durable goods Products with a life of longer than one year.

E

Early retirement effect Social Security's effect of increasing private savings by encouraging earlier retirements.

Earned Income Credit (EIC) A federal income tax credit for eligible low-income working individuals and families. The credit is available whether or not the worker pays federal personal income taxes. State governments may also utilize an EIC for their personal income taxes.

Earnings Money received from labor market activities.

Economic conservative A person who believes in very low levels of government involvement in the economy.

Economic development A multifaceted process that involves improvements in standards of living, reductions in poverty, and growth in GDP per capita.

Economic growth A sustained increase in production, represented by an outward shift of the production possibilities curve. An increase in GDP (or GDP per capita) over an extended time period. Average annual growth in GDP per capita is calculated as the average annual growth in GDP minus the average annual population growth, over some time period.

Economic liberal A person who believes in high levels of government involvement in the economy.

Economic reform Change in policies and institutions that moves economies to freer (more capitalist) markets.

Economies of scale A situation whereby a large amount of a product can be produced at a lower cost per unit than a small amount of the product.

Efficient Using resources in such a way as to maximize the output we desire.

Effluent fees Taxes on production causing water pollution.

Elastic demand Demand in which buyers are relatively responsive to changes in price.

Emissions fees Taxes on production causing air pollution.

Employment discrimination Not hiring certain workers on the basis of some arbitrary characteristic.

Endowments Income-earning investments of a school or other institution.

Enrollment cap A maximum limit on the number of students allowed to enroll in a school.

Entitlement A payment which eligible citizens have a right to receive by law.

Equilibrium A state of balance; a point at which quantity demanded equals quantity supplied.

Equity Fairness.

Euro The common currency of the European Union.

Exchange rate The price of one country's currency in terms of another country's currency.

Excise taxes Taxes applied to the purchase of specific goods or services.

Exclusive franchise Permission by the government (often a local government) for a monopoly firm to exist. (It is normally accompanied by government regulation.)

Exemptions Amounts of money for each household member that can be deducted from household income before personal income tax rates are applied.

Expansionary fiscal policy Fiscal policy that increases aggregate demand, thereby expanding GDP.

Expansionary monetary policy Monetary policy that increases aggregate demand, thereby expanding GDP.

Exports The value of goods and services sold to foreigners.

Export cropping Agricultural production for export, rather than production of food for local consumption.

Externality The cost or benefit of an economic activity that spills over onto the rest of society.

F

Fair market rent An amount determined by HUD to be reasonable rent for low-income housing.

Federal Reserve The U.S. central banking system.

Fee-for-service The charging of a specific fee for provision of a specific health care service.

Fiscal policy The use of government spending and tax policy to shift the aggregate demand curve.

Flexible (floating) exchange rate system A system whereby exchange rates are determined on the basis of international demand and supply for a currency.

Formerly socialist industrialized world The industrialized ex-socialist countries of eastern Europe.

Free rider problem A situation in which individuals who do not pay their share for a good or service nevertheless enjoy its benefits.

Frictional unemployment Temporary unemployment caused by a normal time delay when a person seeks a first job, changes jobs, or reenters the labor force after an absence.

Full employment A situation in which there is no cyclical unemployment; all unemployment is frictional or structural.

Full-employment GDP The level of gross domestic product associated with full employment of the labor force. (It is a hypothetical concept.)

Fully funded Having sufficient reserves to pay all expected liabilities; it is a legal requirement of private insurance.

G

General Agreement on Tariffs and Trade (GATT) An international trade agreement, first negotiated in 1947, that has included efforts to reduce tariff barriers among member countries of the world. It has now been replaced by the World Trade Organization.

Gentrification The conversion of low-cost apartments into middle- and upper-middle-class housing.

GNI per capita   Gross national income per person on average. Calculated by dividing total gross national income by total population.

Government securities   Government bonds and treasury bills.

Gross domestic product (GDP)   A measure of the total output produced in a nation. It is the market value of all final goods and services produced in the economy in a given time period (usually one year).

Gross national income (GNI)   The income generated from the production of a nation's output. Gross national income is the broadest of all income concepts.

Gross national product (GNP)   An alternative measure of the total output produced by a nation. It is the market value of all final goods and services produced *by* the economy in a given time period (usually one year).

Group of Eight (G-8)   A group of eight countries (the United States, Canada, Britain, France, Italy, Germany, Japan, and Russia) that coordinates policies in an effort to influence exchange rates.

H

Health maintenance organizations (HMOs)
Health insurance plans under which the covered care is limited to designated providers and the use of services is coordinated by a patient's primary care physician. HMOs often encourage preventative care.

Home owner's insurance   Insurance that covers the replacement cost of a house and its contents.

Housing voucher   Housing subsidies in the amount of the difference between the fair market rent and 30 percent of a poor family's income.

Human capital discrimination   Anything that prevents certain groups from acquiring the level or quality of education or training to which other groups have access.

Hyperinflation   Extremely high inflation, whereby money becomes almost worthless.

I

Imports   The value of goods and services purchased from foreigners.

Incidence of poverty   Who the poor are and which groups of people have a greater likelihood of being poor.

Income distribution   The division of total income in an economy among people of different income groups.

Income transfer   A cash transfer from the government to an individual for which no good or service is provided to the government in return.

Income   Money received from all sources.

Increasing opportunity costs   As more of one good is produced, society must give up increasingly larger amounts of the alternative good.

Index of dissimilarity   A measure of segregation.

Indigenous   People who are of native-born ancestry in a country.

Indirect cost   The opportunity cost of forgone alternatives.

Individual equity   The principle that benefits received are proportional to amounts paid in.

Indivisible   A characteristic of public goods in that they are impossible to divide into units sufficiently small to be sold in private markets.

Inefficiency   Using resources in such a way as not to maximize the desired output from them.

Inelastic demand   Demand in which buyers are relatively unresponsive to changes in price.

Inequity   Unfairness.

Infant mortality rate   The number of infants who die within their first year of life per 1,000 live births.

Inflation   A rise in the average price level in the economy.

Informal employment sector   An employment sector consisting primarily of service occupations in an unofficial setting.

Infrastructure   Social overhead capital, including facilities for transportation, communication, marketing, and extension services.

In-kind transfers   Transfers of goods or services (or access to goods or services) from the government to an individual for which no good or service is provided to the government in return.

Interest rate   The percentage of borrowed funds that must be paid to the lender (or investor) for the privilege of using the funds.

International Monetary Fund (IMF)   An international organization, largely funded by Western industrialized countries, that provides conditional loans and financial assistance to needy countries.

Inventories   Unsold goods and materials.

Investment in human capital   Spending that is designed to improve the productivity of people.

L

Labor force participation rate   The ratio of the number of people in the labor force to the number of people age 16 or older in the population.

Labor force   All people age 16 and older who are working for pay or actively seeking employment.

Labor productivity Total output per average work hour, calculated as GDP divided by the number of work hours.

Labor-intensive technology Technology utilizing large amounts of labor.

Law of demand There is a negative relationship between price and quantity demanded.

Law of supply There is a positive relationship between price and quantity supplied.

Less-developed world The less-developed countries of the world.

Liberalism A movement toward freer markets.

License A permit to operate in a trade or profession.

Life expectancy The age to which a baby born in a particular year can be expected to live on average.

Literacy rates The percentages of populations that can read and write.

Loanable funds Money that is borrowed and lent.

Luxury good A commodity for which demand is highly sensitive to changes in income.

M

Macroeconomics The study of the total economy.

Macroeconomy The total economy.

Malpractice insurance Insurance carried by health care professionals to protect themselves from large malpractice damage awards.

Marginal cost The additional cost of one additional unit of change (in this case, it refers to the additional cost of reducing one additional unit of pollution).

Market power The ability of an individual firm to influence the market price of its product.

Market price The retail price of a product plus any sales and excise taxes paid by the consumer.

Maternal mortality rate The number of deaths of women for pregnancy-related reasons per 100,000 live births.

Mean Average.

Means-tested A way of determining who is eligible for a program, based on the person's low-income status and/or low asset ownership.

Median The value that is exactly in the middle of a list of all values of some variable, such as earnings, when ranked from highest to lowest.

Medicaid A government program providing medical coverage for eligible low-income people.

Medical savings account A type of insurance in which the purchaser makes payments into an account that can be drawn against in times of illness.

Medicare A government program providing medical coverage largely to elderly people.

Menu costs The costs associated with reprinting menus, revising cost schedules, adjusting public telephones and vending machines, and so on, when inflation occurs.

Mergers The combining of two firms into one.

Microeconomics The study of individual areas of activity within the total economy.

Minimum wage A legally imposed minimum price (wage) for labor.

Minority A group with lesser access to higher positions in society.

Monetary policy Changes made in the nation's money supply to shift the aggregate demand curve.

Money income All household income from any source, including income transfers, calculated before taxes.

Monopolist The single firm in a monopoly market.

Monopoly A market in which only one firm produces a product with no close substitutes.

Mortgage insurance Insurance that pays off a mortgage if the borrower defaults.

N

National debt The total amount of money owed by the federal government. It represents the accumulation of all funds ever borrowed by the federal government that have not yet been repaid.

National health insurance A government program ensuring universal and comprehensive coverage of the population.

Natural monopoly A market with significant economies of scale.

Negative income tax A taxation system that taxes people with incomes above a certain level and pays people with incomes below that level.

Net benefits The excess of benefits over costs.

Newly industrializing countries (NICs) Singapore, South Korea, Taiwan, and other countries achieving rapid growth through industrialization.

Nominal GDP GDP calculated at current prices.

Nondurable goods Products with a life of less than one year.

Nonexcludable A characteristic of public goods in that their benefits cannot be kept from persons who do not pay for the goods' provision in a private market.

Nonrivalrous A characteristic of public goods in that use by one person does not prevent use by others.

Normal retirement age The minimum age at which workers can retire with full Social Security benefits.

North American Free Trade Agreement (NAFTA) An agreement between the United States, Canada, and Mexico allowing more equal access to one another's markets. The agreement went into effect on January 1, 1994.

O

Occupational crowding Crowding some groups of workers into a limited number of jobs.

Occupational discrimination Not hiring some groups of workers for particular jobs, resulting, for example, in men's jobs and women's jobs or minority jobs and white jobs.

Oligopolists Individual firms in an oligopoly market.

Oligopoly A market in which only a few large firms dominate.

Opportunity cost The best alternative forgone in order to produce or consume something else; what you give up to get something else.

Overallocation of resources The production of more than the socially optimum amount of a good or service.

P

Patent A government grant of exclusive rights by the inventor to use or sell a new technology or product for a period of time.

Pay-as-you-go system A program in which current taxes pay current benefits.

Payroll taxes Taxes based on earnings from work, usually deducted directly from workers' paychecks.

Performance standard A regulation that specifies the required level of performance but not the means of compliance.

Personal Responsibility and Work Opportunity Reconciliation Act (PRA) of 1996 Legislation that eliminated AFDC and replaced it with state programs that require work. It also tightened eligibility for and reduced the benefits offered by other social assistance programs.

Petrodollars Money earned from the sale of petroleum. Petroleum prices are denominated in dollars.

Physician sovereignty A medical doctor's control over the demand for medical procedures.

Points Fees charged by a lender at the time it grants a mortgage.

Pollution permits Tradable permits that allow the owners of the permits to produce a given amount of pollution.

Pollution Waste that is not recycled.

Poverty line A level of income below which a household is considered poor.

Poverty rate The percentage of the population that is poor.

Preferred provider organization (PPO) A health insurance plan under which a group of medical providers contract to provide the insured patient's medical care at discounted rates.

Prejudice A prejudgment on the basis of stereotypes and hearsay, plus the refusal to consider evidence that conflicts with the prejudgment.

Premium A payment to purchase and keep in force an insurance policy.

Price ceiling A legally imposed maximum price for a good or service.

Price discrimination Charging different groups of buyers different prices (when price differentials are not justified by cost differences).

Price floor A legally imposed minimum price for a good or service.

Price leadership A form of collusion in which firms follow the price increases of a leading firm.

Price maker A firm that is able to influence the market price of its product.

Price support A legally imposed minimum price of an agricultural good. A price support is a specific example of a price floor.

Price taker A firm that is unable to influence the market price of its product.

Primary commodities Unprocessed raw material and agricultural products.

Private goods Goods provided by business firms.

Private insurance A private program provided by for-profit insurance companies and funded by premiums. Its purpose is the pooling of risk of losses.

Private schools Schools that are not operated by the government and that are mainly financed by student tuition.

Private Individual people and businesses.

Privatization The transfer of government-owned enterprises or responsibilities to the private sector.

Product differentiation The creation of the image that one firm's product is different from or somehow superior to other similar products.

Production possibilities curve An economic concept explaining scarcity and the need for choices; a graph showing alternate combinations of the maximum amounts of two different goods that can be produced during a particular time period if the economy's resources are efficiently and fully employed.

Profit-push inflation Inflation that occurs when businesses use market power to restrict output in order to push up prices and profits.

Programs to reduce supply Policies to decrease the amount produced and offered for sale.

Progressive tax A tax that takes a greater percentage of income from high-income people than from low-income people.

Property taxes Taxes levied by local governments to fund services such as education and police protection.

Proportional tax A tax that takes the same percentage of income from people of all income levels.

Prospective payment A flat rate paid a hospital by Medicare to treat a particular patient having a given diagnosis.

Public assistance Any government program that is targeted to aid low-income people.

Public goods and services Goods and services provided or paid for by the government because their unique characteristics make it unlikely that the private market will provide them in sufficient quantity.

Public housing Housing units owned and operated by a local public housing authority but federally subsidized and often federally regulated.

Public schools Schools that are operated by the government and are financed by tax revenue.

Public Government.

Purchasing power The ability to buy goods and services.

Pure competition A market in which many independent producers compete to sell a standardized product to many independent buyers.

Q

Quota A restriction on the quantity of an imported good; a rigid numerical requirement in hiring or admission.

R

Rate of return The "benefit rate," computed by dividing the net benefit by the amount invested.

Rationing function of price The ability of a flexible market price to clear the market of shortages and surpluses.

Real GDP GDP calculated at constant prices.

Real price The price as adjusted for the effects of inflation. We do this when we consider price changes over time.

Recession A decline in a nation's gross domestic product (output) associated with a rise in unemployment.

Refundable A refund is available even if an income earner does not pay taxes, as long as he or she files a tax form.

Regressive tax A tax that takes a greater percentage of income from low-income people than from high-income people.

Regressivity A situation in which a larger percentage of income is taken from low-income people than high-income people.

Relative poverty A situation in which people are poor in comparison with other people.

Rental ceiling (rent control) A legally imposed maximum rent on an apartment.

Replacement rate The percentage of the worker's last working year's earnings that is replaced by Social Security retirement benefits.

Resources Land, labor, machinery, and other inputs used to produce goods and services.

Retaliation A situation in which one country responds to the trade restrictions of another country by imposing trade restrictions of its own.

Reverse discrimination Discrimination against white males.

Rising marginal cost The rising additional cost of making each additional unit of change.

Rural-urban migration The movement of people from the rural sector to the urban sector, often in search of better living conditions.

S

Savings rate Total savings divided by gross domestic product.

Scarcity Limited resources relative to wants and needs.

Services Activities (such as hair cuts, health care, and education) that are consumed (used) by consumers.

Shortage A situation in which quantity demanded is greater than quantity supplied. This occurs only when the price is lower than the market level.

Six Markets Group (Asian G-6) A group of six (original) countries (the United States, Japan, China, Singapore, Australia, and Hong Kong) that coordinates financial policies.

Social adequacy The principle that benefits are sufficient to provide a minimum level of economic security to the population as a whole.

Social costs of production The total costs of production, including private costs and spillover costs.

Social insurance A program provided by government and funded by payroll taxes of employers, employees, or both. It is targeted to aid certain eligible groups of people. Its purpose is the pooling of risk of losses, and people need not have low income to qualify.

Social Security wealth effect The tendency of the population to substitute Social Security for private saving, thus decreasing private saving.

Social Security A federal program that provides income transfers to retired workers, the survivors of deceased workers, and disabled workers.

Socialism An economic system wherein the economic decisions are made by the public (government) sector and the means of production are owned by the public sector.

Spillover benefit A positive externality in which benefits are shifted from the private market onto society.

Spillover cost A negative externality in which costs are shifted from the private market onto society.

Spillovers Costs or benefits of private market activity shifted onto society at large.

Stagflation Simultaneous inflation and recession.

Standard deduction A fixed amount of money that taxpayers can deduct from their taxable income when calculating their personal income taxes, if other deductions are not claimed.

Standards Maximum levels of pollutants that are acceptable by law.

State Child Health Insurance Program (SCHIP) A federal program providing health care coverage for children in low-income working families.

Statistical discrimination Judging an individual on the average characteristics of his or her group.

Statutory right A right that is specified by law.

Structural unemployment Unemployment that results from structural changes in our economy, such as changes in demand or technology.

Subsidies to developers Government payments to landlords who build housing for the poor.

Subsidies Payments from the government for some given action, such as recycling.

Subsidize The payment of some of the costs of an economic activity by the government.

Subsistence food crops Crops grown primarily as food for the family. A small amount may be marketed.

Supply curve A graph showing the quantities that suppliers are willing to sell at alternative prices during a specified time period.

Supply schedule A table showing the quantities that suppliers are willing to sell at alternative prices during a specified time period.

Supply-side economics The view that conservative economic policies can be used to increase aggregate supply.

Supply-side policy The use of various tools to improve the incentives for workers and businesses to produce more, thereby increasing aggregate supply and GDP.

Surplus A situation in which quantity supplied is greater than quantity demanded. This occurs only when the price is higher than the market level.

T

Target prices A program in which farmers are paid the difference between the target price and the market price.

Tariff A tax on an imported good.

Tax base Income, earnings, sales, property, or other valued items that have a tax rate applied to them. In the case of the personal income tax, the tax base is incremental income. In the case of the social security tax, the tax base is earnings subject to payroll taxes.

Tax credits Amounts of money by which the income taxes payable to the government can be directly reduced. A person or business must meet certain criteria to be eligible for a credit.

Tax rate The percentage of the tax base that must be paid to the government as tax.

Technology forcing Standards that force firms to use specific pollution control technologies.

Technology Ways of using available resources to produce output.

Temporary Assistance for Needy Families (TANF) A block grant from the federal government to state governments to be used in state welfare programs in compliance with federal guidelines. (Pronounced TAN-EF.)

Third-party payment A health care payment made by someone other than the patient or the patient's family.

Tokenism Hiring minorities to comply with the law, not for their abilities.

Trade balance The value of a nation's exports minus its imports.

Trade deficit The amount by which a nation's trade balance is in deficit (imports exceed exports).

Trade embargo Restrictions on trade with another country for political reasons.

Trade surplus The amount by which a nation's trade balance is in surplus (exports exceed imports).

Trickle-down philosophy The view that supply-side policy will generate economic growth and prosperity, the benefits of which will eventually "trickle down" to all.

Trust fund Taxes collected and invested specifically to pay future Social Security benefits.

U

Underallocation of resources The production of less than the socially optimum amount of a good or service.

Underemployment A situation in which people work limited hours or with low productivity.

Unemployed person A person age 16 or older who is actively seeking employment but is unable to find a job.

Unemployment rate The percentage of the labor force that is unemployed.

Unemployment A situation in which resources are not fully used in production.

Universal entitlements Payments (or programs) to which eligible citizens have a right by law.

Usury laws Laws establishing a maximum legal interest rate.

V

Variable rate mortgages Mortgage loans on which interest rates are periodically adjusted.

W

Wage discrimination Paying equally productive workers different wages on the basis of some arbitrary characteristic.

Western industrialized world The industrialized capitalist countries of the world.

World Trade Organization (WTO) The organization that replaced GATT in 1995 and continues to pursue GATT's agenda to reduce barriers to trade among member countries.

INDEX

A

AAI (American Antitrust Institute), 205
Absolute advantage in international trade, 214–215
Absolute poverty, 134–140
  definition, 132
  feminization of, 140
  implications of, 139–140
  incidence of, 136–139
  measuring, 134
  population of poor, 136
  poverty line
    life at, 135
    meaning of, 134–135
    measurement problems, 135
    origins of, 134
  poverty rates of racial and ethnic groups, 138–140
  trends in, 135–136
Acid rain, 64–65
Adverse selection, 316
AFDC. See Aid to Families with Dependent Children (AFDC)
Affirmative action
  access to higher education and, 104–105
  arguments for and against, 122–124
  definition, 122
  and education, 126–128
  policies to eliminate discrimination, 122–124
  University of Michigan and, 126–127
Africa, AIDS problem, 182–183
African Americans
  housing segregation and, 250–252
  as percentage of U.S. populations, 110–111
  poverty rate of, 138
  unemployment rate of, 333
Age group, poverty statistics by, 137, 139
Aggregate demand, 359–362
  definition, 355
  increases and decreases in, 369
  sectors represented by
    businesses, 360–361
    consumers, 359–360
    foreign purchasers, 361–362
    government, 361

shifts in, 362, 378
slope of curve, 375–376
Aggregate demand and supply
  cost-push inflation and, 363–364
  demand-pull inflation and, 363
  profit-push inflation and, 364–365
Aggregate supply, 359–362
  definition, 355
  shifts in, 362
  slope of curve, 376–379
  in Western industrialized countries, 412
Agricultural Adjustment Act (1933), 288
Agricultural development, 173
  access to inputs, extension services, and markets, 173–174
  export cropping, 176
  international role in, 176–177
  land redistribution, 173
  price of products, 174–176
  rural–urban migration effects, 181
Agriculture. See also Farm products
  biotechnological advances, 296–297
  characteristics of, 284–287
    farm income, 285–286
    farm resources, 286–287
    inelastic demand for products, 284
    price instability, 284–285
    technological change, 286
  concentration in, 295
  conservative versus liberal viewpoint, 299
  environmental effects, 295–296
  farm bill of 2002, 294
  farmworkers, 296
  government policy toward, 287–294
    evaluation of, 294–297
    politics of, 298–300
    price supports, 288–291
    programs to increase demand, 292–293
    programs to reduce supply, 291–292
    recent programs, 293–294
  less-developed countries and, 297–298
  "Little House on the Prairie" myth, 290, 295, 299
Aid to Families with Dependent Children (AFDC), 148, 371
  disincentives built into, 148
  elimination of, 149

AIDS in less-developed countries, 182–183
Air Pollution Act (1955), 63
Aleutian Islanders, as percentage of U.S. population, 110–111
Allocation of resources, 82
Aluminum Company of America (Alcoa), 195
Amadou, Hamza, 179
American Antitrust Institute (AAI), 205
American automobile industry, 199
  collusion in, 199
  import competition and, 204
  inefficiency in, 199
  price discrimination in, 200
American Indians, as percentage of U.S. population, 110–111
American Tobacco, 199
Andean Community trade agreement, 228
Antipoverty policies. See also Poverty
  public education as, 81–82
Antitrust, definition of, 201
Antitrust system, 201–203
  Bush administration and, 202
  Clinton administration and, 202
  market power decreased by, 201–203
  Reagan administration and, 202
Appreciation, 233
Arab Oil Embargo, 226, 257, 420–421
Archer Daniels Midland Company, 202
Arctic National Wildlife Refuge, 416
  policies for oil and gas exploration in, 76
ASEAN trade agreement, 228
Ashcroft, John, 40
Asian G-6, 234–235
Asians
  as percentage of U.S. population, 110–111
  poverty rate of, 137, 138
  unemployment rate for, 331–333
Assets, 170
AT&T, 190–191, 201
Average life expectancy, 168

B

Bakke decision (1974), 127
Balanced budget, 400–401

Barriers to entry, 194–197
definition, 188
Barter, 345
Becker, Gary, 123
Behavior of established firms, 196
Benefits. *See also* Spillover benefits
of crime prevention activities, 37
Biotechnology, 296–297
effects on world market, 298
Birthrates, economic development effects on, 180
Births to teenage mothers, poverty rate and, 142–143
Births to unmarried mothers, poverty rate and, 142
Black persons. *See* African Americans
Block grants, 148
Boeing, 202
Bread for the World, 139
Bricklin, 195
Bridges, Tyler, 422
Brown, Lee, 42–43
Brown v. Topeka Board of Education, 125
Budget cuts, as cause of poverty, 143
Budget deficit, 396
Budget surplus, 396
Buffer stock of cereal grains, 176
Bumper crops, 285
Burden of the tax, 391
Bush, George H.W., 416
Bush, George W., 41, 74–77, 87, 89, 92, 105, 126, 133, 152–153, 252, 278, 294, 367, 370–371, 373–374, 383–384, 390, 397, 409, 416
George W. Bush administration
antitrust system and, 202
drug prohibition program, 43
faith-based initiatives, 154
housing voucher funding, 249
opposition to Kyoto Accord, 74–75
polluter fines, 76–77
trade embargoes and, 226
Buyers, responsiveness to price change, 53–55

C

Campbell's Soup, 199
Canada
national health insurance plan, 277
North American Free Trade Agreement and, 227
Capital, increases in, 413–414
Capital flight, 422

Capital gains, 414
definition, 382–383
Capital goods, 8
Capital-intensive technology, 172
Capitalism, 410
global trends toward, 410, 417–418, 424
socialist transition to, 417–418
Capitalist countries, 411–417
Cartel, 198
Carter, Jimmy, 364
Castro, Fidel, 226
Caterpillar Tractor Company, 199
CCC (Commodity Credit Corporation), 290
Cellar-Kefauver Act (1950), 201
CFCs (chlorofluorocarbons), effects of releasing, 58
Charter schools, 88
opposition to, 89–90
Chernobyl nuclear accident, 75
Chevron, 298
Chiapas uprising, 170
Child care availability, effects on employment rate, 140–142, 144
Child labor, 329–330
Children
homeless, 252–253
poverty rate of, 136–140
roles of in less-developed countries, 179
Chile, 227
China and U.S. trade embargo, 226
Chlorofluorocarbons (CFCs), effects of releasing, 58
Chrysler, 199
Cisneros, Henry, 250
Cities
homeless persons in, 252
segregation in, 250–252
Civil Rights Act (1964), 122
Clayton Act (1914), 201
Clean Air Act (1963, 1970, 1977, and 1990), 63, 67
Clean Skies Act (2003), 77
Clinton, Bill, 146, 148, 366–367, 416
Clinton administration
antitrust system and, 202
drug prohibition programs, 42–43
national health insurance proposal, 277
polluter fines, 76–77
Clorox, 196
Cochrane, William W., 290
Coinsurance payment, 270

COLA. *See* Cost-of-living adjustment (COLA)
Collusion, 198–199
in American automobile industry, 199
definition, 198
Commodity Credit Corporation (CCC), 290
Compaq, 202
Comparative advantage
consumption possibilities curve and, 217–218
in international trade, definition, 214–215
opportunity cost and, 214
production possibilities curve and, 216–217
resource costs and, 214
Competition, 188–190
among schools, 88–90
benefits of, 219
definition, 188
import, 204
Competitive market, characteristics of, 188
Composition of GDP, 167, 359
Composition of poverty, 136
Comprehensive Environmental Response, Compensation, and Liability Act (1980), 64
Computer technology, investment in, 415
Concentration
in agriculture, 295
measuring, 192–194
Concentration ratio, 192
Conservation
economics of, 69–71
recycling and, 68–73
Conservation and recycling
conservation economics, 69–71
population strain, 68–69
recycling economics, 71–73
Conservative economics, 411
Conservative Republicans, 411
Conservative views, 409–410, 424
on agriculture, 299
on discrimination, 127
on economic development, 182
on economics, 29
on education, 104
on environment, 76
on fiscal policy, 373
on government borrowing, 402
on health care, 279
on housing, 254

Conservative views (*continued*)
  on illegal drugs, 50
  on inflation, 348
  on international trade, 228
  on macroeconomics, 373
  on market power, 205
  on monetary policy, 373
  on poverty, 154
  on Social Security, 324
  on taxes, 402
  on unemployment, 348
Constant prices, 357
Constitutional rights, drug prohibition
    and, 46
Consumer goods, 8
Consumer price index (CPI), 135
  calculation of, 342–343
  construction of, 351
  inflation rates based on, select
      years, 344
Consumers
  incomes of, 360
  interest rates and, 360
  purchases of, 359–360
Consumption possibilities curve
  comparative advantage and,
      217–218
  definition, 217
Consumption tax, 414
"Contract with America," 148
Contractionary fiscal policy, 365–367
Contractionary monetary policy, 368
  in 1980s, 421
Contractual right, 310
Corporate crime, 35, 40–41
Corporate responsibility law, 41
Corruption
  in formerly socialist world, 419
  of police, 45–46, 51
Cost-benefit analysis
  of crime prevention activities, 37–38
  definition, 37, 68
  of incarceration, 39
Cost containment and health care inef-
    ficiencies, 267
Cost of living, 342
Cost-of-living adjustment (COLA),
    321–322, 344
Cost-push inflation, 348, 363–364
Cost shifting, 267
Costs
  of anticrime activities, 37–38
  of crime, 35–36
  of public education, 84
CPI. *See* Consumer price index (CPI)

Crime
  costs of, 35–36
  definition, 36
  drug prohibition and, 45
  statistics on, 35
  violent crimes against persons, 39
  white-collar crime, 40–41
Crime prevention
  cost-benefit analysis of, 37–38
  by criminal courts, 37
  empirical studies of, 39
  incarceration policy, 39–40
  by police, 37
  by prison system, 37–39
    costs of, 38–39
  production possibilities curve for, 38
  as public good, 36–37
Crime rates, 36
Criminal behavior, drug use and, 43
Criminal justice system, 37
  administration costs, 35–36
  spending on, 38
Crowding out, 395–396
Cuba and U.S. trade embargo, 226
Culture and choice versus discrimina-
    tion, 121–122
Current prices, 357
Cyclical unemployment, 337

D

DeBeer's diamond cartel, 198
Debt crisis, international, 421–423
Declining terms of trade, 223
Decontrol of prices, 418
Deductibles, 270
Defense expenditures and government
    budget, 397
Defensive medicine
  definition, 267
  medical costs and, 267–268
Deficiency payments, 304–305
Deflation, 342
Deforestation
  effects of, 58
  in less-developed countries, 177–178
DeLorean, 195
Demand. *See also* Demand and supply
  aggregate. *See* Aggregate demand
  curve, 9–12
  elasticity of, 48, 53–55
    excise tax impact on, 54–55,
        405–407
    extremes of, 53

  inelasticity of, 53
    legalization of drugs and, 47–48
  law of, 11
  prices and quantity relationship,
      9–10
  schedule, 10–11
  tutoring services example, 9–12
  understanding, 9–12
Demand and supply
  aggregate, 359–362
  combining schedules, 15–18
  distribution and, 9–24
  of education, 82–83
  equilibrium, 16–19
  flexible (floating) exchange rate sys-
      tem and, 231–234
  graphs of, 353
  legalization of drugs and, 46–50
  price ceiling effects on, 174–175
  real world applications, 22–24
  shifts in, 19–22
Demand curves
  definition, 10
  elasticity and, 54
    excise tax impact on, 55
  for legalization of drugs, 46–47
  real-world factors causing shifts
      in, 23
Demand-pull inflation, 348, 363
Demand schedule, 10
Demand-side programs
  for farm products, 292–293
  for housing, 249
Demographic trends, poverty and, 142
Department of Housing and Urban De-
    velopment (HUD), 248, 250
Depreciation, 233
Deregulation, 203–204, 371–372
  market power decreased by, 203–204
Desertification in less-developed coun-
    tries, 177–178
Design standard, 66
Developers, subsidies to, 248
Diagnosis related groups (DRGs), 272
Direct costs
  definition, 97
  of higher education, 97
Discouraged workers, 333–334
Discrimination
  conservative versus liberal view-
      point, 127
  culture and, 121–122
  definition, 113
  diversity of U.S. population and,
      110–112

earnings and, 113–115
  disparities in, 113–116
  and education, 115–116
  and experience, 116
  and income, 113
  and unemployment, 116
educational segregation, 124–126
employment discrimination, 114,
  117–118
explanations of, 116–118
housing segregation, 124–125
human capital discrimination, 115
individual choice and, 121–122
in labor market, 114, 118–121
  economy effects, 118–120
  individuals, effects on,
    120–121
  with and without occupational
    crowding, 117–119
measuring, 121–122
against minorities, 112–113
occupational discrimination, 114
occupational overcrowding discrimination, 117–118
policies to eliminate
  affirmative action, 122–124
  Civil Rights Act (1964), 122
  Equal Pay Act (1963), 122
population growth trends and,
  110–112
poverty, effects on, 146
reverse discrimination, 123
statistical discrimination, 117
types of, 114–115
wage discrimination, 114
Distribution
  demand and supply, 9–24
  economics and, 9–24
  of GNI, 168
  of income. *See* Income distribution
Diversity of U.S. population,
  110–112
Dollar
  debt repayment in, 422–423
  international demand for. *See* Ex-
    change rates
  oil valuation in, 421
  value of, 421
Donaldson, Sam, 298
Down payment, 240–241
Doyle, Jim, 152
DRGs (diagnosis related groups), 272
Drug awareness and education programs, 42
Drug offenders, 39–40

Drug use
  criminal behavior and, 43
  increase with legalization, 47
  public health consequences, 43
  social problems related to, 43
  statistics on, 41
  zero tolerance policy on, 42
Drugs, illegal
  background on legal status of, 41–42
  conservative versus liberal view-
    point, 50
  demand for, 46–48
    decreasing, 42–43
  demand-side prevention programs,
    44, 46, 49
  excise taxes on, 49–50
  international control efforts, 44–45
  legalization of, 41–50
    argument against, 43–44
    argument for, 44–46
    benefits of, 46
    economics of, 46–51
  needle exchange programs and, 46
  organized crime involvement in, 45
  penalties for possession of, 42
  political party involvement in,
    44–45
  prohibition
    costs of, 45–46
    economics of, 46–51
  supply of, 47–48
    decreasing, 42
  supply-side programs, 44–45
  taxing producers of, 46
  War on Drugs, 42–44
Drugs, legal/illegal use of, 50–51
Dumping, 293
Durable goods, 359–360

E

Early retirement effect, 319
Earned Income Credit (EIC), 146,
  342, 383
Earnings
  definition, 113
  full-time worker median annual,
    115–116
  full-time worker median weekly, 114
  worker educational attainment and,
    96–98
EconDebate
  "Do Technological Advances Result
    in Higher Unemployment?" 141

  "Does a Gender Wage Gap Still
    Exist?" 114
  "Does an Increase in the Minimum
    Wage Result in a Higher Unem-
    ployment Rate?" 143, 340
  "Does Foreign Direct Investment
    Hinder or Help Economic Devel-
    opment?" 173
  "Does the U.S. Economy Benefit
    from Foreign Trade?" 214
  "Does the U.S. Economy Benefit
    from the WTO?" 211
  "How Should the U.S. Budget Sur-
    plus Be Used?" 396
  "How Should We Reform the Current
    Tax System?" 386
  "Is Microsoft a Monopoly?" 191
  "Is More Spending on Infrastructure the
    Key to Economic Growth?" 412
  "Is There a Need for Health Care Re-
    form?" 264
  "Is There a New Economy?" 7
  "Is Workfare Working?" 252
  "Should Antipollution Standards Be
    Strengthened?" 65
  "Should Medicare Provide Prescrip-
    tion Drug Coverage?" 271
  "Should There Be a Market for
    Human Organs?" 274
  "What Accounts for the Recent In-
    creases in Income Equality?" 135
  "Will Social Security Survive into the
    Twenty-First Century?" 147, 321
EconLinks
  "A Tale of Two Countries: Hemp
    Farming," 44
  "Coco Leaf Prices Reach a High," 49
  "Ecstasy for Customs in the Drug War
    Would Be Higher Prices," 42
  Panel Study of Income Dynam-
    ics, 244
  "Should Marijuana Be Decriminal-
    ized?" 41
  on tax distribution, 389
  on tax rates, 384
  "The Afghan Opium Drug Policy: Is It
    Poppycock?" 42
  "The Economics of Drug Dealing," 46
  White House Economics Statistics
    briefing room, 285
  World Factbook, 179
EconNews
  "A Supersized NAFTA," 226
  "A Tariff-ic Proposal?" 220
  "All Work and No Play," 314

EconNews (*continued*)

"An International Market in Pollution," 67

"Cell Phones Selling Well," 12

"Child Labor," 329

"College: To Go or Not Go—That Is the Question," 99

"Debt Has Its Virtue," 400

"Do School Vouchers Improve the Quality of Education?" 89

"Education Pays, But Also Costs," 100

"Farmers Dump on Canada for Dumping," 293

"For Richer, for Poorer," 120

"Going Bananas over Steel," 222

"Home, Expensive Home," 238

"Home Improvement—Or Home Investment?" 242

"Hot Gas Prices Cool the Economy," 356

"How Do Some Spell Relief? Lower Debt," 170

"How Should We Reform the Current Tax System?" 90

"Immigration Pluses and Minuses," 180

"Inflation Dips and Economy Smiles," 342

"Is a College Education a Good Investment?" 97

"It's Supposed to Be a Two-Edged Sword," 360

"Looking and Not Liking," 331

"Managed Care Becomes Unmanageable," 276

"No Room at the Top for Women: MIT's Glass Ceiling," 122

"Oldies Are Seen as Golden," 313

"One Farmer's Loss is Another One's Grain," 284

"Output, Income, and Price Level," 357

"Paying the Price of Pollution," 61

"Peak Power Prices," 203

"Poverty Persists," 136

"Precision Plowing," 290

"Reducing Airline Emissions: The Future Is the Past," 68

"Retirees Model the Energizer Bunny: They Keep Going and Going and Going," 314

"Sales Drive Forward," 354

"Slowdown Puts Brakes on Teenage Jobs and Pay," 330

"Steel Supply Strategies," 191

"Students Learn the Hard Way," 17, 101

"Summer Seasonal Shortage," 337

"Sweet Home Improvement Market," 242

"Talking Down the Yen," 232

"The Fall and Rise of PC Prices," 16

"The Taxing Debate," 389

"Tools of Trade," 412

"Trade Wars—In the U.S." 214

"Winn-Dixie Loses in Dixie," 27

"Working Longer and Harder," 416

Economic activity, GDP as indicator of, 357–359

Economic conservative, 51. *See also* Conservative views

definition, 29

Economic development

agricultural development, 173

conservative versus liberal viewpoint, 182

definition, 170–171

economic and political oppression reduction, 171

versus economic reforms, 423

people-oriented strategies for, 183

population growth and, 180

poverty reductions as, 171

standards of living improvements as, 171

women's role in, 178–179

Economic growth

calculation of, 166

for countries around the world, 166–167

decrease in regulation, 415–416

definition, 7, 167

in formerly socialist countries, 417

increase in capital, 413–414

labor productivity improvements, 415

and population growth, 167

technological improvements, 415

trickle-down philosophy of, 153–154

in twenty-first century, 416–417

well-being of people, measuring, 167–168

in Western industrialized world, 411–417

Economic hardship, understatement of, 334

Economic indicators, GDP as, 357–358

Economic liberal, 50. *See also* Liberal views

definition, 29

Economic reform

versus economic development, 423

effects of, 424

in less-developed world, 420–424

Economic systems

capitalistic, 410

socialistic, 410

Economic transition in formerly socialist industrialized world, 417–420

Economic well-being of people, 167–168

Economics

conservative versus liberal viewpoint, 29

distribution and, 9–24

scarcity and, 4–8

Economies of scale, 194–195

"Economy Food Plan" (Department of Agriculture), 134

Education. *See also* Private education; Public education

and affirmative action, 126–128

conservative versus liberal viewpoint, 104

dropout rates, 86–87

and earnings, correlation between, 96–98

equality of, 93

expenditures of federal, state, and local governments on, 84–85

expenditures on as percentage of GDP, 84

federal and state corrective funding, 91

financing of, 91–92

challenges to, 87

higher education, 93–105

K–12 education, 84–93

in less-developed countries, 177

multiculturalism movement in, 105

positive externalities of, 82

property tax funding of, 84–87

reforms of, 90–91

quality of, racial dimension, 86–87

schools

competition between, 88–90

condition of physical facilities, 86

poverty rates and, 92

underfunding of, 85–86

spending on, increasing, 144

spending per student, 86–87, 92–93

spillover benefits of, 82–84

value of, 81

Educational segregation, 124–126

EEOC (Equal Employment Opportunity Commission), 122
Efficiency
    definition, 4
    equity and, 25
Efficient, 25
Effluent fees, 66–67
EIC. *See* Earned Income Credit (EIC)
Elasticity
    market power and, 208–209
    monopoly profits and, 208
    price discrimination and, 208–209
Elasticity coefficient, 53
Elasticity of demand, 53–55
    definition, 48
Electrical equipment conspiracy, 198–199
Emissions fees, 66–67
Employees. *See also* Workers
    on-the-job training, 97–98
    promotability of, 97–98
Employment. *See also* Unemployment
    of working mothers, 329
Employment discrimination, 117–118
    definition, 114
Endowment, 95, 96
Enrollment cap, 100
Enron, 41
Entitlement, 308
Environment
    agricultural production, effects on, 295–296
    concern for quality of, 63
    conservative versus liberal viewpoint, 76
    damage to, types of, 58
    international activists, arguments of, 75
    international aspects of problems in, 74
    legislation on, 63–65
    policies on, 62–63
        criticisms of, 75–76
        effects on U.S. economy, 73–74
        evaluation of, 68
        innovation in, 73
        politics of, 62–63
    pollution along the U.S.–Mexico border, 64
    pollution problem, international aspects of, 74–75
    protection of, 416
        benefits of, 68
        costs of, 68

regulation of, 65–67, 371
    effects on U.S. economy, 73–74
    evolution of, 63
    government and, 64–65
    U.S. policies, criticisms of, 75–77
    Yucca Mountain, Nevada, nuclear waste dumping at, 76
Environmental policy
    criticism of, 75–77
Environmental Protection Agency (EPA), 64
Equal Employment Opportunity Commission (EEOC), 122
Equal Pay Act (1963), 122
Equilibrium
    definition, 16
    in demand and supply, 15–22
Equilibrium price, 49
Equilibrium quantity
    elastic demand and, 48
    inelastic demand and, 48
    supply and, 48
Equity, 26
    definition, 25
    efficiency and, 25
    poverty issues and, 131–132
Eskimos, as percentage of U.S. population, 110–111
Ethnic minorities. *See* African Americans; Asians; Hispanics; Minority groups; Race and ethnicity
EU. *See* European Union (EU)
Euro, 227
Europe. *See also* Western industrialized world
    hyperinflation in, 344–345
European Union (EU)
    antitrust laws and, 202–203
    international trade and, 227–228
Exchange rates
    definition, 231
    determining, 231–234
    economic policy and, 234
    management of, 234–235
Excise tax
    burden of, 55
    definition, 49, 384
    elasticity and, 54–55, 405–407
Exclusive franchise, 195
Exemptions, 382–383
Expansionary fiscal policy, 365–367
Expansionary monetary policy, 368
Export cropping, 176

Exports
    definition, 212
    import quotas and tariffs and, 204
    market competition, 204
    size of, 361–362
    subsidies on agricultural commodities, 293
Externalities
    definition, 58, 82
    of education, 82
    inefficiency resulting from, 82
    inequity resulting from, 82
    negative, 58–59
    positive, 59
    resource allocation and, 82
Exxon, 192

F

Fair market amount, 248
Families
    low-income
        Aid to Families with Dependent Children (AFDC), 148–149, 371
        housing for, 244–245, 247–249
        rental ceilings and, 245–247
        Temporary Assistance for Needy Families, 146
    poverty statistics by, 137–138
Farm bill, 294
Farm incomes, 285–286, 290, 295
    deficiency payments and, 304–305
    inelastic demand, effects on, 302–303
    of large farms and agribusinesses, 295, 298
Farm products
    bumper crops, 285
    dumping of, 293
    foreign demand for, 293
    genetically modified organisms, 296–297
    inelastic demand for, 284, 302–303
    prices
        government regulation of, 174–176
        instability of, 284–285
        market-determined, 175–176
        price ceilings on, 174–175
        supports for, 288–290
    real price of, 286
    surpluses of, 289–290, 292
    target prices for, 304–305
    trade restrictions on, 297–298

Farm subsidies, 293, 297–298
Farmers, productivity of, 283
Farmworkers, 296
Favre, Brett, 51
Federal Bureau of Investigation (FBI), 36
Federal crime bill Truth in Sentencing provision, 40
Federal government. *See also* Government; Government policy
    block grants from, 148
    education expenditures, 84–85, 91
Federal Housing Administration (FHA) loans, 241, 243
Federal Reserve monetary policy, 367–369
Federal taxes. *See also* Taxes
    rates on income levels, 382–383
    revenue from, 382–384
Federal Trade Commission (FTC), 201–202
Federal Water Pollution Act (1972), 64
Fee-for-service
    definition, 266
    versus managed care, 276
Feminization of poverty, 140
    births to teenage and unmarried mothers and, 142–143
FHA. *See* Federal Housing Administration (FHA) loans
Firms
    barriers to entry, 194–197
    behavior of, 196–197
    deregulation of, 371–372, 415–416
    interest rate effects on, 361
    inventories of, 360
    market power of, 364–365
    purchases of GDP, 360–361
    size of, measuring, 192–194
Fiscal policy, 365–367
    conservative versus liberal viewpoint, 373
    expansionary versus contractionary, 365–367
Flexible (floating) exchange rate system, 231–232
Food. *See also* Farm products
    buffer stock of cereal grains, 176
    market-determined prices for, 175–176
    price ceilings on, 174–175, 259
    price stability of, 176–177
Food stamps, 146–147
Ford Motor Company, 192, 199
Foreign currency earnings, 422–423

Foreign food assistance programs, 293
Foreign purchasers of GDP, 361–362
Formerly socialist industrialized world
    economic transition, 417–420
    definition, 410
    effects of, 419–420
    market-determined prices in, 418
    privatization of, 418–419
Fossil fuels, effects of burning, 58
France
    French fries versus "freedom fries," 227
    politically motivated trade relations and, 227
Franchises, exclusive, 195
Free markets, movement toward, 410
Free-rider problem, 37
Free trade, restrictions on, 221–222
Free Trade Agreement of the Americas expanding the, 227–228
"Freedom fries" versus French fries, 227
Freedom to Farm Bill, 293–294
Frictional unemployment, 336
Friedman, Milton, 123, 145
FTC (Federal Trade Commission), 201–202
Full employment, 338
    full-employment GDP, 366
Fully funded, 309

G

G-8 (Group of Eight), 234
GATT. *See* General Agreement on Tariffs and Trade (GATT)
GDP. *See* Gross domestic product (GDP)
General Agreement on Tariffs and Trade (GATT)
    definition, 227–228
    international trade and, 228
    Kennedy Round and, 228
    Uruguay Round and, 228
    World Trade Organization and, 228
General assistance programs, 146–147
General Electric (GE), 198–199
General Motors, 192, 199
Genetically modified organisms (GMOs), 296–297
Gentrification, 244
Global Crossing, 41
Global economy, 428. *See also* World economy

GMOs (genetically modified organisms), 296–297
GNI. *See* Gross national income (GNI)
GNI per capita, 165–166
GNP (gross national product), 356
Goods
    durable and nondurable, 359–360
    environmental quality as a luxury good, 63
    private, 8
Gore, Al, 89, 373, 383
Government. *See also* Federal government; State government
    investments of, 414
    public goods and services provided by, 37
    purchases of, 361
    regulation by, decreases in, 415–416
    savings and dissavings of, 413–414
    taxation by. *See* Taxes
Government borrowing, 392–397
    conservative versus liberal viewpoint, 402
    government budget effects, 396–398
    income distribution effects, 393–394
    interest rate effects, 394–396
    macroeconomy effects, 392–393
    national debt effects, 396–398
Government budget
    defense and war expenditures and, 397
    government borrowing effects on, 396–398
Government policy
    consumer income effects, 360
    cost-benefit analysis of, 37
    for legalized drug regulation, 49–50
    macro policy, 365–374
        fiscal policy, 365–367
        monetary policy, 367–369
        recent, 373–374
        supply-side policy, 369–372
        trickle-down effect of, 372–373
    toward agriculture, 287–297
        effects on less-developed countries, 297–298
        evaluation of, 294–297
        politics of, 298–300
    toward environment, 75–77, 416
    toward home ownership, 243–244
    toward homelessness, 253
    toward pollution regulation, 65–67
    toward poverty, 170

toward research and development, 415
toward unemployment versus inflation, 348–349, 369, 376–379
Government programs
Aid to Families with Dependent Children, 148–149, 371
budget cuts as cause of poverty, 143
food stamps, 146
general assistance, 146
on housing
housing vouchers, 249
public housing, 247–248
rental ceilings, 245–247
subsidies to developers, 248
Medicaid, 146
negative income tax, 145–146
for poor persons, 134–135, 146
for poverty reduction, 146–148
public assistance programs, 146
to reduce supply of farm products, 291–292
Special Supplemental Nutrition Program for Women, Infants, and Children (WIC), 146–147
State Children's Health Insurance Program, 146
Supplemental Security Income, 146
target pricing for farm products, 304–305
Temporary Assistance for Needy Families, 146–148, 150–153
universal entitlements, 144–145
Government securities, 381
Government spending, 361
Government subsidies, 99–100
on agricultural commodities, 293
on education, 95–96
for real estate developers, 248
"Great Stink," 62
Gross domestic product (GDP)
annual growth rates for Western industrialized countries, 411–412
composition of, 167, 359
definition, 28, 262, 355–357
distribution of, 359
education expenditures as percentage of, 84
exports and imports as share of, 212–213
final goods included in, 355–356
flaws of, 357–358
full-employment GDP, 366
market price of output, 356
national debt and, 398–399

nonmarket activities, 358
real versus nominal, 357
supply-side policy effects on, 412
time frame of, 356
underground activities, 358–359
value terms of, 356
Gross national income (GNI), 165
distribution of, 168
Gross national product (GNP), 356
Group of Eight (G-8), 234

H

Hacket, James, 126
Harley-Davidson, 199
Health care
access to/lack of, 269–271
advertising within industry, 275
alternatives for, 274–277
group practices or managed care, 276
medical savings accounts, 275
Medicare and Medicaid, 274
national health insurance, 276–277
privatization, 274–275
conservative versus liberal viewpoint, 279
costs escalation, 262–263, 265–266
financial access
to Medicaid, 270–271
to Medicare, 271–272
to private insurance, 270
international comparisons
of expenditures, 262–265
of health indicators, 264
legislation concerning, 277–279
in less-developed countries, 177
managed care
versus fee-for-service, 276
growth of, 276
market characteristics
consequences of, 268–269
inadequate cost containment, 267
patient attitudes, 267–268
physician sovereignty, 266
rapid technological change, 266–267
third-party payment, 266
"Medigap" insurance, 272
outcomes of expenditures, 264–265
patient attitudes and, 267–268
problems in, 265–272
production possibilities curve and, 262–263

racial and ethnic groups and, 264–265
rationing of, 272–274
recent policies and proposals, 277–279
rise in demand for, 266–267
social significance of expenditures, 262–263
standard of health indicators, 264–265
waste and inefficiency, 268–269
Health maintenance organizations (HMOs), 276
Higher education. See also Education
affirmative action and, 104–105
costs of
direct and indirect, 97–98
opportunity costs, 97–98
decision variables of investing in, 97–98
demand and supply analysis of, 101–103
different tuition for different programs, 101–103
efficiency of, 101
enrollment caps, 100–101
equal access to, 100, 103–105
expenses of institutions, 93–94
financial aid, 99, 103–104
as investment in human capital, 96–99
low-income student access to and financing of, 103–105
multiculturalism movement in, 105
Pell grants for, 103
public and private, 93–96
funding of, 94–95
resource allocation, improving, 101–103
spending per student, 93, 95
state government support of, 99–100
decreases in, 100–101
tax credits for, 103
tuition, 93–96
increases in, 100
user fees, 103
Hispanics
as percentage of U.S. population, 110–111
poverty rate of, 137–139
unemployment rate of, 333
HMOs. See Health maintenance organizations (HMOs)

Home buyers
    affordability criteria for, 242
    income and debt of, 242
    monthly payments of, 241–242
Home owner's insurance, 242–243
Home ownership, 237–244
    government policy toward, 243–244
Homelessness, 252–253
    government policies toward, 253
    population characteristics, 252–253
Hooker Chemical and Plastics Company, 64
Housing
    affordability of, 243
        buyer income and debt, 242
        expenses at time of purchase,
            240–241
        mortgage payments, 241–242
    conservative versus liberal viewpoint, 254
    down payment on, 240–241
    gentrification and, 244
    home owner's insurance, 242–243
    home values, 239
    homelessness and, 252–253
    inventory of, 239
    low-income housing, 244–245,
        247–249
    mobile homes, 243
    owner occupation of, 239
    poor persons, programs for,
        245–250
    prices, 238
        versus household income, 240
        of new housing, 239–240
    property taxes, 242–243
    quality changes in, 240
    rental housing, 239, 244
    segregation in, 124–125, 250–252
    trends in, 239–240
Housing markets, 237–244
    economic growth trends and,
        238–239
    price differentials, 238–239
    regional differences, 238
Housing vouchers, 249
HUD. See Department of Housing and
    Urban Development (HUD)
Human capital
    higher education as investment in,
        95–99
    investment in, 144, 177–178
Human capital discrimination, 115
Human investment programs,
    177–189

Hunger. See also World hunger
    poverty and, 139, 177
Hyperinflation, 344–345

I

IBM, 202
ICC (Interstate Commerce Commission), 203
Illegal drugs. See Drugs, illegal
IMF. See International Monetary
    Fund (IMF)
Immigrants
    eligibility for benefits, 338
    welfare eligibility, 149
Immigration, unemployment effects of,
    338–340
Import competition, 204
Imports. See also Exports
    definition, 212
    import quotas and tariffs, 204
In-kind transfers, 132–133
    poverty line statistics and, 135
Incidence of poverty, 136
Income
    definition, 113
    government borrowing effects on,
        393–394
    government policy effects on, 360
    tax effects on, 387–390
Income distribution, 359
    definition, 132
    equality of, 132–133
        improving, 169–170
    factors affecting, 133
    in foreign countries, 168–170
    graphing data on, 158–161
    international comparisons of, 134
    measuring relative poverty with, 132
    trends in, 132–133
Income redistribution through agricultural price supports, 290
Income tax
    cuts in, 370–372
    home ownership benefits, 243–244
    negative, 145–146
Income transfers
    cuts in, 371–372
    definition, 132
    examples of, 361
    unemployment compensation
        as, 334
Increasing opportunity costs, 32–33
Index of dissimilarity, 250–251

Indigenous populations
    definition, 170
    ownership of land, 170
Indirect costs
    definition, 97
    of higher education, 97
Individual equity, 310
Industrialization
    capital-intensive technology for, 172
    labor-intensive technology contributions to, 173
    population growth and, 180
    strategies for, 172
Inefficiency, 199–200
    in American automobile industry, 199
    definition, 82–83
    from uncertainty about prices,
        346–347
Inelastic demand
    definition, 47, 223
    farm income and, 285–286, 302–303
    farm prices and, 302–303
    for farm products, 284
    price instability and, 284–285
Inequity
    definition, 83
    from externalities, 82
Infant mortality rate
    definition, 168, 264–265
    international comparisons, 264
    worldwide statistics on, 171–172
Inflation, 342–349
    conservative versus liberal viewpoint, 348
    definition, 28, 262, 342
    effects of, 345–347
        international, 347
        menu costs, 347
        redistribution, 345–346
        uncertainty, 346–347
    in formerly socialist world, 419
    housing prices and, 242
    hyperinflation, 344–345
    interest rates and, 242
    types of, 347
        cost-push, 363–364
        demand-pull, 363
        profit-push, 364–365
    versus unemployment, 348–349,
        369, 376–379
Inflation rate
    calculating, 343
    inaccuracy of, 343–344
    of select years, 344

Informal employment sector
definition, 180–181
underemployment in, 180–181
Information technology, investment
in, 415
Infrastructure, 174
Insurance. *See also* Health care
health care coverage, 266
homeowner's insurance, 242–243
Interest rates
definition, 394
effects on businesses, 361
effects on consumers, 360
government borrowing effects on,
394–396
inflation and, 346
monetary policy and, 367–368
price ceilings on, 258–259
prices and, 376
rise in resulting from inflation, 421
International community. *See also* International trade; World economy
agricultural development, role in,
176–177
role in development of low-income
countries, 176–177
International debt crisis, 421–423
International economics
economic policy, 234
exchange rate determination, 231–234
exchange rate management, 234–235
International environmental issues, 74
International Monetary Fund (IMF),
211, 421
conditionality of assistance, 423
International Paper Corporation, 298
International trade
agreements between countries,
227–228
benefits of, 213–219
absolute advantage, 214
basis for advantage, 218
comparative advantage, 214–218
distribution, 219–221
specialization and exchange,
218–219
conservative versus liberal viewpoint, 228
General Agreement on Tariffs and
Trade, 228
importance to U.S. economy, 212–213
less-developed countries
declining terms of trade, 223
and declining terms of trade,
223–226

export diversity need, 223, 225
globalization effects, 225
inelastic demand for commodities,
223–224
overreliance on imports, 225
politics and trade, 226–227
price rise effects, 375
restrictions to, 221–222
United States and, 212–213
Interstate Commerce Commission
(ICC), 203
Inventories, 360
Investment
in human capital, 96, 144, 177
savings rate and, 413–414
Iran and U.S. trade embargo, 226
Iranian Oil Embargo (1979), 226, 421

J

Jackson, Thomas Penfield, 202
Job readiness, 141
improving, 144
Job training, increasing spending on, 144
John Hancock Mutual Life Insurance, 298
Johnson, Lyndon, 363
Judicial system, spending on, 38
Justice Department Antitrust Division,
201–202

K

K–12 education, 84–93. *See also* Education; Public education
financing of, 84–86
improving, 87–92
No Child Left Behind Act (2001),
87, 92
quality of, 86–87
Kellogg, 199
Kennedy, John, 363
Kennedy-Kasselbaum Health Care Reform Bill (1996), 277
Kennedy Round and GATT, 228
Keynes, John Maynard, 365
King, Martin Luther, Jr., 109, 124
Kozol, Jonathan, 86
Kyoto Accord, 74

L

Labor force
definition, 328–329
discouraged workers, 333–334

full-employment GDP and, 366
unemployed persons in, 331
Labor force participation rate, 328–330
for select countries, 329–330
Labor-intensive technology, 173
Labor markets
discrimination against women in, 143
immigration effects on, 338–340
minimum wage and, 340–342
occupational crowding in, 117–119
Labor productivity
improvements resulting in economic
growth, 415
microeconomic policies for relief, 144
poverty and, 141
Land ownership
by indigenous populations, 170
by minority populations, 170
Land redistribution, 173
Latin America, hyperinflation in, 344
Law of demand, 11. *See also* Demand
Law of supply, 13. *See also* Supply
LDCs. *See* Less-developed countries
(LDCs)
Leavitt, Mike, 64
Legal drugs, illegal use of, 49–51
Legalization
of drugs, 41–51
conservative versus liberal viewpoint, 50
of victimless crimes, 51
Less-developed countries (LDCs), 163
agricultural development in,
173–177
local government role in, 173–174
agricultural prices in, 174–176
AIDS in, 182–183
borrowing to finance oil imports, 421
capital flight from, 422
debt crisis, 421–423
debt repayment issues, 422–423
debt-servicing issues, 422
declining terms of trade, 223
deforestation in, 177–178
desertification in, 177–178
export cropping in, 176
export diversity needs, 223
food price ceilings, 259
geographical location of, 163–164
globalization effects on, 225
human capital investments, 177–178
inelastic demand for commodities,
223–224, 225
infrastructure in, 174
literacy rates in, 178

Less-developed countries (*continued*)
  measures of well-being of people
    in, 171
  overreliance on imports, 225
  population concentrations in,
    180–182
  resource development in, 177–178
  underemployment in, 180–181
  U.S. agricultural policy and, 297–298
  water supply in, 177
  women's role in development of,
    178–179
Less-developed world, 420–424
  definition, 410
  economic reform in, 420–424
Liberal views, 410
  on agriculture, 299
  on discrimination, 127
  on economic development, 182
  on economics, 29
  on education, 104
  on environment, 76
  on fiscal policy, 373
  on government borrowing, 402
  on health care, 279
  on housing, 254
  on illegal drugs, 50
  on inflation, 348
  on international trade, 228
  on macroeconomics, 373
  on market power, 205
  on monetary policy, 373
  on poverty, 154
  on Social Security, 324
  on taxes, 402
  on unemployment, 348
Liberalism, 410–411
Liberalization in twenty-first
  century, 420
Libya and U.S. trade embargo, 226
Licenses, 196
Licensing, 196
Life expectancy, 168, 171
  average, 264
  definition, 264
  increase in, 313–314
  worldwide statistics on, 171–172
Limbaugh, Rush, 51
Literacy rates
  definition, 178
  of women versus men, 178
Loanable funds, 394
Local government education expenditures, 84–85
Local taxes. *See* Taxes

Lorenz curve
  definition, 158
  of total money income for United
    States and Canada, 161
  of total money income in 2002, 159
  of total money income in 1981 and
    2002, 160
Love Canal, 64
Low-income countries. *See* Less-
  developed countries (LDCs)
Low-income families
  housing for, 244–245, 247–249
  rental ceilings and, 245–247
Luxury goods, 63

M

Macroeconomic policy, 365–374. *See
  also* Government policy
  fiscal policy, 365–367
  monetary policy, 367–369
  recent, 373–374
  supply-side policy, 369–372
  trickle-down effect of, 372–373
Macroeconomics
  conservative versus liberal view-
    point, 373
  definition, 28, 328
  inflation, 342–349
  unemployment, 328–342
Macroeconomy, 328
  graphing, 353–355
Magnet schools, 88–89
  opposition to, 89–90
Malpractice insurance, 267
Manufacturing industries, concentration ratios for, 192–194
Marginal cost, 67
Marijuana
  decriminalization of, 41–42, 48–49
  health consequences of, 43
  supply of, 44
Market-determined prices, 175–176
  in formerly socialist world, 417–418
Market failures, list of, 25–29
Market power, 364–365
  barriers to entry, 194–197
    behavior of established firms,
      196–197
    control of essential raw materi-
      als, 195
    economies of scale, 194–195
    exclusive franchises, 195
    licensing, 196

  patents, 195–196
  product differentiation, 196
competition, 188–190
concentration
  effects on prices, output, and prof-
    its, 197–198
  measuring, 192–194
  ratio, 192–194
conservative versus liberal viewpoint, 205
definition, 27, 188
effects of, 197–200
  collusion, 198–199
  inefficiency, 199–200
  price discrimination, 200
elasticity and, 208–209
extent of, 204–205
forces decreasing, 201–205
  antitrust system, 201–203
  import competition, 204
  regulation and deregulation,
    203–204
  technological change, 201
monopolies, 190–191
oligopolies, 190–191
trade and, 27
Market price, 188
  of output, 356
Markets, 409–410. *See also* World
  economy
  efficiency of, 409–410
  equity in, 410
  free market, movement toward, 410
  government involvement in,
    409–410
  housing markets, 250–252
  private market, 37
  for recycled products, 73
  special, 27
Maternal mortality rates, 178–179
McAffrey, Barry, 42–43
McDonnell Douglas, 202
Mean, definition of, 96
Means-tested, definition of, 271
Median, definition of, 96
Median earnings, level of education
  and, 96
Medicaid, 140, 146–147
  administration of, 270–271
  change proposals, 278
  cost shifting and, 267
  coverage from, 270–271
  curtailment or elimination of, 274
  definition, 270
Medical savings account, 275

Medicare, 140
    administration of, 271–272
    change proposals, 278
    cost shifting and, 267
    coverage from, 271–272
    curtailment or elimination of, 274
    definition, 270
    regressivity and, 270
"Medigap" insurance, 272
Men
    labor force participation rate of,
        328–330
    unemployment rate for, 331–333
Menu costs, 347
Mercosur trade agreement, participat-
    ing countries, 228
Mergers
    definition, 201
    McDonnell Douglas and Boeing, 202
    Sprint and WorldCom, 202
Methyl-bromide, 75
Metropolitan areas
    index of dissimilarity in, 251
    worldwide, 180–181
Mexico
    environmental pollution along U.S.
        border, 64
    North American Free Trade Agree-
        ment and, 227
    pollution in, 227
    working conditions in, 227
Michigan property tax reform experi-
    ment, 90–91
Microeconomics, 28, 328
Microsoft Corporation, 202–203
Milliken v. Bradley, 125
Minimum wage, 340–342
    definition, 340
    earner income potential and, 143
    increasing, 146
Minorities. See Discrimination
Minority groups. See also Women
    discrimination against, 144
    housing segregation and, 250–252
    unemployment rates for, 333
Mobro garbage barge, 71
Monetary policy, 367–369
    conservative versus liberal view-
        point, 373
    expansionary versus contrac-
        tionary, 368
Money income
    definition, 132
    income transfers as, 132
Money supply, 367–369

Monopolies, 190–191
    characteristics of, 191
    definition, 190
    examples of, 190–191
    profits and elasticity, 208
Monopolistic, definition of, 190
Mortality rates, 168, 171
    maternal, 178–179
Mortgages
    closing costs, 241
    down payment, 240–241
    interest on, 241–242
    monthly payments, 241–242
    mortgage insurance, 241
    points, 241
    variable rate mortgages, 242
Mugabe, Robert, 170
Multiculturalism movement in educa-
    tion, 105

N

Nader, Ralph, 187
NAFTA. See North American Free Trade
    Agreement (NAFTA)
National Center for Victims of
    Crime, 35
National Coalition for the Home-
    less, 244
National debt, 398–401
    balanced budget proposals,
        400–401
    budget deficit and, 396
    definition, 397
    government borrowing effects on,
        396–398
    gross domestic product and,
        398–399
    impact of, 400
    ownership of, 399–400
    proposals for eliminating, 400–401
    size of, 398–399
National health insurance. See also
    Health care
    Canada's plan, 277
    definition, 276–277
    proposals, 276–277
National Household Survey on Drug
    Abuse, 41
National unemployment rate, 331. See
    also Unemployment
Native Americans, agricultural policy
    and, 296
Natural increase, 112

Natural monopolies
    definition, 195
    examples of, 195
Natural resource development,
    177–178
Negative externalities, 58–59
    effects of, 58–59
Negative income tax, 145–146
    definition, 145
Neo-liberalism, 410
Net benefits, 37
Net immigration, 112
Newly industrializing countries (NICs),
    172. See also Less-developed coun-
    tries (LDCs); Less-developed world
Nissan, 204
Nixon, Richard, 42, 248
No Child Left Behind Act (2001), 87, 92
Nominal GDP, 357
Nondurable goods, 359–360
Nonmarket activities, 358
Normal retirement age, 313
North American Free Trade Agreement
    (NAFTA)
    Canada and, 227
    definition, 227
    environmental protections of, 64
    Mexico and, 227
    Traditional Adjustment Assistance
        program and, 227
North Korea and U.S. trade embargo, 226

O

Occupational crowding, 117
Occupational discrimination, 114
Occupational overcrowding discrimina-
    tion, 117–119
Oil crisis in 1970s, 420–421
Oligopolies, 190–191
    definition, 191
Oligopololists, 191
OPEC. See Organization of Petroleum
    Exporting Countries (OPEC)
Opportunity costs. See also Production
    possibilities curve
    comparative advantage and, 214
    definition, 5
    increasing, 32–33
Organization of Petroleum Exporting
    Countries (OPEC), 198, 257,
    364, 420
Organized crime, drug trade benefits, 45
Overallocation of resources, 61

Overpopulation, from an ecological
    viewpoint, 69
Oxfam, 297–298
Ozone depletion, 75

P

Pacific Islanders. *See also* Asians
    poverty rate of, 137–138
Patent protection, 415
Patents, 195–196
    definition, 195
    market power and, 196
Patient attitudes and health care ineffi-
    ciencies, 267–268
Pay-as-you-go system definition, 309
Payment-in-Kind (PIK) program, 292
Payroll taxes, 309, 384
Pell grants, 103
Perfect elasticity, 53. *See also* Elasticity
Perfect inelasticity, 53. *See also* Inelastic
    demand
    of demand, 405
    of supply, 407
Performance standard, 66
Perot, Ross, 227
Personal factors, poverty and, 141–142
Personal income tax, 382–383.
    See also Taxes
Personal Responsibility and Work Op-
    portunity Reconciliation Act
    (PRA), 149–153
Petrodollars, 421
Physician sovereignty
    definition, 266
    and health care inefficiencies, 266
Police, 37
    corruption of, 45–46, 51
    spending on, 38
    vice squads, 51
Polluter fines of Clinton versus Bush
    administrations, 76–77
Pollution
    by consumers, 68–69
    definition, 58
    effects in a single market, 59–61
    environmental quality as a luxury
        good and, 63
    as inefficient resource allocation,
        59–62
    local community standards for, 65
    negative effects of, 64–65
    negative externalities from, 58–59

positive externalities from, 59
problem of, 58–62
regulation of
    marketable permits, 67
    pollution fees, 66–67
    standards approach, 65–66
spillover costs and benefits of, 58–59
types of, 58
Poor countries, 165–166. *See also* Less-
    developed countries (LDCs); Less-
    developed world
Poor persons. *See also* Poverty; Poverty
    rate; World poverty
    composition of poor population,
        137–138
    rental ceilings and, 245–247
Population
    density in urban areas, 181–182
    diversity of, 110–112
    and Social Security, 314–315
Population groups
    absolute poverty rates of, 137–140
    health care and, 264–265
    poverty rates of, 137–140
    unemployment rates of, 331–333
Population growth
    average life expectancy, 168
    and economic growth, 167
    infant mortality rate, 168
    in less-developed countries, 179–180
    trends in the United States, 111–112
Population policy in less-developed
    countries, 180
Population strain, 68–69
Positive externalities, 59
    effects of, 59
Posse Comitatus Act, 42
Poverty
    absolute poverty, 132, 134–140
    causes of, 140–144
    complexity of, 155
    conservative versus liberal view-
        point, 154
    economic growth versus government
        programs and, 153–154
    health care and, 140
    homelessness and, 140, 253
    hunger and, 139, 177
    over- and understatement of, 135
    relative poverty, 132–134
    solutions to, 144–148
    statistics on, 131
    stereotypes of, 131
    student performance and, 92

welfare reform and, 148–153
world hunger and, 297
Poverty line
    definition, 134
    in-kind transfers and, 135
    inflation adjustments, 135
    life at, 135
    meaning of, 134–135
    measurement problems of, 135
    origins of, 134
Poverty rate
    from 1960 to 2002, 136
    of different age groups, 137–139
    of children, 137–139
    definition, 135
    of ethnic minorities, 137–139
    of family groups, 138–140
    health care quality and access corre-
        lation, 265
    of residence groups, 138–139
    of white persons, 137–138
Powell, Colin, 126
PPO (preferred provider organiza-
    tion), 276
PRA (Personal Responsibility and Work
    Opportunity Reconciliation Act),
    149–153
Preferred provider organization
    (PPO), 276
Prejudice, 113
Premium, 270
Prescription drugs
    advertising, 275
    spending on, 267
Price. *See also* Prices
    instability of and international trade,
        223–225
    versus quantity, 24
    rationing function of, 18, 289
Price ceilings
    on agricultural products, 174–175
    examples of, 256–259
    rental ceilings as, 245–247
Price discrimination, 200
    in American automobile industry, 200
    definition, 200
    drug industry and, 200
    elasticity and, 208–209
Price-fixing. *See* Collusion
Price floors
    definition, 288, 340
    minimum wage as, 340
    as price supports, 288
Price leadership, 199

Price makers, 190
Price stability of food products,
   176–177
Price supports
   definition, 288
   for farm products, 288–290, 304
   price floors as, 288
Price takers, 188
Prices
   constant prices, 357
   current prices, 357
   decontrol of, 418
   increases in, effects of, 18
   interest rates and, 376
   international trade effects, 375
   market-determined, 175–176
      in formerly socialist world, 417–418
   market price of output, 356
   purchasing power effects, 375
   target prices, 304–305
   uncertainty about, 346–347
Primary commodities, 223
Prison system, 37
   costs of, 38–39
   drug offenders in, 45
   "get-tough" policies, 39
   imprisonment policy, 39–40
   life sentences, 40
   mandatory sentencing policies, 40
   overcrowding of, 39–40
   prison population, nature of, 39–40
   "three strikes and you're out"
      laws, 40
   Truth in Sentencing provision, 40
Private
   definition, 28
   versus public, 28
Private education
   endowments to, 96
   higher education institutes, 93–96
   sources of revenue, 94–96
Private goods, 8
Private insurance, 270
   characteristics of, 309–310
   definition, 309
   social insurance and, 309–310
Private market. See also Markets;
   World economy
   private versus public goods in, 37
Private schools, 82. See also Education
Privatization
   definition, 274, 307
   in formerly socialist world, 417–419
   partial, 323

Product differentiation, 196
Production possibilities curve
   application to country's resources, 7–8
   assumptions used, 4–5
   comparative advantage and, 216–217
   for crime prevention, 38
   definition, 4
   economic growth and, 7, 412
   health care and, 262–263
   opportunity cost and, 5, 6
      increasing, 32–33
   resource allocation example, 4–6
   unemployment and, 6–7
   for unemployment effects, 335
Profit-push inflation, 348, 364–365
Programs to reduce supply of farm
   products, 291–292
Progressive taxes, 311, 387
Prohibition of drugs, 45–46. See also
   Drugs, illegal
Property taxes, 242–243
   educational funding, 84–87
   reforms of, 90–91
Proportional taxes, 311, 388
Proposition 187, 338
Prospective payment, 272
Public assistance
   definition, 146, 310
   programs for, 146–148, 310–311
Public education. See also Education
   costs of, 84
   financing of, 81
   higher education system, 93–95
      enrollment caps, 100–101
      sources of revenue, 95
      tuition increases, 100
   state government subsidization of,
      95–96, 99–101
Public goods and services, 8
   adequacy of provisions, 25–26
   crime prevention as, 36–37
   definition of, 36
   free-rider problem, 37
   indivisibility of, 36
   nonexcludable nature of, 37
   nonrivalrous nature of, 36
Public housing, 247–248
Public schools, 82
Public versus private, 28
Purchasing power
   inflation effects on, 345
   redistribution of, 345–346
   reductions in, 375
Pure competition, 27

Q

Quantity versus price, 24
Quotas, 123, 221

R

Race and ethnicity. See also Minority
   groups
   births to unmarried mothers and, 142
   poverty statistics by, 136–139
Racial segregation in housing markets,
   250–252
Rate of return
   definition, 98
   of higher education, 98
Rationing function of price, 18, 289
Raw materials, control of, 195
Reagan, Ronald, 42, 153, 327, 364,
   369–371, 416
Reagan administration
   antitrust system and, 202
   government program budget cuts, 143
Real estate developers, subsidies to, 248
Real GDP, 357
Real price
   definition, 286
   of farm products, 286
Recession, 364
   as cause of poverty, 140–141
   definition, 140, 328
   fiscal policy during, 366–367
   1970s worldwide, 421
Recycling
   conservation and, 68–73
   economics of, 71–73
   garbage barge example, 71
   markets for recycled products, 73
   motivation for, 72
   population strain and, 68–69
   problems facing programs, 71–73
Redistribution, 345–346
Refundable, definition, 383
Regressive taxes, 388
   definition, 311
Regressivity
   definition, 270–271
   Medicare and, 270
Regulation, 203–204
   decreases in, 415–416
   market power decreased by, 203–204
   of pollution, 65–67

Relative poverty, 132–134
 definition, 132
 income distribution
  international comparisons of, 134
  trends in, 132–133
  measuring, 132
Rental ceilings, 245–247
Rental housing
 availability of, 244–245
 demand for, 244
Replacement rate, 312
Research and development (R&D), 415
Residence, place of
 home affordability by, 243
 poverty statistics by, 136–139
Resolution Trust Corporation
 (RTC), 250
Resource allocation
 for agriculture, 295
 efficiency of, 59–62
 in higher education, improving,
  101–103
Resources
 agricultural, immobility of, 286–287
 allocation of, 82
 costs and comparative advantage, 214
 definition, 4
 over- and underallocation of, 61, 82
 pollution and inefficiencies
  interdependent market effects,
   61–62
  single market effects, 59–61
 scarcity and the production possibilities curve, 4–8
Retaliation, 222
Retirement age, 322–323
Reverse discrimination, 123
Rich countries, 165–166
Rio Earth Summit
 Brazil (1992), 74
 Japan (1997), 74
 South Africa (2002), 74
Rising marginal cost, 67–68
Risk aversion and uncertainty,
 346–347
Roosevelt, Franklin D., 288
RTC (Resolution Trust Corpora-
 tion), 250
Runge, C. Ford, 290
Rural–urban migration, 180–182
 incentives for, 181
Russia
 price decontrol in, 418
 privatization in, 418–419

S

Savage Inequalities: Children in America's
 Schools (Kozol), 86
Savings rate, 413
 incentives for increasing, 414
 and Social Security, 319
Scarcity
 definition, 4
 economics and, 4–8
SCHIP. See State Children's Health In-
 surance Program (SCHIP)
School systems
 competition between, increasing,
  88–90
 overcrowding in, 87
School vouchers, 89
 opposition to, 89–90
Section 8 project-based housing, 248
Segregation in housing markets,
 250–252
Senior citizens, poverty rate of,
 137–140
Services, 8
Set-Aside program, 292
Sheppard, William, 204–205
Sherman Act (1890), 201
Shortage, 17
Six Markets Group (Asian G-6),
 234–235
Social adequacy, 310
Social conservatives, 51
Social costs of production, 60
Social insurance
 characteristics of and private insurance, 308–310
 characteristics of and public assistance, 310–311
 definition, 146, 308
 programs for, 146–148
Social insurance taxes, 382, 384
Social liberals, 50
Social problems related to
 drugs, 43
Social Security, 146–147
 aging population considerations
  demographic changes implications, 313
  long-run financial viability, 315
  normal retirement age, 313–314
  taxing of benefits, 314–315
  trust fund balances, 314
 "bad buy" argument, 317–318
 benefits of, 312

compulsory versus voluntary argument, 315–316
conservative versus liberal viewpoint, 324
cost of living adjuster, 345–346
 definition, 146
earnings and tax rate, 310–312
entitlement definition, 308
financial viability of, 315
future of system, 320–323
 altering tax proposal, 321
 cutting of benefits proposal,
  321–322
 partial privatization, 323
 retirement age increase effects,
  322–323
 stock market investment proposal, 323
 taxing of benefits proposal, 322
misconceptions about, 320
problems and issues, 313–319
as social insurance program,
 308–310
taxes for, 310–311
treatment of women, 318–319
wealth effect, 319
Social Security Act (1935 and 1983),
 308, 314
Social Security Administration,
 307–308, 312
Social Security wealth effect, 319
Socialism, 410
 price controls, 418
Soil Bank, 292
Sowell, Thomas, 123
Special Supplemental Nutrition Program for Women, Infants, and
 Children (WIC), 146–147
Specialization and exchange concept,
 213–214
Spillover benefits, 59
 definition, 82
 of education, 82–84
 underallocation of resources and, 83
Spillover costs, 58
 definition, 82
Spillovers, 26
 costs and benefits, 58–59, 82
 definition, 26
Sprint, 202
SSI (Supplemental Security Income),
 146–147
Stability, 27–28
Stagflation, 364
Standard deduction, 383

Standards, definition of, 65
Standards approach
    technology forcing, 66
    understanding, 65–66
    using, 65–66
Standards of living
    GDP as indicator of, 359
    measures of, 171–172
    in poor countries, 171–172
State Children's Health Insurance Program (SCHIP), 146–147, 277
State government. See also Government
    block grants for, 148
    criminal justice system expenditures, 36
    education expenditures, 84–85, 87, 91
    public higher education system expenditures, 94
    welfare contributions, 149
State taxes. See Taxes
Statistical discrimination, 117
Statutory right, 310
Stock market, investment of Social Security taxes in, 323
Structural changes in economy
    effects on income distribution, 133
    poverty and, 141
    unemployment and, 336–337
Structural unemployment, 336–337
Subsidies
    on agricultural commodities, 293, 297–298
    definition, 69, 96
    of public higher education, 99–101
    to real estate developers, 248
Subsistence food crops
    definition, 179
    production by women, 179
Sudan and U.S. trade embargo, 226
Sun Microsystems, 202
Superfund, purpose of, 64
Supplemental Security Income (SSI), 146–147
Supply. See also Aggregate supply; Demand and supply
    aggregate, 355. See also Aggregate demand and supply
    curve, 12–15. See also Supply curve
    elasticity of
        excise tax impact on, 405–407
    equilibrium quantity and, 48
    law of, 13
    opportunity cost considerations, 12–13

price and quantity relationship, 13
    schedule, 13–14
    tutoring services example, 12–15
    understanding, 12–15
Supply curve
    definition, 13
    excise tax effects on, 49–50
    for legalization of drugs, 47–48
    real-world factors causing shifts in, 22–23
Supply schedule, 13–14
Supply-side programs, 369–372, 410
    deregulation, 371–372
    desired effects of, 412
    effects of, 371–372
    housing programs, 247–248
    income tax cuts, 370–372
    income transfer cuts, 371–372
    for restricting farm production, 291–292
Surplus, 18

T

TANF. See Temporary Assistance for Needy Families (TANF)
Target prices for farm products, 304–305
Tariffs, 221
    barrier reduction agreements, 228
Tax base
    definition, 85, 310, 383
    federal government, 65
Tax credits
    definition, 383
    Earned Income Credit, 146, 342, 383
Tax cuts, 370–371
    indirect effects of, 133
Tax rate, 85, 310–311, 382
Taxes
    aggregate demand and, 386
    on capital gains, 414
    conservative versus liberal viewpoint, 402
    consumption tax, 414
    evasion of, 41
    federal
        corporate income taxes, 382–383
        estate taxes, 384
        personal income taxes, 382–384
        proposed changes to, 383–384, 390
        rates on income levels, 382–383
        social insurance taxes, 382–383

home ownership benefits and, 243–244
    income distribution effects, 387–390
        of progressive taxes, 387–388
        of proportional taxes, 388
        of regressive taxes, 388–390
    income taxes, 382–383
    on legalized drugs, 49
    macroeconomic effects, 386–387
    microeconomic effects, 390–392
    progressive, 311, 387
    rates, 382–383
    revenue from, 382–384
    Social Security and, 310–312, 389
    state and local, 384–386
        personal taxes, 385
        property taxes, 385
        sales and excise taxes, 384–385
    types of, 382–386
Taxpayers, burden of drug prohibition on, 45
Technological change, 201
    agricultural sector, effects on, 286
    economic growth resulting from, 415
    health care costs, impact on, 266–267
    market power decreased by, 201
    poverty rate effects, 141
Technology
    definition, 415
    patent protection, 415
Technology forcing
    definition, 66
    problems with, 66
Temporary Assistance for Needy Families (TANF), 146–148
    child care provisions, 152
    economic business cycles and, 153
    federal funding of, 152
    mothers working outside home, 152
    state responsibility for, 153
    vocational education provision, 152
    Wisconsin Works program example, 150–152
    work requirements, 152–153
10-year plan, 292
Third-party payment
    definition, 266
    health care inefficiencies and, 266
Third World countries. See Less-developed countries (LDCs); Less-developed world
"Three strikes and you're out" laws, 40
"Thrifty Food Plan" (Department of Agriculture), 134

Tokenism, 123
Toyota, 204
Trade, market power and, 27
Trade balance, 212
Trade deficit, 212–213
Trade embargo, 226
Trade restrictions
    on agricultural commodities,
        297–298
    effects of, 221–222
    purpose of, 221
Trade surplus, 212–213
Transportation, effects on employment
    rate, 141–142, 144
Trickle-down philosophy, 153–154,
    372–373
Trust fund, 314
Turner, Ted, 298
Tyco, 41

U

Uncertainty, 346–347
Underallocation of resources, 62
Underemployment, 180–181. *See also*
    Unemployment
Underground economic activities,
    358–359
Unemployed persons, 331, 334–335
Unemployment, 328–342
    conservative versus liberal view-
        point, 348
    definition, 6
    effects of, 334–335
        macroeconomic, 335
        on persons, 334–335
    full employment and, 338
    homelessness and, 253
    immigration effects on, 338–340
    versus inflation, 348–349, 369,
        376–379
    labor force participation rate,
        328–330
    macroeconomic policies to relieve, 144
    measuring, 334
    minimum wage and, 340–342
    types of, 335–338
        cyclical, 337
        frictional, 336
        structural, 336–337
Unemployment compensation, 334
Unemployment rate, 116, 330–331
    calculating, 116, 330–331
    measurement problems, 333–334

national, 331–333
poverty and, 141
for select groups, 331–333
Union Carbide toxic emissions
    release, 75
United Nations World Food Summit, 297
United States
    environmental pollution along Mexi-
        can border, 64
    gross national income per capita, 427
    international trade and, 212
    NAFTA and, 227–228
    purchasing power of, 345
    savings rate of, 413–414
    trade restrictions
        effects of, 221–222
        purpose of, 221
    unemployment rate in, 116
United States Supreme Court
    affirmative action decisions, 123,
        126–127
    school voucher ruling, 89
    segregation decisions, 125–126
Universal entitlements, 144–145
University of Michigan and affirmative
    action, 126–127
Urban informal employment sector, un-
    deremployment in, 180–181
Urban renewal, rental housing market
    and, 244
Urbanization, 180–182
Uruguay Round and GATT, 228
U.S. Charter School Organization, 88
U.S. military, drug enforcement role, 42
U.S. population. *See* Population
U.S. Post Office, 191
Usury laws, 241, 258

V

Variable rate mortgages, 242
Viagra, 267
Victimless crimes, legalization of, 51
Vietnam and U.S. trade
    embargo, 226
Violent crime rate, 39
Volkswagen, 204

W

Wage discrimination, 114
Wal-Mart, 192
Wall Street Journal, 199

War expenditures and government bud-
    get, 397
War on Drugs, 42–43
    costs of, 45
    demand for drugs, decreasing, 42–43
    successes of, 44
    supply of drugs, decreasing, 42
Water supply in less-developed coun-
    tries, 177
Welfare
    caseload reductions, 149–150
    dependency on, 148–149
    disparity between states, 153
    expense of, 149
    federal and state guidelines for,
        149–150
    outcomes of, 150
    qualification for, 134–135
    state responsibility for, 153
    Wisconsin Works program, 150–152
Welfare reform, 148–153
    disincentives built into, 148
    Personal Responsibility and Work
        Opportunity Reconciliation Act,
        149–153
    welfare dependence and, 148–149
    welfare expense and, 149
Western industrialized world,
    411–417
    aggregate supply and production
        possibilities in, 412–413
    definition, 410
    economic growth, 411–412
        policies toward, 412–416
        in twenty-first century, 416–417
Westinghouse, 198–199
Westvaco Corporation, 298
White-collar crime, 40–41
White persons
    as percentage of U.S. population,
        110–111
    poverty rate of, 137–139
    unemployment rate of, 331–333
Whitman, Christine Todd, 64
WHO (World Health Organization), 235
WIC (Special Supplemental Nutrition
    Program for Women, Infants, and
    Children), 146–147
Women
    with AIDS, 182
    contributions to economy, 358
    development of LDCs, role in, 178–179
    empowerment of, 180
    homeless, 252
    as homemakers, 358

labor force participation rate of,
328–330
labor market discrimination
against, 143
literacy rates of, 178
mandatory sentencing policies
and, 40
as minority group, 113
poverty rate of, 137–140
Social Security and, 318–319
unemployment rate of, 331–334
widows income gap, 318
working mothers, 329
working wives, treatment of,
318–319
Work effort, economic disincentives
for, 148
Worker safety regulations, 371
Workers. *See also* Employees;
Unemployment
job readiness, 141, 144
unemployment effects, 334–335
Working mothers, 329
World Bank, 211

World economy, 428
of formerly socialist world, 417–420
free market, movement toward, 410
inflation effects, 347
of less-developed world, 420–424
of Western industrialized world,
411–417
World Health Organization (WHO), 235
World hunger
biotechnology and, 296–297
food distribution policies and, 297
World market. *See* International trade
World poverty
AIDS and, 182–183
development theories and practices
and, 172–179
economic development and,
170–171
economic growth measurements,
166–170
GNI per capita measurements,
165–166
people-oriented strategies for, 183
population growth and, 179–180

standards of living and, 171–172
statistics on, 165
urbanization and rural-urban migration and, 180–182
World Trade Organization (WTO),
75, 211
definition, 228
GATT and, 228
trade agreements of, 228
WorldCom, 41, 202
WTO. *See* World Trade Organization (WTO)

Y

Youths, unemployment rate of, 331–333
Yucca Mountain, Nevada, nuclear
waste dumping at, 76

Z

Zimbabwe land distribution controversy, 170